THE HARPERCOLLINS
DICTIONARY OF BIOLOGY

THE
HARPERCOLLINS
DICTIONARY
OF

BIOLOGY

W.G. Hale and J.P. Margham

Series Editor, Eugene Ehrlich

Harper Perennial

A Division of HarperCollins*Publishers*

Library of Congress Cataloging-in-Publication Data
Hale, W. G.
    [Collins dictionary of biology]
    Harper dictionary of biology / W.G. Hale, J.P. Margham. —1st U.S. ed., 1st
    HarperPerennial ed.
        p. cm.
    "Originally published 1988 in Great Britain by William Collins Son & Co.
    under the title Collins dictionary of biology" —T.p. verso.
    ISBN 0-06-271503-8—0-06-461015-2 (pbk.)
    1. Biology—Dictionaries. I. Margham, J.P. II. Title.
QH302.5.H34 1991
574′.03—dc20   90-55500

97   RRD   20 19 18 17 16 15 14 13 12

For
Professor Arthur J. Cain
who told us both what a species is!

A

a- *prefix* denoting not, without, away.

A (amino acid) site the location at which specific TRANSFER RNA molecules become attached to RIBOSOMES during the TRANSLATION phase of protein synthesis.

ab- *prefix* denoting from, out of, away, apart.

A-band the dark band of the muscle sarcomere that corresponds to the thick myosin filaments. See MUSCLE CONTRACTION.

abaxial (of a leaf surface) facing away from the stem of the plant.

abdomen the part of the body of vertebrates containing the viscera, that is, the kidneys, liver, stomach, and intestines. In mammals the diaphragm separates the abdomen from the thorax, which contains the heart and lungs. In arthropods the abdomen is the part of the body directly behind the thorax, and in many other invertebrates the abdomen is divided into segments that have a superficial similarity.

abducens nerve the cranial nerve of vertebrates, which supplies the external rectus muscle of the eye (see EYE MUSCLE). It is mainly MOTOR in function.

abductor or **levator** any muscle that moves a limb away from the body. An example of an abductor is the *abductor pollicis*, which moves the thumb outward. Compare ADDUCTOR.

abiogenesis see SPONTANEOUS GENERATION.

abiotic factor any contribution to the environment that is of a nonliving nature, for example, climate.

ABO blood group a classification of blood based on natural variation in human blood types, identified and named by Karl Landsteiner (1868—1943) in 1901. There are four groups: A, B, AB, and O, each classified by a particular combination of ANTIGEN(S) in the red blood cells (see also H-SUBSTANCE) and naturally occurring ANTIBODIES in the BLOOD PLASMA. The relative frequency of the four ABO groups in the GENETIC POLYMORPHISM has been investigated in most human populations and differs widely between races (see Fig. 1).

Antigens and antibodies of the same type cause AGGLUTINATION when mixed, resulting in difficulties in blood transfusion (see UNIVERSAL DONORS and UNIVERSAL RECIPIENTS). Although possessing no A or B antigens, Group O individuals have an H-antigen (see H-SUBSTANCE), which is a precursor to the A and B types. H, A, and B antigens are found

Blood group	Antigen (RBC)	Antibody (plasma)	Typical % frequency in:		
			UK	China	Australian Aborigines
A	A	Anti-B	41	31	57
B	B	Anti-A	9	28	0
AB	AB	none	4	7	0
O	none	Anti-A + Anti-B	46	34	43

Fig. 1. **ABO blood group.** Main features of the ABO blood types.

also in human body secretions, such as saliva and semen, often a useful fact in forensic tests. See SECRETOR CONDITION.

Inheritance of grouping is controlled by a single autosomal gene (see AUTOSOME) on chromosome 9 with three major ALLELES—A, B, and O, sometimes written as I^A, I^B, and I^O. See Fig. 2. Four types of the A group are now known, making six multiple alleles (see MULTIPLE ALLELISM) at this LOCUS.

Genotype	Phenotype
A/A, A/O	Group A
B/B, B/O	Group B
A/B	Group AB
O/O	Group O

Fig. 2. **ABO blood group.** Inheritance of the ABO groupings.

abomasum the true digestive part of the RUMINANT STOMACH, secreting enzymes for digesting food prior to passing it on to the small intestine. The abomasum is HOMOLOGOUS with the monogastric stomach of nonruminants.

aboral away from or opposite the mouth in groups of animals with no clear-cut DORSAL or VENTRAL surfaces.

abortion the spontaneous or induced expulsion of a fetus before it becomes viable outside the uterus or womb.

abscess a collection of pus surrounded by an inflamed area in any tissue or organ of an animal.

abscisic acid a plant hormone. It is called *abscisin* when found in aging leaves, and it is partly responsible for leaf ABSCISSION. It is also called DORMIN when in buds and seeds and causes induction of dormancy. See Fig. 3.

abscission the process by which plant organs are shed. The process occurs in stalks of unfertilized flowers, ripe fruits, and deciduous leaves in autumn, or in diseased leaves at any time. It is due to formation of an *abscission layer* of thin-walled cells in the stalk base that rupture

Fig. 3. **Abscisic acid.** Molecular structure.

under strain, for example, wind. A layer of cork forms beneath the abscission layer to seal the plant surface. Abscission is controlled by plant hormones that are present: a low concentration of AUXIN, high amounts of ETHYLENE, and in some plants a high concentration of ABSCISIC ACID all stimulate production of the abscission layer. See Fig. 4.

Fig. 4. **Abscission.** Abscission layer in a leaf stalk.

absolute refractory period the brief period during discharge of a nerve impulse when the neuron cannot fire again.

absolute zero the lowest possible temperature for all substances, at which their molecules possess no heat energy. $-273.15°C$ is usually accepted as absolute zero.

absorption the process by which energy or matter enters a system passively, for example, take-up of nutrient material from the gut system of animals into the bloodstream, or the process by which chlorophyll absorbs light for photosynthesis. Compare ADSORPTION.

absorption spectrum the part of the light spectrum that is absorbed by a pigment. For example, chlorophyll (see Fig. 9) absorbs red and blue light and thus appears green.

abyssal (of organisms) inhabiting deep water below 1000 meters.

acanth- or **acantho-** *combining form* denoting spine.

Acanthodii an order of placoderm fossil fish, whose members bear spines along the anterior margin of the fins.

Acarina an order of the ARACHNIDA, containing ticks and mites.

acceptor molecule a molecule with high affinity for electrons, usually passing them on to another acceptor molecule in a series, called an ELECTRON TRANSPORT SYSTEM. As each acceptor receives an electron, it becomes reduced and then oxidized as the electron is given up (see REDOX POTENTIAL). Each reduction-oxidation reaction is catalyzed by a different enzyme, energy being gradually released with each electron transfer. Acceptor molecules, for example, CYTOCHROME, are vital in AEROBIC RESPIRATION and PHOTOSYNTHESIS.

accessory nerve a branch of the VAGUS nerve, occurring in TETRAPODS as the 11th cranial nerve.

acclimation see ACCLIMATIZATION.

acclimatization or **acclimation** the process by which a range of adjustments occur in the body, for example, in TEMPERATURE CONTROL and RESPIRATION, when an organism is subjected to unusual environmental stresses. See ADAPTATION, PHYSIOLOGICAL.

accommodation 1. the process by which the focus of the eye changes so that distant and near images can be made sharp. In fish and amphibians, this is achieved by moving the lens backward and forward. In birds, reptiles, humans, and some other mammals the shape of the lens is changed by the CILIARY MUSCLES. When the ciliary muscles contract, the tension lessens on the ligaments and the lens thickens as it rounds off through its own elasticity, enabling the eye to focus on near objects. When the ciliary muscles relax, the ligaments tighten, and the lens becomes stretched and thin and normally focuses on infinity. See Fig. 5.

relaxed ciliary muscle stretches lens which is focused on infinity

contracted ciliary muscle thickens lens and enables focusing on near object

Fig. 5. **Accommodation.** Accommodation in the vertebrate eye.

2. the process by which the sensitivity of excitable membranes to DEPOLARIZATION during a NERVE IMPULSE depends on the rate at which the current increases. As a result, greater depolarizations are required to produce an ACTION POTENTIAL when the current increases slowly than when there is a sudden increase in current.

accrescent (of plant structures such as the CALYX) becoming larger after flowering.

accumulator any plant, such as a nitrogen fixer, that enriches the habitat with nutrients.

acellular (of an organism) having a body that is not composed of cells.

Acellular organisms may have a complex structure differentiated into specialized areas and ORGANELLES. Such organisms are also described as *unicellular,* although this adjective suggests a simple structure, which is not the case.

acentric chromosome a chromosome formed by the joining of two broken pieces of chromosomes that lack CENTROMERES. The acentric chromosome is lost at the next division. Compare METACENTRIC CHROMOSOME.

acephalous without a head.

Acetabularia a genus of marine algae. Individuals may reach a size of 30 mm and are ACELLULAR, with a body consisting of three distinct areas: head, stalk, and a base containing the single NUCLEUS. Experiments by the German biologist Joachim Hammerling (born 1901) using grafts between two species demonstrated that the nucleus alone is responsible for body morphology and produces a chemical substance that can control development. Such results can now be interpreted as indications of the role of DNA and MESSENGER RNA.

acetabulum one of two cup-shaped sockets in the PELVIC GIRDLE articulating with the ball of the FEMUR.

acetic acid or **ethanoic acid** a clear colorless liquid with a pungent odor of vinegar. Formula: CH_3COOH.

acetylcholine (ACh) a TRANSMITTER SUBSTANCE secreted at the ends of CHOLINERGIC nerve fibers on arrival of a NERVE IMPULSE. ACh then passes the impulse across a SYNAPSE and as soon as ACh has depolarized the postsynaptic membrane, it is destroyed by the enzyme CHOLINESTERASE. Compare ADRENERGIC.

acetylcholinesterase the enzyme present in the synaptic cleft that destroys acetylcholine (see END PLATE).

acetylcoenzyme A (acetyl-CoA) an organic compound important in OXIDATION of energy-rich compounds to CO_2 and water. In the presence of oxygen, the three-carbon pyruvic acid produced in GLYCOLYSIS is broken down in the MITOCHONDRIA to produce CO_2, two hydrogen atoms (reducing NAD to $NADH_2$), and an active form of two-carbon acetic acid bonded to *coenzyme A,* called acetylcoenzyme A. Metabolism of fats and proteins also produces acetyl-CoA, either via pyruvic acid or directly. Thus, acetyl-CoA is common to the metabolism of all major types of food, forming a step leading to the KREBS CYCLE. See Fig. 6.

ACh see ACETYLCHOLINE.

achene a small, dry, INDEHISCENT, one-seeded fruit with a thin PERICARP, for example, seen on the surface of strawberries. See Fig. 7.

achlamydeous (of a flower) lacking both petals and sepals.

5

Fig. 6. **Acetylcoenzyme A.** Production of acetyl-CoA from food.

Fig. 7. **Achene.** The achenes of a strawberry.

achondroplasia the most common form of human dwarfism. It results from abnormal cartilage development, producing numerous bone defects: stunted trunk, shortened and deformed limbs, and bulging skull. The condition is controlled by an autosomal dominant gene (see DOMINANCE, GENETIC), so affected children who are born to normal parents must result from a mutation in one or the other parent. About 80% of achondroplastics die in early childhood, but those surviving are fertile, have normal intelligence, and can live more or less normal lives. The typical circus dwarf is achondroplastic.

acid any chemical substance that acts as a proton donor. Acids dissolve in water with the formation of hydrogen ions, which may be replaced by metals to form salts.

acid-base balance the maintenance of a constant internal environment in the body through BUFFER systems maintaining a balance between acids and bases.

acid dyes the dyes that contain an acidic organic component, which stains materials such as cytoplasm and collagen when combined with a metal.

acidophil or **acidophile** or **acidophilic** or **acidophilous 1.** (of a cell such as a leukocyte) having tissues that are easily stainable with acid dyes. **2.** (of organisms, particularly microorganisms) preferring an acidic environment.

acidosis a body condition in which there is excessive acidity in body fluids, normally regulated by the kidney.

acid rain any rain that contains pollutants, for example, dissolved sulfur compounds, and as a result adversely affects plant and animal life on precipitation. The pollutants are released into the atmosphere by the burning of fossil fuels, such as coal or oil.

acinus the terminal sac of an alveolar gland. The gland has a multicellular structure with sac-shaped secreting units.

acoelomate lacking a COELOM, which is the true body cavity. This occurs in some invertebrate groups, such as coelenterates, platyhelminths, nemerteans, and nematodes.

acorn worm a hemichordate, one of the three groups of invertebrate chordates collectively referred to as PROTOCHORDATES.

acoustic pertaining to hearing.

acoustico-lateralis system see LATERAL-LINE SYSTEM.

acquired characters characteristics of an organism that, according to Lamarck (see LAMARCKISM), become well developed through use or through environmental influences during an organism's lifetime and are inherited by its progeny. No clear experimental evidence has yet been found to support the theory. Current opinion is that the environment plays a large part in evolution, but only through NATURAL SELECTION.

Acrania an outdated taxonomic term often used as a synonym for PROTO-CHORDATE, but in some classifications is limited to synonymy with CEPHALOCHORDATE.

Acrasiales a grouping in some classifications within the Myxomyceta that includes slime molds, which are cellular or communal and do not coalesce.

acrocentric (of a chromosome) having the CENTROMERE near one end, making one chromosome arm much longer than the other.

acrocephaly possession of a dome-shaped head, also called *oxycephaly*.

acromegaly a chronic disease characterized by enlargement of the head, hands, and feet. It is caused by excessive secretion of growth hormones.

acropetal 1. (of plant structures, such as leaves and flowers) produced one after another from the base of the stem to the apex. **2.** (of substances, such as water) moving from the base of a plant to the apex.

acrosome a membrane-bound sac derived from the GOLGI APPARATUS, located at the tip of the sperm. The acrosome plays an important role in fertilization. It contains enzymes that, when the sac ruptures on contacting the egg, aid in penetration of the egg membrane, thus enabling transfer of the sperm nucleus to the egg cell. See Fig. 8.

Fig. 8. **Acrosome.** Head of a typical mammalian sperm.

A-C soil see RENDZINA.

ACTH see ADRENOCORTICOTROPIC HORMONE.

actin a contractile protein found in the muscles of all animals from protozoa to vertebrates and in the MICROFILAMENTS of all cells. The energy for contraction is derived from adenosine triphosphate (ATP).

actinomorphic (of regular flowers) divisible into two or more planes to give identical halves. In animals such a structure is referred to as radially symmetrical (see RADIAL SYMMETRY).

Actinomycetes a group of PROKARYOTIC organisms in the form of Gram-positive bacteria (see GRAM'S STAIN) that develop branching HYPHAE (0.5—1.0 μmeter in diameter). The hyphae in turn form a MYCELIUM. Reproduction is either by total FRAGMENTATION of the hyphae and/or by production of SPORES in specialized areas of the mycelium. Most species are SAPROPHYTES, AEROBES, or MESOPHILIC and grow optimally at neutral pH.

actinomycin D a substance that inhibits transcription of RNA from DNA. When isolated from soil bacteria and used pharmaceutically, it acts as an ANTIBIOTIC.

Actinopterygii a class of bony fishes characterized by having fins with rays. They are the most successful group of fishes and are subdivided into two small orders, the Chondrostei (including sturgeons and paddlefishes) and the Holostei (including the garpikes and bowfin), and a third large order called the Teleostei, which are the dominant fishes of the world today and the most numerous of all vertebrates.

Actinosphaerium a PROTOZOAN, known as the *sun animalcule*, which is related to *Amoeba.*

Actinozoa a less common term for the ANTHOZOA.

action potential the electrical potential present between the inside and outside of a nerve or muscle fiber when stimulated. In the resting state (RESTING POTENTIAL), the muscle or the nerve fiber is electrically negative inside and positive outside. With the passage of the impulse, the charges are reversed, and the wave of potential change that passes down the fiber is the most easily observable aspect of an impulse. The impulse (DEPOLARIZATION) lasts for about 1 ms, after which the resting potential is restored. See NERVE IMPULSE.

action spectrum a range of light wavelengths within which a physiological process can occur. For example, the range of wavelength of light in which the chlorophyll in green plants is able to synthesize carbohydrates by photosynthesis corresponds closely to the ABSORPTION SPECTRUM, showing that most of the light absorbed by chlorophyll is actually used in photosynthesis. See Fig. 9.

Fig. 9. **Action spectrum.** The absorption and action spectra of chlorophyll.

activated sludge any material used in sewage treatment, consisting mainly of bacteria and protozoans, that purifies the sewage and increases by multiplication during the process. Part of the new sludge is used in the continuing treatment of the sewage.

activation energy the energy required to initiate a reaction. Chemical bonds holding molecules together are difficult to break, requiring extra activation energy to push the bonded atoms apart. This extra energy makes the bonds less stable, so the molecule releases not only the activation energy but also the energy unlocked when the chemical bonds break, forming an EXERGONIC REACTION.

Activation energy can be applied externally as heat, but this is inappropriate for living organisms. Living organisms rely on biological catalysts (ENZYMES), which decrease the activation energy needed for the reaction to take place. See Fig. 10. See also ENDERGONIC REACTION.

activator any drug that increases the activity level of the person being treated.

active absorption/uptake the uptake of substances through the active

Fig. 10. **Activation energy.** (a) Activation energy required without enzymes. (b) Activation energy required with enzymes. (c) Energy from an exergonic reaction.

metabolism of a plant, often against a concentration gradient, as opposed to *passive uptake* along a concentration gradient.

active center 1. the part of an ENZYME molecule that interacts with and binds the substrate, forming an enzyme substrate. 2. the part of an antibody molecule that interacts with and binds the antigen, forming an antibody/antigen complex.

active immunity see ANTIBODY.

active ingredient the chemically active part of a manufactured product, for example, a HERBICIDE, the remainder being inert.

active site an area of ENZYME surface that has a shape complementary to a particular SUBSTRATE, enabling the enzyme and substrate to become temporarily bonded to form an enzyme—substrate complex. Such a *lock-and-key mechanism* explains the great specificity of enzymes for substrates and also why changes in enzyme three-dimensional shape, by pH or temperature, for example, cause alterations in enzyme activity. See Fig. 11.

Fig. 11. **Active site.** Lock-and-key mechanism of enzyme activity.

active state the condition in which muscle exists immediately before and during contraction, which makes it nonextensible. It is caused by attachment of MYOSIN bridges to ACTIN filaments.

active transport movement of a substance from a region of low concentration to another of higher concentration, that is, against the CONCEN-

TRATION GRADIENT. Such transport typically occurs in cell membranes, which are thought to contain carriers that move molecules from one side of the membrane to the other. Since these processes involve movement up a free-energy gradient, they require expenditure of energy from the breakdown of ATP and are therefore sensitive to factors affecting metabolism—temperature, oxygen, pH, etc. Compare DIFFUSION. See Fig. 12.

Fig. 12. **Active transport.** Active transport across a membrane.

activity the ability of a substance to react with another.

actomyosin a protein formed by interaction of ACTIN and MYOSIN. It is closely connected with the process of MUSCLE contraction.

acuity sharpness of vision; the resolving power of the eye.

acuminate (of leaves) tapering to a point, narrowing sharply toward the tip and then less sharply near the point.

acute 1. (of plant structures such as leaves) sharply pointed. 2. (of a disease) coming quickly to a crisis. 3. (of a radiation dose) applied at a high level in a short space of time. Compare CHRONIC.

ad- *prefix* denoting to, next to.

adaptation, genetic any characteristic that improves chances of an organism transmitting GENES to the next generation, that is, producing offspring. Such beneficial changes are genetically controlled and can be distinguished from alterations occurring within one generation (see ADAPTATION, PHYSIOLOGICAL), which may not lead to genetic change. Adaptations can affect any level of organization, from cells to whole organisms, and their behavior. Adaptions are favored by the process of NATURAL SELECTION.

adaptation, physiological change in the reaction organisms show as a result of prolonged exposure to conditions that normally produce a different or more extensive reaction. For example, altitude sickness— headache, nausea, fatigue—in people passes as they become acclimatized to high altitudes because of adjustments that occur in the respiratory and circulatory systems. See ACCLIMATIZATION.

adaptive enzyme an enzyme produced by an organism, for example, bacteria, only in the presence of its normal substrate or a closely similar substance. Such enzymes are not produced in circumstances to which the organism is not adapted. See OPERON MODEL.

adaptive radiation the evolution from an ancestral form of a wide range of related species occupying and exploiting many different types of available habitats. For example, mammals, evolving from the Tertiary period, have occupied many habitats and now have flying, running, swimming, and burrowing forms, often involving changes in the PENTA-DACTYL LIMB structure.

adaxial (of a leaf) facing the stem.

Addison's disease a disease caused by a deficiency of adrenocorticosteroid hormones, for example, CORTISONEand ALDOSTERONE, produced by cells of the ADRENAL GLAND cortex. Named for Thomas Addison (1793—1860), the English physician who first described it. The major symptoms of the disease are lowered blood pressure, lowered blood-sugar levels, reduced kidney function, loss of weight, extreme muscular weakness, and brownish pigmentation of the skin and mucous membranes.

additive genes those in which more than one gene controls a character, with each allele making a definite and measurable contribution toward the character. There is no DOMINANCE between alleles of one gene and no EPISTASIS between different loci (see LOCUS). Many pigment systems are controlled by additive genes, producing widespread variability.

adductor 1. a muscle that pulls a structure or limb toward the main part of the body. An example is the adductor mandibulae, which closes the jaws in amphibians. Also called a *depressor*. **2.** a muscle that pulls two structures together, for example, the two valves of a shell.

adenine one of four types of nitrogenous bases found in DNA, having the double-ring structure of a class known as PURINES (see Fig. 13).

Fig. 13. **Adenine.** Molecular structure.

Adenine forms part of a DNA unit called a NUCLEOTIDE and always forms COMPLEMENTARY BASE PAIRING with a DNA PYRIMIDINE base called THYMINE (see Fig. 14). When pairing with RNA during TRANSCRIPTION, adenine is complementary to URACIL. Adenine also occurs in RNA molecules, ATP, and AMP.

Fig. 14. **Adenine.** Complementary pairing. P, phosphate group.

adenohypophysis the part of the PITUITARY GLAND derived embryo-logically from the HYPOPHYSIS.

adenosine a nitrogen-containing compound consisting of an ADENINE base attached to a ribose sugar. Adenosine forms part of NUCLEOTIDES making up NUCLEIC ACIDS and ATP.

adenosine diphosphate see ADP.

adenosine monophosphate see AMP.

adenosine triphosphate see ATP.

adenovirus a type of virus responsible for several acute infections of the respiratory system. The name derives from the adenoid tissues, where the virus is often found.

adenyl cyclase the enzyme that catalyzes the formation of cyclic AMP from ATP by removal of pyrophosphate.

ADH (antidiuretic hormone) a hormone secreted by neurosecretory cells of the HYPOTHALAMUS and released by the posterior lobe of the PITUITARY GLAND. ADH stimulates resorption of water through the distal-convoluted tubule of the KIDNEY nephron in mammals, thus limit-ing the water content and overall volume of urine.

adipose tissue a fatty CONNECTIVE TISSUE, the matrix of which contains large, closely packed, fat-filled cells. Adipose tissue is important in en-ergy storage, occurring around the liver and kidneys, and where it occurs in the dermis of SKIN it insulates the body from heat loss.

adjacent disjunction see TRANSLOCATION HETEROZYGOTE.

adjuvant a substance added to enhance a physical or chemical property, for example, adjuvants are commonly added to ANTIGENS, improving the IMMUNE RESPONSE in the recipient and thus increasing production of ANTIBODIES.

adnate (of a structure) joined to an organ of a different kind.

adoral (of an organism) the side on which the mouth is situated.

ADP (adenosine diphosphate) a molecule consisting of an ADENO-SINE unit to which are attached two phosphate groups joined by a high-energy bond. ADP can be converted to ATP by addition of inorganic phosphate and about 34 kJ energy. See Fig. 15. See ATP for molecular structure.

adrenal cortical hormones hormones secreted by the cortex of the

Fig. 15. **ADP.** General structure of ADP and ATP. P, phosphate group.

ADRENAL GLANDS. They are generally of three main types: (a) *mineralocorticoids,* for example, ALDOSTERONE and deoxycorticosterone, which are concerned with salt and water balance; (b) GLUCOCORTICOIDS, for example, CORTISONE and hydrocortisone, which aid in formation of carbohydrates from fat and protein; and (c) *sex hormones,* particularly ANDROGENS, in both male and female mammals.

adrenal gland an endocrine organ consisting of a medulla (central part) secreting ADRENALINE and NORADRENALINE and a cortex (outer zone) secreting ADRENAL CORTICAL HORMONES. The two parts are closely associated in mammals, but sometimes are separated into distinct organs in other vertebrates, for example, in fish.

The activity of the medulla is controlled by the sympathetic nervous system, and that of the cortex by ADRENOCORTICOTROPIC HORMONE secreted by the pituitary gland. Mammals have a pair of adrenal glands, situated anteriorly to the kidneys. Other vertebrates have more than two adrenals.

adrenaline or **epinephrine** a hormone secreted by the medulla (central part) of the ADRENAL GLAND. It prepares the body for emergency action (FIGHT-OR-FLIGHT REACTION). It increases cardiac frequency; constricts the vessels supplying the skin and gut; increases blood pressure; increases blood sugar; dilates the blood vessels of the muscles, heart, and brain; widens the pupils; and causes hair erection. It is usually secreted with NORADRENALINE, whose effects are similar. Both hormones are also secreted by the ADRENERGIC nerve endings of the sympathetic nervous system.

adrenergic (of nerve endings) secreting ADRENALINE and NORADRENALINE on the arrival of a NERVE IMPULSE. These substances then stimulate the effector nerve fibers in the SYMPATHETIC NERVOUS SYSTEM of many vertebrates in much the same way that ACETYLCHOLINE acts as a transmitter substance in CHOLINERGIC nerve fibers.

adrenocorticotropic or **adrenocorticotrophic hormone (ACTH)** or **corticotrophin** a small, proteinaceous hormone secreted by the anterior lobe of the PITUITARY. It controls secretion of other hormones of the cortex of the ADRENAL GLAND.

adsorption the taking up of gas or liquid by a surface or interface. In physical adsorption, molecules are held by VAN DER WAALS' FORCES of attraction. In chemical adsorption, there is exchange or sharing of electrons. Compare ABSORPTION.

adventitious 1. (of a root) growing laterally from a stem rather than the main root, for example, prop roots of corn and clinging roots of climbing vines. **2.** (of a bud) not developing in a leaf axil, as in *Begonia*, where such buds can be produced from leaf wounds.

Aepyornis a very large, flightless, recently extinct bird from Madagascar. It was larger than an ostrich and the egg content was in excess of 9 liters.

aerenchyma cork-like tissue with large air-filled cavities between cells, present in the stems and roots of certain water plants, that enables adequate gaseous exchange even below water.

aerial respiration a process of gas exchange occurring in terrestrial and some aquatic organisms, by which oxygen is absorbed from the air and carbon dioxide is released. Respiratory surfaces are usually internal, for example, MESOPHYLL of leaves, TRACHEAE of insects, BOOK LUNGS of spiders and scorpions, and LUNGS of land vertebrates, although some respiratory organs are external, for example, the SKIN of amphibia. All surfaces rely on a water layer for gas exchange and may also depend on a blood system for transport of gases to and from distant parts of the body.

aerobe any organism, typically a microorganism, that can survive only in the presence of oxygen it requires for AEROBIC RESPIRATION.

aerobic respiration a type of CELLULAR RESPIRATION that requires oxygen. GLUCOSE is broken down to release energy in a series of steps that can be grouped in three main stages:

Stage 1: glucose is converted to PYRUVIC ACID in a process called GLYCOLYSIS, which takes place in the cell CYTOPLASM. A stable glucose molecule is first energized by addition of a phosphate group from two ATP molecules (PHOSPHORYLATION) and then broken down to two molecules of three-carbon phosphoglyceraldehyde (PGAL). Each PGAL molecule is oxidized by removal of two hydrogen atoms, which are picked up by an NAD molecule. Since oxygen is present, NADH can undergo a MITOCHONDRIAL SHUNT to enter an ELECTRON TRANSPORT SYSTEM (ETS). See Fig. 16. Four molecules of ATP are then synthesized in SUBSTRATE-LEVEL PHOSPHORYLATION over several steps, giving a net gain of two ATP molecules per molecule of glucose. Glycolysis is completed with production of two molecules of three-carbon pyruvic acid (*pyruvate*).

Stage 2: oxidation and DECARBOXYLATION of pyruvic acid in the MITOCHONDRIA to form two molecules of two-carbon ACETYLCOEN-

AEROTAXIS

Stage	CO_2 molecules	H atoms	ATP molecules via substrate-level phosphorylation	ATP molecules via ETS		Total ATP	Water molecules via ETS
				FADH	NADH		
1	0	4	4 (2)	0	6	10 (8)	2
2	2	4	0	0	6	6	2
3	4	16	2	4	18	24	8
Total	6	24	6 (4)	34		40 (38)	12

Fig. 16. **Aerobic respiration.** The products of one molecule of glucose undergoing aerobic respiration. Net figures in brackets.

ZYME A (acetyl-CoA). CO_2 is released in this process, together with two hydrogen atoms per molecule of pyruvic acid, picked up by NAD, and then passed down an ETS located on the inner membranes of mitochondrial cristae. Three molecules of ATP are produced per NADH, with oxygen acting as final acceptor of hydrogen, producing water.

Stage 3: entry of acetyl-CoA into the KREBS CYCLE (TCA cycle). Each molecule of acetyl-CoA can turn the cycle once. As each glucose molecule is broken down to two acetyl-CoA molecules, the cycle will turn twice per glucose molecule, yielding 2×2 molecules of CO_2 and 2×8 atoms of hydrogen. Six pairs of hydrogen atoms are picked up by NAD to produce 18 (6×3) molecules of ATP via the ETS. The remaining two pairs of hydrogen atoms are accepted by FAD molecules, which move to the ETS to produce 4 (2×2) molecules of ATP. One molecule of ATP is produced directly by substrate-level phosphorylation for each turn of the cycle. For each molecule of glucose undergoing aerobic respiration, the products are as shown in Fig. 16. The three stages are summarized in Fig. 17.

Note that the net production of ATP per molecule of glucose is 38 molecules, since two were required at the start of glycolysis. Of these 38 ATP molecules, only two (about 5%) are synthesized without oxygen, that is, anaerobically. The other 36 are the product of aerobic respiration.

Fats and proteins can also undergo aerobic respiration, entering the reactions at various stages. See ACETYLCOENZYME A for details.

aerotaxis the movement of an organism with reference to the direction of air or oxygen.

aerotropism plant growth response affected by the presence of air. For example, negative aerotropism is growth away from air, as in the growth of the POLLEN TUBE from stigma to ovary in flowering plants.

afferent neuron a nerve fiber that conducts impulses toward the central nervous system from receptor cells. Compare EFFERENT NEURON.

Fig. 17. **Aerobic respiration.** Summary of products in aerobic respiration.

affinity the relationship of one organism to another in terms of their evolution.

African sleeping sickness a fatal infection of the nervous and lymphatic systems that is endemic in certain parts of Africa and is caused by a flagellate protozoan called *Trypanosoma,* particularly *T. brucei gambiense* (West Africa) and *T. bruceirhodesiense* (East Africa). The vector of the flagellate is the tsetse fly *Glossina,* which also feeds on cattle, the latter acting as a reservoir for the parasite. African sleeping sickness is not to be confused with ENCEPHALITIS, which is caused by a virus.

afterbirth the remains of the placenta and blood that are voided from the uterus of EUTHERIAN mammals after the young is born.

afterripening a period through which apparently fully formed seeds and the spores of some fungi must pass before they can germinate. Afterripening is a form of DORMANCY that may involve production of growth hormones or destruction of growth inhibitors to produce suitable conditions for further development to begin.

agamospermy reproduction that does not involve FERTILIZATION or MEIOSIS but produces an embryo by asexual means other than VEGETATIVE REPRODUCTION.

agar the carbohydrate product of some seaweeds that, on forming a gel with water and allowed to solidify, is used as a culture medium for microorganisms.

agave a semi-woody perennial native of the American continent. Pulque and aquamiel are produced from it as fermented beverages, and mescal and tequila may in turn be distilled from these.

agglutination a clumping together of cells, usually as a result of reaction between specific ANTIGENS and ANTIBODIES in blood and lymph, forming a natural defense against foreign materials, including bacterial cells. Transfusion of blood between persons of different ABO BLOOD GROUPS is also subject to the risk of agglutination (see UNIVERSAL DONOR and UNIVERSAL RECIPIENT).

agglutinin a type of ANTIBODY causing AGGLUTINATION.

agglutinogen a surface antigen that induces formation of agglutinins in cells, including bacteria, and binds them to produce an AGGLUTINATION reaction.

aggregate fruit a fruit consisting of a collection of simple fruits, derived from a flower with several free CARPELS. An example is the blackberry.

aggregation a clumping or clustering of individuals of a population in a nonrandom distribution. Such clumping can occur (a) as a response to local habitat differences, for example, some organisms preferring damp to dry areas; (b) as a response to daily or seasonal weather changes; (c) by reproductive processes, for example, individuals hatching from the same egg batch in some animals, or poor seed dispersal in plants; and (d) as a result of social attraction, for example, colonial nesting in birds.

aggressins enzymes produced by parasitic bacteria. Aggressins dissolve tissues and enable bacteria to enter host tissues.

aggression a type of behavior that includes both threats and actual attacks on other animals, although often limited to threat display. See also AGONISTIC BEHAVIOR.

Agnatha aquatic, jawless, fish-like vertebrates characterized by fewer than two pairs of limbs (fins). The group is often given the status of a subphylum to separate it from other vertebrates with jaws, which are included in the subphylum Gnathostomata. The Agnatha includes lampreys, hagfish, and the fossil OSTRACODERMI.

agonistic behavior a broad grouping of behavior patterns that not only includes all aspects of AGGRESSION, including threat and actual attack, but also the consequent aspects of appeasement and flight.

agouti a fur coloration in which there are alternating light and dark bands of color on the individual hairs, giving a speckled brownish appearance. Such a fur coloration is found in mammals, such as rabbits, rats, and mice.

agranulocyte a type of LEUKOCYTE (white blood cell) with nongranular cytoplasm and a large spherical nucleus. Agranulocytes are produced either in the LYMPHATIC SYSTEM or in the bone marrow. They form about 30% of all leukocytes and are of two types, LYMPHOCYTES and MONOCYTES.

agriculture the cultivation of the soil for any aspect of farming or horticulture.

agronomy the study of the cultivation of field crops, with particular emphasis on improving their productivity and qualitative features.

A horizon the uppermost zone of soil—top soil containing leaflitter at the top, raw humus in the middle, and a dark-colored humus layer at the bottom. See also B HORIZON.

AIDS *acronym for* acquired immune deficiency syndrome, a serious human disease caused by a virus that can destroy the body's natural defense system (see IMMUNE RESPONSE) and cause death when the body becomes unable to fight any infection.

The level of response to infection varies. Not everyone who carries the virus develops AIDS, but all infected individuals can pass it on, by two main methods: (a) through sexual intercourse and (b) by transfer of blood cells, as when drug users share needles. At present there is no known vaccine against the AIDS virus, although several are being developed.

air bladder or **gas bladder** or **swim bladder** a gas-containing sac present in the roof of the abdominal cavity of bony fish that enables the fish to maintain position off the bottom with little or no movement.

airborne pathogen any disease-causing organism that can be transmitted through the air.

air pollution the presence of contaminants in the form of dust, fumes, gases, or other chemicals in the atmosphere in quantities that adversely affect living organisms. See ACID RAIN.

air sac a thin-walled extension to the lungs present in the thorax, abdomen, and bones of birds. Air sacs also occur as diverticula (outgrowths) of the TRACHEA in insects, where they are important in respiration, as they also are in birds. See Fig. 18.

air space any part of the interior of an organism occupied by air.

alanine one of 20 AMINO ACIDS common in proteins. It has a NONPOLAR

Fig. 18. **Air sac.** The air-sac system of a bird (left side).

structure and is relatively insoluble in water. The ISOELECTRIC POINT of alanine is 6.0. See Fig. 19.

Fig. 19. **Alanine.** Molecular structure.

alar pertaining to the wings.

alary muscles a series of small muscles found in the pericardial wall of insects. Their contraction causes blood to flow into the pericardium from the perivisceral cavity and then into the heart.

albinism an inherited condition found in many organisms whose chief feature is a lack of MELANIN pigment in structures that are normally colored. In humans the syndrome of albinism comprises: (a) pinkish skin in which the pigment-containing cells (MELANOPHORES) are present but contain little or no melanin. The pinkish coloration comes from the underlying blood vessels. (b) eyes with a deep red pupil and pink iris, both due to lack of normal pigmentation and heavy vascularization. (c) *photophobia* (fear of light) brought on by excess light entering the eye and reflecting onto the retina. Albinos usually wear dark glasses. (d) pale yellow hair.

Albinism is an INBORN ERROR OF METABOLISM produced by a blockage in tyrosine metabolism due to absence of a functional tyrosinase enzyme. The condition is controlled by a single RECESSIVE GENE on an AUTOSOME. Approximately 1 in 20,000 of the population are albinos. See Fig. 20.

albumen or **egg white** a solution of protein in water that is secreted by the oviduct of birds and some reptiles. Albumen surrounds the embryo and yolk, which it cushions within the shell of the egg. It is eventually absorbed by the embryo as food.

Fig. 20. **Albinism.** Blockage in tyrosine metabolism.

alcohol an organic molecule in which a hydrogen atom of a hydrocarbon is replaced by a hydroxyl group (OH). See Fig. 21.

Fig. 21. **Alcohol.** Molecular structure of an alcohol.

alcoholic fermentation a type of CELLULAR RESPIRATION found in plants and some unicells that does not require oxygen, resulting in the production of ethanol (an alcohol) from GLUCOSE and the release of small amounts of energy. The main details are described under ANAEROBIC RESPIRATION, but it can be said here that fermentation involves GLYCOLYSIS to produce PYRUVIC ACID and then, in the absence of oxygen, the breakdown of pyruvic acid to ethanol via ethanal with the release of CO_2. See Figs. 22 and 34.

$$C_6H_{12}O_6 \longrightarrow 2CH_3CH_2OH + 2CO_2 + 168kJ \text{ energy}$$

Glucose   Ethanol

Fig. 22. **Alcoholic fermentation.** The production of ethanol from glucose.

Alcyonaria a division of the Anthozoa containing the soft corals, for example, sea pens, sea pansies, deadmen's fingers, and precious coral.

aldehyde group any organic compound containing the group CHO, a carbonyl group fixed to one hydrogen and one oxygen atom.

aldose a sugar having an aldehyde group attached to the first carbon atom, for example, D-glyceraldehyde.

aldosterone a hormone of the cortex of the ADRENAL GLAND. It is responsible for the relative concentration of sodium and potassium ions in the body. It promotes reabsorption of sodium ions from the ascending limb of the LOOP OF HENLE in the kidney, with elimination of potassium ions, and increases uptake of sodium ions by the alimentary canal. The concentration of sodium ions in the blood thus rises and potassium ions decrease, enabling ionic regulation of body fluids (see SODIUM PUMP).

aleurone layer a layer of cells just below the TESTA of some seeds, for example, barley. Aleurone releases large quantities of hydrolytic enzymes (AMYLASES, PROTEASES, and NUCLEASES) for digestion of the ENDOSPERM. Thus, food material is made available in soluble form for embryo growth. Enzyme release is brought on by the plant hormone GIBBERELLIN, which is released by the embryo when the seed is soaked in water prior to germination.

aleuroplast a colorless PLASTID that stores protein, found in many seeds.

algae a collective term for several taxonomic groups of plants, namely, Charophyta, Chlorophyta, Chrysophyta, Cyanophyta, Euglenophyta, Phaeophyta, Pyrrophyta, and Rhodophyta. All are relatively simple photosynthetic forms with unicellular reproductive structures. They range from UNICELLULAR organisms to nonvascular filamentous or thalloid plants. Algae occur in both sea water and fresh water, whereas others are terrestrial, living in damp situations on walls, trees, and the like.

algal bloom an extensive growth of algae in a body of water, usually as a result of the phosphate content of fertilizers and detergents.

alien an organism, usually a plant, that is not native to the environment in which it occurs and is thought to have been introduced by people.

alimentary canal or **gut** or **enteric canal** or **enteron** or **gastrointestinal tract** the tubular passage that extends from MOUTH to ANUS. It has several distinct functions:

(a) ingestion of food via the mouth, utilizing teeth and tongue.

(b) DIGESTION of food beginning in the mouth and continuing in the STOMACH and SMALL INTESTINE.

(c) ABSORPTION of nutrients in soluble form, occurring mainly in the small intestine, with water being taken in via the large INTESTINE.

(d) elimination of fecal material via the anus, the fecal material containing a mixture of undigested food and excreted material, for example, BILE SALTS.

See DIGESTIVE SYSTEM.

aliquot a measured portion of the whole; a sample of known size taken from a preparation.

alisphenoid the bone forming in the middle region of the cranium of mammals.

alkali a soluble BASE or a solution of a base.

alkaline having the properties of or containing an ALKALI.

alkaline tide a period when the alkalinity of the body and urinary system is affected by excessive secretion of digestive hydrochloric acid.

alkalinity 1. the quality or state of being alkaline. **2.** the amount of alkali or base in a solution, often expressed in terms of pH.

alkaloids basic organic compounds containing nitrogen that are found in some families of plants, for example, Papaveraceae. Alkaloids have poisonous and medicinal properties. Examples include nicotine, quinine, morphine, and cocaine.

alkalosis the state in which there is excessive body alkalinity.

alkaptonuria see GARROD, A.E.

allantoic chorion the fusion of the ALLANTOIS with the mesoderm of the CHORION, which in eutherian mammals develops into the PLACENTA. See AMNION (Fig. 30) for diagram.

allantoin the heterocyclic end product of purine catabolism in some reptiles and in mammals other than primates.

allantois a membranous growth from the central side of the hind gut of the developing vertebrate embryo that extends outside the embryo proper and is covered by a layer of connective tissue containing many blood vessels. In birds and reptiles, the allantois acts as a respiratory surface with the allantoic cavity (see Fig. 30) being used for storage of excretory materials. In placental mammals, the allantoic blood vessels carry blood to and from the PLACENTA for respiration, nutrition, and excretion. In all groups most of the allantois is detached at birth.

allele a particular form of GENE. Alleles usually occur in pairs, one on each HOMOLOGOUS CHROMOSOME in a DIPLOID cell nucleus. When both alleles are the same, the individual is described as being a HOMOZYGOTE. When the alleles are different, the individual is a HETEROZYGOTE.

The number of allelic forms of a gene can be many (MULTIPLE ALLELISM), each form having a slightly different sequence of DNA bases but with the same overall structure. Each diploid, however, can carry only two alleles at one time. See also DOMINANCE(1).

allele frequency or **gene frequency** the proportion of a particular ALLELE of a gene in a population relative to other alleles of the same gene. For example, if a gene has two alleles, A and a, and the frequency of A is 0.6, then the frequency of a will be $1.0 - 0.6 = 0.4$. The allele frequency can be calculated from the GENOTYPE FREQUENCY. See Fig. 23.

allelopathic substance a secretion or excretion of an organism that has an inhibitory effect on others.

Allen's rule a rule stating that in warm-blooded animals (HOMOIOTHERMS) there tends to be a reduction in size of protruberant parts of the body, such as legs, bill, or tail, in cooler climates. One example is

genotypes:	AA	Aa	aa
frequency:	0.25	0.40	0.35

frequency of A allele = 0.25 + 0.40/2 = 0.45
frequency of a allele = 0.35 + 0.40/2 = 0.55
                        1.00

Fig. 23. **Allele frequency.** Calculation of allele frequency from genotype frequency.

shortened bill length within some species of birds, such as the redshank. This size reduction is an extension of BERGMANN'S RULE and is also a mechanism to reduce heat loss. The rule was devised by J.A. Allen in 1877.

allergen an antigen that produces an allergic response.

allergy the overreaction of the IMMUNE RESPONSE of the body to minute traces of foreign substances (antigens). The reaction is usually visible in the form of rashes, itching, breathing difficulties, and the like. Many of these symptoms can be attributed to specific antigens. For example, in hay fever, ANTIBODIES react against pollen (antigen) and cause local damage with the release of HISTAMINE. *Antihistamine* drugs are one means of counteracting the effects of histamine.

allochronic species species that do not occur together in terms of time, that is, species that occur in different geological times.

allochthonous (of peat) not made in situ, for example, peat deposited from plants grown elsewhere. Compare AUTOCHTHONOUS.

allogamy see CROSS-FERTILIZATION.

allogenic (of vegetational SUCCESSION) affected by outside factors.

allograft a transplant from one individual to another individual of the same species but having a different genotype. The transplant is therefore subject to rejection by the recipient because it contains foreign antigens. Also called *homograft*. See HISTOCOMPATIBILITY.

allometric growth 1. unequal growth rate in different portions of the body of an organism that gives rise to the final shape. **2.** growth of a particular structure at a constantly greater rate than the whole.

allopatric (of a population) being geographically separate, or nearly so, from another population of the same species. Compare SYMPATRIC.

allopatric speciation the genetic differentiation of populations that are geographically separate to the point where they become separate SPECIES.

allopolyploid a type of POLYPLOID in which the number of chromosomes is doubled in a hybrid between two species. The resulting *allotetraploid* or *amphidiploid* is fertile, since HOMOLOGOUS CHROMOSOMES of both types can now pair at MEIOSIS to produce viable GAMETES (see Fig. 24).

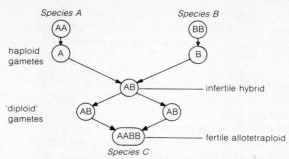

Fig. 24. **Allopolyploid.** The creation of a fertile allotetraploid.

Such a process has been important in the production of new species, particularly in plants. For example, the successful marshland grass *Spartina anglica* is a fertile allotetraploid developed from an infertile hybrid (*S. townsendii*) produced originally by a cross between *S. alterniflora* and *S. maritima*. Compare AUTOPOLYPLOID.

all-or-none law a law stating that certain tissues respond in a similar way to stimuli no matter how strong or weak the stimuli are, that is, they either react by giving a response (all), or do not react and give no response (none). Nerve fibers normally act in this way.

allosteric enzyme a type of enzyme that has two alternative forms: one active with a functional BINDING SITE, the other inactive where the binding site has been altered in shape so as to become nonreactive. Such enzymes have a QUATERNARY PROTEIN STRUCTURE, which becomes changed by addition of a modulator molecule producing the inactive shape, and the process results in NONCOMPETITIVE INHIBITION. See Fig. 25.

Fig. 25. **Allosteric enzyme.** Active (a) and inactive (b) forms.

allosteric inhibitors substances that prevent an enzyme from changing into an active form by combining not with the ACTIVE SITE but with some other part of the enzyme.

allotetraploid a form of polyploidy. See ALLOPOLYPLOID.

allotype one of a range of ANTIBODIES containing different sequences of amino acids but all having an area with an identical amino acid sequence, and thought to be produced by different alleles of the same gene (see MULTIPLE ALLELISM).

allozyme a form of protein coded by a particular ALLELE at a single gene LOCUS that is detectable by ELECTROPHORESIS.

alluvial soil a young soil derived from river, estuarine, or marine deposits and having a high fertility.

alpha helix a twisted polypeptide chain that forms a helical structure in many proteins, with 3.6 amino-acid residues per turn of the helix. Successive turns of the helix are linked by weak hydrogen bonds, and the structure is much more stable than an untwisted polypeptide chain. Long-chain alpha-helix construction is characteristic of structural fibrous proteins, found in hair, claws, fingernails, feathers, wool, and horn. Proteins that are intracellular are usually of the globular type with short segments of alpha helixes.

alpha particle a type of subatomic particle found in the atomic nucleus.

alpha taxonomy the level of TAXONOMY concerned with characterizing and naming a species. See also BETA TAXONOMY.

alternate arrangement (in plants) structures arranged in two rows, but not opposite. The structures may include a spiral arrangement.

alternate disjunction see TRANSLOCATION HETEROZYGOTE.

alternation of generations the occurrence within the life cycle of an organism of a sexually reproducing generation followed by an asexual generation. In some COELENTERATES, such as *Obelia,* the sexual organs are carried on MEDUSAS, and subsequent fertilization gives rise to an asexually producing HYDROID stage; here both generations are DIPLOID. See Fig. 26a.

Among the plants, ferns have a diploid SPOROPHYTE generation, the plant itself. This undergoes MEIOSIS to form spores that give rise to a HAPLOID GAMETOPHYTE generation known as a PROTHALLUS, which reproduces sexually. Male and female GAMETES fuse to form a ZYGOTE, which then develops into a new fern plant, the sporophyte. See Fig. 26b.

Some definitions of alternation of generations require a haploid generation alternating with a diploid generation, thus excluding all animal examples.

altruistic behavior behavior involving unselfish regard for others. In organisms other than humans, altruism probably exists only where the benefits to the individual performing the behavior are greater than those to the individual to whom the particular behavior is directed, that is, *phenotypic altruism.* For example, parental care of the young is

Fig. 26. **Alternation of generations.** (a) Life cycle of *Obelia* (Coelenterata). (b) Life cycle of fern (Pteridophyta). n, haploid number of chromosomes.

clearly of genetic benefit to the individual parent, since it ensures that its genes are transmitted. See also KIN SELECTION.

alveolus (*pl.* alveoli) 1. a small air-filled sac that occurs in large numbers in the LUNGS of vertebrates and whose function is to increase surface area for gaseous exchange (see AERIAL RESPIRATION). 2. groups of secretory cells found at the internal ends of ducts of mammary and other glands. 3. an inflated area of the follicle that surrounds the depressions from which cilia (see CILIUM) arise in some ciliates, for example, *Paramecium.* 4. a tooth cavity in the jaw bone.

amber codon a TERMINATION CODON of messenger RNA (UAG), the first stop signal discovered in the GENETIC CODE.

ambergris a substance, used in the manufacture of perfume, found in the alimentary canal of sperm whales in the form of a gray waxy secretion.

ambient surrounding, prevailing. The term is used most often in connection with temperature levels during experiments.

ambulacrum one of the five radial bands on which tube feet occur on the outside surfaces of ECHINODERMS.

ameba see AMOEBA.

amebic dysentery a form of intestinal infection marked by severe diarrhea and sometimes by bleeding. It is caused by the parasitic ameba *Entamoeba histolytica.* The disease is transmitted by cysts present in feces that are swallowed by a new host.

amebocyte a type of cell found in the blood and other body fluids of invertebrates that is capable of AMOEBOID MOVEMENT within the fluid and often acts as a PHAGOCYTE.

ameboid moving and feeding in the manner of *Amoeba,* by the action of PSEUDOPODIA.

ameboid movement movement by means of PSEUDOPODIA, being a projection of the surface of a cell caused by alternate formation of SOL and GEL protoplasm in the region of the temporarily formed false foot. See AMOEBA.

Ames test a technique devised in the USA by Bruce Ames and an associate, which is designed to screen environmental chemicals for mutagenicity. The test uses histidine-requiring mutant strains of *Salmonella typhimurium* and measures the frequency of BACK MUTATIONS that no longer require histidine supplements in their food supply. The Ames test has been employed widely since 1975 as a check for potential CARCINOGENS, since these chemicals usually act as MUTAGENS.

Ametabola see APTERYGOTA.

amine an organic base formed by replacing one or more of the hydrogen atoms of ammonia by organic groups.

amino acid a building block of protein, containing a carboxyl group (COOH) and an amino group (NH_2), both attached to the same carbon atom. Over 80 amino acids are known to occur naturally, with 20 found commonly in proteins (see Fig. 27), each with a different side chain, called an R group (see Fig. 28). Each of these common amino acids is described under its own heading.

Ala = Alanine	Leu = Leucine
Arg = Arginine·	Lys = Lysine
Asn = Asparagine	Met = Methionine
Asp = Aspartic acid	Phe = Phenylalanine
Cys = Cysteine	Pro = Proline
Gln = Glutamine	Ser = Serine
Glu = Glutamic acid	Thr = Threonine
Gly = Glycine	Trp = Tryptophan
His = Histidine	Tyr = Tyrosine
Ileu = Isoleucine	Val = Valine

Fig. 27. **Amino acid.** The 20 amino acids commonly found in protein.

Many amino acids can be synthesized in the body from other amino acids by a process called TRANSAMINATION, although most organisms have a number of ESSENTIAL AMINO ACIDS that must be taken in with the diet. Each amino acid is coded by at least one triplet of DNA bases (see GENETIC CODE), and the string of amino acids making up a protein is joined by PEPTIDE BONDS to form a POLYPEPTIDE CHAIN. Amino acids are soluble in water but vary considerably in degree of solubility. When

Fig. 28. **Amino acid.** Structure of a generalized amino acid.

in solution, they are ionized (see ZWITTERION) and generally are electrically neutral with a pH known as the ISOELECTRIC POINT. They are amphoteric, that is, they act as acids or bases when the pH is shifted.

amino-acid sequence the order in which AMINO ACIDS are placed along a protein molecule. Secondary and tertiary protein structure is highly dependent on amino-acid sequence in the POLYPEPTIDE CHAIN, which affects the bonding together of the molecule. The blueprint for this sequence is contained in DNA, whose bases contain the amino acid code. Three bases provide the code for each amino acid. By TRANSCRIPTION and TRANSLATION, the DNA-base sequence is mirrored in the amino-acid sequence, there being COLINEARITY between DNA and protein. See Fig. 160 (FRAMESHIFT) for diagram.

aminoacyl-tRNA the molecule produced when an AMINO ACID is activated into its aminoacyl form and attached to its specific TRANSFER RNA molecule, the whole process being catalyzed by a specific aminoacyl-tRNA synthetase enzyme.

aminopeptidase an enzyme that catalyzes the sequential hydrolysis of amino acids in a polypeptide chain from the N-terminal.

amino sugar a MONOSACCHARIDE in which an amino group has replaced a hydroxyl group on one or more occasions.

amitosis nuclear division in a cell that occurs without formation of a SPINDLE or appearance of chromosomes, and from which daughter nuclei with identical chromosome sets are probably not produced. Amitosis occurs, for example, in the protozoan *Paramecium* when the MACRONUCLEUS divides.

ammocete the larva of a lamprey. It feeds by ciliary action similar to the way AMPHIOXUS feeds.

ammonia a colorless gas, the main form in which nitrogen is utilized in living cells. Formula: NH_3.

ammonite a name given to a large group of fossil cephalopod mollusks of late Paleozoic and Mesozoic time that had a spiral shell similar to that of *Nautilus*.

amniocentesis a technique for diagnosing congenital abnormalities before birth. In this procedure a sample of 10—15 cm^3 of amniotic fluid surrounding the fetus is extracted through the abdominal wall, using a surgical syringe usually at about the 16th week of pregnancy. The sloughed-off embryonic cells contained in the fluid can be cultured to enable KARYOTYPE analysis, which shows the number and condition of the chromosomes. The fluid can also be analyzed for the presence of chemicals that indicate biochemical and other defects, for example, spina bifida. See Fig. 29.

Fig. 29. **Amniocentesis.** Sampling amniotic fluid by means of a surgical syringe.

amnion an embryonic, fluid-filled sac occurring in reptiles, birds, and mammals (AMNIOTES). Formed of ECTODERM and MESODERM and containing a coelomic space (see COELOM), the amnion grows around the embryo and eventually roofs over and completely encloses it. It provides a fluid-filled space necessary for development of embryos of land animals, and it also acts as a protective cushion. See Fig. 30.

Fig. 30. **Amnion.** A vertebrate embryo lying within the amnion.

amniote any land vertebrate possessing an AMNION, CHORION, and ALLANTOIS, that is, reptiles, birds, and mammals.

amniotic cavity the space within the AMNION.

Amoeba a genus of unicellular PROTOZOANS in the class Rhizopoda.

Amoebae are characterized by their changing shape brought about by projection of PSEUDOPODIA, which have a locomotory function. *Amoeba* is often wrongly cited as an example of a primitive organism, low on the evolutionary scale. However, as in many PROTISTA, functions that are carried out by organ systems in so-called higher forms are here carried out within a single cell, so they cannot be considered primitive. They are highly evolved over millions of years, albeit on a different scale from higher organisms. See Fig. 31.

Fig. 31. **Amoeba.** General structure.

amorph allele an ALLELE of a gene that appears to code for no detectable product. It can be produced by a DELETION mutation.

AMP (adenosine monophosphate) a molecule consisting of an ADENOSINE unit onto which is attached a phosphate group with a low-level energy bond (see Fig. 32). The molecule is important because it functions as the basic structure for ADP and ATP, both of which contain HIGH-ENERGY BONDS (34 kJ/mole) that serve as a short-term energy store for the cell. See ATP (Fig. 55) for molecular structure.

9.2kJ/mole

Fig. 32. **AMP.** The low-level energy bond of AMP.

amphetamine a drug that stimulates the CENTRAL NERVOUS SYSTEM and inhibits sleep. Its structure is: 1-phenyl-2-aminopropane.

amphi- *prefix* denoting both kinds, around.

amphibian a member of the vertebrate class Amphibia, containing frogs, toads, newts, salamanders, and the burrowing caecilians. Descended from fish-like animals, they colonized the land in the late DEVONIAN PERIOD. They are thought to be the immediate ancestors of the reptiles, though present-day amphibians are little like their Devonian ancestors. Most amphibians, although normally terrestrial animals, return to water during the breeding season. Fertilization is external—the eggs lack a shell and embryonic membranes—and the eggs are usually laid and develop in water.

amphicribral bundle a VASCULAR BUNDLE in which the PHLOEM surrounds the XYLEM, as in some ferns.

amphidiploid see ALLOPOLYPLOID.

amphimixis true sexual reproduction, as opposed to APOMIXIS.

Amphineura a primitive group of mollusks thought to be like the ancestral form. Present-day forms are similar to Ordovician fossils.

Amphioxus the disused scientific, although better-known, name for *Branchiostoma* (the lancet), a PROTOCHORDATE found in many parts of the world. Its embryonic development has been extensively studied and is used in texts as an example of a link between invertebrates and vertebrates. It feeds by ciliary action, trapping food particles in mucus.

amphiploid a POLYPLOID that is generally fertile, formed by the doubling of chromosomes in a species hybrid, for example, *Primula kewensis* (2n = 36) is an amphiploid of *P. floribunda* (2n = 18).

Amphipoda an order of crustaceans that includes shrimps and beach fleas.

amphivasal bundle a VASCULAR BUNDLE in which the XYLEM surrounds the PHLOEM, as in some monocotyledons.

amphistylic a type of jaw suspension in which the upper jaw is attached by two points to the neurocranium, as in some cartilaginous fish.

amphoteric (of chemicals) capable of acting either as bases or acids. Amino acids and some metal oxides, such as zinc, are amphoteric.

amplexicaul (of plants) clasping the stem. For example, the bracts of the henbit, *Lamium amplexicaule,* are amplexicaul.

amplification, genetic the synthesis of many copies of DNA from one master region, a mechanism that ensures rapid production of large quantities of protein when required.

ampulla any small vesicle or sac-like offshoot, particularly the dilation at the end of the semicircular canal of the EAR, which houses sensory epithelium. Other examples include the internal expansion of the echinoderm tube foot, and the pit housing the medusoid stage in the calcareous skeleton of *Hydrocorallina.*

amylase a digestive enzyme that enables the splitting of starch into smaller subunits of MALTOSE, usually in alkaline conditions (see Fig. 33).

   Amylases are found in the saliva of most mammals and were previously called *ptyalin*, but their functioning is limited to the brief time that food remains in the mouth. Once food is swallowed, the acid stomach conditions prevent further amylase activity. The principal location of starch digestion is in the duodenum, where *pancreatic amylase* is

Fig. 33. **Amylase.** The splitting of starch to form maltose.

poured into the gut lumen from the pancreas as part of the pancreatic juice. Pancreatic amylase has a greater digestive efficiency than salivary amylase. Amylases are common in plants, particularly in association with the starch stores of seeds and underground perennating organs such as rhizomes, tubers, and taproots.

amylopectin a carbohydrate polymer of high molecular weight, composed of branched chains of GLUCOSE units.

amyloplast a type of cell inclusion found in many plant tissues, particularly storage organs such as the potato tuber. Amyloplasts contain starch enclosed in a UNIT MEMBRANE, the whole structure being a type of LEUKOPLAST. Besides serving as a storage place for starch, amyloplasts are thought by some scientists to function also as a gravity-seeking device, helping roots push through soil in the correct direction (see GEOTROPISM).

amylose a form of starch composed of unbranched chains of GLUCOSE units.

an- or **a-** *prefix* denoting not, without.

ana- or **an-** *prefix* denoting 1. up, upward. 2. again. 3. back, backward.

anabolism or **synthesis** a type of metabolism in which complex chemicals are synthesized from simpler building blocks, a process that is endergonic, that is, it requires energy.

The classic example of an anabolic process is PHOTOSYNTHESIS, in which solar energy is incorporated into complex compounds such as glucose and its derivatives. Animals also carry out many anabolic reactions, building up complex molecules such as proteins from simpler subunits, the amino acids obtained from heterotrophic nutrition (see HETEROTROPH).

anadromous (of fishes, such as the salmon) migrating up rivers to spawn in the shallow waters near the source. Compare CATADROMOUS.

anaerobe an organism able to metabolize in the absence of free oxygen, obtaining energy from the breakdown of glucose in ANAEROBIC RESPIRATION. Some anaerobes are *obligate,* that is, they cannot survive in oxygen, for example, the bacteria causing food poisoning (see BOTULISM). Others, the majority, can live either in the presence or absence of oxygen and are called *facultative.* When oxygen is present, respiration in these types is of the aerobic type, involving the KREBS CYCLE to release maximum energy. When oxygen is absent, they rely solely on energy released in anaerobic respiration.

anaerobic respiration a type of cell respiration that takes place in ANAEROBES, and in which energy is released from glucose and other foods without the presence of oxygen. The reactions fall into two stages:

Stage 1: GLYCOLYSIS, in which glucose is converted to two molecules of pyruvic acid (pyruvate) in the general cell cytoplasm. The same reactions occur as in AEROBIC RESPIRATION, but in anaerobes the absence of oxygen prevents the two produced molecules of reduced NAD from being oxidized via the ELECTRON TRANSPORT SYSTEM (ETS) in the MITOCHONDRIA. Instead, ATP is produced from ADP by SUBSTRATE-LEVEL PHOSPHORYLATION. Thus, the net output of ATP in anaerobic respiration is two molecules (4 minus 2 used in the initial phosphorylation).

Stage 2: once pyruvate has been produced, two alternative pathways can occur. In plants and many microorganisms the pyruvate is broken down to ethanol via ethanal (acetaldehyde) in a process called ALCOHOLIC FERMENTATION, which requires hydrogen from NADH (see Fig. 34). In animals the pyruvate is changed via a single step into LACTIC ACID, in a process called lactic-acid fermentation, which again requires hydrogen from NADH.

Fig. 34. **Anaerobic respiration.** Breakdown of pyruvic acid to ethanol.

The role of NADH in both fermentations should be noted. Since the amount of NAD present in the cell is limited, glycolysis would quickly come to a halt if anaerobic respiration stopped at pyruvate. By going on to ethanol or lactic acid, NAD is freed in the fermentations to return to glycolysis and thus enable glucose CATABOLISM to continue. The yield of ATP in anaerobic respiration is poor: first, because the ETS cannot be used without oxygen, and, second, because the end products still contain large amounts of energy. As a result, the free energy released and stored is only a fraction of the amount in the complete oxidation of glucose, as shown in Fig. 35.

	Anaerobic respiration		Aerobic respiration
	alcoholic fermentation	lactic acid fermentation	
Free energy available from reactions (kJ/mole)	168	198	2874
Number of ATP molecules synthesized	2	2	38
Total energy stored in ATP (kJ)	2 × 34 = 68	2 × 34 = 68	38 × 34 = 1292
Efficiency of storage	40%	34%	45%
$\frac{\text{Energy stored}}{\text{Total in glucose}} \times 100$	2.4%	2.4%	45%

Fig. 35. **Anaerobic respiration.** Energy release in anaerobic and aerobic respiration.

anagenesis progressive EVOLUTION.

anal pertaining to the anus.

analgesic a substance reducing pain without causing unconsciousness.

analogous structure a structure having the same function as another but different origins, for example, the eye of man and the eye of the octopus. Analogy between structures does not imply evolutionary relationships but may imply CONVERGENCE.

anamniote a vertebrate whose embryo lacks an AMNION.

anandrous (of flowers) lacking stamens.

anaphase a stage of nuclear division in eukaryotic cells (see EUKARYOTE), occurring once in MITOSIS and twice in MEIOSIS. The main process involved is the separation of chromosomal material to give two groups of chromosomes that eventually will become new cell nuclei. This important step is controlled by SPINDLE MICROTUBULES, or fibers, which run from the organizing center at each pole to every chromosome, the point of attachment being the kinetochore of the CENTROMERE (see METAPHASE). Various theories for chromosomal movement have been put forward, including: (a) active repulsion of chromosomes; (b) the idea that when sliding past each other the microtubules may act as tiny muscles, the sliding filament theory; and (c) a suggestion that the microtubules are disassembled at the poles, thus reeling in the attached chromosomes.

anaphylaxis a hypersensitive reaction that can occur after a second exposure to an ANTIGEN. Such anaphylactic shock responses are varied, ranging from reddening and itching of the skin all the way to respiratory failure and death.

anapsid a member of the Anapsida, a group of reptiles in which the skull lacks a temporal FOSSA. The Anapsida include *Seymouria,* tortoises and turtles.

anastomose joining to form loops; interconnecting, as in capillary blood vessels.

anatomy the science of the structure of living organisms.

anatropous (of flowering plants) having the OVULE inverted so that the MICROPYLE points toward the PLACENTA.

andro- *combining form* denoting male.

androdioecious having male and hermaphrodite flowers on separate plants. Compare ANDROMONOECIOUS.

androecium the male parts of an ANGIOSPERM flower composed of two or more stamens, which are concerned with reproduction and so are called *essential* organs.

androgen one of several types of male hormone that stimulate development and maintenance of the male's SECONDARY SEXUAL CHARACTERISTICS. Naturally occurring androgens, for example, TESTOSTERONE, are STEROIDS produced mainly in the testis (see INTERSTITIAL CELLS), but also to a small extent in the OVARY and ADRENAL CORTEX.

andromonoecious having male and hermaphrodite flowers on the same plant. Compare ANDRODIOECIOUS.

anemia a deficiency in the number of red blood cells, their volume, or the hemoglobin content.

anemophily the transfer of pollen from male to female plant organs by means of the wind. The process usually involves cross-pollination between different plants, rather than self-pollination (see POLLINATION). Wind pollination is wasteful of male gametes and fairly rare in ANGIOSPERMS—most have evolved other, more efficient methods in partnership with insects—but common in GYMNOSPERMS. Well-known anemophilous plants include the grasses, a group containing cereals, such as corn, wheat, and barley, and the stinging nettles, docks, plantains, and many types of pine.

Various features of anemophily can be recognized in angiosperms: flowers small and inconspicuous, often green with reduced petals; flowers with no nectar or perfume; stamens often long and pendulous (for example, hazel catkins) or projecting up above the herbaceous plant (for example, plantain and docks) to ensure efficient pollen dispersal; flowers frequently appear early in spring before leaves can interfere with pollination; stigmata are often branched and feathery to catch the airborne pollen. Compare ENTOMOPHILY.

aneuploidy a condition in which more or less than a complete set of chromosomes is found in each cell of an individual. Compare EUPLOIDY. Typically, aneuploids have one extra or one missing chromosome. For example, in DOWN SYNDROME, affected individuals have three number-21 chromosomes rather than the normal two, a condition known as TRISOMY. See CHROMOSOMAL MUTATION.

aneurysm dilation of an artery wall, a sac formed by abnormal dilation of the weakened wall of a blood vessel.

angiosperm any member of the class Angiospermae, in which the seeds are enclosed in an ovary. The class contains the most advanced vascular plants. Each member of the class is either a MONOCOTYLEDON, for example, grasses and tulips, or a DICOTYLEDON, for example, apple and primrose. See PLANT KINGDOM for a more complete classification.

angiotensin a substance produced by the action of RENIN on a GLOBULIN protein molecule found in blood plasma and then stimulates the cortex of the ADRENAL GLAND to release ALDOSTERONE, causing general constriction of smooth muscle.

angular bone in bony fish, reptiles, and birds, a membrane bone of the lower jaw; in mammals it has become separated to form the TYMPANIC BONE.

angustiseptate (of a fruit) having the septum crossing the diameter at its narrowest point.

animal kingdom a category of living organisms comprising all animals. The classification of animals into major groups is now generally agreed on by most biologists, unlike the situation in the PLANT KINGDOM, where there are several alternative systems of classification. However, the Protozoa remain problematical, since in some modern classifications these organisms are placed with unicellular algae in the Protista, which is given the status of a kingdom. The system below places the Protozoa in the animal kingdom.

Subkingdom Protozoa—single-celled animals
Subkingdom Parazoa—sessile, aquatic, porous animals
    Phylum Porifera—sponges
Subkingdom Metazoa—
    Phylum Coelenterata—two-layered, sac-like animals possessing a MESOGLEA and stinging cells
        Class Hydrozoa—hydra, colonial hydroids, siphonophores
        Class Scyphozoa—jellyfish
        Class Anthozoa—corals

Phylum Platyhelminthes—flattened, worm-like animals
  Class Turbellaria—flatworms
  Class Trematoda—flukes
  Class Cestoda—tapeworms
Phylum Nematoda—roundworms
Phylum Nemertea—bootlace worms
Phylum Annelida—segmented worms
  Class Polychaeta—paddle worms
  Class Oligochaeta—earthworms
  Class Hirudinea—leeches
Phylum Mollusca—soft-bodied animals often possessing a shell
  Class Gasteropoda—snails
  Class Lamellibranchiata—bivalves
  Class Cephalopoda—squids and octopus
Phylum Arthropoda—jointed-limbed animals with an exoskeleton
  Class Crustacea—water fleas, barnacles, crabs, etc.
  Class Myriapoda—centipedes, millipedes
  Class Arachnida—mites, ticks, scorpions, spiders
  Class Insecta—insects
Phylum Echinodermata—spiny animals with a penta-radiate
symmetry
  Class Asteroidea—starfish
  Class Ophiuroidea—brittle stars
  Class Echinoidea—sea urchins
  Class Holothuroidea—sea cucumbers
  Class Crinoidia—feather stars and sea lilies
Phylum Chordata—animals possessing a notochord at some stage
during their development
Subphylum Protochordata—sea squirts, *Amphioxus*
Subphylum Vertebrata
  Class Agnatha—jawless fishes, for example, lamprey
  Class Chondrichythyes—sharks
  Class Choanichthyes—coelacanth, etc.
  Class Actinopterygii—bony fish
  Class Amphibia—salamanders, frogs, toads
  Class Reptilia—reptiles
  Class Aves—birds
  Class Mammalia—mammals

animal pole the point on the surface of an animal ovum nearest the
nucleus and normally at the opposite side of the egg to the aggregation
of yolk droplets at the VEGETAL POLE. See Fig. 36.

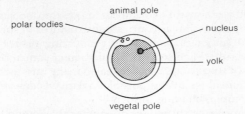

Fig. 36. **Animal pole.** The animal pole in a generalized ovum.

anion a negatively charged ion that is attracted to the ANODE during electrolysis.

aniso- *combining form* denoting unlike or unequal.

anisogamy the state in which the GAMETES are different from each other, that is, male and female. Usually the former is smaller and more active than the latter. Compare ISOGAMETE.

Anisoptera a suborder of the order Odonata containing the larger dragonflies in which the fore and hind wings are of different shapes and the nymphs possess a rectal gill.

ankylostomiasis a human disease in which the lining of the small intestine becomes heavily infested with adults of the hookworm *Ancylostoma,* causing a lethargic, anemic state.

annealing see MOLECULAR HYBRIDIZATION.

annelid a member of the animal phylum Annelida, a group containing the segmented worms, for example, earthworms, polychaete worms, and leeches. Annelids are characterized by the presence of METAMERIC SEGMENTATION, a COELOM, well-developed blood and nervous systems, and NEPHRIDIA.

annual plant any plant that germinates from seed, grows to maturity, and produces new seed all within one year or growing season. Since the life-cycle duration is so short, annuals are usually herbaceous rather than woody. Examples include groundsel and shepherd's purse. See BIENNIAL, PERENNIAL.

annual rhythm any activity or process that an organism experiences on a yearly basis, for example, courtship, migration, shedding of leaves.

annual rings a series of concentric circles found in the heartwood of trees, indicating the approximate age of the tree. Each ring is formed by the contrast in texture between spring wood and autumn wood. Spring wood in ANGIOSPERMS contains a high proportion of large, thin-walled XYLEM vessels and few fibers for maximum water transport when the leaves are newly formed. Autumn wood contains fewer, smaller, thicker-walled vessels with many fibers for greater mechanical support. GYMNOSPERMS show similar contrasting structures in spring wood and autumn wood, although their water-conducting tissues contain TRACHEIDS, not vessels. Microscopic examination of annual rings, a science called DENDROCHRONOLOGY, has revealed many interesting facts about past climates and also makes it possible to date wooden structures accurately, for example, building timbers.

annular (of plants) ring-shaped, as in annular thickening of XYLEM vessels.

annular thickening ring-shaped thickening in the internal wall of XYLEM cells or TRACHEIDS, providing mechanical strength but also allowing longitudinal stretching.

Annulata or **Annelida** the ringed or segmented worms. See ANNELID.

annulus 1. the ring of cells in the moss or fern capsule that splits and allows liberation of spores. 2. a ring of tissue surrounding the stalk in the fruiting bodies of BASIDIOMYCETE fungi.

anode a positively charged electrode to which negatively charged ions move. Compare CATHODE.

Anopleura see LOUSE.

anoxia lack of oxygen in tissues.

ant- or **anti-** *prefix* denoting opposed to, against.

ant any insect of the family Formicidae of the order Hymenoptera, characterized by a narrow abdominal construction. All ants are colonial, and each colony may contain several castes, groups of specialized individuals. The queen is the only egg-laying individual, fertilization taking place during a nuptial flight involving several colonies. The queen then sheds her wings and starts a colony in which workers are wingless. Social activities include tending and milking APHIDS. See Fig. 37.

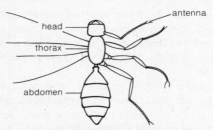

Fig. 37. **Ant.** Winged female ant.

antagonistic muscle any muscle that acts in opposition to another, for example, a contractor to a relaxer or vice versa. See Fig. 38.

Fig. 38. **Antagonistic muscle.** Antagonistic muscles in the arm, biceps, and triceps.

antagonism 1. the inhibiting or nullifying action of one substance or organism on another, for example, the antibiotic effect of penicillin, or the exhaustion of a food supply by one organism at the expense of another. **2.** the normal opposition between certain muscles (see ANTAGONISTIC MUSCLE).

ante- *prefix* denoting before in time or position; in front of.

anteater any of a group of ant-eating mammals that includes the spiny anteater, scaly anteater, Cape anteater (aardvark), and marsupial anteater.

antenna (*pl.* antennae) usually one of a pair of many-jointed, whip-like structures present on the head of many arthropods, particularly insects (first appendage on head) and crustaceans (second appendage). Antennae have a sensory function, though in some crustaceans they are used for attachment or swimming.

antennal gland an excretory organ occurring at the base of the antennae in some crustaceans.

antennule the foremost of two pairs of antennae that occurs in some crustaceans. Most antennae in other arthropods are homologous with the antennules of crustaceans.

anterior 1. (in animals) the part of the animal that proceeds first in forward movement, usually the head. **2.** (in plants) the part of the IN-FLORESCENCE farthest from the main stem. Compare POSTERIOR.

anterior root the VENTRAL ROOT of a nerve.

antesepalous (of plant parts) positioned opposite the insertion of the SEPALS.

antihelminthic (of a drug) removing parasitic worms when administered to the host.

anther the part of the STAMEN of a flower that produces the male GAMETES and is located at the end of a flexible stalk (the filament). Each anther usually has four pollen sacs in which POLLEN GRAINS (HAPLOID) develop by a process of MEIOSIS. The pollen-grain nucleus divides into generative and tube nuclei, representing a truncated version of the GAMETOPHYTE generation found more clearly in lower plants. See Fig. 39.

Fig. 39. **Anther.** Transverse sections of (a) young and (b) mature anthers.

See also EMBRYO SAC.

antheridium (*pl.* antheridia) the male sex organ of bryophytes, pteridophytes, algae, and fungi. See Fig. 40.

Fig. 40. **Antheridium.** Generalized structure, longitudinal section.

antherozoid or **spermatozoid** a mobile male GAMETE having flagella (see FLAGELLUM).

anthesis 1. the opening of a flower bud. 2. the period from flowering to fruit setting.

antho- *combining form* denoting flower.

Anthocerotae a class of the division BRYOPHYTA containing the hornworts.

anthocyanins a group of water-soluble pigments responsible for most reds, purples, and blues in plants, particularly in flowers but also in leaves, stems, and fruits.

anthozoan or **actinozoan** any of the sessile COELENTERATES of the class Anthozoa, including sea anemones, sea pens, and corals, which have no MEDUSOID stage (see MEDUSA) and possess a body cavity more complex than in other coelenterates.

anthrax a fever of the spleen in cattle and sheep caused by toxins released from the bacterium *Bacillus anthracis.* The disease can spread to humans when infected animal products such as wool and bristles are handled, giving rise to malignant skin lesions and pustules.

anthropo- *combining form* denoting man or human.

Anthropoidea a suborder of the primates that includes monkeys, anthropoid apes, and humans. The group is subdivided into Old-World forms (Catarrhini)—for example, baboons, chimpanzees, humans—and New-World forms (Platyrrhini)—for example, marmosets and howler monkeys. Old-World forms have parallel nostrils directed downward and two premolar teeth, and often have cheek pouches. New-World forms have nostrils diverging anteriorly, three premolar teeth, and no cheek pouches.

anthropomorphism the attribution of human characteristics to animals other than man.

anti- see ANT-.

antiauxin any chemical substance that prevents the action of AUXINS.

antibiotic any substance produced by a microorganism that even in low concentrations can inhibit or kill other microorganisms. For example, PENICILLIN produced by the fungus *Penicillium* prevents reproduction of many bacteria by preventing cell-wall synthesis.

Antibiotics are frequently the products of secondary metabolism in that, while not of major importance, their formation presumably offers a selective advantage to the organism. The amount of antibiotic produced per gram of producer can be greatly enhanced by optimal culturing conditions and strong selection pressure over many generations. Unfortunately, most antibiotics are not lethal to viruses. Furthermore, continued use of an antibiotic against a generally susceptible strain of bacteria will favor survival of the few resistant members of the bacterial population, resulting eventually in an antibiotic-resistant strain.

antibody a type of protein called an IMMUNOGLOBULIN that reacts with a specific ANTIGEN and serves as part of a vital body-defense mechanism. Various reactions can occur between antigen and antibody. If the antigen is a TOXIN, as in snake venom, or as produced by bacteria causing, for example, botulism and tetanus, neutralizing antibodies are called *antitoxins*. If the antigen adheres to the surface of a cell, antibodies called *agglutinins* cause clumping, or AGGLUTINATION of cells, while antibodies called *lysins* cause disintegration, or LYSIS, of the cell in conjunction with COMPLEMENT. Other antibodies, *opsonins*, facilitate uptake of antigens by PHAGOCYTES in the blood, while *precipitins* cause soluble antigens to precipitate.

Antibodies are produced in the lymphoid tissues of the body. For example, LYMPH NODES are produced by a type of LYMPHOCYTE called B-CELLS. Most antibodies are produced during exposure to an antigen, such a response being termed *active immunity*. Specific antibodies to rare or synthetic antigens can be manufactured as easily as those to common antigens. A few antibodies are produced even without the apparent presence of the appropriate antigen. Such natural antibodies include several involved in blood grouping, for example, A and B antibodies in the ABO BLOOD GROUP. Young mammals have limited capacity to produce antibodies in the first few weeks of life, but can obtain some *passive immunity* by receiving maternal antibodies via the mother's milk. This fact has been used to encourage human mothers to breast-feed their infants rather than bottle-feed. Most antibodies circulate in the blood and other body fluids, but most if not all body secretions also contain antibodies, mainly of the IgA type.

anticlinal (of plant cell division) along a plane at right angles to the outer surface.

anticoagulant a substance that hinders AGGLUTINATION, or clotting, of blood cells. BLOOD CLOTTING is a vital reaction to damage in the circulatory system, one of the steps in the process being dependent on the presence of calcium ions. However, the tendency of blood to clot can be overcome by suitable chemicals that remove calcium, such chemicals being used as anticoagulants when storage of blood is required. Many blood-sucking parasites such as mosquitoes secrete anticoagulants into the host's bloodstream, thus enabling easy transport of blood into the parasite's digestive system.

anticodon see TRANSFER RNA.

antidiuretic hormone see ADH.

antigen a substance, usually a protein or carbohydrate, that when introduced into the body induces an IMMUNE RESPONSE, including production of specific ANTIBODIES. Antigens can be toxins, as in snake venom, or molecules on cell surfaces, for example, A/B antigens on red blood cells.

antigibberellin any substance causing growth of short thick stems, that is, having an effect opposite to that of GIBBERELLINS. For example, maleic hydrazide is used to retard grass growth and thus reduce the frequency of cutting.

antihistamine see ALLERGY.

antilymphocytic serum a serum produced by injecting LYMPHOCYTES into a horse and collecting the antibodies produced. The serum is capable of destroying the original lymphocytes and allowing grafting of tissues to the animal so treated from another.

antimycin a poison that blocks the flow of electrons from cytochrome b to cytochrome c in the ELECTRON TRANSPORT SYSTEM (see Fig. 141).

antipodal cells the three haploid cells that remain at the nonmicropylar end of the EMBRYO SAC after division of the cells. Once the egg cell is formed, they play little or no further part in seed development.

antisepsis see ANTISEPTIC.

antiseptic literally, a substance that counteracts putrefaction; more usually, a substance that prevents infection in a wound. *Antisepsis* is carried out by disinfection or sterilization using nontoxic, noninjurious substances and has the effect of killing or inactivating microorganisms that cause infection.

antiserum see SERUM.

antisporulant a substance that reduces or prevents spore production by a fungus while enabling vegetative growth to continue.

antitoxin a type of ANTIBODY that neutralizes TOXINS.

anucleate without a nucleus or nuclei.

anuran any amphibian of the order Anura, such as the batrachians, including frogs and toads, which are characterized by large hind legs and lack of a tail.

anus the posterior opening of the ALIMENTARY CANAL, often surrounded by a ring of muscle called the anal SPHINCTER, which is under nervous control (see AUTONOMIC NERVOUS SYSTEM) and regulates the release of gut contents to the outside (DEFECATION).

anvil 1. the INCUS. 2. any stone used by a song thrush to break open land snails such as *Cepaea nemoralis*. Collecting shells at such a site can show which color forms of the snails are selected by the searching thrushes.

aorta the great artery of the mammalian BLOOD CIRCULATORY SYSTEM. It carries oxygenated blood from the left ventricle of the heart around the AORTIC ARCH and along the *dorsal aorta*, which runs the length of the trunk, giving rise to several branches to individual body organs. The ventral aorta is the main artery in fish and lower chordates, which carries blood from the heart to the gills.

aortic arch one of up to six paired arteries that join the ventral and dorsal aorta in vertebrates or their embryos. In fish the arches form the efferent and afferent branchial vessels, and in higher vertebrates the carotid, systemic, and pulmonary arches.

aortic body an area of nerve tissue in the wall of the AORTA, close to the heart, that is sensitive to small changes in blood CO_2 levels. Excess partial pressure of CO_2 triggers nerve impulses from the aortic body to cardiac/respiratory centers in the hindbrain via afferent nerve fibers (see BREATHING). A drop in CO_2 pressure causes inactivation of the aortic body—an example of a negative FEEDBACK MECHANISM.

ap- or **aph-** or **apo-** *prefix* denoting away from, apart.

ape any tailless primate of the family Simiidae, including gorillas, chimpanzees, orangutans, and gibbons.

apetalous (of plants) without petals.

aph- see AP-.

Aphaniptera or **Siphonaptera** the insect order containing the fleas,

APHETOHYOIDEA

whose members are laterally compressed, blood-sucking forms that lack wings but have well-developed hind legs modified for jumping.

Aphetohyoidea or **Placodermi** a group of fossil fish possessing a primitive jaw suspension (ligaments only) and a functional pair of first gill slits.

aphid any member of the family Aphididae, order Hemiptera. Commonly called *green fly*. Aphids feed on plant juices by using piercing and sucking mouthparts and are of considerable economic importance because they can act as vectors of plant viruses. See Fig. 41.

Fig. 41. **Aphid.** Winged female.

aphotic characterized by or growing in the absence of light.

aphotic zone the zone of an ocean or sea into which light does not penetrate and in which, therefore, photosynthesis cannot take place. It is usually below about 100 meters. See also SEA ZONATION.

aphyllous without leaves.

apical of, at, or being the apex.

apical dominance a condition in plants in which the stem apex prevents development of side shoots from lateral buds near the apex. The dominance is controlled by the presence of high concentrations of plant hormones (AUXINS) at the apex, produced by the *apical bud.* Farther down the stem, the auxin concentration is reduced and strong lateral branches are formed. Removal of the apical bud causes lateral branches to develop, for example, after pruning rose bushes.

apical growth growth resulting from an APICAL MERISTEM.

apical meristem a region of dividing tissue at the growing tips of roots and shoots that is responsible for increase in length of the plant body. MERISTEM cells are small, with thin walls and CYTOPLASM containing few vacuoles. They undergo active MITOSIS when growth is occurring, depending on the season, and the new cells look similar to the parental ones but become more vacuolated and elongated. Eventually, farther away from the meristem, the cells undergo CELL DIFFERENTIATION, taking on the appearance of mature plant cells.

Meristematic tissues are delicate and in need of protection. In shoots, the apices are covered by tiny leaves forming apical buds at the tips of the branches and axillary buds at the nodes where the leaves join the stem. Root structures are less complex, each root-tip meristem being protected by a shield of loose cells called a ROOT CAP. Compare CAMBIUM.

apical region a tip of a root or shoot in a plant where growth in length takes place by activity of the APICAL MERISTEM.

aplanospore an asexual, nonmotile spore found in some algae and some fungi.

apnea the absence or suspension of breathing, as occurs in diving mammals.

apo- see AP-.

apocarpous (of an ovary of a flowering plant) having the CARPELS free from each other. Compare SYNCARPOUS.

Apoda or **Gymnophiona** an order of worm-like, burrowing amphibians, caecilians, that lack limb girdles and limbs. They have small, functionless eyes and are found in Southeast Asia, India, Africa, and Central America.

apodeme an inward projection of the exoskeleton of arthropods, which serves as a site for muscle attachment.

apodous lacking legs.

apogamy a form of asexual reproduction found in ferns where the GAMETOPHYTE, which is diploid, gives rise directly to the SPOROPHYTE.

apomict any plant that is produced by APOMIXIS.

apomixis the development of an embryo in plants without FERTILIZATION or MEIOSIS. This method of pseudosexual reproduction is regularly used in plants such as garlic and the citruses. Similar processes occur in animals, where the term used is PARTHENOGENESIS. See also APOSPORY, APOGAMY, and AGAMOSPERMY.

apomorph a derived character.

apophysis a PROCESS of vertebrate bones to which muscles, tendons, or ligaments are attached.

apoplast 1. a PLASTID that lacks CHROMATOPHORES. The adjective *apoplastic* is applied to individual protozoans lacking color in a group that generally is colored. *Apoplasty* occurs when cell division is so fast as to outpace plastid division, producing individuals formed without plastids. **2.** the areas of the plant outside the SYMPLAST, comprising the parts outside the PLASMALEMMA, such as cell walls and the dead tissues of XYLEM.

aporepressor a regulatory protein that inhibits activity of specific genes when in the presence of a COREPRESSOR.

aposematic coloration see WARNING COLORATION.

aposematic selection a type of FREQUENCY-DEPENDENT SELECTION operating on a species that has several morphological forms, at least one of which is a mimic of a different model species that is distasteful. See MIMICRY.

apospory a situation occurring in some plants where MEIOSIS is omitted and an ordinary diploid SPOROPHYTE cell gives rise to the spore that produces a diploid GAMETOPHYTE.

apostatic selection a type of FREQUENCY-DEPENDENT SELECTION occurring in a species with several morphological forms, and classically used in relation to prey species that are visibly POLYMORPHIC. The amount of predation of each type is directly related to the relative MORPH frequencies.

apothecium the fruiting body of some ascomycete fungi (cup fungi) and lichens, containing asci (see ASCUS). Often lightly colored, they can reach up to 40 cm in diameter, but are usually only a few millimeters across.

appeasement display behavior designed to pacify or make peace following a display of aggressive behavior. For example, a defeated dog will turn on its back and present its underbelly to the victor, which then ceases combat.

appendage any projection from the body of an animal, for example, legs, mouthparts, antennae.

appendicularia or **tadpole larva** the larva of tunicates (ASCIDIACEA). It has a tail, NOTOCHORD, and tubular nerve cord and is indicative of the evolutionary relationships of the adults.

appendicular skeleton the part of the skeleton attached to the vertebral column, that is, the limbs or fins.

appendix or **vermiform appendix** a small fingerlike projection from the tip of the CECUM in the mammalian gut. See Fig. 42. In herbivores the cecum and appendix are important, containing bacteria that facilitate digestion of cellulose. In humans and other non-herbivores, the cecum and appendix have no function. The appendix can become infected and must be removed surgically (*appendectomy*) if in this condition.

Fig. 42. **Appendix.** Location of appendix.

apposition growth in cell-wall thickness brought about by successive deposition of layers of material.

apposition image the mosaic image formed in a compound eye (see EYE, COMPOUND).

appressed (of an organ) close to another but not united with it.

Apterygidae the kiwis, primitive flightless birds of New Zealand. They are nocturnal and the feathers are modified to appear hairlike.

Apterygota or **Ametabola** a subclass of primitive insects that have never evolved wings and that undergo little or no METAMORPHOSIS. There is little change in form from INSTAR to instar. The subclass includes silverfish (Thysanura), springtails (Collembola), and Protura. Compare PTERYGOTA.

aptosochromatosis the process of color change without molt in birds, for example, the greenshank, in which fully formed feathers change color without abrasion.

aquaculture the manipulation of the reproduction, growth rates, and mortality of aquatic organisms useful to man to enhance their yield; the aquatic equivalent of AGRICULTURE.

aquatic respiration a process in which freshwater and marine organisms carry out gas exchange with the water that surrounds them. Fully saturated water contains only about 0.02% as much oxygen per unit volume as air. However, since the tissues are in direct contact with the gas-carrying medium flowing past, the system is efficient and often a relatively small respiratory surface is required.

Many aquatic organisms, particularly the less advanced groups, have no special respiratory organs. They rely on a large surface area for gas exchange, for example, protozoa, algae, and nematodes. Others have developed specialized structures that are either external, for example, gills of the ragworm *Nereis*, or internal, for example, fish gills. GILLS are richly supplied with blood vessels for transport to and from the body tissues, and many organisms with gills expend much energy creating a regular flow of water over the respiratory surfaces.

aqueous habitat any habitat in which water is the medium in which the organisms live.

aqueous humor fluid that fills the space between the cornea and the lens of the vertebrate EYE (see Fig. 151).

arable farming the cultivation of land to produce crops, as compared with raising livestock.

arachnid or **arachnoid** any member of the class Arachnida in the phylum Arthropoda. The class contains scorpions, spiders, ticks, mites, and king crabs. They lack antennae, usually have four pairs of walking legs, and with the exception of *Limulus*, the king crab, are air-breathing.

arachnoid 1. the middle of the three membranes (see MENINGES) that cover the brain and spinal cord. **2.** see ARACHNID.

Araneida an order of the class Arachnida, containing the spiders.

arbovirus any virus that is ARTHROPOD-borne, for example, the yellow-fever virus carried by the mosquito *Aedes aegypti*.

arch- or **archaeo-** or **arche-** or **archi-** *combining form* denoting ancient.

Archaeopteryx the earliest known fossil bird, genus *Archaeopteryx*, found in the Jurassic period about 140 million years ago. The bird is characterized by the presence of teeth in the jaws, claws on the wing, and a tail containing vertebrae.

Archaeornithes the order of extinct reptilelike birds that contains ARCHAEOPTERYX, the only known genus.

arche- see ARCH-.

Archegoniatae a nonsystematic grouping of primitive plants, for example, BRYOPHYTA, in which the female reproductive organ is an ARCHEGONIUM.

archegonium (*pl.* archegonia) the female sex organ of BRYOPHYTA, PTERIDOPHYTES, and most GYMNOSPERMS. See Fig. 43.

Fig. 43. **Archegonium.** Mature archegonium of *Marchantia* (Hepaticae).

archenteron the part of the developing embryo of animals (BLASTULA) formed by an invagination of MESODERM and ENDODERM cells into the blastocoel that ultimately forms the gut. The archenteron opens to the exterior via the blastopore. See Fig. 44.

archesporium the cell or group of cells from which SPORES are derived.

archetype the hypothetical ancestral type from which other forms are thought to be derived. It usually lacks specialized characteristics.

archi- see ARCH-.

Archiannelida a class of annelid worms, possibly evolved from the same stock as the POLYCHAETE worms. All are marine and of simplified structure.

(Hepaticae).

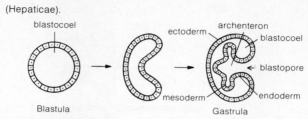

blastocoel
ectoderm
archenteron
blastocoel
blastopore
endoderm
mesoderm
Blastula
Gastrula

Fig. 44. **Archenteron.** Formation of the archenteron in an amphibian embryo.

Archichlamydeae a subclass of the ANGIOSPERMS in which the PERI-ANTH is incomplete or the parts of the COROLLA are entirely separate.

arcuate curved in the form of a bow to the extent of a quadrant of a circle or more.

areolar tissue connective tissue consisting of a gelatinous matrix that includes large fibroblasts. The fibroblasts synthesize COLLAGEN white fibers and yellow elastic fibers, ameboid MAST CELLS that secrete the matrix, fat-filled cells, and phagocytic MACROPHAGES. Areolar tissue occurs beneath skin and between adjacent tissues and organs. See Fig. 45.

elastic fiber
fat cell
macrophage
collagen fiber
mast cell

Fig. 45. **Areolar tissue.** Generalized structure.

arginine one of 20 AMINO ACIDS common in proteins. It has an extra basic group and is alkaline in solution. The ISOELECTRIC POINT of arginine is 10.8. See Fig. 46.

arginine phosphate see PHOSPHAGEN.

arista 1. a bristle at the base of the antenna in insects. In some types, for example, syrphids, it is larger than the rest of the antenna. 2. a bristle-like structure in the flowering GLUMES of grasses, an AWN.

aristate having an ARISTA (2).

Fig. 46. **Arginine.** Molecular structure.

Aristotle's lantern a five-sided, globular structure supporting the mouth and jaws of sea urchins.

arithmetic mean or **mean** a number (symbol: $\bar{x}$) that is computed by calculating the sum of a set of numbers (Σx) and dividing the sum by the number of terms (n). See Fig. 47.

$$
\begin{array}{r}
x\ values \\
13 \\
9 \\
12 \\
\underline{10} \\
\Sigma x = \quad 44 \\
\end{array}
$$

Fig. 47. **Arithmetic mean.** In this example, the mean of 4 values of x is 11.

Arnon, Daniel (1910—) American biochemist. With his coworkers in the 1950s, he first discovered electron passage from one electron acceptor to another in the ELECTRON TRANSPORT SYSTEM of PHOTOSYNTHESIS, particularly the role of ferredoxin.

arsenic a chemical element in the form of a gray metal, more familiar in the extremely poisonous form of arsenic trioxide. It was at one time used in arsenical soap for preservation of animal and bird skins in museums, so particular care should be taken in handling old museum skins.

Artenkreis a SUPERSPECIES.

arterial arch blood vessels that link the lateral dorsal AORTA with the ventral aorta. Six arches are present in vertebrate embryos and 4—6 remain to serve the gills in fish. In higher vertebrates 3, 4, and 6 remain as the carotid, systemic, and pulmonary arches.

arteriole any of the narrow, thin-walled arteries that carry oxygenated blood to tissues from the heart, forming part of the BLOOD CIRCULATORY SYSTEM. Arterioles get progressively smaller as they approach the target tissue, giving off side branches that become capillaries. Some arterioles connect up directly to VENULES via SHUNT VESSELS, particularly in tissues with a constant blood supply, such as the skin. See Fig. 48.

Fig. 48. **Arteriole.** Arterioles, capillaries, and venules.

arteriosclerosis a pathological condition or any of a group of diseases in which there is an increase in the thickness of the arterial walls, a reduction in elasticity of the vessel, and a constriction of diameter that affects the blood flow; the classic hardening of the arteries of the elderly.

artery any of the large vessels with thick, elasticated muscular walls that carry oxygenated blood to the tissues from the heart, or deoxygenated blood to the lungs from the heart, forming part of the BLOOD CIRCULATORY SYSTEM. See Fig. 49. Arteries become less massive as the vessels approach their target organs, eventually becoming reduced to ARTERIOLES. See VEIN.

Fig. 49. **Artery.** Transverse sections.

arthro- *combining form* denoting a joint.

arthropod any member of the animal phylum Arthropoda, containing jointed-limbed organisms that possess a hard EXOSKELETON. It is the largest phylum in terms of numbers of species and includes insects, crustaceans, spiders, centipedes, and many fossil forms.

articular bone a bone present in the lower jaw of birds and reptiles that forms the joint with the skull (*quadrate*). In mammals it forms the MALLEUS.

articulate connect by means of a joint.

articulation see JOINT.

artifact something that appears during preparation or examination of material that is not present in the natural state. Two scientists from the

53

University of Surrey, Harold Hillman and Peter Sartory, have suggested on the evidence provided by solid geometry that some structures described by electron microscopy, for example, Golgi apparatus, nuclear pores, and endoplasmic reticulum, are artifacts of the preparation of material.

artificial classification see CLASSIFICATION.

artificial insemination (AI) the introduction of spermatozoa into the reproductive tract of a female animal without COPULATION in order to achieve fertilization. The method is used routinely in animal breeding to transfer genetic material over large distances and to achieve many fertilizations in different females from one ejaculation of semen. In the case of humans, artificial insemination is used sometimes in attempts to achieve fertilization where normal methods have failed.

artificial parthenogenesis the development of an egg into an embryo stimulated not by fertilization but by artificial means, for example, by cooling, treating with acid, and mechanical damage.

artificial respiration the maintenance of breathing by artificial means. Examples include mouth-to-mouth resuscitation, physical compression and distention of the thorax, and use of a respirator.

artificial selection a SELECTION process in which humans choose particular organisms from which to breed, based on their PHENOTYPE, thus aiming to alter the average GENOTYPE and phenotype of the resulting progeny. This process, a form of DIRECTIONAL SELECTION, is carried out by plant and animal breeders whose job is to enhance certain features of the organisms with which they work, for example, greater resistance to root rot in tomatoes or higher milk yield in cattle. Such selection depends on GENETIC VARIABILITY in the chosen population. See also HERITABILITY.

artio- *combining form* denoting an even number.

Artiodactyla the even-toed ungulates, that is, animals possessing hoofs with two or four toes, such as cattle, pigs, deer, and camels. Compare PERISSODACTYLA.

arum lily the plant *Arum maculatum*. It is a remarkable example of COEVOLUTION in that the shoot is modified to form a large, foul-smelling BRACT attractive to small flies. The bract (or *spathe*) is swollen at its base, which encloses the male and female flowers. Once attracted by the spathe, flies carrying pollen enter the swollen bract chamber searching for nectar, and so pollinate the female flower. CROSS-POLLINATION is ensured by differential maturation times for male and female flowers. When the flies leave, they carry pollen from the male flowers, which ripened while the flies were in the chamber.

Ascaris a genus of parasitic roundworm, phylum Nematoda, that occasionally inhabit the small intestine of man. *A. lumbricoides* can reach a length of 30 cm and when present in large numbers can block the gut and kill the host.

ascending sloping or curving upward, for example, the ascending limb of the loop of Henle in kidney tubules.

ascidian any PROTOCHORDATE of the class Ascidiacea, subphyllum Tunicata, such as the sea squirt, the adults of which are degenerate and sedentary. See also APPENDICULARIA.

asco- *combining form* denoting sac, in the shape of a leather wine flask.

ascocarp the fruiting body of an ASCOMYCETE fungus. See ASCUS.

ascomycete any fungus of class Ascomycetes (now included in the subdivisions Ascomycotina and Deuteromycotina) characterized by formation of ascospores during sexual reproduction. The hyphae are septate, and the asci (see ASCUS) are grouped in a visible fruiting body.

ascorbic acid or **vitamin C** a water-soluble organic compound found in citrus fruits, green vegetables, and tomatoes. Formula: $C_6H_8O_6$. Its best-known role is in the formation of COLLAGEN, the chief component of CONNECTIVE TISSUE. Deficiency in ascorbic acid results in the disease called SCURVY, which is characterized by changes in collagen leading to many further effects.

Ascorbic acid acts as a VITAMIN in man, but rats and most other mammals can manufacture their own supply from D-glucose.

ascospore a HAPLOID spore resulting from MEIOSIS in the ASCUS within the fruiting body of ASCOMYCETE fungi.

ascus or (formerly) **theca** (*pl.* asci) a cell present in the fruiting body of ASCOMYCETE fungi, in which the fusion of HAPLOID nuclei occurs during sexual reproduction. This is normally followed by MEIOSIS, giving rise to four haploid cells, after which MITOSIS produces eight ASCOSPORES. The precise arrangement of ascospores within the ascus enables the events at meiosis to be fully analyzed (see TETRAD ANALYSIS). The asci are usually enclosed within an aggregation of hyphae termed an ASCOCARP, a number of different types being recognized, for example, perithecium, cleistothecium, and apothecium. See Fig. 50.

20 μm

Fig. 50. **Ascus.** Containing ascospores of *Neurospora crassa*.

ASEPTIC TECHNIQUES

aseptic techniques techniques performed in an environment that is as free of disease-causing microorganisms as possible, for example, in a hospital operating room. To achieve this end, the atmosphere is filtered, all instruments and outer clothing are sterilized (usually with high temperatures in an AUTOCLAVE), and the staff wear face masks and gloves. Such techniques should not be confused with the use of ANTISEPTICS.

asexual reproduction a process by which organisms multiply without formation and fusion of GAMETES, specialized sex cells. Each feature of asexual reproduction has advantages and disadvantages. See Fig. 51.

Feature	Advantage	Disadvantage
1. Only involves one individual.	No need to find a partner.	No chance of mixing genes to produce a new combination.
2. Produces individuals that are identical with parent.	When the environment is constant a genetically favored type will spread rapidly.	Genotype may not be able to adjust to a change in environment.
3. Progeny often produced in large numbers near parent.	Environment is suitable since parent survives.	Overcrowding may result. Widespread dispersal is difficult.

Fig. 51. **Asexual reproduction.** Advantages and disadvantages of asexual reproduction.

The genetically identical products of asexual reproduction are called CLONES. Asexual reproduction is a feature of lower animals and occurs in all groups of plants, including ANGIOSPERMS, usually in addition to sexual reproduction. Perhaps the fixed location of many plants makes this type of reproduction particularly suitable. There are several types of asexual reproduction. These are dealt with under their own headings but are summarized here:

(a) fission (see BINARY FISSION), where the entire organism splits into two (for example, bacteria).

(b) BUDDING: new individuals produced as outgrowths of the parent (for example, yeast and *Hydra*).

(c) FRAGMENTATION: mechanical separation of the plant body into segments (some algae).

(d) SPORULATION: producing asexual spores (for example, fungi).

(e) VEGETATIVE PROPAGATION: parts of higher plants producing new whole organisms (for example, potato tubers).

asexual spore or **isospore** a spore that does not arise through sexual reproduction.

asparagine one of 20 AMINO ACIDS common in proteins. It has a polar

R structure and is water soluble. See Fig. 52. The isoelectric point of asparagine is 5.4.

Fig. 52. **Asparagine.** Molecular structure.

aspartic acid or **aspartate** one of 20 AMINO ACIDS common in proteins. It has an extra carboxyl group and is therefore acidic in solution. The isoelectric point of aspartic acid is 2.8. See Fig. 53.

Fig. 53. **Aspartic acid.** Molecular structure.

aspect the direction in which an object faces. For example, a north-facing slope has a northern aspect.

asperous rough to the touch.

asphalt lake a pool formed largely of bitumen (almost entirely carbon and hydrogen, but some oxygen, nitrogen, and sulfur) found mainly in the southern United States and South America, for example, the La Brea tar pits in which trapped animals have been preserved since the Miocene period.

asphyxia suffocation, lack of oxygen.

aspirin or **acetylsalicylic acid** an analgesic.

assimilation the intake by organisms of new materials from the outside and their incorporation into the internal structure of the organism.

association a small natural grouping of plants that live together. The term originally denoted an entire habitat, for example, a pine forest. It now is usually applied to much smaller groupings. Compare CONSOCIA-TION.

association center an area of nerve coordination in invertebrates that distributes stimuli received from sensory receptors.

assortative mating a type of cross in which the choice of partner is affected by the GENOTYPE, that is, mating is nonrandom. For example, human matings are often assortative with respect to racial features, since persons of one racial group may tend to have children by partners of the same group. This choice of mates means that genotypic frequencies predicted by the HARDY-WEINBERG LAW may not be found. See also RANDOM MATING, INTERBREED.

-aster *combining form* denoting a star.

aster a group of blind-ending SPINDLE MICROTUBULES radiating out from the CENTRIOLES of dividing cells in lower plants and all animals. The aster function is uncertain, but does not seem to be concerned with spindle formation. See Fig. 54.

Fig. 54. **Aster.** Generalized form.

Asteroidea a class of star-shaped ECHINODERMS, with a basic pentaradiate shape (five-sided RADIAL SYMMETRY), for example, the starfish.

asynchronous fibrillar muscle see FLIGHT.

atavism the recurrence of a characteristic possessed by an ancestor after an absence for several generations.

athlete's foot or **tinea** or **ringworm** a fungal disease caused by *Epidermophyton floccosum*. The fungus can cause irritation of other parts of the body apart from the feet and is parasitic or pathogenic on nails and skin in general. Athlete's foot is most common in adolescent males, and infection is caused usually by walking barefoot on infected floors.

atlas the first vertebra of TETRAPODS.

atmometer an instrument for measuring the rate of evaporation of water into the air. This is carried out by measuring the level of water in a calibrated cylinder at frequent intervals.

atmosphere the gaseous envelope surrounding a particular structure, or the gaseous content of a given structure or container.

atom the smallest particle of matter possessing the properties of an element.

atomic weight the weight of an atom of an element in relation to hydrogen, which is considered to have the atomic weight one.

ATP (adenosine triphosphate) a molecule consisting of ADENINE and ribose sugar onto which are attached three phosphate groups, two being joined by high-energy bonds (see Fig. 55). HYDROLYSIS of these special bonds results in release of energy. ATP molecules are formed in two main processes, both involving addition of inorganic phosphate to ADP via a high-energy bond:

$$ADP + P + 34 \text{ kJ energy} = ATP + H_2O$$

Fig. 55. **ATP.** The structure of ATP, ADP, and AMP.

ATP can be formed during CELLULAR RESPIRATION, either in the general cytoplasm during GLYCOLYSIS or in the MITOCHONDRIA via the KREBS CYCLE and the ELECTRON TRANSPORT SYSTEM if oxygen is present. ATP is also formed during photosynthesis in the CHLOROPLASTS of green plants, again using an electron transport system. ATP molecules act therefore as short-term biological batteries, retaining energy until required for such processes as active transport, synthesis of new materials, nerve transmission, and muscle contraction. An active cell requires more than two million molecules of ATP per second to drive its biochemical machinery.

atrioventricular node (AVN) see HEART.

atrium (*pl.* atria) a passage or chamber in the body, particularly one or more of the chambers in the heart receiving blood from the body. All vertebrates except fish have hearts with two atrial cavities. See Fig. 56. See also HEART and HEART, CARDIAC CYCLE.

atrophy the reduction in size of an organ or tissue mass, often after disuse.

atropine a poisonous chemical obtained from the deadly nightshade,

Fig. 56. **Atrium.** Primitive heart.

which prevents depolarization of the postsynaptic membrane and therefore prevents synaptic transmission, in a similar way to CURARE. It is used medicinally in preanesthetic medication and to treat peptic ulcers, renal and biliary colic, etc.

attached-X chromosome a single chromosome formed by the joining of two X-chromosomes at a common CENTROMERE. Such a chromosome acts as a single entity so that a carrier has a double-X complement plus another sex chromosome, a form of NONDISJUNCTION.

attachment an enlargement of the base of an algal THALLUS by which the plant is anchored to the SUBSTRATE.

attenuate (of a leaf or plant structure) gradually tapering to a long slender point.

attenuation the loss of virulence of a microbial pathogen so that, although still alive, it is no longer pathogenic. In this state it is able to stimulate beneficial ANTIBODY production when used as a vaccine. Various procedures are used to attenuate the virulence of a pathogen, for example, the aging of cultures, or passing the pathogen through an unnatural host.

attenuator a regulatory NUCLEOTIDE sequence occurring in the LEADER REGION of an operon (see OPERON MODEL) and containing a TRANSCRIPTION stop signal. The attenuator acts as a fine control mechanism for activity of structural genes, sometimes being operative, sometimes not, depending on conditions in the cell.

auditory canal or **external auditory meatus** the canal leading from the PINNA (outer ear) to the eardrum.

auditory capsule the bony or cartilaginous capsule that encloses the middle and inner parts of the ear in vertebrates.

auditory nerve the 8th cranial nerve. It carries sensory impulses from the inner ear.

auditory organ the sense organ that detects sound. In vertebrates it also provides information about the animal's relationship to gravity and its acceleration.

Auerbach's plexus a network of nerve fibers and ganglia in the gut musculature, bringing about PERISTALSIS when stimulated by pressure of food in the gut.

auricle 1. a former term for the ATRIUM of the heart. 2. an alternative term for the PINNA (outer ear). 3. (also called *auricula*) an ear-shaped part or appendage, such as that occurring at the base of some leaves.

Australian fauna See MARSUPIAL.

Australopithecus a genus of early Pleistocene primate that was hominid in some features but apelike in others, such as the skull. Southern African in origin, *Australopithecus* was upright in posture.

autecology the ecology of individual species as opposed to community ecology. Compare SYNECOLOGY.

authority the author of a scientific name usually cited in most taxonomic works, for example, *Tringa totanus* (Linnaeus).

auto- *combining form* pertaining to oneself, independently.

autocatalytic (of a substance) catalyzing its own production. The more substance is made, the more catalyst is available for further production.

autochthonous (of peat) derived from plants that lived on the site of its formation.

autoclave 1. an apparatus in which objects or materials are sterilized using air-free saturated steam under pressure at temperatures in excess of 100°C. 2. a sealed vessel in which chemical reactions can occur at high pressure.

autocoid an alternative name for HORMONE.

autoecious (of parasites, especially the rust fungus) completing the entire life cycle on a single species of host.

autogamy 1. the process by which the two parts of a divided cell nucleus reunite, as in some protozoans. 2. self-fertilization in plants.

autogenic (of VEGETATIONAL SUCCESSION) affected by plant communities, altering their environment themselves.

autograft the grafting on an organism of a part of itself.

autoimmunity a situation in which the immunological defenses of the body become sensitized to parts of the same body, resulting in self-destruction in that area. In other words, one's own ANTIGENS become mistaken for foreign antigens, setting up an IMMUNE RESPONSE. Such an occurrence is dangerous and may be associated with aging. An example is rheumatoid arthritis.

autolysis the breakdown of tissues, usually after death, by their own enzymes.

autonomic 1. pertaining to the part of the nervous system controlling involuntary muscles (see AUTONOMIC NERVOUS SYSTEM). 2. (in plants) pertaining to movements arising from internal stimuli, for example, protoplasmic streaming, spiral growth of stem apices.

autonomic nervous system the part of the nervous system that controls the involuntary activities of the body. There are two main parts:
(a) The *sympathetic nervous system* in which complexes of SYNAPSES form ganglia alongside the vertebrae, and the preganglionic fibers from

the central nervous system are therefore short; the fibers are ADRENER-
GIC.

(b) The *parasympathetic nervous system* in which the ganglia are
embedded in the wall of the effector so that preganglionic fibers are long
and postganglionic fibers short; these are CHOLINERGIC.

The sympathetic and parasympathetic systems innervate the same
end organs, but the effects produced by the two systems generally oppose one another, for example:

Sympathetic system	*Parasympathetic system*
inhibits peristalsis	stimulates peristalis
stimulates contraction in sphincters of bladder and anus	inhibits contraction in sphincters of bladder and anus
inhibits bladder contraction	stimulates bladder contraction
stimulates pacemaker, speeding up the heart	inhibits pacemaker, slowing down the heart
stimulates arterial constriction	inhibits arterial constriction, causing dilation
inhibits contraction of bronchioles, causing dilation	stimulates contraction of bronchioles
inhibits contraction of iris muscle, causing dilated pupil	stimulates contraction of iris muscle, causing reduced pupil

autopolyploid a type of POLYPLOID in which there has been duplication
of the number of each chromosome, all chromosomes coming from the
same original species. For example, in Fig. 57, A represents one complete set of chromosomes. Like an ALLOPOLYPLOID, an autopolyploid is
a mechanism for creating new species, particularly in plants. Allopolypl-
oids are more successful, perhaps because autopolyploid chromosomes
have pairing difficulties at MEIOSIS.

autoradiograph a photographic representation of radioactive areas in
a tissue. Tissues labeled with an ISOTOPE (for example, ^{14}C) are placed
on a photographic plate, which is irradiated in the same way that photographic film is exposed to light. Radioactive areas can be seen in the
photographs.

autosexing a technique by which the sex of an offspring can be determined without examination of the genitalia. For example, the sex of

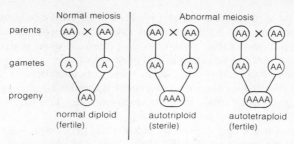

Fig. 57. **Autopolyploid.** Types of autopolyploid compared with normal diploid.

young poultry chicks is difficult to determine anatomically. However, a Barring gene enables the feather color of females (one X-chromosome) to be distinguished from that of males (two X chromosomes).

autosomal gene a gene found on an AUTOSOME.

autosomal inheritance a pattern of transmission of ALLELES, which are located on AUTOSOMES, that is, not on sex chromosomes, so that the sex of the parent does not affect the result of a mating, RECIPROCAL CROSSES giving identical results.

autosome a type of chromosome found in all cells, *not* concerned with SEX DETERMINATION. Chromosomes are of two types: autosomes and SEX CHROMOSOMES. Autosomes carry the major part of genetic information in cells, including information on sexual characteristics. See SEX LINKAGE for a comparison of the inheritance of autosomal and sex-linked genes.

autostylic jaw suspension the attachment of the upper jaw to the skull by a number of attachments called the *otic process,* the *basal process*, and the *ascending process.* It occurs in lungfish and terrestrial vertebrates. Compare HYOSTYLIC JAW SUSPENSION.

autotomy the deliberate casting of part of the body when attacked, as when a lizard casts it tail.

autotroph an organism that can manufacture its own organic requirements from inorganic materials independent of other sources of organic substrates. Autotrophs are either phototrophic (see PHOTOAUTOTROPH) or CHEMOAUTOTROPHIC, energy being derived either by photosynthesis where chlorophyll is present, or from inorganic oxidation where it is absent. For example, hydrogen sulfide is oxidized by sulfur bacteria. Autotrophs are primary producers (see PRIMARY PRODUCTION). Compare HETEROTROPH.

autotrophic pertaining to an AUTOTROPH.

autozooid an independent coelenterate polyp capable of feeding itself.

auxin a type of plant hormone involved in the growth of cells and several other functions. The most important auxin is indolacetic acid (IAA, see Fig. 188), but many other substances have been classified as auxins, using a BIOASSAY method developed by FRITZ WENT.

The effects of auxins depend on their concentration in the plant. They are most concentrated at the shoot tip and least concentrated in the root, except for small amounts at the root tip. The major effects of auxin are summarized below:

(a) Encourages cell growth by elongation, producing a softening of the MIDDLE LAMELLAE of cell walls.

(b) Stimulates cell division in the PHLOEM of the VASCULAR BUNDLES, thus encouraging new growth.

(c) Promotes positive PHOTOTROPISM in shoots by growth of tissues toward the light source.

(d) Promotes GEOTROPISM in all parts of the plant—positive in roots, negative in shoots, due to unequal distributions of the hormone.

(e) Induces APICAL DOMINANCE by suppressing lateral buds.

(f) Induces lateral root formation.

(g) Stimulates fruit development, enabling seedless fruits to be produced artificially.

(h) Suppresses ABSCISSION in leaves and fruit.

(i) Encourages formation of wound tissues in injured or diseased plants.

auxotroph a mutant strain of microorganisms that require growth factors in addition to those required by the WILD TYPE; that is, they will not grow on MINIMAL MEDIUM.

Avery, Oswald T (1877—1955) American physician, who with Colin MacLeod and Maclyn McCarty in 1944 demonstrated that the transforming principle, suggested by GRIFFITH, to explain bacterial transformation was DNA. Thus, DNA alone could cause a heritable change in bacteria, strongly suggesting that DNA, rather than protein, was the basic genetic material of cells.

Aves a class of vertebrates, the BIRDS.

avirulent lacking virulence; that is, the ability of an organism to cause disease is absent.

awn see ARISTA (2).

axenic descriptive of a pure culture, one in which no other organism is present.

axial skeleton the part of the SKELETON containing the SKULL and VERTEBRAL COLUMN.

axil a location on a plant stem that is the angle between the leaf and the upper part of the stem. (See Fig. 58).

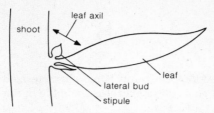

Fig. 58. **Axil.** A leaf axil.

axile (of plant structures) attached to the central axis.

axillary (of plant structures) arising in the angle of a leaf or bract.

axis cylinder an AXON.

axolotl the larval stage of the aquatic American salamander *Amblystoma*. It is capable of breeding in the larval form, thus demonstrating a phenomenon known as NEOTONY.

axon the process of a NERVE cell that conducts impulses from the nerve cell body.

axoneme the complex of MICROTUBULES and associated tubes found in the shaft of a CILIUM or FLAGELLUM.

axoplasm the cytoplasm that occurs within the AXON.

azo dye any of a class of artificial dyes obtained from aromatic amines.

B

baboon a PRIMATE of the genus *Papio* characterized by presence of a doglike muzzle, short tail, and callosities on the buttocks. There are five species in Africa and Asia.

Bacillariophyceae the diatoms, a class within the division Chrysophyta. They are unicellular and occur in both marine and freshwater environments. Their silicified cell walls are preserved in diatomaceous earth and peat. Diatoms are one of the most important PRIMARY PRODUCERS in the sea and are responsible for formation of petroleum deposits.

bacillus the general name for a rod-shaped BACTERIUM, but more specifically a generic name for a group of spore-producing forms, for example, the hay bacillus *Bacillus subtilis.*

backbone see VERTEBRAL COLUMN.

backcross a genetic term describing a mating between a HYBRID organism and one of the original parental types. The results of a backcross depend on the parental type. See Fig. 59. A backcross to the recessive parental is diagnostic, since it reveals the genotype of the hybrid, and is called a TESTCROSS.

Fig. 59. **Backcross.** Results from different parental types.

back mutation an inherited change (MUTATION) in a mutant gene that causes it to regain its WILD TYPE function. Compare FORWARD MUTATION.

bacteria (*singular* bacterium) unicellular or, more rarely, multicellular PROKARYOTE organisms. Some are AUTOTROPHIC, contain BACTERIO-CHLOROPHYLLS and bacterioviridin, carrying out photosynthesis anaerobically. Bacteria have various shapes, occurring as cocci (spherical), bacilli (rod-shaped), and spirilla (helical). They range in size from 1 μmeter to about 500 μmeters, but are usually 1—10 μmeters in diameter. They are present in soil, water, air, and as free-living SYMBIONTS, PARASITES, and PATHOGENS.

While some bacteria are useful in NITROGEN and SULFUR CYCLES,

many cause diseases of plants, animals, and humans, for example, AN-
THRAX and TETANUS. Reproduction occurs asexually, but genetic transfer can take place by CONJUGATION. Other genetic changes can be
brought about by MUTATION or the acquisition of a PLASMID (see Fig. 60.
Identification usually involves biochemical tests rather than visual study,
and classification often involves use of NUMERICAL TAXONOMY.

Fig. 60. **Bacteria.** A generalized bacterium.

bactericide a substance causing death to BACTERIA, for example, an
ANTIBIOTIC.
bacteriochlorophyll a form of CHLOROPHYLL possessed by photosynthetic bacteria (green and purple types). In addition to small amounts
of bacteriochlorophyll, green bacteria mostly possess another type of
chlorophyll, called *bacterioviridin*.
bacteriology the study of BACTERIA.
bacteriophage or **phage** a VIRUS that attacks BACTERIA. Each bacteriophage is specific to one form of bacterium.
bacteriostasis the inhibition of growth in bacteria without killing them.
bacteriostatic (of a substance) inhibiting the growth of bacteria but not
killing them.
balance the maintenance of stability and specific orientation by an organism in relation to the immediate environment. Organs of balance occur
at the end of each SEMICIRCULAR CANAL in the inner ear, where there
is a swelling, called an AMPULLA. This is a RECEPTOR that has a group
of sensory cells, hairs from which are embedded in a gelatinous cap—the
CUPULA. Since the semicircular canals are at right angles to each other,
the ampullae are sensitive to movement in any plane, as the canal fluid
moves the cupula in a direction opposite to that of the movement of the
head. Head position is given by receptors containing calcareous
OTOLITHS in the UTRICLE and SACCULE, and these react to gravity in

BALANCED DIET

relation to the position of the head. Nerve fibers lead to the brain from ampullae, saccule, and utricle.

balanced diet an intake of the various types of food in such proportions as to promote good health.

balanced polymorphism or **stable polymorphism** a GENETIC POLYMORPHISM in which the various morphs are maintained in a stable frequency over several generations due, possibly, to constant NATURAL SELECTION pressures.

balancer see HALTER.

Balanoglossus a genus of wormlike, burrowing PROTOCHORDATE.

baleen or **whalebone** horny plates that hang from the roof of the mouth in some whales (Mystacoceti), for example, right whales and rorquals. The plates filter out krill, small shrimplike crustaceans, from the sea water as it is forced out of the mouth.

Banks, Barbara biochemist who, in the early 1970s, argued that ATP when hydrolyzed required rather than gave up energy to break covalent bonds. Most biologists consider that energy is provided when ATP is hydrolyzed, although currently it is not thought to be stored simply in the terminal phosphate bond.

Banting, Sir Frederick Grant (1891—1941) Canadian physician and Nobel prizewinner. He is known best for his discovery with C.H. BEST of the hormone INSULIN in 1921, during his work on the internal secretion of the pancreas.

banyan tree *Ficus benghalensis,* an Indian tree known best for producing large aerial roots that are let down from its larger branches and, in effect, form secondary trunks. These trunks give extra support and enable the tree to spread.

barbiturate any UREIDE such as phenobarbital, amytal, and seconal. Barbiturates have a depressant effect on the central nervous system, usually producing sleep.

barbs lateral lamellae that project from the quill or calamus of the FEATHER and form the vane.

barbules 1. hooklike processes on the barbs of FEATHERS, which interlock to form the continuous vane. 2. teeth found in the capsules of some mosses.

bark the outer, living part of a woody stem, consisting of three layers:

    (a) an inner layer, called secondary PHLOEM, containing the elements of primary phloem plus horizontal ray cells that function in transporting materials across the stem.

    (b) a middle layer of cork CAMBIUM, a group of meristematic (dividing) cells originating in the PARENCHYMA cells of the outer stem cortex.

As the cells divide, the outer ones develop into cork cells, and the inner ones give rise to parenchyma-like tissue.

(c) CORK, an outer region of cells forming a waterproof and protective layer broken only by LENTICELS.

barnacle the common name for any of the CRUSTACEAN class Cirripedia, most of which are SESSILE, grow on rocky substrates, and have a CALCAREOUS outer covering.

baroreceptor or **baroceptor** a pressure RECEPTOR that responds to changes in blood pressure, found particularly in the carotid sinus and aortic arch.

Barr body sex CHROMATIN particles found in the interphase nucleus of buccal epithelial cells in some female mammals and probably derived from an X-chromosome (see INACTIVE-X HYPOTHESIS). First described by Murray Barr in 1949, Barr bodies can be used as a sex marker, always occurring in numbers one less than the total number of X-chromosomes. Thus, normal human males and TURNER'S SYNDROME females have no Barr bodies, while KLINEFELTER'S SYNDROME males have two. See Fig. 61.

Fig. 61. **Barr body.** Sex chromatin in nuclei from human male and female buccal epithelial human cells.

basal body a structure similar to and homologous with a CENTRIOLE connected to the axial filament of the flagellum and cilium, for example, in sperm.

basal metabolic level see BASAL METABOLIC RATE.

basal metabolic rate (BMR) or **basal metabolic level (BML)** the minimal rate of METABOLISM in a resting organism in an environment with a temperature the same as its own body heat, while not digesting or absorbing food. The rate is commonly expressed in terms of energy per unit surface area per unit time, usually as $kJ\ m^{-2}\ h^{-1}$. See STANDARD METABOLIC RATE, REGULATORY HEAT PRODUCTION.

base a chemical substance that has a tendency to accept protons (H^+). The base dissolves water with the production of hydroxyl ions and reacts with acids to form salts.

base analogue any chemical that has a similar structure, that is, is analogous to one of the purine or pyrimidine bases in DNA or RNA. Such analogues can become incorporated into the nucleic acid and may act

BASE DELETION

as a MUTAGEN. For example, 5-bromouracil (5Bu) is an analogue of thymine and can be incorporated into DNA in place of thymine. In its normal state, 5Bu acts like thymine and pairs with adenine (see COMPLEMENTARY PAIRING), but the analogue sometimes undergoes a chemical change called a *tautomeric shift* and then pairs with guanine. At the next DNA replication, an incorrect base will be incorporated into the DNA, causing a TRANSITION SUBSTITUTION mutation (adenine—guanine). See Fig. 62.

Fig. 62. **Base analogue.** The action of 5-bromouracil on DNA.

base deletion removal of a NUCLEOTIDE base, a purine or a pyrimidine from the DNA structure, producing a DELETION MUTATION that can have serious consequences for the related protein. See FRAMESHIFT.

base insertion addition of an extra NUCLEOTIDE base to a DNA molecule, producing an INSERTION MUTATION that can have serious consequences for the related protein. See FRAMESHIFT.

basement membrane a membrane lying between an EPITHELIUM and its underlying CONNECTIVE TISSUE.

base pairing hydrogen bonding between NUCLEOTIDE bases of DNA. See COMPLEMENTARY PAIRING.

base substitution replacement of a NUCLEOTIDE base in a DNA molecule with another base, possibly producing a SUBSTITUTION MUTATION.

basic dyes dyes with a basic organic grouping that stain when colored with an acid. They are used mainly for nuclear staining, in which they combine with nucleic acids, for example, fuchsin as used in the Feulgen stain for DNA.

basidiomycete any fungus of the subdivision Basidiomycotina, a group containing over 14,000 species. They have a septate mycelium, and many forms, such as mushrooms, produce complex sporophores. Sexually derived spores (basidiospores) are produced externally on basidia, usually in groups of four, and this is characteristic of the group Basidiomycotina. Members are important as food (mushrooms), in plant diseases (rusts and smuts), and in dry rot of timber.

basidium the microscopic structure on which the sexually produced basidiospores of BASIDIOMYCETE fungi are formed during sexual reproduction. See Fig. 63.

Fig. 63. **Basidium.** The basidium of *Scleroderma*.

basifixed (of anthers) joined by the base and not capable of independent movement.

basilar membrane the tissue that bears the auditory hair cells in the COCHLEA of the EAR. See TECTORIAL MEMBRANE.

basipetal 1. (of a stem) producing structures one after the other from the apex down to the base, so that the oldest are at the apex. **2.** (of substances, for example, AUXINS) movement away from the apex to lower parts of the plant.

basipodite the segment of the crustacean limb proximally attached to the coxopodite and distally supporting the exopodite and endopodite.

basophil leukocyte a type of white blood cell, of the GRANULOCYTE group, that takes up the stain of a basic dye. Basophils form about 1% of adult human leukocytes. They are produced in the bone marrow and have a function that is probably associated with the IMMUNE RESPONSE, for example, in chickenpox infection.

bastard wing the part of the wing of a bird attached to the thumb of the forelimb.

bat a flying mammal of the order CHIROPTERA, the only true flying vertebrate apart from the birds.

Batesian mimicry see MIMICRY.

Bateson, William (1861—1926) British pioneer of genetics. He rediscovered Mendelian inheritance in 1900, using, for example, poultry and sweet peas. See MENDELIAN GENETICS.

batrachian see ANURAN.

B-carotene a CAROTENE that is a precursor of vitamin A, producing two molecules of vitamin A per molecule of B-carotene.

B-cell a LYMPHOCYTE formed in the bone marrow of mammals. After stimulation with a particular ANTIGEN, it divides to produce daughter cells that manufacture large amounts of ANTIBODIES, which are passed into the bloodstream.

B-complex or **vitamin B complex** a group of water-soluble VITAMINS that function mostly as COENZYMES in metabolic reactions taking place in animal cells. The complex consists of THIAMINE (B_1), RIBOFLAVIN

(B_2), PANTOTHENIC ACID (B_5), PYRIDOXINE (B_6), BIOTIN, NICOTINIC ACID, FOLIC ACID, and COBALAMIN (B_{12}).

bdelloid leechlike.

Beadle, George Wells (1903—) American geneticist. With Edward Tatum, he began the modern study of biochemical genetics, using the red bread mold *Neurospora crassa*. They investigated nutritional mutants in the fungus (AUXOTROPHS) and coined the ONE GENE/ONE ENZYME HYPOTHESIS.

beak 1. also called *bill*, the jaws and associated horny covering in a bird or turtle. **2.** any pointed projection in plant fruits. **3.** a projecting jawbone in fish such as pike. **4.** the tip of the UMBO in bivalve mollusks. **5.** the jaws of CEPHALOPODS, for example, of an octopus.

bee any member of the Apoidea in the insect order HYMENOPTERA. They possess membranous wings, usually a hairy body, and sucking or chewing mouthparts, for example, *Apis mellifera*, the honey bee.

beetle any member of the insect order COLEOPTERA.

behavior 1. the total activities of a living organism (usually an animal) ranging from simple movement to complex patterns involved with courtship, threat, camouflage, and the like. **2.** the observable response of an organism to stimuli from the environment. See INSTINCT, LEARNING.

Benedict's test a procedure used to detect the presence of REDUCING SUGARS in a solution. *Benedict's solution* consists of a single solution of copper sulfate, sodium citrate, and sodium carbonate in water. The solution is added to the test solution and heated. A red precipitate of Cu(I) oxide indicates the presence of a reducing sugar.

benign nonmalignant, as in a growth.

benthos the organisms that live on the bed of the sea or a lake, ranging from the high-water mark to the deepest trenches. Benthic organisms are subdivided into littoral (to 40 meters deep), sublittoral (41—200 meters), bathyal (200—4000 meters), abyssal (4001—6000 meters), and hadal (>6000 meters). See SEA ZONATION.

Bergmann's rule a rule stating that the individuals from populations of warm-blooded species of animals (HOMOIOTHERMS) that occur in cooler climates tend to be larger on average than individuals of the same species in warmer climates. This is because the *surface area/volume ratio* in large animals is smaller, so heat loss is reduced. The rule is named for the German biologist W. Bergmann and was formulated in 1847. See also ALLEN'S RULE.

beriberi a human disease caused by vitamin B_1 (THIAMINE) deficiency in which affected individuals suffer from wasting of muscles, paralysis, mental confusion, and sometimes heart failure.

Bernard, Claude (1813—1878) French physiologist. He was the father of modern experimental physiology and the first person to appreciate the importance of the internal environment in the functioning of organisms.

berry a type of succulent, fleshy FRUIT produced by some plants, in which seeds are embedded in the pulp. The fruit is formed from the swollen tissue of the PERICARP, for example, tomato, grape, date, gooseberry, citrus fruits.

Best, Charles Herbert (1899—1978) Canadian physician, codiscoverer of INSULIN in 1921 with Frederick G. BANTING. He also discovered histaminase, carried out extensive studies on insulin and diabetes, and worked on heparin and thrombosis, and choline and liver damage.

beta taxonomy the level of TAXONOMY concerned with arranging species into a natural CLASSIFICATION, which logically follows ALPHA TAXONOMY.

B horizon the second main zone of a soil profile that accumulates leeched substances. See also A HORIZON.

bi- *prefix* denoting two.

bibliographical reference a precise form of reference to an organism in taxonomic literature. It must include the name of the author, date of publication of the organism's name, title of the book or journal, and exact page references.

biceps a group of muscles present in the upper forelimb of TETRAPODS, which are flexors of the elbow joint. In the hind limb, the biceps femoris is a flexor of the knee and an elevator of the femur. See ANTAGONISM.

bicollateral bundle a VASCULAR BUNDLE of plants with two phloem groups, one internal and one external to the xylem, for example, marrow and tomato.

bicuspid 1. a type of tooth in which the crown is formed into two distinct points or cusps, found typically in premolar teeth. **2.** (of a plant structure) possessing two points or cusps. **3.** formerly called *mitral.* (of a valve) allowing a flow of blood from the left ATRIUM to the left VENTRICLE.

biennial 1. occurring every two years. **2.** a plant that lives for two seasons or years, germinating from seed and growing to maturity in the first season with food storage in swollen roots for overwintering. In the second season, flowers, fruit, and seeds are produced before death occurs. Such plants are herbaceous rather than woody, for example, Canterbury bell (*Campanula*) and the carrot. See ANNUAL, PERENNIAL.

bifid divided into two, forked.

biflagellate having two flagella, as in *Chlamydomonas*.

bilateral cleavage or **radial cleavage** the type of CLEAVAGE that gives rise to BILATERAL SYMMETRY. It occurs in echinoderms and CHORDATES. Compare SPIRAL CLEAVAGE.

bilateral symmetry an animal body structure with a head and a rear, and with the body organs arranged so that a section through the midline from dorsal (upper) to ventral (lower) surfaces would divide the organism into almost identical right and left halves. Most higher invertebrates (for example, PLATYHELMINTHS, ANNELIDS, ARTHROPODS) and all vertebrates are bilaterally symmetrical. Compare RADIAL SYMMETRY.

bile a thick, brown-green fluid secreted by the liver that is alkaline in its reactions, containing bile salts, bile pigments, CHOLESTEROL, and inorganic salts. Bile is transferred from liver to the DUODENUM via the bile duct, which in many mammals contains a reservoir called the gallbladder. The bile pigments, bilirubin and biliverdin, result from the breakdown of HEMOGLOBIN in red blood cells, giving the bile its coloration, in turn affecting the color of the FECES. The amount of cholesterol excreted in bile depends on blood fat level, cholesterol in the bile normally being kept in solution by the bile salts. Reduction in bile salt concentration can cause cholesterol to be deposited in the gallbladder, contributing to formation of gallstones.

   Although bile contains no digestive enzymes, bile salts are also responsible for EMULSIFICATION of fats in the duodenum, lowering the surface tension of the fatty film surrounding fatty food particles, thus producing a larger surface area on which digestive enzymes (LIPASES) can work. Secretion of bile from the liver is stimulated by the hormone SECRETIN, which is produced in the wall of the duodenum. See Fig. 64. See also CHOLECYSTOKININ-PANCREOZYMIN.

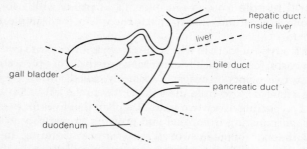

hepatic duct
inside liver

liver

gall bladder

bile duct

pancreatic duct

duodenum

Fig. 64. **Bile.** The human gallbladder and bile duct.

bile duct the duct through which bile passes from the liver or gallbladder to the duodenum.

bile salts the sodium salts secreted in bile, sodium taurocholate and sodium glycocholate, which greatly lower surface tension and are important in emulsifying fats.

bilharziasis or **schistosomiasis** a human disease common in Egypt and other warm parts of the developing world, in which affected individuals suffer from body pains followed by severe dysentery and anemia, leaving them weak and highly susceptible to other diseases. The disease is caused by the MIRACIDIUM larva of the blood fluke *Schistosoma*, which lives as an adult in the abdominal veins and has a water snail as a secondary host, transmission being effected via urine.

bilirubin a BILE pigment.

biliverdin a BILE pigment.

bill see BEAK.

bimodal distribution a statistical pattern in which the frequencies of values in a sample have two distinct peaks, even though parts of the distribution may overlap. For example, the sexual differences between men and women for such characters as height and weight produce a bimodal distribution. See Fig. 65.

Fig. 65. **Bimodal distribution.** The peaks, or modes, represent the character values of height and weight for men and women.

bimolecular leaflet a double layer of LIPID molecules with many of the properties of the PLASMA MEMBRANE and on which Danielli and Davson based their theory of membrane structure.

binary fission an asexual method of cell reproduction (see ASEXUAL REPRODUCTION) carried out by PROKARYOTES and some primitive EUKARYOTES, in which the chromosomal material is replicated and then the cytoplasm splits by CYTOKINESIS. Such processes differ from MITOSIS and MEIOSIS in that the chromosomal separation does not involve cellular MICROTUBULES forming a spindle.

binary system any system in which two alternatives occur, as in some taxonomic keys (see KEY, IDENTIFICATION).

binding site an area of an ENZYME to which other molecules can attach. Such an area can be an ACTIVE SITE for particular substrates or for other molecules, as in COMPETITIVE INHIBITION. Alternatively, some enzymes have two binding sites, one for substrate attachment and the other for attachment of other molecules, as in noncompetitive inhibition and allosteric inhibition (see ALLOSTERIC INHIBITORS).

binocular vision a type of vision in which the image of an object viewed falls on the retinas of both eyes simultaneously. Examples occur in many vertebrates, particularly in primates and predators, such as owls and cats. Such vision facilitates estimation of distance and in this the FOVEA, an area of acute vision, is of particular importance. Binocular vision results in a stereoscopic or 3-D effect, the slightly different positions of the two eyes being important in that they view the object from slightly different angles.

binomial expansion equation an equation stating that $(p + q)^2 = 1.0$, in which p and q are variables. The equation is used in population genetics (see POPULATION sense 2). Expansion of the term produces

$$p^2 + 2pq + q^2 = 1.0,$$

the genotype frequencies expected in a population that has a gene with two alleles at frequencies of p and q, respectively. The equation can be expanded to include additional alleles of a gene (see HARDY-WEINBERG LAW). For example, if a gene has three alleles with frequencies of p, q, and r, the expected genotype frequencies would be:

$$(p + q + r)^2 = p^2 + 2pq + 2pr + q^2 + 2qr + r^2.$$

binomial nomenclature the basis of the present scientific nomenclature of animals and plants, each of which is given a generic name followed by a specific name, in Greek, Latin, or often Latinized English. The generic name invariably has an initial capital letter, and the specific name, even if it is the name of a person, an initial small letter, both names being in italics, or underlined. Thus, the Old World robin is named *Erithacus rubecula*.

All scientific names used before publication of the 10th edition of LINNAEUS'S *Systema Naturae* (1758) are no longer applicable, and the names given since then have priority by date as a rule, the earliest name for an organism being given preference over others. Often, the scientific name is followed by the name of the person allocating the name and the date, for example, *Erithacus rubecula* (L.) 1766. L. is an abbreviation for Linnaeus, and the parentheses indicate a change from the genus in which he originally placed it. Where genera and species are redefined, a change of generic name is allowable. The Old World robin was originally named *Motacilla rubecula* L. 1766. *Motacilla* is now the genus including wagtails, a group not closely related to robins, which were subsequently placed in the genus *Erithacus*.

bio- or, frequently before a vowel, **bi-** *combining form* denoting life or living organisms.

bioassay a technique in which the presence of a chemical is quantified by using living organisms, rather than by carrying out chemical analysis.

For example, the amount of a toxic substance such as an insecticide in a sample could be estimated by comparing mortality in organisms treated with the unknown sample, against an agreed standard figure of mortality in organisms treated with known quantities of the substance.

biochemical evolution the evolutionary processes concerned with formation of biomolecules and attributes of living cells, such as metabolic pathways.

biochemical mutant a mutant with a defect in a biochemical pathway, such as an AUXOTROPH. See also ONE GENE/ONE ENZYME HYPOTHESIS.

biochemical oxygen demand (BOD) an empirical standardized laboratory test designed to measure the oxygen requirements or demands of a given effluent. It is an approximate measure of biochemically degradable organic matter in a water sample. In its simplest form, BOD is measured by taking a water sample of known volume, incubating it in the dark for a known period, usually five days, and measuring the oxygen levels at the start and end of the period. During the test the oxygen levels will have been reduced by bacteria in proportion to the amount of organic matter present.

biochemistry the study of the chemistry of living organisms.

biocide see SYSTEMIC BIOCIDE.

biodegradation the breaking down of inorganic and organic substances by biological action, a process usually involving bacteria and fungi, which are known as SAPROBIONTS when the substrate is biological.

biodeterioration the unwanted breakdown by microorganisms of materials such as foodstuffs, surface coatings, rubber, and lubricants, resulting in significant financial losses in many industries. Compare MICROBIAL DEGRADATION.

biogenesis the principle that life is propagated only by existing life, rather than by SPONTANEOUS GENERATION. The principle's original formulation was that organisms are able to generate only other forms similar to themselves, but where ALTERNATION OF GENERATIONS occurs, the statement is not entirely true. Biogenesis has thus come to mean that a species gives rise only to similar forms, and these forms can only be derived from parents that are similar.

biogeographical region the regions of Earth's surface containing distinctive groups of animals and plants that normally are prevented from moving out of those regions by various natural barriers. See Fig. 66.

biokinetic zone the temperature range over which organisms can survive (5°—60°C).

biological classification the arrangement of organisms into taxa (see TAXON) on the basis of their genetic relationships.

biological clock or **internal clock** an internal mechanism, as yet

Fig. 66. **Biogeographical regions.** The faunal regions of the world: 1a, Palearctic; 1b, Nearctic; 2a, Ethiopian; 2b, Madagascan; 3, Oriental; 4, Neotropical; 5, Notogaea; 6, Wallacea.

poorly understood, by which many plants and animals keep a sense of time, making possible a rhythmic pattern of behavior. Many organisms have such clocks producing activity cycles of approximately 24 hours (CIRCADIAN RHYTHM) which, however, can be affected by external influences that set the clock (*entrainment*). An individual's clock can be reentrained if placed in a new time zone, as happens with rapid long-distance travel.

Biological clocks affect not only whole organism activities, such as sleeping, but also cellular patterns of activity, such as varying META-BOLIC RATES. See also DIURNAL RHYTHM.

biological control a method of pest control using natural predators (harmless to other organisms) to regulate the size of pest populations. The technique has been used mainly against arthropod pests causing economic or medical problems. For example, red spider mites (*Tetranychus urticae*), which in some countries are pests of greenhouse crops, such as cucumbers, but are routinely controlled by application of commercially available samples of predatory mites (*Phytoseilus persimilis*) that feed on the red spider mites, thus reducing their numbers below an economically harmful level.

biological indicator any organism that can be used to characterize particular environmental properties, such as pollution or oxygenation. For example, *Sagitta elegans* characterizes oceanic waters, and *S. setosa* characterizes the continental shelf.

biological magnification the increasing concentration of a substance, such as a pesticide, in organisms from their predecessors in the FOOD CHAIN.

biological oxygen demand (BOD) see BIOCHEMICAL OXYGEN DEMAND.

biological rhythm any regularly occurring sequence of events in living organisms, either internal (ENDOGENOUS), for example, heartbeat, or external (EXOGENOUS), for example, the seasons and tides. See CIRCADIAN RHYTHM.

biological speciation the formation of new species, based on REPRODUCTIVE ISOLATION of the constituent populations.

biological warfare the use of living organisms, particularly microorganisms, or their products to induce illness or death in a population.

biology the study of living organisms.

bioluminescence the production of light of various wavelengths by living organisms, often wrongly termed *phosphorescence*. The phenomenon is found in such divergent groups as bacteria, fungi, fireflies (COLEOPTERA), and various marine organisms. See LUMINESCENCE.

biomass the total mass of organisms in a given ENVIRONMENT or at a certain TROPHIC LEVEL. It is measured as either live or dry weight per unit area, and the alternative used should be stated.

biomass pyramid see PYRAMID OF NUMBERS.

biome a major regional ecological community of organisms usually defined by the botanical habitat in which they occur and determined by interaction of the substrate, climate, fauna, and flora. The term is often limited to denote terrestrial habitats, for example, tundra, coniferous forest, and grassland. Oceans may be considered a single biome, the marine biome, although sometimes this is subdivided, for example, coral reef biome. There is no sharp distinction between adjacent biomes.

biometry or **biometrics** the analysis of biological data by means of statistical or mathematical techniques.

bionomics see ECOLOGY.

biophysics the physics of biological processes and the application of methods used in physics to biology.

biopoiesis the production of living from nonliving material.

biopsy the surgical removal of small amounts of tissue for examination to aid a diagnosis.

biosphere the part of Earth's surface and its immediate atmosphere occupied by living organisms.

biosynthesis the process by which complex molecules are formed from simpler ones by living organisms, for example, PHOTOSYNTHESIS.

biosystematics the part of the study of systematics concerned with variation within a species and its general evolution.

biota the living organisms present in a specific region or area, ranging in size from a small puddle to a BIOME or larger.

biotechnology the use of organisms, or their parts or processes, for manufacture or production of useful or commercial substances. The term denotes a wide range of processes, from using earthworms as a source of protein to genetic manipulation of bacteria to produce human gene products, such as growth hormone.

biotic community all organisms living on and contributing to a specific region (a BIOTA).

biotic factor the influences that occur within an environment, on both the physical environment and the organisms living there, as a result of the activities of living organisms. See EDAPHIC FACTOR.

biotic potential the theoretical maximum rate of increase of a species of organism in the absence of adverse environmental factors, such as predators or disease.

biotin a water-soluble vitamin of the B-COMPLEX present in many foods, including yeast, liver, and fresh vegetables. Biotin acts as a COENZYME in amino acid and lipid METABOLISM. Biotin deficiency, rare in humans, causes dermatitis and intestinal problems.

biotrophic (of microorganisms) feeding on living organisms, parasitic. Compare NECROTROPHIC.

biotype a group of individuals genetically identical, forming a physiologically distinct race within a species.

bipedalism a mode of locomotion found in many primates, particularly humans, and in birds, in which only the hind limbs are used in walking. True bipedalism, that is, where locomotion is normally bipedal, has required evolutionary changes in the vertebral column and pelvis, with their associated musculature. A principal advantage of bipedalism would seem to be that the forelimb can become modified for a nonwalking function, for example, tool handling in humans, flight in birds.

bipolar cell a NEURON cell with two axons emerging from opposite sides of the cell body. Such cells are found in the vertebrate retina.

biramous appendage the forked appendage of CRUSTACEANS formed by the protopodite, coxopodite and basipodite, which is nearest the body; and the two branches, exopodite and endopodite, which may form pincers, mouthparts, or legs. See Fig. 67.

Fig. 67. **Biramous appendage.** A crustacean's biramous appendage.

bird a vertebrate organism belonging to the class Aves and characterized by presence of feathers; forelimbs modified as wings, usually for flying; a bill or beak without teeth in the jaws; internal fertilization; calcareous shelled eggs incubated outside the body; and ability to control body temperature.

birth the act of bringing forth young from the female animal, usually from the uterus of a female mammal, but also denoting the birth of any animal in which eggs develop inside the adult and young are produced as independent organisms, for example, seahorses.

birth control any method used to limit the size of the human population, which usually involves prevention of fertilization of the ovum by the sperm but can also include abortion of the fetus. Behavioral methods include (a) abstention from copulation, (b) the so-called rhythm method, which takes advantage of less fertile phases of the menstrual cycle, and (c) coitus interruptus. Other methods involve use of *contraceptive* devices, pills, hormonal treatment, and sterilization.

Many countries have government-sponsored birth control programs, initiated in an attempt to control the rapidly increasing human population. For example, China not only encourages one child per family but is also attempting to produce a longer period between generations, over 25 years, by favoring marriages at a late date.

birth rate the average number of offspring produced by a female in a given time. This is calculated as the total number of new individuals added to the population during the time in question, divided by the number of mature breeding females in the population at that time.

bisexual of or referring to (a) HERMAPHRODITE individuals, (b) a population that contains both males and females.

biuret reaction a chemical change used as a quantitative method for protein determination. The reaction takes place when dilute copper sulfate solution is added to a protein solution, which then is made alkaline by addition of sodium hydroxide. A copper hydroxide precipitate forms, and a purple/violet color is produced, the strength of which indicates the amount of protein present. The reaction works only if at least two PEPTIDE BONDS are present in the protein. Thus, single AMINO ACIDS and DIPEPTIDES with only one peptide bond will not give a positive biuret reaction.

bivalent (of a pair of homologous CHROMOSOMES) being paired during prophase I of MEIOSIS. Compare MULTIVALENT.

bivalve any marine or freshwater mollusk of the class Lamellibranchiata (Pelecypoda) having two hinged parts to its shell. BRACHIOPODS are also bivalves, in that there are two hinged parts to the shell, but the term is usually restricted to true mollusks.

blackwater fever a rare tropical disease triggered by MALARIA PARASITE infestation, in which there is massive destruction of red blood cells, producing dark red or black urine.

bladder a hollow muscular bag situated in the lower abdominal cavity of mammals serving as a reservoir for urine from the kidneys. The bladder is composed of an internal epithelium surrounded by a coat of smooth muscle running in both circular and longitudinal directions, contraction of which causes complete collapse of the baglike shape. The flow of urine down the URETERS from kidneys to the bladder is continuous, the amount depending on body fluid levels. When the bladder is empty, the opening to the outside is closed by an internal SPHINCTER of smooth muscle which, like the bladder muscle, is controlled by the AUTONOMIC NERVOUS SYSTEM. When full, the internal sphincter relaxes under nervous control and urine enters the URETHRA, the duct to the outside, but is prevented from being voided by contraction of an external sphincter of striated muscle. Regulation of the sphincter, and thus of urine release, or micturition, is under voluntary nervous control. See Fig. 68 and Fig. 69.

opening of left ureter into bladder

internal sphincter of smooth muscle

bladder wall to smooth muscle

urethra ducting urine to outside

external sphincter of striated muscle

Fig. 68. **Bladder.** The mammalian bladder.

Bladder state	Autonomic system stimulation	Bladder muscle	Internal sphincter muscle
Empty	Sympathetic	Relaxed	Contracted
Full	Parasympathetic	Contracted	Relaxed

Fig. 69. **Bladder.** Summary of bladder control.

bladder worm the CYSTICERCUS larva of a tapeworm.

blastema an undifferentiated mass of animal cells that later forms a structure or organ either embryologically or through regeneration, for example, the head of a flatworm.

blasto- *combining form* denoting an embryo or bud or the process of budding.

blastocoel the cavity within the BLASTULA.

blastocyst the BLASTULA of mammals, differing from that of lower vertebrates in that it consists of an outer wall of cells, the TROPHOBLAST, by which the embryo implants in the uterus, and in having an inner cell mass, the embryonic disk, from which the embryo is formed.

blastoderm the layer of cells formed by cleavage of the fertilized egg in the presence of large amounts of yolk, for example, in birds, so that the blastoderm forms on one side of the yolk mass, initially as a small blastodisk.

blastodisk see BLASTODERM.

blastokinesis the movement of an embryo within an egg during the course of development.

blastomere any cell that occurs in the BLASTULA.

blastopore the opening of the GASTRULA.

BLASTOSPHERE

blastosphere see BLASTULA.

blastozooid see OOZOOID.

blastula or **blastosphere** a stage in the development of an embryo in which the embryo consists of a hollow ball of cells with a central cavity (a MORULA) formed by a process of CLEAVAGE. Invagination, the in-pushing of the ball at one side, of cells into the blastula gives rise to the GASTRULA. See ARCHENTERON (Fig. 44). See Fig. 70.

cleavage   morula   micromeres

blastocoel

yolky macromeres

Fig. 70. **Blastula.** Formation of the blastula by cell cleavage.

blending inheritance a pre-20th century theory that the male and female GAMETES each contain essences from the various parts of the parental body, which are mixed at fertilization to produce offspring showing some features of both parents. The theory was backed up by results from crosses involving quantitative characters (see POLYGENIC INHERITANCE) in which there was an apparent mixing of PHENOTYPES due to segregation of polygenes.

The idea of blending was overtaken by the discoveries of MENDEL and his laws of particulate inheritance.

blepharoplast a structure of unknown function that occurs at the base of the flagellum in some Protozoa.

blight any of various plant diseases caused by microorganisms, in which the entire plant is infected and soon dies.

blind spot the point at which the optic nerve leaves the retina of the eye and from which light-sensitive nerve cells, the rods and the cones, are absent.

blood a connective tissue with a liquid matrix called BLOOD PLASMA. Suspended in the plasma are three types of cells that form about 45% of total blood volume: (a) red blood cells, ERYTHROCYTES; (b) white blood cells, LEUKOCYTES; and (c) cell fragments, PLATELETS. See Fig. 71.

blood circulatory system the mechanism by which blood is moved through the body. All vertebrates and a few invertebrates, such as AN-NELIDS, have closed blood circulatory systems involving muscular tubes, BLOOD VESSELS, connecting the heart to all areas of the body. Other invertebrates, notably the ARTHROPODS, have open systems in which a pool of blood is circulated by action of the heart.

Fig. 71. **Blood.** The constituents of blood.

The various vertebrate classes display a fascinating range of circulatory structures thought to relate to their evolutionary history (see HAECKEL'S LAW). The circulatory system of fish is regarded as primitive because blood from the heart goes straight from the respiratory organs (gills) to the body tissues in the systemic circulation. Such a single circulation through two CAPILLARY BEDS in series produces a relatively sluggish flow of blood through the system, which is inefficient. In amphibia, evolution has progressed so that the circulation to the lungs is in parallel with the systemic system, and the heart is partially divided (two atria, one ventricle) to produce a double route. The two separate circuits enable a higher blood pressure to be maintained and thus a more efficient flow of blood.

A truly double circulation system did not occur until birds and mammals evolved from reptiles. In the mammal the heart is divided into two halves, the right half pumping blood to the lungs in the pulmonary circulation, the left half pumping blood to the body tissues in the systemic circulation. (See Fig. 72).

Fig. 72. **Blood circulatory system.** (a) Fish. (b) Amphibian. (c) Mammal (pulmonary and systemic circulation similar to circulation of amphibian). A = atrium, V = ventricle.

BLOOD CLOTTING

Although the circulatory system of the mammal is complex, it is possible to recognize several important features:

(a) in systemic circulation, arteries carry oxygenated blood from the left ventricle of the heart, starting at the AORTA, while veins carry deoxygenated blood, collecting together to form the VENAE CAVAE, which return blood to the right atrium of the heart.

(b) the pulmonary circulation is unusual in that the pulmonary artery carries deoxygenated blood from the right ventricle to the lungs, while the pulmonary vein carries oxygenated blood back to the left atrium of the heart.

(c) while all blood vessels are basically similar, there are large differences among the various types. See ARTERY, VEIN, CAPILLARY.

(d) the blood supply from the gut does not feed directly back to the venae cavae, but via the liver in the HEPATIC PORTAL SYSTEM.

blood clotting a condition in which elements in the BLOOD PLASMA change consistency from a liquid to a gel-like structure, causing a clot to form at the site of damage. The process of clotting is complex, but can be summarized as follows:

(a) damage to the blood circulatory system causes both BLOOD PLATE-LETS and BLOOD VESSELS to secrete *thromboplastin* (see HEMOPHILIA).

(b) thromboplastin, in the presence of calcium ions, causes *prothrombin*, which is a globulin type of plasma protein produced in the liver when vitamin K is present, to change to *thrombin* (see ANTICOAGU-LANT).

(c) thrombin acts as an ENZYME, causing FIBRINOGEN, another type of plasma protein, to be changed to fibrin. When fibrin contracts, it forms a mesh of fibers in which blood cells become trapped. The final result of clotting is a hard lump that can plug the damaged area, if not too large, thus preventing further loss of blood and entry of microorganisms from outside. See Fig. 73.

blood corpuscle a white or red BLOOD cell suspended in a watery matrix, the plasma.

blood film a smear of blood made on a microscope slide, which is subsequently fixed and stained for examination.

blood fluke *Schistosoma*, a close relative of the liver FLUKE, which causes BILHARZIASIS.

blood grouping a method in which blood is characterized by presence or absence of particular ANTIGENS on the surface of red blood cells. The antigens can be recognized by their reaction to specific ANTIBODIES, which causes AGGLUTINATION to occur. Two well-known blood groupings are the ABO BLOOD GROUP and RHESUS BLOOD GROUP systems.

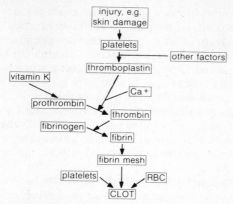

Fig. 73. **Blood clotting.** The process of clotting.

blood islands the beginning of the blood system in the vertebrate embryo in the form of cell masses that later form blood vessels.

blood pigments the complex protein molecules found in blood and other tissues, which contain metal atoms in their structure. Such pigments have a high affinity for oxygen, functioning in oxygen transport, for example, HEMOGLOBIN in vertebrates (containing iron) and HEMOCYANIN in mollusks and arthropods (with copper), and in oxygen storage within tissues, for example, MYOGLOBIN (iron) found in muscle cells. See OXYGEN DISSOCIATION CURVE.

blood plasma the watery matrix of BLOOD in which the blood cells are suspended. Plasma consists of about 90% water, acting as a solvent, and the following solutes:

(a) *plasma proteins.* The largest component, about 7% by weight, which is divided into three groups: albumin (55%), globulin (44.8%), and fibrinogen (0.2%). Plasma proteins are important in maintaining correct blood osmotic potential, regulation of blood pH, and for fibrinogen only, in BLOOD CLOTTING.

(b) NITROGENOUS WASTE substances that are carried from their site of production to the kidneys. These excretions consist mostly of UREA, but also have small amounts of ammonia and URIC ACID.

(c) *inorganic salts* of sodium, calcium, magnesium, and potassium, the most common being sodium chloride. These salts form about 0.9% by weight and are responsible for maintaining correct osmotic pressure and pH in the blood, as well as maintaining the proper physiological balance between tissues and blood.

(d) *organic nutrients.* Among the most important are: (i) blood sugar, mainly glucose, derived from the breakdown of foods, either directly from the gut or from GLYCOGEN stored in the liver (glycogenolysis). The precise level of blood sugar is critical for maintaining homeostatis and is controlled by a negative FEEDBACK MECHANISM in which insulin plays a major part (see DIABETES). (ii) blood LIPIDS such as fats and cholesterol, derived from dietary intake or activity of the liver.

(e) hormones manufactured in the ENDOCRINE GLANDS.

(f) dissolved gases, such as nitrogen (physiologically inert), small quantities of oxygen (mostly carried by hemoglobin in the ERYTHROCYTES), and carbon dioxide carried as bicarbonate (HCO^-_3) in the plasma (see CHLORIDE SHIFT).

blood platelets or **platelets** or **thrombocytes** disklike components of mammalian BLOOD, consisting of unnucleated cytoplasmic fragments of large bone-marrow cells 3 μm in diameter, called *megakaryocytes*, that have entered the blood circulatory system. Platelets play an important part in BLOOD CLOTTING.

blood pressure the force exerted by blood against the walls of the blood vessels, caused by heart contractions forcing a constant volume of blood through a closed system. Strong contraction of the left ventricle (SYSTOLE) ejects blood at high pressure into the AORTA, stretching the arterial walls. When the heart relaxes (DIASTOLE), force is no longer exerted on the arterial blood so pressure drops, although maintenance of pressure is helped by elastic recoil of the arterial walls. These oscillations of blood pressure are largest in the aorta, gradually diminishing as the blood flows along the arteries and becoming nonexistent in the CAPILLARIES.

The level of blood pressure also decreases from heart to tissue and back to the heart, these differences in pressure enabling the flow of blood through the system. See Fig. 74. Blood in the veins is prevented from moving backward by the presence of one-way valves. Venous circulation is also enhanced by activity of the skeletal muscles, so leg and arm movements aid blood flow back to the heart.

Note that although the above comments refer to the systemic circulation, a similar situation applies in the smaller pulmonary system of mammals (see BLOOD CIRCULATORY SYSTEM).

Several factors control the exact level of blood pressure: (a) heart action (rate of heartbeat, force per beat, volume per beat); (b) peripheral resistance to blood flow in the capillary beds, caused by friction; (c) elasticity of arteries; (d) total blood volume (the higher the volume, the higher the pressure); and (e) viscosity of blood (an increase in viscosity causes an increase in blood pressure but a decrease in flow rate).

Fig. 74. **Blood pressure.** The variation of blood pressure in different vessels.

blood serum or **serum** a fraction of the blood consisting of BLOOD PLASMA from which FIBRINOGEN, a clotting factor, has been removed. See Fig 75.

Fig. 75. **Blood serum.** The fractions of blood serum.

blood sugar see BLOOD PLASMA.

blood vessel one of a number of muscular tubes found in higher invertebrates and all vertebrates connecting the heart to the tissues via arteries and capillaries, and the tissues to the heart via veins—altogether forming a BLOOD CIRCULATORY SYSTEM.

bloom an overabundant growth of algae, often resulting from nutrient enrichment.

blubber the thick layer of fat deposited below the DERMIS and acting as a thermal insulation layer in some mammals, for example, whales and seals.

blue baby a rare condition in human infants in which there is incomplete separation of oxygenated and deoxygenated blood in the heart. Some deoxygenated blood enters the aorta rather than the pulmonary artery, resulting in inadequate oxygen supply to the body tissues and a bluish appearance to the skin.

The problem arises because of incomplete closure of two routes, which causes bypassing of the lungs during fetal life: (a) DUCTUS ARTERIOSUS, a blood vessel connecting the pulmonary artery and the aorta; and (b) FORAMEN OVALE, a hole in the septum that divides left and right atria. The condition is a serious one but rectifiable by surgery.

blue-green algae a division of algae-like organisms, Myxophyta or Cyanophyta, whose members are PROKARYOTES and live in marine or fresh water. They are usually blue-green in color and propagate mainly by asexual reproduction. Some blue-green algae are filamentous (see FILAMENT sense 1), with no well-defined nucleus or chromatophores, and reproduce by fission, or by fragmentation if filamentous. Some blue-greens live in inhospitable environments, for example, hot springs, where the temperature is above 85°C. The pigments produced are chlorophyll (green), phycocyanin (blue), and phycoerythrin (red).

BMR see BASAL METABOLIC RATE.

BOD see BIOCHEMICAL OXYGEN DEMAND.

body cavity the space within the body of most animals in which the gut and various organs are suspended. It normally contains fluid and is derived embryologically in different ways in different groups of animals. Absent in PLATYHELMINTHS and NEMERTINE worms, it is derived from the COELOM in vertebrates, the HEMOCOEL in arthropods and mollusks and occurs as an intercellular space in nematode worms.

bog an area of peat formation, typically in upland situations, that supports an extremely OLIGOTROPHIC vegetation. See FEN.

Bohr effect or **Bohr shift** a phenomenon named for its discoverer, the Danish physiologist Christian Bohr (1855—1911), who showed that the oxygen-carrying capacity of blood HEMOGLOBIN varies with pH. At high pH values, hemoglobin has a high affinity for oxygen, but more acid conditions cause hemoglobin to release their oxygen, as in tissues with a high concentration of dissolved carbon dioxide. See OXYGEN DISSOCIATION CURVE.

bolting an unusual lengthening of plant stems, due to elongation of cells, which can be induced by plant hormones called GIBBERELLINS, producing a stem with long INTERNODES. Bolting can occur naturally, as when biennials such as cabbage and sugar beet produce elongated flower stalks in their first year rather than flowering in the second year. The problem arises when such plants are subjected to winter conditions in their first year, usually because they were planted too early in the spring, which induces growth typical of the second year.

bolus a soft mass of chewed food, suitable for swallowing, shaped by the tongue in the BUCCAL cavity.

Bombay blood type a rare blood type in which individuals appear to be Group O (see ABO BLOOD GROUP) and yet can produce offspring of a type normally impossible for a Group O parent. It appears that Bombay types are homozygous (see HOMOZYGOTE) for a pair of recessive *h* alleles that inactivates production of the ABO blood group antigen, even though they have the genes to manufacture these antigens, a form of EPISTASIS. See Fig. 76.

bomb calorimeter a CALORIMETER in the form of a thick-walled con-

Fig. 76. **Bombay blood type.** (a) Normal and (b) Bombay blood group types.

tainer in which organic material is ignited by electricity, burned, and the heat generated then measured. The instrument is used to estimate the energy content of materials per unit weight.

bond 1. the force of mutual attraction that holds atoms together in molecules (see VAN DER WAALS' INTERACTIONS and SULFUR BRIDGE), such as high-energy bonds in ATP, weak hydrogen bonds in DNA, PEP-TIDE BONDS, and the disulfide bond of proteins. 2. also called **pair bond.** The attraction that maintains a male/female relationship, for purposes of breeding, during the life cycle of some animals, mainly warm-blooded vertebrates.

bone the skeletal substance of vertebrate animals, consisting largely of calcium and phosphate, which make up 60% of the weight and give it hardness. This bone salt, together with large numbers of COLLAGEN fibers, forms a matrix in which cells (OSTEOBLASTS) are distributed, and these are connected by delicate channels (canaliculi). Larger channels carry blood vessels and nerves (Haversian canals), and the cells are arranged concentrically around them. Haversian bone is found in the shafts of limb bones and is compact, while spongy bone is found at the epiphyses (ends of bone). See Fig. 77.

Fig. 77. **Bone.** The shaded areas are lacunae occupied by osteoblasts.

bone marrow a modified connective tissue of a vascular nature found in long bones and some flat bones of vertebrates.

bony fish or **Osteichthyes** the ACTINOPTERYGII and CHOENICHTHYES, classes of fish that have a bony skeleton, as compared with cartilage in ELASMOBRANCH fish.

book gill the respiratory organs of aquatic ARACHNIDS, such as the king crab (*Limulus*). Such organs possess numerous leaves, hence the word *book*, through which blood circulates and over which oxygenated water is circulated.

book lung a form of respiratory organ found in spiders and scorpions. The large number of leaflets around which air circulates are contained in the book lung and have the form of book pages, hence the name.

bordered pit a communicating channel between cells, found in the VESSELS(2) and TRACHEIDS of higher vascular plants. See Fig. 78.

Fig. 78. **Bordered pit.** Bordered pits in the tracheids of vascular plants.

botany the scientific study of the plant kingdom, usually including microorganisms.

botryoidal tissue the MESENCHYME of leeches, consisting of dark-colored, tubular cells containing bloodlike fluid.

bottleneck a period in the history of a population during which the number of individuals is sharply reduced, perhaps by disease or extreme environmental conditions. As a result RANDOM GENETIC DRIFT may occur in the population. See also FOUNDER EFFECT.

botulism a dangerous type of food poisoning, caused by toxins from the bacterium *Clostridium botulinum,* an obligate ANAEROBE that grows well in airtight containers, for example, in cans that were not properly sterilized before being filled. The toxin acts against the nervous system, particularly the CRANIAL NERVES, producing weakness and sometimes paralysis. The disease is named after the Latin *botulus* for sausage, a common source of the bacterium.

Bowman's capsule the capsule attached to the end of the uriniferous tubule of the vertebrate kidney, which contains the GLOMERULUS. The capsule performs a process of ultrafiltration so that the composition of the capsular fluid contains all the constituents of the blood in the glomerulus minus the blood cells and plasma proteins. See Fig. 79.

Fig. 79. **Bowman's capsule.** (a) The capsule is a small sac at the end of a kidney nephron. (b) An enlarged section of the uriniferous tubule.

Boyle's law the principle that the pressure of a gas varies inversely with its volume at a constant temperature. Named for Robert Boyle (1627—1691).

BP *abbreviation for* before present, a term used in GEOLOGICAL TIME scales to denote any time before the present.

brachi- or **brachio-** *combining form* denoting an arm.

brachial of or relating to the arm or to an armlike structure.

brachiation the movement of an animal in its arborial habitat by swinging from tree to tree by means of the arms.

brachiopod or **lamp shell** any marine invertebrate animal of the phylum Brachiopoda. They were the dominant marine forms of PALEOZOIC and MESOZOIC times, and a few species survive. See BIVALVE.

brachy- *in Greek, a combining form* denoting something short.

brachycephalic (of humans) having a short broad head, a characteristic common among the Mongolian people, where the breadth of the head is at least equivalent to the length. See CEPHALIC INDEX.

brachydactylic having abnormally short fingers or toes, an inherited characteristic in humans and some other animals, in which the phalanges are short and partially fused, and may even be reduced in number. The condition is controlled by a dominant autosomal gene, which was the first human Mendelian dominant gene discovered (see MENDELIAN GENETICS).

bract a specialized leaf with a single flower or inflorescence growing in the axil. See also SPADIX.

bracteole a small BRACT.

brady- *combining form* denoting slowness.

bradycardia an abnormal reduction in heart rate.

bradykinin a hormone formed from a kininogen in the blood plasma that has the effect of rapid VASODILATION in the skin.

bradymetabolism the pattern of thermal physiology in which an animal exhibits a relatively low BASAL METABOLIC RATE when measured at a body temperature of 37°C. In such animals, a fall in core temperature simply results in a reduction of the basal metabolic rate. Although usually poikilothermic (see POIKILOTHERM) and ectothermic (see ECTO-THERM), many bradymetabolic forms are able to attain varying degrees of homoiothermy (see HOMOIOTHERM). All living lower vertebrates and invertebrates are bradymetabolic.

brain the enlarged part of the CENTRAL NERVOUS SYSTEM beginning at the anterior end of bilaterally symmetrical animals (see BILATERAL SYM-METRY). The enlargement is associated with the aggregation of sense organs at the point that first contacts the changing environment. The brain, together with the rest of the central nervous system, coordinates the body functions. See also HEAD, CEPHALIZATION. See Fig. 80.

Fig. 80. **Brain.** The vertebrate brain.

brain stem the part of the brain in vertebrates that excludes the CERE-BELLUM and CEREBRAL HEMISPHERES.

branched pathway a biochemical PATHWAY in which an intermediate substance serves as a precursor for more than one final product.

branchial arches or **gill bar** the cartilaginous or bony masses supporting the gills of fish. There are usually five pairs of arches. See GILL BAR.

branchial chamber a chamber or cavity containing the gills of fish.

branchial clefts the apertures in the walls of the PHARYNX of fish or young amphibia, four to seven pairs, which allow water entering by the mouth to pass out over the gills.

branchio- or **branchi-** *combining form* denoting a gill.

Branchiopoda the most primitive class of Crustacea, including the fairy shrimp *Chirocephalus* and the water flea *Daphnia*.

brassica any member of the family Brassicaceae or Cruciferae, particularly members of the genus *Brassica*, for example, cabbage and rutabaga.

bread mold the fungus *Mucor* or a related form, *Rhizopus*, which grows on bread. The term can also denote *Neurospora crassa*, a member of the class Pyrenomycetes associated with decomposing or burned vegetation. This organism was used by BEADLE and Tatum in their work on which the ONE GENE/ONE ENZYME HYPOTHESIS is based.

breast-feeding (in humans) the direct feeding of an unweaned child on breast milk from the MAMMARY GLAND, as opposed to *bottle-feeding*.

breathing a process in which air is taken into the lungs (*inspiration*) and then expelled from the lungs (*expiration*). In a mammal such as man the structures involved are as shown in Fig. 81.

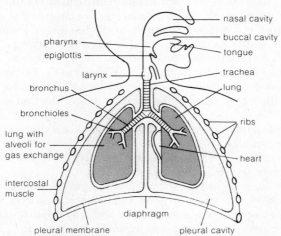

Fig. 81. **Breathing.** The human respiratory system.

BREATHING

Inspiration occurs when the rib cage and the DIAPHRAGM alter shape to increase the volume and reduce the pressure in the thoracic cavity. The ribs are drawn up and outward by contraction of the external INTERCOSTAL MUSCLES (chest breathing), while contraction of the diaphragm causes it to flatten downward (abdominal breathing). Expiration can be a passive process in which the muscles relax, causing the ribs to drop down and inward and the diaphragm to curve upward. These movements reduce the thoracic volume which, along with elastic recoil of the lungs, results in raising the internal pressure so that air is expelled. Forced expiration can also occur when the abdominal muscles force the diaphragm farther up into the thoracic cavity. See Fig. 82.

Fig. 82. **Breathing.** Expansion and relaxation of the chest during breathing.

Control of breathing is by a series of reflex actions so that, although the muscles involved are skeletal and therefore can be controlled voluntarily, respiration movements are automatic to a large extent. The main area of control is a *respiratory center* in the hindbrain, located in the pons and the MEDULLA OBLONGATA. The steps in breathing control are as follows (see also Fig. 83, steps 1—6):

(a) spontaneous nerve impulses are generated in the *inspiratory center* and cause contraction of the intercostal muscle (via the intercostal nerve) and the diaphragm (via the phrenic nerve). The thoracic volume increases.

(b) the *pneumotaxic* and *expiratory centers* are excited by impulses from the inspiratory center.

(c) when sufficiently excited, the pneumotaxic and expiratory centers send inhibitory signals to the inspiratory center.

(d) at the same time as (c), stretch receptors in the walls of the lungs become excited and begin to send inhibitory signals (via the vagus nerve) to the inspiratory center, which eventually stops stimulating the intercostal muscle and the diaphragm so that they relax.

(e) the expiratory center stimulates contraction of the abdominal

Fig. 83. **Breathing.** Steps in breathing control.

muscles. Steps (d) and (e) cause reduction of thoracic volume so that the stretch receptors are no longer stimulated. As a result, the breathing cycle begins again at step (a).

(f) finally, there is a chemical method of control. Excess carbon dioxide in the blood causes a lowering of pH, which is detected in the AORTIC BODY and the CAROTID BODY as well as the respiratory center itself. As a result, the inspiratory center is stimulated to produce deeper breathing and reduce the level of CO_2 in the blood. This negative FEEDBACK MECHANISM thus relies not on oxygen levels but rather on CO_2 levels to control breathing rate. See Fig. 83.

breeding individual an individual in a POPULATION involved in transferring its genes to the next generation via SEXUAL REPRODUCTION. Thus, a population will have two components: breeding individuals and those not breeding, that is, juveniles and individuals that have undergone GENETIC DEATH.

breeding range the geographical area within which a species breeds.

breeding season the period of the year during which the female comes into reproductive condition.

breeding true an organism not genetically variable for a particular character. Thus, crossing two parents, or self-pollinating one parent, of this type would produce offspring that were all identical with the parents. Such types are also known as pure-breeding and were used, for example, by MENDEL in his experiments with the garden pea. In more precise terms, parents breed true when they are homozygous (see HOMOZYGOTE) for a pair of ALLELES of a particular *gene*.

breeding value the economic worth of an individual's GENOTYPE, as judged by the average performance of its offspring. From the amount of the breeding value, it is possible to choose suitable parents for future crosses. See PEDIGREE ANALYSIS.

broad-sense heritability the widest estimate of the role of genes in influencing total phenotypic variability (see HERITABILITY), measured by the ratio of total genotypic variance to total phenotypic variance. Compare NARROW-SENSE HERITABILITY.

bronchiole one of the smaller tubes branching off the two main bronchii in the lungs of higher vertebrates. See BREATHING and Fig. 81.

bronchitis an inflammation of the bronchial tubes.

bronchus one of a pair of tubes (bronchii) linking the trachea to the lungs in mammals. Each bronchus consists mainly of connective tissue and a small amount of smooth muscle, the tubes becoming finely divided into bronchioles within the lungs, forming a bronchial tree. See BREATHING and Fig. 81.

brood pouch a pouch or cavity in certain animals in which eggs are contained and hatched.

brood spot or **patch** a prolactin-induced (see LUTÉOTROPIC HORMONE) bare layer of skin in birds from which feathers are virtually absent and which receives a rich blood supply. Such patches are used to incubate the eggs.

brown fat a special fat layer found between the neck and shoulders of some mammals, for example, bats and squirrels, whose function is to enable production of large amounts of heat, particularly after HIBERNATION. The fat is heavily vascularized (see VASCULAR) and has many mitochondria (see MITOCHONDRION), the latter giving it its brown color due to presence of mitochondrial cytochrome oxidase. Heat is released by very rapid fat metabolism, rather than the more normal fatty acid metabolism, and is rapidly transported away via the large vascular system.

Brownian movement a random movement of microscopic particles suspended in liquids or gases, which results from the impact of molecules in the fluid around the particles. Such movements can be seen in COLLOIDS in a solid state or in a suspension of microorganisms. Named for Robert Brown (1773—1858).

brown rot any fungal or bacterial disease of plants where browning and tissue decay occur.

brucellosis a feverish disease caused by the bacterium *Brucella*, which occurs commonly in cattle, sheep, and goats. Infection of *B. abortus* in cattle can cause spontaneous abortion of calves, and an attenuated live VACCINE has been developed to decrease the prevalence of the pathogen.

Brunner's glands the specialized areas of the inner lining of the DUODE-NUM, lying at the bottom of the CRYPT OF LIEBERKUHN. The glands produce alkaline fluid and mucus but probably few or no digestive enzymes.

brush border see MICROVILLUS.

bryophyte any plant of the division Bryophyta, a division containing the liverworts (see HEPATICA) and mosses (Musci). These plants do not possess a vascular system, and there is always an ALTERNATION OF GENERATION with distinct SPOROPHYTE and GAMETOPHYTE generations.

bryozoan or **polyzoan** or **sea mat** any aquatic invertebrate animal of the phylum Bryozoa. These are small animals superficially resembling hydroid COELENTERATES because of their ciliated tentacles and horny or calcareous exoskeletons. There are two groupings, each sometimes referred to as a class, although by many considered separate phyla—the Ectoprocta and Endoprocta.

bubble respiration respiration by means of a bubble attached to the rear end of an insect, for example, a water beetle, which enables the insect to stay below water until the oxygen in the bubble is used up, at which time the insect surfaces and takes on a new bubble.

buccal relating to the mouth cavity. For example, buccal epithelium lines the inside of the cheeks.

bud an undeveloped embryonic shoot in a plant containing a meristematic area (see MERISTEM) for cell division, surrounded by leaf primordia (immature leaves), often with an outer protective layer of scales formed from modified leaves. The tip of a twig usually carries a terminal bud, while leaves generally have a lateral bud in their AXILS.

budding a method of ASEXUAL REPRODUCTION common in some lower animal groups, for example, in COELENTERATES, in which part of the body wall bulges outward and eventually forms a new individual, which becomes detached from the parent. Budding can also take place in single-celled organisms such as yeasts, but there the process is more akin to MITOSIS, with daughter cells of unequal size produced. The production of plantlets from the leaf margins of *Bryophyllum* is also called budding by some biologists.

buffer a chemical substance with the capacity to bond to H^+ ions, removing them from solution when their concentration begins to rise and releasing H^+ ions when their concentration begins to fall. In this way buffers stabilize the pH of biological solutions and are thus important in maintaining HOMEOSTASIS. HEMOGLOBIN is an excellent example of a buffer, maintaining a stable pH in the ERYTHROCYTE.

bulb a short, specialized underground stem in which nutrients, particularly sugars, are stored in fleshy scale leaves overlapping the stem. One

BULBIL

or more buds are present in the AXILS of the scale leaves, and in the spring these develop into new shoots, utilizing the stored food material. Examples of plants producing bulbs are the onion, tulip, and hyacinth. See Fig. 84.

Fig. 84. **Bulb.** Vertical section.

bulbil a small BULB or tuber that arises on the aerial part of a plant in the axil of a leaf or in an inflorescence.

bulla a bony projection.

bundle end the simplified ending of a VASCULAR BUNDLE in the mesophyll of a leaf.

bundle of His or **atrioventricular bundle** a group of specialized muscle fibers in the mammalian heart carrying electrical signals from the ATRIOVENTRICULAR NODE down the septum between the ventricles and eventually dividing up into Purkinje fibers. See HEART and Fig. 183.

bundle sheath a layer of PARENCHYMA that occurs around a VASCULAR BUNDLE.

bursa copulatrix a depression around the genital aperture of insects that receives the male organ during copulation.

bursicon an insect hormone produced in the central nervous system that tans and hardens the freshly molted cuticle.

bush a low woody perennial plant with branches at or near ground level.

butterfly a diurnal insect of the order LEPIDOPTERA, which has clubbed antennae.

bypass vessel a blood vessel that joins arteries and veins, thus bypassing capillaries. Constriction or dilation regulates blood flow through the capillaries. See ARTERIOLE and Fig. 48.

byssus the threads that attach certain mollusks to the SUBSTRATE(2) or the stalk in some fungi.

C

C_3 and C_4 plants a grouping of higher plants, related to the carbon content of the compound produced when carbon dioxide is fixed during PHOTOSYNTHESIS. In C_3 plants, the more common type, carbon dioxide combines with 5-carbon ribulose diphosphate to produce two molecules of 3-carbon phosphoglyceric acid (PGA).

In C_4 plants, for example, corn, there is a special KRANZ ANATOMY in which mesophyll cells are adjacent to bundle sheath cells containing large chloroplasts. Carbon dioxide combines with 3-carbon phosphenol pyruvate (PEP) in the mesophyll cells to form 4-carbon oxaloacetic acid and malic acid, which are then transported to the bundle sheath cells where carbon dioxide is released to go into the CALVIN CYCLE. The advantage of using PEP is that C_4 plants can fix carbon dioxide even when in low concentration in the atmosphere, for example, in dense tropical vegetation. The system is also used in some XEROPHYTES as a CO_2 source in daytime, when the STOMA is closed. See Fig. 85.

Fig. 85. **C_3 and C_4 plants.** Starch formation in C_4 plants.

cactus the common name for members of the Cactaceae family, all of which, with the possible exception of *Rhipsalis*, are native to the New World. Most cacti are XEROPHYTES and succulents, found in deserts that have infrequent but heavy rainfall. Cacti are absent from deserts with little or no rainfall. *Epiphylum* species and their relatives are found in rain forests and are chiefly EPIPHYTES. Cacti are distinguished from other succulents by having an *areole,* a pin-cushion type of structure from which wool, spines, new shoots, and flowers develop. Other succulents do not possess an areole even though spines may be present.

cadophore a projection from the dorsal side of TUNICATES to which individual, newly separated offspring from the adult attach themselves.

caducous being shed at an early stage in development, as in the sepals of the poppy and the stipules of the lime tree.

caecilian see APODA.

caffeine a bitter purine derivative found especially in coffee beans, tea leaves, and cacao beans, which acts as a stimulant and a DIURETIC.

Cainozoic period see CENOZOIC PERIOD.

Calamites an extinct group of reedlike plants found in the upper Devonian, Carboniferous, and Triassic periods. They are usually classified with EQUISETALES.

calcareous of, containing, or resembling calcium carbonate; chalky.

calcicole a plant usually found on or limited to soils containing free calcium carbonate, such as *Fragaria vesca,* the wild strawberry.

calciferol or **vitamin D$_2$** a compound that has vitamin D properties and is obtained by ultraviolet irradiation of ergosterol.

calcifuge or **oxylophyte** a plant usually absent from soils containing free calcium carbonate, for example, *Calluna,* the heather.

calcitonin a polypeptide hormone secreted by both the THYROID and PARATHYROID glands that lowers the calcium content of the blood.

calcium an essential element for all animals and plants. Symbol: Ca.

callose a thick CARBOHYDRATE plant material deposited in the pores of sieve plates in response to damage or disease, or over a period of time, resulting in blockage of the SIEVE TUBE. Callose is also present in the walls of fungal hyphae.

callus a mass of immature plant cells that can differentiate into mature tissues, depending on the relative concentrations of plant growth hormones present. Callus can develop from EXPLANTS in laboratory tissue culture experiments but also occurs naturally at the end of cut or wounded surfaces of shoots and roots.

calorie the heat required to raise 1 g (1 cm^3) of water through 1°C, for example, from 14.5°C to 15.5°C. A Calorie (with a capital C) is used sometimes to denote a *kilocalorie.* Used as a unit of energy content or output, but now largely superseded by the S.I. unit joule (4.19 J = 1 cal).

calorimeter an instrument for measuring quantities of heat. For example, a BOMB CALORIMETER measures the heat output on burning a sample of material. Calorific values used in energetics are now measured in JOULES rather than CALORIES.

Calvin, Melvin (born 1911) American biochemist best known for his work on CO_2 fixation in PHOTOSYNTHESIS. In his experiment he labeled CO_2 with ^{14}C and, using the Lollipop apparatus for exposing algal cells to light, and CHROMATOGRAPHY of cell extracts after varying time intervals, was able to isolate the various steps from CO_2 to starch, a sequence later called the CALVIN CYCLE. He was awarded a Nobel Prize for this work in 1961.

Calvin cycle a series of chemical reactions, first described by Melvin CALVIN, that take place in the watery matrix of CHLOROPLASTS, where carbon dioxide is incorporated into more complex molecules and eventually carbohydrate. Energy for the reactions is supplied by ATP with NADPH (see NADP) acting as a reducing agent, both having been produced in the light reactions of PHOTOSYNTHESIS. Since light is not required for the Calvin cycle to continue, provided that CO_2, ATP, and NADPH are present, the steps are called the dark reactions. See Fig. 86. Every turn of the cycle fixes one molecule of carbon dioxide by producing two molecules of PGA and then two molecules of PGAL. Three turns are necessary to release one molecule of PGAL (C_3) for the glucose pathway, with the remaining five PGAL molecules staying within the cycle. Thus, six turns produce sufficient quantities of PGAL for producing one molecule of glucose ($C_3 + C_3 = C_6$).

Fig. 86. **Calvin cycle.** The dark reactions of the Calvin cycle.

calyptera a development of the archegonial wall (see ARCHEGONIUM) that in liverworts and mosses provides a hoodlike covering of the capsule.

Calyptoblastea an order of hydrozoan COELENTERATES in which the PERISARC surrounds the hydranths and gonothecae.

calyptrogen a layer of cells covering the growing part of roots that gives rise to the root cap.

calyx the group of SEPALS that usually form a whorl at the base of a flower.

CAM see CRASSULACEAN ACID METABOLISM.

cambium or **fascicular cambium** or **lateral meristem** a group of actively dividing cells found in the VASCULAR BUNDLES of roots and stems. Their function is to produce new plant tissue for lateral growth. INTERFASCICULAR CAMBIUM sometimes occurs between vascular bundles. Compare APICAL MERISTEM.

Cambrian period a geological period that began about 570 to 590 million years ago and ended about 500 million years ago. At that time, for example, the British Isles lay in the southern hemisphere, and the Sahara was at the South Pole and subject to extensive glaciation. Trilobites and Brachiopods flourished and most invertebrate phyla had evolved. The first *graptolites* appeared in the mid-Cambrian, but few traces of plants have been found and these are largely limited to simple algae. See GEOLOGICAL TIME.

camel the common name for a member of the mammalian family Camelidae that also includes dromedaries and llamas. They are even-toed UNGULATES, and the RUMEN of the stomach has numerous pouches and diverticulae capable of storing large amounts of water.

camouflage a disguise resulting from an organism having coloration similar to that of the background, or markings that cause breaking of the outline, so that the organism blends into the background and is hidden from predators. See CRYPTIC COLORATION.

campanulate (of plant structures) bell-shaped, as in the harebell flower, *Campanula rotundifolia.*

campylotropous (of a plant ovule) curved over so that the FUNICLE appears attached to the side between the MICROPYLE and the CHALAZA.

Canada balsam a commonly used microscope slide mounting material for biological specimens. It is miscible with xylene.

canaliculi fine channels, for example, those occurring in bone.

canalization, genetic the progression of a cell down a developmental pathway (see EPIGENETIC LANDSCAPE) as it becomes modified into its final, adult form (see CELL DIFFERENTIATION). Only at certain fixed times in its development (see COMPETENCE) is the cell capable of being induced to move into another developmental pathway and thus becomes a different end type. The process of INDUCTION is thought to be due to chemicals secreted by tissues surrounding the developing cell.

canalizing selection gene selection that stabilizes developmental pathways so that the phenotype is less affected by genetic and environmental disturbances.

cancer a disease affecting the growth rate of affected tissues in which the control mechanisms of cells become altered and the cells divide to form neoplastic growths or tumors. So-called benign tumors consist of well-differentiated cells similar to those in the surrounding tissues and are usually harmless unless located in regions where no operation is possible. So-called malignant tumors are dangerous and usually contain embryonic cells capable of floating away and forming new malignant growths in other sites.

Little is known of the cause of cancer, although exposure to CARCINOGENS, such as nicotine and mustard gas, and the presence of certain microorganisms are possible causes. Radiation, surgery, and chemotherapy are all used in treating various cancers.

canine tooth one of four pointed teeth present in the jaw between the INCISORS and the PREMOLARS in mammals, being particularly prominent in the Carnivora and having a stabbing function.

canker a plant disease giving a limited NECROSIS of affected tissue and caused by bacteria or fungi.

canopy the branches and leaves of a woody plant, particularly trees, forming the uppermost light-restricting area some distance above the ground.

capacitance the property of storing an electric charge by electrostatic means.

capacity the ability to store an electric charge, measured in farads (F).

capillarity the action by which the surface of a liquid, usually water, is elevated when in contact with a solid surface by attraction of molecules between the liquid and solid surfaces. When the liquid is in a narrow container, for example, a capillary tube, the level of water will rise considerably, but capillarity can also occur in such structures as soils, causing a rise in the water table. Capillarity has been suggested as the explanation of why water rises in XYLEM vessels in plants, but it is not considered to exert a significant effect. Compare COHESION/TENSION HYPOTHESIS, ROOT PRESSURE.

capillary one of many minute blood vessels, 5 to 20 μm diameter, that connect ARTERIOLES and VENULES in vertebrate tissues, allowing a high level of exchange of materials between blood and tissues via the interstitial fluid or LYMPH. See Fig. 87. Capillary walls are made up of a single layer of epithelial cells, which are flexible and so allow changes in diameter with changing blood pressure. See Fig. 88.

Capillaries are efficient because: (a) they are thin-walled, with narrow

single layer of
epithelial cells

diameter sufficient
to allow the flow
of red blood cells

Fig. 87. **Capillary.** The structure of a capillary vessel.

cells of tissue

interstitial fluid

capillary wall

capillary contents

Fig. 88. **Capillary.** Exchange route of materials between blood and tissues.

diameters giving a high surface area to volume ratio, (b) they are very numerous, forming a CAPILLARY BED, and (c) blood flow is slow, allowing maximum time for exchange.

capillary bed a fine network of blood CAPILLARIES extending throughout all tissue, enabling efficient exchange of materials between cells and the blood. See ARTERIOLE and Fig. 48.

capillary soil water water held between particles of soil by CAPILLARITY and taken up by plant roots.

capitate headlike.

capitellum a rounded bone articulation. See CAPITULUM(1).

capitulum 1. (in animals) the rounded rib head that articulates with the centrum of the vertebra. 2. (in plants) a head of flowers.

capsid the protein coat of a virus.

capsule a containing structure with a strong outer covering, found in many different groups, for example:

(a) the outer coat of some bacteria (referred to as *encapsulated*) that enhances resistance to the defenses of the host (see TRANSFORMATION for genetic control).

(b) the sporangium of BRYOPHYTES, for example, mosses, consisting of a hard outer layer inside which are developing spores.

(c) a type of fruit in ANGIOSPERMS that splits open when dry (DEHISCENT). Examples include poppy, willowherb, and snapdragon.

(d) a spherical bony structure in some vertebrate skulls, for example, the auditory capsule of the dogfish.

(e) the blind-ending part of the kidney NEPHRON.

carapace the part of the exoskeleton of a CRUSTACEAN that spreads over the head and thorax. In other animals, for example, the tortoise, the carapace is the dorsal covering of bony plates.

carbamate a type of insecticide, related to the organophosphates. Carbaryl, the first of the carbamates was introduced in 1956.

carbaminohemoglobin the compound formed by the reaction of HE-MOGLOBIN with carbon dioxide, which forms one of the methods of transportation of CO_2 in blood.

carbohydrase an enzyme that catalyzes the hydrolysis of carbohydrates.

carbohydrate a family of organic molecules with the general formula $(CH_2O)_x$, ranging from simple sugars, such as glucose and fructose, to complex molecules, such as starch and cellulose. All complex carbohydrates are built up from simple units called MONOSACCHARIDES, which cannot be hydrolyzed to a simpler structure.

The types of carbohydrate are described in detail under their own headings and are summarized in Fig. 89.

Name	Type	Structure	Location
Glucose	Reducing monosacch.	$C_6H_{12}O_6$ (hexose)	sweet fruits
Fructose	Reducing monosacch.	$C_6H_{12}O_6$ (hexose)	honey, fruit juice
Lactose	Reducing disacch.	Glucose + Galactose	milk
Maltose	Reducing disacch.	Glucose + Glucose	germinating grain
Sucrose	Non-R. disacch.	Glucose + Fructose	sugar cane
Starch	Polysaccharide	repeated glucose units (linear)	potato tuber
Glycogen	Non-R. polysacch.	repeated glucose units (branched)	liver
Cellulose	Non-R. polysacch.	repeated glucose units (linear)	cell walls
Ribose	Reducing monosacch.	$C_5H_{10}O_5$ (pentose)	RNA
Deoxyribose	Reducing monosacch.	$C_5H_{10}O_5$ (pentose)	DNA

Fig. 89. **Carbohydrate.** The types of carbohydrate.

carbon the element that is the basis of organic structure. Carbon has a valence of four, each atom forming four covalent bonds in its compounds. Long chains may be formed that give rise to the complexity of many organic compounds.

carbon-14 see CARBON DATING.

carbon cycle the circulation of carbon by the metabolic processes of living organisms in an ECOSYSTEM so that it always returns to an arbitrary starting point. See Fig. 90.

CARBON DATING

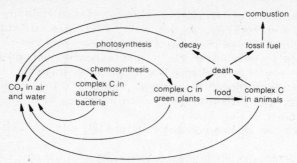

Fig. 90. **Carbon cycle.** The main steps.

carbon dating the dating of organic remains by measuring radioactive carbon content. Atmospheric carbon dioxide contains carbon atoms of two types, ordinary carbon ^{12}C and radioactive carbon ^{14}C. Like other radioactive isotopes, ^{14}C decays with age, so that the proportion of radioactive carbon present, for example, in peat gives an indication of its age, assuming that no more ^{14}C has been incorporated in it since it was a live plant and the amount of ^{14}C in the atmosphere has remained constant.

Dating organic remains by use of ^{14}C is a valuable technique but not entirely accurate, due to variations in atmospheric ^{14}C over long periods of time. Comparisons with tree ring dates (see DENDRO-CHRONOLOGY) have shown errors on the order of 900 years in 5000.

carbon dioxide a colorless, odorless gas, heavier than air, produced in respiration of organisms, and used to form sugars in PHOTOSYNTHESIS. Formula: CO_2.

carbon dioxide exchange see GAS EXCHANGE.

carbonic acid a compound formed by carbon dioxide and water.

carbonic anhydrase an enzyme that accelerates the reaction between carbon dioxide and water to form carbonic acid in the red blood cells.

Carboniferous period a geological period that began about 370 million years ago and ended 280 million years ago. It is often divided at about 325 million BP into Lower and Upper Carboniferous. The coal measures, from which the period derives its name, occurred mainly in the latter period. Club mosses, horsetails, and ferns were the dominant plants during the period, and amphibians were the most common vertebrates, although this was also when the reptiles emerged.

carbon monoxide a colorless, odorless gas formed by incomplete oxidation of carbon; poisonous to animals. Formula: CO.

carboxyhemoglobin a stable compound produced when carbon monoxide combines irreversibly with HEMOGLOBIN in the red blood cells, giving the blood a bright red color. A consequence of the reaction is that hemoglobin is less able to combine freely with oxygen. This can lead to poisoning by lack of oxygen in the blood and eventually to death if there is sufficient carbon monoxide in the atmosphere.

carboxylase an enzyme that assists in CARBOXYLATION or decarboxylation of a SUBSTRATE(3).

carboxylation the addition of carboxyl (COOH) or carbon dioxide into a molecule as, for example, when carbon dioxide is added to ribulose diphosphate (C_5) in the CALVIN CYCLE to give an unstable C_6 product.

carboxyl group the monovalent group, —COOH, found in aldehydes and ketones.

carboxypeptidase an exopeptidase that catalyzes the hydrolysis of amino acids in polypeptide chains from the C-terminal.

carcinogen a substance that is a CANCER-causing agent.

carcinoma a malignant tumor of epithelial tissue. See CANCER.

cardiac 1. of or relating to the heart. 2. see PYLORIC.

cardiac cycle see HEART, CARDIAC CYCLE.

cardiac frequency the rate at which the heart beats.

cardiac muscle a type of vertebrate muscle found only in the HEART that appears to be halfway between INVOLUNTARY MUSCLE and STRIATED MUSCLE in that its fibers are striated but contain a single nucleus (see Fig. 91). The action of cardiac fibers is to produce strong and rhythmic contractions from within, even when removed from the body (see MYOGENIC CONTRACTION). Unlike striated muscle, cardiac muscle does not become fatigued even though it is repeatedly stimulated. The heartbeat is controlled by the AUTONOMIC NERVOUS SYSTEM.

1 nucleus per cell

muscle fibres

muscle cell with striations

intercalated discs

Fig. 91. **Cardiac muscle.** The intercalated disks enable rapid transmission of excitatory waves across the tissue.

cardiac output the total volume of blood pumped out by the heart per unit time.

cardiac sphincter the sphincter at the junction of the vertebrate esophagus and stomach (the heart end). Compare PYLORIC SPHINCTER.

cardial veins paired longitudinal vessels present in fish and vertebrate embryos that collect blood from most parts of the body and return it to the heart via the CUVIERIAN DUCTS.

cardiovascular center a group of nerve cells in the MEDULLA of the brain that controls heartbeat.

care of young a feature of the behavior of mammals and birds in which the young are tended by the adult(s) until the young become independent. The phenomenon is less evident or absent in other groups of animals.

caridoid facies the body arrangement found in shrimps, crayfish, lobsters, and the like (the MALACOSTRACA), in which six body segments are present in the head, eight in the thorax, and six in the abdomen. The animals have a CARAPACE, stalked compound eyes, SWIMMERETS on the abdomen, and a tail fan.

caries progressive decay of a bone or tooth.

carina or **keel** 1. the keel-shaped edge of a leguminous flower, consisting of two fused lower petals. This may have a role in pollination, acting, for example, as a landing platform for bees. 2. the breastbone of a bird.

carnassial teeth the last premolar of the upper jaw and the first molar of the lower jaw, which form cutting edges in carnivorous mammals.

Carnivora an order of EUTHERIAN mammals containing bears, weasels, wolves, cats, and seals. Most have well-developed incisors and canine teeth, for tearing flesh.

carnivore any flesh-eating animal. The term is sometimes restricted to members of the CARNIVORA, although OMNIVORES also eat meat. See also CARNIVOROUS PLANTS.

carnivorous plants plants that obtain at least some of their nutrients by trapping small animals, usually insects. In some countries, such plants may grow in boggy places where nitrogen is difficult to obtain, extra nitrogen being extracted from the bodies of captured prey. The sundew *Drosera* and the bladderwort *Utricularia* are common carnivorous plants.

carotene an orange plant pigment of the CAROTENOID group that is usually present in the CHLOROPLASTS, and sometimes occurs in pigment-containing structures called CHROMOPLASTS, which are found in yellow/orange leaves, vegetables, and fruits. Carotene is necessary for producing vitamin A in humans and has an ABSORPTION SPECTRUM of about 450 nm.

carotenoids a group of yellow/orange pigments found in plants that are subdivided into CAROTENES (orange) and xanthophylls (yellow).

carotid artery either of the two vessels carrying oxygenated blood from the AORTA to the head in mammals and other vertebrates (see Fig. 92). Nervous receptor areas are located in the CAROTID SINUSES and the CAROTID BODIES.

internal carotid artery

external carotid artery

common carotid artery to head

subclavian artery to arm

aorta from left ventricle of heart

Fig. 92. **Carotid artery.** Mammalian carotid artery.

carotid body an area of glandlike tissue situated near the joining of the external CAROTID ARTERY to the common carotid, which acts as a CHEMORECEPTOR (see Fig. 93.) When blood-oxygen concentration levels are low and/or the concentration of carbon dioxide is high, the carotid body is stimulated to produce nervous impulses, which are transmitted to the respiratory center in the hindbrain, thus influencing BREATHING rate.

afferent autonomic nerves to hindbrain

external carotid artery

internal carotid artery

carotid body (O$_2$/CO$_2$ sensor)

carotid sinus (pressure sensor)

right common carotid artery

blood from heart

Fig. 93. **Carotid body.** Location.

carotid sinus a small swelling at the base of the internal CAROTID ARTERIES that contains baroreceptors (pressure receptors) that act as STRETCH RECEPTORS (see CAROTID BODY and Fig. 93). When blood pressure drops below normal, the sinus is stimulated to produce nervous impulses that are transmitted to the cardiovascular center in the hindbrain (see HEART).

carpal any bone present in amphibia, reptiles, birds, and mammals in the part of the forelimb attached to the radius and ulna. They articulate distally (see DISTAL) with the METACARPALS. There are eight carpals in the human wrist. See Fig. 94.

Fig. 94. **Carpal.** The human wrist and hand.

carpel or **pistil** the flask-shaped female reproductive unit of a flower, composed of ovary, style, and stigma. One or more carpels make up the entire female structure, the GYNOECIUM.

carpogonium the female sex organ of red algae, which contains the egg in the swollen base. The male gamete enters the narrower mouth or TRICHOGYNE.

carpospore the sexually produced spore of red algae.

carpus the part of the forelimb of TETRAPODS that contains the CARPALS.

carrier 1. an individual plant or animal that is infected with pathogenic organisms internally or externally without showing signs of disease, and is capable of transferring them to others, thus causing disease. 2. an individual with a GENOTYPE containing a deleterious recessive gene that does not show in the PHENOTYPE. For example, a carrier of PHENYLKE-TONURIA.

carrier molecule a molecule that is lipid-soluble and carries other molecules with a lower mobility within biological membranes. See ACTIVE TRANSPORT.

carrion feeder or **necrophagous feeder** any organism that feeds on dead animals.

carrying capacity the capacity of a particular habitat with reference to the maximum number of organisms the habitat can normally support, for example, the maximum number of wading birds an estuary can support.

cartilage or **gristle** a form of connective or skeletal tissue characterized by presence of rounded cartilage corpuscles (CELLS), surrounded by a matrix of mucopolysaccharide (CHONDRIN) in which, besides the carti-lage cells, there are numerous collagen fibers. Cartilage forms the first parts of the skull, vertebrae, and long bones of the developing embryo but in adult mammals and many other vertebrates is largely replaced by bone. It remains at the ends of bones, in joints, at the ventral ends of the ribs, and in a few other places. The types of cartilage are as follows:

(a) *hyaline cartilage,* bluish-white and translucent and containing some very fine collagen fibers. It is present at rib ends, in tracheal rings, in the nose, in the embryos of all vertebrates, and in the adult stages of cartilaginous fishes.

(b) *elastic cartilage,* containing yellow fibers and present in the ear and EUSTACHIAN TUBE.

(c) *fibrocartilage,* containing few cells and large numbers of fibers, and associated with joints subject to severe strains. It is present as disks between the vertebrae and in the pubic symphysis.

cartilage bone or **replacing bone** any bone that develops from cartilage by means of OSTEOCLASTS breaking down the cartilage, and OSTEOBLASTS replacing it with bony material. Long bones are an example.

cartilaginous fish any fish of the classes Chondrichthyes or Elasmobranchii, including the sharks, skates, and rays, whose skeletons are entirely cartilaginous.

caruncle a wartlike growth present on the seeds of some ANGIOSPERMS.

caryopsis see KARYOPSIS.

casein a phosphoprotein that is the principal protein in cheese.

Casparian strip a waterproof thickening on the radial (side) and end walls of endodermal root cells (see ENDODERM). The strip is thought to influence the route by which water passes from the cortex into the VASCULAR BUNDLE of the STELE. See Fig. 95.

Fig. 95. **Casparian strip.** The strip surrounds the endodermal root cell.

caste a specialized individual among social insects. For example, workers and drones in a bee colony.

castration see EMASCULATION (2).

casual an introduced plant that has not become established in an area but may occur away from cultivation.

catabolism a type of METABOLISM in which biochemical processes taking place in a cell result in the breaking down of complex compounds into simpler ones to release energy. Catabolism usually involves a series of step-by-step reactions, each catalyzed by its own enzyme, for example, AEROBIC RESPIRATION.

catadromous (of fishes such as the eel) migrating down river to the sea to spawn. Compare ANADROMOUS.

catalase an iron-containing ENZYME found in tissues, such as liver and potato tubers, whose function is to catalyze the breakdown of toxic hydrogen peroxide into water and oxygen:

$$H_2O_2 \rightarrow H_2O + \tfrac{1}{2}O_2$$

Catalase has a high TURNOVER RATE and works by reducing the ACTIVATION ENERGY required from about 80 kJ to less than 10 kJ.

catalyst a compound able to increase the speed of a reaction by lowering the ACTIVATION ENERGY needed for the reaction to start. Protein catalysts are called ENZYMES and are found in all living cells.

cataphyll a simplified leaf form, for example, a bud scale, cotyledon, or scale leaf.

catecholamine any catechol-derived compound, such as adrenaline or dopamine, that exerts an action similar to that of the sympathetic nervous system (see AUTONOMIC NERVOUS SYSTEM).

Catharrhini the primate group containing the Old World apes and monkeys and humans. Members of this group have an internasal septum and a bony external ear passage. Compare PLATYRRHINI.

cathepsin the intracellular, proteolytic enzymes that bring about AUTOLYSIS.

cathode a negatively charged electrode to which positively charged ions move. Compare ANODE.

cathode-ray oscilloscope an instrument that gives a video display of small electrical charges. The device is used to record and display electrical impulses from nerves and muscles.

catkin an INFLORESCENCE usually in the form of a pendulous spike of unisexual, much-reduced flowers, for example, a male catkin of hazel.

caudal relating to or in the position of the tail.

cauline (of leaves) borne on the aerial and mainly upper part of the stem of a plant.

C-banding a technique of chromosomal staining in which chromosomes are exposed to alkaline and then acid conditions in order to reveal bands of constitutive HETEROCHROMATIN that are identified with Giemsa stain.

cecum 1. (in animals) also called **hepatic cecum.** a blind-ending sac in the digestive system, which occurs in mammals at the junction of the small and large intestines. In herbivores the cecum contains bacteria that produce CELLULASE, enabling breakdown of cellulose cell walls. See also APPENDIX. **2.** (in plants) a protrusion of the EMBRYO SAC into the endosperm tissue of seeds.

cell the structural unit of most organisms, consisting of a microscopic mass of protoplasm bounded by a membrane and containing one or more nuclei (in EUKARYOTES) or pieces of chromosome material (in PROKARYOTES). Cell size is roughly constant in all tissues and organisms, being limited by the physical restraints of unfavorable surface area/volume ratios as size increases.

cell body the enlarged region of a NEURON containing the nucleus.

cell cycle the series of stages through which a cell progresses when it is actively dividing, consisting of three subdivisions of INTERPHASE (G1, S, and G2) plus MITOSIS. See Fig. 96.

Fig. 96. **Cell cycle.** The interphase stages.

cell differentiation the process by which young cells develop into the various cell types making up the plant or animal structure. All young cells in an organism are thought to contain the same genetic information (DNA) and may become differentiated into any type of cell, the mature cell being produced by GENE SWITCHING rather than loss of DNA. Compare DEDIFFERENTIATION.

cell division the division of a cell into two new cells during growth or reproduction. The new cells are called *daughter cells.* In PROKARYOTES, two identical cells are produced by BINARY FISSION. In EUKARYOTES, cell division is more complicated, because the genetic material is located on CHROMOSOMES inside the nucleus, being composed of two distinct processes that usually occur together: (a) nuclear division (MITOSIS producing two identical nuclei, or MEIOSIS producing four nuclei with a halving of the genetic complement) and (b) cytoplasmic division (CYTO-KINESIS).

cell fusion the fusion of two cells in TISSUE CULTURE.

cell lineage the developmental history of a cell from the ZYGOTE.

cell membrane or **plasma membrane** the outer boundary of cells, the structure of which is visible only under the ELECTRON MICROSCOPE and which is still not clearly understood. Two major models have been proposed for membrane structure: the UNIT MEMBRANE MODEL and the FLUID-MOSAIC MODEL structures. The cell membrane gives shape and some protection to the cell, and also acts as a regulatory filter for transport of materials in and out of the cell (see ACTIVE TRANSPORT, DIFFUSION). Higher plants, fungi, and bacteria have a CELL WALL outside the cell membrane.

cell plate a membrane of differentially staining material in plant cells that appears at the equator of the spindle in TELOPHASE of MITOSIS, and is concerned with formation of the MIDDLE LAMELLA between the two new cells. See CYTOKINESIS.

cell respiration see CELLULAR RESPIRATION.

cell sap a watery liquid contained in the VACUOLES of plant cells that is usually hypertonic (see HYPOTONIC) to the external medium. This causes the vacuoles to take in water by OSMOSIS, maintaining TURGOR in the cell.

cell structure see CELL.

cell theory the idea that all living things are composed of CELLS, first proposed by the German biologists Mattias Schleiden and Theodor Schwann in 1838/39. The cell theory is also used to suggest that all living cells come from preexisting living cells and do not arise by SPONTANEOUS GENERATION.

cellular respiration or **cell respiration** a catabolic process (see CATABOLISM) occurring in cells in which complex organic molecules are broken down to release energy for other cellular processes. Cell respiration usually occurs in the presence of oxygen (see AEROBIC RESPIRATION), but some organisms can respire without oxygen (see ANAEROBIC RESPIRATION).

cellulase an ENZYME capable of splitting CELLULOSE into glucose, used particularly in the softening or digestion of plant cell walls. Most animals are not capable of producing cellulase and therefore of digesting plant material themselves, relying instead on a variety of gut microorganisms to produce the enzyme and then absorbing the glucose product (see CECUM). Cellulase is also produced in large quantities in the ABSCISSION layer formed in leaf stalks of higher plants, causing a weakening of cell walls prior to leaf fall.

cellulose a type of unbranched polysaccharide carbohydrate composed of linked GLUCOSE units that can be hydrolyzed by the enzyme CELLU-LASE. Cellulose is the main constituent of plant cell walls and is the most common organic compound on earth.

cell wall a thick, rigid coat formed outside the CELL MEMBRANE of plants, fungi, and bacteria, which is composed mainly of CELLULOSE secreted by the protoplasm of the cell. Older cells may also produce a secondary wall inside the primary wall that is thicker and contains LIGNIN for extra strength. Such cells often die after producing the secondary wall, for example, XYLEM vessel cells.

cement the spongy bonelike substance surrounding the roots of mammalian teeth, which assists in holding teeth in their sockets. Part of the enamel of the crown of the teeth in some mammals, for example, ungulates, is also covered by cement.

ceno-, caeno-, coeno- or **caino-** *combining form* denoting recent.

cenobium, a colony of algal cells in which the cells are arranged in a constant form and number and are surrounded usually by a gelatinous matrix. They are connected, act as a single functional unit, and are thus regarded as a single organism, for example, *Volvox*.

cenocyte, a multinucleate mass of protoplasm formed when nuclei divide without the division of the cytoplasm of the original cell, as in many fungi.

cenogenetic (of larval features) evolved because of use in the larval stage, being absent in the adult form.

cenospecies all members of an ECOSPECIES related to each other by the ability to breed and exchange genes through hybridization, for example, dogs and wolves.

Cenozoic or **Cainozoic period** a geological era that includes the QUATERNARY PERIOD and TERTIARY PERIOD, beginning some 65 million years ago and extending to the present time. See GEOLOGICAL TIME.

centi- *combining form* denoting a hundred.

central dogma the hypothesis, based on WEISMANNISM, that genetic information flows only in one direction, from DNA to RNA to PROTEIN, and not in the opposite direction. Thus, in general, changes to protein structures produced by external forces are not inherited. See SOMATIC MUTATION.

central nervous system (CNS) the main mass of nervous material lying between the EFFECTOR and the RECEPTOR organs, coordinating nervous impulses between receptor and effector. The CNS is present in vertebrates as a dorsal tube that is modified anteriorly as the BRAIN and posteriorly as the SPINAL CORD, respectively enclosed in the skull and backbone. In invertebrates the CNS often consists of a few large cords of nervous tissue associated with enlargements called ganglia (see GAN-GLION). In some forms, that is, the COELENTERATES, the place of the CNS is taken by a diffuse nerve net. In addition to relaying messages for the sense organs, in higher organisms at least, the CNS takes on an additional activity of its own in the form of memory, which is the storage of past experiences. See also AUTONOMIC NERVOUS SYSTEM.

centric fission the splitting of a chromosome at or near the CEN-TROMERE to produce two chromosomes.

centric fusion the joining together of two ACENTRIC CHROMOSOMES to produce one METACENTRIC CHROMOSOME.

centric leaf see LEAF.

centrifugation a process in which particles in suspension are subjected to centrifugal forces by being spun in a CENTRIFUGE, thus forming a sediment. Subsequent removal of the SUPERNATANT fluid from the sediment and subjecting it to higher speeds of centrifugation can enable particles of different sizes to be separated out and collected. Eventually, the supernatant fluid will contain only soluble materials. See DIFFEREN-TIAL CENTRIFUGATION, ULTRACENTRIFUGE.

centrifuge a rotating machine that separates liquids from solids, or dispersions of one liquid in another liquid, by the action of centrifugal force.

centriole one of a pair of small ORGANELLES lying at right angles to each other just outside the nucleus of lower plants and all animals (see Fig. 97). Centrioles are self-replicating, dividing into two during the S phase of the INTERPHASE of the CELL CYCLE and then separating into two pairs, one pair migrating to each pole of the future mitotic spindle, from which an ASTER forms. The role of centrioles in nuclear division is unclear, since they are absent from most plant cells, and laser-beam irradiation of centrioles has no effect on division.

centrolecithal (of eggs) having the yolk aggregated in the center.

centromere a structure occurring along the length of a CHROMOSOME, often visible under the light microscope as a bump or a constriction whose location can help to identify the chromosome. The centromere contains a complex system of fibers called the *kinetochore*, which becomes duplicated when the chromosomes divide into CHROMATIDS. The kinetochore attaches to SPINDLE microtubules during nuclear division. Damaged chromosomes without centromeres (ACENTRIC CHROMO-SOMES) fail to move normally during nuclear division.

Fig. 97. **Centriole.** Structure and orientation.

centrosome an area of cell CYTOPLASM found near the nucleus, whose function is thought to be the organization of nuclear division, since it is capable of assembling and disassembling MICROTUBULES. When nuclear division begins, the centrosome divides into two organizing centers that migrate to each pole, along with the CENTRIOLES, if present, and the spindle develops between them.

centrum the central part of each VERTEBRA. The centrum lies ventral to the spinal cord and derives embryologically from the NOTOCHORD. Each centrum is joined to the centrum of the next vertebra by COLLA-GEN fibers.

Cepaea a genus of land snail much studied because of its GENETIC POLY-MORPHISM.

cephal- or **cephalo-** *combining form* denoting the head.

cephalic pertaining to the head.

cephalic index an anthropological measurement obtained by dividing the maximum head width by the maximum length (back to front) and expressing it as a percentage.

dolichocephalic	<75%	(long head)
mesocephalic	75–80%	
brachycephalic	>80%	(short head)

The ratios of one index to another vary between populations and have been used in studies of race.

cephalization the development of the head of an organism during evolution. The development is largely associated with a concentration of sense organs at the front of an animal (see BRAIN). The complexity of the head region depends on the habits of the animal. Highly active, free-living animals have the best-developed cephalization, requiring maximum detection of the environment at the front, whereas sedentary forms normally have less developed heads.

Cephalochordata a primitive group of the phylum Chordata that is usually given the status of a class. The group contains only AMPHIOXUS and a few related forms.

cephalopod any member of the class Cephalopoda containing mollusks, such as squids (10 arms) and octopuses (8 arms). They have a well-developed brain, eyes very similar to vertebrate eyes (an example of CONVERGENCE), and can change color rapidly because they possess CHROMATOPHORES.

cephalothorax the fused head and thorax occurring in many ARTHROPODS, particularly CRUSTACEANS.

cerat- *combining form* denoting horn or a hornlike part.

cercaria the last larval stage of the liver FLUKE. It lives in the freshwater snail *Limnaea,* produces a cyst around itself, and develops into the adult fluke after ingestion by a sheep or other primary host.

cerci appendages that are often sensory and occur at the posterior tip of the abdomen in many insects. Cerci may be short, blunt, or long, giving the insect the appearance of having a forked tail.

cere the portion of the base of the upper mandible of the bill in birds that is swollen and appears waxy.

cereal any member of the plant family Gramineae, which produces edible fruits, for example, rice, wheat, corn, oats, and barley.

cerebellum the anterior dorsal part of the HINDBRAIN, which controls muscular coordination. It is best developed in birds and mammals. In the latter there is a cortex of gray matter, and the surface is complexly folded. The folds are lined with PURKINJE CELLS. Removal of the cerebellum unbalances an animal and affects the accuracy of voluntary movements.

cerebral cortex a layer of GRAY MATTER forming the most superficial layer of the roof of the CEREBRAL HEMISPHERES in the forebrain of higher vertebrates. The cerebral cortex consists of millions of densely packed nerve cells and is rich in synapses. It is present in reptiles, birds, mammals, and some lower vertebrates. See BRAIN.

cerebral hemisphere one of a pair of large lobes in the forebrain of vertebrates. In reptiles, birds, and mammals, the coordinating function is dominant and the cerebral hemispheres control most of the activities of the animals. In lower vertebrates, the hemispheres are associated mainly with the sense of smell. In mammals, the enlargements of the cerebral hemispheres, the largest part of the BRAIN, are caused by development of the neopallium, which forms the entire roof and sides of the forebrain. The frontal lobes are particularly developed in humans and are the seat of memory, thought, and a considerable part of what is considered to be intelligence. See Fig. 98.

cerebro- *combining form* denoting the brain.

Fig. 98. **Cerebral hemispheres.** Localization of functions in the human brain.

cerebrospinal fluid (CSF) a solution secreted by the CHOROID PLEX-USES—in humans there is one in the roof of each of the four brain VENTRICLES(2). The solution fills the cavity of the brain and SPINAL CORD and the space between the CENTRAL NERVOUS SYSTEM and its ensheathing membrane. It contains most of the small molecules found in blood, for example, salts and glucose, but little protein and few cells, and serves as a nutritive medium. In humans, the total volume is about 100 cm^3.

cerebrum the part of the forebrain that expands to form the CEREBRAL HEMISPHERES, found in all vertebrates except fishes.

cerumen the wax secreted in the ear of mammals.

cervic- or **cervico-** *combining form* denoting the neck or cervix.

cervical of or relating to the neck or cervix.

cervix the neck of the UTERUS in female mammals that leads into the VAGINA. It contains numerous glands supplying MUCUS to the vagina.

Cestoda a phylum of the Platyhelminthes containing the parasitic tape-worms, the adults of which are intestinal parasites of vertebrates. They have complex LIFE CYCLES, usually involving intermediate hosts that are preyed upon by the primary host, which thus becomes infected.

cetacean or **whale** any aquatic EUTHERIAN mammal of the order Ceta-cea, comprising the porpoises, dolphins, and whales. Cetaceans are com-pletely aquatic, have lost their hind limbs during evolution and have finlike forelimbs, often a dorsal fin and, in marked comparison with fishes, a blowhole and transverse tail fin. The young are large at birth and suckled like other mammals. Cetaceans have an extensive outer layer of fat associated with their marine habit, have a large brain, and are capable of complex communication.

chaeta or **seta** a bristlelike structure, often chitinous (see CHITIN). The structures are found particularly in ANNELID worms, where they occur as projections on most segments, and serve as anchors for that segment during locomotion.

chaeto- *combining form* denoting hair.

chaetognath any small wormlike marine invertebrate of the phylum Chaetognatha, such as the arrowworms, which are INDICATOR SPECIES of water type.

Chaetopoda the ANNELID worms of the classes Polychaeta or Oligochaeta, characterized by the possession of CHAETAE. See OLIGOCHAETE, POLYCHAETE.

chain reaction a chemical or atomic reaction in which the products of each state promote a subsequent reaction. Initially, there is a slow induction period, but as the reaction progresses the reaction rate is accelerated.

chalaza the basal part of the OVULE of a flowering plant to which the FUNICLE (1) is attached, and through which the pollen tube sometimes enters the ovule prior to fertilization.

chalice cell see GOBLET CELL.

chalone one of a group of chemicals (PEPTIDES and GLYCOPROTEINS) occurring in living animal tissues that specifically inhibit MITOSIS.

chamaephyte a plant that bears its perennating buds (see PERENNATION) between soil level and a height of 25 cm. See RAUNKIAER'S LIFE FORMS.

character a genetic feature of an individual that can be assessed in some way. Such features often appear in various alternative forms, each controlled by different ALLELES. For example, the height of a pea plant is a character, with tall plants (2 m high) and dwarf plants (0.3 m high) as alternative forms (see QUALITATIVE INHERITANCE). Characters sometimes display a continuous range of forms, as in human height, which may be influenced strongly by environmental conditions (see POLYGENIC INHERITANCE). See also MULTIPLE ALLELISM.

character displacement the divergence of characteristics (see CHARACTER) in sympatric species (see SYMPATRIC SPECIATION), as a result of the selective effects of competition.

character index a value made up of the sum of the ratings of several GENETIC CHARACTERS that is used in NUMERICAL TAXONOMY to indicate degrees of difference between related taxa. See KEY.

Charophyta a group of the ALGAE, including the stoneworts, which inhabits ponds.

chartaceous (of plant parts) having a papery texture.

Chase, Martha see HERSHEY.

chasmogamous (of a flower) opening before pollination.

checklist a list of the organisms contained within a GROUP that can be used for quick reference in the arrangement of collections, for example, a list of the organisms' presence in various habitats.

cheese a partially fermented, coagulated product of milk. Varieties of cheese are produced by the use of different microorganisms in the fermenting process and by the use of different types of milk.

cheironym an unpublished manuscript name for an organism.

Cheiroptera see CHIROPTERA.

chela the large pincerlike claw of crabs and lobsters, formed from modification of the 5th segment (dactylopodite) and 6th segment (propodite) of the limb.

chelation the binding of a metal ion to an organic molecule from which it can later be released. In complex molecules, chelation results, for example, in zinc binding with amino acids in carboxypeptidase enzymes. The process also enables plants to take up metal ions such as iron that are not readily available in a free state.

cheli- *combining form* denoting claws.

Chelonia the order of reptiles containing the tortoise and turtles.

chemiosmosis see ELECTRON TRANSPORT SYSTEM.

chemoautotrophic or **chemotrophic** (of an organism) capable of manufacturing organic molecules from carbon dioxide and water by a process of CHEMOSYNTHESIS. For example, *Thiobacillus* oxidizes hydrogen sulfide to sulfur in order to produce the energy for chemosynthesis. Chemoautotrophic organisms are one form of AUTOTROPH, the other form displaying PHOTOTROPISM.

chemoheterotroph a CHEMOAUTOTROPHIC heterotroph.

chemoreceptor a RECEPTOR stimulated by contact with molecules and capable of reacting to and differentiating between different chemical stimuli, for example, in taste and smell.

chemostat a growth chamber designed to allow input of nutrients and output of cells on a controlled basis.

chemosynthesis the process of obtaining energy and synthesizing organic compounds from simple inorganic reactions. This is brought about by special methods of respiration involving oxidation of inorganic compounds, such as iron, ammonia, and hydrogen sulfate, and is carried out by several kinds of CHEMOAUTOTROPHIC bacteria. See AUTOTROPH.

chemotaxis the orientation of an animal in relation to the presence of a particular chemical, the response being negative (moving away) or positive (moving toward). For example, the movement of a wasp toward an attractive odor such as that of beer would be positive chemotaxis.

chemotherapy the use of chemical substances to combat disease caused by microorganisms. The term is often extended to include cancer treatment by chemicals.

chemotrophic see CHEMOAUTOTROPHIC.

chemotropism a growth response in plants in relation to a particular chemical. For example, growth of the pollen tube after pollination due perhaps to a chemical substance in the stigma.

chiasma the cross-shaped configuration of chromatids produced during CROSSING OVER in meiosis.

chickenpox an acute, contagious disease distinguished by slight fever and skin vesicles, and caused by the herpes varicella-zoster virus. The same virus can cause shingles in adults, which is a painful inflammation along the path of a major nerve, frequently across the back or sides.

chief cells the gastric epithelial cells that release PEPSIN.

chilo- *combining form* denoting lip.

chilopod any arthropod of the class Chilopoda (centipedes), carnivorous MYRIAPODS distinguished by having one pair of legs on each segment.

chimera 1. also called **graft-hybrid.** an organism, usually a cultivated plant, whose tissues are of more than one genetic type resulting from mutation or grafting. 2. a smooth-skinned cartilaginous deep-sea fish (king of the herrings) of the subclass Holocephali, which were common in the Jurassic.

Chiroptera the order of mammals that includes the bats, the wings of which are formed from a membrane of skin, the patagium, stretched from the front to hind limbs and over the fingers, but not the thumb, of the forewing.

chi-square test a statistical routine that is a test of SIGNIFICANCE, comparing the observed results of an experiment or sample against the numbers expected from a theory or prediction. The test produces a value called chi-square (χ^2) which is:

$$\chi^2 = \text{sum of } \frac{\left(\begin{array}{c} \text{observed no.} \\ \text{in class} \end{array} - \begin{array}{c} \text{expected no.} \\ \text{in class} \end{array} \right)^2}{\text{expected no. in class}} \text{ for each class}$$

The χ^2 number is then converted to a probability value (P) using an χ^2 table. If the P value is larger than 5%, we can conclude that there is no significant difference between the observed results and those expected, any deviation being due to chance. If the probability is less than 5%, however, it must be concluded that there is a significant difference between the observed results and those expected from theory. Note that the χ^2 test can only be used with data that fall into discrete categories, for example, heads or tails, long or short, yellow or orange.

chitin a POLYSACCHARIDE containing nitrogen that has considerable strength because of its long fibrous molecules. It is resistant to chemicals and is found in the cuticle of insects and some other arthropods where the outer parts are impregnated with tanned proteins that give it added strength. Many fungi contain a chitinlike substance in their cell walls.

Chlamydomonas a flagellate, unicellular green alga now normally placed in the division CHLOROPHYTA but in many older texts regarded as a protozoan and placed in the class MASTIGOPHORA. It is characterized by the presence of two flagella (see FLAGELLUM) and, because of the presence of CHROMATOPHORES (1), is referred to as a phytoflagellate and often given subclass status: Phytoflagellata.

Reproduction is by repeated fission or varies between species from an asexual method to a sexual method of CONJUGATION in which ISOGAMETES rather than differentiated male and female gametes are produced. See Fig. 99.

Fig. 99. **Chlamydomonas.** Generalized structure.

chlamydospore an asexually produced, thick-walled fungal spore capable of surviving adverse conditions that are unfavorable to the main body of the fungus.

chloragogen cells the yellow cells surrounding the gut of earthworms that break loose into the COELOM, absorb nitrogenous waste, break up, and are either excreted via nephridial tubes or deposited elsewhere as pigment.

chloramphenicol a BACTERIOSTATIC antibiotic produced by a species of *Streptomyces* that inhibits protein synthesis in a variety of organisms.

Chlorella a microscopic green alga of high-protein content, used commercially as an additive in food and candy.

chlorenchyma plant cells, usually of the PARENCHYMA type, that contain CHLOROPLASTS in their cytoplasm. The cells are found in leaves (see MESOPHYLL) and other plant organs.

chloride secretory cells cells present in the gills of TELEOST fish that actively extrude salts in marine conditions. In fresh water, the cells move salts into the body from the surrounding water.

chloride shift the movement of chloride ions into a red blood cell (see ERYTHROCYTE) from the plasma. The carriage of carbon dioxide results in an accumulation of bicarbonate ions in the red blood cell, but because of permeability of the cell membrane to negative ions they readily diffuse out into the plasma. The red blood cell thus develops a net positive charge, because it retains positive ions, and this is neutralized by inward movement of negative chloride ions from the plasma. This ensures ionic and electrical stability during transport of carbon dioxide. See Fig. 100.

Fig. 100. **Chloride shift.** The entry of chloride ions (Cl^-) into a red blood cell from the surrounding plasma. Carbon dioxide is carried into the cell from respiring tissues.

chlorocruorin a green respiratory pigment closely related to hemoglobin that is present in some polychaete worms.

chlorophyll a group of pigments giving a green coloration to most plants, which are found in any part of the plant exposed to sunlight. The pigments are usually contained in cell organelles called CHLOROPLASTS. Chlorophyll exists in several forms, of which chlorophylls *a* and *b* are the most common, and have the vital function of absorbing light energy for PHOTOSYNTHESIS. See ACTION SPECTRUM.

Chlorophyta the green algae, which constitute the largest division of algae, ranging from microscopic unicellular forms that are not mobile or have flagella (see FLAGELLUM), to large forms with a flattened THALLUS. Reproduction may be asexual (see CELL DIVISION, FRAGMENTATION, ZOOSPORE) or sexual (see ANISOGAMY, ISOGAMETE). They occur terrestrially in damp places, such as tree trunks, in fresh water, and in the marine environment.

chloroplast or **granum** a type of PLASTID containing CHLOROPHYLL found within the cells of plant leaves and stems. The chlorophyll is packed within granules called *quantasomes*, which are located in the walls of flattened sacs called LAMELLAE. The lamellae lie close together in certain areas to form grana and are more separate in the intergranal regions. LIGHT REACTIONS of photosynthesis are thought to take place in the quantasomes, whereas DARK REACTIONS occur in the watery matrix surrounding the lamellae, the *stroma*. See Fig. 101.

Fig. 101. **Chloroplast.** (a) Thylakoid arrangement. (b) An enlarged section of a granum.

chlorosis a yellowing of plant leaves caused by lack of CHLOROPHYLL pigment due to mineral deficiency, for example, magnesium or iron, or due to disease, for example, virus yellows, which results in a decrease of the photosynthetic rate.

choanae the internal nostrils that open into the roof of the mouth in all air-breathing vertebrates.

choanate any vertebrate possessing internal nostrils.

Choanichthyes the class of fishes closely related to the basic stock from which amphibians arose. Common in the Devonian and Carboniferous periods, the group includes present-day lungfish and CoELOCANTHS.

choanocyte or **collar cell** a cell in which the FLAGELLUM is surrounded by a protoplasmic sheath, occurring only in sponges (Porifera) and choanoflagellates.

choanoflagellate or **collar flagellate** any stalked protozoan that occurs either singly or in branching colonies, possessing a FLAGELLUM surrounded by a cuplike structure into which food particles are wafted by flagellar movement. They are very similar to CHOANOCYTE cells.

choice chamber an apparatus used in experiments in animal behavior in which it is possible for an organism to choose between, say, damp or dry, hot or cold, conditions.

cholecystokinin-pancreozymin (CCK-PZ) a single hormone secreted by the wall of the duodenum in mammals when food enters the small intestine. CCK-PZ causes contraction of the gallbladder muscle, resulting in bile being pumped into the duodenum via the bile duct, and stimulates the pancreas to secrete pancreatic juice containing large quantities of digestive enzymes, which enter the duodenum via the lower part of the bile duct. At one time it was considered that cholecystokinin and pancreozymim were separate, different hormones. CCK-PZ causes VASODILATION of the intestinal blood vessels.

cholera a serious human disease caused by gut infection of the bacterium *Vibrio cholerae* that results in severe diarrhea, vomiting, and abdominal cramps. Up to 15 liters a day of fluid may be lost from the gut, resulting in extreme dehydration and even death. Treatment is effected by replacement of the lost body fluids and salts. Cholera is endemic in certain third-world countries, occurring more often where natural resistance of the host is impaired, particularly by malnutrition.

cholesterol a steroid that occurs in the cell membranes of animal cells, but not in plants. Cholesterol is produced in the liver and when in excess is excreted in the bile but is partly reabsorbed by the ileum. It may precipitate gallstones in the gallbladder or bile duct. Alternatively, if there is excess cholesterol in the blood, it may be deposited on the walls of the blood vessels, obstructing them and often leading to an intravascular clot which if it occurs in the region of the heart gives rise to a heart attack or coronary thrombosis. Cholesterol is the precursor of animal steroid hormones and bile acids.

choline an organic base that is a constituent of ACETYLCHOLINE.

cholinergic (of nerve fibers) secreting ACETYLCHOLINE as a TRANSMITTER SUBSTANCE. In vertebrates these include motor fibers to STRIATED MUSCLE, parasympathetic fibers to INVOLUNTARY MUSCLE, and fibers to sympathetic ganglia from the central nervous system. Compare ADRENERGIC.

cholinesterase an enzyme that hydrolyzes and destroys excess ACETYLCHOLINE after it has been liberated and has produced its effect on specific sites on the postsympatic membrane. See NERVE IMPULSE.

chondr- or **chondrio-** or **chondro-** *combining form* denoting cartilage.

Chondrichthyes a class of the phylum Chordata containing the cartilaginous fish, sharks, rays, and chimeras. In some classifications, the term is synonymous with ELASMOBRANCHII. They are the lowest vertebrates with complete and separate vertebrae, movable jaws, and paired appendages. All are predators and virtually all are marine. They are characterized by absence of true bone and presence of CLASPERS(1) in males, and DENTICLES.

chondrin the white, translucent matrix of CARTILAGE.

chondrioclast see OSTEOCLAST.

chondriosome see MITOCHONDRION.

chondroblast a cell that gives rise to CARTILAGE.

chondrocranium the cartilaginous original cranium surrounding the brain of the embryo, most of which is subsequently replaced by bone during further development.

chorda cells cells of the embryo that give rise to the NOTOCHORD.

chordamesoderm the MESODERM and NOTOCHORD of the embryo of vertebrates, which originally form a mass of very similar cells and are conveniently referred to by a single term.

chordate 1. any animal of the phylum Chordata, characterized by presence of a notochord, hollow dorsal nerve cord, and gill slits. The major subdivisions are the PROTOCHORDATES and the VERTEBRATES. 2. of or relating to the Chordata.

chordotonal receptors the sense organs of insects that detect changes in muscle tension.

chorioallantoic grafting an experimental process of culturing tissues in eggs, whereby the tissue is introduced to the surface of the CHORION (2) of a live chick embryo, the blood vessels of which enter the tissue and maintain it after sealing the egg shell.

chorion 1. the superficial outer coat of the insect egg, which is noncellular and secreted by the ovary around the ovum. 2. an embryonic membrane of AMNIOTES formed from an outer ectodermal layer (see ECTODERM) and an inner mesodermal layer (see MESODERM). See AMNION. In birds and mammals it forms the outer membrane covering the amniotic cavity, and in mammals the mesodermal component of the chorion fuses with the allantois to form the chorioallantoic PLACENTA. Here the chorion develops fingerlike outgrowths, the *chorionic villi,* which project into blood spaces in the uterus of the mother. See CHORIONIC BIOPSY.

chorionic biopsy a technique that enables prenatal assessment of a fetus between the 7th and 11th weeks of pregnancy, involving sampling cells from the chorionic villus. These villi are small, fingerlike outgrowths of the CHORION (2) that, at the time of the sampling, are full of rapidly dividing fetal cells. A biopsy of the villus is taken with a small tube inserted through the vagina and cervix. No anesthetic is needed and no amniotic fluid is collected. The large number of dividing fetal

CHOROID

cells in the sample means that chromosomal and biochemical studies can be completed quickly, so that termination, if required, is usually before the 10th week, a significantly less traumatic period of gestation than termination after AMNIOCENTESIS.

choroid 1. a layer behind the retina of the vertebrate eye that contains blood vessels and pigment. 2. resembling the CHORION.

choroid plexus a nonnervous EPITHELIUM that projects into and forms part of the roof of the brain of vertebrates. It secretes the CEREBROSPINAL FLUID.

choroid rete a countercurrent arrangement of arterioles and venules that occurs in the eyes of teleost fish, behind the retina.

chrom- or **chrome-** or **-chromo** *combining form* denoting color.

chromatid one of a pair of duplicated CHROMOSOMES produced during the S phase of the CELL CYCLE, which are joined together at the CENTROMERE. See Fig. 102. During nuclear division, the centromere splits (in anaphase of mitosis, anaphase 2 of MEIOSIS) to produce two separate chromosomes.

Fig. 102. **Chromatid.** (a) Before duplication. (b) After duplication.

chromatid interference the restriction of CROSSING OVER between nonsister CHROMATIDS during prophase 1 of MEIOSIS, due to a prior CHIASMA having already formed. Such interference produces a reduction in the amount of RECOMBINATION and hence an underestimate of the map distance between genes linked on the same chromosomes.

chromatin the part of the cell nucleus that becomes deeply stained with basic dyes. This is now known to be chromosomal material consisting of DNA together with HISTONE and nonhistone proteins.

chromatography a technique designed to separate out the constituent parts of a mixture by taking advantage of the property of molecular substances, which enables them to combine physically with inert material, for example, by electrical charges. An inert substrate, such as paper or silica gel, supports the mixture over which a solvent flows. Components of the mixture will have different affinities for the solvent and be carried to different parts of the substrate and thus separated out. They subsequently can be identified by comparison with the migration pattern of known chemicals.

chromatophore 1. also called **chromoplast.** (in plants) a pigmented PLASTID of plant cells that may be green due to the presence of chlorophyll or differently colored because of the presence of other CAROTENOID pigments. CHROMATOPHORES are often CHLOROPLASTS in which the pigment has broken down, as in the ripening of fruit. **2.** (in animals) a cell with pigment in the cytoplasm, which can be dispersed or concentrated, thus changing the color of the animal as a whole, for example, frog, chameleon, and cephalopod. **3.** (in bacteria and blue-green algae) a LAMELLA carrying photosynthetic pigments.

chromomere one of many densely staining bands across the SALIVARY GLAND CHROMOSOMES of certain insects, each of which is thought to represent the actual location of a different gene.

chromoplast see CHROMATOPHORE (1).

chromosomal mutation any genetic change in the structure of a chromosome, usually of a fairly major type (compare POINT MUTATION) and often causing severely adverse effects. Such mutations are classified into various types: (a) *inversion,* the rearrangement of a chromosomal segment so that it has the reverse sequence, for example, ABCDE → ADCBE; (b) *deletions*, the removal of a segment; (c) *duplication,* the repeating of a segment either next door to the original or elsewhere along the chromosome; (d) *translocation,* the exchange of segments between nonhomologous chromosomes. Sometimes the loss or gain of whole chromosomes occurs, which is an extreme example of chromosomal mutation (see ANEUPLOIDY and EUPLOIDY).

chromosome a coiled structure found in the nucleus of EUKARYOTE cells that contains DNA, the genetic material making up the genes, and basic proteins called HISTONES and nonhistone acidic proteins that may regulate the activity of DNA.

Each species of organism has a typical number of chromosomes, for example, 46 in humans and 20 in corn, which come in identical HOMOLOGOUS pairs in DIPLOID (1) types, although lower types such as some fungi have only one chromosome of each type (see HAPLOID, sense 1). Chromosomes are not visible during the interphase parts of the CELL CYCLE, but during MITOSIS and MEIOSIS they shorten and thicken and, after suitable preparation, can be observed under the microscope. Individual chromosomes can be recognized by their overall length and the position of the CENTROMERES.

In PROKARYOTES, the chromosome consists of an intact DNA molecule lacking a centromere and is often circular. In viruses, the chromosomal material can be DNA or RNA.

chromosome map or **linkage map** or **genetic map** a map on which the position of genes relative to one another is marked on lines representing the separate CHROMOSOMES, the estimation being carried out by GENETIC LINKAGE analysis.

chromosome puffs or **puffs** the cloudy areas visible on specific CHROMMERES of SALIVARY GLAND CHROMOSOMES at certain times, which contain DNA and RNA and are thought to represent gene TRANSCRIPTION. This idea is reinforced by the fact that such puffs occur at regular intervals, suggesting that GENE SWITCHING is in operation.

chronic 1. (of a disease) of long duration, developing slowly but not acute. 2. (of a radiation dose) applied at a low level over a long time, rather than at an ACUTE dose level.

chrys- or **chryso-** *combining form* denoting the color of gold.

chrysalis the pupal stage that ENDOPTERYGOTES, such as moths and butterflies, enter into after the larval stage. It is an immobile, seemingly dormant stage but one in which there is considerable internal activity. Larval structures are broken down and those of the IMAGO formed.

Chrysophyta a division of the algae. The coloring is caused by presence of CAROTENOID pigments along with CHLOROPHYLL. This very diverse group of freshwater and marine forms includes the golden-brown algae (Chrysophyceae), yellow-green algae (Xanthophyceae), and the diatoms (Bacillariophyceae).

chyle the form of food after passage through the mammalian SMALL INTESTINE, forming an alkaline, fluid emulsion.

chymase see RENNIN.

chyme food in the semifluid state after being subjected to the rhythmical contractions of the stomach.

chymotrypsin an enzyme found in the pancreatic juice of mammals that functions as an endopeptidase, catalyzing the hydrolysis of PEPTIDE BONDS. It attacks the carboxyl groups of specific amino acids—phenylalanine, tyrosine, leucine, tryptophan, and methionine—and so produces large peptides. The enzyme works in the alkaline medium of the small intestine and is secreted by the pancreas in an inactive form.

chymotrypsinogen the inactive precursor of CHYMOTRYPSIN.

cichlid fish a group of TELEOST fish that carry the young in the mouth.

cilia see CILIUM.

ciliary body the thickened rim of the CHOROID of the vertebrate eye, which surrounds the lens and iris. It contains the CILIARY MUSCLES and secretes the AQUEOUS HUMOR.

ciliary feeding a method of obtaining food used by animals, such as mollusks, in which cilia (see CILIUM) beat to cause currents that carry food to the gut opening of the organism concerned.

ciliary movement locomotion brought about by the beating of cilia (see

CILIUM) as found in some protozoans (ciliates) and free-living flatworms (Turbellaria). Numerous cilia projecting from the body beat in relays, giving the effect of waves. This is called METACHRONAL RHYTHM. Cilia are rigid on the backstroke, pushing the organism forward, but bend on the forward stroke.

ciliary muscle any muscle contained within the CILIARY BODY surrounding the lens of the vertebrate eye. Through attachment to the lens, the muscles change the shape of the lens and bring about ACCOMMODATION(1).

ciliate any PROTOZOAN of the class Ciliata, usually placed in the subphylum Ciliophora, members of which possess cilia (see CILIUM) during some part of their life cycle for locomotion and/or food capture. Ciliates are said to be the most specialized of the protozoans and have various organelles to perform particular processes. There are more than 5500 species and they are common in both fresh and salt water.

ciliated epithelium a sheet of cells (see EPITHELIUM) that carry cilia (see CILIUM) on the exposed surface. These cilia exhibit METACHRONAL RHYTHM and commonly move fluids about the bodies of animals, for example, in the respiratory passages of terrestrial vertebrates, expelling dust or other foreign matter in microphagous animals. Ciliated epithelium is usually columnar.

Ciliophora a very large subphylum of PROTOZOANS, including the Ciliata and Suctoria, that at some time during the life cycle possess cilia (see CILIUM) and usually a micro- and meganucleus.

cilium (*pl.* cilia) a fine cytoplasmic structure in the form of a thread that projects from the surface of cells. Each cell may bear numerous cilia, which beat constantly in one direction, either moving liquid over the surface of the cells concerned or moving the cell(s) in relation to the liquid, for example, locomotion in PROTOZOANS. They are also present in all Metazoa except the ARTHROPODS and NEMATODES, but in only a few plants, for example, cycads. The cilium has a structure similar to the FLAGELLUM, consisting of an outer membrane surrounding a matrix containing two central MICROTUBULES around which is a ring of nine more microtubules (a 9 + 2 structure). See Fig. 103.

circadian rhythm the basic rhythm with a periodicity of approximately 24 hours that organisms undergo when isolated from the daily rhythmical changes of the environment, for example, when kept entirely in the dark. This rhythm demonstrates the ability of the organs to measure time, but the physiological basis of this is unknown. See DIURNAL RHYTHM, BIOLOGICAL CLOCK.

circular overlap a naturally occurring arrangement of contiguous and

Fig. 103. **Cilium.** (a) Vertical section. (b) Transverse section.

intergrading populations that interbreed, curving around geographically until the beginning and end overlap, and behave as *good species.* A species that behaves in this way is called a *ring species.*

circulatory system see BLOOD CIRCULATORY SYSTEM.

circum- *prefix* denoting surrounding.

circumnutation the spiral path followed by a plant organ as it grows, as seen, for example, in the twining stem of *Convolvulus.*

circumscissile (of a DEHISCENT spore or seed capule) exhibiting transverse dehiscence, the top opening like a lid.

cirriped any marine arthropod of the class Cirripedia, such as the barnacles and the parasite *Sacculina.*

cis-phase an isomer (see ISOMERISM) having similar atoms or groups on the same side of the molecule.

cisterna (*pl.* cisternae) a cellular space enclosed by a membrane, as in the GOLGI APPARATUS.

cis-trans isomerization the conversion of the configuration of a *cis* isomer (see ISOMERISM), with similar atoms or groups on the same side of the molecule to a *trans* form, with the similar atoms or groups on opposite sides.

cis-trans test a genetic COMPLEMENTATION TEST to determine if two mutations have occurred within the same CISTRON or in adjacent cistrons. The test depends on the two mutations being introduced into a cell at the same time. If they complement each other by producing a WILD TYPE phenotype, the mutations are in different cistrons, that is, they are nonallelic. If a mutant phenotype is produced, this shows the two mutations to be noncomplementary and therefore to be located in the same cistron, that is, allelic.

Two arrangements are possible in the *cis-trans* test (see Fig. 104), which can be carried out in a double HETEROZYGOTE individual, that is, a HETEROKARYON in a haploid type. The more important is the transconfiguration, which is diagnostic, since two normal cistrons are present if the mutations are nonallelic, giving wild type, whereas the same cistron is mutant on both chromosomes if the mutations are allelic, giving a mutant phenotype.

	cis-configuration	trans-configuration
if allelic	m1m2 ⎯⎯⎯⎯⎯ ⎯⎯⎯⎯⎯ wild type	m1 ⎯⎯⎯⎯⎯ ⎯⎯⎯⎯⎯ m2 mutant
if non-allelic	m1 m2 ⎯⎯⎯⎯⎯ ⎯⎯⎯⎯⎯ wild type	m1 ⎯⎯⎯⎯⎯ ⎯⎯⎯⎯⎯ m2 wild type

Fig. 104. **Cis-trans test.** The *cis-trans* test configurations—m1 and m2 are mutations. The two lines represent two homologous chromosomes.

cistron or **functional gene** a portion of DNA coding for one POLYPEP-TIDE CHAIN. The one gene/one enzyme hypothesis thus becomes the one cistron/one polypeptide hypothesis.

citric-acid cycle see KREBS CYCLE.

cladistics an approach to CLASSIFICATION by which organisms are ordered and ranked entirely on a basis that reflects recent origin from a common ancestor, similar to a family tree. The system is concerned simply with the branching of the tree and not with the degree of difference. The latter is the concern of evolutionary taxonomists, who oppose the cladistic approach.

clado- or **clad-** *combining form* denoting a twig.

cladoceran any minute crustacean of the order Cladocera, with a laterally compressed carapace and large forked antennae used in swimming.

cladode see CLADOPHYLL.

cladogram a genealogical DENDROGRAM based on the principles of CLADISTICS, in which rates of evolutionary divergence are ignored.

cladophyll or **cladode** a green flattened stem that functions as a leaf. For example, the lateral branches of butcher's broom, *Ruscus aculeatus*, are cladophylls and bear flower buds.

clasmatocyte see HISTOCYTE.

claspers 1. the rodlike projections between the pelvic fins of male ELASMOBRANCH fish, which are utilized in copulation. **2.** the processes at the tip of the male abdomen of insects used to hold the female during copulation.

class a TAXON below the level of phylum and above order. Related classes make up a phylum just as related orders make up a class. See CLASSIFICATION.

CLASSIFICATION

classification the ordering of organisms into groups on the basis of their relationships. The groups are referred to as TAXA, for example, kingdom, phylum (in animals), division (in plants), class, order, family, genus, species. *Natural classification* based on overall evolutionary relationships is the usual form, but *artificial classification* based on nonevolutionary considerations or on one or a few characters is often used in identification. More recently, the CLADISTICS approach has gained favor in some circles.

Classification is not to be confused with identification, which is the placing of individuals by deductive procedures into previously established groups. Most criteria used in classification are structural, but as more becomes known of physiological and biochemical criteria, these will be used in classification, as they are already with many microorganisms. See NUMERICAL TAXONOMY, TAXONOMY.

clavate (of plant or animal structures) club-shaped.

clavicle a bone associated with the ventral side of the shoulder girdle on each side of many vertebrates. In humans it is the collar bone. See Fig. 105.

Fig. 105. **Clavicle.** Location on left side of a primate.

clay soil a soil formed on a clay substrate.

clearing a process used in preparing materials for microscopic examination when, after dehydration using alcohols, clearing in benzene or xylene is carried out as these are MISCIBLE with the mountant and alcohols, whereas the alcohols are immiscible with the mountant.

cleavage the division of the cytoplasm during nuclear division (see MEIOSIS, MITOSIS) following FERTILIZATION of the egg to form the ZYGOTE. *Holoblastic cleavage* occurs in animals where there is little yolk, and there the entire zygote is involved. *Meroblastic cleavage* occurs where the yolky part of the zygote fails to divide, only part of the zygote undergoing cleavage. BILATERAL CLEAVAGE gives rise to a bilaterally symmetrical arrangement of blastomeres, as opposed to spiral cleavage, which gives rise to a spiral arrangement of blastomeres. Bilateral cleavage occurs in chordates, echinoderms, and a few smaller groups, indicat-

136

ing their common origins, whereas most other invertebrate phyla have spiral cleavage. See Fig. 106.

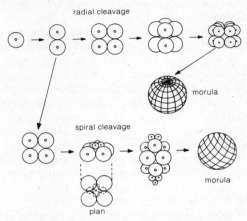

Fig. 106. **Cleavage.** Radial and spiral cleavage.

cleidoic egg an egg that possesses a protective shell.

cleistocarp the fruiting body of some ASCOMYCETE fungi that is completely closed and must be ruptured to release the spores.

cleistogamy the production of small, inconspicuous flowers in which self-fertilization occurs before the flowers open. For example, the violet forms large, showy, cross-pollinating flowers, but also forms cleistogamic flowers late in the summer.

climacteric 1. any critical event. 2. the MENOPAUSE.

climacteric phase a stage preceding senescence in certain fully grown fruits, in which there is a marked increase in respiration rate. Climacteric fruits, for example, apples and bananas, can be prevented from undergoing this respiratory increase by treatment with high levels of carbon dioxide and/or exposure to low temperatures. Exposure to ethylene may then be used to hasten the climacteric phase, so that the fruit is ready for sale. Many fruits such as citrus types do not exhibit the climacteric phase.

climate the general meteorological conditions prevailing in an area.

climax a plant community that has reached stability and is in equilibrium with the climatic conditions prevailing at the time, for example, oak forests. A succession of climaxes resulting from climatic change is called a *clisere*.

cline a gradual and continuous, or nearly continuous, change in a character, such as size or color, in relation to its geographical or ecological distribution. For example, there is an increase in the percentage of bridled forms in some guillemot populations in more northerly latitudes.

clisere see CLIMAX.

clitellum a saddlelike structure present around part of the anterior half of some ANNELID worms that contains glands secreting mucus, forming a sheath around copulating animals and a cocoon around the eggs.

clitoris an erectile structure occurring ventral to the uterus in female mammals that is homologous with the PENIS in the male.

cloaca the terminal part of the gut system of most vertebrates, except higher mammals, into which open the ducts from the kidney and reproductive system. In these types, there is thus only one posterior aperture to the body as compared with two in mammals, the anus and the opening of the urinogenital system. In some vertebrates, such as birds, the cloaca is reversible and forms a penislike structure in the males during copulation.

clock, internal see BIOLOGICAL CLOCK.

clone 1. any of two or more individuals with identical genetic makeup produced from one parent by ASEXUAL REPRODUCTION, for example, daughter plants produced by strawberry RUNNERS and whole plants produced by tissue culture. 2. either of the identical individuals produced by the splitting of a young embryo.

closed community a plant community so dense on the ground that new species cannot colonize.

closed population a population into which there is no gene input from outside, that is, the only possible genetic change is through MUTATION.

cloven-footed herbivore a member of the mammalian order ARTIODACTYLA with two functional toes (numbers three and four) on each foot. While all in this group are herbivorous, some are RUMINANTS— camels, deer, sheep, and cattle— whereas others are not—pigs and hippopotamuses.

club moss any mosslike pteridophyte plant of the order Lycopodiales, having erect or creeping stems covered with small overlapping leaves. The group existed as far back as the Paleozoic era. *Lycopodium* and *Selaginella* are present-day forms.

clustering methods the means by which groups of related or similar species are arranged in species groups or in higher taxonomic groupings.

clypeus the cuticular plate on the head of an insect above the LABIUM.

Cnidaria a subphylum of the phylum Coelenterata in some classifications, where the Ctenophora (sea gooseberries) form the other subphylum (see COELENTERATE). In more modern classifications, the Ctenophora are given the status of a phylum, so that the organisms classified in the Cnidaria—hydroids, jellyfishes, sea anemones, and corals—are the only organisms in the new phylum Coelenterata—making the term Cnidaria obsolete.

cnido- *combining form* denoting a nematocyst.

cnidoblast or **nematoblast** a stinging *thread cell.* See NEMATOCYST.

cnidocil the trigger on a CNIDOBLAST.

CNS see CENTRAL NERVOUS SYSTEM.

co- or **con-** or **com-** *prefix* denoting with, together.

CO_2 acceptor, a molecule (ribulose diphosphate) whose function is to combine with carbon dioxide in the CALVIN CYCLE.

coacervate theory a theory expressed by the Russian biochemist A.I. Oparin in 1936 suggesting that the origin of life was preceded by formation of mixed colloidal units called coacervates. These are particles composed of two or more colloids that can be protein, lipid, or nucleic acid.

Oparin proposed that while these molecules were not living, they behaved like biological systems in the ancient seas and were subject to natural selection in terms of constant size and chemical properties. There was a selective accumulation of material, and the coacervates reproduced by fragmentation. Subsequent work by the American biochemists Stanley Miller and Harold Urey shows that such organic materials can be formed from inorganic substances under the conditions prevailing on prebiological Earth. They synthesized amino acids by passing a spark through a mixture of simple gases in a closed system.

coagulation the separation or precipitation of suspended particles from a dispersed state.

coalescent (of plant structures) joining together.

cobalamin or **cobalamine** or **cyanocobalamin** or **vitamin B_{12}** one of the B-COMPLEX of water-soluble vitamins, containing cobalt and required for red blood cell formation. A deficiency of B_{12} can lead to pernicious anemia, especially in old people. The vitamin is synthesized by bacteria in the gut rather than being obtained from the diet.

coccidiosis a disease caused by SPOROZOAN parasites that occurs in rabbits and poultry.

coccus a bacterium having a spherical or globular form.

coccyx the fusion of the posterior vertebrae to form a single unit, the coccyx. In humans, three to five vertebrae are involved and these form the remnant of a tail.

cochlea a part of the inner ear concerned with detection of the pitch of the sound received by the ear. A projection of the SACCULE (2), it occurs in some reptiles, birds, and mammals. In the mammal it is a coiled tube consisting of three parallel canals and contains the *organ of Corti,* the part that actually responds to sound. See Fig. 107.

Fig. 107. **Cochlea.** Cross section.

cocoon a protective covering of eggs or larvae found in several invertebrate groups. In some cases, for example, ANNELIDS, a cocoon is produced by the adults to contain the eggs and in others, for example,
insects, by the larvae to protect the pupa during development.

codominance the relationship between two different ALLELES of a gene
in the HETEROZYGOTE, producing a PHENOTYPE containing both parental forms of the character. For example, allele *A* of the ABO blood group
is codominant to allele *B,* so that an individual with both alleles (*A/B*)
produces both *A* and *B* antigens. Compare INCOMPLETE DOMINANCE.
See DOMINANCE (1).

codon or **triplet** a group of three DNA nucleotide bases that codes for
a specific amino acid in the related protein. See PROTEIN SYNTHESIS,
GENETIC CODE.

coefficient of the difference the difference of the means divided by
the sum of the STANDARD DEVIATION.

coefficient of dispersion the variance divided by the mean. Where
this value is equal to 1, there is a random or POISSON DISTRIBUTION.
Above 1 there is aggregation or under-dispersion. Below 1 there is an
even distribution or over-dispersion, for example, territoriality in birds.

coefficient of inbreeding the probability that any two gametes fusing
to form a zygote will carry the same allele of a gene from a COMMON
ANCESTOR. Symbol: F.

coefficient of variability the STANDARD DEVIATION as a percentage of
the mean.

coel- *combining form* denoting a cavity.

coelacanth a primitive bony fish with lobed fins, as distinct from ray fins.
Almost all its relatives were freshwater fossil forms dating from the
DEVONIAN PERIOD. *Latimeria* is a living marine form found around the
Comoro Islands off Southeast Africa and collected for the first time in
1938. It is remarkable in that it has remained almost unchanged from

its ancestors in the lower CARBONIFEROUS PERIOD, which existed more than 300 million years ago. See Fig. 108.

Fig. 108. **Coelacanth.** *Latimeria chalumnae.* Length: 1.5 meters.

coelenterate any invertebrate of the phylum Coelenterata, including the hydroids (Hydrozoa), jellyfish (Scyphozoa), and sea anemones and corals (Actinozoa). In some classifications, the sea gooseberries (Cteno-phora) are included as a separate subphylum. See CNIDARIA.

coelenteron the digestive cavity in COELENTERATES, which has only one opening, the mouth.

coelom the main body cavity of most animals with three body layers, being a fluid-filled space between inner and outer layers of MESODERM. The coelom often has tubes connecting to the outside called CO-ELOMODUCTS. See Fig. 109.

Fig. 109. **Coelom.** Location.

coelomoduct any duct leading from the COELOM of an animal to the exterior that can carry either excretory materials or gametes. For example, the oviduct in vertebrates is thought to have evolved as a co-elomoduct.

coenzyme an organic COFACTOR molecule smaller than protein that bonds with a specific ENZYME while the reaction is being catalyzed. Like enzymes, coenzymes are not altered or used up in the reaction and can be used many times, but a minimal quantity is required for normal level of enzyme function and thus normal health. This explains why VITA-

COENZYME A

MINS, which often act as coenzymes, are so essential. See also ACETYL COENZYME A.

coenzyme A see ACETYL COENZYME A.

coevolution the evolution of unrelated organisms that has taken place together because of the special link between them, for example, insects and the flowers they pollinate (see ENTOMOPHILY), parasites and their host, and members of a symbiotic relationship (see SYMBIOSIS). The ARUM LILY is a notable example.

cofactor a substance essential for the catalytic activity of some enzymes, binding to the enzyme only during the reaction. Cofactors can be metallic ions or nonprotein organic molecules (coenzymes), such as vitamins in the B-COMPLEX.

coherent (of plant structures) united at some point but appearing free.

cohesion-tension hypothesis a hypothesis that explains the ascent of water from roots to leaves in a plant as due to a combination of upward pull created by TRANSPIRATION losses producing a tension on the xylem vessels and cohesion of water molecules to each other, aided by the adhesion of water molecules to the sides of the narrow vessels. Evidence for the hypothesis comes from: (a) the long rise in mercury in a column attached to a leafy shoot as compared with mercury rise in a vacuum, and (b) the decrease in tree trunk diameter during the day, due possibly to tension, when transpiration is at its highest level. See DENDROMETER.

coincidence, coefficient of the proportion of double recombinant types observed in a progeny as compared with the number expected. A value below 1.0 indicates that CHROMATID INTERFERENCE has taken place.

coitus the act of copulation between male and female animals during which sperm is transferred from male to female.

colchicine a poisonous alkaloid extracted from the corms of *Colchicum autumnale* that acts as a spindle inhibitor during NUCLEAR DIVISION and can thus be used to produce cells with double sets of chromosomes, due to NONDISJUNCTION.

cold receptor a sensory structure that responds particularly to cold and sometimes to pressure. Such receptors occur in the skin of vertebrates, and in humans are more abundant and occur more superficially than warm receptors. Fibers from cold receptors are active between 10° and 40°C, with a maximum firing frequency between 20° and 34°.

Coleoptera an order of insects, including beetles and weevils. The forewing is thick, leathery, and veinless, and is called an *elytrum*. When closed, elytra meet along the midline and protect the membranous hindwings, which fold forward. Some of the approximately 280,000 species of Coleoptera, however, are wingless. There is a complete META-MORPHOSIS. See Fig. 110.

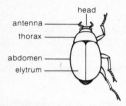

Fig. 110. **Coleoptera.** Generalized structure.

coleoptile a nonchlorophyllous covering over the growing shoot of young plant seedlings in certain MONOCOTYLEDONS, for example, oats. The coleoptile is the first structure to break through soil into the air after germination. As growth proceeds, the coleoptile is ruptured by the first foliage leaf of the enclosed shoot. Oat coleoptiles have been used extensively in experiments with AUXINS.

coleorhiza a structure similar to the COLEOPTILE but located around the radicle of young seedlings.

coliform (of Gram-negative rod bacteria) normally inhabiting the colon, for example, *Escherichia coli, Enterobacter aerogenes,* and *Klebsiella.* See GRAM'S SOLUTION.

colinearity the linear relationship between a piece of DNA coding (a CISTRON) and the POLYPEPTIDE CHAIN (see Fig. 111). Therefore:

$$\frac{A \text{ to } X}{A \text{ to } B} = \frac{C \text{ to } Y}{C \text{ to } D.}$$

collagen a fibrous protein forming the white fibers of vertebrate CON-NECTIVE TISSUE. These, for example, tendons, have high tensile strength but are not elastic. Collagen tissues consist of a glycoprotein matrix containing densely packed collagen fibers.

collagenoblast a type of FIBROBLAST giving rise to COLLAGEN.

collar cell see CHOANOCYTE.

collar flagellate see CHOANOFLAGELLATE.

collateral a minor side branch of a blood vessel or nerve.

collateral bud an accessory bud on a plant stem, lying beside the axillary bud.

Fig. 111. **Colinearity.** The DNA bases are transcribed from left to right.

collateral bundle a plant vascular bundle in which the PHLOEM is on the same radius as the XYLEM and external to it.

collecting duct that part of the renal tubule in a kidney in which water absorption takes place under the control of ADH, producing urine of variable concentration depending on overall water levels in the body.

Collembola an order of small primitive wingless insects comprising the springtails, most of which have a springing organ (*furcula*). They live in soil and leaf litter. See VENTRAL TUBE.

collenchyma a type of plant tissue in which the cells are similar to PARENCHYMA but have cellulose wall thickenings, particularly at the angles when seen in transverse section. Collenchyma acts as a supporting tissue, especially in young stems and leaves. See Fig. 112.

Fig. 112. **Collenchyma.** Transverse section.

colloid a mixture of two substances that are immiscible (see MISCIBLE), but where the particles of one are too small to settle out and so remain suspended indefinitely. Glue is a colloid of animal gelatin in water. The water is defined as the *matrix* and the gelatin as the *inclusion*. Colloid particles measure 1×10^{-4} to 1×10^{-6} mm in diameter, forming either a SOL or GEL structure, which does not diffuse through cell membranes. Colloids are common in cells, where their large surfaces are important for chemical changes constantly in progress.

colon a part of the large intestine of mammals, consisting of a wide tube with folded walls between the ILEUM of the small intestine and the

RECTUM. The main function of the colon is the reabsorption of water from the FECES.

colon bacillus the bacillus *Escherichia coli* found in the colon.

colonial animal an association of animals in which the individuals are connected, as in the Hydrozoa or Polyzoa. The term is not usually attributed to higher animals, such as birds, that live in colonies.

colony 1. an aggregated group of separate organisms that have come together for specific purposes, for example, breeding in birds. 2. a group of incompletely separated individuals organized in associations, as in some hydrozoan COELENTRATES and polyzoans. 3. a localized population of microorganisms, for example, bacteria, derived from a single cell grown in culture.

color blindness a condition in which certain colors cannot be distinguished, due to a lack of one or more color-absorbing pigments in the retina. In humans the most common example is red/green color-blindness, which can be considered as being controlled by a single locus on the X-CHROMOSOME, although at least two closely linked loci are known to influence the character. The normal vision ALLELE is dominant to the color blindness allele. Color-blind females must therefore be HOMOZYGOUS for the color-blindness allele, whereas males will be affected if they carry only one color-blindness allele. Consequently, color blindness is more common in males than females.

color change a process in which certain animals, for example, squid and sole, can alter their colors or shade by changing the concentration of pigment in their pigment cells [(see CHROMATOPHORES (1)] under nervous or hormonal control.

color vision the ability of some animal groups to detect color in an object, due in vertebrates to activity of CONE CELLS in the retina of the eye. Examples of animals with color vision include primates, many fishes, most birds, and the insects. Animals without color vision probably see objects in shades of gray (monochrome vision).

colostrum a yellowish, watery secretion expressed from the breast nipples of female mammals when in late pregnancy and for a few days after birth. Colostrum has a high protein content and is rich in vitamin A and ANTIBODIES, which give the baby an immediate, short-term, passive immunity to foreign ANTIGENS.

columella 1. the sterile central column in the sporangia of mosses and liverworts. 2. the domed structure forming a pillar supporting the sporangium of some fungi, for example, *Mucor*. See Fig. 113. 3. the central area of a root cap, which contains STATOLITHS (1). 4. the central axis of a fruit.

columella auris a bony or cartilaginous rod that connects the eardrum

145

Fig. 113. **Columella (2).** The sporangium of *Mucor.*

to the inner ear in reptiles, birds, and some amphibians. It is homologous with the STAPES of mammals and the HYOMANDIBULA of fishes.

columnar epithelium see EPITHELIUM.

coma a tuft of hairs attached to the TESTA of a seed and used in wind dispersal.

commensal (of an organism) living in close association with another organism of a different species where neither has an obvious effect on the other. For example, some POLYCHAETE worms will live in the tubes of others. See SYMBIOSIS.

Commission short for the International Commission on Zoological Nomenclature.

commissure 1. (in invertebrate animals) a bundle of nerve fibers joining ganglia; in vertebrate animals, a similar bundle of nerve fibers joining left and right sides of the brain or spinal cord. 2. (in plants) the faces by which two CARPELS are joined.

common ancestor a relative occurring in the family trees of both parents in a cross. For example, cousin matings have grandparents as common ancestors.

communication the transmission of information from one individual to another of the same or different animal species, which receives and understands it. Any of the five senses can be used in communication. Many higher organisms use sound, but posturing in specific displays, for example, courtship in birds and primates, dancing in bees, and touch and smell (see PHEROMONE) are other important means of conveying information.

community a naturally occurring group of different species of organisms that live together and interact as a self-contained unit, relatively independent of inputs and outputs from adjacent communities. Ideally, the community is self-contained in terms of food relationships, and usually the only energy required from outside is that of the sun.

companion cell see SIEVE TUBE.

compatibility a state in which two organisms or parts of organisms can be mixed. For example, when two plants can cross-fertilize, or when two tissues can be added together, as in transplant surgery or blood transfusion. Animal compatibility depends on suitable matching of ANTIGENS and ANTIBODIES. See also SELF-INCOMPATIBILITY.

compensation light intensity the level of illumination at which photosynthesis exactly balances respiration in plants. Only at levels greater than this can organic compounds accumulate to give a net gain of plant material.

compensation period the time taken when a plant is removed from darkness to reach the *compensation point* where photosynthesis and respiration proceed at the same rate and there is no net gain or loss in carbohydrate. The compensation period is shorter in shade plants, which are efficient at utilization of low levels of light.

compensation point see COMPENSATION PERIOD.

compensatory hypertrophy the enlargement of a tissue or organ as a result of removal or damage. For example, if one kidney is removed from a human, the other enlarges.

competence 1. a period when a differentiating cell or tissue is capable of switching to an alternative developmental PATHWAY. See INDUCTION, CELL DIFFERENTIATION, GENE SWITCHING, CANALIZATION. 2. a state in bacteria when they are able to receive DNA from other bacteria in a process called TRANSFORMATION.

competition the interaction between organisms striving for the same end. Such interaction may adversely affect their growth and survival. This includes competition for food, living space, and mates. See INTERSPECIFIC COMPETITION, INTRASPECIFIC COMPETITION.

competitive exclusion the principle that two species cannot coexist if they have identical ecological requirements.

competitive inhibition a form of enzyme control in which an inhibitor molecule very similar in structure to the normal SUBSTRATE of an enzyme becomes reversibly bound to the ACTIVE SITE, thus reducing the quantity of enzyme available. However, if excess substrate is present, the inhibitor can be forced out by the substrate molecule that takes its place, and the reaction proceeds. Compare NONCOMPETITIVE INHIBITION.

complement the protein components of blood serum that can bind to antigen/antibody groups already formed on the surface of cells, thus enhancing destruction of the foreign body by PHAGOCYTES.

complemental males those that live attached to their females, which are much larger, for example, angler fish.

complementary base pairing the arrangement of NUCLEOTIDE BASES so that purines bond with pyrimidines, as occurs in the two polynucleotide chains of DNA (adenine with thymine, guanine with cytosine) and between DNA and MESSENGER RNA nucleotides during TRANSCRIPTION. See Fig. 130.

complementation test a genetic test to determine the precise location of mutations in one area of DNA. See CIS-TRANS TEST.

compost heap a pile of vegetable material that is allowed to break down through decomposition by microorganisms, and is subsequently used to improve the fertility of garden soils.

compound (of plant structures) made up of several similar parts, as in a leaf compound of several leaflets. A *simple* structure is one *not* divided into similar parts.

compound microscope see MICROSCOPE.

compressed flattened.

concentration gradient a system set up where the concentration of any SUBSTRATE, usually in the form of ions or molecules, is different with respect to the concentration elsewhere in the system. For example, ionic concentration across cell membranes, solutes in sap.

concentric bundle a vascular bundle in which one tissue surrounds another, for example, phloem around xylem (AMPHICRIBRAL BUNDLE) or xylem around phloem (AMPHIVASAL BUNDLE).

conceptacle the cavity containing the sex organs in some species of brown algae, for example, *Fucus*.

conchiolin a fibrous insoluble protein that forms the basic structure of mollusks.

concolorous having the same color throughout the structure concerned, for example, petals and leaves.

concordance any similar traits occurring in MONOZYGOTIC TWINS or the possessors of similar genes.

condensation reaction a reaction involving removal of water (dehydration) from two or more small molecules to form a new larger compound. For example, the disaccharide carbohydrate sucrose is formed by a condensation reaction between glucose and fructose molecules. Compare HYDROLYSIS.

conditional lethal a mutation that causes death in certain circumstances, for example, in high temperature, but not in others, for example, in low temperature.

conditioned reflex a reflex action modified by experience, so that while the response remains the same, the stimulus is replaced by one different from the original. The classic example is the experiment by the Russian physiologist Ivan Pavlov (1849—1936) with dogs, where the smell, sight, and taste of food caused them to salivate. Pavlov rang a bell immediately before producing food and, after considerable repetition, salivation could be brought about by ringing the bell in the absence of food (a *Pavlovian response*).

conductance 1. the measure of the ability of a conductor to carry a current, measured in siemens (S) (reciprocal of the ohm [Ω]). 2. the ability of heat to flow by conduction across an object under a temperature gradient.

conduction the transmission of an electrical current by a conductor.

conductivity 1. the property of conducting an electric current. 2. the passage of a physiological disturbance through tissue or a cell, as in a NERVE IMPULSE.

condyle the protruberance of a bone that fits into the socket of another bone, thus forming a joint.

cone 1. (in plants) a reproductive structure in the form of a conical mass of scalelike sporophylls surrounding a central axis, found particularly in GYMNOSPERMS but also in other plant groups, for example, horsetails (*Equisetales*). 2. (in animals) a light-sensitive structure in the vertebrate eye. See CONE CELL.

cone cell a light-sensitive nerve cell containing the photochemical pigment IODOPSIN, which is not readily bleached by bright light. Cones are concerned with discrimination of color and are found in the retina of most vertebrate eyes. The highest density of cones is in the FOVEA of the eye, although they are absent in many animals that live in the dark.

There are now thought to be three types of cone cells, each giving maximum response when stimulated by the blue (450 nm), green (525 nm), and red (550 nm) parts of the spectrum. Color vision is a result of differential stimulation of the three types of cone cells so that the color seen results from differential excitation of the three types. This is in accord with the trichromatic theory of color vision, which suggests that all colors can be produced by mixing blue, green, and red. In general, cones have more direct connections to the brain than RODS, and in the center of the fovea each cone has its own optic nerve fiber, whereas groups of rods converge on a single fiber (retinal convergence). Away from the fovea there are more nerve fibers per cone than per rod, thus increasing the precision of cones and the sensitivity of rods.

congeneric (of species) in the same genus.

congenital existing at or before birth and referring especially to defects and diseases that are environmental in origin and not inherited.

conidiophore see CONIDIUM.

conidium a sexual SPORE found in certain fungi and borne on a *conidiophore*, which is a specialized HYPHA.

conifer any GYMNOSPERM tree or shrub of the group Coniferae, including pines and spruces, which are more northerly forms, and cedars, yews, and larches, which are the more temperate forms. Most are tall forest trees, usually evergreen, but some, for example, larches, are deciduous. Usually they are MONOECIOUS and possess separate male and female cones.

conjugant one of a pair of gametes in CONJUGATION.

conjugation a method of sexual reproduction involving fusion of similar GAMETES that are not freed from the parent forms, as in ciliates, where two individuals fuse together, exchange micronuclear material, and then separate. Conjugation also occurs in some algae, for example, *Spirogyra* and fungi, for example, *Mucor*. The partial exchange of genetic material between two bacterial cells may also be regarded as conjugation.

conjunctiva a protective covering over the front of the vertebrate eye and extending to line the eyelids, formed of a layer of MUCUS-secreting epithelium and underlying connective tissue.

connate (of plant organs) originally distinct, but growing together and joining.

connective tissue an animal tissue in which the intercellular matrix forms the major part. Such tissues fall into three main groups: (a) true connective tissue (ADIPOSE TISSUE, AREOLAR TISSUE, LIGAMENTS, and TENDONS), (b) CARTILAGE, and (c) blood, the last differing from the other two in containing no fibers in the matrix (BLOOD PLASMA).

connivent (of plant parts) originally widely separate at the base but growing toward each other apically (see APIX).

consanguineous mating mating between closely related individuals.

conservation the preservation, protection, and management of an environment that take into account recreational and aesthetic needs, in addition to preserving as much as possible of the natural fauna and flora and allowing for harvesting of natural resources and agriculture. This necessitates sensible planning of what is taken from the environment in terms of the yield of plants, animals, and materials, while at the same time maintaining as much natural habitat as possible, and thus the largest possible GENE POOL.

conservative replication model a model of DNA synthesis, now disproved, in which both chains of the original molecule act as a template for a new daughter molecule. The SEMICONSERVATIVE REPLICATION MODEL is now accepted as the correct method of DNA replication.

consociation a climax vegetation in which one species is dominant, as opposed to ASSOCIATION in which there are several dominant species.

conspecific (of animals or plants) belonging to the same species.

constant (C) region an area of an IMMUNOGLOBULIN molecule that shows little variation between molecules with different specificities. Compare VARIABLE REGION.

constitutive enzyme an enzyme made all the time at a constant rate, unaffected by inducers.

consumer any organism that consumes other organisms, for example, HETEROTROPHS or SAPROBIONTS. Macroconsumers (*phagotrophs*) are chiefly animals that ingest other organisms or particulate organic matter (detritus). Microconsumers are chiefly bacteria and fungi, which break down dead organic material, absorb some of the decomposition products, and then release inorganic nutrients—which are then available again to the PRODUCERS—and organic materials, which may provide energy sources to other organisms.

contact insecticide a chemical, for example, DDT and Malathion, lethal to insects when they alight on a surface coated with the poison. Compare SYSTEMIC BIOCIDE.

contagious (of infections) transmitted by contact.

contaminant an organism, usually a microorganism, introduced into a pure culture.

contiguous (of plant parts) touching at the edges.

continental drift the theory originally put forward in 1912 by Alfred Wegener that continental masses were continuously moving over the surface of the globe as though floating on a sea of molten rock. Doubted extensively for many years, the theory is now generally accepted and supported by evidence from geomagnetic studies and the study of PLATE TECTONICS.

Two hundred million years ago, the present continents were joined in a universal land mass called *Pangaea*. Since that time, the continents have drifted apart, and the study of plate tectonics shows that they are still moving. Over a period of 400 million years, for example, Great Britain has drifted from south of the tropic of Capricorn to its present position—over 80° of latitude. Pangaea was probably formed by previously separate continents coming together, and the line of the Appalachian, Caledonian, Greenland, and Scandinavian mountains was probably formed by North America, Europe, and Africa coming into contact. Previous separation would account for the position of the equator and South Pole 440 million years ago. See Fig. 114.

contingency table a method of presenting results so as to show relationships between two characters, which can then be tested statistically by a modified CHI-SQUARE TEST (the *heterogeneity chi-square test*). For example, eye color and hair color might be measured in a sample population and the results presented in a contingency table. See Fig. 115.

Fig. 114. **Continental drift.** The continent of Pangaea 200 million years ago.

Hair color		Eye color			
		Blue	Gray	Brown	total:
	Blonde	96	42	37	175
	Brown	58	61	107	226
	Black	17	32	93	142
	total:	171	135	237	543

Fig. 115. **Contingency table.** A contingency table for eye and hair colors in a sample population.

continuity the principle in taxonomy that continued usage of a particular scientific name should have priority over date of publication. In scientific classification, the date of publication normally has priority.

continuous variation a feature of certain CHARACTERS, for example, height, in which there is a complete spread of forms across a range, often producing a bell-shaped, NORMAL DISTRIBUTION CURVE when sampling in a population. See also POLYGENIC INHERITANCE.

contorted (of PERIANTH lobes) overlapping and appearing to be twisted when in bud.

contour feathers the vaned feathers possessing barbules that chiefly cover the body of a bird and give it a streamlined form. Those that extend beyond the body on the wings and serve for flight are termed *flight feathers*.

contraceptive see BIRTH CONTROL.

contractile vacuole a membrane-surrounded vacuole that periodically fills with liquid, expands, and then voids the contents to the outside of the organism. Particularly found in protozoans and freshwater sponges, the contractile vacuole appears to have an osmoregulatory function. This theory is supported by the relative absence of such vacuoles in marine amoebae, whereas they are common in freshwater forms that take in water along an osmotive gradient because of the higher, that is, less negative, osmotic pressure.

control 1. an experiment carried out to afford a standard of comparison for other experiments. For example, where the effect of a nutrient substance on a plant is being tested, control plants are grown in exactly similar conditions but without the addition of the nutrient substance. **2.** also called **population control.** the limitation by man of numbers of harmful plants or animals by artificial means, for example, spraying with chemicals, poisoning, shooting, or by seminatural means, such as BIO-LOGICAL CONTROL. See also REGULATION (2).

controlling factor any factor that has an increasing effect as population density increases. See DENSITY-DEPENDENT FACTORS.

conus arteriosus the projection from which the pulmonary artery arises on the right ventricle of the heart.

convection the propagation of heat through liquids and gases by movement of the heated particles.

convergence or **convergent evolution** or **parallelism** a form of evolution that results in unrelated organisms independently producing similarities of form, usually because they become adapted to living in similar types of environment. For example, fish and cetaceans have evolved similar streamlined body shapes and fins.

converging (of plant parts) having apices closer together than their bases.

convolute coiled or rolled together.

Cooley's anemia see THALASSEMIA.

cooling see TEMPERATURE REGULATION.

copepod any minute free-living or parasitic crustacean of the subclass Copepoda. Copepods lack a carapace and are extremely common in both freshwater and marine plankton, where they constitute an important food source for larger animals such as fish.

coprodeum the part of the CLOACA into which the rectum opens in birds.

coprophage an animal that feeds on the feces of other animals.

copulation or **coition** the act of coupling of male and female animals in sexual intercourse. In mammals, the male organ (penis) penetrates the female and introduces the male GAMETES. MATING is a term usually restricted to the behavioral aspects of pair formation and this occurs normally before copulation, whereas fertilization takes place only after copulation.

coracoid one of a pair of bones that form the ventral part of the pectoral girdle of many vertebrates. In most mammals they are reduced to small processes on the SCAPULA, and their role is taken over by the CLAVICLES.

coral 1. the calcareous skeleton of certain COELENTERATES. 2. the skeleton together with the animals that live in it and secrete it, the whole structure often forming a reef. The animals, usually anthozoans and hydrozoans, have a POLYP structure.

Cordaitales an extinct order of carboniferous GYMNOSPERMS having the form of tall, slender trees at the top of which was a crown of branches bearing large, elongated leaves.

cordate heart-shaped.

corepressor a substance of low molecular weight that unites with an APOREPRESSOR and reduces the activity of certain structural genes (see OPERON MODEL).

core temperature (T_c) the mean temperature of the tissues of organisms at a depth below that directly affected by a change in the AMBIENT temperature. T_c cannot be measured accurately and is generally represented by a specified body temperature, for example, rectal and cloacal temperatures.

coriaceous (of plant structures) having a leathery appearance.

corium see DERMIS.

cork a plant tissue made up of cells with thick walls impregnated with SUBERIN. Cork cells are dead when mature, forming an outer layer in stems and roots of woody plants that is impervious to water and air. The cork oak *Quercus suber* produces large quantities of cork, which can be removed and used commercially.

cork cambium a specific CAMBIUM that contributes toward production of bark.

corm a modified underground stem found in some MONOCOTYLEDONS that is usually broader than high and contains no fleshy scale leaves (as in the BULB) but rather has its food reserves in the stem. For example, crocus and meadow saffron. See Fig. 116.

cormidium an aggregation of polyps in a SIPHONOPHORE.

corn in many parts of the world, any of various cereal plants, usually the predominant cereal crop of a region, for example, wheat in England, oats in Scotland and Ireland, corn in North and South America.

cornea the part of the SCLERA at the front of the eye of vertebrates overlying the iris and lens. It is a transparent layer of EPITHELIUM and

Fig. 116. **Corm.** Generalized structure.

CONNECTIVE TISSUE through which light enters the eye and is refracted so that the lens can then focus it on the retina.

cornification the formation of KERATIN in the epidermis from epidermal cells, as occurs in the skin when subjected to abrasive stresses.

corolla a collective term for the petals of a flower.

corona a trumpet-shaped outgrowth of the PERIANTH, as in daffodil flowers.

coronary thrombosis the formation of a blood clot (*thrombus*) in a coronary artery.

coronary vessels the arteries and veins supplying the muscles of the heart.

corpus a body.

corpus allatum a gland present in the head of insects that is responsible for the production of *juvenile hormone* and maintains the larval characteristics at each molt until the adult metamorphosis takes place. See Fig. 117.

Fig. 117. **Corpus allatum.** The brain of *Rhodnius* (the kissing bug).

corpus callosum a band of nervous tissue connecting the cerebral hemispheres in the higher mammals.

corpus cavernosum one of a pair of laterally situated masses of erectile tissue in the mammalian penis which, together with the CORPUS SPONGIOSUM, causes erection of the penis when filled with blood.

corpus luteum an endocrine organ formed in mammals in the ruptured GRAAFIAN FOLLICLE after the process of OVULATION. The corpus luteum is responsible for secreting PROGESTERONE under the influence of LH and LTH. If fertilization of the egg occurs, the corpus luteum persists during pregnancy. Otherwise, it degenerates at the end of the ESTRUS CYCLE. It is formed by the action of luteinizing hormone produced by the anterior lobe of the PITUITARY GLAND. Progesterone prepares reproductive organs for pregnancy and maintains the uterine lining.

corpus quadrigemina the four lobes of the mammalian brain.

corpus spongiosum a median mass of erectile tissue in the mammalian penis. See CORPUS CAVERNOSUM.

correlated response a change in the PHENOTYPE resulting from SELECTION for a completely different character, for example, selection for more bristles, which in some insects can also cause sterility.

correlation a statistical association between two variables, calculated as the correlation coefficient r. The coefficient can range from $r = 1.0$ (a perfect positive correlation) to $r = -1.0$ (a perfect negative correlation), with an r value of 0 indicating no relationship between the two variables. Height and weight in humans are positively correlated, since as values for height increase so do values for weight, whereas other variables give a negative correlation, for example, as human age increases so mental agility tends to decrease.

cortex an outer zone of any organ or part, as in the mammalian kidney and brain, or the layer of plant tissue outside the VASCULAR BUNDLES but inside the epidermis.

corticotropin see ADRENOCORTICOTROPIC HORMONE.

cortisol or **hydrocortisone** an adrenocortical steroid with effects similar to those of CORTISONE.

cortisone a GLUCOCORTICOID hormone secreted by the adrenal cortex, whose function is to combat stress. It causes shrinkage of lymph nodes and lowers the white blood cell count, reduces inflammation, promotes healing, and stimulates GLUCONEOGENESIS. Cortisone controls its own production, which is triggered by the ADRENOCORTICOTROPIC HORMONE in a negative FEEDBACK MECHANISM.

corymb a type of RACEME in which the pedicels shorten toward the apex, as a result of which flowers occur at approximately the same level and produce a flat top.

corymbose cyme a flat-topped CYMOSE inflorescence that resembles a CORYMB but is not produced in the same way, in that the oldest parts are in the center (top) of the inflorescence.

cosmic rays a stream of atomic particles entering Earth's atmosphere from outer space at nearly the speed of light. Cosmic rays are thought to be a cause of SPONTANEOUS MUTATIONS.

cosmoid (of the scales of coelacanths and lungfish) consisting of an outer layer of *cosmin*, which resembles dentine, and a mid-layer of spongy bone and a lower layer of bony lamellae. Compare GANOID, PLACOID.

costal of the ribs.

cotyledon 1. a part of the plant embryo in the form of a specialized seed leaf that acts as a storage organ, absorbing food from the endosperm and functioning as a leaf after EPIGEAL germination. Some ANGIOSPERMS have one cotyledon per seed (MONOCOTYLEDONS), whereas others have two (DICOTYLEDONS). 2. a part of the mammalian placenta on which a tuft of villi occurs, particularly in ruminants.

cotype see SYNTYPE.

Coulter counter an electronic particle analyzer, in which two electrodes detect the effect of a passing particle on the impedance. The counter is used to measure the total cell count in a microbiological sample.

countercurrent exchange a biological mechanism designed to enable maximum exchange between two fluids. The mechanism's effect depends on the two fluids flowing in opposite directions, and having a concentration gradient between them.

| fluid ONE | high concentration | → | low concentration |
| fluid TWO | high concentration | ← | low concentration |

Such mechanisms occur, for example, in oxygen exchange between water and the blood vessels in fish gills, and in the ascending and descending tubules of the LOOP OF HENLE in the mammalian kidney.

countercurrent multiplier the amount of cross-transport in a COUNTERCURRENT-EXCHANGE system per unit distance, being a function (= multiplication) of the total distance over which the exchange takes place.

counterflow system the flow of water and blood in opposite directions across the gills of fish ensuring that blood meets water with the highest possible oxygen content. See COUNTERCURRENT EXCHANGE.

coupling an arrangement in a double HETEROZYGOTE in which WILD TYPE alleles of two genes are located on one chromosome with MUTANT alleles of these two genes on the other HOMOLOGOUS CHROMOSOME. Such an arrangement of linked genes is usually referred to as *in coupling* (see Fig. 118). Such arrangements are important when considering the implications of GENETIC LINKAGE. Compare REPULSION.

courtship the aspects of behavior involving displays and posturings in order to bring about copulation.

wild type alleles ———— $a+$ $b+$
mutant alleles ———— a b

pair of homologous chromosomes

Fig. 118. **Coupling.** The arrangement of genes in coupling.

cover glass or **cover slip** a thin piece of glass used to cover a preparation on a microscope slide for microscopic examination.

coxa (*pl.* coxae) the basal segment of the leg of an insect.

crab a decapod CRUSTACEAN, suborder Brachyura, characterized by a large flattened, laterally expanded carapace below which the abdomen is curled forward.

cranial nerve one of 10 (in ANAMNIOTES) or 12 (in AMNIOTES) peripheral nerves that emerge from the vertebrate brain as distinct from the spinal cord.

Craniata see VERTEBRATE.

cranium the skull of vertebrates.

crassulacean acid metabolism (CAM) a method of PHOTOSYNTHESIS found in certain succulent plants, members of the family Crassulaceae, that close their stomata during the day to avoid excessive TRANSPIRATION losses and open them at night. During the night CO_2 is taken in and stored as organic acids, for example, malic acid. During the day the CO_2 is released from the organic acids and used in the CALVIN CYCLE.

crayfish a decapod crustacean, suborder Macrura, that possesses an elongate body of the CARIDOID FACIES type.

creatine phosphate or **phosphocreatine** see PHOSPHAGEN.

creatinine the nitrogenous waste material of muscle creatine. See PHOSPHAGEN.

crenate (of plant leaves) having a notched edge.

Cretaceous period the geological period that began about 135 million years BP and ended 65 million years BP. It is usually divided into Lower (135—95 million years) and Upper (94—65 million years) periods. The dominance of flowering plants began during this period and large reptiles, for example, dinosaurs, and ammonites were extinct by its end. See GEOLOGICAL TIME.

cretin a person suffering or who has suffered from serious reduction in THYROID GLAND activity during development. A cretin shows slow growth, pot belly, gross intellectual deficiency, and retarded sexual development.

Crick, Francis (1916—) English biochemist best known for his work with James WATSON and Maurice WILKINS on the structure of the DNA molecule, for which they shared a Nobel Prize in 1962. They were able to suggest a model for DNA structure and how it replicates that is widely accepted today. Crick also proposed the *wobble hypothesis*, which refers to the fact that the third base of each DNA codon often can be varied without changing the AMINO ACID coded for by that codon.

crinoid any echinoderm of the class Crinoidea, including the present-day feather stars and sea lilies. They are common fossils from the CAMBRIAN PERIOD throughout geological history and are mainly sedentary.

crisped (of plant structures) curled.

crista (*pl.* cristae) a fold in the inner membrane of a MITOCHONDRION on which the electron-transport reactions of AEROBIC RESPIRATION take place.

critical group a taxonomic group in which it is difficult to recognize taxonomic differences.

CRM (cross-reacting material) a protein, usually without an enzymic function, that can be recognized in serological tests.

crocodile any large, tropical, aquatic lizardlike reptile of the order Crocodilia, possessing a four-chambered heart that is unique in reptiles.

crop 1. in vertebrates, particularly some birds, an expanded part of the esophagus where food is stored. **2.** in invertebrates, an expansion of the anterior part of the gut system where food is either digested or stored. **3.** the agricultural or commercial fishery yield. **4.** in ecological terms, the difference between gross annual production and the net production, that is, the material eaten by predators or herbivores, including that taken by humans and that consumed by organisms responsible for decay. See STANDING CROP.

crop growth rate the total dry matter production of a COMMUNITY per unit land area after a known time span.

crop milk pigeon's milk that is secreted by the epithelium of the CROP (1) and fed to nestlings.

crop pruning the removal of old growth to promote new growth and better CROP (3) production.

crop rotation the growing of CROPS (3) in a regular sequence over a number of seasons so as not to exhaust the soil. A simple example is: root crop, oats, leguminous plants, and wheat. The leguminous crop is of particular importance in returning nitrogen to the soil from the atmosphere through the nitrogen-fixing bacteria (see NITROGEN FIXATION) in their root nodules.

crop spraying the treatment of CROPS (3) with chemical sprays to prevent or limit attack by insects and plant pathogens.

cross 1. a mating between a male and a female of a plant or animal species, from which one or more offspring are produced. **2.** a hybrid produced by mating two unlike parents.

crossbreed see INTERBREED (2).

cross-bridge link the connection of the globular head of the MYOSIN cross-bridge with the myosin thick filament in skeletal muscle fibrils.

cross-fertilization or **allogamy** the production of an offspring by the female GAMETE being fused with a male gamete from a different plant. Compare SELF-FERTILIZATION.

crossing over a process occurring in the DIPLOTENE stage of prophase 1 of MEIOSIS in which there is exchange of nonsister CHROMATIDS, producing genetic RECOMBINATION (see Fig. 119). See also UNEQUAL CROSSING OVER.

Fig. 119. **Crossing over.** The exchange of chromatid material.

Crossopterygii a subclass of the class Choanichthyes, an ancient group of mainly freshwater fish, including many fossil forms but only a single living species, the COELACANTH *Latimeria.*

cross-over value an estimation of the number of gametes containing a gene combination produced by CROSSING OVER during MEIOSIS, as a proportion of all gene combinations in the gametes produced. The frequency produced by this calculation is used as a measure of GENETIC LINKAGE, one percent cross-over value being equivalent to one map unit.

cross-pollination the transfer of pollen from the anthers of one flower to the stigma of another by the action of wind, insects, etc., with the subsequent formation of pollen tubes. Compare SELF-POLLINATION. See POLLINATION.

crustacean a member of the class Crustacea in the phylum Arthropoda. The class includes shrimps, lobsters, crabs, and water fleas. Most forms are aquatic, although a few are terrestrial, living in damp places, for example, wood lice.

cryophytes plants that grow on ice or snow—usually algae, mosses, fungi, or bacteria.

cryoturbation the movement of frozen earth sediments as a result of ice formation.

cryptic coloration any coloration that conceals animals in their normal habitats by its resemblance to that of the surroundings (see CAMOU-FLAGE).

cryptic species a sibling species.

crypto- *combining form* denoting hidden.

crypt of Lieberkuhn a narrow pit at the base of a villus in the lining of the DUODENUM and ILEUM that passes secretions from BRUNNER'S GLANDS, PANETH CELLS, and GOBLET CELLS. See Fig. 120.

lumen — villi

goblet cells

crypts of Lieberkuhn

Brunner's gland

Paneth cells

Fig. 120. **Crypt of Lieberkuhn.** A transverse section of the wall of the duodenum.

cryptogam (in obsolete classification schemes) any plant that does not produce seeds, that is, plants placed in the groups Thallophyta, Bryophyta, and Pteridophyta. Whereas in conifers and flowering plants (Phanerogamia) the organs of reproduction are prominent, they are not so in the Cryptogamia—hence the name (secret marriage).

cryptophyte or **geophyte** a hidden plant, one in which the renewal bud is buried.

cryptozoa 1. any animals that live in litter, dark places, and the upper layers of soil. **2.** any animals that *may* exist, such as the Yeti, but whose existence has yet to be positively demonstrated.

CSF see CEREBROSPINAL FLUID.

ctenidium (*pl.* ctenidia) one of the comblike gills present in the mantle of many mollusks, particularly Lamellibranchia.

ctenophore any marine invertebrate of the phylum Ctenophora, including the sea gooseberries, that moves by means of comb rows of cilia. They are sometimes classified with the COELENTERATES but more usually are given the status of a phylum.

cubical epithelium see EPITHELIUM.

cud the food from the first stomach of a ruminant, which is regurgitated into the mouth and rechewed.

cull 1. to take out (an animal, especially an inferior one) from a herd. **2.** to reduce the numbers of a population of animals by killing them, for example, seal culls.

culmen the median longitudinal ridge of the upper mandibles of the bill of a bird.

cultivar a cultivated variety of a plant or animal species that contains unique features and can be propagated sexually or asexually. In horticulture the use of cultivar names is common and is written after the species name, for example, the common ivy cultivar *Hedera helix* (English ivy).

cultivation 1. the preparation of ground for crops. **2.** the planting, care, and harvesting of crops.

culture medium see MEDIUM.

cuneate (of leaves) wedge-shaped.

cuneiform or **cuniform** (of leaves) wedge-shaped with the thin end of the wedge at the base.

cupula 1. any cup-shaped structure. **2.** a structure in the AMPULLA of the ear containing sensory end organs.

curare a paralyzing poison originally extracted from the root of *Strychnos toxifera* by South American Indians and used on arrowheads. Now it is a valuable source of drugs. Its action in paralysis is to prevent ACETYLCHOLINE from depolarizing the postsynaptic membrane, particularly at nerve/muscle junctions, thus preventing passage of the nerve impulse and rendering the victim immobile.

cusp one of a series of projections on the biting surface of a molar tooth in mammals.

cutaneous respiration the exchange of gases through the skin. Many lower organisms in the animal kingdom, provided they are small enough, are able to take up oxygen and lose CO_2 entirely by diffusion. Organisms up to 1 mm in diameter can get all their oxygen supply through mere diffusion on the assumption that they consume about 0.05 $cm^3 \, g^{-1} \, h^{-1} \, O_2$. If their metabolic rate were considerably lower and required less O_2, they could have a larger diameter, but lower O_2 consumptions than this are rare. Thus, animals exceeding 1 mm in diameter must have a special oxygen-transport system to supply internal tissues. However, even organisms with such a system may also carry out gaseous exchange through the skin. Indeed, amphibians have a higher mean oxygen uptake through the skin than through the lungs in temperatures up to 22°C.

cuticle or **cuticula 1.** in both animals and plants, a thin noncellular layer secreted by the epidermis. In higher plants it covers all the exterior, except where stomata and lenticels occur, and prevents water loss (*cuticularization*). In many arthropods, it forms part of the EXOSKELE-TON and is composed of CHITIN and PROTEIN, with a calcareous element in CRUSTACEANS. **2.** the epidermal cells of vertebrates (the *stratum corneum*) that have been converted to KERATIN (as in hair, feathers, scales, nails, claws, hooves, horns, etc.), preventing water loss, bacterial entry, and admission of ultraviolet light.

cutinization the formation of CUTICLE in plants by impregnation of the cell wall with cutin, a fatty substance with waterproofing qualities.

cutting a method of artificial propagation in plants where a small stem, usually with attached leaves, is removed from the parent plant (for example, *Begonia, Geranium*) and placed in water or moist sand. Once ADVENTITIOUS (1) roots have developed, the cuttings are transferred to soil.

Cuvierian duct or **ductus Cuvieri** one of a pair of blood vessels that lead from the sinuses and blood vessels to the sinus venosus of the heart in fish. They are homologous with the venae cavae of higher vertebrates.

cyanide any salt of hydrocyanic acid. Potassium cyanide (KCN) and hydrogen cyanide (HCN) are the most common examples of cyanides, all of which are extremely poisonous. They combine with cytochrome enzymes (for example, CYTOCHROME OXIDASE), which transfer hydrogen atoms in CELLULAR RESPIRATION and thus block production of energy in the cells.

cyanocobalamin see COBALAMIN.

cyanophyte see BLUE-GREEN ALGAE.

cybernetics the study of the comparison of control in the workings of the living body with man-made mechanical systems, such as those used in robots.

cycad any tropical or subtropical GYMNOSPERM of the order Cycadales. Cycads date from the MESOZOIC PERIOD. Present-day forms grow to 20 meters in height and have a crown of fernlike leaves. They live for up to a thousand years.

Cycadofilicales an order of extinct GYMNOSPERMS whose members are of interest from a phylogenetic point of view. They reproduce by seeds but have a fernlike vascular system and develop secondary wood.

cyclic AMP (cAMP, adenine monophosphate) a molecule thought to act as an intermediary between a hormone and the biochemical process of its target cell. The process is thought to be this: (a) the hormone arrives at the target cell and becomes complexed to receptor sites in the cell membrane; (b) the adenyl cyclase enzyme is activated, enabling conversion of ATP to cAMP; and (c) specific cellular enzymes are activated by cAMP starting a chain reaction. See also CYCLIC GMP.

cyclic GMP (cGMP, guanosine monophosphate) a nucleotide that usually produces cell responses opposite to those of CYCLIC AMP. Analogous with cyclic AMP, it is present in much lower concentrations.

cyclic phosphorylation see LIGHT REACTIONS.

cycling matter any material recirculated within a system.

cyclo- *combining form* denoting a cycle.

cyclopia the possession of a single median eye.

cyclosis see CYTOPLASMIC STREAMING.

cyclostome 1. any member of the order Cyclostomata, a group consisting of lampreys and lungfish, characterized by lack of jaws and presence of a suctorial mouth. 2. a suborder of Polyzoa possessing a tubular body wall and lacking an operculum.

cyme a CYMOSE inflorescence.

cymose (of an inflorescence) having growing parts that end in flowers, as a result of which the combined growth depends on production of lateral growing points; the oldest part of the inflorescence is thus at the apex.

cyphonautes larva the larva of a polyzoan, similar to a TROCHOPHORE, with a bivalve shell.

cypris larva the larva of barnacles.

cypsela the fruit of members of the Compositae, similar to an ACHENE and formed from two carpels.

cyst 1. a bladder or baglike structure that may contain the resting stage of an organism. Many groups or organisms have encysted stages, for example, protozoans, nematodes, flukes, and tapeworms. 2. a MORBID structure arising as an outgrowth of the skin, for example, a sebaceous cyst, usually arising from a blocked duct, or an internal growth, for example, an ovarian cyst.

cysteine one of 20 AMINO ACIDS common in proteins that has a polar R structure and is water soluble. See Fig. 121. The ISOELECTRIC POINT of cysteine is 5.1.

Fig. 121. **Cysteine.** Molecular structure.

cysticercoid a larva of tapeworms similar to a CYSTICERCUS but possessing only a small bladder.

cysticercus the larval form of a tapeworm that grows into the adult when eaten by the primary host, and consists of a SCOLEX inverted into a large bladder. When ingested the outer cyst wall is digested, the scolex everts, and the bladder disappears. The scolex attaches to the intestinal wall of the host, and a new tapeworm forms with the growth of proglottides. See Fig. 122.

early proglottids
strobila
sucker
bladder
scolex inside out

Fig. 122. **Cysticercus.** Generalized structure.

cystic fibrosis a disease of humans, affecting one child per 2000 live births, in which various MUCUS-secreting glands, particularly in the pancreas and in the lungs, become fibrous, producing an abnormally thick mucus. Symptoms of the disease include intestinal blockage and pneumonia which, despite modern medicines, can still be fatal.

The condition is inherited as an autosomal recessive gene on the long arm of chromosome 7, so that affected children are homozygous recessive, a MUTANT allele having been passed on by both parents. At present there is no cure for the disease, but in 1986 a gene probe prenatal test was announced involving CHORIONIC BIOPSY of the fetus at 9—11 weeks. If the result of the test is positive, the parents may have a choice of whether to terminate the pregnancy.

cystitis a painful inflammation of the bladder caused by infection with the gut bacterium *Escherichia coli.*

cystocarp a structure produced from the fertilized CARPOGONIUM of a red alga that irritates the CARPOSPORES.

cystolith a structure found in some plants, for example, nettles, formed by an ingrowth of the cell wall and carrying a grain of calcium carbonate at its tip.

cytochrome a protein pigment containing iron that is capable of being alternately oxidized and reduced, acting as an electron carrier in the ELECTRON TRANSPORT SYSTEM of a MITOCHONDRION.

cytochrome oxidase an enzyme acting as the last hydrogen electron carrier in the ELECTRON TRANSPORT SYSTEM, receiving an electron from CYTOCHROME and passing it on to oxygen, with the formation of water.

cytogenetics the study of the inheritance of cells and their chromosomes. Cytogenetic analysis of fetal cells (see AMNIOCENTESIS and CYSTIC FIBROSIS) is used to assess potential risks to the baby.

cytokinesis a part of CELL DIVISION that usually occurs during TELOPHASE of nuclear division. The cytoplasm becomes divided into two parts that are sometimes unequal, for example, the production of ova and polar bodies during OOGENESIS. The mode of splitting differs between organisms. In higher plants, a special membrane-producing area (the CELL PLATE) develops internally and becomes joined to the outer membrane. In lower plants, the cell wall and plasma membrane grow in from outside. In animals, the plasma membrane forms a deep cleft from the outside inward, which eventually divides the cell.

cytokinin or **kinetin** or **kinin** a PLANT HORMONE that promotes cell division (CYTOKINESIS) and cell enlargement by swelling. Several effects are similar to those produced by AUXIN, but others are different. For example, cytokinin promotes lateral bud development and growth, whereas auxin suppresses lateral buds (see APICAL DOMINANCE).

cytology the study of cells.

cytolysis the breakdown of cells.

cytoplasm the part of the cellular PROTOPLASM not located in the nucleus. The range of organelles contained in the cytoplasm varies widely between PROKARYOTE and EUKARYOTE cells.

cytoplasmic inheritance or **extranuclear inheritance** the control of certain characters by genetic factors located in the cytoplasm of EUKARYOTES. These cytoplasmic mechanisms can show themselves as general maternal influences, since the female gamete contains more cytoplasm than the male, as in the control of shell coiling in the snail *Limnaea*. DNA has also been located in several cytoplasmic organelles, such as a MITOCHONDRION or a CHLOROPLAST, that can replicate and function independently of the nucleus.

cytoplasmic streaming or **cyclosis** the movement of cytoplasm from one region of a cell to another, often in definite currents, thought to be controlled by MICROFILAMENTS composed of protein similar to ACTIN. Such streaming has several possible functions: (a) transport of substances from one part of the cell to another, for example, during TRANSLOCATION in SIEVE TUBES; (b) cellular movement, for example, in PSEUDOPODIA of white blood cells; (c) maintenance of optimal temperature; and (d) provision of optimal light conditions for chloroplasts, for example, in MESOPHYLL cells of a leaf.

cytosine one of four types of nitrogenous bases found in DNA, having the single-ring structure of a class known as PYRIMIDINES. Cytosine forms part of a DNA unit called a NUCLEOTIDE and always forms complementary pairs with a DNA purine base called a GUANINE. Cytosine also occurs in RNA molecules. See Fig. 123.

Fig. 123. **Cytosine.** Molecular structure.

cytoskeleton a network of MICROTUBULES and MICROFILAMENTS in the cytoplasm of cells that is thought to give the cell its characteristic shape. The network enables movement of specific organelles within the cytoplasm, as in vesicles produced by the GOLGI APPARATUS, and production of general CYTOPLASMIC STREAMING.

cytosol the soluble portion of the cytoplasm, including dissolved solutes but excluding any particulate matter.

cytostome a mouthlike opening present in many unicellular organisms.

cytotaxonomy a method of classification based on the characteristics of CHROMOSOMES.

D

dactylo- *combining form* denoting finger or toe.

dactylozooid a stinging COELENTERATE polyp, usually possessing long tentacles that serve to collect prey in colonial forms.

damping-off a disease caused usually by the fungus *Pythium* in which young seedlings are attacked at ground level when in overcrowded, damp conditions, causing them to rot and fall over.

damselfly any insect of the suborder Zygoptera, similar to but smaller than dragonflies.

Danielli, James see UNIT-MEMBRANE MODEL.

dark adaptation the increase in light sensitivity of an eye as a result of remaining in the dark.

dark-field microscopy a microscope technique that involves creating a dark background for the subject to be observed under the microscope and viewing this by reflected light. The object thus appears light on a dark background.

dark reactions those processes in PHOTOSYNTHESIS that do not require light energy but can occur in both light and dark conditions. The reactions involve reduction of carbon dioxide to carbohydrate in the CALVIN CYCLE, using ATP and NADPH$_2$ formed in the LIGHT REACTIONS.

dark repair repair of DNA by a mechanism that does not require light.

dart sac a sac branching from the vagina of snails and containing a dart that is shot out prior to copulation between two snails, so the darts from each penetrate the tissues of the other.

Darwin, Charles Robert (1809—1892) English naturalist. His works include: *Voyage of the Beagle* (1839), *On the Origin of Species by Means of Natural Selection* (1859), and *The Descent of Man* (1871). He and WALLACE originated modern evolutionary theory. See DARWINISM.

Darwinism the theory of evolution formulated by Charles DARWIN, holding that different species of plants and animals have arisen by a process of slow and gradual changes over successive generations, brought about by NATURAL SELECTION. The essential points of Darwin's theory are:

(a) in organisms that reproduce sexually, there is a wide range of variability, both within and between species.

(b) all living forms have the potential for a rapid rise in numbers, increasing at a geometric rate.

(c) the fact that populations usually remain within a limited size must indicate a struggle for existence in which individuals unsuited to conditions operating at the time are eliminated or fail to breed as successfully as others (see FITNESS).

(d) the struggle for existence results in natural selection that favors survival of the best-adapted individuals, a process described by Herbert Spencer (1820—1893) as the *survival of the fittest* in his *Principles of Biology* (1865).

Darwin's finches a group of finches that occurs on the Galapagos Islands in the Pacific. The islands are oceanic and were colonized by an ancestral type that has speciated and provides an excellent example of ADAPTIVE RADIATION.

daughter cell see CELL DIVISION.

Davson, H. see UNIT-MEMBRANE MODEL.

day-neutral plant a plant that flowers after a period of vegetative growth, regardless of PHOTOPERIOD. Examples include the dandelion, tomato, and sunflower. Compare SHORT-DAY PLANT, LONG-DAY PLANT.

day sleep the folding of the leaflets of a compound leaf in conditions of bright light so that stomatal surfaces come together, thus reducing water loss.

DDT *abbreviation for* a chlorinated hydrocarbon, *d*ichloro*d*iphenyl-*t*richloroethane, which acts as a powerful insecticide with long-lasting effects. DDT was the first major insecticide in use. Although DDT is cheap to manufacture, it has produced adverse ecological consequences. Its lack of biodegradability and the fact that it tends to accumulate in fatty tissues have resulted in its transfer from one consumer to another up the FOOD CHAIN, becoming further concentrated at each step.

One effect of this has been to endanger the top carnivorous birds, whose eggshells have become paper thin because DDT has prevented mobilization of calcium in the oviduct, thus reducing the reproductive potential of many rare species. While these processes have been occurring, the target insects have been subjected to strong SELECTION pressure from the DDT, with the result that highly resistant populations now exist, making the insecticide useless in many parts of the world.

de- *prefix* denoting from, out or away.

dealation the loss of wings in ants and other insects. For example, the queen ant removes her wings prior to laying eggs after fertilization.

deamination the removal of the amino group (NH_2) from a molecule, as in the release of ammonia (NH_3) from AMINO ACIDS, the residue of which can then enter the KREBS CYCLE, usually via ACETYLCOENZYME A. The amino group then enters the ORNITHINE CYCLE.

death rate see MORTALITY RATE.

deca- *combining form* denoting ten.

decapod a taxonomic name applied unusually to two completely different groups of organisms. **1.** any crustacean of the largely marine order Decapoda, having five pairs of walking limbs, including the crabs, lobsters, shrimps, prawns, and crayfish. **2.** any cephalopod mollusk of the order Decapoda, having a ring of eight short tentacles and two long ones, including the squids and cuttlefish.

decarboxylation the removal of carbon dioxide from a molecule, as in the conversion of oxalosuccinic acid (C_6) to ketoglutaric acid (C_5) in the KREBS CYCLE.

decay the decomposition of dead tissue.

decerebrate rigidity a state in which limb extensor muscles go into tonic contraction and the limbs are held rigidly out from the body. This occurs if the brain is transected immediately behind the ganglionic center (red nucleus) of the midbrain.

decerebration an experimental cutting off of cerebral activity either by sectioning the brain stem or by interrupting the blood supply to the brain.

decidua the part of the lining of the uterus of mammals that, after thickening during pregnancy, is shed as AFTERBIRTH.

deciduous teeth or **milk teeth** the first set of teeth, present in most mammals. These are replaced by a second, permanent set of teeth together with several molars that are absent as deciduous teeth.

deciduous tree any tree in which there is leaf-fall in autumn with new leaves produced in spring after a winter spent in dormancy. Such trees are generally ANGIOSPERMS (for example, oak, ash, and beech) although some CONIFERS are also deciduous (for example, the larch).

decomposer any saprophytic organism, such as bacteria and fungi, that breaks organic materials down into simpler compounds and eventually into inorganic materials. The latter can then be used by PRODUCERS in synthesizing organic compounds.

decomposition 1. the breakup of a chemical substance into two or more simpler substances. **2.** the breakdown of organic material by microorganisms.

decumbent (of stems) lying on the ground and growing upward only at the tip.

decussate (of leaves) at right angles to each other.

dedifferentiation a process in which tissues that have undergone CELL DIFFERENTIATION can be made to reverse the process so as to become a primordial cell again (see GURDON). In theory, all cells should possess this ability since the mature cell does not lose DNA (see TOTIPOTENCY), but reversal has been demonstrated in plants much more easily than in animal cells.

deer any of the ruminant quadrupeds included in the family Cervidae.

defecation the elimination of feces from the alimentary canal via the anus, a process requiring rhythmic contraction of the smooth muscle of the gut wall under autonomic control, and relaxation of the striated muscle of the anal SPHINCTER under voluntary control.

deficiency disease any condition exhibiting abnormalities produced by lack of a particular component in the diet. Examples include BERI-BERI (vitamin B_1), SCURVY (vitamin C), KWASHIORKOR (protein deficiency), and RICKETS (vitamin D). Plants can also exhibit conditions brought about by deficiency of minerals. For example, magnesium is required in the synthesis of CHLOROPHYLL, a lack of the mineral producing CHLOROSIS of the leaves.

deflexed (of bent structures) bent sharply downward.

degeneracy a situation in the GENETIC CODE in which most amino acids are coded by more than one triplet of DNA NUCLEOTIDE bases. For example, ARGININE is coded by CGU, CGC, CGA, and CGG CODONS. See also CRICK.

degeneration the loss or reduction in size of an organ during the lifetime of an organism, or during the course of evolution. The latter process may give rise to a vestigial organ.

deglutition the act of swallowing, which is brought about by a complex series of reflexes initiated by stimulation of the pharynx.

degrees of freedom the number of unrestricted variables in a frequency distribution, a factor of great importance in statistical testing. For example, in a simple CHI-SQUARE TEST the number of degrees of freedom is one less than the number of classes (types) of individuals, one degree of freedom having been lost due to the assumption that a certain proportion of each class is expected. Thus, in testing a 9:3:3:1 ratio there are three degrees of freedom.

dehiscent (of plant structures) spontaneously bursting open to liberate the enclosed contents. The two main dehiscent structures are ANTHERS releasing pollen grains, and certain dry fruits that split open to release seeds, for example, peas, beans, and delphiniums. See also CIRCUMSCISSILE.

dehydration the process by which water is removed from any substance. It is used in freeze-drying for the preservation of materials, and in removal of water from microscopic preparations where it is necessary to use substances immiscible with water.

dehydrogenase an enzyme, such as any of the respiratory enzymes, that catalyzes a reaction in which hydrogen is removed from a molecule, often to be taken up by the ELECTRON TRANSPORT SYSTEM. For example, in the KREBS CYCLE the conversion of succinic acid to fumaric acid is catalyzed by succinate dehydrogenase, the hydrogen released being passed on to FAD.

dehydrogenation the removal of hydrogen atoms from a donor molecule, which is oxidized, to a receptor molecule, which is reduced, a reaction involving DEHYDROGENASES.

deleterious gene an ALLELE of a gene whose effects on the PHENOTYPE are likely to result in reduced FITNESS. Such genes are often recessive, so they can be transmitted through families without being detected unless two occur together in the same individual.

deletion mapping the use of overlapping deletions (see DELETION MUTATION) to locate the position of a gene on a CHROMOSOME MAP.

deletion mutation a type of gene MUTATION in which genetic material is removed from chromosomes (see CHROMOSOMAL MUTATION, POINT MUTATION). The deletion can be as small as a single DNA base, which can cause a misreading of the base sequence during PROTEIN SYNTHESIS (see FRAMESHIFT), to a large piece of chromosome containing many GENES.

delimitation the formal statement in taxonomy that defines and limits the characters of a TAXON.

deltoid triangular.

deme or **local population** a group of individuals within a species largely isolated genetically from other individuals of the species, with clearly definable genetic, cytological, and other characteristics.

demersal (of organisms) living on or near the sea bottom, beyond the tidal zone.

demi- *combining form* denoting half.

demographic transition a theory of demography stating that as a nation industrializes, it goes through populational changes, starting with a decline in infant and adult mortality and followed later by a reduction in birth rate. The time lag between decline in deaths and births produces rapid population growth in developing nations. In developed nations, births and deaths become approximately equal, giving a stable population structure.

demography the study of human populations.

denaturation the breakdown of the bonds forming the quaternary, tertiary, and secondary bonds of PROTEINS, a process that can be caused by various agents, such as excess heat, strong acids or alkalis, organic solvents, and ultrasonic vibration. Usually, denaturation is irreversible as in, for example, the heating of egg albumen to give a solid egg white.

dendr- or **dendro-** *combining form* denoting tree.

dendrite or **dendron** the projections from the nerve cell that branch and conduct impulses to the cell body from other axons with which they have SYNAPSES. See NEURON and Fig. 222.

dendrochronology the study of ANNUAL RINGS in timber to discover the age of the wood and the climatic situation at the time of growth.

dendrogram a diagram illustrating taxonomic relationships in the manner of a family tree.

dendrometer a device for monitoring variations in the girth of a tree trunk, often mentioned in relation to evidence for the COHESION-TENSION HYPOTHESIS.

dendron see DENDRITE.

denitrification the process by which nitrogenous compounds are degraded and nitrogen is returned to the air in gaseous form, for example, the breaking down of nitrates and nitrites to gaseous nitrogen, carried out in the absence of oxygen by soil bacteria. See NITROGEN CYCLE.

denitrifying bacteria the bacteria responsible for DENITRIFICATION.

density-dependent factor any factor that regulates the size of a population under natural circumstances by acting more severely on a population when it is large than when it is small. Such factors can affect either the birth rate or the mortality, but the latter is more usual. At high densities of populations, some organisms have fewer young, or the mortality rate—brought about by predation, disease, or food shortage—may be higher than at low densities. The factors tend to cause population numbers to be maintained at a relatively constant level over long periods of time. See CONTROL, REGULATION (2). Compare DENSITY-INDEPENDENT FACTOR.

density-gradient centrifugation the separation of the components of a homogenate by a process of CENTRIFUGATION, in which each component is moved to a level equivalent to its density in the solute gradient used. See DIFFERENTIAL CENTRIFUGATION, ULTRACENTRIFUGE, EQUILIBRIUM CENTRIFUGATION.

density-independent factor any factor, such as climate, that does not depend on the density of population. Compare DENSITY-DEPENDENT FACTOR.

dent- *combining form* denoting a tooth.

dental formula a formula derived from numbering the incisors, canines, premolars, and molars on one side of the mouth. The formula displays the upper jaw numbers over the lower jaw numbers, for example, the dental formula in humans is:

$$\frac{2.1.2.3}{2.1.2.3}$$

dentary the lower jawbone of mammals.

dentate (of plant structures) having teeth or toothlike projections.

denticle see PLACOID.

dentine the calcified tissue surrounding the pulp cavity of a tooth. Dentine is acellular but like bone in structure. It is penetrated by cellular processes from the central cavity of the tooth that secrete the enamel.

dentition the arrangement, type, and number of teeth in vertebrates.

deoxyribonucleic acid see DNA.

deoxyribose a pentose sugar that is the carbohydrate constituent of deoxyribonucleic acid (see DNA).

dependent differentiation the differentiation of embryonic tissue initiated from other tissue by ORGANIZERS. For example, the eye lens on a frog develops under the influence of organizers from the optic cup. See CELL DIFFERENTIATION.

depolarization the process of reversing the charge across a cell membrane (usually a NEURON), thus causing an ACTION POTENTIAL. In depolarization, the inside of the membrane, which is normally negatively charged, becomes positive and the outside negative. This is brought about by positive sodium ions rapidly passing into the axon. The RESTING POTENTIAL is restored by the SODIUM PUMP mechanism. See Fig. 124.

Fig. 124. **Depolarization.** Depolarization of a nerve fiber.

depressed (of plant structures) 1. sunken, producing a concavity. 2. flattened.

depressor muscle see FLIGHT.

depth distribution the vertical distribution of organisms, for example, in soil or water.

derived character a characteristic that is considerably altered from the ancestral condition.

derm- *combining form* denoting skin.

dermal bone any bone deposited in the lower layer of skin that does not replace existing cartilage. Examples include the clavicle, and bones of the mammalian cranium.

Dermaptera the order of insects that contains the earwigs.

dermatogen superficial layer of cells in the growing point of a plant stem or shoot thought to give rise to the epidermis.

dermis or **corium** the deeper portion of the SKIN of vertebrates that is derived embryologically from the MESODERM, and lies beneath the EPI- DERMIS, which is of ectodermal origin. The dermis contains nerves, blood vessels, muscles, and connective tissue.

Dermoptera the order of insectivorous mammals containing the flying lemurs that have a membrane stretching between wrist, ankle, and tail.

description the formal statement of the characters of a TAXON with particular emphasis on those distinguishing it from other closely related forms.

desert a terrestrial environment characterized by poor soil, climatic extremes of high and low temperatures, and low rainfall, and consequently a scarcity of living organisms, all of which must be specially adapted. See XEROPHYTE, METABOLIC WATER.

desiccation the process by which a substance is dried out and the moisture removed. This is often carried out in a desiccator, which contains a substance that will take up water, for example, calcium chloride.

design of experiments the planning of an experiment so that the results will provide evidence for or against the hypothesis being tested. For example, any experiment that involves sampling should be planned in such a way that the results are sufficient to enable proper statistical testing. Thus, in designing the experiment, it is best first to consult a statistician.

desmognathous (of jaws) having large, spongy maxillopalatine bones, usually united ventral to the vomer. Such jaws are found in swans, geese, ducks, parrots, and some birds of prey.

desmosome a thickened zone in the cell membrane of adjacent eukaryote cells.

detergent a substance that when dissolved in water acts as a cleansing agent for the removal of grease by altering the interfacial tension of water with other liquids or solids. Powerful detergents are used to break up oil spillages at sea.

determination the process by which embryonic tissues become able to produce only one sort of adult organ or tissue.

detoxification the process by which poisonous substances are rendered less harmful. For example, the liver converts ammonia into the less toxic compound urea (see ORNITHINE CYCLE), and hydrogen peroxide is split into water and oxygen by the enzyme CATALASE.

detritivore an organism feeding on DETRITUS.

detritus any organic debris.

deutero- *combining form* denoting second.

Deuteromycotina see FUNGI IMPERFECTI.

deutoplasm the yolk or food material of an egg.

development the proceeding toward maturity of eggs, embryos, or young organisms.

Devonian period a geological period lasting from about 415 to 370 million years ago. Many freshwater fish existed during this period and plants became established on land. True seed plants evolved and lycopods reached the size of trees. Amphibians evolved; the first known insects, spiders, and mites occurred; and most graptolites became extinct. See GEOLOGICAL TIME.

de Vriesianism the hypothesis that evolution has taken place as a result of drastic mutations, particularly at the species level. The hypothesis was suggested *c.* 1900 by the Dutch botanist, H. de Vries (1848—1935), who was also responsible for rediscovery of MENDELIAN GENETICS.

dextrin a polysaccharide carbohydrate that may form an intermediate step in the hydrolysis of insoluble starch to soluble glucose, ready for CELL RESPIRATION, TRANSLOCATION, or further synthesis. See Fig. 125.

starch ⟶ dextrin ⟶ maltose ⟶ glucose

Fig. 125. **Dextrin.** The hydrolysis of insoluble starch to soluble glucose.

dextrorotatory (of a crystal, liquid, or solution) having the property of rotating a plane of polarized light to the right (for example, glucose). Compare LEVOROTATORY.

dextrose see GLUCOSE.

di- *prefix* denoting two, twice.

dia- *prefix* denoting through or across.

diabetes a metabolic disorder, either where there is an increase in the amount of urine excreted (*diabetes insipidus*) or where excess sugar appears in the blood and urine, associated with thirst and loss of weight (*diabetes mellitus*). The former is caused by failure of the pituitary to secrete ADH, and the latter by failure of the ISLETS OF LANGERHANS to produce sufficient insulin.

diadelphous (of stamens) having filaments united and in two groups, or having one separate and the rest united.

diageotropism the phenomenon of growing horizontally in response to gravity, for example, a RHIZOME.

diagnosis a statement that distinguishes the particular TAXON in question from other similar taxa, in terms of the most important characters.

diakinesis the final stage in Prophase I of MEIOSIS, where the chromosomes reach maximum contraction with the HOMOLOGOUS CHROMOSOMES tending to separate from each other. The NUCLEOLUS disappears, the nuclear membrane degenerates, and a spindle is formed of microtubules produced by the CENTROSOMES.

dialysis a process by which small molecules can be separated from larger ones using a fine membrane, for example, collodion, to contain the larger, but which allows the smaller molecules to pass through into the excess water on the other side. The kidney functions by means of this principle, which is also the basis for kidney machines used in cases of kidney disease or failure.

diapause a period of arrested growth and development in insects that is under control of the endocrine system. Diapause is an adaptation to avoid adverse conditions, but does not automatically end with termination of the adverse conditions, since it is genetically determined. However, diapause can be broken by an appropriate environmental change, or artificially by temperature shocks or chemical stimulation.

diapedesis the passage of blood cells through the unruptured wall of a blood vessel by changing in shape.

diaphragm a sheet of tissue present only in mammals that separates the thorax from the abdomen. It consists mainly of muscle and tendons, and its flattening from a convex position projecting into the thorax is an important aspect of the expansion of the lungs as inspiration takes place. See BREATHING.

diaphysis the shaft of a long bone. Compare EPIPHYSIS.

diapsid 1. a vertebrate skull having two fossae, one above the other, behind the orbit. 2. (in some classifications) a reptile of the subclass Diapsida.

diastase an enzyme mixture common in seeds, such as barley, that is responsible for starch hydrolysis. The mixture contains amylases for converting starch to MALTOSE, sometimes via DEXTRIN, and MALTASE for converting maltose to glucose.

diastema a gap between teeth.

diastole see HEART, CARDIAC CYCLE.

diatom a member of the BACILLARIOPHYCEAE.

dicarboxylic acid an organic acid containing two carboxyl (—COOH) groups.

dicentric a chromosome with two CENTROMERES.

dichasium a CYME where the branches are opposite and approximately equal.

dichlamydeous having two whorls on the perianth segments of flowers.

dichogamy the maturation of anthers and ovules in a flower at different times.

dichotomous 1. (of a plant) branching by repeated division into two equal parts. **2.** (of characters) choosing between two possibilities. See KEY, IDENTIFICATION.

dicotyledon any flowering plant of the subclass Dicotyledonae, class Angiospermae. Other ANGIOSPERMS belong to the subclass Monocotyledonae (see MONOCOTYLEDON). See Figs. 126 and 166.

Feature	Dicotyledons	Monocotyledons
1. No. cotyledons/embryo.	two.	one.
2. Leaf vein structure.	pinnate or palmate.	parallel.
3. Stem vascular bundles.	cylindrically arranged.	scattered.
4. Root system.	typically a taproot.	typically fibrous.
5. Cambium in vascular bundle?	Yes.	No.
6. Floral parts.	in fours, fives or multiples.	in threes or multiples

Fig. 126. **Dicotyledon.** The differences between dicotyledons and monocotyledons.

dictyosome see GOLGI APPARATUS.

dictyostele a type of STELE found in some forms of plant, with phloem internal and external to the XYLEM, that is broken up into distinct strands, each surrounded by endodermis.

Didelphia see MARSUPIAL.

didymous (of plant structures) formed of two similar parts that are attached at some point.

didynamous (of stamens) being in two pairs, one pair being larger.

dieback NECROSIS of a shoot, starting at the plant apex and moving downward.

dieldrin a chlorinated hydrocarbon that is a powerful insecticide, with long-lasting effects. It has become ecologically damaging and is banned from many countries. See also DDT.

differential centrifugation a technique in which cell organelles can be separated by spinning a homogenate at various speeds, each speed causing sedimentation of a specific cell fraction. The smaller the organelle, the higher the speed required for sedimentation. See DENSITY-GRADIENT CENTRIFUGATION, ULTRACENTRIFUGE, CENTRIFUGATION.

differential permeability see SELECTIVE PERMEABILITY.

differentiation see CELL DIFFERENTIATION.

diffusion or **passive transport** the movement of molecules of a particular substance from regions of high concentration to regions of low concentration of that substance, that is, down a CONCENTRATION GRADIENT. The rate of diffusion in gases is much greater than in liquids, due to differences in their molecular structure. For example, carbon dioxide will diffuse 10,000 times more rapidly in air than in water.

diffusion pressure deficit (DPD) see WATER POTENTIAL.

digastric 1. (of muscle) having two swollen parts, or bellies, interconnected by a tendon. 2. a muscle concerned with the swallowing reflex in the human neck.

Digenea a subclass or order of trematodes containing the liver FLUKES. Compare MONOGENEA.

digestion a process requiring enzymes in which complex food molecules are broken down by HYDROLYSIS into a state in which they can be absorbed. In some organisms digestion is extracellular, the enzymes being released outside the body and the digested products absorbed, for example, all fungi. In the majority of HETEROTROPHS, digestion takes place in a specialized cavity or internal tube, the ALIMENTARY CANAL, which is usually muscular, with food being squeezed through the DIGESTIVE SYSTEM by a process of PERISTALSIS.

digestive system the ALIMENTARY CANAL together with associated digestive glands (see DIGESTION). Taking mammals as an example, the main areas of digestive activity are:

(a) MOUTH cavity. Starch digestion occurs during chewing, which increases the surface area of food using teeth modified for particular foodstuffs. The pH in the mouth ranges from slightly acid to slightly alkaline.

(b) STOMACH. the site of the start of protein digestion in acid conditions with strong muscular churning movements. Bones are partly digested.

(c) SMALL INTESTINE. the main area of digestion for all types of food, with enzymes secreted by pancreas and intestinal glands. Strong alkaline conditions.

digit 1. a primate finger or toe. 2. any part of the PENTADACTYL LIMB of vertebrates that contains a linear group of PHALANGES.

digitate having fingerlike processes.

digitigrade walking on the toes or fingers, as in most fast-running animals, such as dogs and cats.

dihybrid 1. an organism that carries two different ALLELES of one gene and two different alleles of another gene. For example, character *A* (controlled by alleles $A1$ and $A2$) and character B (alleles $B1$ and $B2$). The dihybrid would have the genotype $A1A2\ B1B2$, that is, a double HETEROZYGOTE. **2.** (of a cross) having two parents that have been mated to produce dihybrids, which then are also mated. A single dihybrid plant is self-fertilized (see SELF-FERTILIZATION). MENDEL formulated his law of INDEPENDENT ASSORTMENT from the results of a dihybrid cross involving pairs of contrasting characters in the pea plant.

dikaryon **1.** a fungal hypha with two types of nuclei in an unfused state in the same cells, so that cytologically they are n+n. When the nuclei are from different genetic strains, the individual or cell is called a HETEROKARYON. **2.** a single animal cell with two nuclei, each from a different species, for example, mouse and man.

dilute make a substance less concentrated by the addition of water.

dimer a molecule made by the joining of two molecules of the same kind, that is, two MONOMERS. Ultraviolet light can induce thymine dimers in DNA, where two thymine bases on one polyneucleotide chain form into a dimer that displaces their position in the helix, preventing normal hydrogen bonding with adenine bases on the opposite polynucleotide chain and so inactivating the DNA molecule.

dimictic lake a lake that has two annual periods of free mixing of water.

dimorphism the occurrence of an organism in two forms, for example, the male and female (see SEXUAL DIMORPHISM). Dimorphism can occur in body form or in color phases, for example, the two-spotted ladybird, which has a brown form with four red spots, and a red form with two dark spots. See GENETIC POLYMORPHISM.

dino- *combining form* denoting frightful or terrifying.

dinoflagellate any of a group of unicellular biflagellate aquatic organisms forming a constituent of plankton now normally placed in the division Pyrrhophyta. They can be regarded as an order of protozoans (Dinoflagellata) or a class of algae (Dinophyceae).

Dinornithidae the moas, large, extinct flightless birds (taller than 3 meters) of New Zealand that probably were hunted to death by humans.

dinosaur any extinct reptile of the orders Saurischia and Ornithischia. Dinosaurs (terrifying lizards) were the dominant form of land vertebrates during the JURASSIC and CRETACEOUS periods.

dinucleotide a compound formed of two NUCLEOTIDES.

dioecious (of plants) the occurrence of male flowers in one individual and female flowers in another individual, for example, the willow. (The term literally means two homes.) Compare MONOECIOUS.

dioxin a chemical byproduct of the manufacture of certain herbicides and bactericides, particularly tetrachlorodibenzo-paradioxin (TCDD), which is extremely toxic.

dipeptide the product of joining together two AMINO ACIDS by a CON-DENSATION REACTION forming a PEPTIDE BOND. See Fig. 127.

Fig. 127. **Dipeptide.** Formation and molecular structure.

diphtheria a serious disease of the upper respiratory tract in humans caused by toxins produced by the bacterium *Corynebacterium diphtheriae*. The toxins cause NECROSIS of epithelial cells in the throat, resulting in production of a grayish EXUDATE that gradually forms a membrane on the tonsils and can spread upward into the nasal passages or downward into the larynx, causing suffocation if not treated.

diplanetism the presence in the life cycles of some fungi of two ZOOSPORE stages.

dipleurula a bilaterally symmetrical larva of ECHINODERMS.

diplo- *combining form* denoting double.

diploblastic (of animals) having a body wall of two layers of cells, the ECTODERM and ENDODERM, an arrangement found only in the COELENTERATES.

diploid 1. (of a cell nucleus) containing two of each type of chromosome in homologous pairs and formed as a result of sexual reproduction. 2. an organism in which the main life stage has cell nuclei with two of each type of chromosome, written as 2n. Diploid stages occur in all EUKARYOTES, apart from certain fungi, and allow a greater degree of genetic variability in individuals than the HAPLOID state, n.

diplonema chromosome structure during the DIPLOTENE stage of meiosis.

diplont an organism in the DIPLOID stage.

diplopod any arthropod of the subclass Diplopoda (class Myriapoda), the millipedes. They have a cylindrical body and two pairs of limbs on each abdominal segment.

diplospondyly the state in which organisms have two vertebrae in each body segment, as in the tails of some fish.

diplotene a stage of MEIOSIS near the end of Prophase 1, in which the CHROMATIDS become separated except at the chiasmata, and the chromosomal material is contracting. The chiasmata indicate that CROSSING OVER is taking place. See CHIASMA.

Dipnoi a subdivision of the CHOANICHTHYES containing the only three living species of lungfish, though the group was common in the DEVONIAN PERIODS and CARBONIFEROUS PERIODS. The air bladder is developed as a lung for air breathing, and this facilitates survival during dry seasons.

dipolarity the possession by a molecule of regions of both positive and negative charge, so that it is positive at one end and negative at the other.

dipteran any two-winged fly of the order Diptera in the class Insecta. Dipterans are ENDOPTERYGOTES and have the hind pair of wings much reduced to form HALTERES that are used for balance in flight. See Fig. 128.

Fig. 128. **Dipteran.** A fly of the family Statiomyidae.

directional selection the SELECTION of a character in one direction, for example, toward larger size, that may occur as a result in a change in environment. For example, if another ice age were imminent, temperatures would fall and the overall size of warm-blooded vertebrates living in a particular region would probably increase. See BERGMANN'S RULE.

disaccharide a double sugar, such as MALTOSE or LACTOSE, with the general formula $C_{12}H_{22}O_{11}$, synthesized by a condensation reaction joining together two MONOSACCHARIDE sugars. See Fig. 129.

disc see DISK.

Discomedusae an order of the class Scyphozoa (COELENTERATES) that contains most of the common disk-shaped jellyfish.

discontinuous distribution a distribution in which populations of related organisms are found in widely separated parts of the world, for example, lung flukes in Australia, Africa, and South America. Such a distribution is thought to indicate the great age of the group, with intermediate populations having become extinct.

Fig. 129. **Disaccharide.** Molecular structure.

discontinuous variation a variation in which different forms of a CHARACTER fall clearly into a particular grouping without overlapping each other and are often controlled by a small number of major genes. For example, white and red eye colors in fruit flies. See also QUALITATIVE INHERITANCE.

discordance any difference in a character between individuals due to genetic differences, as may occur in DIZYGOTIC TWINS, but not usually in MONOZYGOTIC TWINS.

disease an abnormality of an animal or plant caused by a pathogenic organism that affects performance of the vital functions and usually gives diagnostic symptoms.

disease resistance the ability of some organisms to withstand attack by PATHOGENS and remain virtually unaffected. The resistance can occur naturally but may be enhanced in a population by ARTIFICIAL SELECTION, as in plant and animal breeding, for example, the breeding of varieties of tomatoes resistant to certain fungal diseases.

disjunction the separation of HOMOLOGOUS CHROMOSOMES to opposite poles during anaphase of nuclear division, particularly MEIOSIS. Abnormalities in disjunction (see NONDISJUNCTION) can lead to a chromosomal mutation in which daughter cells possess too many or too few chromosomes. In humans, extra AUTOSOMES can result in severely abnormal individuals (see DOWN SYNDROME, PATAU SYNDROME, EDWARDS' SYNDROME). See also TURNER'S SYNDROME and KLINEFELTER'S SYNDROME for disjunction abnormalities affecting the SEX CHROMOSOMES.

disk or **disc** the part of the receptacle surrounding the plant ovary that is fleshy and sometimes nectar-secreting.

dispersal the act of disseminating or scattering the seeds of plants, or the larvae of animals (particularly important in sessile animals), or any movement of adults. Animal larvae may be mobile, but the dispersal of spores, seeds, and fruits is brought about by wind, water, and animals, and in some plants explosive mechanisms are present.

DISPERSION

Many mechanisms exist to aid dispersal: some fruits are hooked, for example, the teasel and burdock, becoming attached to the bodies of animals; the use of vectors, for example, mosquitoes in the case of the malarial parasite, to carry parasitic organisms between hosts; and some larvae of marine animals move to different layers of water where current direction may be different from the level at which the adults live. Dispersal techniques include EMIGRATION, IMMIGRATION, and MIGRATION.

dispersion the distribution of individual organisms once DISPERSAL has taken place. For example, organisms may be randomly dispersed, underdispersed (aggregated), or overdispersed (as in territorial animals). Dispersion should not be confused with DISTRIBUTION, which normally refers to a species as a whole and not to individuals.

displacement activity any animal behavior that takes place outside its normal context, usually in a stress situation. It has been interpreted as being a result of aggression and fleeing drives occurring together. Examples include false brooding in birds, birds picking up nesting material from the ground and throwing it away on being disturbed from the nest, and sticklebacks suddenly digging in the vertical position during a boundary clash. See VACUUM ACTIVITY.

display any ritualized behavior, including posturing, vocalization, and movements that elicit specific reactions in other organisms. Courtship displays, particularly in birds, are often complex, but displays may also be concerned with threat, DISTRACTION, etc.

disruptive selection the selection in favor of phenotypic extremes in a population. Disruptive selection produces divergence between subpopulations. Compare STABILIZING SELECTION.

dissociation a process in which a chemical combination breaks into component parts, as with hemoglobin and oxygen. See OXYGEN-DISSOCIATION CURVE.

distal farthest from the body in any structure, or farthest from the center of the system concerned. For example, the finger is at the distal end of the human arm. Compare PROXIMAL.

distal-convoluted tubule see KIDNEY.

distance receptor a RECEPTOR that detects stimuli from an animal's environment and thus enables the animal to become oriented with respect to the stimuli.

distichous (of plant structures) arranged in two rows that are diametrically opposite.

distraction a display by animals, generally in response to a predator that threatens eggs or young, for example, feigning injury or engaging in behavior directed at a predator with the aim of diverting attention.

distribution the occurrence of a species over the total area in which it occurs, that is, its range or geographical distribution. In aquatic organisms or soil organisms, or even organisms living on mountains, vertical distribution is also important. In some organisms, vertical distribution may vary seasonally, as does geographical distribution, particularly in migratory forms. See also FREQUENCY DISTRIBUTION, DISPERSION.

disulfide bridge the covalent bond between two sulfur atoms, particularly in peptides and proteins.

diuresis the increased output of watery urine by the kidneys. See ADH.

diuretic a substance that enhances DIURESIS.

diurnal rhythm a pattern of activity based on a 24-hour cycle, in which there are regular light and dark periods. See also CIRCADIAN RHYTHM.

divaricate diverging widely.

divergent evolution EVOLUTION from a common ancestral form.

diversity the variety of species richness of a COMMUNITY.

diversity (D) region a sequence of amino acids unique to particular IMMUNOGLOBULINS, enabling the molecule to act as an ANTIBODY against specific ANTIGENS.

diversity index a single integrated measure that expresses the diversity of a particular community of organisms, for example, freshwater invertebrates. The index can be related to the level of pollution in an ecosystem, and the greater the diversity, the less the pollution.

diverticulum any sac or pouch formed by herniation of the wall of a tubular organ or part, especially the intestines.

division 1. a major grouping in plant classification (see PLANT KINGDOM). **2.** the process of formation of daughter cells from a parent cell (see CELL DIVISION).

dizygotic twins or **fraternal twins** a pair of children born at the same time to the same mother but each developing from a different egg. Such twins are therefore nonidentical, being equivalent to normal SIBLINGS, and can be of the same or different sexes. Compare MONOZYGOTIC TWINS.

DNA (deoxyribonucleic acid) a complex NUCLEIC ACID molecule found in the chromosomes of almost all organisms that acts as the primary genetic material, controlling the structure of proteins and hence influencing all enzyme-driven reactions.

(a) *structure.* The model proposed by WATSON and CRICK in 1953 has now become universally accepted. DNA is considered to consist of two POLYNUCLEOTIDE CHAINS joined together by hydrogen bonds between NUCLEOTIDE bases, with COMPLEMENTARY BASE PAIRING between specific bases ensuring a parallel-sided, stable structure: ADENINE pairing with THYMINE (2H bonds), and CYTOSINE with GUANINE (3H bonds). See

Fig. 130. The two polynucleotide chains have opposite polarities due to the way the phosphates are attached to the sugar, and the entire molecule is twisted into a *double helix* shape, with a complete turn every 10th base. See Fig. 131.

Fig. 130. **DNA.** Complementary base pairing.

Fig. 131. **DNA.** The double-helix shape produced by coiling.

(b) *replication* (see SEMICONSERVATIVE REPLICATION MODEL). The molecule unzips through enzymic breakage of the hydrogen bonds between polynucleotide chains. Each chain acts as a template for attachment of free nucleotides under the influence of various DNA POLYMERASES working in the 5' to 3' direction only. See Fig. 132. DNA replication occurs in the S phase of the CELL CYCLE prior to nuclear division.

Fig. 132. **DNA.** Replication.

(c) *location.* DNA is found in all chromosomes except those of certain viruses, for example, tobacco mosaic virus (TMV), in which the heritable material is RNA. In PROKARYOTES, DNA is in the form of a single coiled molecule in a continuous loop and may also occur as extrachromosomal material in the cytoplasm. In EUKARYOTES, the DNA is also highly coiled but is complexed with basic and acidic proteins. There is probably only one very long DNA molecule per chromosome. DNA is also found in CHLOROPLASTS and MITOCHONDRIA of eukaryote cytoplasm (see CYTO-PLASMIC INHERITANCE).

(d) *DNA as a genetic material.* There are several pieces of evidence to suggest the role of DNA in inheritance: (i) TRANSFORMATION experiments with *Pneumococcus* in 1928, by F. GRIFFITH; (ii) identification of the transforming principle as DNA by AVERY, MacLeod, and McCarty in 1944; (iii) the fact that the wavelength of ultraviolet light that causes most mutations in various prokaryotes and eukaryotes matches the AB-SORPTION SPECTRUM of nucleic acids (260 nm); and (iv) HERSHEY and Chase's experiment with labeled BACTERIOPHAGE.

DNA has several features that make it an ideal genetic material: great stability (see *structure* above); accurate replication so that all cells contain an identical copy of information; four nucleotide bases that provide storage of coded information (see GENETIC CODE); ability to mutate by altering the base sequence; ability to rejoin after breaking to form new genetic combinations (see RECOMBINATION); and stored information accurately readable by other cell molecules (see TRANSCRIPTION).

DNA ligase an enzyme that catalyzes the formation of covalent bonds between adjacent parts of a broken DNA POLYNUCLEOTIDE CHAIN (5′ to 3′), thus helping in repair.

DNA polymerase a group of three types of enzymes responsible for attachment of free NUCLEOTIDES onto the unzipped DNA molecule during DNA replication. The first DNA polymerase was discovered by A. Kornberg in 1957, for which work he received the Nobel Prize, although it now appears that this enzyme is not the main one in the group, but rather helps to repair DNA after damage.

dogfish any small cartilaginous fish of the family Scyllidae; a small shark.

dolicho- *combining form* denoting long.

dolichocephalic (of humans) having a long head. See CEPHALIC INDEX.

Dollo's law of irreversibility a principle formulated by the Belgian paleontologist L. Dollo, stating that a structure once lost in evolution cannot be regained.

dominance 1. a genetic interaction in which one ALLELE of a gene masks expression of an alternative allele in the HETEROZYGOTE, so the PHENOTYPE is of the form controlled by the dominant allele. For example, gene A has two alleles $A1$ and $A2$:

$$A1/A1 = \text{black phenotype}$$
$$A2/A2 = \text{white phenotype}$$

but when heterozygous, $A1/A2$ = black phenotype. Thus, $A1$ is dominant to $A2$, with $A2$ recessive to $A1$. In molecular terms, the $A1$ allele is coding for a protein of such quality and quantity to allow the normal amount of black pigment to be produced, even though the $A2$ allele is not coding for a normal enzyme. See also CODOMINANCE, INCOMPLETE DOMINANCE. **2.** the preponderance of one species within an ecological COMMUNITY, for example, oaks in oak forests.

dominance hierarchy a phenomenon in animal societies in which some members are subordinate to others, giving a reproductive advantage to the less subordinate members. See PECKING ORDER.

dominant epistasis a form of EPISTASIS in which dominant ALLELES of one gene can cause a masking effect on the expression of alleles at another locus. Such an interaction would produce a DIHYBRID (1) ratio of 12:3:1 instead of the more normal 9:3:3:1. Compare RECESSIVE EPISTASIS.

dominant species the most common species in a COMMUNITY.

Donnan equilibrium an electromechanical equilibrium set up when two solutions are separated by a membrane that is impermeable to some of the ions in solution.

donor an individual supplying tissue, for example, bone marrow, to a recipient. See COMPATIBILITY, ABO BLOOD GROUP, UNIVERSAL DONOR/ RECIPIENT.

DOPA (dihydroxy phenylalanine) a precursor in the biochemical PATHWAY leading to MELANIN formation in animals. DOPA is not metabolized in individuals with ALBINISM.

dopamine the decarboxylation product of DOPA. Formula: $C_8H_{11}O_2N$.

dormancy a state in which seeds and other structures, such as underground stems, reduce their metabolic activities to a minimum level during unfavorable conditions, for example, low temperature or drought, so as to survive until conditions improve. In fungal spores, dormancy can be EXOGENOUS, requiring an external stimulus for germination, for example, presence of nutrients; or ENDOGENOUS, when dormancy is controlled by an innate property of the spore and is unaffected by the ambient environment in this state. See GERMINATION for events that occur when seed dormancy is broken.

dormin a growth-inhibiting substance found in buds of plants undergoing DORMANCY, with a chemical structure identical with that of ABSCISIC ACID.

dorsal 1. (of an animal) the part that normally occurs uppermost. The back of an animal is called the *dorsal surface*. The dorsal side is normally directed upward, as in *dorsal fin*, but backward in primates in the upright position. **2.** (of a plant) of, or situated on the side of, an organ that is directed away from the axis. See also DORSIVENTRAL LEAF.

dorsal fin any unpaired median fin on the backs of fishes and some other aquatic vertebrates. The fin maintains balance during locomotion.

dorsal lip the part of the rim of the BLASTOPORE that in further development becomes the dorsal side.

dorsal root a nerve trunk containing only sensory axons that enters the SPINAL CORD near the dorsal surface.

dorsifixed (of ANTHERS) attached at the back.

dorsiventral leaf the leaf type found mainly in DICOTYLEDONS, with a structure that changes from dorsal (upper) surface to ventral (lower) surface. The major areas are an upper EPIDERMIS with no stomata, a palisade MESOPHYLL layer below which is spongy mesophyll with large intercellular spaces, and a lower epidermis with irregularly spaced STOMATA. Such leaves are generally held horizontally.

dosage compensation a genetic mechanism in which ALLELES of a gene automatically regulate the amount of a useful product produced, so that homozygous-dominant GENOTYPES produce the same amount of gene product as heterozygotes. In this way the two genotypes cannot be distinguished. Dosage compensation occurs regularly in female mammals, in which one X-chromosome in each cell is thought to become inactivated, leading to equal amounts of gene products in males and females. See INACTIVE-X HYPOTHESIS.

dose the known amount of chemical or other treatment received by an organism.

double circulation the type of circulation found in mammals and birds, in which the pulmonary and systemic circulations are completely separate. See BLOOD CIRCULATORY SYSTEM.

double cross a method of plant breeding in which four different inbred lines are crossed together (A × B and C × D) and the progenies crossed again ((A × B) × (C × D)) to produce a four-way hybrid seed with good vigor.

double crossover two separate CROSSING-OVER events occurring between CHROMATIDS. In a TEST CROSS involving three genes, progeny that have carried out this process can be identified and usually form the least-frequent type of offspring.

double fertilization the situation in flowering plants in which a male nucleus combines with the egg nucleus, and another male nucleus combines with the primary endosperm to form an endosperm nucleus. See EMBRYO SAC.

double helix see DNA.

double recessive a GENOTYPE in which both ALLELES of a gene are of the recessive type, that is, HOMOZYGOUS. See DOMINANCE(1).

doubling time (in microbiology) the time it takes for the number of cells in a population to double.

down the soft, small feathers lacking BARBULES that cover the body of a bird and aid heat retention.

Down syndrome or formerly **mongolism** a human abnormality caused by presence of an extra AUTOSOME (number 21) in the chromosome complement of each cell (see ANEUPLOIDY). The main features of the syndrome are mental retardation, short stature with stubby fingers, characteristic slanting eyes, and heart defects. The abnormality arises in the mother's egg as a rule, with older mothers having a far higher chance of producing abnormal ova than younger mothers. This may be because the mother's eggs have been part-way through Prophase 1 of MEIOSIS since birth, so that eggs of older mothers have been at risk of NONDISJUNCTION much longer than those of younger mothers. Down syndrome is the most common chromosomal abnormality in humans, with an incidence of 1 in 600 live births.

drainpipe cells any epithelial cells (see EPITHELIUM) with an intracellular lumen in the form of a drainpipe joined end to end, as in the TRACHEOLES of insects and excretory ducts of flatworms.

drift see RANDOM GENETIC DRIFT.

Drosophila or **fruit fly** any small dipterous fly (see DIPTERAN) of the genus *Drosophila,* which has been used extensively in genetic investigations. *D. melanogaster* is probably the best-understood animal in terms of inheritance studies.

drought tolerance the ability of plants to resist drought. See XEROPHYTE.

drug 1. any substance used as an ingredient in medical preparations. 2. any substance that affects the normal body functions.

drupe a type of succulent, fleshy fruit produced by some plants in which the seed is enclosed in a hard, woody stone. The fruit is formed from the swollen tissue of the PERICARP. Examples include peach, plum, cherry, olive, apricot.

dryopithecine any extinct Old World ape of the genus *Dryopithecus.*

dry rot 1. a rotting of timber caused by the fungus *Serpula lacrymans*, in which infected timber shows characteristic cubic cracking. Only damp wood is attacked initially, although other, drier wood can be attacked later via long water-conducting structures. 2. any general symptoms of plant disease in contrast to WET ROT, for example, dry rot of gladioli.

dry weight the weight or mass of biological material dried at 105°C until no further water loss takes place. Because water content varies considerably between individuals, dry weight is the most commonly used method of assessing weight in plants and animals. See BIOMASS.

ductless gland see ENDOCRINE GLAND.

ductus arteriosus a blood vessel found in fetal mammals that connects the pulmonary artery to the AORTA and thus creates a bypass to the lungs. See Fig. 133. The vessel closes soon after birth so that all blood is then sent through the lungs for oxygenation. Occasionally, the vessel does not close completely, which may cause a condition called BLUE BABY.

Fig. 133. **Ductus arteriosus.** Location in mammals.

ductus Cuvieri see CUVIERIAN DUCT.

Duffy blood group a red blood cell ANTIGEN found in certain human racial groups, controlled by a single autosomal gene on chromosome 1. About 65% of Caucasians and 99% of Chinese are positive for the antigen, being either homozygous or heterozygous for the allele Fy $^+$, while 92% of West Africans are not, being homozygous for Fy $^-$ alleles.

duodenum the part of the SMALL INTESTINE connecting the stomach to the ileum. It is about 25 cm long in humans. The wall is highly folded internally with microscopic projections called VILLI, which increase the surface area for digestion and absorption. Within the wall are BRUNNER'S GLANDS and PANETH CELLS which, together with secretions from the pancreas entering the duodenum via the bile duct, produce a whole range of enzymes to complete digestion.

duplication, chromosomal a type of CHROMOSOMAL MUTATION in which part of a chromosome is replicated, thus producing extra copies of those genes contained in the duplicated segment. For example, the Bareye mutation in *Drosophila* is due to duplication of a segment along the X-CHROMOSOME.

dura mater the connective tissue that covers the brain and spinal cord of vertebrates. See MENINGES.

dwarfism a form of body malfunction in which the adult individual does not reach the normal height and may sometimes have other abnormalities. Such conditions can be due to a deficiency of GROWTH HORMONE secreted by the anterior pituitary, or to cartilage abnormalities due to genetic defects (see ACHONDROPLASIA). Compare GIGANTISM.

dyad a chromosome consisting of two sister CHROMATIDS joined at their centromere, which is produced after DISJUNCTION.

dynamic equilibrium a balanced state of continual change, for example, water and water vapor, where particles are constantly passing from one phase to the other.

dysentery a severe disorder of the ileum and colon caused by the bacterium *Shigella dysenteriae* and several other species, resulting in abdominal cramps, diarrhea, and fever. The disease—spread by food, feces, fingers, and flies—can be controlled by sanitary precautions.

dysgenic of or relating to a deleterious genetic change. See also TURNER'S SYNDROME.

dyslexia or **word blindness** impairment of the ability to read, due to a brain disorder.

dysplasia abnormal growth or development, as may occur in organs or cells.

dyspnea labored breathing, with breathlessness.

E

e- or **ex-** *prefix* denoting out of, without.

ear the sense organ of vertebrates concerned with reception of sound (hearing), BALANCE (detecting position with respect to gravity), and acceleration. The external ear is absent in amphibia and some reptiles, where the eardrum is at the skin surface. In other forms the external ear consists of an AUDITORY CANAL and the pinna, a projection of skin and cartilage. The *middle ear*, or *tympanic cavity*, not present in some amphibians and some reptiles, lies between the eardrum and the auditory capsule. The EUSTACHIAN TUBE connects the middle ear to the pharynx. It contains the ear ossicles and lies within the bulla, which is a projection of the skull. The inner ear, or *membranous labyrinth*, is contained in the auditory capsule. The utricle gives rise to the semicircular canals (for balance), and from the saccule the hearing organ arises in the form of the COCHLEA in some tetrapods. See Fig. 134.

Fig. 134. **Ear.** The human ear.

Hearing results from sound waves striking the tympanic membrane and causing it to vibrate. The vibrations are transmitted to the oval window by means of the ear ossicles, which magnify them. This disturbs the fluid in the vestibular canal of the cochlea and causes movement in

REISSNER'S MEMBRANE, which then results in displacement of the fluid of the middle canal. This moves the basilar membrane and then disturbs the fluid in the tympanic canal, which stretches the membrane covering the round window. Movement of the basilar membrane stimulates the organ of Corti (see COCHLEA), and impulses are fired in the auditory nerve. Loud sounds cause greater movement of the basilar membrane and a higher frequency of impulses from the organ of Corti. Pitch of a sound determines the frequency of movement of the basilar membrane.

eardrum see TYMPANIC MEMBRANE.

ear ossicle the COLUMELLA AURIS of lower vertebrates and the MALLEUS, INCUS, or STAPES of mammals. See EAR.

earthworm any ANNELID of the order Oligochaeta.

ecad a plant form that results from the habitat in which the plant occurs and is not brought about genetically. See PHENOTYPIC PLASTICITY.

ecdysis the process of molting the cuticle in insects, usually in the preadult stage. The old cuticle is split and cast off to reveal a new, soft cuticle underneath. The insect increases in size, often by intake of air, and the new cuticle hardens. Each larval stage is referred to as an INSTAR, so the first instar is terminated by the first ecdysis, the second instar by the second ecdysis. Ecdysis is initiated by the MOLTING HORMONE.

ecdysone see MOLTING HORMONE.

ecesis the germination and subsequent establishment of a plant colonizing a new habitat.

ECG (electrocardiogram) a recording of the electrical changes occurring as the heart beats (see HEART, CARDIAC CYCLE), which can be used in diagnosing heart malfunction. To obtain an ECG, electrodes are attached to various parts of the body surface, usually both arms and the left leg. Also called *EKG*. See Fig. 135.

echidna any of the spine-covered MONOTREME mammals of the family Tachyglossidae, found in Australia and New Guinea. They have a long snout and claws for digging out ants.

echinoderm any member of the phylum Echinodermata, including sea urchins, starfish, brittle-stars, sea cucumbers, feather stars, and sea lilies. The phylum is characterized by a pentaradiate structure (a five-sided RADIAL SYMMETRY) and the presence of tube feet in most forms.

echinoid any of the ECHINODERMS of the class Echinoidea, including the sea urchins.

eclipse 1. the period during which a virus exists as a free nucleic acid in the host cell. **2.** (of plumage in birds) occurring for a short time after the breeding plumage is molted, particularly in ducks.

Fig. 135. **ECG.** A tracing of the electric currents that initiate the heart-beat. The broken line indicates diastole, the solid line systole.

ecogeographical rules see BERGMANN'S RULE, ALLEN'S RULE, GLOGER'S RULE.

ecological equivalent one of two species from the same ancestral stock, evolved in similar environments and showing the same adaptive characters.

ecological isolation the separation of organisms (usually) within the same geographical region because of their preference for different types of habitats. For example, the toads *Bufo fowleri* and *B. americanus* both live in the same areas but breed in different places, the former in large, still bodies of water, such as ponds, the latter in puddles or in pools within brooks. Compare GEOGRAPHIC ISOLATION. See also SPECIATION.

ecological niche 1. the physical space occupied by an organism. 2. the organism's functional role in the community, for example, TROPHIC LEVEL. 3. other conditions of the organism's existence, such as preferred temperature, moisture, and pH.

ecological pyramid a graphic means of illustrating the trophic structure or trophic function of communities. They are of three general types:

(a) the PYRAMID OF NUMBERS, which illustrates the numbers of organisms at each TROPHIC LEVEL (see Fig. 256).

(b) the pyramid of BIOMASS, based on DRY WEIGHT or, occasionally, live weight at each level.

(c) the pyramid of energy, which shows the energy flow between each level. See Fig. 136. See FOOD CHAIN.

ecological race a localized form that has evolved characteristics as a result of the selective effect of a specific environment.

ecology or **bionomics** the study of plants and animals in relation to their total environment.

Fig. 136. **Ecological pyramid.** A hypothetical ecological pyramid for standing crop on tropical grassland. Figures in Kcal m^{-2} yr^{-1}.

ecophenotype a modification—not heritable—of the phenotype of an organism resulting from environmental influences. See PHENOTYPIC PLASTICITY.

ecospecies a species of plant or animal that can be divided into several ECOTYPES (see CENOSPECIES) able to exchange genes freely without loss of fertility or vigor in the offspring.

ecosphere the parts of Earth and its atmosphere where life can exist.

ecosystem an ecological system that includes all the organisms and their environment within which they occur naturally.

ecotone the transition zone between two major ecological communities where one does not merge gradually into the other, for example, that between grassland and woodland. Such steep gradients between communities are usually man-made.

ecotype the product arising as a result of the response of the GENOTYPE of an organism to the particular habitat in which it lives. For example, *Plantago maritima* has a height of about 17.5 cm in waterlogged mud and 56 cm in fertile meadow. See also PHENOTYPIC PLASTICITY.

ecto- or **ect-** *combining form* denoting outer *or* outside.

ectoblast see ECTODERM.

ectoderm or **ectoblast** the germ layer lying on the outside of the developing embryo that eventually gives rise largely to the EPIDERMIS, but also to nervous tissue and, where present, to nephridia (see NEPHRIDIUM). Compare ENDODERM.

ectoenzymes enzymes secreted across the body wall of a SAPROPHYTE into the materials they have invaded, thus facilitating absorption.

ectoparasite see PARASITE.

ectoplasm the outer layer of cytoplasm as distinct from the ENDOPLASM of a cell. It is often much more gel-like (see PLASMA GEL) than the liquid endoplasm, but there is no clear line of distinction between the two. Ectoplasm is important in the movement of unicellular animals such as *Amoeba*.

Ectoprocta see BRYOZOAN.

ectotherm see POIKILOTHERM.

ectotroph any HETEROTROPH that absorbs food materials directly from outside the body. Examples include bread mold and tapeworms. In contrast, an *endotroph* is a heterotroph that absorbs food material from a gut cavity. Examples include humans and *Hydra.*

eczema a blistery skin rash usually due to an allergy.

edaphic factor any characteristic of the environment resulting from the physical, chemical, or biotic components of the soil.

edaphic race an ECOPHENOTYPE resulting from the properties of the SUBSTRATE rather than other environmental factors.

edema a swelling of tissues caused by the capillary blood vessels passing out water into the surrounding tissues, and so increasing the intercellular fluid content.

edentate any of the placental mammals that constitute the order Edentata. Edentates are primitive mammals, lacking teeth or having only peglike teeth from which enamel is absent, for example, sloths, anteaters, and armadillos.

edentulous without teeth.

Edwards' syndrome a human genetical abnormality in which there are multiple congenital malformations: elongated skull, low-set ears, webbed neck, and severe mental retardation. The condition is caused by TRISOMY of chromosome 18 and, like DOWN SYNDROME, is related to maternal age. Ninety percent of cases die in the first six months after birth.

EEG (electroencephalogram) a recording of the electrical changes occurring in the brain, produced by placing electrodes on the scalp and amplifying the electrical potential developed. The EEG shows three main types of wave, called *alpha, beta,* and *delta*, which differ in their rates of production. Delta waves are the slowest and are found normally only during sleep.

eel any TELEOST fish of the Anguilliformes, having a smooth, shiny skin, a long, snakelike body, and reduced fins.

eelworm any plant-parasitic or free-living NEMATODE.

effector a structure or organ that brings about an action as a result of a stimulus received through a RECEPTOR that can come from the central nervous system or from a hormone.

efferent neuron a nerve fiber carrying impulses away from the central nervous system to effector cells. Compare AFFERENT NEURON.

egestion the evacuation of feces or unused food substances from the body.

egg 1. see OVUM. **2.** a structure produced by insects, birds, and reptiles whose function is to enable embryonic development outside the female on land without use of water as a growth medium. The vertebrate egg consists of an outer shell—hard in birds, leathery in reptiles—four types of embryonic membranes, a food supply in the yolk sac and surrounding albumen (egg white), and the embryo, which develops from an OVUM fertilized before the shell is deposited. Domestic birds can produce unfertilized eggs in which the embryo does not develop.

egg cell see OVUM.

egg membrane any membrane, shell, or jellylike layer surrounding and protecting the EGG, including primary mechanisms secreted by the OVUM or OOCYTE, secondary membranes secreted by cells of the ovary, and tertiary membranes secreted by glands of the oviduct, for example, albumen and egg shell.

egg tooth a small horny projection at the tip of the bill in birds used to pierce the egg shell.

eglandular without glands.

ejaculation the process by which SEMEN is expelled from the penis by strong muscular contractions of the urethral wall.

elasmobranch any cartilaginous fish of the subclass Elasmobranchii (class CHONDRICHTHYES), including fish such as sharks, dogfish, skate, and rays—the entire class except for the chimeras. In some classifications the term is synonymous with Chondrichthyes.

elastic cartilage see CARTILAGE.

elastic fiber any of the highly extensible fibers found scattered in CONNECTIVE TISSUE in vertebrates, occurring particularly in the lungs and artery walls.

elastin the protein found in ELASTIC FIBERS.

elater 1. a cell in which the wall is reinforced by spiral bands of thickening, whose function is to assist in discharging spores in liverworts in response to high humidity. 2. an appendage of horsetail spores, whose function is similar to that of definition 1.

elaterid any COLEOPTERAN of the family Elateridae, including the click beetles, fireflies, and wireworms.

electric organ an organ capable of giving an electric shock to any organism coming in contact with it, and occurring particularly in ELASMOBRANCH fish, such as rays.

electrocardiogram see ECG.

electroencephalogram see EEG.

electromagnetic spectrum the entire range of wavelengths of electromagnetic radiation, most of which are not detectable by the human eye except in the *visible spectrum* from about 400—700 nm wavelength. Wavelengths shorter than the visible spectrum contain large quantities of energy that can be harmful to living material. See Fig. 137. See X-RAY, GAMMA RADIATION, ULTRAVIOLET LIGHT.

Fig. 137. **Electromagnetic spectrum.** The wavelength ranges of the electromagnetic spectrum.

electron microscope (EM) a microscope that produces high-resolution images by the interaction of electrons with the specimen, the electrons being guided by electromagnetic lenses. There are two major types of electron microscopes:

(a) *transmission (TEM)*. The beam of electrons passes through the specimen, for example, thinly sectioned tissues, and is focused onto a fluorescent screen or a photographic film. Magnifications well above × 250,000 are possible, with a RESOLUTION of less than 1 nm.

(b) *scanning (SEM)*. The specimen—an entire cell or tissue—is bombarded with high-energy electrons causing generation of low-power, secondary electrons from the specimen surface. These electrons are collected to form an image of the surface. Magnifications above × 100,-000 are possible, with a resolution of about 5 nm. See Fig. 138.

Fig. 138. **Electron microscope.** The movement of electrons through the transmission electron microscope (TEM) and the scanning electron microscope (SEM).

electron transport system (ETS) a series of biochemical steps by which energy is transferred in steps from a higher to a lower level. Each

ELECTRON TRANSPORT SYSTEM (ETS)

step involves a specific electron carrier that has a particular energy level, or REDOX POTENTIAL, with the carriers organized in a sequence of decreasing energy. See Fig. 139.

Fig. 139. **Electron transport system.** The role of electron carriers.

Thus, the oxidation of X releases more energy than is required to reduce Y. The released energy can be used to produce ATP in MITO-CHONDRIA and CHLOROPLASTS, probably by a process of *chemosmosis.* This mechanism, proposed by P. Mitchell (born 1920, Nobel prize-winner in 1978), involves hydrogen ions (H^+) being pumped in or out of the membranes containing the ETS, generating a *proton motive force* that enables ATP synthesis from ADP and P.

Electron transport is vital in both PHOTOSYNTHESIS and AEROBIC RESPIRATION:

(a) *photosynthesis.* Two ET systems are used during the LIGHT REAC-TIONS in the grana of the chloroplasts. One ETS enables production of ATP by PHOTOPHOSPHORYLATION, and the other enables production of reduced NADP. See Fig. 140.

Fig. 140. **Electron transport system.** Photosynthesis.

(b) *aerobic respiration.* A molecule of NADH from GLYCOLYSIS or the KREBS CYCLE is passed to the cristae of mitochondria, where it is oxidized in the *respiratory ETS,* the final products being water and three molecules of ATP (= OXIDATIVE PHOSPHORYLATION). See Fig. 141. The free energy of NADH is approximately 220 kJ. Of this, about 102 kJ is stored in the three ATP molecules (3×34 kJ). The remaining energy is lost as heat, a conversion efficiency of about 46%. FADH enters the ETS at a lower energy level than NADH, yielding only two ATP molecules, not three.

Fig. 141. **Electron transport system.** Aerobic respiration.

electro-osmosis a type of OSMOSIS in which the SEMIPERMEABLE MEMBRANE has a potential difference across it so that charged solvents move from the negative to the positive side.

electrophoresis a method for separating particles with different electrical charges, for example, proteins. The apparatus consists of a supporting medium soaked in a suitable buffer with an electrical field set up across it. The mixture to be separated, for example, blood proteins, is placed on the supporting medium. The components with different charges then separate from each other, and their eventual position is compared with the position of known standards.

element a substance that cannot be destroyed by normally available heat or electrical energy.

elephantiasis an abnormality of the human lymphatic system in which blockage of the lymph ducts causes gross swelling in surrounding tissues, often resulting in limbs that appear like those of an elephant. The condition can be caused by bacterial infection, but in tropical regions is caused most often by nematode FILARIAL WORMS, for example, *Wucheria bancrofti*.

elevator muscle see FLIGHT.

elimination the removal of waste and undigested materials from the body through defecation and through exhalation of CO_2 during breathing.

elytron see COLEOPTERA.

emarginate (of plant structures) notched shallowly toward the apex.

emasculation 1. (in plants) the removal of stamens from hermaphrodite flowers before pollen is liberated, thus enabling artificial CROSS-POLLINATION. 2. (in animals) also called **castration** or **gelding**. Removal of the testicles.

embedding the process of sealing a specimen in wax that is to be sectioned, usually with a microtome.

Embioptera an order of hemimetabolous insects (see EXOPTERYGOTA). The males have four wings, and the females are wingless. They are social animals, living in silken tunnels below bark or stones.

embryo 1. (in animals) the stage immediately after the beginning of CLEAVAGE up to the time when the developing animal hatches, or breaks out of egg membranes, or is born. **2.** (in plants) the partly developed SPOROPHYTE, which in ANGIOSPERMS is protected within a seed. At one end of the embryo axis is the RADICLE, or ROOT, and at the other the apical MERISTEM, or PLUMULE in some forms, and one or two young leaves (COTYLEDONS).

embryology the study of the developing EMBRYO in animals or plants.

embryonic membrane or **extraembryonic membrane** any of the protective membranes surrounding the developing embryo in animals that are involved in the respiration and nutrition of the developing organism. They derive from the zygote, lie outside the embryo proper, and form the CHORION, ALLANTOIS, AMNION, and YOLK SAC.

embryophyte any plant of the nontaxonomic group Embryophyta, possessing an embryo and multicellular sex organs. Examples include mosses, liverworts, ferns, and seed plants.

embryo sac the female GAMETOPHYTE of flowering plants, consisting of a sac-like structure inside the OVULE in which are found six HAPLOID cells (without cell walls) and two haploid nuclei. See Fig. 142.

Fig. 142. **Embryo sac.** Vertical section.

The name "embryo sac" comes from the fact that the plant embryo develops from within the sac. Two MALE GAMETE NUCLEI enter the embryo sac from the POLLEN TUBE and carry out a double fertilization. One male nucleus fuses with the egg cell to give a DIPLOID zygote, the future plant. The other male nucleus fuses with two polar nuclei giving a triploid (3n) ENDOSPERM nucleus, the future food supply in some species.

emendation the correction of a previously published misspelled scientific name.

emigration the movement of animals away from a specific area. Compare IMMIGRATION.

emphysema a pulmonary disorder involving overdistention and destruction of the air spaces in the lungs.

emulsification a process in which an emulsion is formed, an emulsion being a liquid containing droplets of another liquid that do not together form a solution, for example, fats in milk. BILE is an important emulsifier in the mammalian digestive system.

enamel a substance consisting mainly of a calcium phosphate-carbonate salt, bound together by KERATIN, found on the crowns of teeth and the denticles of fish. It is formed from the EPITHELIUM of the mouth. See TOOTH.

enation an outgrowth on a leaf produced by a virus infection resulting in the multiplication of leaf cells.

encephalitis or **sleeping sickness** an inflammatory viral disease of the human CENTRAL NERVOUS SYSTEM that is ENDEMIC in parts of North America. Encephalitis is not to be confused with AFRICAN SLEEPING SICKNESS, which is caused by a trypanosome protozoan.

encystment a process found in the life stages of some organisms in which they surround themselves with a CYST. Encystment is usually a protective stage in the life history and occurs, for example, in *Euglena* and in a larval stage of FLUKES.

endangered species any species at risk of extinction as a result of human activity.

endemic (of organisms or disease) occurrence limited to a particular geographical area, such as an island.

endergonic reaction or **endothermic reaction** a reaction requiring free energy, for example, heat, from an outside source to begin the reaction. See also ACTIVATION ENERGY.

endo- *combining form* denoting within.

endoblast see ENDODERM.

endocardium the inner lining of the HEART.

endocrine gland or **ductless gland** the glands of internal secretion, which shed their secretions (HORMONES) directly into the blood system.

endocrinology the study of ENDOCRINE GLANDS and their secretions.

endocytosis an active process by which some cells can enclose a smaller body, for example, food particles, forming a membrane-bound vesicle. Compare EXOCYTOSIS. See PHAGOCYTOSIS, PINOCYTOSIS,

endoderm or **endoblast** the embryological germ layer in animals that gives rise to the gut system and its association organs. It arises initially as a result of GASTRULATION from cells that have moved in from the surface of the BLASTULA. Compare ECTODERM.

endodermis a one-cell layer of tissue found outside the vascular areas in many ANGIOSPERMS that is particularly important in the roots, where endodermal cells are thickened with CASPARIAN STRIPS for control of water transport.

endogamy pollination of a flower by another flower on the same plant. Compare EXOGAMY.

endogenous (of growth or production) from within the body, for example, the development of new roots from the PERICYCLE of the old ROOT. Compare EXOGENOUS.

endolymph the fluid contained in the membranous labyrinth of the vertebrate ear.

endometrium the lining of the uterus in female mammals, being a glandular MUCUS membrane that undergoes changes during the ESTROUS CYCLE, when it builds up in preparation to receive the fertilized egg. When fertilization does not occur, the endometrium regresses or—in the case of humans, anthropoid apes, and Old World monkeys—suddenly breaks down, producing bleeding. See MENSTRUAL CYCLE.

endomitosis the doubling of the chromosome number without subsequent cell division, so producing a POLYPLOID.

endonuclease restriction enzymes bacterial ENZYMES capable of cleaving DNA at points where specific NUCLEOTIDE sequences occur, a function thought to be important in defending an organism against invasion by foreign DNA. Such enzymes have been used extensively to map the base sequences of DNA controlling, for example, the structure of HEMOGLOBIN molecules.

endoparasite see PARASITE.

endopeptidase or **proteinase** a type of protein-splitting enzyme that hydrolyzes peptide bonds between amino acids located *inside* the chain, but not at the ends. There are three major endopeptidases in the mammalian gut: PEPSIN (stomach), TRYPSIN, and CHYMOTRYPSIN (pancreas). Such enzymes are responsible for the first stage of protein digestion. Other proteases (protein-splitting enzymes), called EXOPEPTIDASES, complete the digestion of protein in the ILEUM.

endoplasm any cytoplasm present within the plasma membrane and ECTOPLASM of a cell. It is often more liquid (see PLASMA SOL) than the ectoplasm and is important in locomotion of some PROTOZOANS. It contains more granules than the ectoplasm, from which it is difficult to distinguish, as there is no distinct boundary between the two.

endoplasmic reticulum (ER) a series of interconnected, flattened cavities lined with a membrane about 4 nm thick, which is continuous with the NUCLEAR MEMBRANE. When it is covered with RIBOSOMES, it is referred to as *rough ER*. When ribosomes are absent, the ER is known as *smooth ER* and gives rise to the GOLGI APPARATUS.

Endoprocta see BRYOZOAN.

Endopterygota or **Holometabola** a subclass of the class Insecta, containing insects that have a marked METAMORPHOSIS in which a larval form pupates and gives rise to an adult (imago) with a very different body form from the larva. Examples include DIPTERANS and LEPIDOPTERA.

end organ a single or multicellular organ situated at the end of a fiber of the peripheral nervous system (outside the CNS). It is either a receptor or a means of transferring a nerve impulse to an effector, as in a motor endplate (see ENDPLATE, MOTOR).

endorphin a small protein produced in the nervous system of vertebrates exhibiting actions similar to those of morphine.

endoskeleton a skeleton present within the body of an organism, for example, the vertebrate skeleton. Compare EXOSKELETON.

endosperm a TRIPLOID (1) tissue found in many angiosperm seeds, for example, castor oil, and serving as a food source for the embryo developing within it. Nonendospermic seeds, for example, the runner bean, store their food substances within the cotyledons. See EMBRYO SAC for origin.

endospore a very resistant bacterial SPORE that develops by a process called SPORULATION, from a vegetative cell.

endostyle a ciliated groove on the ventral wall of the pharynx of urochordates, cephalochordates, and the ammocete larva of the lamprey, which passes food by ciliary action backward to the gullet.

endothelium a layer of flattened cells one cell thick that lines the heart, blood vessels, and lymph vessels of vertebrates.

endothermic reaction see ENDERGONIC REACTION.

endothermy the ability of an organism to produce sufficient metabolic heat to raise its CORE TEMPERATURE above that of its surroundings. It may be maintained continually or for limited periods only, as during activity.

endotroph see ECTOTROPH.

endplate, motor the modification of the muscle fiber membrane at a nerve muscle junction to which the DENDRITE is attached, forming an END ORGAN. ACETYLCHOLINE released from the nerve ending diffuses across the junction and depolarizes the endplate, thus giving rise to an endplate potential which, as it builds up, may give rise to an ACTION POTENTIAL and initiate muscle contraction. See Fig. 143.

end-product inhibition a type of FEEDBACK MECHANISM in which the

ENERGY

postsynaptic membrane
presynaptic membrane
mitochondrion
axon
myelin sheath
synaptic vesicle
synaptic cleft (acetylcholinesterase)
myofibril
sarcoplasm
muscle

Fig. 143. **Endplate.** Vertical section.

movement of substances along a biosynthetic PATHWAY is prevented by the end product of the pathway, resulting in self-regulation.

energy the capacity of a body or system to do work. The most important energy forms, as far as living organisms are concerned, are heat, radiant, chemical, and mechanical energy. Energy units of importance are:

1 calorie = heat to raise 1 g of water through 1°C

$$1 \text{ erg} = \frac{\text{energy to raise 1 g through 1 cm against gravity}}{981}$$

1 joule = 10^7 ergs
1 Calorie = 1 kcal (= 1000 cals)
1 calorie = 4.2×10^7 ergs
1 calorie = 4.2 joules

The amount of solar energy entering Earth's atmosphere is 64.3×10^8 J m^{-2} yr^{-1}. The SI UNIT of energy is the Joule (J). In plants and animals, energy is stored in ATP (short-term storage) and in starch and FAT (long-term storage).

energy acceptor a molecule, for example, CYTOCHROME, capable of receiving energy, usually in the form of electrons, and of passing it on to another acceptor, as in an ELECTRON TRANSPORT SYSTEM.

energy donor the molecules that give up the energy to drive an ENDERGONIC REACTION.

energy flow the movement of energy through an ECOSYSTEM. The energy is usually trapped first as *radiant energy* (from the sun) by PRODUCERS, which are then eaten by HERBIVORES that might in turn be consumed by PREDATORS. There is considerable loss of energy, both material energy and heat, back into the ecosystem and out of it at each level.

enrichment culture a technique for isolating an organism from a mixed culture by manipulating the growth conditions in its favor and to the detriment of other organisms.

enteric canal see ALIMENTARY CANAL.

entero- *combining form* denoting intestine.

enterocrinine a gastrointestinal hormone that controls secretion of intestinal juice.

enterogastrone a hormone secreted by the MUCOSA of the duodenum that decreases gastric secretions and movement in response to the ingestion of fat.

enterokinase an ENZYME secreted by the wall of the small intestine whose function is to catalyze conversion of inactive trypsinogen in the pancreatic juice to active TRYPSIN.

enteron see ALIMENTARY CANAL.

Enteropneusta see HEMICHORDATA.

entire (of plant structure) not toothed or cut.

ento- *combining form* denoting within.

entomo- *combining form* denoting insect.

entomogenous (of fungi) parasitic on insects.

entomology the study of insects.

entomophily the POLLINATION of plants by insects. Such animal pollinators are one of the two main mechanisms for transporting pollen to the stigma, the other being ANEMOPHILY. In entomophilous flowers, the colors are adapted to their pollinators. For example, moths are mainly active at dusk and at night and they visit flowers that are mostly white. Bees cannot see red and will visit mainly blue or yellow flowers. Many flowers have patterns visible only with ULTRAVIOLET LIGHT, which insects but not mammals can detect. Deep flowers are pollinated by insects with long mouthparts, and short flowers by insects with short mouthparts, an example of COEVOLUTION of plants and insects.

entropy the amount of disorder or the degree of randomness of a system. For example, when a protein is denatured by heat (see DENATURATION), the molecule, which has a definite shape, uncoils and takes up a random shape, producing a large change in entropy.

envelope any enclosing structure, such as a membrane or skin. In bacteria, it is the part of the cell enclosing the cytoplasm, that is, the cytoplasmic membrane cell wall and capsule. In VIRUSES, it is the outer lipid-containing layer of some virions.

environment the surroundings of any organism, including the MEDIUM, SUBSTRATE, climatic conditions, other organisms (see BIOTIC FACTORS), light, and pH.

ENVIRONMENTAL RESISTANCE

environmental resistance the collective effect on population growth of predators and competition for food and space.

environmental temperature the temperature at which an inanimate body of the same shape and size as a given organism will come to equilibrium with its surroundings when placed at the same point in space as the organism. The temperature includes radiative and convective influences on the organism.

environmental variation see PHENOTYPIC PLASTICITY.

enzyme a protein molecule that catalyzes a biochemical reaction by lowering the ACTIVATION ENERGY required for the reaction to proceed. Enzymes are usually specific to particular substrates (see ACTIVE SITE) and are sensitive to environmental conditions, such as pH and temperature (see Fig. 144 and Q_{10}). ALLOSTERIC ENZYMES exist in inactive and active forms, while others can be inhibited by nonsubstrate molecules (see COMPETITIVE INHIBITION, NONCOMPETITIVE INHIBITION). Protein-splitting enzymes (PROTEASES) are produced in nonactive forms in the mammalian digestive system to minimize the risk of self-digestion. For example, TRYPSIN is produced as inactive trypsinogen.

Fig. 144. **Enzyme.** The effect of pH activity.

enzyme induction the process in which a structural gene is activated by a substrate binding with a repressor substance, thus enabling production of an enzyme that will catalyze metabolism of the substrate. See OPERON MODEL.

enzyme inhibitor a molecule that prevents an enzyme from catalyzing a reaction. Such inhibitors can compete with the normal substrate (see COMPETITIVE INHIBITION) or can block the active site, preventing entry of the substrate (see NONCOMPETITIVE INHIBITION). Enzyme inhibitors often form part of a FEEDBACK MECHANISM to regulate a biochemical pathway.

eobiont a hypothetical chemical precursor of a living cell.

Eocene a geological epoch lasting from 54 to 38 million years ago; a subdivision of the TERTIARY PERIOD. During this time extensive planktonic populations of Foraminifera laid down rock beds, from which the pyramids of Egypt were built, and many groups of mammals appeared for the first time, for example, rodents, whales, and carnivores. See GEOLOGICAL TIME.

eosinophil leukocyte a type of white blood cell of the GRANULOCYTE group that takes up the stain of an acid dye. Eosinophils make up about 4% of adult human leukocytes. They are produced in the bone marrow, and their function is probably connected with the IMMUNE RESPONSE, particularly ALLERGIES.

ep- or **epi-** or **eph-** *prefix* denoting upon, on, over, *etc.*

ephemeral (of organisms) having a very short life cycle. The term is used specifically to describe plants that have more than one generation a year, as opposed to ANNUAL, BIENNIAL, PERENNIAL.

Ephemeroptera an order of the class Insecta, containing the mayflies. They are EXOPTERGYOTES and spend the great majority of their life in the nymphal stage and only a few minutes or hours in the nonfeeding, adult stage. See Fig. 145.

Fig. 145. **Ephemeroptera.** *Ephemera* sp.

ephyra the free-swimming larva of a COELENTERATE jellyfish that results from STROBILATION of a scyphistoma larva (see SCYPHOZOAN).

epi- see EP-.

epiblem the outermost layer of PARENCHYMA cells in the root, which becomes the functional outer layer when the piliferous layer sloughs off as roots increase in age.

epiboly the process by which a BLASTULA is converted into a GASTRULA by growth of ectoderm over the endoderm.

epicalyx a CALYX-like structure that occurs outside and around the true calyx, as in the strawberry flower.

epicardium the external covering of the HEART wall.

epicotyl the axis, or stem, of the shoot in a young germinating seedling, located above the COTYLEDON. See GERMINATION and Fig. 166.

epidemic the occurrence of many cases of a disease within an area.

epidemiology the study of the incidence, distribution, and control of an EPIDEMIC disease in a population.

epidermis 1. (in plants) the tissue, usually one cell thick, that surrounds young roots, stems, and leaves. In stems and leaves, the epidermal cells secrete a CUTICLE (1). In roots, they do not. In older roots and stems the epidermis is often replaced by CORK tissue. 2. (in animals) the outer layer of the skin derived from embryonic ECTODERM. In vertebrates, the epidermal layer is usually made up of stratified EPITHELIUM with an outer layer of dead cells that become keratinized (see KERATIN), forming a protective layer. The invertebrate epidermis is normally one cell thick and often forms a protective cuticle.

epididymis the long, coiled narrow tube running from the TESTIS to the VAS DEFERENS in the higher vertebrates. It functions to store sperm.

epifauna the part of the BENTHOS living on the mud surface.

epigamic character any secondary sexual character brought into existence by hormone action and used in courtship display.

epigeal of or relating to seed GERMINATION, in which the COTYLEDONS are carried above ground and form the first green foliage leaves of the plant, for example, string beans (*Phaseolus vulgaris*).

epigenesis the formation of entirely new structures during development of the EMBRYO.

epigenetic landscape a concept related to the developmental PATHWAYS along which a cell passes during differentiation. See CANALIZATION.

epiglottis a thin flexible structure, made of CARTILAGE with a leaflike shape, which guards the entrance to the larynx (the *glottis*) and prevents food material from entering the TRACHEA during swallowing. See Fig. 146.

Fig. 146. **Epiglottis.** The left-side cervical region in humans.

epigynous see GYNOECIUM.

epilepsy a nervous condition due to abnormalities in the brain cortex that results in seizures ranging from a sense of numbness in certain body areas (*petit mal*) to extreme muscular convulsions and seizures (*grand* *mal*). Epileptics exhibit large, abnormal brain waves that can be detected on an EEG.

epimere the dorsal part of the mesoderm of a vertebrate embryo, consisting of a series of SOMITES.

epinasty the increased growth of the upper surface of a structure, such as a leaf, resulting in its being curved downward.

epinephrine see ADRENALINE.

epipelagic zone see EUPHOTIC ZONE.

epipetalous (of plant structures) inserted on the COROLLA, as in the stamens of the primrose.

epiphysis the ossified part of the end of a mammalian limb bone or vertebra which, during growth, is separated by a plate of cartilage from the rest of the ossified bone. When growth is complete, the epiphysis fuses with the rest of the bone. Compare DIAPHYSIS.

epiphyte a plant, for example, certain mosses and orchids, that grows attached to another and uses it solely for purposes of support, there being no parasitic association.

epiphytotic (of plant diseases and parasites) affecting plants over a wide geographical region.

episome a circular DNA molecule found in bacterial cells that can exist independently in the cell or can become integrated into the main CHROMOSOME. In recent times, episomes have been added to a general group of extrachromosomal factors called PLASMIDS.

epistasis a form of genetic interaction in which one gene interferes with the expression of another gene, for example, if genes A and B code for enzymes active in the same PATHWAY. See Fig. 147. If both ALLELES of gene A code for a nonfunctional version of enzyme A, then the pathway will shut down irrespective of which B alleles are present, that is, gene A is epistatic to gene B. Compare DOMINANT EPISTASIS, RECESSIVE EPISTASIS.

Fig. 147. **Epistasis.** The interaction of genes A and B.

epithelium 1. (in animals) a layer of covering cells that is normally one cell thick and usually covers connective tissue embryologically derived from the ECTODERM. The cells often have a secretory function, and their shape gives rise to names descriptive of the cells, for example, *columnar, cubical, squamous* (see Fig. 148). Where the epithelium is more than one cell thick, it is described as *stratified*. Similar cells can be derived from MESODERM and are referred to as *mesothelium* when lining the COELOM, and as ENDOTHELIUM when lining blood vessels. 2. (in plants) a layer of cells lining cavities and secretory canals, for example, resin canals.

squamous   cuboidal   columnar   stratified

Fig. 148. **Epithelium (1).** Types of epithelium.

epizoite any animal that lives attached to another and uses it for protection or means of locomotion, there being no parasitic relationship.

epizootic (of a disease) suddenly and temporarily affecting a large animal population.

equal weighting a taxonomic procedure in which all characters are regarded as equally important. The procedure is commonly used in NUMERICAL TAXONOMY.

equatorial plate an arrangement of chromosomes lying in one plane at the equator of the spindle in METAPHASE of MITOSIS or MEIOSIS.

equilibrium centrifugation a process of DENSITY-GRADIENT CENTRIFUGATION that continues until there is no net movement of the molecules, each molecule having come to rest when its density equaled that of the solution.

equilibrium of population see GENETIC EQUILIBRIUM.

Equisetum any pteridophyte plant of the genus *Equisetum,* comprising the horsetails. The plant is herbaceous, has rhizomes and a vertical stem with whorls of scale leaves, and is often found growing in water and damp conditions. It is the last living representative of the order Equisetales.

eradicant any biocide, for example, a fungicide, used to cure an established infection.

erection, penis the hardening and lengthening of the mammalian penis in order to bring it into condition for copulation. An erection is brought about by engorgement of blood in the CORPUS SPONGIOSUM and CORPUS CAVERNOSUM, causing them to become turgid.

erector-pili muscle a small muscle found in the DERMIS of a mammal, which is connected to a hair and controls the position of the hair in relation to the skin surface for temperature regulation.

erepsin a mixture of PROTEOLYTIC ENZYMES secreted by the small intestine of mammals.

ergot 1. a disease caused by the ascomycete *Claviceps purpurea* in cereals and grasses. **2.** a SCLEROTIUM forming in place of a grain in a diseased grain head. Ergots contain substances that are poisonous and sometimes are used medicinally.

erose (of plant structures) having the appearance of being gnawed, with irregular notches.

erosion the wearing away of geological formations such as rock and soil. For example, deforestation may cause soil erosion.

erythro- *combining form* denoting red.

erythroblastosis fetalis a hemolytic disease of newborn children brought about when a rhesus negative mother produces a rhesus negative child (see RHESUS BLOOD GROUP). In late pregnancy, Rh $^-$ cells may pass into the mother, who produces antigens that pass back across the placenta and adversely affect the child.

erythrocyte or **red blood cell (RBC)** a vertebrate cell that carries some carbon dioxide as HCO_3 — from tissues to lungs (see also CHLORIDE SHIFT), and contains HEMOGLOBIN pigment for oxygen transport from lungs to tissues. Unlike other vertebrate cells, mammalian RBCs are nonnucleated and have definite biconcave shape. See Fig. 149. Compare LEUKOCYTE.

$\leftarrow$7.2 μm$\rightarrow$ $\leftarrow$$\rightarrow$$\leftarrow$—2.2 μm

(a)   (b)

Fig. 149. **Erythrocyte.** (a) Surface view. (b) Vertical section.

erythromycin an antibiotic produced by a strain of STREPTOMYCIN that includes protein synthesis, particularly in organisms that are Gram-positive (see GRAM'S SOLUTION).

escape 1. any cultivated plant growing in the wild that is not well naturalized. **2.** any organism that is normally captive but has been freed into the natural environment.

escape response any flight reaction elicited in an animal as a result of a threat.

Escherichia coli (E. coli) a bacterium common in the human gut, used extensively in biochemical and genetical studies.

eserine a plant alkaloid capable of blocking CHOLINESTERASE.

esophagus the part of the alimentary canal of vertebrates that lies between the PHARYNX and the STOMACH. No digestive juices are produced here, but PERISTALSIS takes place, often moving the bolus upward from the lowered head to the stomach.

essential amino acid an AMINO ACID that must be taken in via the diet, as distinct from nonessential amino acids, which can be synthesized by the organism itself in a process called TRANSAMINATION using the essential amino acids as a source. In humans there are 10 essential amino acids: ARGININE, TRYPTOPHAN, ISOLEUCINE, METHIONINE, THREONINE, LYSINE, LEUCINE, VALINE, HISTIDINE, and PHENYLALANINE.

essential element or **mineral element** an element without which normal growth and reproduction cannot take place. In plants, there are seven major essential elements: nitrogen, phosphorus, sulfur, potassium, calcium, magnesium, and iron. There are also TRACE ELEMENTS required in much smaller quantities, for example, manganese, boron, and chlorine. Animals also have requirements for elements, the list being similar to that for plants.

essential fatty acid see LINOLEIC ACID.

ester a compound formed from an alcohol and an acid.

esterification the formation of an ESTER.

estivation 1. (in animals) a state of dormancy during summer or dry season. Compare HIBERNATION. 2. (in plants) the arrangement of the parts of the bud of a flower.

estradiol an ESTROGEN produced by the follicle cells of the vertebrate ovary. It promotes estrus, the development of the endometrium, and stimulates ICSH secretion.

estrogen a hormone produced by the OVARY of the female vertebrate that maintains the female SECONDARY SEXUAL CHARACTERS and is involved in repairing the uterine wall after menstruation (see MENSTRUAL CYCLE). It is also produced by the female PLACENTA and in small quantities by the ADRENAL CORTEX and the male TESTIS.

estrous cycle a reproductive cycle caused by cyclic production of gonadotrophic hormones by the PITUITARY GLAND. It occurs in adult female mammals and is only complete when pregnancy does not occur, lasting from 5 to 60 days, depending on the species.

Initially, follicle growth occurs in the ovary as a result of secretion of FOLLICLE-STIMULATING HORMONE (FSH) by the anterior pituitary. This results in increased ESTROGEN production and thickening of the uterus lining. The build-up of estrogen causes the anterior pituitary to produce LUTEINIZING HORMONE, which in turn brings about ovulation with the formation of a CORPUS LUTEUM, development of the uterine glands, secretion of PROGESTERONE by the corpus luteum (which inhibits FSH production), and a consequent decrease in estrogen production.

Fertilization may occur at this stage and, if it does, pregnancy results.

If not, there is a regression of the corpus luteum and a feedback to the anterior pituitary to produce FSH as progesterone decreases. New follicles are formed, the lining of the uterus thins, menstruation (see MENSTRUAL CYCLE) occurs in human females and some other primates, and there is a cessation of progesterone secretion and a continued decrease of estrogen. The cycle then begins again as new follicles grow. Only during the initial period of the cycle, when ovulation takes place, will the female of most mammalian species copulate. This is the period of heat, or estrus.

estrus the period of heat or rut in mammals.

estuary the point at which a river meets the sea, with a consequent mixture of saline and freshwater conditions, often with areas of tidal mudflats and salt marsh. Because of the varying salinity and tidal cover, there often is a specific flora and fauna associated with such areas.

ethanoic acid see ACETIC ACID.

ethanol an alcohol produced in ALCOHOLIC FERMENTATION.

ethene see ETHYLENE.

ethology the study of animal behavior in the natural habitat of the animals concerned.

ethylene or **ethene** a simple hydrocarbon with the formula $CH_2 = CH_2$ that can act as a PLANT HORMONE even when present in very low concentrations, down to 1 ppm. Ethylene inhibits elongation in most growing tissues and promotes leaf ABSCISSION and fruit ripening in some plants. Plant cells produce ethylene from the amino acid METHIONINE.

etiolation the range of symptoms developed by plants when grown in the dark. Examples include pale yellow or white color due to lack of chlorophyll, long internodes, small and rudimentary leaves, and poor development of lignified tissue.

etiology or **aetiology** the study of causes, usually of a disease.

ETS see ELECTRON TRANSPORT SYSTEM.

eu- *combining form* denoting true, well, *or* good.

eucarpic (of an adult fungal THALLUS) having clear distinction between vegetative and reproductive parts.

eucaryote see EUKARYOTE.

euchromatin a chromosome material that stains heavily in METAPHASE but hardly at all in INTERPHASE, when it is relatively uncoiled and undergoes TRANSCRIPTION. Compare HETEROCHROMATIN.

eugenics the study of ways of improving the hereditary qualities of a population, especially the human population, by application of social controls and guided by genetic principles.

Euglena a genus of large, green flagellates (division Euglenophyta) common in both fresh and salt waters. Euglenoids produce a polysaccharide storage molecule called PARAMYLUM and, unlike other flagellates, do not possess a cell wall, but produce a flexible PELLICLE instead.

Euglenophyta a division of the algae, sometimes classified by zoologists in the class Flagellata. They normally possess chlorophyll *a* and *b,* but this may be lost. Colorless forms do not regain their chlorophyll, and no members of the division are completely AUTOTROPHIC.

eukaryote or **eucaryote** any member of a group of organisms that contains all plants and animals apart from bacteria and blue-green algae, which are PROKARYOTES. Eukaryotes are distinguished by the fact that their cells possess a membrane-bound nucleus containing the genetic material, but there are also other differences from the prokaryotes. See Fig. 150.

Procaryotes	Eukaryotes
1. No true nucleus.	Nucleus with NUCLEAR MEMBRANE.
2. Single chromosome made up of nucleic acid.	Several CHROMOSOMES with nucleic acid complexed with protein.
3. Cell organelles absent.	GOLGI APPARATUS, ENDOPLASMIC RETICULUM LYSOSOMES, MITOCHONDRIA present.
4. If present, chlorophyll not in chloroplasts.	If present, CHLOROPHYLL in chloroplasts.
5. Flagella lack 9 + 2 structure.	FLAGELLA with 9 + 2 structure.
6. Cell division by BINARY FISSION.	Cell division by MITOSIS AND MEIOSIS.

Fig. 150. **Eukaryote.** A comparison of prokaryotes and eukaryotes.

Eumycota or formerly **Mycophyta** the true fungi (see FUNGUS), a division of the kingdom Mycota.

euphausiid any small, pelagic, shrimplike CRUSTACEAN of the order Euphausiacea. Euphausiids are an important constituent of *Krill,* the main food of whalebone whales.

euphotic zone or **photic zone** or **epipelagic zone** the top 100 meters of the sea, into which light can penetrate and in which PHOTOSYNTHESIS takes place. See SEA ZONATION.

euploidy the condition of a cell, tissue, or organism that has one or more multiples of a chromosome set, for example, a TRIPLOID (3n). Euploids with more than two sets of chromosomes are POLYPLOIDS.

eupnea the normal, quiet breathing of an animal at rest.

euryhaline (of organisms) capable of tolerating a wide variety of salinity in the surrounding medium.

eurypterid any large extinct scorpionlike aquatic arthropod of the order Eurypterida, found in the SILURIAN PERIOD.

eurythermous (of organisms) able to tolerate a wide range of environmental temperatures.

eusporangiate (of sporangia) arising from a group of parent cells and having a wall consisting of at least two layers of cells.

Eustachian tube a tube passing from the pharynx to the middle ear in higher vertebrates, serving to equalize pressure on either side of the TYMPANIC MEMBRANE.

euthanasia the act of painless killing to relieve human suffering from an incurable disease.

eutherian any placental mammal of the subclass Eutheria, characterized by the embryo developing in the uterus of the female, where it obtains food and exchanges gases through the attached PLACENTA.

eutrophic (of a body of water) rich in organic and mineral nutrients, either naturally or by fertilization.

eutrophication a process by which pollutants cause a body of water to become overly rich in organic and mineral nutrients, so that algae grow rapidly and deplete the oxygen supply.

e value the solar energy present on other planets expressed as a percentage of Earth's solar energy.

E_0 values a numerical series indicative of the REDOX POTENTIAL of molecules. Protons are accepted by a molecule from any other molecule with a more positive E_0 value.

evaporation the physical change when a liquid becomes a gas. Since such a change usually requires heat as an energy source, heat is drawn from the immediate environment, which produces a significant cooling effect. The size of the cooling effect depends on the *latent heat of evaporation* of the liquid. Evaporation of water is used by mammals in temperature regulation, through sweating, and occurs in plants from the surface of the mesophyll cells during TRANSPIRATION.

evergreen a type of tree or shrub that possesses leaves in all seasons. Most CONIFERS are evergreen, as are many ANGIOSPERMS, for example, laurel and privet.

eversible (of structures) capable of protruding from an organism by being turned inside out. Examples include the eversible proboscis in some worms, and the eversible cloaca in some birds that can be protruded to form a penislike structure used in copulation.

evocation the induction of embryonic tissue by a chemical stimulus. For example, ECTODERM produces neutral material in the vertebrate embryo due to an evocator (see ORGANIZER REGION) from the underlying CHORDAMESODERM.

evocator region see ORGANIZER REGION.

evolution an explanation of the way in which present-day organisms have been produced, involving changes taking place in the genetic makeup of populations, which have been passed on to successive generations. According to DARWINISM, evolutionary MUTATIONS have given rise to changes that, through NATURAL SELECTION, either have survived in better adapted organisms (see ADAPTATION, GENETIC) or died out.

Evolution is now generally accepted as the means that gives rise to new species, as opposed to SPECIAL CREATION, but there is still debate about exactly how it has taken place and how rapidly changes can take place. See LAMARCKISM.

evolutionary tree a diagram showing relationships between a group of organisms and their evolution from an ancestral stock.

excision the removal of a DNA fragment from a chromosome.

excision repair the removal of damaged polynucleotide segments from DNA, for example, thymidine DIMERS produced by ultraviolet light, and replacement with a correct segment using DNA POLYMERASE and DNA LIGASE.

excitability any change in membrane conductance as a response to stimulation.

excitation the process by which electrical stimulation of a surface membrane results in contraction of the muscle, or by which it brings about secretion of a transmitter substance at a nerve ending.

excitatory postsynaptic potential (EPSP) a reduction in the RESTING POTENTIAL of a postsynaptic cell caused by arrival of TRANSMITTER SUBSTANCE from the presynaptic cell. The reduction takes the membrane potential close to the THRESHOLD and, therefore, nearer to itself forming an ACTION POTENTIAL. See FACILITATION.

excitor neuron a neuron that directly excites a muscle or other organ.

exclusion principle the principle that two species with the same ecological requirements cannot exist together.

excretion any elimination from an organism of unwanted materials, for example, carbon dioxide and nitrogenous substances produced in METABOLISM. It is worth noting that excretory materials must be *produced* by the organism rather than just pass through it; thus, feces in mammals contain a mixture of undigested gut contents and excreta, for example, bile pigments.

exergonic reaction or **exothermic reaction** a reaction that releases free energy, as in a spontaneous change.

exine the outer coat of a POLLEN GRAIN, which often has protuberances, spines, and the like. The exine also has one or more areas where the wall is thin, forming a pore through which the pollen tube will protrude.

exobiology the study of possible extraterrestrial organisms.

exocytosis an active process in which vesicles containing excretory or secretory materials are actively carried to the periphery of the cell, and released to the outside when the vesicle membrane fuses with the cell membrane. Compare ENDOCYTOSIS. See PHAGOCYTOSIS, PINOCYTOSIS.

exodermis a layer of cortical cells that replaces the piliferous layer in the older parts of roots.

exogamy mating between unrelated individuals. Compare ENDOGAMY.

exogenous 1. originating from or due to external causes. 2. developing near the surface of an organism, as in the development of axillary buds in plants.

exon or **extron** the DNA segments of a EUKARYOTE gene, which are transcribed into mRNA and then into protein. Exons occur along the length of the gene and are separated by segments called INTRONS, whose sequences are also transcribed into mRNA. The intron mRNA segments are then excised, leaving behind exon mRNA segments, which join up to form a functional piece of mRNA in a process called RNA SPLICING.

exonuclease an enzyme that removes a terminal NUCLEOTIDE (3' or 5') in a POLYNUCLEOTIDE CHAIN. Exonucleases remove the nucleotides in a successive way, one by one, and are highly specific in their action.

exopeptidase a type of protein-splitting ENZYME that hydrolyzes the terminal PEPTIDE BONDS rather than those bonds within the chain. There are three main types of exopeptidases in the mammalian gut, each attacking a particular area of the protein: *carboxypeptidase* attacks the carboxyl end of the chain, *aminopeptidase* attacks the amino end of the chain, and *dipeptidase* breaks the bond between DIPEPTIDES. Such enzymes complete digestion of protein prior to absorption into the bloodstream. Compare ENDOPEPTIDASE.

exophthalmic goiter a human condition resulting from overproduction and release of THYROXINE. The thyroid gland becomes swollen, producing a goiter. Symptoms are elevated metabolism, nervousness, irritability, and loss of weight, and the eyes are prominent and staring, with protrusion of the eyeballs. The abnormality can be treated with antithyroid drugs, radioactive iodine, and surgical excision of part of the gland.

Exopterygota or **Heterometabola** or **Hemimetabola** a subclass of the class Insecta, including insects that do not have a marked METAMORPHOSIS, and in which nymphal stages gradually approach the form of the imago at each molt. Examples include EPHEMEROPTERA, ODONATA.

exoskeleton a skeleton present on the outside of an organism, as in ARTHROPODS or MOLLUSKS. Some vertebrates possess an exoskeleton in addition to an ENDOSKELETON, for example, armadillos and turtles. The exoskeleton may lie outside the EPIDERMIS, as in the arthropods, or inside, as in vertebrates such as scaly fish and tortoises.

exothermic reaction see EXERGONIC REACTION.

experimental cytology the study of cells, utilizing microscopy and electron microscopy in conjunction with biochemical and biophysical experimental techniques.

expiration see BREATHING.

expiratory center see BREATHING.

explant any actively dividing plant tissue that can be induced to produce CALLUS tissue in tissue culture.

exploitation the situation in which one organism gains at the expense of another.

exponent a number or quantity placed as a superscript to the right of another number or quantity, indicating how many times the number is to be multiplied by itself. For example, 10^6.

exposure 1. the aspect of a particular location with respect to the points of the compass. For example, some garden plants prefer a southern exposure. **2.** a rock outcrop. **3.** a soil section.

expressivity the degree to which a particular gene exhibits itself in the PHENOTYPE of an organism, once it has undergone PENETRANCE. Thus, for example, a penetrant baldness gene in humans can have a wide range of expressivity, from thinning hair to complete lack of hair.

exserted (of plant structures) protruding.

exsiccata (*sing.* exsiccatum) the preserved material of a herbarium.

exstipulate lacking STIPULES.

extensor a muscle that extends or straightens a limb.

exteroceptor any sensory organ that detects stimuli from outside the organism.

extinct (of an animal or plant species) having died out, no longer present in the world population.

extinction 1. the act of making EXTINCT or the state of being extinct. **2.** the elimination of an allele of a gene in a population, due to RANDOM GENETIC DRIFT or to adverse SELECTION pressures. **3.** any periodical catastrophic event resulting in abrupt death of a species or larger taxonomic group at a point in geological history. Such extinctions are thought to be cyclical, occurring every 28.4 million years, and have been attributed to cosmic activity, such as showers of large asteroids or comets, although neither the periodicity nor its causes are at present universally accepted.

extra- *prefix* denoting outside.

extracellular situated or occurring outside the cell, as in extracellular digestion, where cells secrete enzymes to break down food material, which then is absorbed.

extraembryonic lying outside the embryo, for example, EMBRYONIC MEMBRANE.

extranuclear inheritance see CYTOPLASMIC INHERITANCE.

extrapolation the estimation of a value beyond a given series, for example, extension of the line of a graph beyond calculated points.

extrorse (of anthers) opening toward the outside of the flower.

exudate the material that comes from a cut pore or break in the surface of an organism, such as sweat or cellular debris.

eye the light-receptor organ of animals. Such organs range in complexity from the *ocellus* with a single lens, found in insects and some other invertebrates, to the vertebrate eye, in which light is focused by a lens onto a retina consisting of light-sensitive cells in the form of RODS and CONES (2). See Fig. 151. The front of the vertebrate eye is covered by the CORNEA, behind which is the IRIS, controlling the size of the pupil and thus determining the amount of light entering the eye. The shape, and thus the focus, of the lens is controlled by the INVOLUNTARY MUSCLES of the ciliary body under control of the AUTONOMIC NERVOUS SYSTEM. Light is focused on the retina. See COLOR VISION, ACCOMMODATION, BINOCULAR VISION, and EYE, COMPOUND.

Fig. 151. **Eye.** Vertical section of the mammalian eye.

eye, compound a type of light-receptor organ, found particularly in insects and crustaceans, which is formed from numerous OMMATIDIA each of which can form a separate image.

Movement of the pigment between the ommatidia forms either (a) an *apposition image*, where light enters each ommatidium parallel to its long axis, thus forming a mosaic image; or (b) a *superposition image*, where pigment is withdrawn, allowing in light to the sides of the ommatidia and giving a brighter, less sharp, overlapping series of images. See Fig. 152. The latter occurs in nocturnal insects, the former in diurnal insects, and change from one to the other gives rise to dark adaptation. In many insects the image is either apposition or superposition, and there is no dark adaptation.

Fig. 152. **Eye, compound.** (a) Apposition image. (b) Superposition image.

Ommatidia are larger than rods and cones, so fewer can be packed into the same space. Consequently, the detail of the image is not as good as that in the vertebrate eye. For example, the honeybee has a visual acuity that is 1% of human capacity, and most other arthropods are worse than this. However, the compound eye of insects can detect movement over a large field, and since the reaction time is small, insects are capable of reacting to movement rapidly.

eye muscle 1. one of six muscles that move the eyeball, the so-called extrinsic eye muscles, a pair of oblique muscles situated anteriorly, and four rectus muscles situated posteriorly. 2. one of the intrinsic eye muscles inside the eyeball that are associated with the iris, lens, and ciliary body. See EYE.

eye spot 1. a light-sensitive organelle present in unicellular organisms, green algae, zoospores, and some gametes. 2. a pattern on the wings of some insects, particularly moths, that appears eyelike (see WARNING COLORATION).

F

F₁ the first generation of filial offspring of a particular cross. The number can be changed to indicate the generation. For example, F_3 would be the great-grandchildren of a particular pair of individuals.

facial nerve the 7th cranial nerve, a dorsal root that in mammals is mainly motor in function, supplying facial muscles, salivary glands, and front-of-tongue taste buds.

facilitated transport any carrier-mediated transport (see CARRIER MOLECULE) in a membrane where diffusion is aided by the molecule to enhance mobility of the diffusing substance, but in which there is no ACTIVE TRANSPORT.

facilitation a residual effect that enables or facilitates a second impulse to be transmitted across a junction between a nerve cell or effector cell when a first impulse has failed to cross it. There is thus an increase in responsiveness, resulting from the SUMMATION of impulses, and this is called facilitation.

factor, genetic a term used by early geneticists, for example, R.C. PUNNETT, to describe an ALLELE of a gene.

factorial experiment an experiment in which all treatments are varied together rather than one at a time, so the effect of each or combinations of several can be isolated and measured.

facultative (of an organism) capable of adopting an alternative style of life from the normal one. In this context, the word 'facultative' is followed by the *unusual* style of life. Thus, a facultative PARASITE is one that is normally saprophytic but is occasionally parasitic. A facultative SAPROPHYTE is one that is normally parasitic but can become saprophytic. A facultative ANAEROBE is an organism that is normally aerobic but can exist in anaerobic conditions. Compare OBLIGATE.

FAD (flavin adenine dinucleotide) an electron carrier similar in action to NAD, picking up hydrogen from succinic acid in the KREBS CYCLE. The hydrogen is transported to the mitochondrial lamellae, where it enters an ELECTRON TRANSPORT SYSTEM at a lower point than NAD, with release of only two molecules of ATP rather than three ATP molecules when NAD is the carrier.

falcate sickle-shaped.

Fallopian tube a tube forming part of the OVIDUCT present on either side of a female mammal that transmits eggs from the peritoneal cavity to the uterus and is the usual site of FERTILIZATION. Ciliary action is involved in the egg movement, and muscular action facilitates the upward movement of sperm from the vaginal tract, where they have been deposited after copulation.

family the TAXON between ORDER and GENUS that normally contains more than one genus. Family names of animals usually end in -idae, and of plants in -ceae, for example, Ursidae, the bear family, and Rosaceae, the rose family.

family planning see BIRTH CONTROL.

farmer's lung a human disease in which lesions of minor blood vessels develop in the lungs. The disease is produced as a result of an IMMUNE RESPONSE to the presence of fungal spores in hay. Similar symptoms have been recorded in other occupations, for example, malt workers, pigeon breeders, and cheesemakers.

fascia sheets of CONNECTIVE TISSUE.

fasciation the growing together of branches or stems to form abnormally thick growths.

fascicular see CAMBIUM.

fat a type of simple LIPID found in almost all organisms that is an important energy-storage molecule, containing twice as much energy per gram as carbohydrates. It can also aid in heat insulation, cushioning, and protection. Fats are produced by a combination of one glycerol molecule and three fatty acid molecules—which need not all be the same—forming a *triglyceride*. See Fig. 153.

$$\text{glycerol} + 3 \text{ fatty acids} \underset{\text{hydrolysis}}{\overset{\text{condensation}}{\rightleftharpoons}} \text{fat} + H_2O$$

Fig. 153. **Fat.** The formation of a triglyceride.

Fats are abundant in plant seeds and are also found in roots, stems, and leaves, forming about 5% of the total dry weight. In animals, fats are stored in specialized cells making up ADIPOSE TISSUE. See also BROWN FAT.

fat body 1. (in amphibians and lizards) a structure in the form of finger-like growths immediately in front of the gonads. The fat body stores fat as ADIPOSE TISSUE and is largest just before hibernation. It is of special importance in males, which take little or no food in the breeding season, after which the fat body is greatly reduced in size. 2. (in insects) a loose network of tissue in spaces between organs and around the gut, storing fat, proteins, glycogen, and uric acid. It is found especially in juvenile insects before METAMORPHOSIS.

FECES

fate map a map of an embryo at an early stage of development, showing the regions in which future structures will form.

fatigue exhaustion in muscles resulting from exertion or overstimulation following a period of activity.

fat-soluble vitamin any of several vitamins, including A, D, E, and K, that are soluble in organic solvents but insoluble in water.

fatty acids a range of molecules with the general formula $C_nH_{2n+1}COOH$ that occur naturally in many organisms, often combined with glycerol to form FATS. Fatty acids are of two main types: *unsaturated,* with at least one carbon-to-carbon double bond, and *saturated,* with no such bonds.

The greater the proportion of unsaturated fatty acids in a fat, the lower its melting point, with many unsaturated fats being liquid oils at room temperature. There is evidence that excess consumption of saturated fats can lead to hardening of the arteries, but the facts are disputed, particularly by butter manufacturers.

fauna the grouping of animals present in any one place or at any one time in geological history.

favism a human disease characterized by destruction of red blood cells, resulting in severe anemia. The disease is triggered by consumption of raw fava beans (*Vicia faba*), inhalation of fava bean, pollen, or several other chemicals such as naphthalene, found in moth balls. The condition is due to a deficiency of the enzyme glucose-6-phosphate dehydrogenase found in red blood cells, the trait being controlled by an X-linked gene rare in most caucasian populations and more common in black populations. Since the condition is sex-linked, it is more prevalent in males, although heterozygous females can be shown to have a deficiency of dehydrogenase enzyme.

F⁺ cell a bacterial cell having an F FACTOR.

F⁻ cell a bacterial cell that receives the F FACTOR from an F⁺ cell during conjugation, becoming F⁺ in status.

feather any of the flat light waterproof epidermal structures forming the plumage of birds, several types of which form the body covering of birds. The principal types of feather are *remige* (wing feather), *rectrice* (tail feather), CONTOUR FEATHER (covering the outside of the bird), DOWN (the soft covering of the body), and *filoplume* (hairlike feathers occurring between the contour feathers). Feathers consist of a central RACHIS that supports BARBS which, except in down feathers, are connected to form a lamella by means of BARBULES.

feces the bodily waste material formed in the large intestine and eliminated via the anus. Feces contain a mixture of excretory material from the liver, for example, bilirubin, which gives the feces their characteristic color, food material that has passed straight through the gut, dead bacteria, dead cells, and mucus.

Fechner's law see WEBER-FECHNER LAW.

fecundity the numbers of young produced by an organism during the course of its life. Compare FERTILITY (3). See REPRODUCTIVE POTENTIAL.

feedback mechanism a mechanism by which the products of a process can act as regulators of that process. Many biochemical processes are controlled by *negative feedback* mechanisms. See Fig. 154.

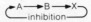

Fig. 154. **Feedback mechanism.** Excess production of X causes shutdown of the process by inhibition of the first step from A to B.

Mammals utilize negative feedback mechanisms to maintain HOMEOSTASIS in several systems, for example, blood thyroxine levels, body temperature, and blood osmotic pressure. *Positive feedback* occasionally occurs. This is a disruptive process, in which products of a process cause further ACTIVATION. For example, excess core heat in mammals will in turn encourage a higher metabolic rate that produces still more heat and eventually death.

feeding phase the phase of life history during which food is taken in, for example, the nymphal stage in mayflies.

Fehling's test a procedure used to detect the presence of REDUCING SUGARS in an unknown solution. Two solutions are mixed: Fehling's solution A, containing copper tartrate (Cu(II)); and Fehling's solution B, containing sodium hydroxide. The mixture is then added to the test solution and boiled. An orange-red precipitate of copper oxide (CU(I)) indicates the presence of a reducing sugar.

femur 1. the thigh bone of TETRAPODS. **2.** the insect leg joint between the trochanter (2nd segment) and tibia (4th segment).

fen a plant community on alkaline, neutral, or slightly acid peat that is wet and usually low-lying.

fenestra ovalis and rotunda the membrane-covered windows leading from the middle ear to the inner ear. See EAR.

fenestration the presence in an organism of windowlike openings, as in the palate of marsupials.

feral (of plants and animals) existing in a wild state, outside human cultivation or habitation.

fermentation 1. see ALCOHOLIC FERMENTATION. **2.** any industrial process involving large-scale culturing of cells in either aerobic or anaerobic conditions, using fermenters.

fern any pteridophyte plant of the class Filicinae, subdivision Pteropsida of the division Tracheophyta, at one time classified in the division Pteridophyta. The ferns constitute the great majority of species in the division and possess large, conspicuous aerial DIPLOID (2) stems. Sporangia are borne on the underside of leaves, and the HAPLOID (2) spores usually give rise to homosporous prothalli that carry both ANTHERIDIA and ARCHEGONIA. There is a small group of heterosporous aquatic ferns (see HETEROSPORY).

ferredoxin an important iron-containing protein acting as an electron carrier in the ELECTRON TRANSPORT SYSTEM that operates in the LIGHT REACTIONS of PHOTOSYNTHESIS, particularly in NONCYCLIC PHOTO-PHOSPHORYLATION.

ferritin a conjugated, electron-dense protein concerned in absorption of iron through the intestinal mucosa. It serves as a storage protein for iron in the liver and spleen.

fertility 1. the readiness with which the gamete of an organism may fuse with a GAMETE of the other sex. 2. the capability of a sperm or ovum of, in the case of the egg, being fertilized or, in the case of the sperm, of fertilizing an egg and so giving rise to a viable ZYGOTE. 3. the capability of an organism, particularly a hybrid (see HETEROSIS), of producing more fertilized ova than others. When such organisms give rise to more young, they are also more fecund (see FECUNDITY), a term with which fertility is often confused. 4. a measure of the productiveness of soil.

fertility factor see F FACTOR.

fertilization the fusion of male and female GAMETES to give rise to a ZYGOTE, which subsequently develops into a new organism. See ACROSOME for further details of animal fertilization. See EMBRYO SAC for details of double fertilization of flowering plants.

fertilization membrane a membrane that appears at the surface of the egg after FERTILIZATION. It is effectively a thickened VITELLINE MEMBRANE that may separate from the surface of the egg. It prevents entry of additional sperms.

fertilizer a fertilizing agent added to agricultural soils, in the form of an added chemical or manure.

fetal membrane the EXTRAEMBRYONIC MEMBRANES of the mammalian FETUS.

fetus the EMBRYO of mammals at the time when it achieves the main features of the adult form. This is usually at the time of the formation of the AMNION, which is after about eight weeks of pregnancy in women. See AMNIOCENTESIS and Fig. 29.

Feulgen, Robert (1884—1955) German physiologist and chemist best known for his discovery of a selective staining technique for DNA, the *Feulgen reaction,* which is based on the reaction of an aldehyde group with leucofuchsin. The intensity of the purple color in the cell nucleus is used as a measure for quantitative estimation of nuclear DNA.

Feulgen reagent a deep purple dye that stains the deoxyribose sugar of DNA in cell nuclei.

F factor or **fertility factor** or **sex factor** an EPISOME that confers donor status on an F$^+$ CELL, so that the F$^+$ cell transfers a copy of the F factor and a small piece of bacterial DNA to an F$^-$ CELL during CONJUGATION, the recipient becoming F$^+$.

fiber a slender fiber in the form of an element of SCLERENCHYMA in plants or of COLLAGEN, RETICULIN, or ELASTIN in animals.

fibril a small FIBER.

fibrillar muscle see FLIGHT.

fibrillation or **ventricular fibrillation** very rapid, irregular contractions of the ventricular muscle of the HEART that cause blood circulation to stop immediately. Under suitable circumstances, ventricular fibrillation can be stopped by passing an electric current through the heart, using a cardiac defibrillator.

fibrin see FIBRINOGEN.

fibrinogen or **fibrin** a large, soluble protein found in BLOOD PLASMA that is formed in the liver and converted to insoluble fibrin during BLOOD CLOTTING.

fibroblast a connective tissue cell that may differentiate into CHONDROBLASTS, COLLAGENOBLASTS, or OSTEOBLASTS.

fibrocartilage see CARTILAGE.

fibrous protein see PROTEIN.

fibrous root system a root system composed mainly of branches rather than of one principal root. Such fibrous systems are found in many herbaceous PERENNIALS, especially the grasses.

fibula a bone present in the posterior limb of TETRAPODS lying slightly posterior to and parallel with the tibia. See PENTADACTYL LIMB.

fight-or-flight reaction a defense reaction or alerting response in higher animals, involving an increase in blood pressure and heart rate and a redistribution of the blood away from the viscera toward the STRIATED MUSCLE. These changes result from integrated nerve pathways in the brain known as defense centers, and from the secretion of ADRENALINE.

filament 1. the stalk of a STAMEN bearing the ANTHER at its apex. 2. a type of cellular organization consisting of a threadlike row of cells, as found in certain algae, for example, *Spirogyra*.

filarial worm a NEMATODE worm that is parasitic on vertebrate animals and has an intermediate ARTHROPOD host. For example, adults of the nematode worm *Wucheria bancrofti* obstruct lymph vessels in humans and cause the disease ELEPHANTIASIS, with nocturnal mosquitoes as the intermediate host.

Filicales the order that includes the FERNS in the old classification of PTERIDOPHYTES.

Filicinae see FERN.

filiform threadlike.

filter feeder any marine or freshwater animal that feeds on microscopic organisms and creates currents, usually by ciliary action, so that food particles are carried into the body cavity, as occurs, for example, in the sea squirt. In other filter feeders, food particles are carried across the gills, where they are trapped in MUCUS carried also by ciliary action into the entrance to the gut system, for example, the freshwater clam *Anodonta*. Filter feeders are described as MICROPHAGOUS.

fimbriate (of plant structures) having a fringe on the margin.

fin a flattened limb found in aquatic animals and used for locomotion.

fin rays the skeletal structures that give rise to the shape of fins in fish. They may be cartilaginous, bony, or fibrous.

first-division segregation the segregation of a pair of different alleles of a gene into different nuclei at the first division or MEIOSIS. In TETRAD ANALYSIS of an ASCUS, such segregation would be detected by four adjacent ascospores carrying one allele type and the other four ascospores carrying the other type.

first law of thermodynamics see THERMODYNAMICS.

first-order reaction a reaction in which the rate of reaction is directly proportional to the concentration of one of the reactants, either product or substrate.

fish any of a large group of cold-blooded, finned aquatic vertebrates. Fish are generally scaled and respire by passing water over gills. Fish were formerly placed in a single grouping, class Pisces. It is now recognized that there are four distinct classes: ACTINOPTERYGII, ray-finned fishes; CHOANICHTHYES, fins with central skeletal axis, collectively sometimes classed as Osteichthyes (see BONY FISH); CHONDRYCHTHYES, sharks; and APHETOHYIDEAN, extinct, primitive, jawed fish.

fission see BINARY FISSION.

fitness the ability of an organism to transfer its genes to the next generation. Organisms favored by SELECTION, whether natural or artificial, have a high fitness, while those subjected to adverse selection pressure have a low fitness. Thus, under conditions of insecticide treatment, resistant members of an insect population will have a high fitness and produce more offspring compared with susceptible individuals that have a low fitness.

fixation a genetic situation in which all members of a population are HOMOZYGOUS for one particular ALLELE of a gene, so that no alternative alleles of that LOCUS exist in the population. Fixation often occurs in small populations. See also EXTINCTION (2).

Flagellata see MASTIGOPHORA.

flagellate any organism carrying a FLAGELLUM.

flagellum (*pl.* flagella) a fine, hairlike process of a cell associated with locomotion in unicellular organisms. It is similar in structure to the CILIUM, but it can be distinguished from cilia by its occurrence in smaller numbers and by generally being longer. Flagella occur in the flagellates, in most motile gametes, in ZOOSPORES, and occasionally in METAZOANS, as in the ENDODERM of some COELENTERATES. Its structure is similar to that of the CILIUM (see Fig. 103).

flame cell a specialized cell that contains a central cavity with several beating cilia. These create a current in the tubules to which they are connected. The tubules usually open to the exterior, and flame cells control the water content of the body. The flame cell and tubule is known as a *protonephridium* and is found in PLATYHELMINTHS, NEMERTINES, rotifers, ANNELIDS, the larvae of mollusks, and AMPHIOXUS. See Fig. 155.

Fig. 155. **Flame cell.** General structure.

flatworm see PLATYHELMINTH.

flavin adenine dinucleotide see FAD.

flavin mononucleotide see FMN.

flavoprotein a protein that is combined with flavin prosthetic groups and acts as an intermediate carrier in respiratory chains between dehydrogenases and cytochromes. See ELECTRON TRANSPORT SYSTEM.

flea any small wingless parasitic blood-sucking insect of the ENDO-PTERYGOTE order Aphaniptera (Siphonaptera).

Fleming, Sir Alexander (1881—1955) Scottish bacteriologist and Nobel prizewinner (1945) who discovered the ANTIBIOTIC penicillin (1928).

flexor any muscle that brings about the bending of a limb.

flexuous (of a stem) bending or wavy.

flight any locomotion through air, either active or passive (gliding). Active flight is brought about by movement of wings by muscles as in birds and insects. Gliding involves a minimum of muscular effort and is found only in some larger birds and certain mammals adapted for flight, such as the flying lemur or flying fox.

In birds, muscles are attached directly to the wings and are of two main types: *depressor muscles*, which produce the downstroke and run from the humerus to the STERNUM, and *elevator muscles*, which produce the upstroke and are attached to the upper surface of the HUMERUS by a tendon that runs through the pectoral girdle to the sternum.

In insects such as bees, wasps, flies, beetles, and bugs, the muscles raising and lowering the wing are attached to the walls of the thorax (*indirect flight muscles*) and not to the wings and are called *asynchronous fibrillar muscles*. *Direct flight muscles* attached to the wings alter the angle and adjust the wings to the resting position. In other insects, for example, the dragonflies, the flight muscles are called *synchronous muscles*, being attached directly to the wings. Asynchronous wing beats are much slower than synchronous ones.

flight feathers see CONTOUR FEATHERS.

flightless (of certain birds and insects) unable to fly, having secondarily lost the ability. The term is usually applied to birds, such as RATITES and penguins.

floccose (of plant structures) covered in small hairs giving a downlike appearance.

flocking the active coming together of animals to form a flock. In most organisms this usually takes place outside the breeding season. The term is normally limited to birds and mammals. Fish are usually described as *schooling*, and insects as *swarming*. Such groupings may serve as a defense against predators, or as a means of transferring information on food supplies, where one member of the group may follow another to a known good feeding area.

flora 1. the plant life characteristic of a particular geographical area. 2. a botanical manual from which plants can be identified by the use of KEYS.

floral diagram a diagram illustrating the number and position of the parts in each set of organs making up the flower. See FLORAL FORMULA.

floral formula an expression giving the information set out in the FLORAL DIAGRAM. For example, a buttercup has the formula $K_5 C_5 A\infty$ $\overline{G}\infty$, indicating five sepals in the calyx (K), five petals in the corolla (C), and the androecium (A) and gynoecium (G) of an indefinite number of stamens and carpels. $\overline{G}$ indicates a superior GYNOECIUM.

florigen a hypothetical plant hormone that may be produced in leaves after suitable light treatment (see PHOTOPERIODISM) and moves to the buds to stimulate flowering.

floristics the branch of botany concerned with the study of vegetation in terms of the number of different species present in the flora.

flower the sexual reproductive structure of ANGIOSPERMS, consisting usually of four types of organs: SEPALS, PETALS, STAMENS, and one or more CARPELS. See Fig. 156. Some plants have unisexual flowers. When these are found on the same plant, the plant is described as MONOE-CIOUS. When found on different plants, the plants are called DIOECIOUS. Many plants produce their flowers in clusters called INFLORESCENCES.

Fig. 156. **Flower.** A vertical section of a typical flower.

fluid-mosaic model a hypothetical model of the structure of CELL MEM-BRANES as observed with the ELECTRON MICROSCOPE. The model proposes two phospholipid layers with proteins sandwiched in the middle and sometimes projecting into the outer layer in a haphazard mosaic pattern. See Fig. 157. The membrane structure is not static. Lipid molecules can move laterally due to weak bonds between molecules, as can the protein molecules to a lesser extent. Some membrane proteins function as carriers in ACTIVE TRANSPORT. See UNIT-MEMBRANE MODEL.

fluke any parasitic flatworm, such as the BLOOD FLUKE or liver fluke, that inhabits the organs of vertebrates and in some causes serious disease. See BILHARZIA.

fluorescence the property of giving out light when molecules are excited by incident light. Emitted light is always of a shorter wavelength than the incident light.

Fig. 157. **Fluid-mosaic model.** Cell membrane structure.

fluorescent antibody technique or **immunofluorescence** a technique used to show the presence of a particular ANTIGEN, in which an antibody is labeled with an ultraviolet fluorescent substance that combines with the antigen and is subsequently located by its FLUORESCENCE.

fluoridation the addition of a fluoride, usually sodium fluoride, to drinking water in a concentration of about 1 ppm, in order to reduce tooth decay. Teeth may also be treated directly with a fluoride gel by the dentist, and this is usually undertaken as a treatment for children.

fluoride a compound of fluorine that replaces hydroxyl groups in teeth and bones and reduces the tendency to tooth decay. Its therapeutic use was discovered accidentally at Bauxite, Arkansas, when water containing fluoride was replaced by water lacking fluoride, resulting in an increase of dental cavities in children. See FLUORIDATION.

flush wet ground, often on hillsides, that is typified by presence of *Sphagnum* moss, where water comes to the surface but does not form a stream bed.

flux the rate of flow of matter or energy.

fly see DIPTERAN.

flying fish a species of fish, *Cypselurus californicus*, in which the pectoral fins are enlarged and act as airfoils when the fish leaps out of the water, enabling it to glide up to 50 meters, possibly to escape predators.

FMN (flavin mononucleotide) a COENZYME produced when RIBOFLAVIN is phosphorylated. It is necessary in biosynthesis of fats.

focus or **primary focus** an area containing a high concentration of diseased plants or animals and from which the disease probably spreads.

foliar feeding a method of supplying plants with nutrients by spraying an aqueous solution of ESSENTIAL ELEMENTS and other nutrients, for example, urea, onto the leaves where they are absorbed through the CUTICLE.

folic acid or **vitamin M** or **vitamin B$_c$** a member of the B-COMPLEX group of vitamins, which is synthesized by microorganisms in the mammalian gut, but is also required in the normal diet. Folic acid is involved in the synthesis of NUCLEIC ACIDS as well as red blood cells, and a deficiency causes reduced growth and anemia.

follicle 1. any small cavity or sac (see GRAAFIAN FOLLICLE, HAIR FOLLI-CLE, OVARIAN FOLLICLE). 2. a dry fruit formed by a single carpel splitting along a line, usually ventral, to liberate its seeds.

follicle-stimulating hormone (FSH) a glycoprotein secreted by the anterior lobe of the PITUITARY GLAND of vertebrates. The hormone stimulates growth of the OVARIAN FOLLICLES and OOCYTES in the OVARY and SPERMATOGENESIS in the seminiferous tubules of the TESTIS.

follicular phase the part of the ESTROUS CYCLE in which GRAAFIAN FOLLICLES are formed and their secretions begin.

fomite any inanimate object through which pathogenic organisms can be transferred, although it does not support their growth, for example, a book.

fontanelle a gap in the skull bone where the brain is covered only by skin. Human babies possess a parietal fontanelle between frontal and parietal bones on top of the head.

food a substance containing or consisting of chemicals that can be used in the body of an organism to build structures and provide energy to sustain life. Most plants are AUTOTROPHS and require only ESSENTIAL ELEMENTS in their food, but animals are HETEROTROPHS so their food must contain certain carbohydrates, fats, and proteins as well as vitamins and essential elements.

food chain a sequence of organisms arranged in such a way that the second grouping, for example, HERBIVORES, feeds on the first, for example, PRIMARY PRODUCERS, and the third, for example, CARNIVORES, feeds on the second. See Fig. 158.

primary producer $\longrightarrow$ primary producer $\longrightarrow$ secondary consumer
(P_1)   (herbivore: H_1)   (carnivore: C_1)

Fig. 158. **Food chain.** A simple food chain.

Each organism in the chain feeds and derives energy from its predecessor in the chain, the relative energy value at each TROPHIC LEVEL often being assessed by construction of ECOLOGICAL PYRAMIDS. In practice, such simple systems rarely exist and the nutritional relationships between organisms normally constitute a *food web*. See Fig. 159.

food poisoning an ACUTE (2) disorder of the gut caused by food contaminated with bacteria or their toxins, for example, BOTULISM, or by some chemical.

food pollen infertile pollen, produced by special ANTHERS, that attracts insects to the flower where they also collect fertile pollen.

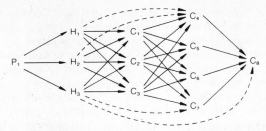

Fig. 159.**Food chain.** A complex *food web* of producer (P), herbivore (H), and carnivore (C).

food production the growth of animal and plant material, and subsequent cropping for human consumption.

food test a method by which certain components of a food mixture can be detected, for example, FEHLING'S TEST for reducing sugars.

food vacuole a fluid-filled space in the cytoplasm of a cell. It is formed by the plasma membrane of the cells invaginating to form a flasklike depression around a food particle and then the neck of the flask closing off, thus sealing the food within the cell—a process known as PHAGOCYTOSIS.

food web see FOOD CHAIN.

foot 1. the part of the leg of vertebrates that contacts the ground in the standing position. **2.** the locomotive organ in invertebrates, for example, the foot of a mollusk or the tube feet of an echinoderm.

foramen an opening.

foramen ovale an embryonic opening in the septum that divides the left and right atria of the mammalian heart, providing a bypass to the lung circulation. Failure to close the aperture at birth can lead to a BLUE BABY condition.

Foraminifera ameboid PROTOZOANS that possess chitinous, calcareous, or siliceous shells that are usually multichambered. Calcareous Foraminifera are the main constituent of chalk.

forb any herbaceous plant other than grass.

Ford, E.B. (1901—) English entomologist famous for his work on the genetics of LEPIDOPTERA and GENETIC POLYMORPHISM.

forebrain the part of the brain that gives rise to the CEREBRAL HEMISPHERES olfactory lobes, PINEAL GLAND, PITUITARY GLAND, and OPTIC CHIASMA, which carries nerve fibers from the eyes to the midbrain. It is marked by a constriction in the developing embryo, where the brain appears to be three-lobed: forebrain, MIDBRAIN, and HINDBRAIN.

foreskin the glandular and vascular fold of skin surrounding the tip of the mammalian penis.

forespore a stage in the process of SPORULATION that can be identified as a refractile body not yet resistant to heat.

forest an extensive wood or tract of wooded country.

form 1. a neutral term for (a) a uniform sample of individuals or (b) any taxon. **2.** the place in which hares lie and may give birth to young.

formation any of the main natural vegetation types extending over a large area that are created by the nature of the climate. Examples include tundra, steppe, rain forest, and coniferous forest.

formenkreiss an aggregation of ALLOPATRIC SPECIES or SUBSPECIES.

forward mutation a genetic change in which a WILD TYPE piece of DNA is altered to a MUTANT sequence. Compare REVERSE MUTATION.

fossa a depression, pit, or cavity.

fossil the remains of a once-living organism preserved in the rock strata.

fossil record the remains of organisms, or traces of their existence, such as footprints, present in the rock strata and forming a history of the development of life from its origins on Earth. The record is largely incomplete, due to the comparative rarity with which fossils are formed, but provides evidence of evolution having taken place, particularly where long series of a particular form can be traced over an extended period of time.

founder effect the result of starting a new population with a low number of individuals, or founders, so that their GENE POOL may not contain the same proportions of ALLELES for a particular LOCUS as in the original population. For example, instead of containing three alleles of the ABO BLOOD GROUP locus, Australian aborigines contain no B alleles and thus no Group B or Group AB individuals are produced, a situation probably caused by a founder effect. Such small founder populations are subject to RANDOM GENETIC DRIFT.

fovea an area in the center of the retina of the eye in which CONES are concentrated and RODS are absent (see Fig. 151). The fovea takes the form of a shallow pit about 1 mm in diameter in humans, there being no layer of nerve fibers over it as there is in the rest of the retina. It occurs in primates, diurnal birds, and lizards. It is an area of acute vision, and in BINOCULAR VISION the image of the object observed is focused on both foveae.

Fox, Sidney W. (born 1912) American biochemist and educator, famous for his work on the origin of life. His work was mainly on proteins—their structure, evolution, and synthesis, particularly in connection with the role they played in the initiation of life on Earth.

fragmentation a type of ASEXUAL REPRODUCTION found in some lower plants, such as *Spirogyra* or blue-green algae, where there is separation of the threadlike FILAMENTS (2), each segment of which can grow into a mature organism. Fragmentation is caused by such mechanical forces as wind, wave action, and rain.

frameshift an altered reading of the GENETIC CODE during the TRANS-LATION stage of PROTEIN SYNTHESIS caused by a change in the nucleotide base sequence of DNA and RNA due to an insertion or deletion in a POINT MUTATION. Figure 160 shows an example of a DNA base insertion between bases 4′ and 5′. When the sequence is read from left to right, the first amino acid is unchanged, but the second and subsequent amino acids will be altered, producing a mutant protein.

Fig. 160. **Frameshift.** The effect of inserting an extra DNA base into the nucleotide base sequence.

fraternal twins see DIZYGOTIC TWINS.

free energy the amount of energy available for work when released in a chemical reaction. For example, when a molecule of ATP is hydrolyzed to ADP + P, the free energy released is about 34 kJ.

freemartin a female twin born with a male, in which normal female sexual development has been adversely affected by hormones produced by the male twin.

freeze-drying a process by which biological material can be preserved by removal of water under a vacuum while the material is frozen.

freeze-etching the process by which a piece of tissue is frozen and then sectioned for examination under the ELECTRON MICROSCOPE.

frequency-dependent selection any SELECTION in which the FITNESS of genotypes is directly related to the proportions of the various PHENOTYPES present in a population, so that the frequency of the more common types is decreased and that of the less common types is increased. Such selection pressure often produces a stable GENETIC POLYMORPHISM, and when it involves predation is referred to as APOSTATIC SELECTION.

frequency distribution an arrangement of statistical data in order of the frequency of each size of the variable. For example, the numbers 2, 3, 5, 3, 4, 2, 1, 3, 4 would have the frequency distribution shown in Fig.

161. Data from a large sample often produce a NORMAL DISTRIBUTION CURVE.

Fig. 161. **Frequency distribution.** Based on nine numbers (see this entry).

fresh water an aquatic environment such as streams, rivers, and lakes, where there is little dissolved mineral matter and which results directly from precipitation (rain), as opposed to salt water (the seas and oceans).

Frisch, Carl von (1886—) Austrian behaviorist famous for his research on the language, orientation, and direction-finding of bees, and winner of the Nobel prize for physiology (1973). He also carried out extensive research on the color sense of bees and fishes and their senses of hearing, smell, and taste.

frog see ANURAN.

frond 1. the megaphyllous leaf of a fern, which can be subdivided into pinnae and pinnules. 2. the thallus of a seaweed or a lichen.

frontal bone one of a pair of dermal bones present at the front of the head, such as the human forehead.

frontal lobe the anterior part of a cerebral hemisphere in mammals.

fructose a carbohydrate considered to be an atypical KETOSE sugar because it acts as a reducing sugar in FEHLING'S TEST. See MONOSACCHARIDE and Fig. 218.

fruit a plant structure consisting of one or more ripened ovaries, with or without seeds, together with any flower parts associated with the ovaries. Many fruits, such as the berry and drupe, are succulent, but often they contain no fleshy tissue (for example, ACHENE, NUT). See also PERICARP.

fruit fly see DROSOPHILA.

fruiting body a special fungal structure that bears sexually or asexually derived spores. The HYPHAE and the spores borne by them constitute the structure that has a specific name in different groups of fungi. Examples include ascocarp, conidiophore, coremium, and pycnium.

frustule the hard, silica-containing wall of a DIATOM.

FSH see FOLLICLE-STIMULATING HORMONE.

fucoxanthin a brown CAROTENOID pigment found in brown algae and diatoms that is present together with CHLOROPHYLL *c*.

Fucus a genus of algae, typically having greenish-brown slimy FRONDS (2), such as *Fucus vesiculosus,* the bladderwrack.

fugacious (of plant organs) withering and falling quickly.

fungicide any substance, such as captan or benomyl, that kills FUNGI.

Fungi Imperfecti or **imperfect fungi** or **Deuteromycotina** an artificial grouping of fungi with no known perfect (sexual) stages. These fungi apparently do not produce reproductive structures of any kind, but merely fragment. Imperfect fungi contain stages of some ASCOMYCETES and BASIDIOMYCETES.

fungistasis the inhibition of further fungal growth.

fungus (*pl.* fungi) an organism that may be unicellular or made up of tubular filaments (HYPHAE) and lacks CHLOROPHYLL. Fungi live entirely as SAPROPHYTES or PARASITES. There are two main divisions: the EUMYCOTA, the true fungi; and the MYXOMYCETA, the slime molds. Each of these is now given the status of division, but in older classifications were grouped with algae in the Thallophyta.

funicle 1. the stalk of an OVULE by which it is attached to the placenta in plants. 2. the joints of the antenna of some HYMENOPTERA between the second joint and the distal joint or club.

furanose ring a monosaccharide having a five-membered ring structure.

furca any forklike structure, such as that formed by the last two abdominal segments in some arthropods, or the one supporting the two spongy pads on the proboscis of some insects.

furcula 1. the wishbone (clavicle) of birds. 2. the forked springing organ of COLLEMBOLA.

fusiform (of plant structures) spindle-shaped.

G

G1 stage the first growth phase of the CELL CYCLE.

G2 stage the second growth phase of the CELL CYCLE.

gain 1. (in physiological experiments) an increase in signal as a result of amplification. 2. a shift in the progeny mean relative to the mean of the original population brought about by DIRECTIONAL SELECTION. Gain is used to estimate HERITABILITY of characters.

galactose a monosaccharide CARBOHYDRATE that does not occur freely in nature, but is combined with GLUCOSE to form LACTOSE a disaccharide sugar found in milk.

galactosemia a rare INBORN ERROR OF METABOLISM in which the breast-fed human infant is literally poisoned by the mother's milk. The affected individuals are unable to metabolize the milk sugar GALACTOSE which normally is converted to glucose ready for oxidation and the release of energy. Instead, affected infants store the galactose in various tissues, including the brain, resulting in severe malnutrition along with mental retardation.

Galactosemia is due to blockage of the step galactose-1-phosphate to glucose-1-phosphate, because the enzyme uridyltransferase is absent or inactive. The condition is controlled by an autosomal gene, probably on chromosome 9, affected individuals being homozygous for the recessive alleles. The transferase enzyme can be detected in fetal cells from AMNIOCENTESIS before birth and, if newborn infants are given a special diet, development will be normal.

galactosidase the inducible enzyme that catalyzes hydrolysis of galactosides (see GLYCOSIDE) formed from the reaction of GALACTOSE with alcohol.

Galapagos Islands a group of 15 islands in the Pacific Ocean situated on the equator some 900 miles west of Ecuador. In 1835, Charles DARWIN visited the islands during his voyage on the Beagle, and the fauna particularly influenced his views on evolution.

According to his theory, GEOGRAPHICAL ISOLATION has influenced divergence of different forms so that, for example, DARWIN'S FINCHES have all probably evolved from a common ancestor and now occupy numerous niches on the islands due to absence of competition from other birds. Marine iguanas and giant tortoises are other interesting animals found there; and, in the absence of palms and conifers, the normally small prickly-pear cactus has reached treelike proportions.

galea the outer lobe of the MAXILLA in insects.

gall an abnormal growth of plant tissue caused by insects, mites, eel worms, or fungi.

gallbladder a baglike reservoir, of about 50 cm^3 capacity in humans, that lies at the edge of the liver closest to the gut and whose function is to store bile produced by the liver. The contents of the gallbladder are squirted into a gut lumen under the influence of the hormone CHOLE-CYSTOKININ-PANCREOZYMIN. See BILE and Fig. 64.

gallstones calcareous concretions formed in the GALLBLADDER.

gametangium the organ in which the GAMETES are produced in lower plants.

gamete or **germ cell** a specialized HAPLOID cell that fuses with a gamete from the opposite sex, or mating type, to form a diploid ZYGOTE. In simple organisms, the process is called isogamy (see ISOGAMETE), and OOGAMY in more complex organisms. In animals in which oogamy occurs, male gametes are called sperm and female gametes are called eggs. The situation in higher plants is more complicated, but essentially the male gamete is the generative nucleus found in the POLLEN GRAIN, while the female gamete is the egg cell found within the EMBRYO SAC.

gameto- or **gamo-** *combining form* denoting gamete.

gametocyte an animal or plant cell that develops into gametes by meiosis. See GAMETOGENESIS.

gametogenesis the process in which haploid GAMETES are produced from diploid cells by meiotic division (MEIOSIS). See Fig. 162 for animal cells and Fig. 163 for plant cells.

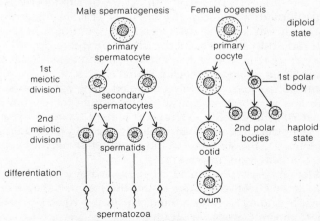

Fig. 162. **Gametogenesis.** In animals.

GAMETOPETALOUS

Males	Females
one of many microspore pollen mother cells (2n).	one of many megaspore (embryo sac) mother cells (2n).

1st meiotic division

| two cells forming microspore dyad (n). | two cells forming megaspore dyad (n). |

2nd meiotic division

| four cells forming microspore tetrad (n). | four cells forming megaspore tetrad (n). |

maturation

four pollen grains	one embryo sac (n) and three degenerate cells (n).
two mitotic divisions.	three mitotic divisions.
male gamete nucleus in pollen tube	egg cell (n) in embryo sac.

Fig. 163. **Gamotogenesis.** In plants.

gametopetalous or **sympetalous** (of flowers) having a structure in which the petals are fused to form a tubelike shape, as in the primrose and convolvulus. Other flowers, such as the buttercup and tulip, have petals that are completely free, that is, *polypetalous*.

gametophyte the part of the life cycle of plants having HAPLOID nuclei and giving rise to the sex cells that on fusing produce a DIPLOID stage, usually the SPOROPHYTE. See ALTERNATION OF GENERATIONS.

gamma globulin a member of a group of proteins found in BLOOD PLASMA that may act as an ANTIBODY. See IMMUNOGLOBULIN.

gamma radiation electromagnetic radiation of shorter wavelength and higher energy than X-RAYS. See ELECTROMAGNETIC SPECTRUM.

gamosepalous (of flowers) having united SEPALS.

ganglion (*pl.* ganglia) a structure composed of the CELL BODIES of neurons that in vertebrates is usually found outside the central nervous system (CNS), but which may form part of the CNS in invertebrates, in which such structures are usually well developed in the head region. In vertebrates, ganglia are found in the PERIPHERAL nervous system and the AUTONOMIC NERVOUS SYSTEM.

ganoid (of fish) possessing ganoid scales, typified by a hard shiny layer of ganoin, an enamel-like substance, and the fact that they increase in thickness by adding layers all around, ganoin above and laminated from below. Compare COSMOID, PLACOID.

Garrod, Archibald E. (1857—1936) English physician who between 1900 and 1910 described the first demonstrable case of a human disease that is inherited according to the laws of MENDELIAN GENETICS. The condition is *alkaptonuria* which is controlled by a single autosomal recessive gene. Garrod proposed that the enzyme that catalyzes the breakdown of homogentisic acid to acetoacetic acid is nonfunctional in alkaptonurics. This results in buildup of acid in the urine, which turns black on exposure to air and is readily observed in an infant's diaper. It was not until 1958 that absence of a functional homogentisic-acid oxidase enzyme was demonstrated in the liver of a patient with alkaptonuria. Garrod went on to explain several other human conditions, such as ALBINISM, as INBORN ERRORS OF METABOLISM.

gas analysis a comparison of atmospheric air and expired respiratory air, in which, for example, in a resting human being at sea level, oxygen constitutes only 16.4% (20.95% in atmospheric air), carbon dioxide 4.1% (0.04 in atmosphere), and nitrogen 79.5% (79% in atmosphere).

gas bladder see AIR BLADDER.

gas carriage see GAS EXCHANGE.

gas exchange or **gas carriage** the transfer of gases between an organism and the environment. In RESPIRATION oxygen is taken in and carbon dioxide given out. Photosynthesis in plants complicates this system in that during the process carbon dioxide is required by the plant and oxygen given off (see COMPENSATION PERIOD). In plants and small animals, such as PROTOZOANS and PLATYHELMINTHS, gas exchange occurs by DIFFUSION. In higher animals, special respiratory surfaces have been developed, for example, internal and external gills, lungs, and trachea.

gas loading see GAS EXCHANGE, OXYGEN DISSOCIATION CURVE.

gastric of or relating to the stomach.

gastric gland any gland in the stomach wall that produces components of the GASTRIC JUICE.

gastric juice the fluid secreted by glands of the stomach, containing PEPSIN, RENIN, and hydrochloric acid.

gastric mill a structure in the proventriculus or stomach of CRUSTACEANS, formed of a series of cuticular teeth that assist in breaking down food.

gastrin a hormone produced by gastrin cells of the pyloric gland that induces gastric secretion.

gastroenteritis an inflammation of the intestinal tract, resulting in diarrhea, vomiting, and nausea.

gastrointestinal tract see ALIMENTARY CANAL.

gastrolith a mass of CALCAREOUS material occasionally found in the proventriculus of crustaceans. It is probably formed as a result of calcium withdrawal from the exoskeleton prior to molting.

gastropod any member of the class Gastropoda in the phylum Mollusca, including MOLLUSKS, such as slugs, snails, pteropods, limpets, winkles, whelks, and sea slugs. Some forms lack a shell, but where a shell is present it is in the form of a single valve, often spiral. Marine, freshwater, and terrestrial forms occur, and there is usually a distinct head, bearing a pair of tentacles and eyes.

gastrotrich any minute aquatic multicellular animal of the phylum Gastrotricha, comprising unsegmented, wormlike organisms whose locomotion is brought about by epidermal cilia. They have some affinities with ROTIFERS and NEMATODES.

gastrozooid a feeding polyp in colonial COELENTRATES.

gastrula a stage in embryonic development in which the BLASTULA has invaginated, giving rise to a two-layered embryo by a process of gastrulation. See ARCHENTERON.

gastrulation the process by which the BLASTULA forms the GASTRULA.

Gause's law a law stating that no two species with identical ecological requirements can exist together in the same environment. Named after the German anatomist G.F. Gause.

Gaussian curve see NORMAL DISTRIBUTION CURVE.

G banding a method of treating chromosomes with Giemsa stain to show areas of the chromosomes with light and heavy staining. Such patterns are different for each chromosome type and thus are useful when arranging chromosomes in KARYOTYPE analysis.

gel a semirigid COLLOID as distinct from the more liquid SOL.

gelding see EMASCULATION.

gemma (*pl.* gemmae) a small group of cells that serves as a means of vegetative reproduction in some mosses and liverworts. These cells become detached from the main THALLUS and often occur in cuplike structures referred to as *gemma cups*. Each gemma is capable of developing into a new plant.

gemmation 1. the process of forming a GEMMA or gemmae. 2. any budding, as in *Hydra*, where a new organism is produced as an outgrowth of the parent.

gemmule a bud formed in sponges as an internal group of cells that gives rise to a new sponge after overwintering (in freshwater forms) and the decay of the parent.

gene the fundamental physical unit of heredity that transmits information from one cell to another and hence one generation to another. Genes consist of specific sequences of DNA nucleotides that can code for the structure of polypeptide chains (see CISTRON), tRNA molecules, and rRNA molecules (see TRANSCRIPTION, TRANSLATION). Individual genes can be recognized through the existence of variable forms, or ALLELES, which form the basis of GENETIC VARIABILITY. Organisms can be considered as gene carriers, being controlled by genes in such a way as to maximize the chances of survival of the genetic material.

gene amplification a process in which many copies are made of some genes at one time, while other genes are not replicated. The replicated genes enable enhanced manufacture of product in a short time. For example, rRNA genes are amplified about 4000 times in oocytes of the clawed toad *Xenopus laevis* to assist in protein production during egg development.

gene bank 1. a collection of clones containing all the genes of a particular organism, such as *E. coli*. **2.** a collection of many lines of a particular crop plant, used as a genetic resource by plant breeders.

gene bridge the means by which a plant pathogen can survive between the main host-growing seasons by living on host plants grown out of the normal season. Thus, for example, a cereal pathogen can often transfer in September from a mature, spring-sown host to newly sown winter cereal plants.

gene cloning the technique of genetic engineering in which specific genes are excised from host DNA, inserted into a vector plasmid, and introduced into a host cell, which then divides to produce many copies (clones) of the transferred gene.

genecology the study of plant populations in relation to habitat and genetical structure.

gene exchange new combinations of genes in offspring resulting from normal sexual reproduction within a breeding population where genes are contributed by both parents.

gene flow or **gene migration** the movement of genes, via GAMETES, from one population to another.

gene-for-gene concept the theory that genes for PATHOGEN resistance in a host plant are matched by corresponding virulence genes in the attacking pathogen.

gene frequency see ALLELE FREQUENCY.

gene induction the activation of an inactive gene so it can carry out TRANSCRIPTION. See OPERON MODEL.

gene locus see LOCUS.

gene migration see GENE FLOW.

gene mutation see POINT MUTATION.

gene pool the sum total of all the genes of all BREEDING INDIVIDUALS in a population at a particular time, represented by their GAMETES. Note that individuals too young to breed (juveniles) or that have undergone GENETIC DEATH do not contribute to the gene pool.

generation 1. a group of organisms of approximately the same age, usually derived from the same parents, referred to as the first filial generation (F_1). 2. the act of propagating a species or bringing about the formation of new individuals.

generation time 1. also called **division time**. the time required for a population of cells to double in number. 2. the time required for a generation of individuals to be born, reach sexual maturity, and reproduce. Generation time is a critical factor in population growth rates, and efforts are being made, particularly in China, to extend the human generation time so as to slow down the rate of population increase.

generative nucleus one of two HAPLOID nuclei found within POLLEN GRAINS of flowering plants, which enters the pollen tube when it is produced, divides by MITOSIS, and becomes the male gamete nucleus that fuses with the female egg cell at FERTILIZATION.

generator potential the nonconducted electrical charge developed when the sensitive part of a RECEPTOR is stimulated. The magnitude of the potential depends on the intensity of the stimulus; and when it reaches a certain threshold, it may give rise to an ACTION POTENTIAL.

gene repression the deactivation of an active gene that causes a shutdown of TRANSCRIPTION. See OPERON MODEL.

generic of or belonging to a genus.

gene switching the process in which genes are activated or deactivated during development, so that there is a sequential output of gene products, some taking part in current biochemical pathways and others acting as inducers and/or repressors of other genes (see JACOB). See also CHROMOSOME PUFFS for physical evidence of gene switching.

genetic of or relating to genes.

genetic background 1. any genes other than those of special interest in a study. 2. any effects in an experiment that can alter the main results in different crosses.

genetic code a collection of CODONS of DNA and RNA that contains information about POLYPEPTIDE CHAIN sequencing during TRANSLATION, each triplet usually coding for one AMINO ACID. See FRAMESHIFT and Fig. 160. A triplet code with four letters (*C*ytosine, *G*uanine, *A*denine, and *T*hymine bases) gives $4^3 = 64$ combinations. Each codon has been shown to have a specific function. See Fig. 164.

Note that the code shows DEGENERACY and that there is one triplet for initiating polypeptide chain production (AUG), and there are three triplets for terminating production (UUA, UAG, and UGA). The code is

Second base

First base (5' end)	U	C	A	G	Third base (3' end)
U	UUU ⎱ Phe UUC ⎰ UUA ⎱ Leu UUG ⎰	UCU ⎱ UCC ⎰ Ser UCA ⎱ UCG ⎰	UAU ⎱ Tyr UAC ⎰ UAA ⎱ Stop UAG ⎰	UGU ⎱ Cys UGC ⎰ UGA · Stop UGG · Trp	U C A G
C	CUU ⎱ CUC ⎰ Leu CUA ⎱ CUG ⎰	CCU ⎱ CCC ⎰ Pro CCA ⎱ CCG ⎰	CAU ⎱ His CAC ⎰ CAA ⎱ Gln CAG ⎰	CGU ⎱ CGC ⎰ Arg CGA ⎱ CGG ⎰	U C A G
A	AUU ⎱ AUC ⎰ Ileu AUA ⎰ AUG Met (start)	ACU ⎱ ACC ⎰ Thr ACA ⎱ ACG ⎰	AAU ⎱ Asn AAC ⎰ AAA ⎱ Lys AAG ⎰	AGU ⎱ Ser AGC ⎰ AGA ⎱ Arg AGG ⎰	U C A G
G	GUU ⎱ GUC ⎰ Val GUA ⎱ GUG ⎰	GCU ⎱ GCC ⎰ Ala GCA ⎱ GCG ⎰	GAU ⎱ Asp GAC ⎰ GAA ⎱ Glu GAG ⎰	GGU ⎱ GGC ⎰ Gly GGA ⎱ GGG ⎰	U C A G

Fig. 164. **Genetic code.** The mRNA codons of the genetic code arranged in a GENETIC DICTIONARY (see Fig. 27 for the AMINO ACID abbreviations).

more or less universal, the same proteins being produced from a particular base sequence in both *E. coli* and mammals.

genetic death a sexually mature individual that is alive but unable or unwilling to breed and thus transmit his or her genes to the next generation via the GENE POOL. Genetic death is fairly rare in most populations of plants and animals, but in developed countries the amount of genetic death among humans is increasing, not only in terms of individuals surviving to old age but also because of those who practice BIRTH CONTROL.

genetic dictionary a construction showing the relationship between the triplets in MESSENGER RNA and each amino acid. See GENETIC CODE.

genetic drift see RANDOM GENETIC DRIFT.

genetic engineering the modification of the genetic complement of an organism to the benefit of humanity. The term applies to a wide range of genetic techniques—for example, plant and animal breeding—to improve physiological performance by SELECTION, but recently the term has become associated with the deliberate transfer of genetic material from one organism to another where it is not normally found.

For example, a gene can be removed from human cells and transferred to microbial cells, using BACTERIOPHAGE or PLASMID vectors, where the foreign gene can control formation of useful products. Industrial production of INSULIN and INTERFERON is now possible using such methods. In the near future, it may be possible to transfer pieces of microbial genetic material to higher organisms. For example, genes from nitrogen-fixing bacteria could be introduced into the genomes of nonleguminous crop plants to supplement their nutrition.

genetic equilibrium or **equilibrium of population** a state that occurs when GENE FREQUENCIES are constant in a population for several generations. Such equilibrium may also be found where SELECTION is operating to produce a stable GENETIC POLYMORPHISM. See also HARDY-WEINBERG LAW.

genetic homeostasis the property possessed by a population for resisting sudden change and maintaining a steady genetic composition.

genetic isolation a form of REPRODUCTIVE ISOLATION in which hybrids from two different species are unable to produce fertile GAMETES and thus are sterile. For example, a horse crossed with a donkey produces a sterile mule. See ISOLATION.

genetic linkage the association between genes located, or linked, on the same chromosome, thus producing proportions of gametes that are not those expected by INDEPENDENT ASSORTMENT although, unless there is very close linkage, the same TYPES of gametes will be produced. Instead, there tends to be association of particular alleles together in the gametes, the parental types, in the same combination as the parent, with other combinations being less frequent (see RECOMBINATION and CROSSING OVER).

By convention the amount of recombination between linked genes is a direct measure of their distance apart along the chromosome, 1% recombination being equivalent to the MAP UNIT. The amount of recombination occurring is best measured in a TESTCROSS calculated from the total number of recombinant types in the testcross progeny as a proportion of the total progeny. For example, a testcross with genes in COUPLING produced the PHENOTYPES in Fig. 165, in which the amount of recombination would be:

$$\frac{33 + 42}{280} \times 100 = 26.8\%$$

and the genes A and B could be represented on a GENETIC MAP as:

testcross: $\dfrac{A\ B}{a\ b} \times \dfrac{a\ b}{a\ b}$

progeny
phenotypes:

A B	108	} parental types
a b	97	
A b	33	} recombinant types
a B	42	
	280	

Fig. 165. **Genetic linkage.** The phenotypes produced by a testcross.

Had the two genes been independently assorting, that is, on different chromosomes, roughly equal numbers of each phenotype would have been expected in the progeny (about 70). Similarly, since the maximum expected amount of recombination between two genes is 50%, if two genes are located more than 50 map units apart on the same chromosome, they will appear to be independent of each other.

genetic load a measurement of the number of harmful genes in a population, calculated as the average number of lethal equivalents per individual.

genetic map see CHROMOSOME MAP.

genetic polymorphism or **polymorphism** the presence in a population of two or more MORPHS, produced when different alleles of a gene occur in the same population, and the rarest allele is not maintained merely by repeated MUTATION, that is, it has a frequency higher than, say, 0.05%. Such a definition excludes continuously variable characters, such as height or skin color in humans, but the human blood groups are classic examples, in which single genes have two or more alleles producing different antigenic phenotypes. A genetic polymorphism can be maintained by several mechanisms, such as heterozygous advantage or FREQUENCY-DEPENDENT SELECTION, and can be stable over several generations (BALANCED POLYMORPHISM) or may become transient as when the environment changes. See, for example, SICKLE CELL ANEMIA.

genetic population see POPULATION.

genetic recombination see RECOMBINATION.

genetics the science that investigates patterns of inheritance between generations, together with how genes express themselves within the lifetimes of individual organisms.

genetic variability a range of phenotypes for a particular CHARACTER produced by alternative alleles of one or more genes, the range containing discrete groups (see QUALITATIVE INHERITANCE) or a continuous spectrum of types (see POLYGENIC INHERITANCE). Genetic variability arises initially by MUTATION and is maintained by sexual reproduction involving CROSSING OVER in MEIOSIS. Such variation is the raw material for NATURAL SELECTION to act upon, ensuring that the best-adapted variants are most likely to reproduce.

geniculate (of plant structures) bent abruptly, kneelike.

genitalia the reproductive organs and their accessory parts.

genitourinary system the excretory and reproductive organs and functions of animals. The two often are grouped together because they are closely associated, particularly in male animals in which the URETHRA is a common duct for urine and sperm.

genome the complete complement of genetic material in a cell or carried by an individual.

genotype the genetic constitution of an individual, usually referring to specific CHARACTERS under consideration. Thus, the two alleles of the human albino gene can be written A and a, with three possible genotypes: a/a, A/a, and A/A. See DOMINANCE (1) for the expression of the genotype in the PHENOTYPE.

genotype frequency the proportion of a particular genotype among all the individuals in a population. Thus, if a population sample contains 5 albinos and 95 normally pigmented individuals, the genotype frequency for albinos (a/a) will be 0.05 or 5%. Note, however, that it is not possible to be certain of the frequency of A/a and A/A genotypes among the normal individuals, since both genotypes have the same PHENOTYPE due to dominance, although their frequencies can be predicted using the HARDY-WEINBERG LAW.

genus a TAXON immediately above that of a SPECIES and usually containing a group of closely related species. The name of a genus, or the generic name, is written or printed with an initial capital letter and in BINOMIAL NOMENCLATURE precedes the specific name, which invariably has a small initial letter.

geobotany the part of botany related to ecology and the geography c plants.

Geoffroyism the belief that there is an adaptive response of the genotype to the demands of the environment, that is, an environmental induction of appropriate genetic changes. Named for the French naturalist Hilaire Geoffroy (1774—1844).

geographical distribution see DISTRIBUTION.

geographical isolation the effective isolation of a GENE POOL by geographical barriers. For example, oceanic islands are isolated because of the difficulty of the sea-crossing for many organisms. The evolution of new species takes place through prevention or limitation of GENE FLOW, and various isolating mechanisms may play a part in this, one of the most important being geographical isolation. Compare ECOLOGICAL ISOLATION. See SPECIATION.

geographical speciation see SPECIATION.

geographical variation any variation that occurs in spatially separated populations of species.

geologic time the period beginning with the formation of Earth and ending in the present day. It is often tabulated beginning with the Cambrian period, since the majority of fossil forms date from then. Precambrian time began with the formation of Earth about 5 billion years ago.

Dating of rocks is usually carried out by the measurement of radioactive decay. The older the rock, the less radioactive it is. Organic remains are dated by CARBON DATING. See Appendix A.

geophyte see CRYPTOPHYTE.

geotaxis a type of animal movement, not growth, in which the body becomes oriented in relation to the force of gravity. For example, fruit flies exhibit negative geotaxis, moving upward in the culture bottle, away from the gravitational force.

geotropism a plant growth movement that occurs in response to gravity. Thus, roots are positively geotropic, growing downward, while shoots are generally negatively geotropic, growing upward.

Gephyrea a class of large, marine ANNELID worms that possess little or no segmentation and few or no chaetae, for example, *Echiuroidea* and *Sipunculoidea.*

German measles or **rubella** a mild human disease whose main feature is a rash on the body occurring about 18 days after infection. Caused by the rubella virus, the condition is highly contagious and is spread by direct contact via nasal secretions. The virus can be transmitted from mother to fetus and may cause serious damage in many fetal tissues and even death. The major period of risk to the child is the first 3 months of pregnancy, when there is at least a 30% risk of abnormality. For this reason many Western countries have a routine immunization program for young females, either as babies or between the ages of 10—14 years.

germ cell see GAMETE.

germicide a substance that kills microorganisms.

germinal epithelium a cell layer found on the outer surface of the vertebrate OVARY and lining the seminiferous tubules of the TESTIS. It gives rise to follicle cells in females and to spermatogonia in males. In males it also produces SERTOLI CELLS, which nourish the developing sperms.

germinal vesicle the meiotic PROPHASE nucleus of the oocyte during growth of cytoplasm in animals.

germination the beginning of the growth of a seed, spore, or other structure that is dormant. Seed DORMANCY can be broken by several factors, depending on the species:

(a) the removal of a germination inhibitor, which can be leached out by water.

(b) a period of cold temperature (STRATIFICATION).

(c) exposure to the correct wavelength of light to stimulate PHYTO-CHROMES in the seed. For example, lettuce seeds require red light for germination and are inhibited by far-red light.

(d) rupture of a thick testa by (i) microbial breakdown; (ii) abrasive action of soil, as in desert plants; (iii) heat from bush fires; and (iv) the effect of digestive juices, as when eaten by birds, or by the softening action of water.

Once dormancy is broken, a regular sequence of events takes place. Water is imbibed that hydrates the tissues, increasing enzymic action in the ALEURONE layer, when present. The process is aided by release of GIBBERELLIN from the embryo. Food stores are mobilized in the ENDO-SPERM or within the COTYLEDONS. AUXINS and CYTOKININS are formed, which promote cell division and enlargement, causing the embryo to grow and burst through the testa. See Fig. 166.

shoot developed from the plumule — epicotyl — pair of cotyledons — hypocotyl — roots developed from the radicle

Fig. 166. **Germination.** A typical seedling.

There are two main types of germination, depending on whether the seed cotyledons are carried above the soil (EPIGEAL) or remain below ground (HYPOGEAL).

germ layer any of the three embryonic layers of cells—ECTODERM, ENDODERM, or MESODERM—that can be distinguished during development of the GASTRULA and for a short period after its formation.

germ line a group of cells that give rise to the GONADS becoming differentiated from the somatic cells early in embryonic development. Only these cells have the potential to undergo MEIOSIS, and a MUTATION event in them may well be transmitted to the offspring, unlike genetic change in somatic cells (see SOMATIC MUTATION).

germ plasm theory a concept put forward by August Weismann (1834—1914), who suggested that the sex cells are produced by the germ plasm, which is passed on intact from generation to generation and gives rise to body cells in each individual. Today we consider DNA to be the molecular equivalent of the germ plasm.

gestation the development of the embryo in the uterus of mammals. The gestation period is the time elapsing from fertilization and the implantation of the embryo to birth. This takes 60 days in the domestic cat, 9 months in humans, and 18 months in the Indian elephant.

giant fiber a large nerve axon found in some invertebrates such as ARTHROPODS and ANNELIDS. Such fibers can transmit impulses faster than normal fibers due to a reduction in internal longitudinal resistance.

gibberellic acid a crystalline acid that occurs in plants having growth-promoting effects similar to those of a GIBBERELLIN.

gibberellin one of a range of growth regulators in plants that stimulate stem elongation but, unlike AUXINS, do not inhibit root growth. Gibberellins can be used to induce BOLTING in immature plants and to remove dwarfness in mature plants. Unlike auxins, gibberellins can move freely around the plant. Compare ANTIGIBBERELLIN.

gibbon a long-armed anthropoid ape of the genus *Hylobatea.*

gibbous (of a solid object) having a projection in the form of a rounded swelling.

gigantism a rare human condition in which excess production of GROWTH HORMONE by the anterior PITUITARY GLAND during childhood and adolescence causes overelongation of bones, producing a *pituitary giant.* Compare DWARFISM.

gill 1. the respiratory organ of aquatic animals. External gills, as in tadpoles, are produced by the embryonic ECTODERM. Internal gills, as in fish, are developed from the pharynx and are thus endodermal (see ENDODERM). Gills are usually well supplied with blood vessels, and interchange of oxygen and carbon dioxide takes place across the extensive surface area (see COUNTERCURRENT EXCHANGE). Gills also occur in many invertebrates, for example, in insects such as the caddis fly larva and mollusks such as oysters. Occasionally, unusual structures act as gills, for example, the walls of the rectum in certain dragonfly nymphs, water being pumped in and out via the anus. 2. the spore-carrying lamellae in basidiomycete fungi, located underneath the cap, or pileus.

gill bar the tissue that separates the GILL CLEFTS, consisting of skeletal material, nervous tissue, blood vessels, etc.

gill book see BOOK GILL.

gill cleft or **gill slit** an inpushing of the epidermis in the region of the GILLS in developing CHORDATE embryos, including humans. The gill clefts normally meet similar outpushings from the endoderm of the pharynx, and in fish and occasionally in terrestrial vertebrates such as amphibians, break through to the exterior to form the gill slits.

gill fungus a BASIDIOMYCETE, the fruiting bodies of which possess a series of lamellae on the pileus, which carries the spore-bearing hymenium.

gill pouch outgrowths of the pharynx in early embryos that give rise to gills in fish and in amphibian larvae. In higher vertebrates, they usually disappear in further development.

gill slit see GILL CLEFT.

gingivitis an inflammatory disease of the gums associated with an accumulation of plaque containing bacteria of several types, for example, *Streptomyces sanguis*. While painful and unpleasant, the condition usually does not lead to tooth loss.

Ginkgoales an order of the GYMNOSPERMS now represented by only a single species *Ginkgo biloba*, the maidenhair tree. Its ancestors flourished during the MESOZOIC PERIOD.

girdle a bony structure to which the limbs of vertebrates are attached. See PECTORAL GIRDLE, PELVIC GIRDLE.

gizzard a portion of the anterior part of the alimentary canal in which food materials are broken up before digestion. The gizzard usually has strong muscular walls and in invertebrates has internal projections. In some birds, such as the curlew, the gizzard lining is regularly renewed and the old lining cast out in the form of a pellet.

glabrous (of plant structures) without hairs.

glaciation one of the so-called ice ages; a period of ice cover.

gland an organ producing substances that then are secreted to the outside of the gland, sometimes by means of a duct, as in the exocrine glands, for example, the salivary, mammary, lachrymal glands, but also in the case of ENDOCRINE GLANDS directly into the blood system. Occasionally, individual cells act as glands, for example, gland cells of *Hydra* producing digestive enzymes.

glandular cells cells that produce a secretion.

glandular epithelium a layer of cells with a secretory function, the secreted products entering the space lined by the epithelium, for example, the lining of the vertebrate intestine.

glandular fever or **infective mononucleosis** an ACUTE infectious disease, probably caused by the Epstein-Barr virus, that affects primarily the lymphoid tissue throughout the body, resulting in abnormal blood lymphocytes (hence, infective mononucleosis); enlarged lymph nodes and spleen; and sometimes fever and sore throat. The disease is thought to affect teenagers mainly from affluent backgrounds and is prevalent therefore among students. No control measure is available at present.

glaucous (of plant structures) bluish.

glenoid cavity 1. the hollow in the scapula into which the humerus fits. **2.** the depression of the squamosal bone into which the joint of the mammalian lower jaw fits.

glia or **neuroglia** the web of undifferentiated cells that packs and supports nerve cells in the brain and spinal cord.

globigerina ooze the CALCAREOUS mud that occurs on the sea bed as a result of the aggregation of the shells of dead Foraminifera, *Globigerina* being the most common genus of shell present.

globular protein a type of PROTEIN.

globulin a group of proteins soluble in salt solution and coagulated by heat. They occur in blood plasma and antibodies and are the main proteins of plant seeds.

glochidium a lamellibranch larva possessing a small bivalve shell and a tentacle-like sucker for attachment to a fish.

Gloger's Rule a biological rule stating that populations of species that occur in warm, humid areas are more heavily pigmented than those in cool, dry areas.

glomerular filtrate a filtrate that has passed through the GLOMERULUS in the vertebrate kidney.

glomerular filtration rate the total amount of filtrate produced per minute by glomeruli of all nephrons in both kidneys of an individual.

glomerulus a bunch of capillaries found in the vertebrate kidney, enclosed in the BOWMAN'S CAPSULE. Substances such as water and dissolved materials filter from the blood, across the endothelium of the capillaries and the epithelium of the capsule, into the tubules leading to the LOOP OF HENLE.

glossopharyngeal nerve the 9th CRANIAL NERVE of vertebrates; a dorsal root nerve. It is concerned with the swallowing reflex and the back of the tongue taste buds in mammals.

glottis see EPIGLOTTIS.

glucagon a polypeptide of 29 amino acids produced by the cells in the ISLETS OF LANGERHANS of the pancreas of vertebrates. Glucagon acts as a hormone, having an effect opposite to that of INSULIN, in causing breakdown of liver GLYCOGEN and release of glucose into the blood.

glucocorticoid a steroid endocrine secretion produced by the adrenal cortex, influencing the metabolism of carbohydrates and proteins, for example, cortisol (hydrocortisone) and corticosterone.

gluconeogenesis the formation of GLUCOSE or GLYCOGEN in the liver from noncarbohydrate precursors, such as certain AMINO ACIDS, GLYCEROL, and LACTIC ACID.

glucose or **dextrose** an important hexose sugar with an ALDOSE structure that occurs in two forms, alpha and beta. It has the general formula $C_6H_{12}O_6$ and is found in sweet fruits, especially ripe grapes. Glucose is formed in the CALVIN CYCLE of PHOTOSYNTHESIS and acts as a primary energy supply for both plant and animal cells, although usually it is converted to an insoluble form for long-term storage: STARCH in plants, GLYCOGEN in animals. See MONOSACCHARIDE for structure.

glucose-6-phosphate dehydrogenase (G-6-P.D.) an important enzyme in the PENTOSE PHOSPHATE PATHWAY for carbohydrate metabolism, catalyzing the oxidation of glucose 6-phosphate in the presence of NADP coenzyme, giving 6-phosphogluconolactone and NADPH. G-6-P.D. of blood erythrocytes is of particular interest, because a decrease in its activity can lead to the condition called FAVISM.

glume the chaffy scale that encloses the spikelets of grass or the flowers of sedges.

glutamate the dissociated form of the amino acid GLUTAMIC ACID.

glutamic acid one of 20 AMINO ACIDS common in proteins that has an extra carboxyl group and is acidic in solution. See Fig. 167. The ISOELECTRIC POINT of glutamic acid is 3.2.

Fig. 167. **Glutamic acid.** Molecular structure.

glutamine one of 20 AMINO ACIDS common in proteins that has a polar R structure and is soluble in water. See Fig. 168.

glyceraldehyde phosphate see PGAL.

glyceraldehyde 3-phosphate (GALP) see PGAL.

glycerate 3-phosphate (GP) see PGA.

glyceric acid phosphate see PGA.

glycerol or **glycerin** a simple LIPID that is a basic component of fats. See

Fig. 168. **Glutamine.** Molecular structure.

Fig. 169. Glycerol contains large amounts of energy that can be released in metabolism. See GLYCOLYSIS.

Fig. 169. **Glycerol.** Molecular structure.

glycine one of 20 amino acids common in proteins that is soluble in water even though it has a nonpolar R structure. See Fig. 170. The isoelectric point of glycine is 6.0.

Fig. 170. **Glycine.** Molecular structure.

glycocalyx a mass of filaments up to 3 μm thick produced by the membrane of intestinal brush-border microvilli, consisting of acid mucopolysaccharide and GLYCOPROTEIN, and thought to be associated with digestion of small food molecules. Other animal cells also have a glycocalyx on their cell coat, providing a mechanism that enables cells to recognize each other, an important process in embryonic development.

glycogen the principal carbohydrate storage molecule of animals, being produced from glucose in the mammalian liver (see PHOSPHATASE) and muscles when blood sugar levels are too high, a process called *glycogenesis* that is under the influence of INSULIN. Glycogen in the liver can be broken down to glucose when blood sugar levels are low, a process

GLYCOGENESIS

called *glycogenolysis* that is under the influence of GLUCAGON. See Fig. 171. Glycogen in the muscle, however, is broken down to LACTIC ACID, not glucose, in GLYCOLYSIS.

Fig. 171. **Glycogen.** Formation and breakdown of glycogen in the liver.

glycogenesis see GLYCOGEN.
glycogenolysis see GLYCOGEN.
glycolipid any of a group of LIPIDS containing a carbohydrate.
glycolysis the first stage of CELLULAR RESPIRATION, occurring with or without the presence of oxygen, in which glucose is converted to two molecules of pyruvic acid. See Fig. 172. See also AEROBIC RESPIRATION.

Fig. 172. **Glycolysis.** The individual steps of glycolysis.

glycophorin a glycopolypeptide found in human erythrocytes.
glycoprotein any PROTEIN containing sugars as part of the molecule.
glycoside an acetal derivative of a sugar that, on hydrolysis by enzymes or acids, gives rise to a sugar. Glycosides containing glucose are called *glucosides*. Those with galactose are called *galactosides*. They render unwanted substances chemically inert or form food reserves, for example, GLYCOGEN.

glycosidic bond or **glycosidic link** a bond between the anomeric carbon of a carbohydrate and another group or molecule.

glycosuria the condition in which glucose is excreted in the urine because the blood sugar level is above normal (*hyperglycemia*). Glycosuria is one of the symptoms of DIABETES.

glycosylation the addition of a CARBOHYDRATE to an organic molecule, such as a PROTEIN.

Gnathostomata the vertebrates that possess true jaws, that is, all true fish—not lampreys or hagfish—amphibia, reptiles, birds, and mammals.

-gnathous *combining form* denoting having a jaw.

Gnetales an order of GYMNOSPERMS whose members have true vessels in the secondary wood and an absence of archegonia in the ovule. In these features, they resemble ANGIOSPERMS.

goblet cell or **chalice cell** a cell shaped something like a wineglass, which is present in the columnar epithelium of the mammalian intestine and secretes MUCIN.

goiter an abnormal swelling of the thyroid gland due to lack of iodine in the diet.

Golgi apparatus or **dictyosome** a series of cell ORGANELLES consisting of a stack of membrane-lined vesicles called CISTERNAE, first described by Camillo Golgi in 1898 but only clearly defined from studies with the ELECTRON MICROSCOPE. See Fig. 173.

stack of cisternae

secretory vesicles

Fig. 173. **Golgi apparatus.** The secretory vesicles carry products from the apparatus to the edge of the cell, where they may be released.

The membranes of the Golgi apparatus are often linked temporarily to the ENDOPLASMIC RETICULUM, and secretory vesicles are formed by the apparatus which move to the periphery of the cell and may carry out EXOCYTOSIS. The apparatus is thought to have a storage role as well as enabling assembly of simple molecules into more complex ones. For example, carbohydrates and proteins are packaged into glycoprotein.

gon- or **gono-** *combining form* denoting sexual.

gonad the OVARY or TESTIS of an organism.

gonad hormones sex hormones produced by the GONADS.

gonadotrophin or **gonadotrophic hormones** hormones secreted by the anterior lobe of the PITUITARY GLAND and in some mammals, once pregnancy is under way, by the PLACENTA. FSH and LH are produced by all TETRAPODS, although FSH appears to be absent in fish. LTH (Luteotrophin) is present in rats and maintains the CORPUS LUTEUM, although it is absent in other mammals. Prolactin is present in some vertebrates and controls milk production. (LTH is a form of prolactin.) Pituitary output is controlled by the hypothalamus. Gonadotrophins influence other glands connected with reproduction, controlling the activity of the gonads, onset of sexual maturity, ESTROUS CYCLES, breeding rhythms, and LACTATION. See also HCG.

Gondwana or **Gondwanaland** the southern group of continents at the end of the TRIASSIC PERIOD that split from the northern group (LAURASIA). It consisted of South America, Africa, India, Australia, and Antarctica.

gonochorism the possession of GONADS of only one sex, either male or female, in an individual.

gonophore any structure bearing gonads but particularly the specialized polyp of colonial COELENTERATES, which bears the gonads and is shaped like a sessile medusa—a form of GONOZOOID.

gonorrhea a contagious inflammation of the mucus membranes in human reproductive organs, characterized by discharge of mucus and pus from the urethra or vagina and caused by the gonococcal bacterium *Neisseria gonorrhoeae.* Gonorrhea is probably the most prevalent communicable bacterial disease among humans today and, although a VENEREAL DISEASE, is a condition distinct from SYPHILIS.

gonotheca the chitinous cup of perisarc surrounding the reproductive structures of colonial COELENTERATES.

gonozooid a specialized polyp in colonial coelenterates that bears the gonads (see GONOPHORE).

goodness-of-fit an assessment of the similarity between the observed results from an experiment and those expected from theory and supported by a stated NULL HYPOTHESIS. An example of such a statistic is the CHI-SQUARE TEST.

Graafian follicle a structure in the ovary of a female mammal, consisting of an OOCYTE surrounded by granular FOLLICLE cells that enclose also a large, fluid-filled cavity, the entire structure being encased in a wall of connective tissue. See Fig. 174.

The Graafian follicle begins to form deep inside the ovary, stimulated by FSH as the ESTROUS CYCLE develops, gradually enlarging and maturing as it moves to the surface, eventually appearing like a blister on the surface, just prior to release of the egg (*ovulation*) by rupture of the wall.

Fig. 174. **Graafian follicle.** General structure.

After ovulation, the follicle becomes a CORPUS LUTEUM. Further ovulation is normally prevented by the corpus luteum secreting PROGESTERONE, which in turn inhibits FSH production by the PITUITARY GLAND, so no further follicles develop. The presence of the cavity distinguishes the Graafian follicle (named after Regner de Graaf) from the OVARIAN FOLLICLES of other vertebrates.

grade a group of organisms having a similar level of organization.

graded response a response that increases with the amount of energy supplied as opposed to the reaction brought about by the ALL-OR-NONE LAW.

graft the transfer of a small part of an organism to a relatively larger part, where it is transplanted. This may take place from one part of an organism to another part (see AUTOGRAFT), or from one organism to another (see ISOGRAFT, HOMOGRAFT, HETEROGRAFT). Many embryological studies have involved grafting, and from a medical point of view, skin grafting, particularly after serious burns, is commonplace. Organ grafts such as heart transplants are now relatively common, although rejection by an animal of the tissues of another may still be a serious problem (see IMMUNE RESPONSE). In animals the graft comes from a donor and is transferred to the recipient. In plants, grafts are used often in horticulture, where a *scion*, the plant to be cultivated, is attached onto a STOCK (1), the rooting portion.

graft-hybrid see CHIMERA.

Gram-negative or **Gram-positive** see GRAM'S SOLUTION.

Gram's solution a stain taken up by *Gram-positive* bacteria that differentiates them from bacteria that fail to take up the stain (*Gram-negative* types). The initial stain is crystal violet/iodine complex, and Gram-negative bacteria are decolorized with alcohol while *Gram-positive* bacteria retain a blue/purple color.

grandfather method a procedure for estimating the amount of RECOMBINATION between X-linked genes in an individual, which depends on the arrangement of genes in the maternal grandfather. For example, if a mother is known to be heterozygous, her genes could be in COUPLING or in repulsion. This uncertainty can be removed if the phenotype of her father is known, since he has only one X-chromosome. For example, if he was *Ab,* his heterozygous daughter must be *Ab/aB,* thus ensuring that her children are properly identified as parental or recombinant type (see GENETIC LINKAGE).

granulocyte a type of white blood cell (LEUKOCYTE) that possesses granules in the cytoplasm and is formed in the bone marrow. Granulocytes form about 70% of all leukocytes and are of three types: EOSINOPHILS, BASOPHILS, and NEUTROPHILS.

granum see CHLOROPLAST.

graptolite any extinct Paleozoic colonial pelagic animal of the class Graptolithina. Branching forms are found in later strata and up to Carboniferous times.

grass any member of the family Gramineae, all of which have jointed tubular stems, sheathing leaves, and flowers enclosed in GLUMES. Examples include cereals, reeds, and bamboos.

gravity the force by which masses are attracted to each other.

gray matter the material from the CENTRAL NERVOUS SYSTEM of vertebrates containing the nerve cell bodies that give the material a gray color as distinct from the white color of the FIBERS (compare WHITE MATTER). Gray matter also contains the DENDRITES of the nerve cells, with no myelin sheath; blood vessels; and glial cells, which have a supportive function. Gray matter of the spinal cord is internally arranged in an H shape in cross section, unlike the arrangement in the brain, where gray matter is external. Coordination occurs in the gray matter of the CNS.

green gland one of a pair of excretory organs of crustaceans with openings at the antennal base.

greenhouse effect 1. an effect occurring in greenhouses in which the glass transmits short wavelengths but absorbs and reradiates longer wavelengths, thus heating the interior. 2. the application of this effect to Earth's atmosphere. Infrared radiation tends to be trapped by carbon dioxide and water vapor in Earth's atmosphere, and some of it is reradiated back to Earth's surface.

green-island effect a localized increase of photosynthesis in plant tissues immediately surrounding a lesion caused by a biotrophic pathogen.

green revolution the process by which humans have exploited new hybrid varieties of food crops such as barley, rice, corn, and wheat to meet their requirements. New varieties have been produced by crossing and selection. The green revolution has had particularly dramatic effects on developing countries. For example, wheat yields in Mexico have increased by about 300% since introduction of a new dwarf variety in 1960. However, the attempts at plant improvements have not always been of benefit to the peasant farmer.

greeting display a form of behavior in animals, particularly indulged in by some birds, where display arises upon arrival of the mate, say, at a nest site bearing food.

Griffith, Frederick English medical bacteriologist who, in 1928, published a paper showing it was possible to convert one type of *Streptococcus pneumoniae* bacterium into a new type. More specifically, Griffith worked with two strains of bacteria:

Type R	*Type S*
rough outer coat, nonvirulent in mice	smooth outer coat, virulent in mice

His results are summarized in Fig. 175. Griffith proposed that in experiment 4 the heat-killed S type somehow converted the living R type to virulent S types, in a process he called TRANSFORMATION. It was shown later that the transforming principle was DNA.

Experiment	Type of bacterium injected into mice	Mouse reaction	Type of bacterium recovered from mouse
1	Live Type R	Survive	—
2	Live Type S	Die	—
3	Dead Type S	Survive	—
4	Dead Type S plus Living Type R	Die	Live Type S

Fig. 175. **Griffith, Frederick.** Griffith's results.

gristle see CARTILAGE.

ground state the condition of a molecule when at its lowest energy level.

group a collection of closely related taxa (see TAXON), particularly an assemblage of closely related species.

growth the process of increase in size, which has three distinct components: (a) cell division, (b) assimilation, and (c) cell expansion. The basis of growth is CELL DIVISION, but in order to increase in size, cells must be able to synthesize new structures that are manufactured from raw materials derived from their immediate environment. This is assimilation and it results in increase in cell size. Growth during development can be continuous but allometric (see ALLOMETRIC GROWTH), as in humans, or can be discontinuous, as in insects where growth occurs at each ECDYSIS.

growth curve the graphic representation of the growth of a population, which could be *exponential* where, theoretically, the density would eventually be increasing at an infinite rate, or could be logistic (see LOGISTIC CURVE), where the density would stabilize near the CARRYING CAPACITY of the population. See Fig. 176. Populations of microorganisms tend to go through a classic four-stage growth curve (see Fig. 177).

Fig. 176. **Growth curve.** (a) Exponential. (b) Logistic.

Fig. 177. **Growth curve.** A growth curve in a microbial culture.

The *lag* phase is a time of adaptation to the new environment, where such processes as ENZYME INDUCTION take place and reproduction rate equals death rate. The *log* phase is a period of exponential growth, with reproduction rate much greater than death rate. The *stationary* phase is a time of equilibrium, representing the response to a limiting factor, such as nutrient source, while little or no reproduction occurs during the *death* phase, so the population declines.

growth, grand period of the entire time during which a cell, organ, or plant part increases in size, slowly at first, then faster, and more slowly again until it is mature.

growth habit a characteristic manner of growth in plants.

growth hormone or **somatotrophic hormone (STH)** a hormone secreted by the anterior PITUITARY GLAND mainly in the growth period, in which it stimulates lengthening of the long bones in TETRAPODS, induces protein synthesis, and inhibits INSULIN, thus raising the level of blood sugar. Oversecretion during development produces GIGANTISM but excess later in life gives rise to ACROMEGALY, in which a massive forehead, nose, and lower jaw are produced. Deficiency of the hormone results in DWARFISM.

grub an insect larva lacking legs.

guanine one of four types of nitrogenous bases found in DNA, having the double-ring structure of a class known as PURINES. Guanine forms part of a DNA unit called a NUCLEOTIDE and always forms complementary pairs with a DNA pyrimidine base called CYTOSINE. Guanine also occurs in RNA molecules. See Fig. 178.

Fig. 178. **Guanine.** Molecular structure.

guano the white nitrogenous dried excrement, high in uric acid content, that is produced by birds and reptiles. Guano is a valuable fertilizer and has been extensively harvested from guano bird (cormorant) colonies in South America.

guard cells one of a pair of specialized epidermal cells forming a pore (stoma) at the leaf surface. See STOMA for a description of how the stomatal aperture is regulated.

guild a group of species exploiting the same class of environmental resources in a similar way.

Gurdon, J.B. (1933—) British experimental embryologist who demonstrated that a nucleus taken from the differentiated gut cell of a clawed toad and injected into an enucleated egg can produce a normal adult. In other words, he demonstrated that a fully differentiated cell still contains the genetic information to direct development of the cells in the entire animal (see TOTIPOTENCY).

gustation the act of tasting or the faculty of taste. This is brought about by the effect of ions and molecules in solution, stimulating specialized sensory epithelial receptors.

gustatory sensillum a taste bud.

gut see ALIMENTARY CANAL.

guttation the emergence of water from the endings of leaf veins, usually occurring at night, when TRANSPIRATION is low or absent. Guttation is thus a method of exuding excess water and involves special water pores called HYDATHODES at leaf tips. Unlike normal STOMATA, hydathodes are not able to control their aperture size. The process is common in low-growing plants such as grasses. See Fig. 179.

epidermis

sheath preventing water moving into inter-mesophyll areas

loose parenchyma of hydathode

water pore with fixed aperture

xylem

sheath

stoma with adjustable aperture

spongy mesophyll

Fig. 179. **Guttation.** Transverse section of a saxifrage leaf.

gymno- *combining form* denoting naked *or* bare.

Gymnophiona see APODA.

gymnosperm any member of the class Gymnospermae, comprising the CONIFERS and their allies. Gymnosperms derive their name from the fact that the ovules are borne without a covering on the surface of the megasporophylls, which usually take the form of cones.

gynandromorph any animal exhibiting both male and female features, often with the body divided into equal portions of the two sexes. For example, the left-hand side may be male and the right-hand side female.

gynobasic (of a STYLE) appearing to be inserted at the base of the ovary because of the folding of the ovary wall.

gynodioecious (of female and hermaphrodite flowers) occurring on separate plants, an attribute thought to promote cross-pollination, for example, in thyme.

gynoecium or **gynaecium** or **pistil** the female part of a flower composed of one or more CARPELS. When there are several carpels, they can be completely fused to form a compound ovary, stigma, and style. Each carpel can be quite separate, or there can be stages in between the two extremes. See Fig. 180.

When other flower parts arise below the gynoecium, the flower is described as *hypogynous* and the ovary is said to be *superior*. Alternatively, when other flower parts arise above the gynoecium and the RECEPTACLE encloses the ovary, the flower is described as *epigynous* and the ovary is said to be *inferior*.

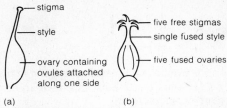

(a)   (b)

Fig. 180. **Gynoecium.** (a) A simple type, for example, a bean. (b) A complex type, for example, a geranium.

gynogenesis the parthenogenetic development of an egg after the egg membranes have been penetrated by a male gamete. There is no nuclear fusion, and stimulation of development can be purely mechanical.

gynomonoecious (of female and hermaphrodite flowers) occurring on the same plant, for example, the daisy.

H

habit the general appearance and form of branching in plants. For example, depending on location, dandelions can have an erect or prostrate habit. See PHENOTYPIC PLASTICITY.

habitable zone the area around a star, such as the sun, in which sufficient energy is present to sustain life.

habitat the part of the environment occupied by an animal or plant, for example, stream, meadowland, or salt marsh.

habitat selection the selection by a dispersing organism (see DISPERSAL) of a suitable habitat.

habituation the progressive loss of a behavioral response as a result of continuing stimulation.

Haeckel's law of Recapitulation or **palingenesis** or **von Baer's law** the belief that ONTOGENY recapitulates PHYLOGENY, meaning that an organism will go through embryonic stages similar to those gone through during its evolutionary development. For example, mammals have a fishlike stage in their embryology. The law was formulated by the German biologist Ernst Haeckel (1834—1919).

hair 1. (in plants) a filamentous outgrowth from an epidermal cell that may have a secretory function—in glands, an absorbing function—in root hairs), or a function in trapping and preventing air movement of the leaf surface, thus lowering the rate of TRANSPIRATION. **2.** (in animals) a filamentous structure of mammalian skin formed of cornified epidermal cells that multiply in the hair follicle.

hair cell a sensory epithelial cell of vertebrates that acts as a mechanoreceptor, possessing either one nonmotile cilium (*kinocilium*) or many nonmotile ciliumlike projections of the surface (*stereocilia*). Such cells are found in the LATERAL-LINE SYSTEM and the ear.

hair follicle a FOLLICLE in the epidermis of mammals through which hair projects into the dermis. The follicle is supplied by a sebaceous gland and erectile muscles for the hair.

half-life the time required for half of the mass of a radioactive substance to disintegrate. For example, the half-life of ^{14}C is 5570 years. See Fig. 181.

hallux the first digit on the hind foot of vertebrates, analogous to the big toe in humans.

halolimnic living in or on salt marshes.

Fig. 181. **Half-life.** X = half-life. Note that the time taken to reach zero amount is *not* 2 × X.

halophyte a plant tolerant of high concentrations of salt in the soil and atmosphere and normally found close to the sea, for example, the marsh samphire, or glasswort, *Salicornia europaea.*

halter (*pl.* halteres) or **balancer** one of a pair of structures found in DIPTERANS. They are thought to be modified hind wings, normally small, clubbed organs very much smaller than the forewing. Halteres are probably associated with maintaining equilibrium during flight.

hammer see MALLEUS.

hamulus (*pl.* hamuli) a hook or hooklike process, as in the barbules of interlocking feathers, or on the forewings of bees, linking with the hind wing.

haplo- *combining form* denoting single.

haplochlamydeous see MONOCHLAMYDEOUS.

haploid, 1. (of a cell nucleus) containing one of each type of chromosome. 2. a haploid organism in which the main life stage has cell nuclei with one of each type of chromosome, written as n. Such organisms, for example, fungi and many algae, usually have a brief DIPLOID (2) phase (2n), returning to the haploid state via MEIOSIS. See ALTERNATION OF GENERATIONS.

haplont an organism in the haploid stage.

haplotype see HLA SYSTEM.

hapten a substance that can combine with specific antibodies but does not produce them unless attached to a large CARRIER MOLECULE.

haptotropism see THIGMOTROPISM.

Hardy-Weinberg law a law stating that in a randomly mating large population the frequency of ALLELES will remain constant from generation to generation. Proposed in 1908 by G.H. Hardy in England and W. Weinberg in Germany, the law explains how the various alleles of a gene could remain constant in a population and yet be inherited by the rules of MENDELIAN GENETICS. The law shows, for instance, why dominant PHENOTYPES are not necessarily in excess of recessive ones in a population. If a gene has two alleles, *A* and *a*, with a frequency of p and q, respectively, the genotypic frequencies would have the proportions:

$$AA \quad Aa \quad aa$$
$$p^2 + 2pq + q^2 = 1.0$$

This equation is derived from the BINOMIAL EXPANSION $(p + q)^2 = 1.0$. Such GENETIC EQUILIBRIUM only occurs under conditions of zero selection and mutation, no emigration or immigration, random mating, and a large population size. However, selection pressures can produce stability (see GENETIC POLYMORPHISM), and selection and mutation effects might cancel each other out.

Harvey, William (1578—1657) English physician who discovered the mechanism of human blood circulation, in which blood flows away from the heart in arteries and toward the heart in veins.

Hatch-Slack pathway an alternative pathway to the CALVIN CYCLE of photosynthesis, thought to operate in some tropical grasses and some dicotyledons. Phosphoenolpyruvate is carboxylated to form oxaloacetate as the first product.

Hatscheck's pit a mucus gland in the oral hood of AMPHIOXUS.

haustorium 1. a specialized development of the end of a HYPHA in parasitic fungi, penetrating a cell of the host and forming a food-absorbing organ. 2. (in other parasitic plants) the organ that penetrates the host and acts as a food-absorbing organ.

Haversian canal one of many channels formed within bone by the development of OSTEOBLASTS in concentric rings around them, and whose function is to facilitate linking of the living parts. Each canal may contain an artery, a vein, and a nerve, and the canals ramify throughout the bone, communicating with the bone marrow and the PERIOSTEUM. The Haversian systems are mainly longitudinal, but cross-connections are present.

hay fever an allergic reaction to atmospheric dust and pollen. Hay fever causes watery eyes, sneezing, and other symptoms due to inflammation of the mucous membranes of the eyes and nose.

HCG (human chorionic gonadotrophin) a HORMONE secreted by the TROPHOBLAST of developing fetal tissues. It maintains the CORPUS LUTEUM during the first 3 to 4 months in pregnancy, thus ensuring a supply of PROGESTERONE for maintaining the uterus lining and preventing MENSTRUATION. HCG begins to be secreted as soon as the trophoblast implants in the uterine wall, and it is at its highest concentration between the 7th and 10th weeks of pregnancy. The urine of women in the first month of pregnancy contains enough HCG to be easily detected by chemical means. After reaching its peak, HCG falls to low concentrations and its only known function is to stimulate production of TESTOSTERONE by the testes of the male fetus. HCG has almost the same combined properties as LH and LUTEOTROPIC HORMONES.

head 1. the upper or front part of the body in vertebrates, which contains and protects the BRAIN, eyes, mouth, nose, and ears when present. There is usually a concentration of sense organs in the head, such as eyes, tentacles, antennae, and mouth parts. The head has probably developed because of forward locomotion, as a well-developed head is absent in organisms lacking unidirectional movement, for example, the sea urchin. 2. the corresponding part of an invertebrate animal. See also CEPHALIZATION.

heart the muscular pump of the BLOOD CIRCULATORY SYSTEM. In invertebrates that possess a heart for example, ARTHROPODS, ANNELIDS, MOLLUSKS, and ECHINODERMS), the heart is composed of several chambers and lies dorsal to the gut. In vertebrates the heart is made of special CARDIAC MUSCLE and lies in a ventral position surrounded by the PERICARDIUM. The five classes of vertebrates show an increasing complexity of structure, from the simple S-shaped heart with one ATRIUM and one VENTRICLE (2) found in fish, through the amphibians and most reptiles, where the heart is divided into two atria but retains a single ventricle, and on to the birds and mammals, where the heart shows complex separation into two sides with two atria and two ventricles. The main features of the human heart are:

(a) the right side pumps blood through the pulmonary (lung) circulation for oxygenation, the left side pumping blood through the systemic (body) circulation where it becomes deoxygenated.

(b) blood from the body enters the right atrium via the superior vena cava (upper body) and inferior vena cava (lower body). A coronary sinus also drains into the right atrium, bringing blood from the heart itself. The right atrium squeezes blood through the atrioventricular (AV) opening into the muscular right ventricle. Finally, blood is ejected into the single opening of the pulmonary artery, which splits to go to the two lungs.

(c) blood enters the left atrium from four pulmonary veins and passes through the left AV opening into the left ventricle. This has a much thicker wall than the right ventricle, reflecting its requirement for greater power. Blood leaves the left ventricle by one great vessel, the AORTA, which supplies all parts of the body, including the heart.

(d) flow of blood through the heart is in one direction only, due to the presence of various valves. Backflow from ventricles to atria is prevented by AV valves, the *tricuspid* valve on the right side with three flaps, and the BICUSPID (3) *valve* on the left side with two flaps. Both valves are held in place by cords of connective tissue, the *chordae tendinae*. Backflow from arteries to the ventricles is prevented by semilumar valves.

(e) various nerve areas connected with contraction are located in the heart (see HEART, CARDIAC CYCLE): (i) the *sinoatrial node (SAN)*, or pacemaker, located in the wall of the right atrium near the entry of the venae cavae; (ii) the *atrioventricular node (AVN)* at the junction of all four heart chambers; and (iii) a network of *Purkinje tissue* and other fibers spreading out from the AVN across the walls of both ventricles. See Fig. 182.

Fig. 182. **Heart.** Nerve centers in the mammalian heart.

Other nerve areas are situated in or near the heart: (i) *baroreceptors* in the walls of the heart, in the aortic arch, the carotid sinus, venae cavae, and pulmonary veins where they enter the atria. Such sensory receptors are stimulated by stretching of the structure in which they are found, resulting in a decrease in blood pressure. (ii) *chemoreceptors* sensitive to blood CO_2 levels are found in the AORTIC BODY and CAROTID BODY.

heart, cardiac cycle the muscular contractions that squeeze blood through the chambers of the heart and through the blood circulatory system. The return of blood into the heart differs in ARTHROPODS from the mechanism in all other groups. In arthropods blood is drawn into the heart from the pericardial cavity by a sucking motion. In other animals blood flow into the heart depends on venous pressure being higher than in the relaxed heart, thus pushing blood inward.

The features of the cardiac cycle in the mammals are as follows:

(a) CARDIAC MUSCLE has a rhythmic beat that arises in the heart itself. MYOGENIC CONTRACTION occurs at about 72 beats per minute in humans, although the rate is higher in smaller mammals. The rate is regulated by two nerves connected to the sinoatrial node (SAN). Sympathetic nerves from the spinal cord accelerate the heartbeat, and the vagus nerve from the brain medulla slows it down.

(b) when the heart is relaxed (the *diastole* phase), pressure from the venae cavae causes blood to enter the atria and, to a lesser extent, the ventricles. Once the atria are full of blood, a wave of electrical energy, originating in the SAN, spreads across the atria, causing a sharp muscular contraction, or *systole*, which forces blood into the relaxed ventricles.

(c) the electrical energy from the atria collects in the atrioventricular node and then spreads over the ventricular walls via the bundle of His and Purkinje fibers, causing ventricular systole. Meanwhile, the atria are starting diastole, ready to receive further blood from the veins. These changes are illustrated in Fig. 183, which shows a highly simplified heart structure.

(a)   (b)   (c)

Fig. 183. **Heart, cardiac cycle.** (a) Atrium and ventricle diastole. (b) Atrium systole and ventricle diastole. (c) Atrium starting diastole, ventricle systole.

heartwood the central mass of wood in trees, serving only for mechanical support and in which there are no living cells.

heat exhaustion the failure of cooling mechanisms resulting from excessive rise in body temperature in warm-blooded animals, characterized by cramp and dizziness.

heat gain a rise in temperature of a body when obtaining heat by radiation or conduction from an outside source, leading to an increase in METABOLIC RATE in all organs. See TEMPERATURE REGULATION.

heath a lowland plant community that is dominated by heathers on a sandy soil or shallow peat.

heat-labile destroyable by heat.

heat-loss the removal of heat from a body by radiation, evaporation, conduction, and convection during TEMPERATURE REGULATION.

heavy chain see IMMUNOGLOBULIN.

heavy isotope a stable atom in which there are more neutrons than in the normal isotope of the element, giving it a greater mass. For example, ^{15}N is the heavy isotope, ^{14}N the common form.

heavy metal any element with an atomic number greater than 20.

heavy-metal pollution pollution by HEAVY METALS, often found in sewage sludge.

hedgerow a row of shrubs that forms a habitat similar to that of a natural woodland edge, planted to form a division between two pieces of land.

Heidelberg man, *Homo erectus heidelbergensis,* who lived some 550,-000 BP and became extinct some 400,000 BP. Heidelberg man, Java man *(Pithecanthropus),* Peking man *(Sinanthropus),* and *Atlanthropus* are usually all regarded as *Homo erectus.*

HeLa cell a cell type used in tissue culture that is grown as a standard in research laboratories all over the world. The culture is derived from a cervical carcinoma obtained from *Henrietta Lacks* in 1951.

helical of or shaped like a HELIX.

helico- *combining form* denoting spiral.

helicotrema an opening at the apex of the COCHLEA connecting the scala tympani and the scala vestibuli.

helio- *combining form* denoting sun.

heliotropism a type of PHOTOTROPISM in which the flowers of a plant turn toward the sun during the day.

helix *(pl.* helixes or helices) a form of spiral in which any point is at the same distance from the central axis. RNA molecules have a single helix, and DNA is a double helix.

helminth a PLATYHELMINTH worm.

helminthology the study of parasitic worms.

helophyte an herb in which the perennating bud is formed in mud.

helper T-cell see T-CELL.

hematin an iron-containing pigment derived from breakdown of HEMO-GLOBIN.

hematoblast the parent cell of red blood corpuscles.

hematocrit the percentage of blood volume occupied by red blood cells. The percentage is 40.5% in humans.

hematocyte a blood corpuscle.

hematopoiesis or **hemopoiesis** the process leading to red blood cell production.

heme a ringlike chemical structure containing an atom of ferrous iron that is bound as a PROSTHETIC GROUP to each POLYPEPTIDE CHAIN within HEMOGLOBIN and MYOGLOBIN, giving blood and muscle their characteristic red color.

hemerythrin an iron-containing proteinaceous red pigment found in the blood plasma of some ANNELIDS and several minor invertebrate groups. Like HEMOGLOBIN, the pigment can become oxygenated, but in this case oxygen uptake involves a change in valence from Fe(II) to Fe(III).

hemi- *combining form* denoting half.

hemibiotroph a pathogen, usually fungal, that has both a BIOTROPHIC phase and a NECROTROPHIC phase in the course of one life cycle. Examples include apple SCAB and scald of barley (*Rhynchosporium secalis*).

hemicellulose or **hexosan** a polysaccharide associated with cellulose and LIGNIN, found in plant cell walls.

hemichordate any small wormlike marine animal of the subphylum Hemichordata or Enteropneusta, a division of the PROTOCHORDATES that contains wormlike forms, such as *Balanoglossus*.

hemicryptophyte an herb in which the perennating bud is at soil level, where it is protected by litter or soil.

Hemimetabola see EXOPTERYGOTE.

hemiparasite an organism that derives part of its sustenance from other organisms.

hemipteran any EXOPTERYGOTE of the order Hemiptera, containing the true bugs, including leaf hoppers, cochineal insects, scale insects, bed bugs, and aphids. They can cause considerable economic damage and contain both plant and animal parasites sucking plant sap or blood by means of piercing mouthparts. Normally, they have two pairs of wings, the forewings being at least partially hardened, like the elytra (see COLEOPTERA) of beetles.

hemizygous (of a DIPLOID (2) organism) possessing only one allele of a gene, rather than the normal two. For example, male mammals have only one copy of each gene on the single X-chromosome. See SEX LINKAGE.

hemo- or **hem-** or **hemato-** *combining form* denoting blood.

hemocoel the body cavity within many invertebrates, including arthropods and mollusks, which is an expansion of part of the blood system. In contrast with the COELOM, the hemocoel never opens to the exterior nor does it contain germ cells. See Fig. 184.

Fig. 184. **Hemocoel.** Transverse section of an insect, showing the positions of the heart, hemocoel, and blood flow.

hemocyanin a respiratory pigment found in the blood plasma of many mollusks and crustaceans, which performs the same function as HEMOGLOBIN in other animals. The metallic radicle of its PROSTHETIC GROUP is copper rather than iron, however, giving the molecule a bluish color.

hemoglobin a large PROTEIN molecule with a quaternary structure of four POLYPEPTIDE CHAINS, two alpha and two beta chains, each of which is complexed to a separate HEME group. About 300 million molecules of hemoglobin occur in each red blood cell of the mammalian circulation, with each molecule binding to a maximum of four oxygen molecules, one per heme group (= oxygenation). See OXYGEN-DISSOCIATION CURVE for an explanation of oxygen carriage.

Hemoglobin is found in all vertebrates and many invertebrates. In mammals the fetal hemoglobin (HbF) has a different polypeptide combination from that in postnatal adult hemoglobin (HbA), consisting of two alpha and two gamma chains, with different oxygen-carrying characteristics, up to 30% more at low oxygen tension. An altered beta chain in HbA produces SICKLE CELL ANEMIA.

hemolysis the disintegration of red blood cells, with release of HEMOGLOBIN. The process can occur (a) when the cells take in excess water by OSMOSIS, (b) when there is an antigen-antibody reaction involving the cells, as in RHESUS HEMOLYTIC ANEMIA, and (c) as a result of an abnormality such as FAVISM. Addition of glacial acetic acid to a blood sample causes hemolysis of the red blood cells, making it easier to observe and count the white blood cells.

hemophilia a rare human blood disorder in which BLOOD CLOTTING is deficient, resulting often in severe internal and external bleeding. The condition is due to lack of fibrin in the blood and is controlled by two closely linked genes on the X-CHROMOSOME, which are responsible for producing various clotting factors. Hemophilia A individuals lack antihemophilic globulin (AHG), while hemophilia B individuals lack plasma thromboplastin. Males carrying the mutant ALLELE of either locus or, much more rarely, females homozygous for the recessive mutant alleles of either locus will be affected, although heterozygous females have normal blood. Hemophilia A is by far the more common form of the disease, about 80%, and can be treated by transfusions of AHG.

hemopoiesis see HEMATOPOIESIS.

hemorrhage an escape of blood from the blood vessels, due to a wound or disease.

hemosporidian any protozoan parasite of the order Coccidiomorpha, found in the blood corpuscles of vertebrates and transmitted by invertebrate mites. See MALARIA PARASITE.

Henderson-Hasselback equation the formula for calculating the pH of a buffer solution, which states that:

$$pH = pK + \log \frac{(H^+ \text{ acceptor})}{(H^+ \text{ donor})}$$

where pK is the dissociation constant of an acid. The variable term is really a ratio of concentration values and can be taken as being proportional to the amount of acid and base added in the buffer. For example, when 30 cm^3 of 0.1 M NaOH is added to 100 cm^3 of 0.1 M acetic acid, and the pK for acetic acid is 4.73, we can estimate:

$$pH = 4.73 + \log \frac{30}{(100 - 30)}$$
$$= 4.73 + \log 0.429$$
$$= 4.36.$$

Henle, loop of see LOOP OF HENLE.

heparin a mucopolysaccharide molecule produced in the liver that acts as an anticoagulant, inhibiting transformation of prothrombin to thrombin, a vital stage in BLOOD CLOTTING.

hepatic of the liver.

Hepaticae a class of the BRYOPHYTA, a division that contains the liverworts. Liverworts are found in damp and wet conditions and vary in form from species that have a fleshy THALLUS up to 1 cm wide to leafy liverworts, which are very MOSS-like. Reproduction in liverworts may be vegetative, by means of GEMMAE, or sexual, ANTHERIDIA and ARCHEGONIA being present. The male gametes are motile, and fertilization results in development of a capsule containing diploid spore-mother cells. Each spore-mother cell carries out meiosis and produces haploid spores that may develop into a PROTONEMA, which in turn gives rise to the new haploid adult gametophyte.

hepatic cecum see CECUM.

hepatic portal system the part of the BLOOD CIRCULATORY SYSTEM of vertebrates in which blood from the alimentary canal is taken through CAPILLARIES in the liver before transport to the heart. Such a system of veins enables some materials absorbed from the gut to be stored or filtered out during passage through the liver.

hepatitis a serious disorder of the liver that leads to severe jaundice, liver degeneration, even death. The condition is caused by two viruses: hepatitis A virus, which produces *infective hepatitis* transmitted by the intestinal-oral route, and hepatitis B virus, which produces *serum hepatitis* transmitted via infected blood or its products. Although these two viral types can be distinguished in tests, the acute diseases caused by each may be clinically indistinguishable, the chief difference being that type A usually has a shorter incubation period than type B. No specific therapy is available for hepatitis, although vaccines are being developed.

hepato- or **hepat-** *combining form* denoting liver.

hepatocyte a liver cell.

herb 1. any seed-bearing nonwoody vascular plant whose aerial parts do not persist above ground at the end of the growing season. 2. any of various plants, such as rosemary, that are used in cookery and medicine.

herbaceous (of a plant) nonwoody.

herbarium a reference collection of preserved plants.

herbicide any chemical that kills plants. Herbicides can be highly selective. For example, 2,4-D only kills DICOTYLEDONS (broad-leaved plants), leaving MONOCOTYLEDONS unharmed.

herbivore any animal feeding on plant matter.

heredity the transmission of characteristics from one generation to another via a mechanism involving GENES and CHROMOSOMES.

heritability (h^2) the proportion of all phenotypic variance in a population due to genetic differences, which can be assessed in two main ways, BROAD-SENSE HERITABILITY and NARROW-SENSE HERITABILITY. Heritability is thus a general measure of genetic variation without which natural and artificial SELECTION could not proceed. It is used widely by plant and animal breeders to predict the likely effect of selection. For example, if heritability values for a character are low, this indicates high environmental variability and suggests that response to selection would not be rapid.

hermaphrodite 1. any plant possessing stamens and carpels in the same flower. 2. any animal possessing both male and female sex organs. The condition is usual in many plants and lower animals, but may occur in some unisexual organisms as an abnormality.

heroin a white crystalline powder, manufactured from morphine, used as a sedative and narcotic in the hydrochloride form.

herpes simplex a common virus of humans that can persist in a quiescent or latent state for long periods and then become active at irregular intervals, producing local blisters in the mucous membranes or in the skin, where local multiplication occurs. A common result of infective activity is the appearance of cold sores around the mouth and nose, but one form of the virus causes genital herpes, a painful and persistent infection of the genital and anal regions that is transmitted by sexual contact.

Hershey, Alfred (1908—) American scientist who in 1951 with his colleague Martha Chase showed, by means of differential radioactive labeling, that the DNA of T$_2$ BACTERIOPHAGES, rather than their protein, was necessary for formation of new phages within the host bacterium, *E.*

coli. The experimental results are taken as a demonstration that DNA functions as the genetic material.

hertz (Hz) the SI UNIT of frequency, measuring cycles per second.

hetero- *combining form* denoting different *or* other.

heterocercal fin the type of tail fin found on sharks where the ventral lobe is large and the dorsal lobe small.

heterocercal tail see HETEROCERCAL FIN.

heterochlamydeous (of flowers) having dissimilar sepals and petals in two whorls in the PERIANTH.

heterochromatic (of chromosomal preparations) staining differently from the major chromosome parts.

heterochromatin any chromosomal segments or whole chromosomes that appear darkly stained during interphase of the CELL CYCLE (as compared with EUCHROMATIN) due to tight condensation, which may indicate genetic inactivity. Heterochromatin may be condensed at all times (*constitutive*) or only at certain times (*facultative*). See C-BANDING.

heterodont (of an animal) possessing teeth of different kinds, such as incisors or molars.

heteroduplex (of a molecule) possessing double-stranded nucleic acid in which the two POLYNUCLEOTIDE CHAINS come from a different source, either two different DNA strands or a DNA/RNA duplex, and are held together by COMPLEMENTARY PAIRING.

heteroecious (of rust fungi) having different spore forms on different host plants.

heterogametic sex the sex of a particular organism that contains within each nucleus one X-chromosome and one Y-chromosome (or just one X-chromosome), and therefore produces two different types of gametes with respect to the SEX CHROMOSOMES. The male is usually the heterogametic sex, but in some organisms, for example, birds, it is the female. Since the sex chromosomes usually are responsible for SEX DETERMINATION, the heterogametic parent controls the sex of the offspring.

heterogamy the alteration of forms of sexual reproduction. See HETEROGAMETIC SEX.

heterogeneity chi-square test see CONTINGENCY TABLE.

heterograft or **xenograft** a transplant from one species to another.

heterokaryon a cell containing nuclei from two different sources, or in fungi a hyphal cell, spore, mycelium, or organism that contains genetically different nuclei. See COMPLEMENTATION TEST.

Heterometabola see EXOPTERYGOTA.

heteromorphic 1. (of an organism) having morphologically different forms in the life history, for example, where there is ALTERNATION OF GENERATIONS. 2. (of pairs of homologous chromosomes) differing in size or form.

heteropteran any HEMIPTERAN insect of the suborder Heteroptera, having forewings in the form of hemielytra. The suborder includes water boatmen, water scorpions, bed bugs, and most plant bugs.

heterosis or **hybrid vigor** the superiority of a HYBRID produced from crossing two different types of parents having one or more inferior characteristics. Thus, two different inbred lines of cereals when crossed together can produce hybrids with a far higher yield and general vigor than either parental line.

heterosome see SEX CHROMOSOME.

heterospory the formation of more than one sort of SPORE, usually MICROSPORES and MEGASPORES in ferns and seed plants, giving rise to distinct male and female GAMETOPHYTE generations. The terms 'megaspore' and 'microspore' were first used in connection with PTERIDOPHYTES, in which differences in spore size occur. Later, because of how the structures are formed, these terms were used in reference to seed plants, in which such size differences are rarer. In seed plants, the microspore is the pollen, and the megaspore is the cell that gives rise to the EMBRYO SAC.

heterostyly a combination of morphological and physiological mechanisms that promote cross-pollination in flowering plants. Structurally, there are usually two flower forms, for example, the pin and thrum forms of the primrose, which ensure that the pollen collected from the stamens of one type is deposited on the stigma of the other (see ENTOMOPHILY). There is also SELF-INCOMPATIBILITY between pollen and stigma from the same flower type, although there is compatibility between flowers of different types. Compare HOMOSTYLY.

heterothallism (in algae and fungi) a situation in which sexual reproduction occurs only where two self-sterile thalli take part. See THALLUS.

heterotherm see POIKILOTHERM.

heterotrichous (of an algal thallus) prostrate and creeping, and from which branching filaments project.

heterotroph an organism dependent on obtaining organic food from the environment because it is unable to synthesize organic material. All animals, fungi, many bacteria, and a few flowering plants, such as insectivorous plants, are heterotrophs. They obtain almost all their organic material either directly or indirectly from the activity of AUTOTROPHS.

heterotroph hypothesis a hypothesis suggesting that the first organisms were HETEROTROPHS.

heterozygote an individual containing two different allelic forms of the same gene in all DIPLOID (1) cells. Thus, if gene A has two alleles, $A1$ and $A2$, the heterozygote will contain both alleles $(A1/A2)$. Compare HOMOZYGOTE.

hexa- *combining form* denoting six.

hexacanth the six-hooked spherical embryo found in certain tapeworms.

hexapod see INSECT.

hexosan see HEMICELLULOSE.

hexose monophosphate shunt see PENTOSE PHOSPHATE PATHWAY.

hexose sugar a sugar containing six carbon atoms, for example, glucose $(C_6H_{12}O_6)$. Hexose sugars are the basic building blocks for more complex CARBOHYDRATES.

Hfr strain a strain of *E. coli* bacteria that has the ability to transfer a chromosome to an F^- cell and shows a *h*igh *f*requency of *r*ecombination. The F FACTOR is integrated into the Hfr cell chromosome.

hibernation a state of dormancy entered into by many animals during winter, particularly those in cold latitudes. Some temperate and arctic mammals, reptiles, and some amphibians hibernate. In this state, the METABOLISM is slowed down and the body temperature falls. Hibernation is generally triggered by cold weather; and while body temperatures in mammals normally are maintained at the usual level, they may fall much lower and close to the freezing point, for example, in the hamster, or the body temperature may fall to that of the surroundings, for example, in the bat.

True hibernators tend to be midsized animals, as these can have sufficient food reserves without too large a surface area for heat loss. Bears are not true hibernators, in that their body temperature does not drop and they are able to awaken quickly from their winter sleep. In temperate situations, rises in temperature may cause some animals to come out of hibernation temporarily. Compare ESTIVATION (1).

hierarchy (in CLASSIFICATION) the system of ranking in a graded order from species to kingdom. See HIGHER CATEGORY.

high-altitude adjustment the physiological adjustment to atmospheric pressure that occurs when an animal moves into high altitudes from a lower one, including changes in the respiratory and circulatory system, causing an increase in red blood cells and hemoglobin content of the blood. See ACCLIMATIZATION and ADAPTATION, PHYSIOLOGICAL.

high-energy bond a chemical bond containing several times more stored energy than is usual. See AMP, ATP.

higher category (in CLASSIFICATION) any category higher—nearer to kingdom—than to the rank of species. See HIERARCHY.

higher taxon (in CLASSIFICATION) any TAXON higher—nearer to king-dom—than the one in question.

Hillman and Sartory see ARTIFACT.

Hill reaction a reaction in which oxygen and hydrogen are produced from water when CHLOROPLASTS are illuminated in the presence of a strong oxidizing agent, such as a ferric salt, reported by R. Hill in 1936. Hill was unable to achieve assimilation of carbon dioxide by chloroplasts (see CALVIN CYCLE). We now know that his experiments were an indica-tion that PHOTOSYNTHESIS is a two-stage process and that he was demonstrating LIGHT REACTIONS.

hilum 1. a scar located down one side of a seed indicating the point of attachment of the OVULE to the ovary. **2.** a notch on the concave side of the mammalian kidney through which pass the blood vessels and nerves.

Himalayan rabbit a strain of rabbit in which the coat color is white, but all body extremities are black: nose tip, paws, ears, and tail. The condi-tion is controlled by a single autosomal gene with MULTIPLE ALLELISM, one for AGOUTI, one for ALBINISM, and the third for Himalayan. The dominance relationship between the three alleles is agouti > Hima-layan > albino. The Himalayan allele is temperature-sensitive, coding for an enzyme that catalyzes black pigment formation wherever the skin is cooler, the enzyme becoming inactive at higher temperatures.

hindbrain the part of the brain forming the medulla and cerebellum, derived embryologically from the rear third of the brain. See FORE-BRAIN, MIDBRAIN.

hip girdle see PELVIC GIRDLE.

hirsute covered with long hair.

Hirudinea a class of the phylum Annelida that includes the leeches and annelid worms that lack chaetae or parapodia, have an apparent exter-nal segmentation much greater than the small number of internal seg-ments, and possess suckers for attachment. Most species feed on blood.

His, bundle of a group of special cardiac muscle fibers that run from the atrioventricular node down to the septum between the ventricles and, with the Purkinje fibers, transmit electrical energy over the ventricular walls, causing ventricular systole. See HEART CARDIAC CYCLE.

hispid (of plant tissues) possessing coarse, stiff hairs.

histamine a chemical ($C_5H_9N_3$) produced by LEUKOCYTES and other cells, for example, MAST CELLS, which causes blood capillaries to become more permeable and so lose fluids into the tissues, thereby producing local swelling. Histamines are released when foreign ANTIGENS are pre-sent. See ANAPHYLAXIS, IMMUNE RESPONSE.

histidine one of the 20 AMINO ACIDS common in proteins. It carries an extra basic group making it alkaline and is soluble in water. See Fig. 185. The ISOELECTRIC POINT of histidine is 7.6.

specific 'R' group

Fig. 185. **Histidine.** Molecular structure.

histo- *combining form* denoting tissue.

histochemistry the study of the distribution of substances in tissues by using staining methods on preparations, such as sections or whole mounts.

histocompatibility the acceptance by a recipient of tissue transplanted from a donor, a state that is determined by histocompatibility ANTIGENS.

histocyte or **clasmatocyte** a large phagocyte of irregular shape that occurs in blood, lymph, and connective tissue. Histocytes are similar to MONOCYTES but take up stain.

histogen a distinct tissue zone found in many plants in the apical meristem, particularly in the root-apical meristem.

histogenesis the formation of tissues and organs from undifferentiated cells.

histogram a diagram showing a frequency distribution by means of rectangular areas. See FREQUENCY DISTRIBUTION and Fig. 161.

histology the study of tissue.

histolysis tissue breakdown.

histone a type of simple protein that is usually basic and tends to form complexes with nucleic acids (for example, DNA) forming NUCLEOSOMES. CHROMOSOMES of EUKARYOTES contain large quantities of histones, which may regulate DNA functioning in some way. The five major histones are represented as: H1, H2A, H2B, H3, and H4.

HLA human leukocyte A system a major HISTOCOMPATIBILITY complex of four genes, perhaps five, called HLA-A, HLA-B, HLA-C, and HLA-D, with the D locus nearest the centromere on the shorter arm of chromosome 6. Each gene has up to 35 alleles, the particular combination of alleles of the four genes on a chromosome being called the *haplotype.* Since humans are diploid organisms, we have two haplotypes, these being determined by testing a person's white blood cells for the specific HLA antigens.

Although these large numbers of alleles would appear to make the system a complex one in terms of possible combinations in each individual, the situation in fact is simpler than it seems. The four loci within the HLA system are so tightly linked together that there is little CROSSING OVER between them. Thus, each haplotype tends to be passed on to an offspring as a block rather than as four individual genes. Given no recombination between the four genes, four rearrangements would be expected to occur in the progeny of a mating. Any child of a cross, therefore, has a one-in-four chance of inheriting precisely the same HLA combination as another sibling. Since the success of organ transplantation depends on a close match of HLA alleles—even one allele difference can cause the foreign organ to be rejected—the chance of matching HLA types is highest within closely related individuals.

holandric (of genes) carried on the Y-SEX CHROMOSOME and transmitted via the HETEROGAMETIC SEX. In mammals, holandric genes are passed on from father to son.

holdfast the basal part of the stripe (stalk) of large sea weeds, such as *Fucus* and *Laminaria*, attaching the plant to the substrate.

holistic viewing a whole as more than the sum of its parts.

holo- *combining form* denoting whole *or* entire.

holoblastic cleavage see CLEAVAGE.

holocarpic (of the entire adult thallus of a fungus) becoming a reproductive structure.

Holocene, the or **Recent Epoch** the part of GEOLOGICAL TIME that has elapsed since the last ice age ended; the last 10,000 years of the QUATERNARY PERIOD.

Holocephali a subclass of the CHONDRICHTHYES, including fish having a compressed head and flattened teeth for crushing mollusks. The only present-day representative is CHIMERA (2).

holocrine 1. (of a form of cell digestion, particularly in insects) characterized by self-disintegration to produce the digestive fluid. 2. (of gland secretion) characterized by self-disintegration in releasing its product, as in sebaceous glands.

holoenzyme an entire conjugated enzyme consisting of a protein component (an *apoenzyme*) and a nonprotein component (a *coenzyme* or an *activator*).

hologamete a gamete formed by a full-size ordinary individual PROTOZOAN that fuses with another similar individual to form a ZYGOTE.

Holometabola see ENDOPTERYGOTA.

holophytic (of plants) using the energy of the sun to synthesize organic compounds by means of chlorophyll. See AUTOTROPH.

holothurian any ECHINODERM of the class Holothuroidea, including the sea cucumbers.

holotroph an organism capable of ingesting other whole organisms.

holotype the specimen designated by the author of a scientific name as the TYPE specimen at the time of the original publication.

holozoic (of an organism) feeding on solid organic material derived from the bodies of other organisms. This is mainly the method of feeding adopted by animals, though a few specialized plants, such as insectivorous plants, obtain nutrient matter in this way.

homeo- *combining form* denoting similar.

homeostasis the maintenance by an organism of a constant internal environment, such as regulation of blood sugar levels by insulin. The process involves self-adjusting mechanisms in which the maintenance of a particular level is initiated by the substance to be regulated. See also FEEDBACK MECHANISM.

homeotherm see HOMOIOTHERM.

homeotic mutant the mutational change of one structure to another in insects, such as wing to halter, arista to leg.

home range the area in which an animal normally restricts its movements in search of food or a mate, and in which it cares for its young. Compare TERRITORY.

homing (modifier) relating to the ability to return to a place of origin. See NAVIGATION.

hominid any member of the family Hominidae, which includes human and humanlike fossils from the Pleistocene EPOCH.

Homo any primate of the hominid genus *Homo*. Only one species exists at present, *Homo sapiens*, although several extinct species are recognized, such as *H. erectus, H. habilis*.

homo- *combining form* denoting same.

homocercal fin a type of fish tail fin that is symmetrical in shape, that is, the upper and lower lobes are of similar size.

homocercal tail see HOMOCERCAL FIN.

homochlamydeous (of flowers) having PERIANTH segments that are not distinguishable as separate sepals and petals in two whorls.

homodont (of most nonmammalian vertebrates) having teeth of a similar type.

Homo erectus see HEIDELBERG MAN.

homogametic sex the sex that contains in its nuclei similar sex chromosomes, for example, XX, and produces gametes all with the same type of SEX CHROMOSOME. Compare HETEROGAMETIC SEX.

homogamy the state of having anthers and stigmas maturing at the same time.

homogentisic acid see GARROD.

homograft see ALLOGRAFT.

homoiotherm or **homeotherm** or **homotherm** any warm-blooded animal (mammal or bird). A homoiotherm can maintain its body temperature within a narrow range, usually above that of its surroundings (see CORE TEMPERATURE) despite large variation in environmental temperature. It may be maintained continually or for limited periods only. Compare POIKILOTHERM.

homokaryon a cell or mycelium of a fungus, containing identical haploid nuclei.

homologous (of organs, or structures) deriving from the same evolutionary origins. For example, the forelimb of a quadruped, the human arm, and the wing of a bird are said to be homologous (see PENTADACTYL LIMB). Similarities are usually seen best in embryonic development and are regarded by taxonomists as indications of relationships between present-day organisms.

homologous chromosomes those CHROMOSOMES containing identical genetic loci, although possibly different allelic forms. In DIPLOID organisms, the chromosomes occur in homologous pairs, one member of each pair from a different parent and the pair becoming separated during MEIOSIS and giving rise to genetic SEGREGATION.

homology the condition of being HOMOLOGOUS.

homonym a specific or generic name that has been used for two or more different organisms. The homonym published first is designated as senior, and junior if published most recently.

homopteran any insect of the suborder Homoptera, order HEMIPTERA, in which the forewings are of a uniform nature throughout. Examples include plant bugs, froghoppers, and aphids.

homosporous (of an organism) exhibiting HOMOSPORY.

homospory the possession of only one form of SPORE. This gives rise to a single GAMETOPHYTE generation carrying both male and female reproductive organs.

homostyly the possession of styles of only one length in flowers of a particular species. This is a more common condition than HETEROSTYLY.

homothallism the situation in algae and fungi in which sexual reproduction occurs in a colony arising from a single spore, each thallus being self-fertile.

homotherm see HOMOIOTHERM.

homozygote an individual containing two identical forms of the same GENE in all DIPLOID (1) cells that is capable of *pure breeding*. Thus, if gene A has two alleles, $A1$ and $A2$, two homozygous types are possible: $A1/A1$ and $A2/A2$. Compare HETEROZYGOTE.

honeybee *Apis mellifera*, the species of bee (see HYMENOPTERAN) kept by man to produce honey.

honeycomb a structure of waxy hexagonal cells produced by HONEY BEES and in which young are reared and honey stored.

honeydew the sugary waste substance passed out by aphids and similar insects.

hookworm a NEMATODE parasite of humans that gives rise to anemia and mental and physical retardation. See ANKYLOSTOMIASIS.

hoof a horny casing of the toe produced by hardened epidermal cuticle (*keratin*), found particularly in ungulates.

horizon any layer of soil that is distinguishable when soil is examined in vertical sections.

horizontal classification the type of CLASSIFICATION that stresses the grouping of species at a similar level of evolution rather than the position on the same phyletic line. Compare VERTICAL CLASSIFICATION.

horizontal resistance see NONRACE-SPECIFIC RESISTANCE.

hormone a chemical produced in the body of a plant or animal, sometimes in very small quantities, and which when transported, usually by the bloodstream in animals, to another part of the organism, elicits a particular response. Hormones are thus chemical messengers. In animals the ductless glands that secrete hormones are called ENDOCRINE ORGANS. Animal hormones that influence other endocrine glands are called *trophins* (or *tropins*) as in GONADOTROPHINS. See also PLANT HORMONE.

horsetail see EQUISETUM.

host the organism on which a PARASITE lives.

H-substance or **H-antigen** the carbohydrate precursor of the A and B antigens found in red blood cells (see ABO BLOOD GROUP) and in various tissue fluids (see SECRETOR STATUS), recognized by an anti-H-reagent made from gorse seeds.

human chorionic gonadotrophin (HCG) a gonadotrophic hormone secreted by the PLACENTA (1) that has an effect similar to that of a luteinizing hormone (see LH).

humerus the bone of the vertebrate forelimb, or arm, nearest to the body, to which it is attached at the shoulder. It is attached distally to the RADIUS and ULNA at the elbow.

humoral of or relating to a body fluid, as in humoral immunity produced by antibodies carried in lymph.

humus the organic material derived from the breakdown of plant and animal material occurring in the surface layers of the soil. Humus is colloidal in nature and improves the fertility of soil in several ways: (a) in acting as a reservoir of numerous nutrients that it prevents from leaching deeper into the soil layers; (b) in increasing the water-holding capacity of the soil; and (c) in improving soil texture, or friability.

humus-carbonate soil see RENDZINA.

Huntington's chorea an incurable degeneration of the human nervous system characterized by involuntary movements of the head, face, and/ or limbs, leading eventually to death. The disorder is caused by a single autosomal dominant gene on chromosome 4 (see DOMINANCE) that shows delayed penetrance, fewer than 5% of cases being seen before the age of 25. Thus, many individuals carrying the dominant allele have reproduced before their own gene shows itself. In turn, their progeny may have to wait until middle age to discover whether they have inherited the condition. Named after the American neurologist George Huntington (1851—1916).

hyal- or **hyalo-** *combining form* denoting glass.

hyaline transparent.

hyaline cartilage see CARTILAGE.

hyaloid canal a canal found in the vertebrate eye that passes through the vitreous humor from the lens to the blind spot.

hyaluronidase an enzyme present in snake venom and bacteria that catalyzes the hydrolysis of hyaluronic acid, making it ineffective in stopping the spread of invading microorganisms and other toxic substances.

hybrid an offspring of a cross between two genetically unlike individuals. See also HETEROZYGOTE, HETEROSIS.

hybrid DNA a nucleic acid produced by joining together, or annealing, POLYNUCLEOTIDE CHAINS of DNA from different sources. See HETERODUPLEX.

hybridization see MOLECULAR HYBRIDIZATION.

hybrid sterility the inability of some HYBRIDS to form functional gametes, due to chromosomes mispairing during MEIOSIS. This is a form of REPRODUCTIVE ISOLATION.

hybrid swarm a group of genetically variable organisms resulting from hybridization of two previously distinct and separate populations. Subsequent crossing and backcrossing results in a very variable population as a result of segregation. Often the genetical variability appears as morphological variability, such as different color forms. Where different color forms of an animal occur in different parts of the range, the hybrid swarm is characterized by presence of all or a wide range of these forms.

hybrid vigor see HETEROSIS.

hydathode a gland occurring on the leaf edges of many plants and secreting water. See GUTTATION.

hydatid cyst the bladderlike larva of some tapeworms, such as *Echinococcus* that produces an enormous bladder up to five liters in capacity, which may bud off many smaller cysts. In mammals, cysts occurring in the brain produce symptoms of epilepsy.

Hydra a genus of the coelenterate class Hydrozoa. Most species are found in fresh water and are unusual members of the Hydrozoa in that they do not have an ALTERNATION OF GENERATIONS.

hydranth the normal COELENTERATE polyp, having a mouth surrounded by tentacles, found in most colonial forms.

hydration the process of chemical combination with water to form a compound referred to as a *hydrate*.

hydro- or **hydr-** *combining form* denoting water.

hydrocele 1. the water vascular system of echinoderms, which has branches to the tube feet and is concerned to this extent with locomotion. 2. an accumulation of serous fluid in humans, usually about the testes.

hydrogen acceptor any substance, for example, CYTOCHROME OXIDASE, that can become reduced by addition of hydrogen, thus enabling transfer and release of energy, as in the ELECTRON TRANSPORT SYSTEM.

hydrogen bond the attractive force between the hydrogen atom of a molecule and that of another molecule, forming a noncovalent bond. These weak bonds are relevant to the biological function of particular compounds, being formed in the secondary structure of proteins and between complementary base pairs in NUCLEIC ACIDS.

hydrogen carrier system see ELECTRON TRANSPORT SYSTEM.

hydrogen ion concentration see PH.

hydroid a member of the COELENTERATE class Hydrozoa. Most are colonial forms that grow in a marine environment on rocks and seaweeds, such as *Obelia*. Usually, there is an ALTERNATION OF GENERATION (not in HYDRA) in which the MEDUSA (free-swimming) stage carries the sex organs. The sedentary, nonsexual stage of this life cycle is itself referred to as the POLYP or, less commonly, the *hydroid stage*.

hydrolase an enzyme that mediates hydrolytic reactions.

hydrolysis a chemical reaction in which large molecules are broken down by addition of water, for example, fat to fatty acids and glycerol, MALTOSE to glucose, and DIPEPTIDE to two amino acids. The reactions are usually activated enzymically. Compare CONDENSATION REACTION.

hydrolytic enzyme see HYDROLASE.

hydromedusa the MEDUSA of a HYDROZOAN.

hydrophilic having an affinity for water.

hydrophobic having an aversion for water.

hydrophyte a plant that inhabits wet places and whose perennating buds lie in water. Compare MESOPHYTE, XEROPHYTE.

hydroponics the science of growing plants without soil, in which the roots are suspended in aerated water containing known quantities of chemicals that can be adjusted to suit changing conditions. The method is increasingly common in the greenhouse cultivation of, for example, tomatoes and cucumbers.

hydrorhiza the rootlike base of a colonial COELENTERATE that fixes it to the substrate.

hydrosere a plant succession originating in water.

hydrosphere the aqueous envelope of Earth, including underground water and atmospheric water vapor.

hydrostatic skeleton a liquid, usually water, that maintains the shape of an organism by filling internal spaces. See SKELETON.

hydrotheca the cuplike part of the perisarc of colonial COELENTERATES that surrounds and protects the polyp.

hydrotropism the growth of plant roots in a particular orientation with respect to water, usually toward moisture.

hydrozoan any colonial or solitary COELENTERATE of the class Hydrozoa, including most of the species that exhibit an ALTERNATION OF GENERATIONS between HYDROID and medusoid (see MEDUSA) forms.

hymen a fold of mucous membrane stretched across the entrance to the vagina in some mammals. There is normally a small opening in it, and the hymen is ruptured during the first copulation.

hymenium a layer of spore-producing structures present in the fruiting body of BASIDIOMYCETES and ASCOMYCETES.

hymeno- *combining form* denoting membrane.

Hymenoptera an insect order of the subclass ENDOPTERYGOTA, including some of the most important social insects, such as ants, bees, and wasps. They are characterized by the presence of two pairs of membranous wings that are connected together, and often there is a marked constriction (wasp waist) between the abdomen and thorax. Apart from the social insects, the order also contains many solitary bees and wasps and the ichneumon flies, the larvae of which are often parasitic on other insects. See Fig. 186.

Fig. 186. **Hymenoptera.** A winged female ant.

hyoid arch the visceral skeletal arch that lies directly behind the mandibular arch and supports the floor of the vertebrate mouth.

hyomandibula a bone or cartilage present at the end of the hyoid arch that forms part of the jaw structure in fish and the STAPES in higher vertebrates.

hyostylic jaw suspension a form of jaw suspension in which the upper jaw is articulated to the skull only by means of ligaments and the hyomandibula, as in the dogfish.

hyper- *prefix* denoting over.

hypercalcemia having excessive levels of calcium in the plasma.

hypercapnea having excessive levels of carbon dioxide in the plasma.

hyperemia an increased blood flow to an organ or tissue.

hyperglycemia see GLYCOSURIA.

hypermetropia see HYPEROPIA.

hyperopia or **hypermetropia** or **far-sightedness** an inability to see nearby objects clearly, due to their image being focused behind the retina because the eye lens power is insufficient for the size of eye. Compare MYOPIA.

hyperparasite an organism parasitic on another parasite.

hyperplasia an increase in tissue mass caused by an increase in cell number.

hyperpnea an increased ventilation of the lungs.

hypersensitivity the process of localized plant cell death that occurs immediately after entry of a cell by a plant pathogen. Such a reaction can act as a host-resistance mechanism, since the cell death often prevents further growth of biotrophic pathogens, for example, powdery mildews or rusts.

hyperthyroidism a medical condition in which overproduction of the thyroid hormone causes nervousness, sensitivity to heat, and insomnia.

hypertonic see HYPOTONIC.

hypertrophy the excessive growth or development of an organ or tissue.

hyperventilation 1. an increase in air inhalation into the lungs. 2. the depth or rate of breathing.

hypha (*pl.* hyphae) a filament of the plant body of a fungus, the total of which makes up the nonreproductive part of the organism, as opposed to the fruiting body. Hyphae may be *septate*, having internal septae as in some *Phycomycetes,* or *nonseptate* as in most other groups. However, even in the septate stage, pores are present in the septae so there is a continuity of cytoplasmic material throughout the hypha. See also HAUSTORIUM.

hypo- *prefix* denoting under.

hypocotyl the shoot in a young germinating seedling, located below the cotyledon. See GERMINATION and Fig. 166.

hypodermis the layer of cells immediately under the epidermis of plant leaves. The layer is sometimes used for water storage or for mechanical strengthening for extra protection.

hypodigm all the material available to a taxonomist.

hypogeal (of seed GERMINATION) the COTYLEDONS (2) remaining underground within the seed coat, with the young shoot and root growing out from the seed, for example, the lima bean (*Phaseolus limensis*).

hypoglossal nerve the 12th CRANIAL NERVE of higher vertebrates, the motor nerve supplying the floor of the mouth and the tongue.

hypogynous see GYNOECIUM.

hyponasty the more rapid growth of the lower side of an organ, compared with the upper side, that results in curving.

hypopharynx a chitinous structure having its origin in the floor of the mouth in insects and normally carrying the salivary apertures. In blood-sucking insects, the structure extends into the proboscis.

hypophysectomy the removal of the pituitary GLAND.

hypophysis 1. the pouch formed in front of the buccal cavity in the embryo which, together with the INFUNDIBULUM, forms the pituitary. 2. a loose term for PITUITARY GLAND.

hypopnea decreased ventilation of the lungs.

hypostasis a relationship between two genes whose products act in the same biochemical PATHWAY, in which the functional effect of one gene is masked by another. The enzyme coded by the hypostatic gene operates later in the pathway than the enzyme produced by the epistatic gene. See EPISTASIS.

hypostome any structure around or below the mouth, such as the oral cone in *Hydra*.

hypothalamus the part of the sides and floor of the brain derived from the forebrain. Associated with the control of body temperature, it also partially controls the PITUITARY GLAND and contains centers controlling sleep and wakefulness, feeding, drinking, speech, and osmoregulation, the last by secretion of ADH from neurosecretory cells. It is also associated with aspects of reproductive behavior.

hypothermia an abnormally low body temperature that reduces the metabolic rate to a dangerous level and can lead to death, often occurring in elderly people subjected to cold weather. Hypothermia is sometimes induced in medical treatment in order to reduce metabolic activity.

hypotonic (of a fluid) having a less-negative WATER POTENTIAL or a lower solute concentration than another fluid, which is *hypertonic* to it. See Fig. 187. See also PLASMOLYSIS.

Fig. 187. **Hypotonic.** The movement of water from a hypotonic fluid to a hypertonic one.

hypoxia the reduction of oxygen levels.

hypsodont (of teeth) having open roots that continue to grow as fast as they are worn down. They are common in herbivorous animals such as ungulates and rodents.

H zone the lightish area in the middle of a muscle SARCOMERE where MYOSIN and ACTIN filaments do not overlap.

I

IAA (indole-3-acetic acid or **indolacetic acid)** the most thoroughly investigated type of AUXIN, which has been extracted from various natural sources. See Fig. 188.

Fig. 188. **IAA.** Molecular structure.

IAN (indole-3-aceto nitrile) a plant growth-regulating hormone.

I-band or **isotropic band** a light band that in electron micrographs can be seen traversing skeletal muscle myofibrils barely visible on the highest power of the light microscope as fine threads running the length of the muscle fiber. Each myofibril is made up of a series of sarcomeres in the form of a chain (see SARCOMERE and Fig. 265). In electron micrographs, the fibrils can be seen to have dark and light bands. Each I-band is traversed by a darker Z-membrane and is made up of thin filaments of ACTIN. See MUSCLE and Fig. 219.

ichthyo- *combining form* denoting fish.

ichthyosaur a large extinct reptile that existed from the TRIASSIC PERIOD to the CRETACEOUS PERIOD. It had paddle-shaped limbs, a head with long toothed jaws, and a fishlike tail.

identical twins see MONOZYGOTIC TWINS.

identification the determination of the taxonomic identity of an individual. See KEY.

idio- *combining form* denoting proper to one.

idioblast a cell distinct from others in the same tissue.

idiogram a diagrammatic representation of a KARYOTYPE.

ileum the part of the intestine lying between the duodenum and the colon, where digestion is completed by enzymes that break down carbohydrates, fats, and proteins (see SMALL INTESTINE). Absorption of food also occurs there.

ilium the dorsal bone of the PELVIC GIRDLE, which is joined to the SACRAL VERTEBRAE.

imaginal disk a structure found in the pupae of ENDOPTERYGOTES, formed by a thickening of the epidermis and underlying tissue and which, on metamorphosis, gives rise to an adult structure.

imago the sexually mature, adult insect.

imbibition the uptake of water, for example, by a dry seed, that causes GERMINATION to begin. The process is due not to SELECTIVE PERMEABILITY through a membrane, but rather to the property of water ADSORPTION by colloidal particles, such as cellulose, pectin, and cytoplasmic proteins, using chemical and electrostatic attraction.

imbricate (of plant parts in bud) overlapping at their edges like roof tiles.

immigration the movement of organisms into a specific area. Compare EMIGRATION.

immune response an antagonistic host reaction in response to foreign ANTIGENS, involving formation of ANTIBODIES by B-CELLS, or a cell-mediated response by T-CELLS. When such antibodies are present in the body, the individual is said to possess IMMUNITY against the specific antigen that stimulated the antibody production. The immune response is a vital defense mechanism but creates severe problems with, for example, kidney transplants from donors. In these cases the tissues are matched for *tissue compatibility* and the recipient is treated with chemicals that reduce the immune response.

immunity resistance to foreign ANTIGENS such as viruses. Immunity can be either *active*, in which the body produces its own IMMUNE RESPONSE after exposure to a vaccine, or *passive*, in which ready-made antibodies are supplied in a serum or obtained naturally from the mother.

immunization the administration of an ANTIGEN, in the form of a vaccine, to produce an IMMUNE RESPONSE to that antigen and so protect against future exposure to the antigen. See ATTENUATION.

immunofluorescence see FLUORESCENT ANTIBODY TECHNIQUE.

immunoglobulin a protein, such as gamma globulin, made in B-CELLS that possesses ANTIBODY activity and is made up of four POLYPEPTIDE CHAINS: two identical *light chains* and two identical *heavy chains* joined by disulfide bonds. There are five main classes of human immunoglobins, differentiated principally by their heavy chains:

Type	IgG	IgM	IgA	IgD	IgE
Heavy chain	gamma	mu	alpha	delta	epsilon
M.W. (x 1000)	144	160	144	156	166

IMMUNOLOGICAL TOLERANCE

Each heavy and light chain consists of a CONSTANT REGION of amino acids that is virtually the same in all antibodies of that class, and a VARIABLE REGION containing a sequence of amino acids that makes the antibody specific to a particular ANTIGEN. See Fig. 189.

Fig. 189. **Immunoglobulin.** Molecular structure. S = sulfur bonds.

immunological tolerance the failure to respond to a potential antigen.

immunotoxin an antibody attached to a specific toxic agent that is used to destroy specific cancer cells. Although experimental at present, these so-called magic bullets hold out great hope as a new form of cancer CHEMOTHERAPY.

impedance any resistance to the flow of fluids moved by a series of pulses, such as blood flow.

imperfect fungi see FUNGI IMPERFECTI.

implantation the act of attachment of the mammalian embryo to the uterus wall of the mother.

impressed sunk below surface level.

imprinting an aspect of learning in which there is rapid development of a response to a particular stimulus at an early stage of development. Young animals recognize the first object they see, such as a mother figure, and they can be imprinted on objects other than their own species. For example, Konrad LORENZ imprinted young graylag geese on himself as a mother figure. Imprinting also occurs in other areas of experience—for example, bird song, where young, inexperienced birds have adult calls imprinted on them.

inactive-X hypothesis or **Lyon hypothesis** an explanation for DO-SAGE COMPENSATION in the X-chromosomes of mammals, including humans, proposed by Mary Lyon. The main features of the hypothesis are that only one X-chromosome is active in a mature mammalian cell, all other X-chromosomes present having been inactivated during embryological development. Different X-chromosomes are thought to be inactivated in different cells, which may produce a MOSAIC phenotype in heterozygous individuals. BARR BODIES are thought to indicate the presence of inactive X-chromosomes.

inborn error of metabolism an inherited biochemical abnormality in humans due to enzymic deficiencies. The term was coined in the eraly 1900s by Archibald GARROD, who theorized that various conditions he had studied in hospital cases were due to defective enzymes, causing breakdown of biochemical pathways and buildup of intermediate chemicals in the body. Garrod's work was not recognized as important until the ONE GENE/ONE ENZYME HYPOTHESIS was proposed in the 1940s.

inbreeding any mating between relatives, which can lead to general lowering of viability due to accumulation of deleterious genes passed on through both parents from a common ancestor. Compare OUTBREEDING.

inbreeding depression a reduction in viability resulting from increased homozygosity through INBREEDING.

incisor a front, chisel-shaped tooth in mammals, normally used for cutting or gnawing. In some species incisors continue to grow throughout life. For example, gnawing rodents and rabbits have so-called persistent pulps, with the pulp cavity remaining open throughout life. In other species, the incisors are modified as tusks.

inclusion a particle or structure contained within a cell or organ.

inclusion body a body present in the nuclei or cytoplasm of cells infected by viruses or other intracellular parasites.

incompatibility see SELF-INCOMPATIBILITY.

incomplete dominance a pattern of inheritance in which a cross between two phenotypically different parents produces an offspring different from either parent but containing partial features of both. The classic instance cited is flower color. Crossing white and red parents, for example, produces a pink offspring. Compare CODOMINANCE. See also DOMINANCE (1).

in coupling see COUPLING.

incubation 1. the process of brooding or incubating in birds. 2. the period between infection by a pathogen and appearance of disease symptoms. 3. the maintenance of microbiological cultures at specific temperatures for a given time.

incurved (of plant structures) gradually bent inward.

incus or **anvil** the anvil-shaped bone of the middle EAR, the central bone of the three ear ossicles, situated between the MALLEUS and STAPES.

indehiscent (of a plant organ) not opening to release spores or seeds.

independent assortment the random arrangement and separation of chromosomes during MEIOSIS, giving all possible combinations in equal frequency, unlike the situation with GENETIC LINKAGE.

The process is important in understanding MENDELIAN GENETICS and explains the random distribution in the gametes of genes or non-homologous chromosomes. For example, take two pairs of HOMOLO-GOUS CHROMOSOMES in a DIPLOID (1) cell. During anaphase 1, there are two ways in which the chromosomes can become separated (see Fig. 190). Independent assortment of the chromosomes in the figure gives four types of possible gametes $(1 + 3)$, $(2 + 4)$, $(1 + 4)$, and $(2 + 3)$. In fact, the number of combinations is 2 to the power of the number of pairs of chromosomes, $2^2 = 4$ in the above example. A human with 23 pairs of chromosomes would produce $2^{23} = 8,388,608$ combinations by independent assortment alone.

Fig. 190. **Independent assortment.** Separation of chromosomes.

indicator community an association of species characteristic of particular conditions or habitats. For example, a range of CALCICOLE plants indicates a base rich soil.

indicator species any species indicative of particular conditions or habitats. For example, the leech *Erpobdella testacea* is found only in alkaline or polluted waters, the arrowworm *Sagitta setosa* is characteristic of continental shelf water, and *S. elegans* is characteristic of oceanic water.

indigenous native, not introduced by humans.

indirect selection the selection of mutant organisms (microorganisms) by determining those that do not grow on particular media.

individual variation the variation found in a population of the same species.

indolacetic acid see IAA.

inducer a small molecule that inactivates the repressor of an OPERON, usually binding to the repressor and so preventing the repressor from binding with the operator of the operon.

inducible enzyme an enzyme that is produced in response to presence of its substrate, the inducer. See OPERON MODEL.

induction 1. (in biochemistry) the synthesis of new enzyme molecules in response to a stimulus, usually another chemical. See OPERON MODEL. **2.** (in embryology) the formation of an alternative cell type during CELL DIFFERENTIATION under the influence of an inducer molecule. **3.** (in microbial genetics) the release of a PROPHAGE for the bacterial chromosome, initiated by, for example, ultraviolet light.

indumentum a total hairy covering.

indurated toughened and hardened.

indusium the covering of a sporangium or several sporangia.

industrial melanism a phenomenon found in several groups, notably moths, in which a heavily pigmented variant (a MORPH) becomes the most frequent type in an area with heavy, man-made atmospheric pollution. Melanism is an excellent example of MICROEVOLUTION, in that rapid evolutionary change has been brought about by strong forces of natural selection acting in favor of a dominant allele for melanism. The agents of selection against moths are birds, which seek out most heavily those types of moths that rest against an inappropriate background, for example, poorly pigmented forms resting on sooty tree trunks.

The proportion of melanics to nonmelanics in an area is correlated with the level of pollution, although neither type appears to be completely absent in any environment, creating a GENETIC POLYMORPHISM. See also KETTLEWELL.

infauna the burrowing portion of the BENTHOS.

infection the invasion of tissues by microorganisms with or without disease production.

infective hepatitis see HEPATITIS.

inferior ovary an ovary in which the perianth is inserted on top of the ovary, and which appears fused with the receptacle.

inflammation a local response to injury or damage, including dilation of blood vessels, and invasion of blood proteins, blood fluid, and LEUKOCYTES into the tissues to combat invading bacteria.

inflexed bent inward.

inflorescence a specialized branching stem bearing flowers, for example, a male CATKIN.

influenza an acute respiratory disease affecting the upper respiratory tract, with symptoms of fever, chills, and generalized aching, caused by a number of influenza viruses, particularly types A and B. Influenza outbreaks occur frequently and can have a worldwide distribution, often being associated with secondary bacterial complications. Over 20 million people died in the PANDEMIC outbreak of 1918—1919, principally young adults who may have been exposed previously to an unusually virulent form of virus.

information theory the study of the measurement and properties of codes and messages.

infra- *prefix* denoting below.

infrared the electromagnetic radiation in the region between red light and radio waves. See ELECTROMAGNETIC SPECTRUM.

infraspecific within a species.

infrasubspecific within a subspecies.

infundibulum the part of the PITUITARY GLAND that is produced by a downgrowth of the posterior region of the forebrain.

infusion the liquid extract of any substance that has been soaked in water.

infusoria any organisms found in INFUSIONS of organic material, such as Protozoa and Rotifers. The term is sometimes restricted to the CILIATES.

ingestion the act of taking food into the gut system, where it is then subjected to DIGESTION.

inheritance 1. the acquisition of characteristics by transfer of genetic material from ancestor to descendant. 2. the total of characters in the fertilized ovum.

inherited abnormality any genetically determined malfunction. These fall into two main types:

(a) Those controlled by single genes in which, for example, a biochemical process is disrupted by faulty enzymes coded by abnormal alleles, such as those causing ALBINISM (see also INBORN ERRORS OF METABOLISM). In other cases, such as SICKLE-CELL ANEMIA, a molecule is produced that does not function in the normal way.

(b) Those produced by chromosomal changes (see CHROMOSOMAL MUTATION). Here, loss or addition of parts or of whole chromosomes can have serious effects. Changes in autosomal chromosomes (see DOWN SYNDROME) often produce more severe effects than in sex chromosomes (see KLINEFELTER'S SYNDROME).

inhibiting factor see RELEASING FACTOR.

inhibition a state in which an enzyme is unable to catalyze reactions. See COMPETITIVE INHIBITION and NONCOMPETITIVE INHIBITION.

initial the cell or group of cells that differentiate to give rise to other tissues or organs, such as a MERISTEM.

initiation codon a triplet of bases in mRNA with the sequence AUG, which acts as a start signal for TRANSLATION, specifying the first amino acid at the N-terminus of the POLYPEPTIDE CHAIN. See GENETIC CODE.

ink sac a sac opening into the rectum of some CEPHALOPODS that, when stimulated, releases dark brown fluid, which acts as a smoke screen.

innate behavior any behavior exhibited by animals reared in isolation that appears to be inherited, and thus instinctive, in some interpretations of the meaning of this word. Innate behavior develops independently of any experience of the behavior in other animals. See INSTINCT, IMPRINTING.

innate reflex any behavioral response, such as a reflex action (see RE-FLEX ARC), that is automatic and not learned.

innervate 1. supply nerves to (a bodily organ or part). 2. stimulate (a body organ or part) with nerve impulses.

innominate 1. a short artery arising from the AORTA that gives rise to the subclavian and carotid arteries. 2. the fusion of ilium, ischium, and pubis to form a single bone forming half of the PELVIC GIRDLE.

inoculation the introduction of biological material (the *inoculum*) into a medium such as a living organism, synthetic substrate, or soil.

inoculum see INOCULATION.

inotropic affecting or controlling the strength of heart contractions. Chemicals that increase the force of contraction, for example, have a positive inotropic effect.

input load the quantity of inferior alleles in the gene pool resulting from mutation and immigration.

in repulsion see REPULSION.

insect any small air-breathing arthropod of the class Insecta, containing organisms that in the adult normally have six legs, three distinct regions to the body (head, thorax, and abdomen), one pair of antennae, and one or two pairs of wings.

Mouthparts are often adapted to the method of feeding, such as biting, piercing, and sucking (see Fig. 191).

Fig. 191. **Insect.** (a) Vertical section and (b) front view of insect mouthparts.

Abdominal appendages are absent except in the more primitive groups, such as springtails. Most insects have a distinct juvenile stage, a nymph (see EXOPTERYGOTA) or a larva (see ENDOPTERYGOTA). These undergo METAMORPHOSIS to form the adult. Insects comprise about five sixths of all known animal species. The class contains the following groups:

Subclass: APTERYGOTA (wingless)
Orders: Protura
         Collembola—springtails
         Diplura—japygids
         Thysanura—bristletails
Subclass: PTERYGOTA (normally winged)
         EXOPTERYGOTA (HETEROMETABOLA or HEMIMETABOLA)
Orders: Odonata—dragonflies
         Ephemeroptera—mayflies
         Orthoptera—grasshoppers
         Dermaptera—earwigs
         Plecoptera—stoneflies
         Isoptera—termites
         Embioptera—embiids
         Mallophaga—biting lice
         Anoplura—sucking lice
         Psocoptera—book lice
         Zoraptera
         Hemiptera—bugs
         Thysanoptera—thrips
         ENDOPTERYGOTA (HOLOMETABOLA)
         Mecoptera—scorpion flies
         Neuroptera—lacewings
         Trichoptera—caddisflies
         Lepidoptera—butterflies and moths
         Diptera—flies
         Siphonaptera—fleas
         Coleoptera—beetles
         Strepsiptera—stylops
         Hymenoptera—ants, bees, and wasps

The more important insect orders are described under separate headings.

insecticide any substance that is used to kill insects. See also PESTICIDE.

insecticide resistance the ability of a member of an insect population to withstand the toxic effects of an insecticide to the point where it now resists control with that chemical. The genes controlling resistance are thought to be present in low frequencies within a generally susceptible

population before application of the chemical. After treatment, susceptible members of the population are removed and the survivors thrive,
becoming common in the population, which then is described as resistant.

insectivore any member of the insect-eating mammalian order Insec-
tivora, a group comprising shrews, moles, and Old World hedgehogs.

insemination any means by which male sperm is introduced to the
female prior to FERTILIZATION. See ARTIFICIAL INSEMINATION.

insertion 1. a point of attachment of an organ, such as a leaf or muscle.
2. the point of application of force by a muscle.

insertion mutation a POINT MUTATION in which one or more bases are
inserted into DNA, causing a FRAMESHIFT reading error during TRANS-
LATION.

insight learning the production of a new and adaptive response as a
result of insight. For example, presented with a bunch of bananas that
is too high to reach, chimpanzees will pile up boxes or fit two sticks
together in order to get them.

inspiration see BREATHING.

inspiratory center see BREATHING.

instantaneous speciation the production of an individual or individuals reproductively isolated from their parents and capable themselves of
reproducing and establishing a new population.

instar a larval stage of insect development. The first instar hatches from
the egg and after the first molt (see ECDYSIS) becomes the second instar.
Thus, a third instar larva is one that has completed two molts.

instinct aspects of behavior that are not learned, but appear to be inherited, that is, appear to be INNATE BEHAVIOR. It is not now used commonly as a scientific term because of the difficulty of distinguishing
between some aspects of learning and some aspects of so-called instinctive behavior.

instinctive behavior any behavior pattern that is inherited and not
clearly learned.

insulin the hormone controlling the amount of blood sugar, which is
secreted by the beta cells of the ISLETS OF LANGERHANS in the pancreas.
Insulin has three targets: the liver, muscles, and adipose tissue, where
its action helps reduce the blood sugar level in the following ways:

(a) It stimulates absorption of glucose from the blood into muscle and
adipose cells by altering cell-wall permeability.

(b) It stimulates conversion of glucose into GLYCOGEN in the liver and
muscles, reducing the supply of free glucose.

(c) It promotes conversion of glucose into fats in the liver and adipose
cells (LIPOGENESIS).

(d) It inhibits GLUCONEOGENESIS.

(e) It promotes GLYCOLYSIS of glucose in all cells.

Underproduction of insulin causes diabetes, resulting in an increase in blood sugar (hyperglycemia) and sugar appearing in the urine (see GLYCOSURIA). The condition can be fatal if untreated, treatment being by injection of insulin into the bloodstream. The hormone cannot be taken orally as, being a protein, it would be digested. Insulin was discovered by BANTING and BEST in 1921. The control of blood sugar, in which a change in its level automatically brings about the opposite effect, is a good example of a negative FEEDBACK MECHANISM.

integrated control the use of chemical, biological, cultural, and legislative methods in a complementary way to control PESTS and PATHOGENS.

integration the insertion of DNA from one organism into the recipient chromosome of another.

integument 1. (in flowering plants) the covering of the central tissue (*nucellus*) of the OVULE that contains the EMBRYO SAC. Most flowering plants possess both an inner integument and an outer integument, which on hardening form the TESTA of the seed. 2. (in insects) the cuticle.

intelligence the ability to understand and create abstract ideas. Tests designed to measure intelligence are rather unreliable, since it is not possible to separate completely environmental influences, such as schooling and social background, from innate ability. Nevertheless, such tests are widely used, producing a measure called the intelligence quotient (I.Q.) which is:

$$\frac{\text{mental age}}{\text{actual age}} \times 100.$$

Thus, if some people have average mental ages for their age groups, they will have I.Q. scores of 100. The HERITABILITY of intelligence is thought to be between 0.5 and 0.7.

inter- *prefix* denoting between, among.

interbreed 1. breed within a single family or strain to produce particular characteristics in the offspring. 2. (also called **crossbreed**) breed using parents of different races or breeds.

intercellular fluid see INTERSTITIAL FLUID.

intercostal muscles the muscles lying between the ribs of vertebrates that, with the ribs, form the walls of the thorax. Contraction of external intercostal muscles brings about rib movement upward and outward, thus expanding the thoracic cavity, reducing thoracic pressure, and drawing air into the lungs. See BREATHING.

interfascicular cambium an area of meristematic tissue (see MERISTEM) in plant stems and roots, which develops from PARENCHYMA cells between the VASCULAR BUNDLES forming a complete ring of CAMBIUM and carries out rapid division to produce SECONDARY THICKENING.

interference see CHROMATID INTERFERENCE.

interferon a glycoprotein produced by cells in response to viral attack, whose function seems to be that of triggering *viral interference* defense mechanisms in uninfected cells of the same species in which it was produced. Since it has been suggested that interferon might prove effective against viral diseases by inhibiting viral multiplication, and even some forms of cancer, strenuous efforts have been made to isolate sufficient quantities with which to run clinical trials. The problem of production has now been solved by GENETIC ENGINEERING, but the results of trials so far are inconclusive.

intergranum see CHLOROPLAST.

interleukins a group of peptides that signal between cells involved in the immune system. See T-CELL.

internal clock see BIOLOGICAL CLOCK.

internal environment the medium in which all body cells are bathed and that maintains a constant environment (see HOMEOSTASIS), in terms of pH, osmotic pressure, and the like.

international code of zoological nomenclature the official regulations dealing with the scientific names and taxonomy of animals.

interneuron a connecting nerve cell between two others.

internode the portion of a stem found between two successive NODES.- See also BOLTING.

interoceptor a receptor that detects stimuli originating inside the body.

interpetiolar situated between the petioles.

interphase a stage of growth in the CELL CYCLE in which METABOLISM occurs without visible evidence of nuclear division.

interrenal bodies the endocrine organs that lie between the kidneys in fish and are homologous with the mammalian ADRENAL CORTEX.

interrupted gene a EUKARYOTEgene or one of its viruses consisting of sequences of INTRON and EXON segments.

intersex an individual with characteristics intermediate between those of a male and female.

interspecific behavior any act of behavior occurring between species.

interspecific competition any limited competition between two or more different species populations for a resource such as food. All populations involved are negatively affected by the competition and may exhibit increased mortality or decreased birthrate.

interstitial cells 1. any cells packing an area between other tissues. 2. See LEYDIG CELLS.

interstitial fluid or **intercellular fluid** a liquid, also called *lymph* when inside lymphatic vessels, bathing all the cells of the body, acting as a connecting link between blood and cells. An average human male with 42 liters of total body water would have about 7 liters of interstitial fluid.

interstitium the tissue space between cells.

intestine the part of the alimentary canal that lies between the stomach and anus. It is usually coiled, and the internal surface is greatly increased by the presence of folds and projections (*villi*) to enable efficient digestion and absorption. Anteriorly, the intestine is lined with an EPITHELIUM containing enzyme- and mucus-secreting glands, and in higher vertebrates it is referred to as the *small intestine*. The posterior, so-called *large intestine* dehydrates the feces that are stored there until voided in *defecation*.

intine the thin inner coat of a pollen grain, composed of cellulose.

intra- *prefix* denoting within.

intracellular within a cell.

intracellular tubules any tubules that occur within a cell, such as DRAINPIPE CELLS.

intrafusal fibers the muscle fibers within a MUSCLE SPINDLE.

intrapetiolar between the stem and the petiole in plants.

intraspecific within the species.

intraspecific competition any limited competition within the same species population for a resource, such as food. Not all members of the population may be negatively affected by the competition, resulting in differential ability to survive and reproduce (see FITNESS).

intravaginal 1. (of plants) inside the sheath. 2. (of animals) within the VAGINA.

introduced species one that does not naturally occur in the area and has been brought in accidentally or intentionally by man, for example, rabbits in Australia, which were introduced originally to the British Isles from Spain.

introgressive hybridization the spread of genes of one species into the germ plasma of another species as a result of hybridization.

intron a segment of DNA from EUKARYOTES, which is transcribed into mRNA but is then excised from the RNA, leaving behind the EXON sequences to be translated into polypeptide.

introrse (of a flower) opening to its middle.

intussusception the growth in the surface area of a cell wall by inclusion of additional particles in the wall.

inulin a complex polymer of FRUCTOSE that is soluble in water and occurs in the cell sap of such storage organs as dahlia TUBERS and dandelion TAP ROOTS.

invagination an inpushing of a layer of cells, as in GASTRULATION or in formation of the PROCTODEUM.

invasion the entry and colonization of a host by an organism.

inversion a CHROMOSOMAL MUTATION in which a segment becomes reversed and, although there is no loss or gain of genetic material, there may be a positive or negative POSITION EFFECT on the phenotype.

invertase see SUCRASE.

invertebrate any animal that does not possess a backbone.

in vitro (of biological processes or reactions) made to occur outside the body of an organism in an artificial environment (vitro = glass). For example, fertilization of human eggs in vitro is accomplished in the laboratory prior to reimplantation in the mother. Compare IN VIVO.

in vivo (of biological processes or experiments) occurring in the living organism. Compare IN VITRO.

involucre 1. a calyxlike structure formed by bracts below the base of a condensed INFLORESCENCE. 2. a growth of the tissue of the thallus in liverworts (see HEPATICA) that covers and protects the ARCHEGONIUM.

involuntary muscle or **visceral muscle** or **smooth muscle** a type of muscle termed involuntary because it is innervated by the AUTONOMIC NERVOUS SYSTEM. It is also termed visceral because it is found in the alimentary canal, the blood vessels, CILIARY BODY, respiratory passages, and URINOGENITAL SYSTEM. It is also called smooth because the MYOFIBRILS lack striations. Involuntary muscle contracts slowly and takes a long time to fatigue. Compare STRIATED MUSCLE.

involuntary response a reaction of INVOLUNTARY MUSCLE brought about by mechanisms not under the control of will.

involution (of plant organs) having rolled-up margins.

iodopsin a photochemical pigment thought to be of three types found in the CONES of the retina of the eye. It is not readily bleached even by high-intensity light. See also RHODOPSIN.

ion an atom that carries a charge due to loss or gain of electrons.

ionic bond an electrostatic bond.

ionizing radiation a beam of short-wavelength electromagnetic energy that can penetrate deeply into tissues, leaving a track of unstable atoms that have lost electrons (IONS). Such radiations, X-rays and gamma rays, are powerful MUTAGENS.

iris the pigmented part of the vertebrate eye. It consists of a thin sheet of tissue, attached at its outer edge to the CILIARY BODY, which has radiating muscles that can increase the size of the central pupil and a central ring of muscle around the pupil that, on contraction, causes a decrease in its size. The iris thus regulates the amount of light entering the eye. See ALBINISM for photophobia.

irreversibility see DOLLO'S LAW OF IRREVERSIBILITY.

irrigation moistening or pouring water over a preparation.

irritability the responsiveness of organisms to changes in their immediate environment.

ischium the ventral bone of the PELVIC GIRDLE in vertebrates, bearing the weight of a sitting human.

islets of Langerhans a group of cells found scattered in the pancreas of jawed vertebrates that secretes the hormones INSULIN and GLUCAGON. Named after the German histologist P. Langerhans.

iso- *combining form* denoting equal.

isoalleles alleles with so little phenotypic expression that special techniques are necessary to demonstrate their presence.

isobilateral having a similar structure on each side, as in the leaf of a monocotyledon.

isoelectric focusing the separation of molecules by differences in their charge, each molecule migrating to the point in a PH gradient where it has no net charge.

isoelectric point the PH of an AMPHOTERIC solution when at electrical neutrality, the ionic state of an AMINO ACID at the isoelectric point being a ZWITTERION.

isogamete a GAMETE that is usually motile and appears similar to the gamete with which it unites at fertilization. Such sexual reproduction, called *isogamy*, occurs in several primitive plant groups, for example, many ALGAE.

isogamy see ISOGAMETE.

isogenic having an identical set of genes.

isograft a transplant from one individual to a closely related individual of the same genotype, such as those between MONOZYGOTIC TWINS, or between members of the same inbred line, as in rodents.

isohyet a line drawn on a map connecting places with the same rainfall.

isolate 1. to separate a microorganism from fresh material and establish it in pure culture. 2. a single pure culture of a microorganism.

isolation 1. any geographical separation from other populations of the same organism. 2. a form of genetic isolation, in which gene transfer is limited or entirely prevented by geographical separation. Such isolation can be termed behavioral, ecological, seasonal (different breeding seasons), and physiological. The prevention of gene transfer results in new lines of EVOLUTION.

isolating barrier any structure that limits the movement of organisms to the extent of preventing gene flow. Examples include oceans, deserts, mountain ranges, salinity, and temperature.

isolating mechanism any mechanism preventing successful breeding between two populations.

isoleucine one of 20 AMINO ACIDS common in proteins. It is nonpolar in structure and insoluble in water. The ISOELECTRIC POINT of isoleucine is 6.0. See Fig 192.

Fig. 192. **Isoleucine.** Molecular structure.

isomerase a group of enzymes that convert organic compounds from D- to L-, or L- to D- forms.

isomerism the phenomenon of two chemical compounds having the same formula but a different arrangement of atoms.

isomerous (of plants) having the same number of parts in different floral whorls, such as a plant possessing five stamens and five carpels.

isomorphic (of organisms, usually plants) having morphologically similar forms in different parts of the life history, for example, where there is ALTERNATION OF GENERATIONS in which the generations are similar.

isopod any crustacean of the order Isopoda, containing the wood lice and pill bugs.

Isoptera the insect order containing the termites, which live in colonies and have a complex system of castes.

isosmotic (of two solutions) having the same OSMOTIC PRESSURE.

isospore see ASEXUAL SPORE.

isostatic (of Earth's crust) movements resulting in sea level changes caused by ice loading from glacier formation during the Ice Age.

isotonic (of a liquid) having a fluid state with the same WATER POTENTIAL as another liquid. See HYPOTONIC and Fig. 187.

isotope any of the forms of an element having the same number of protons (atomic number) but a different number of neutrons (atomic mass). Some isotopes of an element may be *radioisotopes* (for example, ^{12}C is not radioactive, while ^{14}C is) and yet can function normally in

ISOZYME

biological material. Isotopes can thus be tagged, using suitable detection devices, such as Geiger counters, as biochemical processes occur. See HALF-LIFE, AUTORADIOGRAPH.

isozyme or **isoenzyme** one of several forms of an enzyme found in an individual or a population, each form coded by a different allele of a gene. An isozyme is a type of ALLOZYME.

iter (inter a tertio ad quartum ventriculum) the passage between the third and fourth ventricles of the vertebrate brain.

IUD (intrauterine device) any device, such as a coil, that is introduced into the female uterus as a means of preventing either fertilization of the egg or implantation of the embryo. See BIRTH CONTROL.

J

Jacob-Monod hypothesis see OPERON MODEL.

Java man a primitive form of human, *Homo erectus.*

jaw the mandibles of any animal. The term is usually restricted to the bones surrounding the mouth of vertebrates, the upper jaws being referred to as the *maxillae* and the lower as the *mandible*. These bones carry the teeth where present and are often used for crushing purposes.

jaw articulation the joint of the bones forming the skeleton surrounding the mouth of vertebrates, between the upper jaw (maxilla) and lower jaw (mandible).

jejunum a part of the SMALL INTESTINE between the duodenum and the ileum.

jellyfish 1. any large medusa of the class Scyphozoa. 2. the medusoid stages of any coelenterate.

Jenner, Edward (1749—1823) English physician who discovered that cowpox lymph matter could be safely used as an inoculum, or VACCINE, to prevent smallpox. The first vaccination was carried out in 1796.

Johannsen, Wilhelm (1857—1927) Danish botanist who, in the early 1900s, carried out selection experiments with beans (*Phaseolus vulgaris*), which showed selection to be a passive process that eliminates, but does not produce, variations. Johannsen is, however, chiefly remembered for coining the terms GENE, GENOTYPE, and PHENOTYPE.

Johnston's organ an organ situated at the base of the insect antenna consisting of a group of CHORDOTONAL RECEPTORS, probably associated with movement of the antenna. Named for C. Johnston, American physician, who died in 1891.

joint or **articulation** a contact between two separate bones.

joule an SI unit of energy equal to 10^7 ergs or 0.239 cals. Named for the physicist J.P. Joule (1818—1889) who determined the mechanical equivalent of heat and showed that 4.2×10^7 ergs = 1 calorie (4.2 joules = 1 calorie).

jugular of or relating to the throat or neck, particularly the jugular veins, internal and external, which carry blood from the head to the anterior vena cava and hence to the heart.

junior homonym the more recently published of two or more identical names for the same or different taxa.

junior synonym the more recently published of two or more synonyms for the same taxon.

Jurassic period a period of the MESOZOIC ERA that extended from 200 to 135 million years ago, during which time the birds evolved. Cycads, ferns, and conifers were widespread. Dinosaurs were dominant, and the earliest fossil moth recorded dates from this period. *Pangaea* began to break up.

juvenile hormone a hormone present in juvenile insects and secreted by the CORPUS ALLATUM of the brain. As long as it is produced, the cuticle maintains the characteristics of the nymphal or larval form at each molt. Only when it ceases to be present or the level falls below a threshold value does the insect molt to the adult form. Juvenile hormones have been used as an effective means of controlling insects, for example, in preventing development of adult ants during hospital infestations.

juxta-glomerular complex a group of cells lining the efferent glomerular vessels of the kidney that detect changes in blood volume. The cells secrete the enzyme RENIN when blood volume decreases, with subsequent release of ALDOSTERONE from the adrenal cortex, resulting in increased sodium retention. When the blood osmotic concentration increases, release of ADH occurs, and both these factors reverse the decrease in blood volume, an example of a FEEDBACK MECHANISM.

K

K a symbol indicating the maximum number of individuals in the LOTKA-Volterra equations.

K selection selection proceeding in such a way as to maximize K and reduce R, thus optimizing the use of environmental resources without expending excess energy in converting food into offspring.

kappa particles the bacteria that inhabit the cytoplasm of the ciliate *Paramecium aurelia*. Kappa-free Paramecia are sensitive to toxins produced by the particles and die when exposed to them, after CONJUGATION. Kappa carriers, called *killer stocks*, are immune to the toxin.

karyo- *combining form* denoting nucleus of a cell.

karyokinesis the division of the cell nucleus.

karyological of or relating to the structure or number of chromosomes.

karyoplast a nucleus surrounded by a thin layer of cytoplasm and membrane.

karyopsis an ACHENE in which the ovary wall and seed coat are united.

karyosome a chromatin aggregation in the resting nucleus.

karyotype the CHROMOSOME complement of a cell or organism, characterized by the number, size, and configuration of the chromosomes as seen during metaphase of MITOSIS.

keel see CARINA.

kelp a large, coarse seaweed.

Kelvin scale an absolute scale of temperature in which a range of 1° kelvin (K) is equal to a range of 1°C. 0°K = −273.15°C or −459.67°F.

keratin a hard, fibrous, sulfur-containing protein with an alpha-helix structure, found in the epidermis of vertebrates, mainly in the outermost layers of skin. Keratin can have several forms: in scales, feathers, hooves, horns, claws, and nails it is hard; in wool and hair it is soft and flexible.

ketone an organic molecule in which a C = O group is contained within the molecule rather than at one end. Ketones are highly varied in structure, ranging from the simple *acetone* (see Fig. 193) to FRUCTOSE, a KETOSE sugar.

Fig. 193. **Ketone.** The molecular structure of acetone.

ketose a MONOSACCHARIDE with a ketonic structure (see KETONE).

Kettlewell, H.B.D British biologist who in the mid-1950s carried out a series of elegant field and laboratory experiments using light-colored and melanic forms of the peppered moth *Biston betularia*. He was able to show that the selective forces operating against the moths were due to visual predation by birds, which attacked preferentially those forms resting on a noncryptic background. See also INDUSTRIAL MELANISM.

key a character of special significance in an organism. Such characters are used in a system for determining the identity of an organism on the basis of the presence or absence of a succession of characters. Such keys usually are DICHOTOMOUS (2), that is, at each step there is a choice between two possibilities. Keys may have more than two characters at each step, however, and there is a gradual elimination of absent characters until identification is made.

kidney an organ, found in pairs in a dorsal situation in vertebrates, that serves the dual purposes of EXCRETION and OSMOREGULATION. See Fig. 194. Ultrafiltration takes place in the glomerulus, where the glomerular filtrate contains all constituents of blood except for blood cells and plasma proteins. Pores of about 0.1 μm diameter allow passage of the filtrate under pressure caused because the efferent blood vessels from the glomerulus are narrower than the afferent vessels. The filtrate is modified in its flow along the tubule and eventually emerges from the kidney as urine.

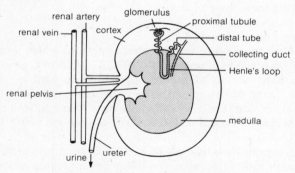

Fig. 194. **Kidney.** General structure.

The LOOP OF HENLE employs the principle of a hairpin COUNTER-CURRENT MULTIPLIER. Active transfer of salt (NaCl) takes place from the ascending limb to the descending limb, thus raising the concentration in the latter. This results in a region of high salt concentration deep in the medulla of the kidney through which the collecting duct passes.

Water is extracted by osmosis from the *distal-convoluted tubule* and collecting duct, thus concentrating the urine (see ADH). Over 99% of kidney fluid is reabsorbed in this way by the kidney tubules. See NEPHRON.

kinase an enzyme that catalyzes the transfer of a phosphoryl group from ATP to another compound.

kinesis any orientation behavior in which the organism does not move in a particular direction relative to the stimulus, but instead moves at an increasing or decreasing rate until it ends up nearer or farther from the stimulus. For example, when a woodlouse finds itself drying out, it begins to move about a great deal until it encounters a moist spot, where it may settle. Compare TAXIS.

kinesthetic capable of detecting movements, as in the sense organs of muscles, tendons, and joints.

kinetin see CYTOKININ.

kineto- *combining form* denoting movement, movable, *or* moving.

kinetochore see CENTROMERE.

kinetodesmata the threads connecting KINETOSOMES in ciliates.

kinetoplast see KINETOSOME.

kinetosome or **kinetoplast** the BASAL BODY of a CILIUM.

kingdom the highest grouping (taxon) in biological classification. See ANIMAL KINGDOM, PLANT KINGDOM.

kinin *see* CYTOKININ.

kinomere a spindle attachment in the region of a chromosome.

kin selection a form of selection favoring altruistic (self-sacrificing) behavior toward relatives. Such a process ensures that even if the chances of an individual surviving are reduced, some of his or her genes will survive in the relative.

Klinefelter's syndrome a human chromosomal abnormality in which there is an extra X chromosome, making a complement of 44 autosomes plus XXY (47 in all). The affected individuals are male, showing the SEX DETERMINATION role of the Y chromosomes, but with much reduced fertility, and a number of female secondary sexual characteristics, such as breasts, often occur. About 1 in 1000 liveborn males are affected by this condition, which arises from NONDISJUNCTION in one or other parent, more probably the female where there is a distinct positive age effect, as in DOWN SYNDROME.

klinostat see CLINOSTAT.

klinotactic response a positive orientation movement of an organism, resulting from a stimulus.

knockdown a measure of biocide effect that is used when it is difficult to assess actual mortality. The measure, used particularly in biocide tests on insects, has been shown to produce results similar to actual mortality counts. Knockdown is often measured as the inability to respond to a stimulus such as light or touch. See KNOCKDOWN LINE.

knockdown line a graphical representation of the rate of response to a biocide as measured by KNOCKDOWN (y-axis) against time or dose (x-axis). Strains of organisms such as insects are characterized by the slope and position of their knockdown lines relative to other strains.

Koch, Robert (1843—1910) German bacteriologist who first introduced the method of making bacterial smears and fixing them with heat. He worked on bubonic plague and sleeping sickness and discovered how they are transmitted. He also developed means of culturing bacteria and rules for properly identifying the agents of various diseases. He is most famous for establishing a series of criteria necessary to establish whether a specific microorganism causes a specific disease. These criteria are known as *Koch's Postulates:*

(a) The microorganisms must be present in every case of the disease.

(b) The microorganisms must be isolated from the diseased organism and grown in culture.

(c) The disease must be reproduced when a pure culture is reintroduced to a nondiseased, susceptible host.

(d) The microorganism must be recoverable from the experimentally infected host.

Kranz anatomy the special structure of leaves in C4 PLANTS, for example, corn, in which the tissue equivalent to the spongy mesophyll cells is clustered in a ring around the leaf veins, outside the bundle-sheath cells. (*Kranz* means wreath or ring in German). The bundle-sheath cells contain large CHLOROPLASTS, whereas the spongy mesophyll cells have few if any chloroplasts, unlike their counterparts in C3 plants (see MESOPHYLL). See Fig. 195.

Fig. 195. **Kranz anatomy.** Transverse section through leaf.

Krebs cycle or **tricarboxylic acid cycle (TCA cycle)** or formerly **citric-acid cycle** a circular series of reactions occurring in the matrix of MITOCHONDRIA and forming part of CELL RESPIRATION in the presence of oxygen. The steps of the cycle were deduced by Sir Hans Krebs (1900—1981), for which he received a Nobel Prize. The reactions leading up to the cycle by which ACETYLCOENZYME A is produced, together with the overall role of the cycle in the breakdown of complex molecules, are described fully under AEROBIC RESPIRATION.

Each turn of the cycle releases 2 molecules of carbon dioxide, 8 hydrogen atoms that produce 11 molecules of ATP via the ELECTRON TRANSPORT SYSTEM, and 1 molecule of ATP produced by SUBSTRATE-LEVEL PHOSPHORYLATION. Two turns of the cycle are needed to complete the breakdown of one glucose molecule. See Fig. 196.

Fig. 196. **Krebs cycle.** The major steps of the Krebs cycle.

krill see EUPHAUSIID.

Kupffer cells the phagocytic cells that form part of the RETICULOENDO-THELIAL SYSTEM, destroying old red blood cells and removing foreign particles from blood flowing through the liver. Named for the German anatomist K. Kupffer.

kwashiorkor the most widespread and serious human nutritional disease, brought on by acute protein starvation. The condition is characterized by apathy, impaired growth, skin ulcers, swollen hands and feet, and enlarged liver. If untreated, it is fatal. Kwashiorkor typically affects children in the early stages after weaning.

kymograph the revolving drum used in investigating the physiology of nerves and muscles. Usually, it is capable of rotating at different known speeds and carries graph paper on which a trace is produced by a lever connected to the physiological preparation.

L

label any marker, often a radioactive atom, that makes it possible to locate and monitor a particular molecule or organism.

labella (*pl.* labellae) an oral lobe present on the distal end of the insect proboscis. Labellae are purely sensory in the mosquito, but are modified for sucking up fluids by means of pseudotrachaea in the blowfly.

labio- *combining form* denoting lip.

labium (*pl.* labia) the lower lip of insects, lying immediately behind the maxillae. The labium is formed by fusion of paired appendages underneath the rear of the head. See Fig. 191.

labrum a cuticular plate at the front of the insect head, forming an upper lip. The labrum lies immediately below the clypeus, with which it is hinged, and in front of the MANDIBLES. See Fig. 191.

labyrinth, membranous see EAR.

labyrinthodont any primitive amphibians of the order Labyrinthodontia, which existed from the Devonian to the Triassic. They are related to Crossopterygian fish, and some are close to the reptiles.

Labyrinthulales a group of aquatic, mainly marine organisms that secrete slimy filaments in the form of a net plasmodium over which cells can glide. The group is a member of the slime molds, Myxomycophyta.

lacerate having the appearance of being torn.

lacertilian any reptile of the suborder Lacertilia, containing the lizards.

lachrymal gland the tear gland that lies below the upper eyelid of mammals and serves to moisten and cleanse the surface of the eye by secreting sterile and antiseptic liquid. Excess fluid is drained away through the lachrymal duct in the corner of the eye, which leads eventually into the nasal cavity.

lac-operon the genetic system of *E. coli* that is required to metabolize lactose and on which the OPERON MODEL is based.

lactase an enzyme that splits the disaccharide LACTOSE into galactose and glucose, secreted as part of the intestinal juice by glands in the SMALL INTESTINE wall. Lactase is also produced in ENZYME INDUCTION by bacteria (see OPERON MODEL).

lactation the production of milk by the adult female mammal from the mammary gland, with which it suckles its young. Lactation is induced by LUTEOTROPIC HORMONES from the anterior PITUITARY GLAND.

lacteals the central lymph vessels in the villi of the vertebrate intestine into which neutral fat is passed from the columnar epithelium, where it has been resynthesized from fatty acids and glycerol. The fat is in the form of a white emulsion of minute globules, giving lymph a milky, or lacteal, appearance. The fat is carried to all parts of the body.

lactic acid an organic acid ($CH_3CH(OH)COOH$) produced from pyruvic acid as a result of ANAEROBIC RESPIRATION in microorganisms (see LACTOSE) and in the active muscles of animals (see OXYGEN DEBT), the hydrogenation of pyruvate being catalyzed by lactic dehydrogenase (LDH). In animals the acid can be oxidized back to pyruvate, using LDH again when sufficient oxygen is available. Most of the conversion takes place in the liver.

lactogenesis the production of milk.

lactogenic hormone see LUTEOTROPIC HORMONE.

lactose or **milk sugar** a DISACCHARIDE carbohydrate found in the milk of mammals. Lactose is produced by CONDENSATION REACTION between galactose and glucose. See Fig. 197.

Fig. 197. **Lactose.** The condensation reaction between galactose and glucose.

The sugar can be broken into its component monosaccharides by LACTASE. Souring of milk is due to conversion of lactose to LACTIC ACID by microorganisms present in milk.

lactose synthetase an enzyme that catalyzes the synthesis of lactose from glucose.

lacuna one of many small spaces between the lamellae of bones that are occupied by individual bone cells. Small canals (*canaliculi*) radiate from the lacunae and in these are small protoplasmic processes that connect with the osteoblasts in other lacunae. See HAVERSIAN CANAL.

lacunate divided into narrow segments in a deep and irregular manner.

lag phase 1. the stage of growth of microbial cells in which nucleic acids and proteins are synthesized, but in which there is no cell division. **2.** an adaption stage. See GROWTH CURVE

Lamarck, Jean-Baptiste Pierre Antoine de Monet (1744—1829) French naturalist best known for his theory of inheritance of acquired characters (see LAMARCKISM). While this theory is now generally discredited, Lamarck deserves recognition for being effectively the founder of modern invertebrate zoology. He was one of the first true scientists to give real consideration to the evolutionary development of life.

Lamarckism the theory of inheritance of ACQUIRED CHARACTERS, which suggests that the structures developed through use during the lifetime of an organism are passed on as inherited characters to the next generation. Evolutionary change might thus be achieved through transmission of these acquired characters.

This theory, proposed by Jean Baptiste de LAMARCK, is now generally discounted in favor of DARWINISM, in which favored characters of utility to a particular organism are maintained by selection, whereas unfavorable characters are selected out. Thus, Lamarck might have claimed that blacksmith's sons were brawny because of their father's profession, whereas Darwin would have said that the reason why the father was a blacksmith was that he was brawny, and brawny men tend to have brawny offspring. LYSENKO attempted unsuccessfully to apply Lamarckian theory to the development of crop plants in the USSR in the 1930s.

lambda phage a TEMPERATE PHAGE of *E. coli*.

lamella or **thylakoid** a thin layer or plate. The term is used in the plural (*lamellae*) for:

(a) the sheetlike membranes that occur within the CHLOROPLAST, each of which consists of a pair of membranes with a narrow space between. Some 3000 occur in each chloroplast, and their function is to maintain the CHLOROPHYLL molecules within the quantasomes in such a position as to receive the maximum amount of light.

(b) the gills of a basidiomycete fungus that radiate out from the stalk beneath the cap of the fruit and bear the spores.

(c) the layers in which the calcified matrix of bone occurs, each about 5 μm thick.

lamelli- *combining form* denoting lamella.

lamellibranch see BIVALVE.

lamina a thin, flat structure such as a leaf or petal.

lampbrush chromosomes the giant chromosomes in vertebrate oocytes, mainly amphibians, that have hairlike lateral extensions in the form of loops with a DNA core.

lamprey a jawless fish of the class AGNATHA.

lamp shell see BRACHIOPOD.

lanceolate (of plant structures) tapering to a point.

Landsteiner, Karl (1868—1943) Austrian pathologist who migrated to the United States, where he spent most of his career working on human blood groups. In 1901 he found that all humans could be divided into one of four ABO BLOOD GROUPS. In 1928 he and Philip Levine discovered another set of blood antigens, which came to be called the MN group, and in 1940 Landsteiner and Weiner found the Rhesus factor (see

RHESUS BLOOD GROUP), important in hemolytic disease of the newborn (see RHESUS HEMOLYTIC ANEMIA).

languets small tonguelike processes.

lanugo the hair on the human embryo that is lost before birth.

lapsus calami a slip of the pen, particularly a spelling error in nomenclature.

large intestine see COLON.

larva (*pl.* larvae) the preadult form of many animals, usually morphologically different from the adult and which in many cases takes up the larger part of the life history. The larva usually is not sexually mature, but in cases of PEDOGENESIS, of which the AXOLOTL is an example, breeding may take place at this stage. Often the larva is a dispersal phase, as in many marine invertebrates among which larvae occur in the PLANKTON and the larvae usually feed in a different manner than do adults and so do not compete.

larynx a dilation of the upper part of the TRACHEA of TETRAPODS (Adam's apple in humans), occurring in the front part of the neck. It is triangular in shape with base uppermost and is made up of nine cartilages moved by muscles. It contains the vocal cords, which are elastic ligaments embedded in two folds of mucous membrane.

Lassa virus a highly contagious virus first isolated in 1969 in Nigeria, which can cause a general malaise leading to severe chest infections and even death.

latent infection an infection that does not produce visible signs of a disease, but may be transmitted to another host.

latent period or **reaction time** the first period of a simple muscle contraction, being the interval between the stimulus being applied and the contraction occurring, usually about 0.01 second. See Fig. 198.

lateral at the side of.

lateral inhibition the reciprocal suppression of excitation brought about by neighboring neurons of a sensory network.

lateral-line system or **acoustico-lateralis system** a complex system of receptors found in fishes and amphibians, occurring in a line along the length of the body and in a complex pattern on the head. The receptors occur in pores or canals and can detect small changes in pressure in the surrounding medium, such as vibrations. When the animal is moving, impulses from efferent nerve fibers to the receptors prevent the latter from responding, so they do not react to the animal's own movement. The inner ear of vertebrates is thought to have evolved from a receptor of the lateral-line system.

lateral meristem see CAMBIUM.

Fig. 198. **Latent period.** A KYMOGRAPH tracing of the twitch of a frog's gastrocnemius muscle.

lateral plate the mesoderm in the ventrolateral position in the vertebrate embryo.

lateral root or **secondary root** the branches that develop from deep inside the plant root (that is, they are ENDOGENOUS), where cells of the PERICYCLE become meristematic (see MERISTEM) and produce a growing point that differentiates into mature tissues. Such branching occurs behind the root hair zone and is initiated by AUXIN.

latex a milky plant juice.

latiseptate having a septum across the widest diameter, as on some fruits.

Laurasia the northern supercontinent of the MESOZOIC ERA, including North America, Greenland, and Eurasia. PANGAEA gave rise to Laurasia and in the south GONDWANA. See also CONTINENTAL DRIFT.

law of mass action a law stating that the rate of progression of a chemical reaction is proportional to the concentration of the reactants.

LD$_{50}$ see LETHAL DOSE.

leaching the process by which nutrients are removed from the soil by percolation of water through it.

leader region a region of DNA between the promoter region and the structural genes in a bacterial operon (see OPERON MODEL). The leader sequence is not translated into protein and may contain an ATTENUATOR.

leaf the principal photosynthetic organ of vascular plants, which typically consists of a flattened lamina joined to the stem by a stalk, or petiole, at which junction an axillary bud can be found. There are numerous types of leaves.

    (a) *dorsiventral* leaves are held horizontally with the upper half of the lamina containing the majority of photosynthetic cells (see MESOPHYLL for diagram). Typically, the lower epidermis contains the majority of STOMATA through which gas exchange and transpiration take place. Leaf veins are usually arranged in a net venation with principal veins called *midribs*. The lamina can be indented to form a compound leaf or remain as a simple structure. See Fig. 199. Dorsiventral leaves are typical of DICOTYLEDONS.

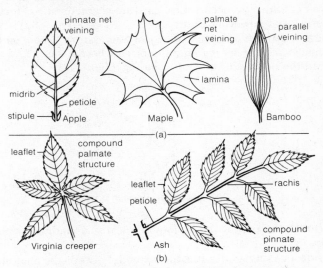

Fig. 199. **Leaf.** (a) Simple leaves. (b) Compound leaves.

(b) *isobilateral* leaves grow erectly with a swordlike shape and are typical of MONOCOTYLEDONS. Both epidermal surfaces contain stomata with palisade mesophyll tissue packed underneath. Isobilateral leaves have a parallel venation and are not divided into compound structures. See also KRANZ ANATOMY.

(c) *centric* leaves are more or less cylindrical, with a central region containing the vascular bundles surrounded by mesophyll tissue. Examples are onion leaves and pine needles.

Some leaves have special modifications. For example, water storage leaves are found in many plants living in dry conditions, for example, cacti. In other plants the leaves are modified into tendrils for climbing (for example, the pea), while in some the leaves have become spines (for example, gorse).

LEAF-AREA DURATION

leaf-area duration the LEAF-AREA INDEX over a period of time. Due to the leaf-area duration changing with time, it is proportional to the area under the line in a graph of leaf-area index plotted against time.

leaf-area index the total area of leaves (one side) in relation to the ground area below them.

leaf blade the part of the leaf in which photosynthesis takes place.

leaf gap the region of the vascular cylinder above the LEAF TRACE where PARENCHYMA occurs. Leaf gaps are characteristic of ferns, gymnosperms, and flowering plants.

leaf scar a scar left on a stem after leaf ABSCISSION. Visible on the scar are smaller scars, each marking the place where a VASCULAR BUNDLE entered the petiole of the LEAF. See Fig. 200.

Fig. 200. **Leaf scar.** Position on stem.

leaf sheath the part at the bottom of a leaf surrounding a stem, as in grasses.

leaf trace a VASCULAR BUNDLE that extends between the main stem and the leaf base.

learning an adaptive change in behavior resulting from experience. Learned behavior is distinct from innate BEHAVIOR and may begin in the embryo. For example, a chick learns to peck because the heartbeat moves the head forward and causes the bill to open. Learning has been classified by the English behaviorist W.H. Thorpe (born 1902) as follows:

(a) *habituation,* in which an animal is subject to repeated stimulation and may cease to respond.

(b) *classical conditioning* resulting in a CONDITIONED REFLEX action.

(c) *trial-and-error learning,* as in rats learning to follow the correct route through a maze.

(d) *latent learning,* as in rats being allowed to run a maze without a final reward. When given a reward later, the rats' performance rapidly reaches that of rats rewarded throughout, so they must have learned something (latently) during the nonreward period.

It must be stressed that these categories overlap and that other classifications of learning are also accepted.

lecithin any of a group of phospholipids, composed of choline, phosphoric acid, fatty acids, and glycerol, found in animal and plant tissues.

lectotype one of a series of SYNTYPES used by the taxonomist when a organism was named, and which was subsequently designated the TYPE.

leech an aquatic annelid of the order Hirudinea.

legionnaires' disease a rare human pneumonial condition, caused by the bacterium *Legionella pneumophila,* that can lead to death. The disease was named after an outbreak at an American Legion convention in a Philadelphia hotel in 1976, the bacteria eventually being traced to the air-conditioning plant of the hotel. A number of cases have been reported since then in connection with recirculating water systems. There is no evidence of person-to-person transmission.

legume any member of the pea family (Leguminosae). These plants have fruits that are pods containing one or more seeds, for example, pea, bean, lupin, and laburnum. Most legumes have root nodules and so can grow in soils deficient in nitrogen (see NITROGEN FIXATION).

leishmaniasis a human disease caused by infection with the protozoan flagellate *Leishmania.* There are several forms of leishmaniasis. A major type found in tropical and subtropical areas is called *cutaneous* in which severe pimpling and ulceration can cover face, arms, and legs. Another species of *Leishmania* causes a lethal *visceral* form of the disease in Africa and Asia, in which infection of the spleen, liver, and other organs occurs, producing symptoms of kala-azar and dumdum fever.

lemma a grass bract with the appearance of a GLUME and bearing a flower in its axil.

lemur a primitive primate that is arboreal and nocturnal. Lemurs are Old World forms with opposable thumbs, prehensile tail, and stereoscopic vision.

lens a transparent body at the front of the vertebrate eye, the main function of which is ACCOMMODATION and *not* refraction, though the latter does take place. The CORNEA is the most important refractive structure.

lentic of or relating to standing waters, such as ponds, lakes, and reservoirs, rather than moving waters, such as rivers and streams.

lenticel a small pore found on the surface of stems and roots in higher plants. Lenticels usually arise below the STOMATA of the original epidermis, where loose packing tissue becomes waterproofed with SUBERIN, leaving large intercellular spaces through which gas exchange can take place. Lenticels are surrounded by a CORK layer. See Fig. 201.

Fig. 201. **Lenticel.** Transverse section of the outer stem.

lenticular having the appearance of a double convex lens, circular in outline, convex on both sides.

lepido- *combining form* denoting scale.

Lepidodendron an extinct genus of treelike giant club moss of the class Lycopodiopsida.

Lepidoptera the ENDOPTERYGOTE order of insects containing butterflies and moths, characterized by the presence of scales on the wings and body. Butterflies and moths are no longer classed as separate taxa. The larvae are caterpillars, which feed mainly on plant tissues. The winged adults are usually nectar feeders and are important in pollination. See Fig. 202.

Fig. 202. **Lepidoptera.** General structure.

Lepidosiren a genus of South American lungfish that differs from the Australian lungfish by having two lungs rather than one.

leprosy a chronic disease characterized by mutilating and disfiguring lesions, with loss of sensation in fingers and toes, caused by infection with the bacterium *Mycobacterium leprae*. Although leprosy is not highly contagious, about 3 million people are affected worldwide, the condition being transmitted by contact between an affected area in the donor and skin abrasion in the recipient. Therapy with sulfone drugs over long periods can produce gradual improvement.

lepto- *combining form* denoting thin, slight.

leptocephalus the transparent oceanic larva of eels of the genus *Anguilla*, which crosses the Atlantic and becomes adult in fresh water on the European continent.

leptosporangiate derived from a single cell and having a wall one cell thick.

leptotene the first stage of PROPHASE I of MEIOSIS, in which each chromosome resembles a thin thread as it emerges from INTERPHASE. The chromosomes have divided into CHROMATIDS but these are not usually visible at this stage.

lesion a localized area of diseased tissue.

lethal allele or **lethal mutation** a mutant allele causing premature death in heterozygotes if dominant and in homozygotes if recessive.

lethal dose (LD) the amount of a treatment, for example, viral inoculation or insecticide, that induces death in a laboratory animal in a standard time. Because the response to treatment is often nonlinear, it is more conventional to measure the amount of a treatment that causes 50% mortality in a standard time, the so-called LD_{50}. In some tests the treatment dosage is fixed and the duration of the treatment period is varied, producing an estimate of lethal time and an LT_{50}.

lethal gene a gene whose effect on the PHENOTYPE is sufficiently drastic to kill the individual. Death from lethal genes may occur at any time from fertilization of the egg to advanced age. Lethal genes can be either *dominant*—for example, HUNTINGTON'S CHOREA, a progressive nervous disorder that usually occurs about middle age—or *recessive*—for example, SICKLE CELL ANEMIA, a disorder of HEMOGLOBIN causing death in adolescence.

leucine one of 20 amino acids common in proteins. It has a NONPOLAR R structure and is relatively insoluble in water. See Fig. 203. The ISOELECTRIC POINT of leucine is 6.0.

Fig. 203. **Leucine.** Molecular structure.

LEUCO-

leuco- see LEUKO-

leucosin a food reserve (see POLYSACCHARIDE) found in the Chrysophyceae, yellow-brown algae.

leukemia a form of cancer in LEUKOCYTES, resulting in uncontrolled increase of immature white blood cells in body organs and often in the blood itself.

leuko- or **leuco-** *combining form* denoting white *or* white blood cell.

leukocyte or **leucocyte** or **white blood cells** any of the large unpigmented cells in the blood of vertebrates. There are several types, formed both in lymph glands and bone marrow. See Fig. 204.

Fig. 204. **Leukocyte.** The types and relative frequencies of leukocytes.

Leukocytes are a primary defense against invading organisms and other foreign material, using two main methods: PHAGOCYTOSIS and the IMMUNE RESPONSE. The leukocyte count is usually about 10,000 cells per mm^3 of blood. This is not the total body count, because leukocytes are found as much in tissues such as thymus, spleen, and kidney as in blood. The cells generally have a short life span, 2 to 14 days, although the antibody-producing types (B-CELLS) tend to last up to 100 days. Compare ERYTHROCYTE. See also individual entries for the cells in Fig 204.

leukocytosis the presence of large numbers of leukocytes in the blood, usually resulting from injury to tissue or infection.

leukophyte a nonphotosynthetic, colorless alga.

leukoplast a colorless PLASTID of plant cells in which starch is often formed (see AMYLOPLAST). Leukoplasts may develop chlorophyll and function as CHLOROPLASTS as, for example, when potato tubers are lifted and exposed to light.

levorotatory (of a crystal, liquid, or solution) having the property of rotating a plane of polarized light to the left, for example, fructose. Compare DEXTROROTATORY.

Leydig cells or **interstitial cells** the cells of the testes that secrete TESTOSTERONE when stimulated by LUTEINIZING HORMONE.

LH (luteinizing hormone) or **ICSH (interstitial cell-stimulating hormone)** a glycoprotein hormone produced by the anterior PITUI-

TARY GLAND. In females it brings about ovulation on the stimulus of increasing ESTROGEN from the ovarian tissues, and causes a change in the GRAAFIAN FOLLICLE to form a CORPUS LUTEUM. LH also stimulates the corpus luteum to produce PROGESTERONE, which in turn inhibits production of LH and thus the subsequent production of progesterone—an example of a FEEDBACK MECHANISM. Menstruation then occurs. In males it causes ANDROGENS to be secreted by the testis.

liana a climbing, tropical plant with a ropelike stem.

lichen a plant formed by the symbiotic association (see SYMBIOSIS) of algal cells, which are surrounded by fungal hyphae. The algae are green (Chlorophyta) or blue-green (Cyanophyta), and the fungus is usually an ASCOMYCETE or sometimes a BASIDIOMYCETE. The fungus gains oxygen and carbohydrates from the alga, and the alga gains water, CO_2, and mineral salts from the fungus. Lichens reproduce vegetatively by means of soredia (hyphal cells enclosing algae) and sexually by means of the fungal apothecia or PERITHECIA. When no algae of the usual association occur, the germinating fungal spore dies. Lichens are common on trees and rocks in unpolluted areas and can be used as an INDICATOR SPECIES.

life cycle the serial progression of stages through which an organism passes from FERTILIZATION to the stage producing GAMETES. In higher animals and plants, the life cycle lasts from fertilization until the resulting individual produces gametes itself, but in many organisms there are asexual stages. See ALTERNATION OF GENERATIONS.

life table a table giving details of the mortality of a species or organism and all stages of the life history.

ligament a band of elastic CONNECTIVE TISSUE that joins bones. Ligaments are composed of tightly packed elastic fibers and are ideally suited to withstanding sudden stresses applied to the joints.

ligand a molecule able to bind to a specific ANTIBODY and used to differentiate very similar types of antibodies.

ligase an enzyme that catalyzes the joining of short molecules into longer ones, for example, DNA LIGASE.

light the part of the ELECTROMAGNETIC SPECTRUM visible to the human eye, between about 400 nm (blue) and 770 nm (red).

light chain see IMMUNOGLOBULIN.

light compass reaction the ability of some organisms, particularly insects, to orient themselves in relation to the position of the sun. This involves an internal timing mechanism that is not clearly understood.

light-dependent reaction a photosynthetic reaction or sequence of reaction that requires the presence of light. Compare LIGHT-INDEPENDENT REACTION.

light-independent reaction a photosynthetic reaction or sequence of reaction that takes place in the absence of light. Compare LIGHT-DEPEN-DENT REACTION.

light intensity the amount of light present.

light reactions those processes of PHOTOSYNTHESIS requiring light energy in which ATP and NADPH are formed, to be incorporated later into the CALVIN CYCLE. Various constituents are necessary for light reactions to occur:

(a) CHLOROPLASTS (in higher green plants) within parenchyma cells, particularly the MESOPHYLL tissue of leaves.

(b) Various pigments on the inner membranes of the chloroplasts responsible for trapping light energy. Chlorophyll *a* and one or more types of accessory pigment, such as chlorophyll *b* and various carotenoids, surround a single molecule of specialized chlorophyll *a* (P_{680} and P_{700}), forming a photosystem. *Photosystem I* (PSI) contains P_{700} and *photosystem II* contains P_{680}.

(c) Two ELECTRON TRANSPORT SYSTEMS (see Fig. 140).

(d) Water.

Two separate processes of PHOTOPHOSPHORYLATION occur:

(i) *cyclic photophosphorylation*, in which the various pigments in PSI collect light striking the chloroplast, passing the energy on to P_{700}, which undergoes PHOTOACTIVATION. An electron with raised energy levels is accepted by ferredoxin and passed on to an ETS, where ATP is produced as the energy level falls back to the starting point.

(ii) *noncyclic photophosphorylation*. Here the initial source of electrons is water, which releases electrons by separation of charge (previously thought to be by means of PHOTOLYSIS), and these are passed on to PSII, and then on to plastoquinone at a higher level. As in cyclic photophosphorylation, ATP is produced via the ETS, with the electron energy dropping down to PSI. Then, however, light causes the energy level of the electron to become high enough to be accepted by ferredoxin. At this stage a second ETS is entered, leading to production of NADPH, with hydrogen coming from separation of water into ions. Two photosystems are involved in reduction of NADP, because there is insufficient energy in light to energize the electrons from water straight to NADP.

Thus, the products of these two types of light reactions are ATP, NADPH, and oxygen. The first two products enter the DARK REACTIONS of photosynthesis, where they become involved in the CALVIN CYCLE and the synthesis of PGAL and eventually of GLUCOSE. See Fig. 205.

light year the distance light travels in 1 year, or 5.9×10^{12} miles.

lignase a group of enzymes that catalyzes the condensation of two molecules.

lignin a complex, noncarbohydrate polymer found in cell walls whose

Fig. 205. **Light reactions.** The main chemical pathways in the light reactions of photosynthesis.

function is to provide stiffening to the cell, as in xylem VESSELS, and bark fibers. Such cells are said to be lignified and, since lignin forms an impermeable barrier, the cells are dead.

ligulate strap-shaped.

ligule a small, scalelike outgrowth from a leaf, found in club mosses and some grasses.

limb 1. an articulated projection from the body of an animal that is used for locomotion, such as a leg or wing. **2.** a branch of a tree. **3.** the flattened part of a calyx or corolla, where the base is tubular.

liming the addition of calcium compounds to the soil, producing three main effects: (a) provision of the major element calcium, (b) neutralizing of acid soils, and (c) promotion of flocculation, or clumping, of clay particles into larger crumbs, so as to encourage aeration and drainage.

limiting factor 1. (in chemical processes) a component that limits the amount of the product that can be formed or its rate of formation. For example, light intensity can be a limiting factor in PHOTOSYNTHESIS. **2.** (in ecology) a factor that restricts the numbers of a population, such as food supply or nesting sites.

limnology the study of freshwater bodies, such as ponds, lakes, and streams, and their inhabitants.

limpet a marine gastropod MOLLUSK of the genus *Patella* that has a single, conical shell. When exposed at low tide, it attaches itself firmly to the substrate, usually rocks.

Limulus the horseshoe crab, or king crab, an aquatic arachnid that has maintained a similar body form since the TRIASSIC PERIOD.

lincomysin a bacteriostatic antibiotic produced by *Streptomyces* that inhibits synthesis of protein.

line a subpopulation with certain characteristics in common. Thus, a population of insects might be divided into several lines, depending on their tolerance to insecticides, and each line inbred further.

linear narrow or slender, particularly with reference to plant parts.

linear regression analysis a statistical method that aims to define the relationship between two variables, producing a value b, the regression coefficient. Several assumptions have to be made in carrying out the analysis, particularly: (a) that there is an independent variable x, for example, time, that can be measured exactly, and also a dependent variable y, for example, metabolic rate; and (b) that for every value of x there is a true value of y.

Linear regression analysis enables the fitting of a straight line to a scatter graph, using the equation $y = a + bx$, the a value being the point at which the regression line crosses the y-axis (the intercept).

linear scale a scale in which equal intervals represent equal increments in the quantities concerned, such as a temperature scale on a thermometer, as opposed to say a LOGARITHMIC SCALE. See Fig. 206.

seconds	10	60	600	6,000
numbers	0.5	1.4	3.3	6.4

Fig. 206. **Linear scale.** The lack of observations as the curve flattens renders the shape of the curve at this point uncertain.

line precedence the occurrence of a taxonomic name earlier on a page of print than another.

lingual of or relating to the tongue.

lingulate (of plant structures) tongue-shaped.

linkage disequilibrium a nonrandom association of alleles at different loci in a population, as is produced when two loci are closely linked and selection operates to keep certain gene combinations together.

linkage, genetic see GENETIC LINKAGE.

linkage map see CHROMOSOME MAP.

linkage unit see MAP UNIT.

Linnaeus, Carolus (1707—1778) Swedish biologist, author of *Systema Naturae* (1753), in which he outlined the binomial system of classifying organisms (see BINOMIAL NOMENCLATURE). He is thus regarded as the founder of modern systematics. Linnaeus was a highly competent biologist who for a long time supported the idea that species were fixed, an anti-evolutionary view. However, he probably changed his views on this in later life. (Linnaeus' Swedish name was Carl von Linné.)

linoleic acid or **essential fatty acid** an unsaturated fatty acid that cannot be synthesized by humans and is therefore described as essential. Deficiency of linoleic acid in the diet results in increased metabolic activity, failure in growth, and even death.

lip 1. (of an embryonic BLASTOPORE) the rim of the blastopore. 2. (of a flower perianth) a group of perianth segments united to a greater or lesser extent and forming a distinct grouping, thus divided from the rest of the perianth. 3. (of vertebrates) one of two fleshy parts (upper and lower) supporting the mouth.

lipase the enzyme that breaks fat down into fatty acids and glycerol. The main source is the PANCREATIC JUICE.

lipid a biological compound containing carbon, hydrogen, and oxygen together with other elements such as nitrogen and phosphorus. Lipids, or fats, are structural components of cell membranes and nervous tissue and are important sources of energy, being stored in various parts of the body (see ADIPOSE TISSUE). Their large molecular size makes lipids insoluble in water, but they are soluble in organic solvents such as acetone and ether.

lipin a complex fat containing nitrogen and frequently phosphorus or sulfur.

lipo- *combining form* denoting fat.

lipogenesis the formation of fats from nonfatty sources.

lipoid any substance with fatlike properties, including true FATS, STEROIDS, and LIPINS.

lipophilic having an affinity for LIPIDS.

lipoprotein a water-soluble molecule made up of a protein containing a lipid group. It is found, for example, in protoplasm, where it is involved in transport of lipids in a soluble form.

liquid feeder any organism that feeds exclusively on liquids, such as a mosquito.

lithosere a plant succession that originates on a rock surface.

lithotroph any organism that makes use of an inorganic electron donor.

LITTER

litter 1. any material aggregated on the surface of soil from vegetation growing above ground. 2. the offspring produced at any one time by a mammal.

littoral zone the shore, or intertidal area of a beach, being the region bounded on its landward side by the extreme high-water mark of spring tides, and on its seaward side by the extreme low-water mark of the same tides.

liver the largest and most complex organ of the vertebrate body, with a wide range of functions (see below), several of which are vital for life to continue. In mammals the liver receives a double blood supply, about 70% coming from the HEPATIC PORTAL SYSTEM and 30% from the arterial system. The liver:

(a) removes excess glucose from blood and stores it as GLYCOGEN.

(b) converts glycogen back to glucose when blood sugar levels are low.

(c) converts food substances to other types, for example, carbohydrates into fats, amino acids into carbohydrates or fats.

(d) deaminates amino acids, converting the ammonia produced into urea via the ORNITHINE CYCLE, releasing nitrogenous wastes into the blood.

(e) transaminates amino acids (see TRANSAMINATION) from one type to another via keto acids.

(f) detoxifies many harmful compounds.

(g) manufactures fats, including cholesterol.

(h) manufactures many plasma proteins, including FIBRINOGEN and PROTHROMBIN.

(i) stores several important substances, for example, iron and fat-soluble vitamins.

(j) excretes bile pigments.

(k) manufactures bile salts.

(l) destroys worn-out red blood cells.

liver fluke see FLUKE.

liverwort see HEPATICA.

lizard any member of the reptilian order Lacertilia, the majority of which possess a long scaly body and tail and four obvious limbs.

loam a soil formed of sand and clay and having an organic or humus content.

lobed (of leaves) divided but not into separate leaves.

lobule of liver one of several lobes or divisions of the liver.

local population see DEME.

loci see LOCUS.

lock-and-key mechanism see ACTIVE SITE.

locomotion the progressive movement of an organism.

loculicidal (of an ovary) being split down the middle of each cell.

locus (*pl.* loci) the position of a gene along a chromosome.

lodicule the small perianth that, in the flowers of grasses, swells and exposes the pistil and stamens by forcing open the surrounding bracts.

lod score a statistical method of estimating linkage between human genes by calculating the odds of a particular frequency of births having been produced by GENETIC LINKAGE as compared with INDEPENDENT ASSORTMENT. Lod is an acronym for *log* of *o*dds.

loess a fine-grained windblown silt characteristic of temperate areas, where thick layers of it were distributed during the retreat of ice after the most recent glaciation.

logarithmic scale a scale in which the values of a variable are expressed as logarithms. Such transformations of data are often employed to simplify the drawing of lines on a graph, where the variable values are spread over a wide range. See Fig. 207. A good example of the use of log scales is seen in Fig. 177, where the LOG PHASE of a microbial GROWTH CURVE is illustrated. Compare LINEAR SCALE.

Fig. 207. **Logarithmic scale.** Note the smoothness of the curve as compared with the LINEAR SCALE curve, for which the data are the same.

logistic curve an S-shaped curve of numbers plotted against time that represents the growth in numbers of a population of organisms in a limited environment. See GROWTH CURVE.

log phase the exponential phase of growth in a bacterial culture. Plotting the log of the number of cells against time gives a straight line. See LOGARITHMIC SCALE and Fig. 207.

log-probit analysis a technique for presenting results of an exposure test on a graph, in which, for example, the dose of a chemical is represented on the x-axis as a log scale, and the mortality is represented on the y-axis as a probability scale. The plotted log-probit line is transformed into a more linear shape as a result of the new scales, making it easier to compare results from different tests.

lomasome an INVAGINATION that occurs in cells of fungal hyphae and sporing structures.

lomentum a form of legume seed in which constrictions between seeds result in their falling singly.

long-day plant one that requires a day length exceeding a certain minimum value for the induction of flowering to take place. The term is somewhat misleading in that such plants, for example, lettuce and clover, are really sensitive to periods of darkness rather than daylight, requiring a night length of no more than a certain maximum duration, so long-day plants might better be called *short-night plants*. Compare SHORT-DAY PLANT, DAY-NEUTRAL PLANT.

loop of Henle the U-shaped, nonconvoluted part of the tubule that leads from a BOWMAN'S CAPSULE to the central cavity of the kidney, the pelvis, and where the urine is concentrated. Together, the capsule and tubule form a NEPHRON. Animals in arid climates have very long loops of Henle and produce small quantities of highly concentrated urine.

lophophore the ring of ciliated tentacles around the mouth in polyzoans and brachiopods.

Lorenz, Konrad (1903—) Austrian biologist, the pioneer of modern ETHOLOGY, who founded the school of behavioral studies, which regards animal behavior as a product of adaptive evolution. He is perhaps best known for two of his books, *King Solomon's Ring* (1952) and *Man Meets Dog* (1954), and also for his work on IMPRINTING.

lotic of or relating to an aquatic environment where there is fast moving water.

Lotka, Alfred James (1880—1949) American biologist, author of *Principles of Physical Biology* (1925), who derived mathematical expressions governing the results of competition between populations and interactions between predator and prey. V. Volterra published similar expressions in Italy independently in 1926. See K.

louse any wingless insect of the order Mallophaga (bird lice or biting lice) or the order Anopleura (sucking lice).

lower critical temperature the environmental temperature defining the lower limit of the THERMONEUTRAL ZONE of a tachymetabolic animal (see TACHYMETABOLISM). Below the lower critical temperature, the animal must undergo REGULATORY HEAT PRODUCTION in addition to its BASAL METABOLIC RATE to maintain homoiothermy (see HOMOIO-THERM).

LSD (lysergic acid diethylamide) a hallucinogenic drug prepared from lysergic acid.

LTH see LACTOGENIC HORMONE.

luciferase an oxidizing enzyme that, acting on the bioluminescent substance luciferin, causes luminosity in glow worms and other insects. See LUMINESCENCE.

lugworm the common name for the marine annelid *Arenicola*.

lumbar vertebra one of the vertebrae present between the thoracic vertebrae and the sacral vertebrae, in the region of the waist in mammals. See VERTEBRAL COLUMN.

lumen any cavity enclosed within a cell or structure, such as the lumen of the gut.

luminescence the production of light by living organisms that is brought about by oxidation of the protein luciferin. The reaction requires ATP and is catalyzed by LUCIFERASE. See also BIOLUMINESCENCE.

luminosity the amount of light emitted or reflected; brightness.

lumper a taxonomist who tends to group organisms together and then form large taxa, as distinct from one who forms many taxa—a SPLITTER.

lung the organ that enables an animal to breathe air (see AERIAL RESPIRATION). In mammals the paired lungs are each supplied by a bronchus that divides, treelike, into bronchioles. Each bronchiole ends in an atrium from which arise numerous alveoli that contact a vast capillary system. The surface area of the alveoli in humans is about 70 m^2, so there is a large surface area over which gaseous exchange can take place. See BREATHING.

lungfish see DIPNOAN.

luteal phase the phase of the ESTRUS CYCLE in which the CORPUS LUTEUM forms in the ovary. Secretion of PROGESTERONE takes place, followed by development of uterine glands and falloff in ESTROGEN secretion.

luteal tissue the tissue derived from follicle cells that fills the ruptured Graafian follicle and forms the CORPUS LUTEUM.

luteinizing hormone see LH.

luteotropic hormone (LTH) or **lactogenic hormone** or **prolactin** a proteinaceous hormone secreted by the anterior PITUITARY GLAND of vertebrates that has a range of functions, including acting as a GONADOTROPHIN. LTH influences the onset of lactation, stimulates PROGESTERONE secretion by the CORPUS LUTEUM in mammals (in tandem with LUTEINIZING HORMONE), and stimulates maternal behavior in all vertebrates.

luxuriance the somatic vigor of hybrids that does not add to their capability to compete.

lyase an enzyme that catalyzes (a) the addition of groups to double bonds and (b) the removal of groups to form double bonds.

Lycopodiales an order of the TRACHEOPHYTA containing the club mosses.

Lycopsida a subdivision of the TRACHEOPHYTA, including the club mosses *Lycopodium* and related species.

Lyell, Charles (1797—1875) British geologist who made extensive studies of PALEONTOLOGY, but from a biological point of view is best known for arranging for publication of the views of Darwin and Wallace on the origin of species.

lymph the INTERSTITIAL FLUID found in the LYMPHATIC SYSTEM and around the tissues of vertebrates. Although its composition varies with location in the body, lymph is typically a clear, transparent fluid (95% water) which, like blood, will clot when removed from lymph vessels, since it contains clotting agents similar to those in blood, except for platelets. Lymph also contains protein, glucose, and salts with large numbers of LEUKOCYTES, mainly LYMPHOCYTES.

lymphatic capillary see LYMPHATIC VESSEL.

lymphatic node see LYMPH NODE.

lymphatic system a system of tubules in vertebrates that drains excess tissue fluid (LYMPH) from the tissue spaces to the blood system. Unlike blood CAPILLARIES, lymph capillaries are blind-ending in the tissue spaces, gradually joining up to larger and larger vessels with two major lymphatic ducts entering the venous system in the upper thoracic cavity. Lymph is not moved along by heart contractions but, as in veins, by the action of skeletal muscles. Lymph vessels contain one-way valves to prevent backflow of fluid to the tissues.

Mammals and some birds possess clumps of lymphatic tissue, called LYMPH NODES, that act as filters and are also sites of LYMPHOCYTE formation. Nodes are especially prevalent in the neck, armpit, and groin, becoming swollen when adjacent to an infection. Besides returning excess water and protein to the blood system and being active in combatting infection, lymph (rather than blood) transports fats from the gut wall, the lymph vessels being called LACTEALS, since their contents are milky white.

lymphatic vessel or **lymphatic capillary** a vessel that carries LYMPH.

lymph heart an enlarged lymphatic vessel that is capable of pumping lymph. It is present in most vertebrates but not in birds and mammals.

lymph node or **lymphatic node** a mass of lymphoid tissue, important in producing antibodies containing macrophages, which remove foreign bodies from the lymph. It is present only in mammals and birds.

lymphocyte a type of LEUKOCYTE (white blood cell) of the AGRANULOCYTE group that is formed in the bone marrow. From there, lymphocytes differentiate into either B-CELLS or T-CELLS. The typical size is about the same as that of a red blood cell, about 8 μm in diameter. Lymphocytes are not themselves motile, but are capable of destroying foreign ANTIGENS in the IMMUNE RESPONSE. Lymphocytes collect in the spleen and lymph nodes, which may become swollen in a severe attack. The two types of lymphocytes react in different ways, T-cells destroying the antigen themselves (*cell-mediated immunity*) and B-cells producing ANTIBODIES.

lymphoid tissue tissue composed largely of LYMPHOCYTES, such as the thymus or lymph nodes.

lymphokine a soluble mediator released by lymphocytes on contact with specific antigens.

lymphoma a tumor of lymphoid tissue.

lyrate shaped like a lyre.

lysergic acid see LSD.

Lyon hypothesis see INACTIVE-X HYPOTHESIS.

Lysenko, Trofim Denisovitch (1898—1976) Russian plant biologist who attempted to apply Lamarckian theory to the development of crop plants. See LAMARCKISM.

lysigenous (of tissues) producing cavities by the breakdown of cells, as in the secretory organs of some plants.

lysin a type of ANTIBODY.

lysine one of 20 AMINO ACIDS common in proteins, having an extra basic group and being alkaline in solution. See Fig. 208. The ISOELECTRIC POINT of lysine is 10.0.

Fig. 208. **Lysine.** Molecular structure.

lysis the rupturing of a cell with release of its contents. For example, a bacterial cell may burst and release BACTERIOPHAGES; in HEMOLYSIS, a red blood cell will burst (see RHESUS HEMOLYTIC ANEMIA).

lysogenic bacterium a bacterium that carries a prophage of a temperate virus.

lysogeny a state in a living bacterium when it carries a nonvirulent TEMPERATE PHAGE (virus). In this condition, the phage DNA is integrated into the bacterial chromosome.

lysosome a cytoplasmic organelle of EUKARYOTE cells that contains hydrolytic enzymes and is thought to be produced by the GOLGI APPARATUS. The saclike structure is surrounded by a single-layered membrane that is impermeable and resistant to the enzymes inside. Lysosomes can act as the digestive system of the cell. When the sac ruptures, the enzymes are released into a food vacuole produced by PHAGOCYTOSIS, thus enabling breakdown of ingested materials.

lysozyme an enzyme that breaks down bacterial cell walls and provides protection against bacterial invasion in the skin, mucous membranes, and many body fluids.

lytic cycle the life cycle of a BACTERIOPHAGE in which many new phages are reproduced and the host bacterial cell undergoes LYSIS, the phages entering new bacterial hosts.

M

McCarty, Maclyn see AVERY.

MacLeod, Colin see AVERY.

macro- *combining form* denoting large, long, great.

macrobiotic prolonging life.

macrobiotics a dietary system advocating a diet of whole grains and vegetables grown without chemical additives, and in which foods are classified according to the principles of Yin and Yang.

macrocephalic having a large head.

macrocyte see MONOCYTE.

macroevolution any evolutionary change taking place at a level above the species, resulting in formation of such groups as genera and families.

macrofauna 1. a widely distributed fauna. 2. any animals visible to the naked eye.

macrogamete the female gamete, so designated because of its larger size. See ISOGAMY, ANISOGAMY.

macrolepidoptera the larger butterflies and moths. The term has no taxonomic significance.

macromere a large cell from the vegetative pole of a developing egg. Such a cell contains yolk and gives rise to the ENDODERM of the embryo.

macromolecule a very large molecule, composed of many atoms and having a very large molecular weight. Examples include nucleic acids and proteins.

macronucleus or **meganucleus** the larger of two nuclei found in some PROTOZOANS and concerned with cell division (see MICRONUCLEUS). It disappears during CONJUGATION and is afterward reformed from material of micronuclear origin, from the zygote nucleus. It appears to have mainly vegetative functions.

macronutrient any element required in large quantities for growth, such as nitrogen or potassium in plants. Compare MICRONUTRIENT.

macrophage a type of cell widely distributed in large numbers in vertebrate tissues and is derived from MONOCYTE blood cells. Its function is to remove debris, which it engulfs by PHAGOCYTOSIS, and it is capable of movement by means of PSEUDOPODIA. Macrophages occur in connective tissue, lymph, and blood, and one of their important roles is the digestion of old and damaged red blood cells in the spleen. Some macrophages are free-moving, and others are located in fixed locations, for example, KUPFFER CELLS. The entire arrangement forms the RETICULO-ENDOTHELIAL SYSTEM.

macrophagous (of animals) feeding on food particles large relative to the size of the animal.

Macropodidae the family of MARSUPIALS containing the kangaroos and wallabies. They are jumping mammals with long hind legs and a balancing tail.

macropterous having large wings, as in some castes of termites and ants.

macrosporangium see MEGASPORANGIUM.

macrospore see MEGASPORE.

macrosporophyll see MEGASPOROPHYLL.

macrurous having a large tail. The term is usually applied to long-bodied CRUSTACEANS, such as the lobster, in which the tail projects backward as opposed to being beneath the abdomen, as in the crab.

macula an area of acute vision on the retina of many vertebrates that lack a FOVEA.

madreporite the porous opening to the hydrocele in ECHINODERMS.

maggot any insect larva lacking appendages and an obvious head, usually the larva of a member of the order Diptera.

magnetite an iron oxide found in some animals, which may play a part in geomagnetic orientation because of its magnetic properties.

maize the British name for Indian corn, *Zea mays*, possibly the most intensively investigated higher plant.

major histocompatibility complex (MHC) a cluster of tightly linked genes on chromosome 6 in humans. These genes code for protein molecules that are attached to the surface of body cells and are used by the body's immune system to recognize its own or foreign material. The proteins of the MHC most easily recognized are found on the surface of leukocytes and are known as the HLA SYSTEM.

Malacostraca the crustacean group containing crabs, lobsters, shrimps, crayfish, etc. See also CARIDOID FACIES.

malaria see MALARIA PARASITE.

malaria parasite the PROTOZOAN *Plasmodium* that causes malaria in people. It is transmitted by the *Anopheles* mosquito, which takes in *Plasmodium* GAMETOCYTES when feeding on humans. The gametocytes develop into male and female gametes in the mosquito stomach, and after fertilization the ZYGOTE bores through the stomach wall, encysts, and gives rise to thousands of sporozoites, which then migrate to the salivary glands. The sporozoites are transferred to people at a subsequent blood meal during which anticoagulants are injected with the saliva.

Sporozoites invade the human liver and give rise to merozoites that invade red blood corpuscles. Further production of merozoites occurs in the red blood corpuscle, and their release into the bloodstream gives rise to bouts of fever. Gametocytes arise from merozoites that invade additional red blood corpuscles, grow within them, and are withdrawn by the mosquito during feeding, to complete the life cycle.

male gamete nuclei two HAPLOID (1) nuclei of flowering plants that arise from mitotic division of the generative nucleus inside the POLLEN GRAIN, which enter the pollen tube and eventually the EMBRYO SAC, becoming involved in the double fertilization.

malic acid or **malate** a four-carbon organic acid that is an intermediate step in the KREBS CYCLE, formed by HYDROLYSIS of fumaric acid (see Fig. 209). Malic acid is also important in C_4 PLANTS, such as sugar cane, in which carbon is captured from CO_2 to form malic acid and other C_4 acids in MESOPHYLL cells before being transferred to the CALVIN CYCLE taking place in the CHLOROPLASTS of special cells nearby. See KRANZ ANATOMY.

$$COOH - \underset{\underset{H}{|}}{\overset{\overset{OH}{|}}{C}} - \underset{\underset{H}{|}}{\overset{\overset{H}{|}}{C}} - COOH$$

Fig. 209. **Malic acid.** Molecular structure.

malignancy a structure such as a tumor or a condition such as a fever, the progressive version of which is threatening to life.

malleus or **hammer** the hammer-shaped bone that is the outermost of the three ear ossicles.

Mallophaga see LOUSE.

Malpighian body or **Malpighian corpuscle** a structure for filtering blood in the vertebrate kidneys that is formed from the BOWMAN'S CAPSULE with its associated GLOMERULUS.

Malpighian layer the layer of EPIDERMIS in the mammalian skin lying immediately above the DERMIS, which is continuously dividing by MITOSIS to replace outer epidermal cells that wear away due to friction.

Malpighian tubules the excretory organs of some ARTHROPODS, such as insects and arachnids, that collect wastes from the body fluids and discharge them into the hind gut. They are tubular glands that open into the anterior part of the hind gut, the other end being closed and bathed in the animal's blood in the HEMOCOEL.

The slender tubules are muscular and capable of movement, taking up soluble potassium urate, water, and carbon dioxide from the blood into the tubule cells. There they react together to form potassium hydrogen carbonate and uric acid. The $KHCO_3$ and some water are reabsorbed from the tubules into the blood. Additional water is absorbed by the rectal gland, and crystals of uric acid are voided into the gut for excretion.

maltase an enzyme that hydrolyzes MALTOSE to glucose. In mammals it is produced in the CRYPT OF LIEBERKUHN in the SMALL INTESTINE and is present in the *succus entericus*. Maltase is also present in many seeds.

Malthus, Thomas Robert (1766—1834) English political economist whose ideas on population growth influenced the evolutionary theory propagated by Charles DARWIN and Alfred WALLACE. His most interesting observation was that the human population, if unchecked, would grow geometrically while the food supply would grow only arithmetically, thus giving rise to mass starvation. He considered that the only checks on population growth were disease, war, famine, and abstinence from sex, the last one being considered the most reliable method of BIRTH CONTROL at the time.

maltose a disaccharide CARBOHYDRATE consisting of two GLUCOSE units linked by a GLYCOSIDE bond and common in germinating barley (see Fig. 210). The barley seeds are soaked in water, initiating release of large amounts of AMYLASE, a hydrolytic enzyme that breaks down stored starch into maltose, a reducing sugar.

Fig. 210. **Maltose.** Molecular structure.

mammal any animal of the class Mammalia, a group often regarded as the most highly evolved animals. There are three living subclasses:

(a) Monotremata—MONOTREMES, primitive egg-laying mammals such as the duck-billed platypus and *Echidna,* the spiny anteater.

(b) Marsupialia—MARSUPIALS, which transfer their young to pouches for the latter part of their early development.

(c) Eutheria—EUTHERIANS, which have a placenta.

Mammals are characterized by the presence of hair, a DIAPHRAGM used in AERIAL RESPIRATION, milk secretion in the female (LACTATION), presence of the left systemic arch only in the blood circulatory system, three auditory ossicles in the ear, and a lower jaw of a single pair of bones. In all classes except the monotremes, the young are born alive.

mammary gland or **milk gland** a gland present in female MAMMALS that produces milk used to suckle the young (see LACTATION). It probably evolved from a modified sweat gland and at least two are normally present, although in many mammals more than two are developed, usually concentrated on the underbelly beneath the pelvic girdle. In most mammals the size of the gland is determined by the state of the ESTROUS CYCLE.

mandible the part of the mouthparts of an animal that does most of the crushing of food materials. In vertebrates, the term usually denotes the lower jaw. In insects and other arthropods, the mandibles are one of a pair of mouthparts used for crushing food (see Fig. 191).

mantle the part of the EPIDERMIS of a mollusk that secretes the shell and covers the dorsal and lateral surfaces.

manubrium 1. any handlelike elongated process. 2. the tubular mouth of a jellyfish. 3. the anterior segment of the sternum in mammals. 4. the first segment of the springing organ in COLLEMBOLA.

manus the hand or forefoot of a TETRAPOD.

manuscript name a scientific name that has not been published.

map unit or **linkage unit** a unit of distance between genes along a chromosome. The number of map units is directly correlated with the amount of RECOMBINATION between loci; that is, 1% recombination is equal to 1 map unit. See CROSS-OVER VALUE, GENETIC LINKAGE.

marker gene a gene whose location and characteristics are well known, so it is used to investigate other genes. For example, it can be used to determine the location of any gene relative to the marker gene.

marram grass *Ammophila arenaria* a grass found on coastal sand dunes. It is a XEROPHYTE that is capable of rolling its leaves to prevent loss of water during a drought. It has deep-running stems (RHIZOMES) and roots that bind the sand in the dunes and thus is often planted to stabilize dune systems.

marrow the pulplike content of the cavities of larger bones that produces red and sometimes white blood corpuscles.

marsh an area of wet or periodically wet land where the soils are not peaty.

marsupial any member of the subclass Marsupialia, also called Didelphia or Metatheria, that contains mammals characterized by presence of a pouch to which the young, born in an undeveloped state, migrate during early development. The pouch contains the mammary glands, which vary in number between species, and the young complete their development in it. The group at one time was widespread but now is restricted to Australasia and South America. In Australasia, marsupials, free from competition from EUTHERIAN (placental) mammals, have radiated to occupy most niches elsewhere occupied by placental forms.

marsupium the pouch of a MARSUPIAL mammal.

mass flow a hypothesis to explain the movement of solutes in a plant by means of an hydrostatic pressure gradient. The idea is that in one part of the plant (the *source*), solute particles are actively secreted into sieve cells of PHLOEM, producing a high osmotic concentration that attracts water by OSMOSIS. In another part of the plant (the *sink*), solute particles are leaving the phloem, thus lowering osmotic concentration and causing water to leave also. Therefore, a pressure gradient is set up between the source (for example, a leaf) and the sink (for example, a root), and fluids flow from one to the other down the gradient. See TRANSLOCATION (1).

mass selection a method of producing new plant and animal varieties in which many suitable individuals contribute their genes to the new variety, all inferior types in the population having been removed (*selected out*) by the breeder.

mast cell a type of large, ameboid cell found in the matrix of CONNECTIVE TISSUE that produces HEPARIN and HISTAMINE and is probably important in rapid responses to ANTIGENS. See IMMUNE RESPONSE.

mastication the process of chewing and breaking down food particles before swallowing.

mastigoneme a projection found in numbers along the length of some flagella that serves to increase the surface area.

Mastigophora or **Flagellata** a group of flagellate PROTOZOANS, sometimes given the status of a class (= Flagellata). The group contains both holozoic and holophyte forms.

mastodon a relative of the elephant that existed in MIOCENE and PLIOCENE times. It was elephantlike, having a short trunk and long tusks.

mastoid process or **mastoid bone** the part of the periotic bone that in humans forms a projection behind the ear.

material the sample available for any study in TAXONOMY.

maternal effect an environmental phenomenon in which the phenotype of an offspring is influenced by the maternal tissue. One example is the adverse influence of maternal smoking on the weight of the unborn baby.

maternal inheritance a form of CYTOPLASMIC INHERITANCE in which genes are passed to the offspring from the female only.

mating 1. any reproduction involving two sexes. **2.** (in lower organisms) reproduction between types that differ in physiology but not in physical form. **3.** (in birds and mammals) the behavioral process of pair formation rather than of copulation leading to sexual reproduction.

mating system the social relationship between sexes during the breeding cycle that ranges from pair formation to forms of polygamy. The pattern of mating can be RANDOM MATING or ASSORTATIVE MATING.

mating types the equivalent of sexuality in lower organisms, where physiological differences rather than physical ones distinguish the types, the mating system usually being inherited.

matrix a ground substance in which other materials or cells are embedded, for example, the matrix of CONNECTIVE TISSUE containing fibers, or blood plasma forming a matrix in which are various blood cells.

matroclinous inheritance a system in which all offspring of a cross have the PHENOTYPE of the mother. See CYTOPLASMIC INHERITANCE. Compare PATROCLINOUS INHERITANCE.

matter that which constitutes the substance of physical forms, has mass, occupies space, and can be quantified.

maturation of germ cells the final stage of development of eggs and sperm in the process of GAMETOGENESIS, producing mature GAMETES capable of FERTILIZATION.

maturation (viral) the collection of infective VIRIONS produced in the host cell.

maxilla 1. (in vertebrates) the bone of the upper jaw, carrying all teeth except the incisors. The term is occasionally used to denote the entire upper jaw. **2.** (in arthropods) the part of the mouthparts lying behind the jaws. See LABRUM, LABIUM.

maxillipede any limb modified for feeding, normally found immediately in front of the legs, particularly in crustaceans.

maxillule one of the first MAXILLAE (2) of a crustacean.

maze a labyrinth of winding passages, used in behavioral experiments involving LEARNING.

MD see MUSCULAR DYSTROPHY.

mean see ARITHMETIC MEAN.

mean body temperature the CORE TEMPERATURE actually attained by behaviorally thermoregulating bradymetabolic animals (see BRADYMETABOLISM) under natural conditions.

measles an acute disease of human childhood in which red circular spots appear all over the body, accompanied by a dry cough, low grade fever, and sore throat. The condition is caused by the *Morbilli* virus. It is highly contagious, being spread in respiratory secretion, but once infected the individual is immune for life. Control is by use of attenuated live virus vaccine given to children.

meatus any natural opening or passage, particularly the external auditory meatus leading to the TYMPANUM in the ear.

mechanical tissues the tissues that serve to support a plant, such as COLLENCHYMA and SCLERENCHYMA.

mechanoreceptor a sensory structure that receives mechanical stimuli, such as sound, pressure, and movement.

Meckel's cartilage one of a pair of cartilages forming the lower jaw of cartilaginous fishes, such as sharks and skates. In fish, reptiles, and birds it forms the ossified articular bone and in mammals, the MALLEUS.

meconium the gut contents of a mammalian fetus, formed of swallowed amniotic fluid and the secretions of glands into the gut.

Mecoptera an order of insects containing the scorpion flies.

median 1. (of a structure or character) describing a location along the line of bilateral symmetry. **2.** (in statistics) the middle value in a frequency distribution, on either side of which lie values with equal total frequencies.

mediastinum the space in the chest of mammals containing the HEART, TRACHEA, and ESOPHAGUS.

medium a substance on or in which microorganisms and other small organisms can be cultured. A medium can be liquid or solid. If solid, it frequently contains agar, a stiffening agent extracted from seaweed. Culture media can contain all necessary nutrients and trace elements for normal growth (a *minimal medium*) but can also be supplemented. For example, ANTIBIOTICS can be added to test for antibiotic resistance in bacteria.

medulla 1. the central part of an animal organ, such as the brain, adrenal gland, or kidney. **2.** see PITH.

medulla oblongata the posterior part of the hindbrain of vertebrates that connects with the spinal cord. Ventrally thick-walled and containing groupings of nerve cells called nuclei, the thin-walled posterior CHOROID PLEXUS is situated on its dorsal side. The medulla contains several important areas of nervous control not influenced by conscious action. The respiratory and cardiovascular centers control respiration and heartbeat and organs of the LATERAL-LINE SYSTEM. The ear, taste, and touch receptors also have their impulses coordinated in the medulla.

medullary plate the neural plate of the vertebrate embryo.

medullary ray an area of the stem between the vascular bundles, containing PARENCHYMA cells initially but which can become converted into meristematic tissue. See INTERFASCICULAR CAMBIUM.

medullated nerve fiber see MYELIN SHEATH.

medusa (*pl.* medusae, medusas) the jellyfish (*medusoid*) stage of the

COELENTERATE life cycle, usually free-swimming and propelled by pulsations of the bell. Medusae usually reproduce sexually, giving rise to a POLYP stage from which the medusae are produced asexually. Medusae form the dominant phase of the life history of members of the class Scyphozoa, but are often absent or of lesser importance in other classes of the phylum.

medusoid see MEDUSA.

mega- see MEGALO-.

megagamete the larger of the two GAMETES, usually the female OVUM.

megakaryocytes see BLOOD PLATELETS.

megalo- or **mega-** *combining form* denoting large, great, grand.

meganucleus see MACRONUCLEUS.

megaphyll the type of leaf found in ferns and seed plants, in which the lamina is thought to have developed from a flattened branch and contains VASCULAR BUNDLES.

megapode any of the mound birds of Australia and Southeast Asia that bury their eggs in mounds of earth so that the eggs develop without incubation.

megasporangium or **macrosporangium** the organ in which MEGASPORES are formed—in flowering plants, the OVULE.

megaspore or **macrospore** the larger of two types of SPORES produced by many ferns and seed plants. The megaspore gives rise to a female GAMETOPHYTE in ferns and in seed plants, and in flowering plants becomes the EMBRYO SAC. Compare MICROSPORE.

megasporophyll or **macrosporophyll** 1. the modified leaf that carries the MEGASPORANGIUM. 2. the CARPEL of flowering plants.

meiosis a type of nuclear division associated with sexual reproduction, producing four HAPLOID (1) cells from a single DIPLOID (1) cell, the process involving two cycles of division. Although meiosis is a continuous process, it has been divided into numerous stages, given below. Further details of each stage can be obtained by referring to individual entries.

PROPHASE I: homologous chromosomes pair, split into CHROMATIDS, and carry out CROSSING OVER. The nuclear membrane disintegrates.

METAPHASE I: chromosomes migrate to the spindle equator, to which they become attached by their CENTROMERES.

ANAPHASE I: HOMOLOGOUS CHROMOSOMES separate to opposite poles.

TELOPHASE I: new nuclei form, in which there is only one type of each chromosome, although each is divided into two chromatids.

PHOPHASE II: nuclear membrane goes.

METAPHASE II: chromosomes attach to spindle.

ANAPHASE II: chromatids separate to poles.

TELOPHASE II: four haploid nuclei are produced, each with one of each type of chromosomes.

Meiosis has two major functions: (a) it halves the number of chromosomes to prevent a doubling in each generation and (b) it produces a mixing of genetic material in the daughter cells by INDEPENDENT ASSORTMENT and RECOMBINATION. Note that the second point is true only if variability already is present in the parent cell.

Meiosis occurs at different stages of the life cycle in haploid and diploid organisms. See Fig. 211. See also MITOSIS, GAMETOGENESIS, and Figs. 162 and 163.

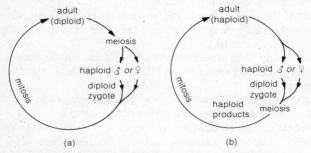

Fig. 211. **Meiosis.** (a) Prezygotic meiosis, for example, humans. (b) Postzygotic meiosis, for example, fungus.

meiospore a spore formed as the result of MEIOSIS.

meiotic drive a mechanical phenomenon during MEIOSIS that results in the two types of gametes produced by a heterozygote occurring in unequal numbers. Meiotic drive can have an important impact when it produces unequal sex ratios, so it has been used in attempts at insect control by producing excess males and few females.

Meissner's corpuscle a light-pressure receptor in nonhairy mammalian skin.

melanin a dark brown or black pigment found in skin or hair. See ALBINISM, DOPA.

melanism a condition in which excess dark pigment produces dark color or blackness in scales, skin, or plumage. See INDUSTRIAL MELANISM.

melanoma an epithelial cancer in which the cells contain dark pigment.

melanophore or **melanocyte** a type of pigment cell, or CHROMATOPHORE, that contains the pigment melanin, usually found in the skin of animals. It has a protective or camouflage function.

melanophore stimulatory hormone a hormone in the form of a PEP-

TIDE produced the ADENOHYPOPHYSIS. It causes color changes in fish, amphibians and reptiles by changing melanin distribution within the cells (see MELNOPHORE).

melatonin a hormone of the pituitary gland thought to inhibit reproductive activities.

melting the denaturation of DNA.

melting point the temperature at which a solid liquefies.

membrane a thin set of tissue.

membrane carrier protein or an enzyme that combines with a substance and transport it across a biological membrane.

membrane potential the potential difference between the two sides of a cell membrane.

membranous (of plant) being dry and flexible but not green.

membranous labyrin see EAR.

memory 1. the recollection of past events or previously learned skills after passage of time. (in computing) the capacity of a computer usually expressed in bys or Ks, where K = 1024 bytes.

menarche the onset of menstruation, which occurs at puberty.

Mendel, Gregor (1822–884) Austrian monk and mathematician who, working with strains of the garden pea (*Pisum sativum*), managed to deduce several primary facts about how genes are transmitted between generations (see MENDELN GENETICS). Mendel's work was published in 1866 but remained unnoticed until 16 years after his death.

Mendelian genetics or **Mndel's laws** the basic laws of inheritance, first published by Gregor MENDEL in 1866 to explain the results he obtained from experiment with the garden pea. Working without detailed knowledge of cell structure or nuclear division he suggested that:

(a) each character, for example, height, is controlled by two *factors*. We would now state this idea as each gene having two alleles, one on each HOMOLOGOUS CHROMOSOME.

(b) each factor segregates in the egg and pollen grains. We would now state that MEIOSIS separates allelic forms of genes (Mendel's first law— see SEGREGATION).

(c) factors for different characters show INDEPENDENT ASSORTMENT. We would now state that genes are assorted independently during meiosis (Mendel's second law) unless linked on the same chromosome.

(d) factors do not cause blending, but are either dominant (see DOMINANCE (1)) or recessive. We know now that we can explain dominance in terms of enzyme activity, and that sometimes two alleles code for enzymes giving an intermediate phenotype when together (see INCOMPLETE DOMINANCE).

(e) the distribution of factors in the egg cells and len grains obeys basic statistical laws giving ratios in the progeny th are predictable.

(f) results from crosses are the same whether th ominant form of the character belongs to the female parent or the n parent. We now know that this statement is true only if the gene is ated on an AUTO-SOME (see SEX LINKAGE).

Mendel's laws see MENDELIAN GENETICS.

meninges (*sing.* meninx) the three membranes ARACHNOID, DURA MATER, PIA MATER—that cover the CENTRAL NER US SYSTEM of verte-brates. See MENINGITIS.

meningitis inflammation of the MENINGES cause by infection.

meniscus 1. the top of a liquid column made ei r concave or convex by capillarity. **2.** an intervertebral disk of fibro tilage.

menopause or **climacteric** the time at which omen stop ovulating, with the result that the normal MENSTRUAL CLE no longer occurs. This is usually at about 45—50 years of age.

menstrual cycle the modified ESTROUS CYCL f most primates, which results in periodic destruction of the mucosa the uterine wall at the end of the LUTEAL PHASE. This results in a d harge of blood known as *menstruation,* the shedding of the ENDOM RIUM, every 28 days in women.

menstruation see MENSTRUAL CYCLE.

mental prominence the projection of the wer jaw; the chin.

mentum a structure found on the head of i insect below the labium.

mericarp one seeded portion of a dry fruit SCHIZOCARP split off from a SYNCARPOUS ovary at maturity.

meristele a distinct vascular strand surro ded by an endodermis that occurs in some ferns and results in brea p of the STELE.

meristem or **meristematic tissue** a re n of a plant in which active cell division (MITOSIS) occurs, the cells c he meristem being undiffer-entiated into a specialized form. Merist atic tissues occur at the root and shoot tips (see APICAL MERISTEM) g ng growth in length. Increase in girth of the plant is produced by the MBIUM of VASCULAR BUNDLES and the INTERFASCICULAR CAMBIUM. te that such specialized divid-ing zones are not found in animals, were cell division occurs in most tissues.

meristematic tissue see MERISTEM.

meristic variation numerical variati in taxonomic characters, such as numbers of bristles, vertebrae, and ots.

mero- *combining form* denoting pa, partial.

meroblastic cleavage see CLEAV E.

merogamete any protozoan GAM E formed by fission of parent cell.

meromatic (of lakes) stratified so that surface and bottom waters never mix.

-merous *combining form* denoting having parts.

mes- see MESO-.

mescaline a psychoactive drug that produces hallucinatory effects in humans, probably by interfering with NORADRENALINE at nerve synapses.

Meselson, Matthew see SEMICONSERVATIVE REPLICATION MODEL.

mesencephalon see MIDBRAIN.

mesenchyme a loose, cellular animal tissue that arises from the embryonic mesoderm and functions as packing around internal organs. Mesenchyme can be thought of as the animal equivalent of PARENCHYMA in plants.

mesentery 1. the layers of PERITONEUM that attach the gut system and its associated organs, for example, the SPLEEN, to the dorsal surface of the peritoneal cavity in mammals. The blood lymph and nerve supplies to the gut are contained in the mesentery. **2.** one of the filaments dividing the body cavity of sea anemones and corals.

meso- or **mes-** *combining form* denoting middle.

mesocephalic (of humans) having a medium-sized head. See CEPHALIC INDEX.

mesoderm the layer of embryonic cells lying between the ECTODERM and ENDODERM in all higher animals—all METAZOA except COELENTERATES—giving rise to muscle, the blood system, connective tissues, the kidneys, the dermis of the skin, and the axial skeleton. The mesoderm is often split into two layers with the COELOM in between.

mesodermal pouches the segmentally arranged blocks of mesoderm that occur on each side of the NOTOCHORD of the vertebrate embryo and subsequently give rise to SOMITES.

mesoglea the jellylike material lying between the ectoderm and endoderm of COELENTERATES. In the HYDROZOA it is relatively thin, but it is much thicker in the other two major groups, SCYPHOZOA and ACTINOZOA. It is acellular and is secreted by the ectoderm and endoderm.

Mesolithic the period from approximately 14,000 years ago to 5500 years ago, in some parts of Europe characterized by use of small flint implements.

mesonephros or **Wolffian body** the middle part of the embryonic kidney, which in fish and amphibia is the functional kidney, but which gives rise embryologically to the tubules of the testis in mammals, birds, and reptiles. See also WOLFFIAN DUCT.

mesophilic (of microorganisms) having an optimal growth temperature from 20°C to 45°C.

mesophyll the internal tissue of a plant leaf, except the VASCULAR BUN-
DLES. In dorsiventral leaves, the mesophyll is differentiated into an
upper *palisade mesophyll* and a loosely packed, lower *spongy mesophyll.* In isobilateral leaves, there are upper and lower palisade meso-
phylls and a central spongy area. In C_4 PLANTS there is yet another
arrangement, called KRANZ ANATOMY.

All mesophyll cells contain CHLOROPLASTS, for PHOTOSYNTHESIS,
which lie close to the edge of the cell in order to gain maximum light
and gas supply. Mesophyll tissue contains numerous intercellular spaces,
which communicate with the atmosphere outside the leaf via STOMATA.
See Fig. 212.

upper epidermis
with cuticle

palisade mesophyll
with chloroplasts

spongy mesophyll
with fewer chloroplasts
and larger air spaces

lower epidermis

guard cell with chloroplasts — stoma

Fig. 212. **Mesophyll.** Transverse section of a dorsiventral leaf.

mesophyte a plant growing in soil with a normal water content. Compare HYDROPHYTE, XEROPHYTE.

mesoplankton the part of the PLANKTON that occurs below 100 fath-
oms.

mesosome a structure with properties similar to those of a MITOCHOND-
RION that is formed in the cell membrane of bacteria by invagination.

mesothorax the middle of the three thoracic segments of insects.

mesotrophic (of plants) having a moderate level of requirement of soil
nutrients.

Mesozoic era the geological era that began about 225 million years ago
and lasted about 155 million years. It includes the CRETACEOUS PERIOD,
JURASSIC PERIOD, and TRIASSIC PERIOD. During this era GYMNOSPERMS
became dominant plants, dinosaurs became the dominant animals, reptiles (Pterosaurs) conquered the air, and birds and mammals evolved.

messenger RNA (mRNA) a single-stranded type of POLYNUCLEOTIDE
molecule that contains four types of bases: ADENINE, GUANINE, CYTO-
SINE, and URACIL. The function of mRNA is to carry a coded sequence
of instructions about protein structure from DNA in the nucleus to RIBO-

SOMES attached to the ENDOPLASMIC RETICULUM, a process called TRANSCRIPTION.

metabolic intensity the metabolic rate of a unit mass of living tissue.

metabolic pathway the sequence of enzyme reactions followed in the formation of one substance from another. See METABOLISM.

metabolic rate the rate at which an organism carries out METABOLISM, and which is closely linked to temperature. The relationship between metabolic rate and temperature can be expressed in terms of a value called Q_{10}. See also BASAL METABOLIC RATE.

metabolic waste any waste substance produced during the metabolism of an organism, such as nitrogen in the form of urea.

metabolic water water formed by a type of METABOLISM called CATABOLISM, in which complex molecules are broken down to release their stored energy, with water as a by-product. In certain insects and desert mammals, which feed primarily on dry seeds, the water conservation mechanisms are so efficient that metabolic water alone is sufficient to replace the normal water loss, so free water is not required in the diet.

metabolism the total of the chemical processes occurring in cells by which energy is stored in molecules (ANABOLISM) or released from molecules (CATABOLISM), life being maintained by a balance between the rates of catabolic and anabolic processes. All metabolic reactions occur in steps in which compounds are gradually built up or broken down. Each step of the metabolic pathway is catalyzed by a different enzyme whose structure is coded by a specific gene, the end product being called a *metabolite*. A special energy-carrying molecule called ATP is involved in these processes. See BASAL METABOLIC RATE.

metabolite see METABOLISM.

metacarpal any one of the series of bones forming the palm of the hand or flat part of the forefoot in vertebrates. See CARPAL.

metacarpus a bone of the forelimb of TETRAPODS that occurs between the wrist (CARPAL) and fingers (PHALANGES). In humans the metacarpus is the hand. See PENTADACTYL LIMB.

metacentric chromosome a chromosome having the CENTROMERE located about halfway along. Compare ACENTRIC CHROMOSOME.

metachromatic having more than one color produced by the same stain. For example, methylene blue stains the diphtheria bacterium *Corynebacterium diphtheriae* blue with red inclusions.

metachronal rhythm the beat of cilia (see CILIUM) or consecutive limbs, as in the ragworm, where a wave appears to pass forward through them in much the same way that wind causes the movement of corn in a field. See Fig. 213. The result of these actions is that the effective movement of liquid over their surface is backward, and the organism moves forward.

beat of cilia ⟶   pellicle of cell

anterior   posterior

⟵ movement of animal

Fig. 213. **Metachronal rhythm.** The wave pattern of metachronal rhythm.

metameric segmentation the division of the body of an organism, for example, the earthworm, into a series of similar or identical units recurring along the length of the body. These units are known as *segments* or *metameres*. In each metamere there is a pattern of muscle blocks, blood vessels, excretory organs, epidermal structures, and elements of the nervous system.

metamorphosis the change in an organism from larval to adult form, which is often quite rapid, as in tadpole to frog, and caterpillar to butterfly. Metamorphosis is said to be incomplete where there is gradual development of a NYMPH to an adult, as in the EXOPTERYGOTA (Heterometabola or Hemimetabola). It is complete where a pupa occurs, as in the ENDOPTERYGOTA (Holometabola).

metanephros the functional kidney in adult reptiles, birds, and mammals that replaces the MESONEPHROS in the developing embryo.

metaphase a stage of nuclear division in EUKARYOTE cells, occurring once in MITOSIS and twice in MEIOSIS. The main process involved is the organization of CHROMOSOMES at the equator of a spindle, forming a *metaphase plate.* Each chromosome is divided into two CHROMATIDS, joined at a CENTROMERE. The chromosomes are densely staining and highly condensed, properties that make them suitable for producing KARYOTYPES. The spindle MICROTUBULES become attached to an area of the centromere called the *kinetochore,* the precise arrangement of chromosomes appearing to be random (this has important genetic implications, see INDEPENDENT ASSORTMENT) and different in mitosis and meiosis (see Fig. 214). The metaphase plate in the second cycle of meiosis is at right angles to the equator in metaphase I.

metaphase plate see METAPHASE.

metaphloem the typical PHLOEM that develops from the procambium next to the *protophloem,* toward the stem center. It has normal SIEVE

Fig. 214. **Metaphase.** Position of chromosomes in mitosis and meiosis.

TUBES, in contrast with the small simplified sieve tubes of protophloem, which lack companion cells.

Metaphyta a TAXON, often given the status of kingdom, that includes all multicellular plants.

metaplasia the transformation of a tissue to another form.

metaplasm the lifeless constituents of protoplasm.

metapneustic (of insects such as mosquito larvae) having SPIRACLES only at the posterior end of the abdomen.

metarhodopsin the substance produced when RHODOPSIN is affected by light.

metastasis the process of cancerous tissue spreading to various parts of the body.

metatarsal any bone of the METATARSUS.

metatarsus the skeleton of the foot between the toes and tarsus of a TETRAPOD, consisting of the five bones of the hind limb. In humans this forms the middle and hind part of the foot. See PENTADACTYL LIMB.

Metatheria see MARSUPIAL.

metathorax the posterior of the three thoracic segments in insects.

metaxylem the parts of the xylem tissue of plant roots and stems that are produced last by the cambium, tending to have larger cells than the PROTOXYLEM, the elements formed first.

metazoan any animal of the group Metazoa, whose bodies are multicellular, as distinct from the PROTOZOANS, in which the bodies are unicellular. Sponges (see PARAZOAN) are the only nonprotozoan group excluded from the Metazoa. Metazoans except for the COELENTERATES have a three-layered body structure with an outer ECTODERM, a middle MESODERM, and an inner ENDODERM.

metazoite one of a large number of cells formed by multiple asexual fission of some Protozoa.

methionine one of 20 AMINO ACIDS common in proteins. It has an R group with a nonpolar structure and is relatively insoluble in water. See Fig. 215. The ISOELECTRIC POINT of methionine is 5.7.

metric character a quantitative character, such as human height, in

Fig. 215. **Methionine.** Molecular structure.

which there is a continuous spread of variability. Such characters are controlled by a system of POLYGENIC INHERITANCE.

micelle an elongated thread of protein or other material present within the cell protoplasm.

Michaelis-Menten constant K_M the concentration in moles per liter of a substance at half the maximum velocity of an enzymic reaction.

micro- *combining form* denoting small, small in relation to other members of the same species. In the metric system of measurement micro- means one millionth with a symbol, as in liters (1×10^{-6} L). See SI UNITS.

microaerophile any organism requiring little oxygen for growth.

microbe any microscopic organism. The term is sometimes restricted to pathogenic microorganisms, such as BACTERIA and VIRUSES.

microbial degradation the beneficial activities of microbes in carrying out biodegradation, for example, in sewage disposal. Compare BIODETERIORATION.

microclimate the immediate climate in which an organism lives, such as the climate around a leaf, within the vegetation layer, or within an adjacent part of the soil.

microdissection the dissection of very small structures, often carried out with the help of a micromanipulator, an instrument that significantly negates hand tremors.

microevolution the small-scale changes resulting from genetic adaptation, which usually are expressed as changes within a species rather than formation of a new species. See INDUSTRIAL MELANISM.

microfauna 1. the microscopic animals of a microhabitat. 2. any microscopic animals not visible to the naked eye.

microfibril a group of some two thousand cellulose chains massed together in the CELL WALL. Microfibrils are embedded in an organic matrix that gives the cell wall great strength.

microfilament a fine, subcellular structure about 5—8 nm in diameter, composed of ACTIN or a similar protein and found in the cytoplasm of

EUKARYOTE cells. Microfilaments are able to contract and are also involved in CYTOPLASMIC STREAMING and PHAGOCYTOSIS.

microgamete the smaller of two gametes. It is usually motile and called the male.

microgeographic race a race restricted to a very small geographical area.

microhabitat a subdivision of a HABITAT that has its own particular properties, such as a MICROCLIMATE.

Microlepidoptera a LEPIDOPTERAN subgroup that no longer has any taxonomic significance. The subgroup includes forms only a few millimeters in length.

micromere any of the small BLASTOMERES formed at the animal pole of a developing egg. These eventually give rise to the ECTODERM.

micron a unit of length equal to 10^{-6} m. Symbol: μm.

micronucleus the smaller of two nuclei found in some protozoans that is concerned with cell division. Compare MACRONUCLEUS.

micronutrient any TRACE ELEMENT or compound required in only minute amounts by organisms. Compare MACRONUTRIENT.

microorganism any unicellular organism such as a PROTOZOAN, BACTERIUM, or VIRUS. The term is often extended to include fungi.

microphagous (of an aquatic organism) collecting very small particles suspended in water and consuming them as food. See FILTER FEEDER.

microphyll a tiny leaf with no vascular tissues that is found in certain mosses.

micropinocytic vesicle a flasklike invagination of the cell plasma membrane that eventually cuts off at the neck to form a cellular vacuole. See PINOCYTOSIS.

micropinocytosis see PINOCYTOSIS.

micropyle a small canal in the integument surrounding the ovule of a flowering plant, through which the POLLEN TUBE usually enters the ovule on the way to the EMBRYO SAC. Water enters the seed via the micropyle prior to GERMINATION.

microscope an instrument for magnifying the perceived size of an object. The simple microscope is the hand lens, but the instrument commonly used is the *compound microscope*, which has two sets of lenses: eyepiece and objective. The compound microscope can magnify 600—1000× using an oil interface between lens and slide (see OIL-IMMERSION OBJECTIVE LENS), and with suitable eyepieces objects can be viewed up to a magnification of 1500×, the maximum power of the normal light microscope. Higher magnification can be obtained with an ELECTRON MICROSCOPE.

microsomal fraction a collection of tiny subcellular particles, invisible with the light MICROSCOPE, that are produced during DIFFERENTIAL CENTRIFUGATION. Under the ELECTRON MICROSCOPE, these *microsomes* can be seen to consist mainly of membranes and RIBOSOMES from the ENDOPLASMIC reticulum.

microsome see MICROSOMAL FRACTION.

microsphere small bodies of matter formed by the combinations of proteins produced in experiments attempting to simulate the creation of life on Earth.

microsporangium the sporangium from which the microspores are formed, which in higher plants is the pollen sac. See ANTHER.

microspore the smaller of the two types of SPORE produced by ferns and higher plants, giving rise to the male GAMETOPHYTE. In TRACHEO-PHYTES the microspore is the POLLEN GRAIN. Compare MEGASPORE.

microsporophyll the structure bearing the microsporangia, that is, a leaf or modified leaf, and in flowering plants, the STAMEN.

microtome an instrument used for cutting very thin sections for microscopic examination.

microtubule or **neurotubule** a hollow filament about 20—25 nm in diameter found in EUKARYOTE cells, composed of ACTIN-like protein called *tubulin*. Microtubules are thought to make up the CYTOSKELE-TON of the cell, the spindle fibers of MEIOSIS and MITOSIS (see also COLCHICINE), and, in some cells of plants and animals, form the 9 + 2 structure of the CILIUM and FLAGELLUM.

microvillus a minute fingerlike process found in numbers projecting from the cell surface where, in epithelium, they form a *brush border*. Microvilli are found, for example, on the villi lining the small intestine.

micturition the release of urine from the body. See BLADDER.

midbrain or **mesencephalon** the part of the brain lying between the forebrain and hindbrain. It contains the optic lobe and is particularly concerned with hearing and sight. See FOREBRAIN, HINDBRAIN.

middle ear see EAR.

middle lamella (*pl.* lamellae) the thin membrane separating two adjacent plant cells, whose function is to cement them together. It consists of varying amounts of PECTIN, depending on IAA concentration (see Fig. 216).

midgut the middle portion of the ALIMENTARY CANAL.

midparent value the average value of a METRIC CHARACTER from two parents. When compared with values of their offspring, midparent values give a direct measure of NARROW-SENSE HERITABILITY.

midriff 1. the middle part of the human body between chest and waist. 2. (in anatomy) the DIAPHRAGM.

cellulose cell wall — middle lamella

air space

Fig. 216. **Middle lamella.** Transverse section through several cell walls.

migration any cyclical movements (usually annual) that occur during the life history of an animal at definite intervals and always include a return trip from where they began. The outward journey is termed EMIGRATION, and the inward journey IMMIGRATION.

mildew 1. a plant disease caused by a fungus. 2. any fungus, such as *Erysiphe,* that causes cereal mildew. 3. a fungus in the mycelial state, growing over a substrate without obvious fruiting bodies.

milk 1. a whitish fluid secreted by the mammary gland in mammals that serves to nourish the young. 2. any white fluid, such as coconut milk.

milk gland 1. see MAMMARY GLAND. 2. a nutrient gland in the uterus of viviparous species of insects, such as the tse-tse fly.

milk teeth see DECIDUOUS TEETH.

Miller, Stanley see COACERVATE THEORY.

milli- *combining form* denoting thousand. In technical terminology, it denotes one thousandth of the base unit.

millipede or **millepede** any member of the subclass Diplopoda, class MYRIAPODA, cylindrical in shape, having two pairs of limbs on each of some 70 segments, herbivorous, and terrestrial.

Millon's test a test for the presence of protein in a mixture, involving use of Millon's reagent, which contains mercuric nitrate and nitrite. On heating a proteinaceous solution with a few drops of Millon's reagent (using a fume exhaust hood), a purplish precipitate is formed. The test is less commonly used today because of the danger associated with handling mercuric salts, the BIURET REACTION being employed instead.

mimetic (of an organism) having evolved to resemble another species. See MIMICRY.

mimicry the adoption by one species of any of the properties of another, such as color, habits, and structure. Particularly common in insects, two main forms of mimicry are recognized:

(a) *Batesian mimicry,* in which two species have the same appearance, often warning colors, but one of them, the model, is distasteful to predators. The mimic gains advantage because predators learn to associate appearance with bad taste and leave both model and mimic uneaten.

(b) *Mullerian mimicry,* in which both model and mimic are distasteful to predators and both gain from the other's distastefulness since the predator learns to avoid all similar-looking forms, whichever it eats first.

mineral deficiency a lack of minerals in the food intake of an organism.

mineral element see ESSENTIAL ELEMENT.

mineralization the conversion of organic matter to inorganic matter.

mineralocorticoids see ADRENAL CORTICAL HORMONES.

mineral requirement the minerals required to maintain an organism in a normal, healthy state.

mineral salt any inorganic homogeneous solid, such as sodium, potassium, phosphorus, or chlorine.

minimal medium a food source containing the minimum requirement for microbial growth. These are carbon inorganic salts and water. Such media are used in screening for AUXOTROPHS. See ONE GENE/ONE ENZYME HYPOTHESIS.

Miocene epoch a division of the TERTIARY PERIOD, lasting from 26 million until 7 million years ago. In this epoch mammals acquired their present form. The European flora became more temperate, and grasslands increased.

miracidium (*pl.* miracidia) the first larval form of a liver fluke, which develops from the egg as a flat free-swimming, ciliated larva.

miscarriage the expulsion of a fetus before it is viable outside the womb.

miscible (of liquids) having the ability to mix.

mismatch of bases the noncomplementary pairing of nucleotide bases in a DNA molecule, perhaps following on from a SUBSTITUTION MUTATION event. The error may be corrected at the next replication of the DNA molecule, producing one mutant and one normal molecule.

mis-sense mutation a change to the base sequence of a DNA CODON so that it encodes a different amino acid. For example, a SUBSTITUTION MUTATION in the first base of a triplet might produce the following mis-sense mutation: CCU (pro) ACU (thr). See GENETIC CODE.

Mitchell, P. see ELECTRON TRANSPORT SYSTEM.

mite any member of the order Acarina, ARACHNIDS possessing clawed appendages in front of the mouth (chelicarae). They may be free-living (many thousands per meter^2 in soil) or parasitic.

mitochondria see MITOCHONDRION.

mitochondrial shunt a transfer (shunt) in the presence of oxygen of reduced NAD produced in the cytoplasm by GLYCOLYSIS to a MITOCHONDRION. It enters the ELECTRON TRANSPORT SYSTEM on the mitochondrial inner lining.

mitochondrion (*pl.* mitochondria) a subcellular, cylindrical organelle found in EUKARYOTES, of about 0.2—0.5 μm in length. Under the ELECTRON MICROSCOPE, the mitochondrion is seen to consist of a double membrane surrounding a matrix, with the inner membrane folded into projections, called CRISTAE. The walls of the cristae are the site of ELECTRON TRANSPORT SYSTEMS producing ATP, while the reactions of the KREBS CYCLE take place within the matrix. Mitochondria have thus been called the powerhouses of the cell and are especially prevalent in cells with a high energy requirement. Mitochondria are self-replicating and contain DNA by which they can control synthesis of some of their own proteins.

mitogen a growth factor in the form of a small protein found in blood serum that often has a specific target organ in which it induces MITOSIS.

mitogenetic rays hypothetical rays of short wavelength emanating from tissues that, according to theory, stimulate MITOSIS in other tissues.

mitosis a type of nuclear division by which two daughter cells are produced from one parent cell with no change in chromosome number. Mitosis is associated with asexual growth and repair and, although it is a continuous process, has been divided into four main stages, given below. Further details of each stage may be obtained by referring to individual entries.

(a) PROPHASE: chromosomes contract and become visible as threads. Each chromosome divides into two CHROMATIDS, and the nuclear membrane disintegrates.

(b) METAPHASE: chromosomes migrate to the equator of a spindle and become attached to the spindle microtubules by their CENTROMERES.

(c) ANAPHASE: chromatids separate and go to opposite poles.

(d) TELOPHASE: nuclear membrane reforms; chromosomes lengthen and cannot be distinguished.

See also MEIOSIS.

mitospore a SPORE resulting from MITOSIS.

mitotic crossing over a recombination between HOMOLOGOUS CHROMOSOMES in a diploid cell undergoing MITOSIS, producing diploid daughter cells that have a different combination of alleles than the original parental cell. See Fig. 217.

Fig. 217. **Mitotic crossing over.** Recombination between homologous chromosomes.

mitral valve see BICUSPID (3).

mixed nerve a nerve containing both EFFERENT NEURONS and AFFERENT NEURONS.

ml *abbreviation for* milliliter, represented as cm^3.

moa a large, extinct, flightless bird of New Zealand, up to 3 meters in height that became extinct in historical times. Eggs are still found preserved in boggy conditions.

mobile genetic element see TRANSPOSABLE GENETIC ELEMENT.

mobility, electrical a measurement of the migration rate of an ion in an electric field.

mobility, mechanical a measurement of the rate at which a molecule diffuses in a liquid phase.

mode (statistics) the most frequently observed value in a series of observations, that is, the peak of a FREQUENCY DISTRIBUTION.

modifier gene any gene that alters the phenotypic expression of a nonallelic gene. See GENETIC BACKGROUND.

molality the number of MOLES of a solute present in a kilogram of pure solvent.

molarity the number of moles of a solute present in a liter of solution.

molar teeth the crushing teeth that occur at the back of the jaw of mammals. Each molar has a complicated pattern of cusps and ridges and several roots. The molars have no preceding milk teeth.

mold see MILDEW (3).

mole the basic SI unit of amount of substance. One mole of any substance contains 6.023×10^{23} (*Avogadro's number*) molecules, atoms, or ions of an element or compound equal to the relative molecular mass in grams. Symbol: mol.

molecular biology the study of structures and properties of molecules found in cells.

molecular hybridization or **hybridization** or **annealing** the artificial creation of duplex polynucleotide molecules by annealing complementary single strands of RNA and DNA together. Such techniques enable estimation of complementarity between DNA/DNA, DNA/RNA, and RNA/RNA polynucleotide chains. See COMPLEMENTARY BASE PAIRING.

molecule the smallest chemical unit of matter that has the characteristics of the substance of which it forms a part.

mollusk any member of the phylum Mollusca, including the snails (GASTROPODS), BIVALVES, the squids and octopuses (CEPHALOPODS), and two minor classes, the Amphineura and Scaphopoda. Most have one or more shells and an unsegmented body structure with a COELOM. Some are terrestrial, but the majority are aquatic.

molt (of birds, mammals, reptiles, and arthropods) to shed (feathers, hair, skin, or cuticle). See ECDYSIS, MOLTING HORMONE.

molting hormone or **ecdysone** a hormone secreted by the thoracic gland of insects that brings about molting of the cuticle and subsequent growth (ECDYSIS). It raises the metabolic rate and increase buildup of proteins from AMINO ACIDS in growing tissue.

mol. wt. *abbreviation for* molecular weight.

monachasium a CYMOSE inflorescence in which the branches are alternate or spirally arranged, or where one branch is developed more strongly than the other.

monadelphous (of STAMEN filaments) united into a single bundle.

Monera the kingdom that contains the BACTERIA and BLUE-GREEN ALGAE.

mongolism see DOWN SYNDROME.

monkey any long-tailed primate excluding the tarsiers and lemurs, comprising the Old World and New World monkeys and marmosets.

mono- *combining form* denoting alone, single, one.

monoaminoxidase an enzyme that inactivates NORADRENALINE by oxidation in ADRENERGIC nerves.

monocarpic (of plants) flowering once during life.

monochlamydeous or **haplochlamydeous** (of flowers) having only a single whorl of perianth segments.

monoclonal antibody an ANTIBODY produced by a CLONE of cells derived from a single, selected cell. Such antibodies are extremely pure, and monoclonal techniques have enabled production of specific antibodies to tumorous cells.

monocotyledon any flowering plant of the group Monocotyledonae. See DICOTYLEDON for comparative table (see Fig. 126).

monocyte or **macrocyte** a type of LEUKOCYTE (white blood cell) of the AGRANULOCYTE group that is produced from stem cells in the bone marrow and is 12—15 μm in diameter. Monocytes remain in the blood for a short time and then migrate to other tissues as MACROPHAGES, moving particularly to areas that have been invaded by bacteria and other foreign materials, where they ingest large particles by PHAGOCYTOSIS. See also HISTOCYTE, LYMPHOCYTE.

monoecious (of plants) having both male and female organs occurring on the same plant, in unisexual flowers such as corn and hazel. Monoecious literally means one home. Compare DIOECIOUS.

monogamy a state in which a single male pairs with a single female in a partnership that may last for several seasons or life. Monogamy is common in birds, for example, among swans, but it is rare in mammals.

Monogenea a group of ectoparasitic trematode FLUKES with only one host and parasitic on fish and amphibia. They are distinguished from the DIGENEA, which have at least two hosts. See also BILHARZIA.

monogenic of or relating to an inherited characteristic that is controlled by one gene.

monograph a publication relating normally to a higher TAXON that includes an exhaustive treatment of all aspects of the biology of the group insofar as they relate to its taxonomy and classification.

monohybrid an organism that carries two different ALLELES of one gene. For example, character A, controlled by alleles $A1$ and $A2$, would produce a monohybrid GENOTYPE of $A1A2$, that is, a HETEROZYGOTE.

A monohybrid cross is one in which two parents are crossed to produce monohybrids, which then are mated, or one in which a single monohybrid plant is self-fertilized (see SELF-FERTILIZATION). Mendel formulated his law of SEGREGATION from the results of a monohybrid cross involving single characters in the pea plant.

monohybrid inheritance a pattern of results from crosses, indicating that a single gene is responsible for controlling a particular character. See MONOHYBRID.

monokaryon or **monocaryon** a fungal hypha, characteristic of BASIDIOMYCETES, that contains cells each of which has only one HAPLOID (1) nucleus.

monolayer see MONOMOLECULAR FILM.

monomer any molecule that can exist alone or with other similar molecules to form a polymer.

monomolecular film or **monolayer** a single layer of lipid molecules with their hydrocarbon chains at right angles to the surface, as when a lipid is allowed to spread over the surface of pure water. See UNIT MEMBRANE and FLUID-MOSAIC MODEL.

mononuclear phagocyte system or **reticuloendothelial system** a mammalian defense system against foreign bodies, consisting of MACROPHAGE cells located in the lymph nodes (see LYMPHATIC SYSTEM), liver, spleen, and bone marrow.

monophyletic (of a group of individuals) descended from a common ancestor.

monoploid an organism or cell in which there is one set of chromosomes instead of the normal two.

monopodial (of a stem) having the same apical growing point responsible for consecutive years' growth.

monopodium a structure, such as a tree trunk, that has increased in length by apical growth.

monosaccharide a carbohydrate MONOMER, a simple sugar with the formula $(CH_2O)_n$, for example, $C_6H_{12}O_6$ glucose and fructose. See Fig. 218. Such carbohydrates are generally white crystalline solids with a sweet taste and are usually soluble in water. The carbon chain forming the backbone of such sugars can be of varying lengths. Some monosaccharides contain only three carbons (triose types such as glyceraldehyde) and others contain five carbons (pentose types such as the deoxyribose sugar of DNA). Those with six carbons (hexose types such as glucose) are the most important since they can be joined together by CONDENSATION REACTIONS (loss of water) to form DISACCHARIDES and POLYSACCHARIDES.

Fig. 218. **Monosaccharide.** Molecular structures of (a) glucose and (b) fructose.

monosomic having one chromosome of a diploid set of somatic chromosomes missing. For example, TURNER'S SYNDROME. See ANEUPLOIDY.

monotreme any mammal of the primitive subclass Monotremata, including the duck-billed platypus and spiny anteater. Monotremes differ from other mammals in laying eggs, and in having a single opening (CLOACA) for the passage of eggs or sperm, feces, and urine. They inhabit Australia and New Guinea.

monotypic (of a TAXON) containing only one subordinate taxon. For example, a genus with only one species, a species with only one subspecies.

monozygotic twins or **identical twins** or **uniovular twins** siblings that develop from one egg, contain identical genetical information, and are (usually) of very similar appearance. Any physical and mental differences detected between identical twins must arise, therefore, from environmental differences, both before and after birth. Such twins are examples of a CLONE and are always of the same sex. Compare DIZYGOTIC TWINS.

moor an upland habitat usually dominated by heather growing on peat that is not normally waterlogged.

morbid diseased, as in morbid anatomy, the study of structural changes due to disease.

Morgan, Thomas Hunt (1866—1945) American zoologist who was a founder of modern genetics. He first used the fruit fly *Drosophila* as an experimental animal, discovering SEX LINKAGE in 1910, together with a simple method of mapping genes on the same chromosome (see GENETIC LINKAGE), the units of distance being called *centimorgans* originally.

morph any individual variant that constitutes a form of a polymorphic species.

morphine a white crystalline narcotic alkaloid drug obtained from opium. Formula: $C_{17}H_{19}NO_3$.

morphogenesis the development of the form or structure of an organism during the life history of the individual.

morphogenetic movement the reorientation of masses of cells during embryonic development.

morphology the study of the shape, general appearance, or form of an organism, as distinct from ANATOMY, which involves dissection to discover structure.

morphospecies a species recognized solely on the basis of its MORPHOLOGY.

mortality rate or **death rate** 1. the percentage of a population dying in a year. 2. the ratio of the number of human deaths per 1000 of population.

morula a solid ball of cells resulting from cleavage of a fertilized ovum. It is formed of a mass of BLASTOMERES that subsequently forms a BLASTULA.

mosaic any organism exhibiting a mixture of cells of different genetic makeup, such as a GYNANDROMORPH. See INACTIVE-X HYPOTHESIS. Plants showing this phenomenon are known as CHIMERAS (1).

mosaic egg any egg with clearly definable zones that develop into particular tissues and organs at a later stage.

mosaic evolution a form of evolution in which various characters or structures of a particular phenotype have different rates of change.

mosquito a DIPTERAN fly that acts as a vector of numerous tropical diseases, such as MALARIA and YELLOW FEVER.

moss any bryophyte of the class Musci. Usually these are small plants (less than 5 cm high) attached to moist or wet substrates by rhizoids; this is the SPOROPHYTE generation. The sexual organs are borne on a GAMETOPHYTE generation, and the ANTHERIDIA and ARCHEGONIA are on separate leaf rosettes. The male gametes are motile and, after fertilization, a diploid sporophyte is produced within which haploid spores are developed, each spore giving rise to a *protonema* from which the new gametophyte develops.

moth a LEPIDOPTERAN that is mainly nocturnal, lacks knobbed antennae, and folds its wings flat at rest. The term has no taxonomic status.

motility motion.

motivation the internal state of an animal prior to a specific behavioral act.

motor relating to the stimulus of an EFFECTOR organ.

motor cortex the part of the cerebral cortex of the brain that controls the motor functions.

motor neuron a nerve cell, the fiber from which connects with STRIATED MUSCLE under voluntary control and conducts the stimulus from the CENTRAL NERVOUS SYSTEM to the effector, which then is stimulated into activity.

mountain sickness fatigue, headache, and nausea in humans resulting from the lack of oxygen above about 4000 meters.

mouth the anterior opening of the ALIMENTARY CANAL of animals through which food is taken into the body. It is often surrounded by mouthparts or tentacles that facilitate feeding. See DIGESTIVE SYSTEM.

mouthbreeder any of various African cichlid fish that retain eggs and young in the mouth, where they are hatched and protected.

mouthpart any of the paired appendages in arthropods that surround the mouth and are associated with feeding.

mRNA see MESSENGER RNA.

mucin a MUCOPROTEIN that forms MUCUS when in solution.

mucopolysaccharide any polysaccharide, such as hyaluronic acid or heparin, that contains either an amino sugar or a derivative.

mucoprotein a complex of protein and polysaccharide.

mucosa any EPITHELIUM that secretes MUCUS, such as the MUCOUS MEMBRANE lining the alimentary canal.

mucous membrane the lining of the gut system and the urinogenital system of animals, consisting largely of moist EPITHELIUM overlying CONNECTIVE TISSUE. GOBLET CELLS in the epithelium secrete MUCUS.

mucronate (of a leaf) having a short narrow point.

mucus 1. any slimy or sticky material secreted by invertebrate animals or plants. 2. a viscous slimy solution of the protein MUCIN secreted by the MUCOUS MEMBRANES of vertebrates.

muddy shore a coastal stretch where deposition of alluvium and detritus has occurred, as opposed to sandy or pebbly shores where beaches are formed. Characterized by development of SALT MARSH.

Mullerian duct the duct from the embryonic PRONEPHROS, which in later development in mammals becomes the oviduct in females and disappears in males. Named for the German anatomist and physiologist Johannes Müller (1801—1858).

Mullerian mimicry see MIMICRY.

multi- or **mult-** *combining form* denoting much, many.

multicellular composed of many cells. See ACELLULAR.

multifactorial (of a character) controlled by several genes.

multinucleate having more than one nucleus.

multiple allelism the occurrence of more than two ALLELES of a gene, although only two may be present together in an individual at any one time. For example, the ABO BLOOD GROUP gene has at least six alleles. In practice it seems likely that all genes possess many alternative alleles but these often remain undetected since no noticeable alteration of PHENOTYPE is observed.

multiple factors or **multiple genes** genes that collectively produce a particular characteristic, such as height in humans.

multiple fission the splitting of the nucleus several times before division of the cytoplasm, as happens in some PROTOZOANS.

multisite activity the action of chemicals— copper, for example—in biological systems where they can disrupt a wide range of biochemical pathways.

multivalent (of chromosomes) forming an association during prophase I of MEIOSIS. Compare BIVALENT.

multivariate analysis (statistics) an analysis involving several variables simultaneously.

mumps an acute, contagious viral disease of humans, particularly of children, characterized by a swelling of the parotid salivary glands lying beneath the ear and caused by a paramyxovirus. The mumps virus is spread by droplets of saliva and respiratory secretions that enter a new host via the respiratory tract. The disease appears most often during winter and early spring and in adults can lead to MENINGITIS. It may cause sterility in males. Once affected, the individual is usually immune to mumps for life. Vaccination is possible using attenuated virus.

murein the cross-linked mucopeptides that form the rigid framework of bacterial cell walls.

muricate (of plant structures) having a surface roughened by short, sharp projections.

muscarine a poisonous alkaloid occurring in certain mushrooms.

muscarinic (in physiological terminology) having acetylcholine receptors that are sensitive to muscarine but not to nicotine.

muscle the fleshy part of any animal that consists of tissue made up of highly contractile cells serving to move parts of the body relative to each other.

A muscle is composed of many fibers or muscle cells. In STRIATED MUSCLE, every cell contains a bundle of MYOFIBRILS, each exhibiting a banding pattern and being made up of a number of SARCOMERES arranged end to end. The sarcomere is the unit of contraction, and the banding visible over its surface results from the fact that the longitudinal filaments making up the myofibril are of two types, thick (dark) and thin (light). These filaments overlap as shown in Fig. 219. The thick filaments are composed of the protein MYOSIN and the thin filaments of ACTIN. H.E. Huxley and K. Harrison found that on contraction the light zones (I-BANDS) were comparatively narrow; on relaxation of the muscle the I-bands were broad. Where very strong contraction takes place, the H-zone disappears and the thin filaments overlap.

Fig. 219. **Muscle.** A sarcomere.

Huxley and Harrison proposed the *sliding filament hypothesis* to account for their observations. Bridges occur between thick and thin filaments and in contraction the bridges pull thin filaments past the thick ones using a ratchet mechanism. Some filaments are retained in this pulled-past position while others detach then reattach and repeat the pulling-past action. ACTOMYOSIN is formed at the point of contact of bridge and thin filament. For each bridge to go through its cycle of attachment, contraction, and reattachment, the splitting of one molecule of ATP is required, the cycles occurring between 50 and 100 times a second. The supply of ATP comes from MITOCHONDRIA between the fibrils. Calcium ions are released from vesicles in the sarcoplasmic reticulum, by the ACTION POTENTIAL passing along the surface of the fiber, and these ions split the ATP. Troponin activated by the calcium displaces tropomyosin, which prevents myosin bridges from binding with actin fibrils. Once binding takes place, this activates ATPase and on hydrolysis of ATP the bridge goes through its cycle of movement.

muscle fiber a muscle cell consisting of numerous MYOFIBRILS.

muscle spindle a PROPRIOCEPTOR found in skeletal muscle in the form of a capsule containing specialized muscle cells and nerve endings. Changes in length or tension of muscle cells stimulate the spindle.

muscular dystrophy (MD) a disease characterized by progressive wasting of muscles and eventual death. One type, called *Duchenne MD*, is controlled by a recessive sex-linked gene (see SEX LINKAGE) and, as a result, affects more boys than girls. The disease first shows itself between 1 and 6 years, progressing until the patient is confined to a wheelchair by the early teens with death resulting by the late teens in most affected individuals. Other forms of the disease are controlled by autosomal genes, both dominant and recessive, and they are equally frequent in males and females.

muscularis mucosa a thin layer of small muscle cells in the outermost layer of the mucosa of the alimentary canal.

musculoepithelial cell a type of cell found particularly in COELENTERATES that is columnar in shape, occurs with ectoderm or endoderm cells, and has two contractile processes extending into the mesoglea.

musculoskeletal system the basis of locomotion in vertebrates, which is the contraction of MUSCLES against a skeleton.

mushroom the common name for the fruiting bodies of the class Basidiomycetes of the family Agaricaceae.

mussel the bivalve mollusk *Mytilus edulis*.

mutagen an agent capable of increasing the MUTATION rate in an organism, for example, X-rays, ultraviolet light, mustard gas.

mutant 1. any gene that has undergone a MUTATION. **2.** an individual showing the effects of a mutation, with a phenotype that is not WILD TYPE.

mutant site the area within a gene where a POINT MUTATION has taken place.

mutation a change in genetic material of an organism. If the alteration affects gametic cells, the change is a genetic, or POINT MUTATION, and can be inherited. If body cells (nonsexual) are affected, the mutation is called *somatic mutation* and will not normally be inherited. Mutations can be at two levels: (a) alterations to a single gene (point mutation) producing a different ALLELE and (b) alterations to the structure and/or numbers of chromosomes. See also SPONTANEOUS MUTATION, CHROMOSOMAL MUTATION.

mutation breeding a breeding technique in which MUTAGENS are used to produce new genetic forms of useful agricultural species. While novel types can be successfully made in this way, most MUTATIONS are harmful and, being random occurrences, it is difficult to control the changes produced, many of which will upset the delicate balance of genes in a particular strain.

mutation frequency the proportion of mutants in a population as compared with normal WILD TYPE individuals.

mutation rate the number of mutations per gene in a fixed time. In sexual organisms this is often measured as the number of mutations per gamete. Rates vary considerably between genes and between organisms, but a typical rate is 1 mutation per locus per 100,000 gametes.

muton the smallest part of a gene that can undergo a MUTATION. It is now known that a muton is the size of a DNA nucleotide base.

mutualism see SYMBIOSIS.

mycelium the total mass of HYPHAE of a FUNGUS, which constitutes the vegetative body as opposed to a fruiting body.

Mycetozoa see MYXOMYCETA.

myco- and **-mycete** *combining forms* denoting mushroom.

mycology the study of fungi.

Mycophyta see EUMYCOTA.

mycoplasmas a group of minute PROKARYOTES that resemble bacteria but do not possess a cell wall and thus have a variable morphology.

mycorrhiza an association between a FUNGUS and the roots of a higher plant. The fungus may be located on or in the root, and in some cases it breaks down PROTEINS or AMINO ACIDS that are soluble and can be absorbed by the higher plant. In most cases, only nitrogen and phosphorus compounds result from fungal activity. Carbohydrates synthesized by the higher plants are absorbed by the fungus, so the relationship is a form of SYMBIOSIS. Some plants that lack chlorophyll, such as the bird's nest orchid, rely on mycorrhizas for carbohydrates in addition to protein.

mycosis an animal disease caused by fungal infection.

Mycota the plant kingdom containing the fungi and slime molds.

mycotrophic (of plants) having mycorrhizas associated with the root system.

myel- or **myelo-** *combining form* denoting marrow.

myelin a white phospholipid. See MYELIN SHEATH.

myelin sheath or **medullated nerve fiber** a sheath of fatty substance associated with protein that surrounds larger nerve fibers of vertebrates (see DENDRITE). The white lipid coating is produced by SCHWANN CELLS. The sheath permits a greater current flow and thus speeds transmission of nerve impulses. Constrictions in the myelin sheath, known as *nodes of Ranvier,* indicate the division between one Schwann cell and another. Nonmyelinated fibers occur commonly in invertebrates, internally in the spinal cord of vertebrates, and in the AUTOMATIC NERVOUS SYSTEM of vertebrates. Myelinated fibers, white in appearance, occur outside the spinal cord of vertebrates. See Fig. 220.

myelitis inflammation of the MYELIN SHEATH surrounding the spinal cord.

Fig. 220. **Myelin sheath.** Cross section of a myelinated nerve fiber.

myeloid tissue the tissue producing blood cells in vertebrates, normally located in bone marrow.

myeloma a cancerous tumor of the bone marrow.

Mymaridae an order comprising the fairy flies (HYMENOPTERA), the smallest known insects. They are related to chalcid wasps and are exclusively egg parasites.

myo- *combining form* denoting muscle.

myoblast a cell that gives rise to a muscle fiber.

myocardium the muscular wall of the vertebrate heart.

myocoel the part of the coelomic cavity that exists within each muscle block or MYOTOME.

myofibril a microscopic contractile unit of STRIATED MUSCLE, made up of a series of SARCOMERES. The myofibril is made up of numerous longitudinal filaments of two forms, thick (MYOSIN) and thin (ACTIN). (See MUSCLE, I-BAND.) Relatively little is known of the contraction of smooth muscle, where so-called contractile elements are thought to contain both actin and myosin.

myogenic contraction contractions that are initiated in the muscle itself rather than by impulses from nerves. For example, in CARDIAC MUSCLE the heart continues to beat under the influence of the PACE-MAKER after removal from the body.

myoglobin a relatively small globular protein (mol. wt. = 17,000) consisting of 153 amino acids in a POLYPEPTIDE CHAIN and one HEME group. The molecule is found in the muscles of vertebrates and some invertebrates, giving the muscles a red color, and has a high affinity for oxygen.

myoneme the contractile fibril that occurs in some PROTOZOANS, such as *Stentor* and *Vorticella*.

myopia or **nearsightedness** an inability to see distant objects clearly, due to their image being focused in front of the retina because the cornea and lens form too powerful an optical system for the size of the eye. Compare HYPEROPIA.

myoplasm the cytoplasmic SOL content of a muscle cell.

myosin a protein found in the thick filaments of the SARCOMERES OF

MUSCLE. Myosin combines with ACTIN to produce ACTOMYOSIN during contraction.

myostatic reflex see STRETCH REFLEX.

myotome a muscle block that is repeated in each METAMERIC SEGMENT. Segmentation becomes much modified in the head region and where paired limbs are developed.

Myriapoda the class of ARTHROPODS containing centipedes (Chilopoda) and millipedes (Diplopoda).

myrmecophily the use of ants by other insects, usually beetles, as a source of food or a place (an ant nest) in which to live.

myxameba a cell produced on the germination of spores. It is found in slime molds and some simple fungi, and is capable of ameboid movement.

myxedema the condition occurring in adults due to undersecretion of THYROXINE. There is a decrease of METABOLIC RATE, an increase in subcutaneous fat, a coarsening of the skin, and mental and physical sluggishness.

Myxomyceta or **Mycetozoa** or **Myxomycophyta** or **slime mold** fungus-like organisms (see PLASMODIUM) having a naked mass of protoplasm and living and feeding on dead, decaying, or living plants. They reproduce by spores and are capable of ameboid movement. The group is now normally classified in the division Myxomyceta of the Kingdom Mycota. See MYXAMEBA.

Myxomycophyta see MYXOMYCETA.

Myxophyta see BLUE-GREEN ALGAE.

Myxosporidia a group of SPOROZOANS parasitic on freshwater fish, to which they attach themselves by structures having a superficial resemblance to coelenterate NEMATOCYSTS.

N

nacreous layer the pearly, innermost layer of the shell of a mollusk, secreted by the mantle epithelium.

NAD (nicotinamide adenine dinucleotide) a COENZYME that readily accepts or gives up hydrogen.

$$NAD \rightleftharpoons NADH$$
$$oxidized \quad reduced$$

NAD acts as an energy carrier in the cell. Reduced NADH transports electrons to the ELECTRON TRANSPORT SYSTEM during AEROBIC RESPIRATION. See also FAD.

NADP (nicotinamide adenine dinucleotide phosphate) a COENZYME that readily accepts hydrogen from an ELECTRON TRANSPORT SYSTEM in PHOTOPHOSPHORYLATION, passing the electrons on to the CALVIN CYCLE of PHOTOSYNTHESIS.

$$NADP \rightleftharpoons NADPH$$
$$oxidized \quad reduced$$

nail a horny, keratinized layer protecting the distal end of each finger and toe in humans and most other primates. In other terrestrial vertebrates the nail is shaped into a claw.

naked (of a plant structure) without hairs or scales.

nanometer one billionth of a meter (10^{-9} m). Abbreviation: nm.

narco- *combining form* denoting torpor.

narcotic any chemical substance that induces a state of stupor or unconsciousness, such as opium.

nares see NOSTRIL.

narrow-sense heritability the proportion of variance among PHENOTYPES in a population that can be attributed to additive genetic variance, the latter being the sum of the average effects of all genes carried in the population that affect a particular character. Narrow sense-HERITABILITY is concerned with how much of a parent's phenotype is inherited by its offspring and often is estimated from results of selection experiments. Compare BROAD-SENSE HERITABILITY.

nasal cavity a system of chambers above the hard palate of mammals through which air passes from the nostrils to the pharynx and on to the lungs. During inspiration, air is filtered, warmed, moistened, and smelled.

nastic movement or **nastic response** a growth movement in plants that takes place in response to a diffuse, or nondirectional, stimulus, for example, the opening and closing of *Crocus* flowers due to changes in temperature.

nastic response see NASTIC MOVEMENT.

national park any relatively large area of countryside or wilderness that is (a) not materially altered by human presence or exploitation, (b) protected by legislation to preserve the characteristics for which it was designated, and (c) made accessible to visitors under special conditions for cultural and recreative purposes. This definition is the international meaning adopted by the International Union for the Conservation of Nature and Natural Resources (IUCN) in 1969.

native a species that has colonized an area without human aid.

native protein a naturally occurring protein.

natural classification see CLASSIFICATION.

natural immunity immunity due to possession of suitable genetic characteristics rather than immunity produced in response to a vaccine or serum.

natural order an obsolete term for a FAMILY of flowering plants.

natural selection the mechanism proposed by Charles DARWIN by which gradual evolutionary changes take place. Organisms that are better adapted to the environment in which they live produce more viable young, increasing their proportion in the population and, therefore, being selected. Such a mechanism depends on the variability of individuals within the population. The variability arises through MUTATION, the beneficial mutants being preserved by NATURAL SELECTION.

nature and nurture see PHENOTYPE.

nauplius the typical crustacean larva, which has a single eye, three pairs of limbs, and a rounded, transparent body.

nautiloid any mollusk of the subclass Nautiloidea, a group of cephalopods related to the fossil ammonites, which produce a large spiral chambered shell, in the last chamber of which lives the animal.

navigation or **orientation** a process of direction-finding. Many animals are capable of navigation, particularly those performing long MIGRATIONS. Birds are now known to find their way home (see HOMING) by means of the sun and stars in addition to landmarks. Bees and other ARTHROPODS use the pattern of polarized light in the sky, from which they deduce the direction of the sun. Other organisms may use chemical gradients to trace a route. For example, salmon find their specific river for breeding purposes by following a scent in from the sea.

Neanderthal man a primitive form of human: *Homo sapiens neanderthalus,* who lived some 100,000 years ago.

necrosis the localized death of plant and animal tissue, for example, the response of a leaf to invasion of a pathogen. An affected area is described as being necrotic. See DIPHTHERIA.

necrotrophic or **saprophytic** (of microorganisms and plants) feeding on dead tissue (see SAPROPHYTE). Compare BIOTROPHIC.

nectar a sugar-containing liquid secretion of the NECTARY of many flowers. It attracts insects, thus bringing about pollination.

nectary an area of tissue in a flower that secretes sugary nectar, serving as an attraction for visiting insects. Nectaries are frequently deep inside the corolla so that the pollinator both deposits and carries off pollen. See ENTOMOPHILY.

negative feedback see FEEDBACK MECHANISM.

nekton the population of free-swimming animals that inhabits the PELAGIC zone of oceans. Compare PLANKTON.

nemato- *combining form* denoting thread or threadlike.

nematoblast see CNIDOBLAST.

nematocyst a structure formed of a hollow thread within a bladder in the CNIDOBLAST, or thread cell, of COELENTERATES. On stimulation, for example, by prey, the thread is everted. Several types exist, such as stinging cells that inject poisonous substances into the prey through the thread, and sticky cells that exude a sticky substance, causing the prey to adhere to the coelentrate tentacle. Enormous numbers are present on the tentacles of some forms, and nematocysts are responsible for the jellyfish sting.

Such cells can be used by other organisms, for example, flatworms preying on coelenterates. The nematocysts migrate to the surface layer of a flatworm that has fed on a coelenterate and are used by the flatworms in exactly the same way that coelenterates use them. See Fig. 221.

nematode any member of the phylum Nematoda, containing roundworms such as ASCARIS.

nemertean any member of the phylum Nemertea, containing the ribbon worms, for example, *Lineus,* the bootlace worm of rocky shores.

neo- *combining form* denoting new or recent.

neo-Darwinism a view of evolutionary theory that combines MENDELIAN GENETICS with DARWINISM. See CENTRAL DOGMA.

Neogene the upper part of the TERTIARY PERIOD, including the Pleistocene, Pliocene, and Miocene epochs.

Neognathae one of the two major groups of living birds, including the

Fig. 221. **Nematocyst.** Nematocysts of *Hydra*. (a) Discharged penetrant. (b) Undischarged glutinant.

flying forms. The group is distinguished by having a small prevomer bone, which does not touch the pterygoid bones. Compare PALEOGNATHAE.

neo-Lamarckism a modern attempt—for which there is scant evidence—to add genetic support to LAMARCKISM, which emphasizes the supposed influence of environmental factors on genetic change.

Neolithic 1. the period of the new Stone Age which began approximately 10,000 years ago in the Middle East. The period marks the beginning of plant cultivation and domestication of animals by humans. **2.** *adj.* relating to this period.

neonatal (of newborn offspring, particularly human) the first month of independent life.

neontology the study of life of recent living organisms. Compare PALEONTOLOGY.

neopallium a nerve mass that forms the main part of the cerebrocortex in humans, and the roof of the cerebral hemispheres in other vertebrates. The neopallium is associated with general muscular coordination and intelligence.

neoplasm an autonomous growth of tissue in the body that has no apparent physiological function, such as a TUMOR.

neoplastic disease an abnormal condition produced by a NEOPLASM.

Neornithes the group containing all birds with the exception of *Archaeopteryx*.

neoteny see PEDOGENESIS.

neotype a specimen selected as the TYPE subsequent to publication of the original description when the original types have been lost, destroyed, or otherwise invalidated.

nephridiopore the external opening of a NEPHRIDIUM.

nephridium (*pl.* nephridia) a primitive excretory organ present in many invertebrates, for example, the earthworm, in the form of a tube that opens at one end to the exterior. The other end may open into the COELOM or may terminate in a FLAME CELL.

nephromyxium a combination of COELOMODUCT and NEPHRIDIUM forming an excretory tubule such as occurs in many ANNELIDS.

nephron the MALPIGHIAN BODY and the associated tubule of the vertebrate kidney. In each human kidney there are about a million nephrons, making a total for both kidneys of about 50 miles of tubules.

nephrostome the internal opening of a NEPHRIDIUM or NEPHROMYXIUM.

neritic of a region of shallow sea water near the coast.

nerve 1. (in animals) a bundle of nerve fibers, usually containing both afferent neurons (to the CENTRAL NERVOUS SYSTEM), and efferent neurons (away from the central nervous system), together with associated connective tissue and blood vessels, situated in a common sheath of CONNECTIVE TISSUE and lying outside the central nervous system. 2. (in plants) a characteristic leaf structure consisting of fine strands that are conductive and/or strengthening in function.

nerve cell see NEURON.

nerve cord a strand of nervous tissue that forms part of the CENTRAL NERVOUS SYSTEM of invertebrates.

nerve ending the tip of a nerve fiber either in the form of an END ORGAN or small branching structure.

nerve fiber the AXON of a NERVE (1) together with its surrounding membranes.

nerve impulse the message conducted along the AXON of a NERVE (1). The impulse is a propagated negative charge on the outside of the membrane that results from a wave of DEPOLARIZATION passing along an axon. The RESTING POTENTIAL is reversed and becomes an ACTION POTENTIAL, and this passes down the axon at a speed between 1 and 100 ms, depending on the diameter of the fiber, presence of a MYELIN SHEATH, temperature, species of animal, and other factors.

Once an impulse is initiated, it progresses without degeneration, and the strength or nature of the stimulus does not affect it. It either is generated or is not (ALL-OR-NONE LAW). Varying stimuli produce varying numbers of impulses (see SUMMATION). After each impulse there is a REFRACTORY PERIOD during which a second impulse cannot pass.

nerve net a system of interconnecting nerve cells, in the form of a net, found in groups of invertebrates that lack a CENTRAL NERVOUS SYSTEM, such as COELENTERATES and ECHINODERMS. In other groups the nerve net is almost nonexistent. Conduction is slow across the net and is often in all directions, as the synapses are not usually unidirectional.

nerve ring the ring of nerves surrounding the mouth of ECHINODERMS.

nerve root the points at which a spinal nerve arises from the spinal cord. Each has two roots: a DORSAL ROOT and a VENTRAL ROOT.

nervous system the main means by which METAZOAN animals coordinate their activities through quick, short-duration reactions. (The ENDOCRINE GLAND system also has a coordinating function, but this is slower and longer lasting.) Receptors receive stimuli and pass them on to effector organs by means of nerve cells. Nerve cells are linked by SYNAPSES and may connect with other nerve cells, receptors, or effectors. Complex connections occur that give rise to complex reactions, and coordination takes place in the CENTRAL NERVOUS SYSTEM, where synapses are present in profusion. Coordination is brought about by transmission of NERVE IMPULSES.

nervous tissue NERVE cells, together with their AXONS and accessory cells.

net assimilation rate a measurement of plant growth (weight increase per unit of time) by assessing change in a particular part of the plant, usually leaf area, rather than in the overall plant.

net primary production see PRIMARY PRODUCTION.

neural relating to nerves or to the nervous system.

neural plate the part of the ectoderm that sinks below the surface of the developing vertebrate embryo and forms the spinal cord.

neurenteric canal an embryonic structure joining the gut with the neural canal when the BLASTOPORE is roofed over by neural folds.

neurilemma a thin membrane surrounding the MYELIN SHEATH of myelinated nerve fibers. It is part of the SCHWANN CELL, lying close to the axon.

neurin a filamentous protein, similar to muscle ACTIN, that is attached to the inner wall surface of brain cells and may have a role in EXOCYTOSIS.

neurocranium the part of the vertebrate skull forming the brain case and sense capsules.

neuroglia see GLIA.

neurohumor a hormone secreted by a NERVE ENDING.

neurohypophysis see PITUITARY GLAND.

neuromuscular junction the area of contact between a MOTOR NEURON and a MUSCLE FIBER.

neuron or **nerve cell** the structural unit of the nervous system, usually consisting of the cell body and cytoplasmic extensions. Long single extensions, known as AXONS, carry impulses from the cell body to other nerve cells or effectors. Short multiple extensions known as DENDRITES receive impulses. Axons may be myelinated (with MYELIN SHEATHS) or nonmyelinated, but in the former the transmission of impulses is quicker as action potentials jump from one node of Ranvier to another. See Fig. 222.

Fig. 222. **Neuron.** A vertebrate motor nerve cell.

neuron theory the theory that the nervous system is formed of numerous separate NEURONS that contact only through synapses and not through a continuity of protoplasm.

neuropeptid see ENDORPHIN.

neurophysiology the study of the physiology of NERVES.

neuropil the mass of DENDRITES and AXONS surrounding the cell bodies of the central nervous system.

Neuroptera the order of ENDOPTERYGOTE insects containing the alderflies and lacewings, possessing two pairs of similar, membranous wings.

neurosecretion the process of secretion of hormones by nerve cells.

neurotransmitter see TRANSMITTER SUBSTANCE.

neurotubule see MICROTUBULE.

neurula the stage of a vertebrate embryo when gastrulation is largely finished and a neural plate is forming, ending with formation of the neural tube.

neuston organisms supported on the water surface.

neuter an organism having nonfunctional or absent sexual parts. In plants, a neuter is one without male and female flower parts, for example, ray florets of a sunflower. A neuter in animals is one that is sexually undeveloped or sterile, for example, the female worker in a bee colony, or a castrated or spayed animal.

neutral allele a form of a gene that when carried in an organism in no way alters the FITNESS of that individual to survive and reproduce.

neutral term any term used in taxonomy, such as form or group, that has no reference to any formal category of taxonomic hierarchy.

neutrophil the most common type of white blood cell (LEUKOCYTE) formed in the bone marrow and with a normal count in human blood of between 2500 and 7500 cells per mm^3. Neutrophils are PHAGOCYTES and are important in combatting bacterial infections.

nevus 1. any birthmark, usually a sharply defined reddish patch on the skin. **2.** a pigmented mole on the skin.

niacin see NICOTINIC ACID.

niche the sum of the characters that determine the position of an organism in its ECOSYSTEM. This includes all chemical, physical, spatial, and temporal factors required for survival of that species and which limit its distribution and growth. A niche is characteristic of a SPECIES, and no two species occupy the same niche in the same environment in the presence of the other. However, a different species may occupy the same niche in the absence of the normal occupant from that habitat.

nick a single-stranded cut or break in a DNA molecule. Nicking of DNA may form part of a DNA repair mechanism, which occurs after damage caused by ultraviolet light.

nicotinamide a crystalline basic amide of the vitamin B complex.

nicotine an alkaloid derived from tobacco.

nicotinic acid or **niacin** a vitamin of the B COMPLEX found, for example, in meat, yeast, and whole wheat. Niacin is converted into nicotinamide in the body, becoming incorporated into NAD, an important coenzyme in cellular respiration. A deficiency of niacin leads to a condition called *pellagra*, with symptoms of dermatitis, muscle weakness, and mental disturbance, among others.

nictitating membrane the third eyelid that occurs in birds, reptiles, and some mammals, sharks, and amphibians. It is transparent and flicks over the eyeball from the inner (anterior) corner of the eye to clean and moisten the eyeball without shutting out the light. In diving birds, such as the auks, there is a lens-like window in the membrane that adjusts the focus of the eye under water.

nidicolous (of young birds, for example, songbirds) hatching in a relatively undeveloped stage and remaining in the nest for the fledging period.

nidifugous (of young birds, for example, waders) hatching in a condition allowing departure from the nest within a few hours after birth. Such birds spend the fledging period away from the nest.

nipple a conical projection at the center of a mammary gland on which the milk ducts have outlets.

Nissl granules or **Nissl bodies** granules that occur in the cell bodies of NEURONS. They are formed of a nucleoprotein combined with iron and are concerned with protein synthesis.

nit the egg of the human louse *Pediculus humanus*, which is found attached to hair.

Nitella a genus of green algae.

nitrification the conversion by soil bacteria of organic nitrogen into inorganic nitrates that plants can take up. Decay of animal and plant proteins gives rise to ammonium compounds, which the bacteria *Nitrosomnas* and *Nitrococcus* oxidize to nitrate. *Nitrobacter* oxidizes nitrites to nitrates. See NITROGEN CYCLE.

nitrogen cycle the circulation of nitrogen in the environment as a result of activity of living organisms. 80% of the atmosphere is made up of nitrogen, and this is maintained by the balancing action of the cycle. See Fig. 223.

Fig. 223. **Nitrogen cycle.**

nitrogen deficiency a supply of nitrogen below an organism's requirements.

nitrogen fixation the utilization of atmospheric nitrogen in synthesizing AMINO ACIDS by some bacteria and blue-green algae. Such PROKARYOTES can be free living (for example, *Azotobacter,* an aerobe; *Clostridium,* an obligate anaerobe), whereas others (for example, the bacterium *Rhizobium*) live in association with plants, occupying swellings in the root called *root nodules.* The latter relationship is one of SYMBIOSIS, in that the plant gains nutrients and thus can live in nitrogen-poor soils, and the nitrogen fixer obtains carbohydrates from the plant. The nitrogen is reduced to ammonia in the microbes by action of the enzyme nitrogenase: $N_2 + 3H_2 = 2NH_3$, the ammonia then reacting with keto acids to form amino acids.

nitrogen-fixing bacteria see NITROGEN FIXATION.

nitrogenous waste the waste nitrogen produced during METABOLISM. Initially this is often in the form of AMINO ACIDS, but few animals can excrete these directly. Many invertebrates and aquatic vertebrates eliminate nitrogen as ammonia, but this would be toxic if excess water were not available. Marine teleost fish excrete TRIMETHYLAMINE OXIDE, which is nontoxic and requires little water for elimination. Mammals, turtles, and amphibians excrete UREA; land reptiles, snails, insects, and birds excrete URIC ACID from which water is removed before voiding it.

nm *abbreviation for* NANOMETER (10^{-9} m).

Noctuidae a family of moths—the owlet moths—whose larvae are known as cutworms and cause damage to crop plant roots.

node the part of a plant stem where leaves are attached or may develop from buds. See also INTERNODE.

nodes of Ranvier see MYELIN SHEATH.

nodule 1. any small spherical swelling. 2. short for *root nodule* (see NITROGEN FIXATION).

nomenclature see BINOMIAL NOMENCLATURE.

nomen conservandum a name officially prescribed by the COMMISSION for Zoological Nomenclature.

nomen dubium a name given to an organism for which the evidence is insufficient to recognize the species to which it has been applied.

nomen oblitum a name that has lost its validity.

nominal taxon a named taxon objectively defined by its TYPE.

nominate (of a TAXON) bearing the same name as its immediately superior taxon and which is its type. For example, in the redshank, an Old World sandpiper, *Tringa totanus, totanus* is the nominate form of the species.

noncompetitive inhibition a form of enzyme control in which the enzyme has two kinds of ACTIVE SITES, one for an inhibitor, the other for the enzyme substrate. The inhibitor prevents catalytic activity of the enzyme, perhaps by changing the shape of the substrate active site. Compare COMPETITIVE INHIBITION. See also ALLOSTERIC ENZYME.

noncyclic photophosphorylation one of two main processes occurring in the light stage of PHOTOSYNTHESIS, involving chlorophyll photosystems I and II in the formation of ATP and reduced NADP. See LIGHT REACTIONS.

nondimensional (of a species) characterized by noninterbreeding of two coexisting populations, uncomplicated by considerations of space and time.

nondisjunction the failure of chromosomes to go to opposite poles during nuclear division, leading to unequal numbers of chromosomes in the daughter cells (see ANEUPLOIDY). See Fig. 224. Nondisjunction produces abnormal numbers of both AUTOSOMES (for example, DOWN SYNDROME) and SEX CHROMOSOMES (for example, TURNER'S SYNDROME).

Fig. 224. **Nondisjunction.** (a) Normal disjunction. (b) Nondisjunction.

nonessential amino acid any amino acid that is not an ESSENTIAL AMINO ACID.

nonhomologous (of chromosomes or chromosomal segments) containing different genes not pairing during meiosis. Compare HOMOLOGOUS CHROMOSOMES.

non-Mendelian genetics a mechanism or theory of inheritance that does not obey Mendel's laws about SEGREGATION of genes or their INDEPENDENT ASSORTMENT. For example, GENETIC LINKAGE between genes produces frequencies of progeny different from those predicted from independent assortment.

nonpolar (of a substance) bearing no charge or hydroxyl groups, and thus not combining with water.

nonrace-specific resistance or **horizontal resistance** a situation in which a large number of genes (POLYGENES) in the host plant confer a general level of resistance to a wide range of attacking organisms— pathogens or parasites. Such a system usually can withstand genetic changes in the attacking organism and thus yield stable production of crops. Compare RACE-SPECIFIC RESISTANCE.

nonrandom mating any mating in a population in which crosses between various types of individuals do not occur in the frequencies expected by chance. Two major types of nonrandom mating can be distinguished: between individuals that are related (see INBREEDING), and between individuals with similar phenotypes (see ASSORTATIVE MATING).

nonreducing sugar see SUGAR.

nonsense codon or **termination codon** or **stop codon** a triplet of MESSENGER RNA bases, such as the OCHER CODON, that does not code for an AMINO ACID and causes termination of polypeptide synthesis during the translation phase of PROTEIN SYNTHESIS. There are three nonsense codons in the GENETIC CODE.

nonsense mutation an alteration in a DNA POLYNUCLEOTIDE CHAIN that results in a NONSENSE CODON when transcribed onto mRNA.

noradrenaline a transmitter substance produced at the nerve endings of ADRENERGIC nerves giving effects similar to those of ADRENALINE. After transmission, it is inactivated by monoaminoxidase in order to prevent a buildup. The action of noradrenaline can be inhibited by various drugs, such as mescaline, which produce hallucinatory effects.

normal distribution curve or **Gaussian curve** the bell-like shape produced when a normal population is sampled for a continuously varying character (for example, height in humans) and the FREQUENCY DISTRIBUTION is plotted on a graph. The curve is theoretically exactly symmetrical, so that the shape on each side of the mean is the mirror image of the other, with an equal area. See Fig. 225. Thus, the MODE, MEDIAN, and MEAN are all at the center of the distribution.

Fig. 225. **Normal distribution curve.** The curve shows the frequency of recorded height in a so-called normal population of humans.

normalizing selection a form of STABILIZING SELECTION in which less fit individuals at both extremes of a distribution are eliminated, reducing the genetic variability in the population.

nose the projecting part of the head of higher vertebrates that usually carries the nostrils and is associated with the sense of smell.

nostril or **nares** an external opening of the nose leading into the nasal cavity.

noto- *combining form* denoting the back.

notochord the longitudinal axial support (skeleton) of the embryos of all chordates, which lies ventral to the nerve cord and dorsal to the alimentary canal. Remnants of the notochord usually remain in the adult between the vertebrae, which come to surround it.

nucellus the tissue within the OVULE of a plant, surrounded by INTEGUMENTS (1) and containing the EMBRYO SAC.

nuclear division a part of the cell cycle. See MITOSIS, MEIOSIS.

nuclear membrane an envelope surrounding the nuclear material of eukaryotic cells that consists of two unit membranes (see UNIT-MEMBRANE MODEL) with a distinct space in between. At intervals the membrane is perforated by large pores, allowing exchange of materials between nucleus and cytoplasm. The nuclear membrane connects up with spaces inside the ENDOPLASMIC RETICULUM.

nuclear pore one of many perforations in the NUCLEAR MEMBRANE of cells.

nuclease any enzyme that promotes hydrolysis of NUCLEIC ACIDS, for example, DNase, which catalyzes the breakdown of DNA into individual DNA NUCLEOTIDES.

nucleic acid a molecule composed of strings of NUCLEOTIDES forming a POLYNUCLEOTIDE CHAIN. Nucleic acids act as the genetic material of cells and occur as either DNA (two chains) or RNA (one chain).

nucleolar organizer an area of nuclear DNA containing genes that code for RIBOSOMAL RNA. The area is associated with the NUCLEOLUS.

nucleolus (*pl.* nucleoli) an organelle found within the nuclei of EUKARY-OTES that contains RIBOSOMAL RNA and is associated with the part of the chromosome that codes for rRNA. Each nucleus contains one or more nucleoli, which appear darkly stained in preparations.

nucleoplasm the contents of the cell nucleus inside the NUCLEAR MEM-BRANE.

nucleoprotein a type of protein found especially in the nucleus, such as the various types of HISTONE found complexed with DNA in the nucleosomes of eukaryote cells.

nucleoside a chemical compound in which a nitrogenous base is attached to a sugar. Such a structure occurs in DNA nucleotides, where a phosphate group is attached to the deoxyribose sugar of the nucleoside.

nucleosome the basic structural unit of the eukaryote chromosome, being composed of four pairs of HISTONE proteins (H2A, H2B, H3, and H4) that are combined to form an octomer around which are wrapped about 150 nucleotide pairs of DNA.

nucleotidase an enzyme that catalyzes hydrolysis of a nucleotide to a nucleoside and orthophosphate.

nucleotide a complex organic molecule forming the basic unit of NU-CLEIC ACIDS, with a structure made up of three components: a pentose sugar (ribose, or deoxyribose with one less oxygen atom); an organic base (PURINE type: ADENINE and GUANINE, or PYRIMIDINE type: CYTOSINE, THYMINE, and URACIL); and a phosphate group (see Fig. 226). The three elements are linked together by two condensation reactions between the 1' sugar carbon and a base forming a NUCLEOSIDE, and the 5' sugar carbon and the phosphate (see Fig. 227). The nucleotides are formed into POLYNUCLEOTIDE CHAINS.

nucleotide pair two NUCLEOTIDES of opposite strands of DNA joined by

Fig. 226. **Nucleotide.** Basic units of (a) deoxyribose sugar and (b) phosphate. Each carbon atom is numbered (1 prime, 2 prime, and so on.).

Fig. 227. **Nucleotide.** Linkage of the three nucleotide elements.

weak hydrogen bonds (see Fig. 228). See COMPLEMENTARY BASE PAIRING.

Fig. 228. **Nucleotide pair.** Complementary base pairing. P = phosphate, S = sugar, A = adenine, T = thymine.

nucleus 1. an organelle of eukaryotic cells that is bounded by a NUCLEAR MEMBRANE and contains the chromosomes whose genes control the structure of proteins within the cell. 2. (anatomy) the mass of nerve cell bodies, connected by tracts of nerve fibers, that occur in the vertebrate brain.

null allele a form of a gene whose product is either absent at the molecular level, or is present but has no measurable phenotypic function. For example, in a heterozygote with INCOMPLETE DOMINANCE, one gene form is a null allele and is inactive, while the other allele is unable to compensate for the null allele and so produces an intermediate phenotype.

null hypothesis a statement that a certain relationship exists that can be tested with a test of statistical SIGNIFICANCE. A typical null hypothesis is the statement that the deviation between observed and expected results is due to chance alone. In biology, a probability of greater than 5% that the null hypothesis is true ($P > 5\%$) is considered acceptable.

nullisomic (of a mutant condition) the absence of a pair of HOMOLOGOUS CHROMOSOMES giving a genetic complement of $2n - 2$.

numerical phenetics the hypothesis that the relationships between taxa can be determined by calculating an overall, unweighted similarity value.

numerical taxonomy the study of the relationships between organisms by means of determining the number of characteristics they have in common. See also CHARACTER INDEX.

nunatak see REFUGIUM.

nut a type of fruit with one seed and a hard woody outer layer, the PERICARP, such as the walnut.

nutation the continuous movement of the growing part of a plant during growth, which usually follows a spiral course, as in the stem of a convolvulus.

nutrient any material that organisms take in and assimilate for growth and maintenance.

nutrient cycle the passage of a nutrient through an ECOSYSTEM so that it eventually becomes available once again to the PRIMARY PRODUCERS.

nutrition the process of promoting the continued existence and growth of living organisms by taking in materials from the environment. Different organisms have different nutritional requirements. For example, the bacterium *E. coli* can synthesize all necessary AMINO ACIDS, COENZYMES, PORPHYRIN structures (for example, in HEMOGLOBIN), and NUCLEIC ACIDS. By contrast, humans need to take in amino acids, VITAMINS, CARBOHYDRATES, and FATTY ACIDS, in addition to water and many ESSENTIAL ELEMENTS.

nyct- *combining form* denoting night.

nyctinasty the so-called sleep movements of plants in which the leaves regularly droop at night in a form of DIURNAL RHYTHM. The activity is particularly common in plants with compound leaves, such as *Oxalis acetosella,* the wood sorrel.

nymph the immature stages of any EXOPTERYGOTE, such as the mayfly. It has compound eyes and mouthparts like the adult, but usually lacks wings—traces are sometimes present—and is sexually immature. See METAMORPHOSIS, ENDOPTERYGOTE.

nystatin a rod-shaped antibiotic molecule that allows passage of molecules smaller than 0.4 nm by creating channels through membranes.

O

ob- *prefix* denoting to, toward, against, etc.

obdiplostemous (of plants) having the stamens in two whorls, where the outer ones are opposite the petals and the inner ones opposite the sepals.

objective synonym any synonym based on the same TYPE specimen.

obligate (of an organism) being able to live only parasitically. Compare FACULTATIVE.

oblong 1. (of a plant) having one axis longer than the other. **2.** (of a leaf) being elliptical.

obtuse blunt.

Occam's razor or **Ockham's razor** the maxim stating that when a selection has to be made from various hypotheses, it is best to start with the hypothesis that makes fewest assumptions. Named for William of Ockham (died *c* 1349).

occipital condyle a projection of bone at the back of the vertebrate skull that articulates with the vertebral column. It is absent in most fish.

occipital lobe the posterior area of the CEREBRAL HEMISPHERE lying behind the parietal lobe and responsible for interpreting visual stimuli from the retina.

occiput or **occipital region 1.** the hard region of the vertebrate cranium. **2.** the dorsilateral plates on the head of an insect.

oceanic occurring in the sea where the depth exceeds 200 meters.

ocellus a single eye with a single lens found in insects and some other invertebrates.

ocher codon one of three NONSENSE CODONS in the GENETIC CODE consisting of the mRNA bases UAA.

ochrea or **ocrea** a sheath formed by fusion of two stipules around a stem to form a tube.

Ockham's razor see OCCAM'S RAZOR.

oct- or **octo-** *combining form* denoting eight.

octad the eight ascospores contained in a fungal ASCUS.

octoploid a cell or an individual having eight sets of chromosomes (8n), that is, four times the DIPLOID (1) number.

octopod any cephalopod mollusk of the order Octopoda, including eight-armed mollusks, such as the octopus.

oculo- *combining form* denoting the eye.

oculomotor nerve the third cranial nerve of vertebrates, which innervates the muscles that move the eyeball.

Odonata the order of insects that includes the dragonflies and damselflies.

odonto- and **-odont** *combining forms* denoting teeth.

odontoblasts the cells that give rise to dentine in vertebrate teeth and to simple teeth in invertebrates.

odontoid process a projection of the second vertebra (the axis), enabling the ATLAS to rotate and thus move the head around.

Oedogonium a genus of filamentous algae.

official index a list of taxonomic names declared invalid by the COMMISSION for Zoological Nomenclature.

oil any fat that is liquid at room temperature.

oil-immersion objective lens an objective lens used to examine objects at very high optical power (at least $1000 \times$). When in use, the small gap between the lens and the object is filled with oil of a high refractive index, preferably identical with that of the lens itself. In these circumstances no refraction takes place until light leaves the objective lens. See MICROSCOPE.

olecranon process a projection of the mammalian ulna forming a process for attachment of the triceps muscle and other muscles used to straighten the arm.

oleic acid an unsaturated, oily liquid found in almost all natural fats, and used in cosmetics, lubricating oils, and soaps.

olfaction the sense of smell, in which there is chemoreception of molecules suspended in the air.

olfactory pertaining to the sense of smell.

olfactory lobe a projection of the frontal lobe of a cerebral hemisphere that is well developed in most vertebrates, but reduced in humans, from which arises the olfactory nerve. It is associated with the sense of smell.

oligo- *combining form* denoting few or little.

Oligocene epoch an epoch of the TERTIARY PERIOD occurring between 38 and 26 million years ago, when modern fauna and flora appeared and the rise of birds and mammals continued. See GEOLOGICAL TIME.

oligochaete any ANNELID worm of the class Oligochaeta, including the earthworms. They occur mainly in nonacidic soils and in fresh water, and are distinguished from the other major order of CHAETOPODS, the POLYCHAETES, by a lack of PARAPODIA (projections from the body), few CHAETAE, and lack of a well-developed head. Fertilization is internal (external in polychaetes).

oligolectic (of bees) collecting pollen from only a few kind of flowers.

oligomer a protein consisting of only a small number of identical POLY-PEPTIDE subunits.

oligophagous feeding on only a few species of food plants.

oligosaccharide a carbohydrate composed of a small number of mono-saccharide residues.

oligotrophic 1. (of water bodies such as lakes) having a poor nutrient supply and relatively little production of organic material. See EU-TROPHIC. 2. (of plants) associated with low levels of nutrition.

omasum one of four chambers in the RUMINANT STOMACH, lying between the fermentation section and the true stomach.

ombrogenic or **ombrogenous** (of peat bogs) dependent on rainfall.

ombrotrophic (of plants or plant communities) associated with a rain-fed substrate poor in nutrients.

ommatidium (*pl.* ommatidia) any of the numerous facets making up the compound eyes of insects and other arthropods. Each ommatidium has its own lens and a group of retinal cells surrounded by pigment cells. The light-sensitive part of the ommatidium is the RHABDOM. When it receives a stimulus, a photochemical reaction takes place that results in impulses being sent to the optic nerve.

omnivore an organism feeding on both animals and plants. For example, humans have teeth adapted to chewing both types of material. See also CARNIVORE.

onchosphere an embryonic form of a tapeworm (Cestoda), which consists of a spherical chitinous shell containing a hexacanth embryo.

oncogene a viral gene causing cancer generation (ONCOGENESIS) in the host.

oncogenesis the generation of cancer, sometimes by an ONCOGENE.

one gene/one enzyme hypothesis a proposal put forward by George BEADLE and Edward Tatum in 1941 to explain the results of their experiments with the fungus *Neurospora crassa*. By developing mutant strains (AUXOTROPHS) that would not grow on a MINIMAL MEDIUM but would grow on a supplemented medium, and by detecting the accumulation of metabolites, they were able to show that each of the different enzymes catalyzing a step in a particular biochemical pathway was controlled by a different gene. See also CISTRON.

onomatophore see TYPE.

ontogeny the entire development of an organism from fertilization to completion of the life history. See HAECKEL'S LAW.

Onychophora a small subphylum of primitive arthropods containing the single genus *Peripatus*. They are wormlike, each segment having clawed limbs, and are probably descended from ancestors of the arthropods that diverged at an early and intermediate stage between annelids and arthropods.

oo- *combining form* denoting egg.

oocyte an early stage in GAMETOGENESIS of female animals, primary oocytes being DIPLOID (1) and secondary oocytes HAPLOID (1), having undergone the first meiotic division. Human females are born with the primary oocytes already formed, which may increase the risk of NONDISJUNCTION of chromosomes. See also DOWN SYNDROME.

oogamy a condition in which male and female GAMETES of an organism are morphologically different, with the male gamete being motile and the female gamete nonmotile and often larger.

oogenesis the process of GAMETE production in female DIPLOID (2) animals. See GAMETOGENESIS.

oogonium 1. An early DIPLOID (1) stage in GAMETOGENESIS of female animals giving rise to the OOCYTES. **2.** (in algae and fungi) the female sex organ containing the OOSPHERES.

oosphere the large, nonmotile female GAMETE formed in an OOGONIUM.

oospore the thick-walled spore found, in some fungi, for example, and arising from fertilization of the OOSPHERE derived from an OOGONIUM.

oostegites the thoracic limb plates found in some crustaceans that form a brood pouch.

oozooid a unit of a colonial organism derived from an egg as opposed to a *blastozooid* derived from a bud. Oozooids occur in TUNICATES.

opal codon one of the three NONSENSE CODONS in the GENETIC CODE, consisting of the mRNA bases UGA.

open population a population into which GENE FLOW is freely possible.

open reading frame a sequence of NUCLEOTIDE bases between an INITIATION CODON and a NONSENSE CODON.

operator see OPERON MODEL.

operculum 1. the lid of a MOSS capsule. **2.** a hard bony flap covering the gills of fishes. **3.** the plate of exoskeletal material on the foot of a gastropod mollusk with which it closes off the entrance to the shell.

operon see OPERON MODEL.

operon model or **Jacob-Monod hypothesis** a concept of gene regulation proposed by the French biochemists François Jacob and Jacques Monod in the late 1950s. Using strains of *E. coli* mutant at the lac locus, they demonstrated that production of lactate occurs only in the presence of lactose, an example of ENZYME INDUCTION, and proposed a new organization of related genes. The model has the following components: an *operon* consisting of at least one *structural gene* coding for primary enzyme structure, and two regulatory elements, one called the *operator* and the other called the *promoter*, which binds with RNA POLYMERASE. The model proposes the presence of a *regulator gene* producing a repressor substance that binds with the operator, thus preventing TRANSCRIPTION of the structural genes.

When a state of *enzyme repression* is in operation, the operator inactivates the structural genes, preventing formation of MESSENGER RNA from the structural genes because the RNA polymerase enzyme cannot move past the operator site (see Fig. 229). However, introduction of a suitable inducer substance, for example, the substrate of the enzyme coded by the structural gene, causes an inducer—repressor complex to be formed that cannot bind to the operator. The operator site thus is no longer blocked, and RNA polymerase can move from promoter to structural gene(s), which then are transcribed, producing a piece of POLYCISTRONIC MRNA, a process called *enzyme induction* (see Fig. 230).

Fig. 229. **Operon model.** Enzyme repression.

Fig. 230. **Operon model.** Enzyme induction.

When the inducer level falls, having been metabolized by the enzyme, the operator becomes blocked again by the repressor so that the structural genes are now repressed, an example of a negative FEEDBACK MECHANISM. The operon model has been extended to encompass a

OPHIDIA

system of enzyme repression where structural genes are active normally, becoming repressed only when too much product is present. Furthermore, although the operon model was developed from bacterial studies, the system has been incorporated into general ideas about CELL DIFFERENTIATION in eukaryotes, in which GENE SWITCHING occurs in an orderly manner throughout development, as may be seen in the sequences of CHROMOSOME PUFFS that occur in some insects.

Ophidia 1. a suborder of the Squamata, comprising the snakes. **2.** (in some classifications) a separate order of the Reptilia.

Ophiuroidea a class of ECHINODERMS, comprising the brittle stars.

ophthalmic of or relating to the eye.

opiate a narcotic substance derived from opium.

opposite (of two plant organs, such as leaves) located at the same height on the plant but at opposite sides of the stem.

opsin a protein occurring in rods and cones of the RETINA of the eye, which combines with retinal$_1$ or retinal$_2$ to form visual pigments.

opsonin a type of ANTIBODY that binds to ANTIGENS, increasing their susceptibility to phagocytosis by other antibodies.

optic of or relating to the eye or to vision.

optic chiasma a point under the hypothalamus of the brain where the two optic nerves meet and cross over, so that a stimulus from either eye is interpreted in the OPTIC LOBE of the opposite side of the brain.

optic lobe one of a pair of lobes found as swellings on the dorsal side of the midbrain of some lower vertebrates. The lobes integrate sensory information from the eyes and certain auditory reflexes. In mammals, the *corpora quadrigemina* are the equivalent of the optic lobes.

optic vesicle an embryological structure formed by the outpushing of the forebrain of vertebrates, which eventually gives rise to the optic cup.

oral of or relating to the mouth or to its uses.

oral groove a depression leading to the mouth in some invertebrates.

orbicular rounded.

orbit the body cavity or socket in the vertebrate skull containing the eyeball.

order a TAXON that occurs at a level of classification between a class (which may contain several orders) and a family (several of which may be found in an order). See CLASSIFICATION.

Ordovician period a period of the PALEOZOIC ERA that occurred between 515 and 445 million years ago. Algae, particularly calcareous, reef-building forms, were common as were graptolites, corals, and brachiopods. The first armored fish evolved in the Ordovician.

organ any multicellular structural or functional unit of an animal or

plant, often composed of different tissues that perform specific roles, such as the liver, leaf, or eye.

organelle any part of a cell that has a particular structural or functional role, such as a FLAGELLUM or a MITOCHONDRION. Organelles are analogous with organs in the bodies of multicellular organisms.

organism any living animal or plant.

organization effect an interaction that occurs between adjacent loci as a result of some features of chromosome organization.

organizer any part of a developing embryo that exerts a morphogenetic stimulus on adjacent parts. See INDUCTION (2).

organizer region an area in the animal embryo that appears to control differentiation of cells in that region. For example, the dorsal lip of the *blastopore* plays a major part in determining the shape of the early embryo.

organochlorine an organic chlorine compound, particularly any of a group of insecticides, for example, DDT.

organ of Corti see COCHLEA.

organogenesis the period during embryonic development of an animal when the main body organs are formed.

organophosphate a phosphate with insecticidal properties. Organophosphates are probably the most commonly used group of insecticides.

organotroph an organism that uses organic compounds as electron donors.

orientation 1. the response of an organism in taking up a particular position in relation to a particular stimulus. 2. see NAVIGATION.

original description the statement of the characteristics of an organism in the proposal of a name for a new taxon.

origin of life the process by which biomolecules, subcellular structures, and living cells have come into existence.

ornithine cycle or **urea cycle** a circular biochemical pathway in liver cells with three major steps, in which excess ammonia produced from the breakdown of amino acids and carbon dioxide react together to give UREA, which is filtered out by the kidneys and excreted. The reaction is essentially:

$$2NH_3 + CO_2 = CO(NH_2)_2 \text{ (urea)} + H_2O.$$

See Fig. 231.

Ornithischia a large herbivorous order of dinosaurs, most of which were bipedal. They were characterized by a birdlike pelvic girdle, which possessed a postpubic bone stretching on each side below the ischium.

Fig. 231. **Ornithine cycle.** The main steps of the cycle.

ornitho- *combining form* denoting bird.

Ornithorynchus the duck-billed platypus. See MONOTREME.

ortho- *combining form* denoting straight, upright, correct.

orthokinesis any random movement in response to a stimulus.

orthologous genes any genes found in different species that, while nonidentical, can be traced back to a common ancestor.

Orthoptera an order of the EXOPTERYGOTA, containing grasshoppers, locusts, stick insects, and in some classifications cockroaches. Most are good runners or jumpers and some have lost the power of flight. Most forms possess biting and chewing mouthparts and have hardened forewings, which are used in creating sounds by movement against the hind leg (STRIDULATION). See Fig. 232.

Fig. 232. **Orthoptera.** General structure.

orthostichy 1. an imaginary vertical line connecting a row of leaves on a stem. 2. the possession of parallel cartilaginous rays in the fins of fossil sharklike fish, such as *Cladoselache*.

orthotropous (of the angiosperm ovule) having the MICROPYLE directed away from the placenta and erect on the FUNICLE.

os 1. the technical name for a bone. 2. a mouth or mouthlike part.

osculum the large aperture in sponges through which water passes out.

osmic acid see OSMIUM TETROXIDE.

osmium tetroxide or **osmic acid** a substance used in fixing cytological preparations that is characterized by the small amount of distortion it causes.

osmometer an instrument used for measuring OSMOTIC PRESSURE of a solution.

osmoreceptor any of the group of structures sited in the HYPOTHALAMUS that responds to changes in osmotic pressure of the blood by means of neurohypophyseal antidiuretic hormone.

osmoregulation the control of OSMOTIC POTENTIAL, or WATER POTENTIAL, in organisms. When separated by a differentially permeable membrane, water molecules tend to move from an area of high osmotic or high water potential (low osmotic pressure) to an area of low osmotic potential or low water potential (high osmotic pressure). Where cells are bathed in a solution, water tends to cross the cell membrane in order to equalize the water potential on either side.

In a dry atmosphere or the marine environment, organisms tend to lose water to their surroundings. In a wet atmosphere or in fresh water, organisms may have difficulty in losing water, so various means are employed to maintain a correct water balance. Xerophytic plants (see XEROPHYTE) may reverse the normal stomatal rhythm, develop a waxy cuticle, fold leaves, store water (succulent plants), or survive dry periods as spores or seeds. Excess water may be removed by GUTTATION in some plants and by CONTRACTILE VACUOLES in some unicellular organisms. In mammals osmoregulation is carried out by the kidney, water passing out of the bloodstream into the kidney tubule via the BOWMAN'S CAPSULE and reabsorbed, where necessary, in the tubule itself. Marine fish, reptiles, and birds are able to eliminate salt through special excretory cells. Different groups of animals remove NITROGENOUS WASTE in different ways—all associated with osmoregulation. Many marine organisms have blood that is ISOTONIC with sea water and so do not have an osmoregulatory problem.

osmosis the movement of a solvent, usually water in biological systems, through a differentially permeable membrane from a solution with high water concentration and low solute concentration, to one with low water concentration and high solute concentration.

osmotic potential a measure of the tendency of a solution to withdraw water from pure water by OSMOSIS across a differentially permeable membrane. Pure water has an osmotic potential of zero at one atmosphere pressure. The osmotic potential of any solution is always negative. *Osmotic pressure* is a measure of the tendency for water to move into a solution by osmosis and is expressed as a positive value. See Fig. 233.

differentially
permeable
membrane

higher concentration · · · lower concentration
of solutes · · · of solutes

higher osmotic · · · lower osmotic
pressure · · · pressure

H_2O

lower (more negative) · · · higher (less negative)
osmotic potential · · · osmotic potential

Fig. 233. **Osmotic potential.** Osmosis through a differentially permeable membrane.

osmotic pressure see OSMOTIC POTENTIAL.

ossicle any of the bones in the middle ear connecting the eardrum to the oval window. In mammals there are three ossicles (MALLEUS, INCUS, and STAPES). In reptiles, birds, and many amphibians, only a single bone—the COLUMELLA AURIS—is present.

Ostariophysi a superorder of freshwater TELEOSTS, including the carp and the minnow. The group has several primitive features, including the WEBERIAN OSSICLE.

Osteichthyes see BONY FISH.

osteo- *combining form* denoting bone.

osteoblast a cell that produces the calcified intercellular material of bone. See also PERIOSTEUM.

osteoclast 1. a multinucleate ameboid cell that breaks down bone during growth and remodeling. 2. also called **chondrioclast** a cell of the same kind that breaks down cartilage in the transformation to bone.

Osteolepis an extinct genus of Crossopterygian fish that possessed casmoid scales and was closely related to the ancestors of land vertebrates.

Osteostraci an order of jawless fishlike vertebrates, possessing a large dorsal head shield, found in the SILURIAN PERIOD and DEVONIAN PERIOD.

ostiole a pore through which spores are discharged from the fruiting bodies of some fungi, or from which gametes are passed out from the conceptacles of brown algae.

ostium any of numerous openings present in sponges through which water is drawn in.

Ostracodermi a class of jawless fossil fish usually classified, together with the CYCLOSTOMES, in the Agnatha. They existed from the ORDOVICIAN PERIOD through to the DEVONIAN PERIOD and were heavily armored.

otic of or relating to the ear.

otoconium see OTOLITH.

otocyst an invertebrate organ, containing fluid and OTOLITHS, that is believed to have an auditory function.

otolith or **otoconium** a granule of calcareous material, several of them occurring in the inner ear of vertebrates, where they are attached to processes associated with sensitive cells, and register gravity. By means of such sense organs, vertebrates are able to assess their position with respect to gravity.

outbreeding a mating system in which matings between close relatives do not usually occur. Compare INBREEDING.

oval window a membranous wall at the junction of the middle ear and inner ear that connects the stapes with the vestibular canal of the COCHLEA.

ovarian follicle the group of cells that surrounds, envelops, and probably nourishes the developing oocyte in most animals. See GRAAFIAN FOLLICLE. In vertebrates the ovarian follicle produces ESTROGEN.

ovary the organ that produces the female gametes by a process called GAMETOGENESIS. In mammals, it also gives rise to the CORPUS LUTEUM from the GRAAFIAN FOLLICLE after ovulation, and in vertebrates generally produces the female hormones estrogen and progesterone. In plants, the ovary occurs at the base of the CARPEL and contains one or more OVULES. See GYNOECIUM for inferior and superior ovaries.

ovate (of a leaf) shaped like the longitudinal section of an egg, with the broader end at the base.

overall similarity (in numerical taxonomy) a value of similarity calculated by considering several characters collectively.

overdominance a phenotypic condition in which the HETEROZYGOTE expresses a stronger manifestation of the trait than does either HOMOZYGOTE. Overdominance produces heterozygous advantage that can maintain GENETIC POLYMORPHISM in a population.

overfishing the removal of fish from a population beyond the point at which the population is able to maintain its numbers and goes into decline.

overshoot the stage of an ACTION POTENTIAL in which the voltage rises from zero to the positive peak.

overwintering the process of passing the winter. For example, some insects overwinter in a pupal stage, and some migratory birds overwinter outside the normal breeding area.

oviduct a tube that carries the egg to the exterior or, in the case of mammals, to the lower part of the tube, the UTERUS, where it becomes implanted in the wall lining (ENDOMETRIUM) if FERTILIZATION has oc-

OVIPAROUS

curred. Usually oviducts are paired, but only one is present in birds. In higher mammals it is divided into an upper FALLOPIAN TUBE, which is ciliated, and into which the egg passes from the COELOM, a middle uterus, where the embryo develops, and a vagina leading to the exterior. See Fig. 234.

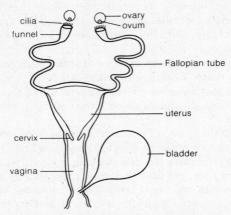

Fig. 234. **Oviduct.** The mammalian oviduct.

oviparous (of an animal) laying eggs in which the embryo develops after egg laying, as in birds and most reptiles. Compare OVOVIVIPAROUS, VIVIPAROUS (1).

ovipositor an organ of female insects, usually present at the tip of the abdomen, through which the egg is laid. The ovipositor is sometimes developed to enable piercing of tissue, particularly where eggs are laid inside other animals and plants.

ovoid egg-shaped.

ovotestis the organ of some HERMAPHRODITES (2) that functions both as a testis and as an ovary, as in snails.

ovoviviparous (of certain fish, reptiles, and many insects) having the embryo developing within the mother, but from which it rarely derives nutrients. The mother and embryo are separated by egg membranes, and there is no PLACENTA. Compare OVIPAROUS, VIVIPAROUS (1).

ovulation the bursting of the OVARIAN FOLLICLE (see also GRAAFIAN FOLLICLE) on the surface of the ovary with the release of an egg, which then normally passes into the OVIDUCT.

ovule a structure found in higher plants that contains an egg cell and develops into a seed after FERTILIZATION. In ANGIOSPERMS, the ovule develops within the ovary of a carpel and consists of an inner EMBRYO SAC containing the egg cell surrounded by the NUCELLUS, which in turn is enclosed within two INTEGUMENTS. The ovule is connected to the ovary wall by the FUNICLE. See Fig. 235.

Fig. 235. **Ovule.** General structure.

ovum (*pl.* ova) or **egg** or **egg cell** a functional egg cell of an animal, produced by GAMETOGENESIS. Ova are frequently packed with nutritive yolk granules and are usually immobile (see OOGAMY). The human egg is about 0.14 mm in diameter, which is some 50,000 times larger than the human sperm.

oxaloacetic acid a dicarboxylic acid that condenses with acetylcoenzyme A, forming citric acid and CoA, thus initiating the KREBS CYCLE.

oxidase an enzyme that catalyzes a reaction in which oxygen is added to a substance (X) with hydrogen removed and water formed. Thus:

$$O_2 + X - H_2 \xrightarrow{\text{oxidase}} H_2O + X - O$$

Most oxidases are proteins with metallic groups attached. For example, cytochrome oxidase contains iron and oxidizes cytochrome *a* in the ELECTRON TRANSPORT SYSTEM of aerobic respiration:

$$O_2 + \text{reduced cyto. } a \xrightarrow[\text{oxidase}]{\text{cytochrome}} H_2O + \text{oxidized cyto. } a.$$

oxidation 1. the addition of oxygen to a substance to increase the proportion of oxygen in its molecule. Oxidation can be achieved without oxygen by the removal of hydrogen (dehydrogenation). **2.** any reaction involving loss of electrons from an atom. For example,

$$Fe(II) \rightarrow Fe(III).$$

oxidation-reduction reaction a reversible chemical process in which electrons are transferred from one molecule to another.

oxidative deamination a deamination that also involves an oxidation, for example, an alpha amino acid to an alpha keto acid.

oxidative decarboxylation a decarboxylation (removal of CO_2 from an organic carboxyl group) that also involves oxidation.

oxidative phosphorylation a process that takes place in the ELECTRON TRANSPORT SYSTEM of aerobic respiration, in which ATP molecules are synthesized from ADP and inorganic phosphate. The process is the major means by which aerobic organisms obtain their energy from foodstuffs.

oxidoreductase one of a group of enzymes that catalyze OXIDATION-REDUCTION REACTIONS.

oxycephaly see ACROCEPHALY.

oxygen a colorless, tasteless gas forming about 21% of Earth's atmosphere and capable of combining with all other elements except the inert gases. Oxygen is particularly important in physical combustion processes and in AEROBIC RESPIRATION.

oxygen cycle the PATHWAY followed by oxygen through the metabolism of organisms that leads back to regeneration of any given organism.

oxygen debt a condition that arises in very active muscles when insufficient oxygen is supplied by the lungs, causing the muscle tissue to respire anaerobically with the production of LACTIC ACID. When muscular activities slow down, the rate and depth of breathing remain at high level until the lactic acid has been oxidized. Oxygen debt can be measured as the difference between the amount of oxygen required after strong muscular activity and the amount required in a resting state. In trained athletes, the debt can be as high as 18 liters of oxygen.

oxygen dissociation curve a curve derived from plotting the percentage saturation of blood with oxygen, against the oxygen tension (the *oxygen exchange*). See Fig. 236.

The curve is S-shaped and shows that HEMOGLOBIN has a high affinity for oxygen. Blood can become saturated at relatively low oxygen tensions, but a small drop in oxygen tension brings about a big fall in the saturation of the blood. If tissues use up oxygen, then hemoglobin responds by giving it up.

Where CO_2 is present, hemoglobin has to be under higher oxygen tension in order to become fully saturated. However, under these circumstances it releases O_2 at higher oxygen tensions. CO_2 affects the efficiency of oxygen uptake by hemoglobin but increases its efficiency in releasing it. The capability of blood to carry oxygen is also affected by pH (see BOHR EFFECT).

Fig. 236. **Oxygen dissociation curve.** The characteristic S-shaped curve of oxygen dissociation.

oxygen exchange see OXYGEN DISSOCIATION CURVE.

oxyhemoglobin HEMOGLOBIN that is oxygenated.

oxylophyte see CALCIFUGE.

oxyntic cell or **parietal cell** any of the glandular cells lying in pits within the wall of the vertebrate stomach. Their function is to secrete hydrochloric acid, giving the gastric fluids a pH of about 2.0.

oxytocin a hormone secreted by the posterior lobe of the PITUITARY GLAND, causing contraction of the uterine muscle. The hormone is important to parturition.

P

P see PARENTAL GENERATION.

pacemaker the sinoatrial node of the right atrium. See HEART.

pachyderm any large, thick-skinned, hoofed mammal, such as an elephant, hippopotamus, or rhinoceros.

pachytene the stage in prophase I of MEIOSIS in which paired HOMOLOGOUS CHROMOSOMES each split into two CHROMATIDS, the whole structure being called a TETRAD.

Pacinian corpuscle a heavy-pressure RECEPTOR in mammalian skin.

page precedence the occurrence of a scientific name on an earlier page of the same publication in which a synonym or homonym occurs.

pain a conscious sensation produced in the brain and stimulated by pain receptors in, for example, the skin. Pain has a protective function and often produces a reflex action (see REFLEX ARC) in response.

pair bond a relationship established between the male and female of higher vertebrates for breeding purposes. In some cases, such as swans, it may last for life.

Palaeoniscus a genus of extinct bony fish of the PALEOZOIC ERA possessing bony head plates and GANOIDscales. *Palaeoniscus* probably arose from the same stock as the CHOANICHTHYES from which land animals eventually evolved. Present-day relatives include POLYPTERUS.

palate the roof of the mouth in vertebrates formed anteriorly by a bony projection of the upper jaw and posteriorly by the fold of connective tissue (*soft palate*). Mammals possess a *false palate*, which has been formed below the original palate and results in the opening of the nasal cavity at the back of the mouth (in the throat), enabling chewing and breathing at the same time.

palea a GLUME-like bract found on the axis of individual flowers in grasses.

palearctic region the part of the Holarctic region comprising the landmass of the Eurasian continent (Europe and Asia) from its northern border to the Sahara and Himalayas. see BIOGEOGRAPHICAL REGION.

paleo- *combining form* denoting old or ancient.

paleobotany the study of fossils plants, particularly fossils of pollen grain, which are used in reconstructing past environments.

Paleocene epoch the first epoch in the TERTIARY PERIOD, lasting from 65 to 54 million years ago. (See GEOLOGICAL TIME.) This was the time of explosive evolution of placental mammals.

paleoecology the study of the ecology of past environments through fossil organisms.

Paleognathae the more primitive of the two major groups of living birds, containing the RATITES and the tinamous. In contrast with the NEOGNATHAE, the jaw structure contains a large prevomer (see VOMER) bone that contacts the pterygoid, or winglike, bones.

paleolimnology the study of past environments, particularly lake ecosystems, from evidence found in lake muds.

Paleolithic the period of the emergence of primitive people, from *c* 600,000 to 14,000 years ago. Stone tools were used, and existence was solely by hunting and gathering, with no cultivation.

paleontology the study of fossil animals and plants. Compare NEONTOLOGY.

Paleozoic era an era of 350 million years duration, from the beginning of the CAMBRIAN PERIOD to the end of the PERMIAN PERIOD, lasting from 590 to 240 million years ago.

palindrome a region of a DNA POLYNUCLEOTIDE CHAIN where a sequence of bases is followed by a base series so that COMPLEMENTARY BASE PAIRING can occur when the chain is folded back. See Fig. 237.

base sequence: TGAC·GTCA   folded: GTCA
                                    CAGT
                          complementary pairing

Fig. 237. **Palindrome.** Complementary base pairing.

palingenesis see HAECKEL'S LAW OF RECAPITULATION.

palisade mesophyll see MESOPHYLL.

pallium 1. the tissue next to the shell of mollusks. **2.** the roof of the vertebrate CEREBRUM.

palmate (of a leaf) having at least three leaflets joined to the PETIOLE at the same place. See Fig. 238.

Fig. 238. **Palmate.** A palmate leaf.

palp a type of appendage having a tactile function associated with the head of invertebrate animals, usually in the mouth region. In some crustaceans, palps perform a locomotory function and in others are associated with feeding, as they are in bivalve mollusks where they produce feeding currents. In insects, palps are found on the first and second maxillae, where they are thought to be associated with olfaction.

pancreas a gland situated in the mesentery of the DUODENUM of jawed vertebrates that has both an exocrine and an endocrine function. The pancreatic duct carries digestive enzymes (see PANCREATIC JUICES) from the gland into the duodenum, secretion being stimulated by (a) the vagus nerve, (b) the hormone SECRETIN, and (c) PANCREOZYMIN.

Groups of cells known as ISLETS OF LANGERHANS secrete two hormones into the blood system: large alpha cells secrete GLUCAGON, while smaller beta cells secrete INSULIN.

pancreatic amylase see AMYLASE.

pancreatic juice the clear alkaline secretion of the PANCREAS that is released into the duodenum and contains the following digestive enzymes:

(a) pancreatic AMYLASE, which breaks down STARCH to MALTOSE.

(b) pancreatic LIPASE, which breaks down fat into fatty acids and glycerol.

(c) NUCLEASES, which break down NUCLEIC ACIDS into nucleotides.

(d) PEPTIDASES, which break down POLYPEPTIDE CHAINS to free amino acids.

(e) a group of closely related protein-splitting enzymes, such as TRYPSIN in the form of inactive trypsinogen.

pancreatin an extract of the pancreas that contains pancreatic enzymes.

pancreozymin see CHOLECYSTOKININ-PANCREOZYMIN.

pandemic occurring over a wide geographical area, as with a disease, such as malaria.

Paneth cells the cells that occur at the bases of the CRYPTS OF LIEBERKUHN. They persist for only about two weeks and then disintegrate. It is thought that they remove ions of heavy metal and secrete AMINO ACIDS and LYSOZYME—an antibacterial enzyme controlling the amount of bacteria in the gut. It is also possible that they secrete enzymes, such as peptidases and lipases.

Pangaea see CONTINENTAL DRIFT.

panicle 1. a branched RACEME. 2. any complex branched inflorescence.

panmixis see RANDOM MATING.

Pantopoda a class of ARACHNIDS, including the sea spiders.

pantothenic acid or **vitamin B₅** a water-soluble organic acid ($C_9H_{17}O_5N$) present in all animal tissues, especially the liver and kidney. Pantothenic acid forms part of coenzyme A which, when bonded to acetic acid, forms ACETYLCOENZYME A. The vitamin is present in almost all foods, especially fresh vegetables, meat, eggs, and yeast. A deficiency causes nervous disorders and poor motor coordination.

papilla (*pl.* papillae) a projection from the surface of a structure, such as tongue papillae, which carry the taste buds.

papilloma a benign wart.

pappus a circle of hairs formed from a modified CALYX found on the seeds of plants of the family Compositae. The pappus assists in dispersal of the seeds by wind, acting as a kind of parachute, for example, in dandelion and thistle seeds.

parabiosis the connecting together of two animals in an experiment so as to allow their body fluids to mix. The technique is used, for example, in the study of the role of insect hormones.

paracentric inversion a chromosomal mutation involving INVERSION of a segment of one arm of a chromosome, not involving the CEN-TROMERE.

parallelism see CONVERGENCE.

paralogous genes genes with a HOMOLOGOUS structure located at different sites on the chromosomes of the same individual, which are probably derived by a process of gene duplication.

Paramecium a genus of freshwater PROTOZOAN, having an oval body covered with cilia and a ventral ciliated groove for feeding. See Fig. 239.

Fig. 239. **Paramecium.** General structure.

paramylum a starchlike substance that occurs as a food reserve in flagellate protozoans and algae, such as EUGLENA.

parapatry any nonoverlapping geographical contact between separate populations or species, without interbreeding.

parapodium (*pl.* parapodia) any of the numerous paired, segmentally arranged projections of the bodies of polychaete worms, containing musculature and often bearing chaetae. The parapodium is locomotory in function.

parasexual reproduction a form of asexual reproduction that involves somatic cell fusion and random loss of individual chromosomes.

parasite an organism that lives in association with, and at the expense of, another organism, the host, from which it obtains organic nutrition. Parasites that live on the outside of the host, such as ticks, are called *ectoparasites,* whereas others that live inside the host, such as tapeworms, are called *endoparasites.* Parasites can be FACULTATIVE or OBLIGATE and have a range of effects, from inflicting minimum harm to the host, which continues to live and reproduce normally (these are the best-adapted parasites, for example, tapeworms), to causing the death of the host (for example, the malaria parasite). COEVOLUTION may occur between host and parasite. See also BIOTROPHIC, NECROTROPHIC.

parasitoid any of the alternately parasitic and free-living wasps and flies, such as the ichneumon fly, the larvae of which parasitize and often kill members of the host species.

parasympathetic system see AUTONOMIC NERVOUS SYSTEM.

parathyroid an endocrine gland in higher vertebrates that is situated in or near the thyroid gland and controls the calcium level of the blood. When too little (Ca^+) is present in the blood, parathyroid hormone is secreted. It (a) reduces the OSTEOBLAST activity and thus the amount of bone-matrix formation, (b) increases (Ca^+) uptake from the gut into the bloodstream, and (c) acts on the kidney tubules, decreasing calcium and phosphate excretion. Undersecretion of this hormone results in a fall of blood calcium and causes TETANY.

paratype any specimen cited by the author of a scientific name other than the HOLOTYPE.

parazoan any multicellular invertebrate of the group Parazoa, comprising the sponges. Compare METAZOAN.

parenchyma 1. a tissue composed of parenchyma cells, which are thin-walled general purpose plant cells that often have a packing function. Parenchyma cells remain alive at maturity and can become meristematic, as in INTERFASCICULAR CAMBIUM (see SECONDARY THICKENING). See Fig. 240. 2. the loose, vacuolated cells that form much of the body tissue of platyhelminths. 3. any specific organ cells apart from connective tissues and blood vessels.

parental gamete a gamete that has a genotype identical with one of the HOMOLOGOUS CHROMOSOMES in the original diploid cell. See GENETIC LINKAGE.

parental generation (P) the members of a cross between PURE BREEDING LINES, giving rise to offspring called the F_1.

parietal 1. (of plant organs) joined to a wall, as in parietal ovules attached to the wall of the ovary. 2. of or relating to the bones of the top of the

Fig. 240. **Parenchyma.** Cross section of cells.

skull, which have a membranous structure and lie behind the frontal bones. 3. (of coelomic lining) covering the body wall as distinct from visceral organs (see also OXYNTIC CELL).

pars intercerebralis the dorsal part of the insect brain containing neurosecretory cells.

parthenocarpy the development of fruit without seeds due to lack of pollination, fertilization, or embryo development.

parthenogenesis the development of an individual from an egg without fertilization by a sperm. The process occurs mainly in lower invertebrates, particularly insects. The egg cell can be HAPLOID (1) to produce, for example, male honeybees (drones), or DIPLOID (1) as produced in wingless female aphids which, during summer, produce diploid eggs by MITOSIS that develop into female adults, only forming haploid gametes by MEIOSIS in autumn, prior to normal sexual reproduction.

partial dominance a form of INCOMPLETE DOMINANCE in which the heterozygote resembles one homozygote more than the other.

partial inflorescence a part of a branched inflorescence.

partial pressure the total pressure of the mixture of gases within which a gas occurs, multiplied by the percentage of the total volume the gas occupies. Thus, if the normal total pressure of the atmospheric gases is 760 mm Hg and there is 21% oxygen in this mixture, the partial pressure of O_2 is: $760 \times 0.21 = 160$ mm Hg.

parturition the act of giving birth to an offspring.

passage cell any endodermal plant cell that remains unthickened and allows passage of materials between the cortex and the vascular bundle.

passerine any member of the avian order Passeriformes—singing or perching birds— which includes about half of the known species of birds.

passive immunity see ANTIBODY.

passive transport see DIFFUSION.

Pasteur, Louis (1822—1895) French bacteriologist who was effectively the founder of microbiology as a science. He put forward the theory that disease was caused by microorganisms and established that SPONTANEOUS GENERATION does not occur. He established that inoculation with attenuated forms of microorganisms (see ATTENUATION) provided immunization against virulent forms, and showed that rabies was caused by microscopic agents, which could not be seen, thus leading to discovery of viruses. He introduced heat treatment to destroy microorganisms in perishable products, such as milk (see PASTEURIZATION).

pasteurization a method devised by Louis PASTEUR of partially sterilizing certain foods such as milk, by heating to 62°C for 30 minutes before distribution. Heating destroys many harmful bacteria, including those responsible for tuberculosis.

patagium 1. a membrane of skin stretched on the wing of a bird or bat, or between the forelimbs and hindlimbs of a flying squirrel to form the parachute. 2. (in some insects) a projection on each side of the prothorax.

Patau syndrome a rare human condition characterized by gross developmental malformations and caused by TRISOMY of chromosome 13. The average survival of affected individuals is 6 months.

patella 1. the kneecap bone, which is present in most mammals and in some birds and reptiles, protecting the front of the joint from injury. 2. the generic name of the LIMPET, *Patella*.

pathogen any organism that causes disease, such as viruses or bacteria.

pathogenic acting as a PATHOGEN.

pathology the study of the structural and functional changes caused by disease.

pathotoxin a toxin produced by a PATHOGEN, capable of causing symptoms of disease. See BOTULISM.

pathway any defined route followed by a series of reactions leading to a specific product, for example, a biochemical pathway.

patroclinous inheritance a form of inheritance in which all offspring have the PHENOTYPE of the father. Compare MATROCLINOUS INHERITANCE.

Pauling, Linus Carl (1901—) American biochemist and Nobel laureate who determined the crystal structure of several molecules by means of X-ray diffraction analysis and, with coworkers, discovered the structure of abnormal HEMOGLOBIN, responsible for SICKLE CELL ANEMIA, using the technique of ELECTROPHORESIS.

Pavlovian response see CONDITIONED REFLEX.

peat an accumulation of dead plant material formed in wet conditions in bogs or fens in the absence of oxygen so that decomposition is incomplete. It is usually acidic.

pecking order the gradation of behavioral dominance between individuals in active groups of mammals and birds. The leader is dominant and thus at the top of the pecking order, getting the best food and mates. The least dominant animal is at the bottom of the order. Birds often show bald patches where they have been pecked by dominant individuals.

Pecora an infra-order of the ARTERIODACTYLA, including ruminants such as cattle, sheep, goats, deer, and giraffe, possessing a placenta having villi in small tufts.

pecten any comblike structure or organ. Examples include the oxygenating structure in the eye of a bird, and the organ used by some insects for STRIDULATION.

pectin a complex POLYSACCHARIDE often found as calcium pectate in plant cells, where it is a component of the MIDDLE LAMELLA of the cell wall. When heated, pectin forms a gel that can set, a feature used in making jam.

pectinate (of plant structures) with comblike lobes.

pectoral fin one of a pair of propellant/steering organs attached to the PECTORAL GIRDLE of fish.

pectoral girdle or **shoulder girdle** the skeletal support for the anterior limbs of vertebrates that transmits power from limbs to the body and also serves to protect and support the organs in the thorax. It normally is a U-shaped structure and is attached to the vertebrae by muscles. See Fig. 241.

Fig. 241. **Pectoral girdle.** Basic plan.

pedal of or relating to the foot, particularly the feet of mollusks.

pedate (of leaves) divided in a PALMATE fashion with further divisions.

pedicel the stalk of a flower.

pedigree analysis a technique in which patterns of inheritance are traced through several generations.

pedipalp either member of the second pair of head appendages of arachnids, specialized for different functions in different forms. Examples include seizing prey in scorpions, locomotion in king crabs, fertilization in male spiders (where the tip becomes a specialized container for sperm transfer), squeezing, chewing food, and for sensory purposes.

pedo- *combining form* denoting child.

pedogenesis sexual reproduction in the larval or juvenile stage that may persist either temporarily or permanently, as in an axolotl. Humans resemble the juvenile stages of apes in several features, such as lack of hair, and pedogenesis may well have played an important part in the evolution of *Homo sapiens*. Some structures are said to be *neotonic* if the juvenile appearance persists in adults, as in the downy feathers of an ostrich.

peduncle the stalk of an inflorescence or a flower.

pelagic 1. (of organisms) swimming actively in the mass of sea water (NEKTON) rather than living at the bottom, or drifting with the currents in the surface waters (PLANKTON). 2. (of birds) spending most of their lives at sea.

pelecypod see BIVALVE.

pellagra see NICOTINIC ACID.

pelletizing the coating of a seed with material, which may include pesticides, to produce a uniform size of seed for sowing.

pellicle a thin membrane.

peltate (of a plant structure) flattened and with the stalk attached to the center of the lower surface, not the edge.

pelvic fin one of a pair of propellant/steering organs attached to the PELVIC GIRDLE of fish.

pelvic girdle or **hip girdle** the skeletal support for posterior limbs of vertebrates that transmits power in locomotion from the hind limbs to the body. See Fig. 242.

Fig. 242. **Pelvic girdle.** Basic plan.

penetrance the percentage of individuals with a particular GENOTYPE that display the genotype in the PHENOTYPE. For example, a dominant gene for baldness is 100% penetrant in males and 0% penetrant in most females, because the gene requires high levels of the male hormone for expression, an example of SEX LIMITATION. Once a gene shows penetrance it may show a range of EXPRESSIVITY of phenotype.

penicillin an antibiotic produced by the mold *Penicillium*, which is toxic to a number of bacteria, both pathogenic and nonpathogenic. In 1928 it was observed by Sir Alexander FLEMING that the mold inhibited growth of bacteria, and that a substance extracted from it still had this antibiotic property.

penis or **phallus** the copulatory organ of a male animal, which conveys the sperm to the genital tract of the female.

Pennatulacea a COELENTERATE family, including the sea pens.

penta- *combining form* denoting five.

pentadactyl limb a limb bearing five digits (fingers or toes), which is present in amphibia, reptiles, birds, and mammals. The limb is thought to have evolved largely for life on land and consists of three main parts: (a) the humerus (anterior limb) or femur (posterior limb); (b) the radius and ulna (anterior), or tibia and fibula (posterior); and (c) a hand or foot made up of carpals (anterior) or tarsals (posterior), metacarpals or metatarsals and phalanges. In many forms the limb is much modified for activities, such as flying, running, or swimming.

pentaploid a POLYPLOID individual having five sets of chromosomes.

pentosan a polysaccharide of pentoses.

pentose a monosaccharide with five carbon atoms.

pentose phosphate pathway (PPP) or **pentose phosphate shunt** or **hexose monophosphate shunt** or **phosphogluronate pathway** a PATHWAY for metabolism of glucose. PPP is particularly important in animal cells, in which it functions as an alternative to GLYCOLYSIS and the KREBS CYCLE, although both mechanisms occur together.

In the PPP, glucose (a hexose sugar) in the form of glucose phosphate molecules is oxidized by removal of hydrogen and decarboxylated, producing pentose sugars, carbon dioxide, and hydrogen atoms, which are transferred to the coenzyme NADP to form $NADPH_2$. In a second stage the pentose sugars are rearranged to produce hexose again, although in a smaller quantity than at the start. Unlike NADH, NADPH is not involved in producing ATP via an ELECTRON TRANSPORT SYSTEM, but transfers hydrogen atoms and electrons to sites where molecules are being assembled.

The $NADPH_2$ molecules are particularly active in cells carrying out fat metabolism, such as cells of adipose tissue, liver, adrenal cortex, and mammary gland tissue.

pentose phosphate shunt see PENTOSE PHOSPHATE PATHWAY.

pentose sugar a MONOSACCHARIDE with a five-carbon ring, particularly sugars such as ribose and deoxyribose found in NUCLEOTIDES.

peppered moth the moth *Biston betularia,* which has been extensively studied. Its coloration is of two main types: peppered (a mixture of white and gray) and melanic (dark brown), the relative proportion of the two color types in an area being related to the amount of atmospheric pollution. The color forms are an example of GENETIC POLYMORPHISM controlled by a single gene with two ALLELES, the allele for melanism being dominant. See INDUSTRIAL MELANISM.

pepsin an enzyme secreted in the inactive form PEPSINOGEN by chief or peptic cells in the gastric pits of the stomach of vertebrates. Pepsin breaks down proteins in acid solution into short polypeptide chains, which are subsequently broken down further by PEPTIDASES.

pepsinogen a precursor of PEPSIN in the vertebrate stomach. In the presence of hydrochloric acid, also secreted by the OXYNTIC CELLS in the stomach wall, pepsinogen gives rise to more active pepsin, which itself activates pepsinogen. The reaction is thus autocatalytic.

peptidase an enzyme present in PANCREATIC JUICE that releases free AMINO ACIDS from POLYPEPTIDE CHAINS. EXOPEPTIDASES split off terminal amino acids, whereas ENDOPEPTIDASES split links with the chain.

peptide any of a group of compounds consisting of two or more amino acids linked by chemical bonding. See PEPTIDE BOND, DIPEPTIDE.

peptide bond a chemical compound joining two AMINO ACIDS together, produced by a condensation reaction (see DIPEPTIDE). See Fig. 243.

Fig. 243. **Peptide bond.** Molecular structure. R = special group unique to each amino acid.

peptidyl site a TRANSFER RNA binding site on the RIBOSOME at which a PEPTIDE BOND occurs.

peptone a soluble product resulting from protein hydrolysis. See PEPSIN, PEPTIDASE.

per- *prefix* denoting through, thoroughly, utterly, very.

perennation the survival of an organism from one season to the next, usually with a period of reduced activity between seasons. See PERENNIAL.

perennial a plant that lives from year to year. Plants with woody stems are generally perennials (for example, trees, shrubs, and woody vines), but so too are many herbaceous plants (for example, dandelion, daisy, and plantain), in which the aerial parts die back during winter leaving perennating organs (for example, tubers, corms, and bulbs) underground.

perfusion the passage of a liquid through an organ or tissue.

peri- *prefix* denoting about *or* around.

perianth the organs of a flower outside the sex organs, consisting of the CALYX and COROLLA; the floral envelope.

perianth segment the individual leaves of the PERIANTH.

periblast the tissue surrounding the BLASTODERM in meroblastic eggs.

pericardial cavity 1. the part of the coelom surrounding the heart of vertebrates. 2. the part of the HEMOCOEL surrounding the heart in arthropods.

pericardial membrane the membrane surrounding the heart.

pericarditis an inflammation of the PERICARDIUM.

pericardium a sac-like envelope surrounding the vertebrate heart and the pericardial cavity in arthropods and mollusks.

pericarp the wall of a fruit, developing from the ovary wall after fertilization has occurred. The pericarp is made up of three distinct layers, an outer exocarp, a central mesocarp, and an inner endocarp. In dry fruit the pericarp is firm and often rigid (for example, poppy capsule, strawberry ACHENES); in succulent fruits the pericarp is swollen, often with a high sugar content in the mesocarp (for example, grape, peach).

periclinal (of planes of cell division in plants) parallel with the surface of the plant.

pericycle the layer of plant cells between the ENDODERMIS and the PHLOEM, consisting mainly of PARENCHYMA, from which lateral roots originate. See STEM and ROOT for diagrams.

periderm a protective tissue formed in roots and stems that has undergone SECONDARY THICKENING, consisting of an outer cork zone, an underlying phellogen (cork cambium), and with a phelloderm (secondary cortex) beneath that.

perigynous (of flowers) having a flat or concave structure on which are borne the sepals, petals, and stamens.

perilymph the fluid separating the bony labyrinth from the membranous labyrinth of the inner ear.

perineustic (of insects) having a respiratory system in which spiracles occur laterally on all abdominal segments.

periosteum the CONNECTIVE TISSUE surrounding the bones of vertebrates and to which are connected the MUSCLES and TENDONS. OSTEOBLASTS are present in the periosteum and are important in bone repair after breakage.

periostracum the outermost of the three layers of the shell of mollusks or brachiopods, composed of CONCHIOLIN. On the inner side lie the prismatic layer and the nacreous layer.

peripheral of or relating to the outside or extreme edge of a structure. For example, the peripheral nervous system is the NERVOUS SYSTEM as a whole with the exception of the CENTRAL NERVOUS SYSTEM.

peripheral isolate an isolated population at or beyond the normal range of the species.

perisarc the horny covering of hydrozoan coelenterates of the orders Gymnoblastea, Calyptoblastea, and Hydrocorallinae. In the last of these, the perisarc is massive and impregnated with calcium.

perisperm a nutritive tissue found in some seeds that is derived from the NUCELLUS of the ovules.

perispore a spore membrane.

Perissodactyla the odd-toed ungulates, such as horses. Compare ARTIODACTYLA.

peristalsis the alternate contraction and relaxation of circular and longitudinal muscle producing waves that pass along the intestine and other tubular systems of animals, moving the tube contents in one direction.

peristome any structure that occurs around the mouth or opening of an organ.

perithecium a type of fruiting body found in the ascomycete fungi, containing numerous asci (see ASCUS).

peritoneum the thin membrane of mesodermal origin that lines the body cavity, covers the heart, and forms mesenteries.

peritrophic membrane an inner lining of the gut found in some insects and crustaceans that may serve to protect the gut cells from injury by food particles. There is evidence that in insects harmful substances may be removed from the body by extrusion of the membrane from the anus.

perivisceral cavity the body cavity surrounding the viscera.

permafrost permanently frozen ground of which only a thin layer thaws in summer, as in the Arctic and Antarctic.

permanent teeth the second set of teeth in mammals.

permeability of membranes a theoretical concept of the permeability of a cell membrane, in which the membrane structure is thought to contain pores through which solutes can sometimes pass down a CONCENTRATION GRADIENT by DIFFUSION (see FLUID-MOSAIC MODEL). Many membranes, however, are differentially permeable to certain molecules. For example, SELECTIVE PERMEABILITY enables OSMOSIS to take place. Other membranes will allow movement against a concentration gradient by ACTIVE TRANSPORT. One example of this is the removal of sodium by cells surrounded by a higher sodium concentration.

permease a protein thought to act as a carrier in ACTIVE TRANSPORT within membranes.

Permian period the last period of the Paleozoic era, which lasted from 280 to 240 million years ago. Amphibians declined in numbers, reptiles increased, and conifers became more common during this period. Many extinctions occurred, including that of the trilobites. Mammal-like reptiles appeared, and the first beetles and insects evolved.

pernicious anemia a severe condition in which there is a progressive decrease in the number of red blood cells together with an increase in their size, producing poor color, weakness, and digestive disorders. The condition can be fatal but may be treated by dosing with vitamin B_{12}.

peroxidase an enzyme such as CATALASE that catalyzes oxidation of various substances by peroxides.

peroxisome an organelle of EUKARYOTE cells that is surrounded by a single unit membrane. Peroxisomes contain PEROXIDASES and may be concerned with production of molecular oxygen from the breakdown of hydrogen peroxide. They are located near MITOCHONDRIA and plant CHLOROPLASTS and appear to be involved in CELLULAR RESPIRATION.

persistence the period of time between acquisition of a virus by a VECTOR and its transference to a new host.

pest any organism that causes nuisance to humans, either economically or medically. Our classification of pests is constantly changing and depends on economic circumstances. For example, the fungus causing apple scab is treated as a pest in some countries because it disfigures the fruit. In poorer countries, however, such cosmetic qualities of apples are less important, and the fungus is not considered a pest.

pesticide any agent that causes the death of a pest. The general definition is usually restricted to chemicals with pesticidal properties, such as herbicides, insecticides, acaricides (mite killers), and fungicides. Pesticide application can produce many problems, for example:

(a) destruction of organisms useful to people (nontarget species).

(b) directly harmful effects to people if used incorrectly.

(c) accumulation and concentration in food chains leading to toxicity in animals at a higher TROPHIC LEVEL.

petal any of the separate parts of the corolla of a flower. Often brightly colored, the petal is a modified leaf and is important in flowers pollinated by insects (see ENTOMOPHILY).

petaloid (of plant structures) looking like a petal.

petiole the stalk of a leaf, containing vascular tissue that connects with the VASCULAR BUNDLES of the stem. The base of a petiole, where it joins the stem, may have small leaflike structures called STIPULES and axillary buds. See AXIL.

petri dish see PLATE.

PGA (phosphoglyceric acid) or **glyceric acid phosphate** or **glycerate 3-phosphate** a three-carbon molecule produced from PGAL (see Fig. 244) in GLYCOLYSIS. PGA is a molecule with a structure similar to that of PGAL, except that a hydroxyl (OH) replaces a hydrogen atom at one point. PGA is also a vital molecule in photosynthesis, being produced in the CALVIN CYCLE from an unstable six-carbon molecule formed when ribulose diphosphate and carbon dioxide combine.

PGAL (PHOSPHOGLYCERALDEHYDE)

Fig. 244. **PGAL.** Molecular structure.

PGAL (phosphoglyceraldehyde) or **triose phosphate** or **glyceral-dehyde phosphate** a three-carbon molecule produced from fructose diphosphate in GLYCOLYSIS (see Fig. 244). PGAL is also a vital molecule in PHOTOSYNTHESIS, being produced in the CALVIN CYCLE from the phosphorylation and reduction of PGA by ATP and NADPH, respectively, which are produced in the LIGHT REACTIONS. Via a series of steps, two molecules of PGAL are rearranged to form six-carbon GLUCOSE.

pH a measure of the *hydrogen ion concentration* in an aqueous solution. The formula is:

$$\frac{1}{\log (H^+)}$$

The formula produces a value in which the greater the number of H^+ ions, the lower the pH reading. The scale of pH values is from 1.0 (highly acid) to 14 (highly alkaline) with 7.0 as the neutral point. Since the pH is logarithmic, each change of one pH unit means a tenfold change in the number of hydrogen ions. pH can be measured by using indicators that change color with changing pH, or by electrical means using a pH meter.

Phaeophycae a class of algae, comprising the brown algae. The class is sometimes raised to the status of a division called Phaeophyta. The algae are mostly marine and their green pigment is masked by fucoxanthin, a yellow pigment. Some members of the group are the largest algae known and may reach several meters in length, for example, *Laminaria*.

Phaeophyta see PHAEOPHYCAE.

phage see BACTERIOPHAGE.

phago- *combining form* denoting eating, devouring.

phagocyte a cell capable of flowing around and engulfing material from its surroundings. Such cells can discriminate between different particles. For example, phagocytic white blood cells will engulf only certain BAC-TERIA. Phagocytes form an important defense mechanism in higher animals, particularly against bacteria, which are engulfed and digested. See MACROPHAGE.

phagocytosis the ingestion of materials (subcellular particles, cells) from outside a cell into its interior, forming a cytoplasmic vacuole.

phalange any of the finger or toe bones associated with the PENTADAC-TYL LIMB. The proximal bone of the phalanges articulates with the METACARPAL or METATARSAL.

Phalangeridae a family of arborial marsupials possessing prehensile tails. The flying phalangers possess a PATAGIUM (1).

phallus see PENIS.

phanerophyte a woody plant bearing buds more than 25 cm from the ground.

pharynx the canal leading from the mouth to the esophagus in vertebrates. In humans, the upper pharynx includes the nasal section divided off by the soft palate, and the lower pharynx includes the mouth and throat. In protochordates it is the part of the gut system into which the gill slits open internally.

phasic transient.

Phasmidae the family of stick and leaf insects (see ORTHOPTERAN).

phenetic ranking an arrangement into categories based on degree of similarity.

phenocopy a disorder or change that appears to be genetic in origin but actually is produced by environmental effects. An example is deafness in an infant that is caused by the GERMAN MEASLES virus rather than by an inherited condition. The distinction can be important since it affects the chances of an affected individual transmitting the condition to the next generation.

phenogram a diagram illustrating the degree of similarity between taxa.

phenon a sample of specimens of similar appearance. See PHENOTYPE.

phenotype the observable features of an individual organism that result from an interaction between the GENOTYPE and the environment in which development occurs. The interaction is that between *nature and nurture*. Variations due to nature are the inherited aspects of the organism, the genotype. Nurture denotes the usually not inherited effects of the environment on the organism.

Sometimes two different genotypes give the same phenotype due to DOMINANCE (1) masking a recessive ALLELE. It is correct to say, however, that the closer we look at the effect of an allele the more likely we are to detect a special phenotype unmasked by dominance. For example, an allele may code for a nonfunctional enzyme and thus be hidden in a heterozygote (classifying the allele as recessive) but its effects may be detected by such methods as ELECTROPHORESIS, which can identify different forms of a protein.

phenotypic plasticity or **environmental variation** the ability of an organism to greatly alter its PHENOTYPE depending on environmental conditions. The phenomenon is seen most clearly in plants, perhaps because they are fixed in the ground. For example, a dandelion will produce an erect habit with long flower stalks if it is in a garden border with other plants. Another dandelion with a similar genotype will produce a PROCUMBENT habit with short flower stalks if it is grown in a lawn.

phenotypic variance the amount of variation in a phenotypic trait among individuals in a population.

phenylalanine one of 20 AMINO ACIDS common in proteins. It has a NONPOLAR R structure and is relatively insoluble in water. See Fig. 245. The ISOELECTRIC POINT of phenylalanine is 5.5. See PHENYLKETONURIA.

Fig. 245. **Phenylalanine.** Molecular structure.

phenylketonuria (PKU) an INBORN ERROR OF METABOLISM in humans in which there is inability to convert PHENYLALANINE to tyrosine, due to absence of a functional phenylalanine hydroxylase enzyme. The condition is controlled by the recessive allele of an autosomal gene, probably on chromosome 1, so affected individuals are recessive homozygotes, having received one recessive allele from each parent, both of whom are usually heterozygous carriers.

The effects of PKU are many and extremely serious. Perhaps the principal problem is abnormal accumulation of phenylalanine in blood and other tissues, which adversely affects nervous tissue to such an extent that 90% of affected individuals have an IQ of less than 40 and thus are classified as severely mentally retarded. There is microcephaly (reduced brain size) in two thirds of all PKU cases, and 75% show tailor's posture, a condition in which muscular hypertonicity causes contraction of leg and arm muscles so that individuals sit cross-legged with their arms drawn into the body.

The condition can be treated if discovered in very early childhood. Treatment consists of a diet low in phenylalanine. (Some of this amino acid must be present in the diet, since it is an ESSENTIAL AMINO ACID). In some countries, a small blood sample is taken from every newborn baby and the sample undergoes a Guthrie test, in which high levels of phenylalanine in the blood are detected by inhibition of bacterial growth.

pheromone a chemical substance used in communication between organisms of the same species. Pheromones are found mainly in animals, but they occur in some lower plant groups in which a chemical is secreted into water by female gametes to attract male gametes. In some animals, pheromones are transmitted in the air, for example, by female moths of certain species, which secrete a chemical attractive to males over large distances, or by male dogs marking out their territory with urine. Insect pheromones have been used to trap females of serious pests.

philopatry the tendency of an animal to remain in its home area or return to it in the case of migrants.

phloem a transport tissue characterized by presence of sieve tubes and companion cells, found in the VASCULAR BUNDLES of higher plants. Phloem functions in the transport of dissolved organic substances (for example, sucrose) by TRANSLOCATION.

phloroglucin a dye that, with hydrochloric acid, stains LIGNIN bright red in sections of plant material.

Phocidae the family of carnivorous mammals containing the seals. The hind limbs are united with the tail and point backward, and there are no external ears.

phosphagen a type of chemical found in the muscles of all animals whose function is to pass on high-energy phosphate to ADP to form ATP. Phosphagens thus act as energy-storage molecules and are especially useful when cellular respiration is not providing enough ATP molecules, for example, when sudden muscular activity takes place. Phosphagens are of two types: *creatine phosphate*, also called *phosphocreatine*, found in vertebrates and echinoderms, and *arginine phosphate*, also called *phosphoarginine*, found in many other invertebrates.

phosphatase an enzyme that catalyzes release of phosphate from a molecule. For example, in the mammalian liver, phosphorylated glucose can be broken down to glucose with a phosphatase enzyme. See GLYCOGEN.

phosphate any salt or ester of any PHOSPHORIC ACID.

phosphoarginine a phosphagen found in many invertebrates.

PHOSPHOCREATINE

phosphocreatine a compound used in producing ATP from ADP in muscles, being converted to creatine with the release of inorganic phosphorus.

phosphoenolpyruvic acid (PEP) a high-energy compound that, when dephosphorylated to pyruvic acid, gives rise to synthesis of ATP from ADP in GLYCOLYSIS.

phosphogluconate pathway see PENTOSE PHOSPHATE PATHWAY.

phosphoglyceraldehyde see PGAL.

phosphoglyceric acid see PGA.

phospholipid a compound fat molecule in which there are two FATTY ACIDS and a phosphate group attached to the glycerol, located mostly in cell membranes. Phospholipids in the blood are responsible for transport and utilization of fats in the body.

phosphorescence see BIOLUMINESCENCE.

phosphoric acid an important component of NUCLEIC ACIDS, connecting the pentose sugars to form a POLYNUCLEOTIDE CHAIN.

phosphorylation the process in which one or more phosphate groups are added to a molecule. Such reactions occur regularly in biological systems. For example, in AEROBIC RESPIRATION glucose is phosphorylated in GLYCOLYSIS; ADP is phosphorylated to ATP at the substrate level and via the ELECTRON TRANSPORT SYSTEM; in plants ATP is produced by PHOTOPHOSPHORYLATION.

photic zone see EUPHOTIC ZONE.

photo- *combining form* denoting light.

photoactivation the excitation of atoms by light energy so that electrons become temporarily raised to a higher energy level. The process is the starting point of PHOTOSYNTHESIS, when light strikes a CHLOROPHYLL molecule. See LIGHT REACTIONS.

photoautotroph a type of AUTOTROPH that uses light as an energy source to synthesize organic compounds from inorganic materials. Green plants are photoautotrophs.

photolysis chemical decomposition using light energy, literally splitting by light. In 1933, Cornelius van Niel (born 1897) proposed that the initial step in PHOTOSYNTHESIS was photolysis of water, leading to release of oxygen ions (forming oxygen gas) and hydrogen ions involved in reduction of NADP during LIGHT REACTIONS. Recently it has become more common to explain the breakdown of water as a separation of charge, a fast spontaneous ionic reaction with water splitting into hydrogen (H^+) and hydroxl (OH^-) ions. The end result is the same as photolysis, but light is not thought to be involved in the process.

photon a quantum of radiant energy with a wavelength in the visible range of the ELECTROMAGNETIC SPECTRUM.

photooxidation a chemical reaction occurring as a result of absorption of light in the presence of oxygen.

photoperiod the length of daylight as compared with the length of darkness in each 24-hour cycle. See PHOTOPERIODISM.

photoperiodism the response observed in an organism to the length and timing of light periods. While all organisms can be affected by PHOTOPERIODS (see also BIOLOGICAL CLOCK), the term is most commonly used in connection with higher plants, particularly their flowering. The regulation of flowering is rather complex and difficult to generalize about, but it is possible to divide plants into three categories: LONG-DAY PLANTS, SHORT-DAY PLANTS, and DAY-NEUTRAL PLANTS— the last being unaffected by photoperiod.

Plants appear to detect the photoperiod with the pigment PHYTO-CHROME, which can exist in two forms in the leaves, P^{660} in red light and P^{725} in infrared light. If P^{660} is present in excess in a short-day plant, or P^{725} is present in excess in a long-day plant, then flowering is induced by production of the hormone *florigen*, changing a vegetative apical MERISTEM to a flowering one.

Phytochromes are also present in the seed coat, the correct balance of P^{660} and P^{725} stimulating enzyme activation and hence GERMINA-TION. See also FLORIGEN.

photophase the light phase of a dark/light cycle. Compare SCOTO-PHASE.

photophosphorylation the production of ATP from ADP, with light as the energy source. The process takes place during the light reactions of PHOTOSYNTHESIS, which also result in production of reduced NADP. The details of ATP and NADPH formation are given under LIGHT REAC-TIONS.

photopigment a pigment molecule that can be excited by light, such as CHLOROPHYLL.

photoreceptor a structure or pigment sensitive to light. In animals such structures are called eyes. They contain sensitive pigments and activate the nervous system when stimulated by light. In plants photoreceptors tend to be pigments of various sorts. For example, PHYTOCHROMES sensitive to red light (see PHOTOPERIODISM) and flavoproteins sensitive to blue light trigger AUXIN production, leading to PHOTOTROPISM.

photorespiration the part of the respiration of plants that occurs in light and during photosynthesis. Mitochondria are not involved, and there is no yield of ATP.

photosynthesis the process by which plants convert carbon dioxide and water into organic chemicals using the energy of light, with the release of oxygen. Photosynthesis occurs in green plants, which are known as AUTOTROPHS. See LIGHT REACTIONS, CALVIN CYCLE.

photosystems I and II see LIGHT REACTIONS.

phototaxis the movement of a whole organism in response to a directional light stimulus. For example, movement of unicellular algae or fruit flies toward a source of light is *positive* phototaxis. Movement away from light if the stimulus is too strong is called *negative* phototaxis.

phototropism a bending growth movement of parts of a plant in response to a light stimulus. The movement produced by unequal growth is due to differences in AUXIN concentration. For example, most seedlings are *positively* phototropic, growing toward a light stimulus, because there is a greater concentration of auxin on the side farthest from the light, giving greater growth on this side. Roots, on the other hand, are often *negatively* phototropic, growing away from a light source.

phragma one of the parts of the insect skeleton projecting inward in the dorsal region, which serves for attachment of muscles and other organs.

phragmocone the internal shell of a cuttlefish or other cephalopod made up of several chambers.

phycocyanin a blue plant pigment with a photosynthetic function found in blue-green and red algae, with an absorption peak of 618 nm (see ABSORPTION SPECTRUM).

phycoerythrin a red pigment with a photosynthetic function found in red algae and some blue-green algae, with absorption peaks at 490, 546, and 576 nm (see ABSORPTION SPECTRUM).

phycomycete any filamentous fungus of the class Phycomycetes, now included in two separate subdivisions of the Eumycota (see PLANT KINGDOM), which usually lack cross walls, that is, are nonseptate.

phyletic of or relating to a line of descent.

phyletic correlation a correlation of phenotypic characters that reflects a well-integrated ancestral gene complex.

phyletic weighting the assessment of taxonomic importance on the basis of PHYLETIC CORRELATION.

phyllo- *combining form* denoting leaf.

phyllode an unusual type of leaf in which the lamina is absent but the petiole is so flattened as to appear to be a normal leaf, and there is still an axillary bud in the leaf node. Phyllodes are found, for example, in the grass vetch, *Lathyrus nissolia*.

phylloplane the surface of the leaf in plants.

phyllopodium a broad flattened crustacean limb used for swimming or for creating respiratory currents.

phylloquinone see VITAMIN K.

phyllotaxy the arrangement of leaves on a stem.

phylogenetic tree a diagram illustrating lines of descent derived from morphological and paleontological evidence.

phylogeny the entire evolutionary history of a species or other taxonomic group of organisms. See HAECKEL'S LAW OF RECAPITULATION.

phylogram a treelike diagram showing the degree of relationship of different TAXA.

phylum a major grouping (TAXON) into which kingdoms, for example, the animal kingdom, are divided and which is composed of a number of CLASSES.

physiological drought a state in which plants are unable to absorb water even though water may be freely available. The condition can be caused by a high ionic concentration in the water, so OSMOSIS cannot occur, or by low water temperature.

physiology the study in animals and plants of internal processes and functions associated with life.

physo- *combining form* denoting bladder.

phyto- *combining form* denoting plants.

phytoalexin a defensive chemical produced by higher plants that is often fungicidal in action (see PLANT DISEASE). Phytoalexins are specific to particular attacking organisms; about 30 types have been identified in various plants, particularly the Leguminosae.

phytochrome a type of plant pigment that occurs in two forms: P_{660}, which absorbs red light, and P_{725}, which absorbs infrared light. P_{725} is biologically active in that it stimulates enzymic reactions, whereas P_{660} is biologically inert. Conversion of one form into the other and vice versa occur simultaneously. See Fig. 246.

$$\text{red light} \rightsquigarrow P_{660} \rightleftarrows P_{725} \rightsquigarrow \text{far-red light}$$

Fig. 246. **Phytochrome.** The simultaneous conversion of red light into infrared light.

Daylight contains a mixture of red and infrared light, with an excess of red light. During the day the proportion of P_{725} builds up relative to P_{660}, whereas during the night there is a gradual conversion of P_{725} to P_{660}. Thus, phytochrome provides the plant with a method of detecting day and night, with P_{725} predominant when it is day, and P_{660} predominant when it is night. This mechanism is the basis of PHOTOPERIODISM.

phytophagous (of animals) feeding on plants.

phytoplankton the part of the plankton made up of plant life. Compare ZOOPLANKTON.

pia mater a thin, inner membrane or *meninx* surrounding the brain and spinal cord. See MENINGES.

pigeon's milk a crop secretion fed to the young pigeon.

piliferous layer a zone of epidermal cells behind the root tip producing root hairs.

piloerection the standing up of hairs on the skin to increase thermal insulation.

pilomotor (of autonomic control of smooth muscle) causing erection of body hair.

pilose (of plant structures) bearing hairs.

pilus an extension of the cell wall in bacteria that can be converted into a tube for CONJUGATION to take place.

pineal body or **pineal gland** an outgrowth of the roof of the forebrain. The posterior part (EPIPHYSIS) has an endocrine function and secretes melatonin, which concentrates the melanophores of fishes and amphibians, inhibits development of the gonads, and is involved in control of CIRCADIAN RHYTHMS. Exposure to light inhibits production of melatonin. The anterior part forms an eyelike structure (third eye) in some lizards; it is vestigial in the lamprey and absent in other vertebrates.

pineal gland see PINEAL BODY.

pinna 1. the primary division of a leaf. 2. a wing or fin. 3. the projecting part of the external ear of mammals.

pinnate (of compound leaves) made up of leaflets arranged in two rows on opposite sides of the axis, or RACHIS.

pinnatifid (of leaves) having a LAMINA cut into lobes that reach about halfway toward the midrib.

pinnatisect (of leaves) having a lamina that is PINNATIFID in shape but with lobes cut very deep, almost to the midrib.

Pinnipedia a suborder of aquatic carnivores, including the seals, sea lions, and walruses.

pinnule a subdivision of a leaf pinna, often bearing SPORANGIA in ferns.

pinocytosis or **micropinocytosis** the active engulfing of very small particles or liquids by cells; a form of ENDOCYTOSIS. The particles become surrounded by the cell membrane on all sides, which eventually forms a channel from which vesicles are pinched off and move within the PROTOPLASM before their contents can be transferred into the cell proper.

pistil see CARPEL.

pit a thin area of the cell wall in higher plants where no secondary wall develops. If two cells have pits in adjacent parts of the wall, there are often fine protoplasmic connections called PLASMODESMATA between the cells. Pits sometimes have a more complex structure, as in BORDERED PITS of seed plants.

pitfall trap a trap, for example, a jar sunk into the ground, into which mobile animals may fall and from which they are unable to escape.

pith or **medulla** the core of a DICOTYLEDON stem, containing PAREN-CHYMA cells that have a storage function.

Pithecanthropus an early type of genus of man from the PLIOCENE EPOCH. It possessed a larger cranial capacity than apes and probably walked erect. See HEIDELBERG MAN.

Pithecinae a family of New World monkeys lacking a prehensile tail.

pituitary gland or **pituitary body** or **pituitary** an ENDOCRINE ORGAN derived from a downgrowth of the infundibulum of the brain (pars nervosa) and an upgrowth of the *hypophysis* (pars distalis and pars intermedia). The pars distalis, usually referred to as the anterior pituitary, produces FOLLICLE STIMULATING HORMONE (FSH), luteinizing hormone (LH), LUTEOTROPIC HORMONE (LTH), ADRENOCORTICO-TROPIC HORMONE (ACTH), THYROTROPIC HORMONE, and GROWTH HORMONE.

The pars intermedia and pars nervosa (*neurohypophysis*) form the posterior pituitary. The former produces intermedin in fish, amphibians, and reptiles (absent in birds and mammals), which is associated with change in skin color. The latter secretes oxytocin and ADH, which are produced in the hypothalamus and stored in the pars nervosa. The pituitary controls the functioning of other endocrine organs.

placebo 1. any inactive substance given to satisfy a patient's psychological need for medication. 2. a control in an experiment to test the effect of a drug.

placenta 1. (in animals) the structure formed from tissues of embryo and mother at the point of attachment of the embryo to the mother, through which the embryo is nourished. In placental mammals the embryonic blood supply may be from the ALLANTOIS (allantoic placenta) or the yolk sac (yolk sac placenta). Small molecules of oxygen and food materials pass to the embryo through the placenta, and urea and CO_2 pass out from the embryo. The placenta itself produces the hormones ESTRO-GEN, PROGESTERONE, and GONADOTROPHIC HORMONE. At birth the fetus is ejected from the uterus first, the umbilical cord is broken, and the placental afterbirth is discharged last, except in abnormal circumstances. See Fig. 247. 2. (in plants) a part of the wall of the ovary on which OVULES are borne.

placentation the arrangement of PLACENTAS (2) in the plant ovary, which can be classified into several categories, including: (a) apical, at the ovary apex; (b) basal, at the ovary base; (c) parietal, on the ovary wall; and (d) free-central, on a column growing up from the ovary base.

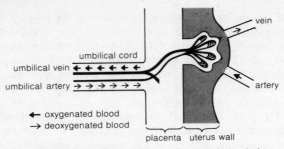

Fig. 247. **Placenta.** Section showing blood circulation.

Placodermi see APHETOHYOIDEA.

placodont a fossil reptile from the Triassic period, which possessed flat crushing teeth and probably fed on mollusks.

placoid or **denticle** 1. a toothlike structure of enamel covered with dentine. 2. (*adj.*) platelike. Compare COSMOID, GANOID.

plankton the organisms inhabiting the surface layer of a sea or lake, drifting with the current. Many planktonic organisms are capable of locomotion but are not sufficiently strong swimmers to move against the currents. Members of the plankton vary in size from unicellular organisms to large jellyfish, 1 meter or more in diameter. Compare NEKTON.

plant see PLANT KINGDOM.

plant breeding the science that aims to improve the quality and yield of plants by genetic engineering of varieties. The main tool of the plant breeder is SELECTION, by which it is possible to alter the genetic constitution of a plant type, provided that genetic variability is present in the original strains. Another method of improvement is the crossing together of inbred lines to produce HETEROSIS in the hybrids (see GREEN REVOLUTION). Plant breeding has led to great improvement in crop yield, better harvesting (for example, with dwarf varieties), and improvements in the natural resistance of plants to pathogens. Recently, cell and tissue cultures using EXPLANTS have begun to be used by plant breeders, to produce: (a) multiple copies (CLONES) of sterile types; (b) development of forms with new chromosome combinations; and (c) HAPLOIDS (2) that can be induced to become fertile DIPLOIDS (2), the latter forming PURE BREEDING LINES.

plant community see COMMUNITY.

plant disease the disruption of normal growth and metabolism in plants leading to reduced viability and even death. Plant diseases may begin with physical attack of the plant by pests, such as insects, slugs, mites, birds, and other animals, some of which may be VECTORS of plant PA-

THOGENS. Often, however, pathogens enter the plant via wounds caused by animal pests. Other pathogens, such as cereal rusts, are able to penetrate plant tissue on their own, often via leaf stomata. Many plants produce special chemicals called PHYTOALEXINS in response to injury, which have an effective defensive function.

plant hormone any of several chemical substances produced in very low concentrations in plants that control growth and development. Plant HORMONES are produced in active MERISTEMS (for example, root and shoot apices) from where they diffuse to other parts of the plant. A distinct contrast with animal hormonal systems is the fact that plants do not possess specific tissues for hormone production, nor a well-defined distribution system equivalent to the blood system.

Plant hormones are classified generally into several groups, discussed under separate headings: ABSCISSIC ACID, AUXINS, CYTOKININS, and GIBBERELLINS.

plantigrade walking on the entire sole of the foot, as in humans and bears.

plant kingdom a category of living organisms comprising all members of the kingdom Plantae. Plants lack locomotive movement, have cell walls, and have no obvious nervous or sensory organs. Most plant groups include members with CHLOROPHYLL. The system in which the plant kingdom is organized is given here.

planula the ciliated larva of coelenterates, which lacks a body cavity.

plaque a clear area in a lawn of a bacterial colony, in which the bacteria have undergone LYSIS due to BACTERIOPHAGE infection.

plasma 1. the cellular PROTOPLASM inside a plasma membrane. **2.** see BLOOD PLASMA.

plasma gel an area of cytoplasm with a GEL structure.

plasma gene a self-replicating particle found in cellular cytoplasm and showing CYTOPLASMIC INHERITANCE.

plasmalemma the CELL MEMBRANE that also lines the connecting PLASMODESMATA between living cells.

plasma membrane see cell membrane.

plasma proteins see BLOOD PLASMA.

plasma sol an area of cytoplasm with a SOL structure.

plasmid a circular piece of DNA found in the cytoplasm of bacterial cells that replicates independently of the host chromosome. Plasmids can be important in public health, since some types possess genes for antibiotic resistance and can quickly be transferred to different types of host cell, thus spreading resistance rapidly. Plasmids are used extensively in GENETIC ENGINEERING of microorganisms. See also EPISOME.

plasmo- *combining form* denoting plasma.

plasmodesmata narrow strands of cytoplasm (see SYMPLAST) that pass through pores in plant cell walls and join the cells to one another. They facilitate movement of material between cells and play an important part in plants in the deposition of cellulose during thickening of secondary cell walls.

plasmodium 1. any parasitic sporozoan protozoan of the genus *Plasmodium*, especially *P. vivax*, which causes malaria. **2.** the vegetative phase of slime molds (see MYXOMYCETE).

plasmolysis the shrinkage of plant cell contents due to loss of water, resulting in the CELL MEMBRANE pulling away from the cell wall, leaving a space filled with fluid. Plasmolysis occurs when plant cells are placed in a hypertonic (see HYPOTONIC) medium so that they lose water by OSMOSIS. See Fig. 248.

Fig. 248. **Plasmolysis.** (a) Isotonic medium. (b) Hypertonic medium, showing plasmolysis.

plastid an organelle of plant cells, with a double membrane. Plastids are large (between 3 and 6 μm in diameter) and have either a photosynthetic function (CHLOROPLAST) or a storage function (AMYLOBLAST).

plate 1. also called *petri dish*, a flat dish used to culture microorganisms. **2.** to spread cells over the surface of a medium in a culture plate.

platelet see BLOOD PLATELETS.

plate tectonics the study of the movement of the large crustal plates that form the surface of Earth on continental land masses and beneath oceans. See CONTINENTAL DRIFT.

platyhelminth or **flatworm** any invertebrate of the phylum Platyhelminthes, containing the TAPEWORMS (Cestoda), FLUKES (Trematoda), and planarians (Turbellaria). The Turbellaria are free-living flatworms that are aquatic and inhabit moist places on land. The two other groups are parasitic. They possess only an anterior opening to the gut system, there is no blood system, and the animals show BILATERAL SYMMETRY.

Platyrrhini the New World monkeys, distinguished from those of the Old World by having a broad cartilaginous nasal septum and a long, usually prehensile tail. Compare CATHARRHINI.

Plecoptera the insect order containing the stoneflies, which are hemi-metabolous and similar to mayflies.

pleiotropism a state in which one gene affects two or more aspects of the PHENOTYPE that are apparently unrelated. For example, the vestigial wing mutation of *Drosophila* not only controls the size and shape of the wings but also affects several other features, including reduced FECUNDITY.

Pleistocene epoch a division of the Quaternary period lasting from 2 million years ago until 10,000 years ago. The epoch contained four major glaciations, and *Homo sapiens* evolved during this time. See GEOLOGICAL TIME.

Pleistocene refuge the areas south of the great ice sheets of the PLEISTOCENE EPOCH in which animals and plants survived during periods of glaciation.

pleomorphic (of cells) having several shapes.

plesiomorphic (of characters) primitive or ancestral.

pleura the membrane that covers the lung and lines the innermost wall of the thorax.

pleural cavity a coelomic cavity surrounding the lungs of mammals that is separated from the rest of the perivisceral coelom by the DIAPHRAGM. The cavity is small and filled with fluid, as the lungs and body wall are in close proximity to each other.

pleuron the lateral plate on either side of the arthropod SOMITE.

Pleuronectidae a family of TELEOST fish, such as the flounder, that start life normally symmetrical but undergo a development as a result of which the eyes come to be on one side, the head is twisted, and the fish in a resting position lies on the bottom on its other side.

plexus a network of interlaced blood vessels or nerves.

Pliocene epoch the last epoch of the TERTIARY PERIOD, lasting from the end of the Miocene 7 million years ago to approximately 2 million years ago. Early people evolved during this period, some 3 million years ago.

ploidy the number of chromosome sets making up the total genome of an organism. Thus, the ploidy of normal humans is two and is written 2n. See DIPLOID (1).

plumule 1. (in plants) the embryonic shoot of a germinating seedling, which develops into an EPICOTYL and leaves. 2. (in animals) a down feather of birds.

pluteus a larva of ECHINODERMS that has ciliated arms, sometimes supported by calcareous rods.

PLUVIAL

pluvial 1. of, relating to, or due to the action of rain. **2.** any period during which the climate was wetter than now, usually applied to periods during the PLEISTOCENE EPOCH.

pneumaticity (of bones) the presence of air spaces that connect with the air sacs and lungs, particularly in birds.

pneumatophore the bladderlike polyp of SIPHONOPHORES that enables them to float. It is usually the uppermost polyp of the CORMIDIUM.

pneumonia a human lung disease caused by a number of bacterial and viral pathogens, particularly *Streptococcus pneumoniae.*

pneumostome a small aperture allowing passage of air, such as that leading into the respiratory cavity of snails.

pneumotaxic center see BREATHING.

podsol or **podzol** a forest soil characterized by a surface accumulation of humus, a strongly leached profile, one or more enriched layers in the SUBSOIL, and vegetation consisting predominantly of conifers.

poikilotherm or **ectotherm** or **heterotherm** any animal whose body temperature follows that of the surrounding environment. Poikilotherms are described as *cold-blooded,* but the body temperature may be quite high. Aquatic poikilotherms follow the environmental temperatures closely, but terrestrial forms may warm up from the sun's irradiation or cool through evaporation to an extent varying with the temperature of the surrounding air. All animals apart from mammals and birds are poikilothermous. Compare HOMOIOTHERM.

point mutation or **gene mutation** a genetic change affecting a single LOCUS, producing an alternative ALLELE of the gene, but not a gross structural change to the chromosome. The genetic change consists of an altered sequence of DNA bases, which can be of three main types: (a) a SUBSTITUTION MUTATION, (b) a DELETION MUTATION, and (c) an INSERTION MUTATION, the latter two often causing a major change in the amino acid sequence of the protein structure. Compare CHROMOSOMAL MUTATION.

Poisson distribution (statistics) the frequency of sample classes containing a particular number of events (0,1,2,3 ... n), where the average frequency of the event is small in relation to the total number of times that the event could occur. Thus, if a pool contains 100 small fish, each time a net is dipped into the pool up to 100 fish can be caught and returned to the pool. In reality, however, only none, one, or two fish are likely to be caught each time. The Poisson distribution predicts the probability of catching 0,1,2,3 ... 100 fish each time, producing a FREQUENCY DISTRIBUTION graph that is skewed heavily toward the low number of events.

polar body or **polar nucleus** or **polocyte** a small haploid cell, produced during OOGENESIS in female animals, that does not develop into a functional OVUM. During such GAMETOGENESIS three polar bodies are produced, along with one large ovum. A similar situation arises in the development of the egg cell of higher plants, in which only one fertile gamete is produced from MEIOSIS. See EMBRYO SAC.

polarity the morphological and/or physiological difference between the two ends of an axis, such as root and stem.

polarization the act of changing an ordinary light beam consisting of billions of wave trains, each vibrating in a different direction, to a beam in which only those wave trains vibrating in a particular plane are allowed to continue in the beam, which is then less bright.

Light from the sun is scattered by molecules in the upper atmosphere in such a way as to result in light arriving at Earth's surface being partially polarized. The extent of polarization at any point depends on the position of the sun, so there is a pattern of polarization of the sky for any particular position of the sun. Bees and probably many other arthropods are capable of navigating by this pattern when the sun is obscured as long as some blue sky can be seen (see NAVIGATION). Polarization can be brought about by naturally occurring crystals, such as calcite, or by Polaroid sheets.

polar nucleus see POLAR BODY.

polar substance any organic substance that combines readily with water. This is due to the presence of side groups of organic molecules that contain the electrical charge of hydroxyl groups.

poliomyelitis a paralytic disease in which cells of the CENTRAL NERVOUS SYSTEM become destroyed by the polio virus, leading to crippling, although most infections are not serious and the patient usually recovers full health. The disease can be kept in check by the administration of vaccines, the most popular being a live, attenuated type. In Western countries, administration of such vaccines is now routine and the disease is rare.

pollen see POLLEN GRAIN.

pollen basket the part of the hind leg of a honeybee modified for carrying pollen. In some leaf-cutting bees, the pollen basket lies below the abdomen.

pollen grain a small structure of higher plants that contains haploid male gamete NUCLEI and is surrounded by a double wall, the EXINE and INTINE. As the pollen grain ripens in the pollen sacs of the ANTHER, the nucleus divides by MITOSIS, and the now-two nuclei, called the generative nucleus and the tube nucleus, have different functions (see POLLEN TUBE). Pollen grains are transported from the male stamen to the female stigma in a process called POLLINATION.

POLLEN TUBE

pollen tube a slender structure produced from a POLLEN GRAIN after POLLINATION. The tube protrudes from a pore in the EXINE and grows down through the stigma, style, and ovary of the CARPEL, entering the ovule usually by the micropyle. See Fig. 249.

Fig. 249. **Pollen tube.** Section of grain, showing tube.

Within the tube, the haploid generative nucleus divides by MITOSIS to give two MALE GAMETE NUCLEI that have an important function in the double FERTILIZATION process of higher plants (see EMBRYO SAC). The growth of the tube appears to be controlled by the tube nucleus, and there is some evidence that the tube shows negative AEROTROPISM. The stimulus for the original germination of the pollen grain comes from a sugary fluid secreted by the stigma. Sometimes, however, germination is prevented by SELF-INCOMPATIBILITY factors in the stigma cells and pollen grain, which prevent self-pollination in some plants.

pollen tube nucleus see POLLEN TUBE.

pollination the transfer of pollen from male to female reproductive organs in higher plants, for example, microsporangium to ovule in GYM-NOSPERMS, and anther to stigma in ANGIOSPERMS. In flowering plants the flowers show a strong link between structure and the method of pollination (see ANEMOPHILY, ENTOMOPHILY).

Many angiosperms carry out CROSS-POLLINATION. Some of these types, such as brassicas, have SELF-INCOMPATIBILITY systems to prevent self-pollination. Self-pollination, however, is common in certain plants, such as groundsel or chickweed.

pollinium a mass of POLLEN GRAINS stuck together and carried as a whole during POLLINATION.

pollution the contamination of an environment by any substance or energy. Heavy metals, oil, sewage, noise, heat, radiation, and pesticides are common pollutants that can affect the environment adversely.

polocyte see POLAR BODY.

poly- *combining form* denoting many or much.

polyandry a system of POLYGAMY in which the female has several mating partners at one time. Compare POLYGYNY.

polychaete any marine ANNELID worm of the order Polychaeta, including both *errant* (moving) and *tubicolous* (living in tubes, therefore mainly sedentary) forms. They are characterized by the presence of CHAETAE carried on parapodia (projections from the body), and in errant forms the head is well developed. Fertilization is external. The group includes nereids (bristle worms such as the ragworm), tube worms, and fan worms.

polycistronic mRNA a MESSENGER RNA molecule found in many PROKARYOTES that contains information transcribed from two or more CISTRONS and translated into two or more polypeptides.

polyembryony 1. (in plants) the formation of more than one embryo within the TESTA of a seed. 2. (in animals) the development of more than one embryo from a single egg as occurs, for example, in certain parasitic HYMENOPTERA that use this phenomenon to rapidly increase the numbers of juveniles within the host.

polygamy a mating system of animals in which one sexual partner mates with several of the opposite sex (see POLYANDRY, POLYGYNY). Polygyny is the most common form and would seem to be present when one parent, usually the male, does not play a large part in rearing the young.

polygenic characters see POLYGENIC INHERITANCE.

polygenic inheritance or **quantitative inheritance** a genetic system in which three or more genes are involved in control of a character, the character being described as quantitative in that it shows a wide range of variability that can be measured (see HERITABILITY). Each polygene in the system has only a small effect on the character and cannot be detected individually. The expression of a polygenic character is strongly affected by the environment in which the individual exists. For example, human height is affected by diet, and human intelligence scores are affected by social background.

polygyny a system of POLYGAMY in which the male has several female mating partners at one time. Compare POLYANDRY.

polymer a compound of high molecular weight formed of long chains of repeating units (MONOMERS).

polymerase an enzyme that catalyzes the joining of DNA or RNA nucleotides.

polymorphism see GENETIC POLYMORPHISM.

polynomial nomenclature a system of nomenclature involving more than two names, such as *Parus major minor*, in which *minor* represents the subspecies.

polynucleotide chain a sequence of NUCLEOTIDES joined together to form a string. RNA consists of one polynucleotide chain, whereas DNA consists of two chains bonded between the bases in a system of complementary pairing: adenine with thymine, guanine with cytosine.

POLYP

The sequence of bases along the chain acts as a GENETIC CODE for the structure of PROTEINS. Polynucleotide chains show polarity based on the position of the bonds in relation to the sugar component. One end of the chain will end at the 3' position, the other at the 5' position. See Fig. 250. The two chains of DNA show opposite polarities. (See Fig. 130.)

Fig. 250. **Polynucleotide chain.** General structure. P = phosphate, S = ribose or deoxyribose sugar, B = one of four bases.

polyp the asexually reproducing, normally sedentary form of COELENTERATES such as the sea anemone (see MEDUSA). In the class Anthozoa, the polyp stage is the dominant part of the life history, but in the Scyphozoa (jellyfish) it is often absent.

polypeptide chain a sequence of AMINO ACIDS joined together by PEPTIDE BONDS, forming a PROTEIN, the sequence being determined by the order of bases along the POLYNUCLEOTIDE CHAINS of DNA in the form of a GENETIC CODE. See PROTEIN SYNTHESIS for details.

polypetalous see GAMOPETALOUS.

polyphenism the presence of several phenotypes in a population that are not the result of genetic differences.

polyphyletic (of a group of organisms) having been derived from more than one source, that is, not of a single line of evolution.

polyploid 1. (of cells or organisms) having three or more complete sets of chromosomes. 2. an individual or cell of this type. See TRIPLOID, TETRAPLOID.

Polypterus a primitive freshwater fish of Central Africa derived, with sturgeons, from Devonian paleoniscid stock. See PALAEONISCUS.

polyribosome or **polysome** two or more RIBOSOMES joined by a molecule of messenger RNA during PROTEIN SYNTHESIS. Such an arrangement ensures that the mRNA is read at maximum speed.

polysaccharide a large carbohydrate molecule with a chainlike or branched structure, made up of many MONOSACCHARIDE units joined together by CONDENSATION REACTIONS. Although most polysaccharides have a terminal monomer present as a REDUCING SUGAR, this forms only a small part of the molecule and thus most polysaccharides do not act as reducing sugars. Polysaccharides are insoluble and unsweet and are important as storage molecules (for example, STARCH, inulin, and GLY-

COGEN) and as reinforcing materials (for example, CELLULOSE of plant cell walls, CHITIN of crustacean and insect cuticles).

polysome see POLYRIBOSOME.

polytene chromosome see SALIVARY GLAND CHROMOSOME.

polythetic (of a taxon) where each member possesses a majority of a set of characters.

polytocous (of animals) producing many young at birth.

polytopic (of a subspecies) having geographically separate but phenotypically similar populations.

polytypic (of a taxon) containing two or more immediately subordinate taxa, for example, a species with several subspecies. A polytypic species is also called a *Rassenkreiss.*

polyuracil a synthetic polynucleotide chain formerly used as MESSENGER RNA for synthesis of phenylalanine. See GENETIC CODE.

polyzoan see BRYOZOAN.

pome a false fruit, such as an apple, in which the main part is developed from the RECEPTACLE and not the OVARY.

population 1. the total number of the individuals of a particular species, race, or form of animal or plant inhabiting a particular locality or region. 2. (in genetics) the total number of BREEDING INDIVIDUALS of a species in a particular location.

population control see CONTROL (2).

population dynamics the processes that contribute to the size and composition of a population.

population genetics the study of heredity at the population level, for example, gene frequencies, mating systems.

population growth an increase in the size of a population as a result of the birth rate exceeding the death rate.

pore any small opening in the skin or epidermis or any structure.

Porifera see SPONGE.

porphyrin an organic compound consisting of four pyrrole rings linked by CH bridges with a heavy metal in the center. Porphyrins form part of several important biological molecules. Examples include the heme group of HEMOGLOBIN and MYOGLOBIN (see Fig. 251), chlorophyll (with magnesium), and cytochromes (with iron).

porrect (of plant structures) extending outward and forward.

portal vein any vein that carries blood from one set of capillaries to another, such as renal-portal and hepatic-portal veins.

position effect an alteration in the expression of a gene due to a change in its location within the GENOME.

positive feedback see FEEDBACK MECHANISM.

Fig. 251. **Porphyrin.** Compound structure.

post- *prefix* denoting behind or later.

postsynaptic membrane the excitable membrane of the dendrite next to the axon at a synapse.

potential energy any stored energy that can be released to do work.

potometer an instrument designed to measure the rate of absorption of water by a cut shoot and hence, indirectly, the rate of TRANSPIRATION by the shoot in a particular set of conditions, which can be varied. See Fig. 252. At the start of the experiment, an air bubble is introduced into the tubing adjacent to the graduated scale. Reservoir A supplies water to replace the water lost by the shoot, the amount taken up being indicated by the movement of the air bubble along the scale. Opening the stopcock at the end of a time period causes water from reservoir B to force the air bubble along the tube, ready for a fresh start.

Fig. 252. **Potometer.**

PPP see PENTOSE PHOSPHATE PATHWAY.

preadaptation the possession by an organism of characteristics that permit a move into a new NICHE or habitat.

Precambrian era all geological time prior to the beginning of the CAMBRIAN PERIOD, 570 million years ago. Very few fossils are known from this time, and the fossil record effectively begins with the trilobites and brachiopods of the Cambrian. However, impressions of soft-bodied animals, such as medusae, sea pens, annelids, and some arthropods, have been found in Precambrian rocks dated between 640 and 570 million years old. Bacteria may have existed for up to 3800 million years and blue-green algae (Cyanophyta) for 3500 million years.

precipitin see ANTIBODY.

predation see PREDATOR.

predator any animal that lives by preying on other animals (usually) from a lower TROPHIC LEVEL.

predictive values the capacity to make predictions on new characters or newly created taxa within a classification.

preferred body temperature the CORE TEMPERATURE of behaviorally thermoregulating bradymetabolic (see BRADYMETABOLISM) animals in an artificial temperature gradient.

preformism the now discredited theory that an egg or sperm contains a preformed adult.

prehensile adapted for holding or grasping, as in the tails of many New World monkeys.

pre-Linnaean name any taxonomic name published prior to January 1, 1758.

premolars the cheek teeth in mammals that occur between the molars and the canines. They have a grinding function.

premorse (of plant structures) appearing as if bitten off at the end.

prepuce the foreskin or fold of glandular and vascular tissue surrounding the tip of the mammalian penis.

presbyopia a loss of ACCOMMODATION (focusing ability) in the eye that occurs frequently in older humans due to loss of elasticity in the lens. Affected individuals require two corrective lenses, one for close work, the other for viewing distant objects.

pressure potential or (formerly) **turgor pressure** a measure of the tendency of a cell to push water out of the cell, usually a positive value. Compare WALL PRESSURE.

presumptive area a part of a developing embryo formed of cells that will become a particular organ or structure, for example, presumptive mesoderm.

presynaptic membrane the excitable membrane of the axon terminal next to the dendrite at a synapse.

prey any animal species that is fed upon by another (the PREDATOR).

prickle a hard, pointed plant structure containing no VASCULAR BUNDLE structure.

Priestley, Joseph (1733—1804) English chemist who discovered oxygen, observed that carbon dioxide (fixed air) was produced in FERMENTATION, and oxygen is produced by green plants in sunlight.

primary consumer any organism that feeds directly on plant material, being the second tier of the PYRAMID OF NUMBERS (biomass). Primary consumers feed directly on primary producers (see PRIMARY PRODUCTION) and are fed upon themselves by SECONDARY CONSUMERS.

primary egg membrane see VITELLINE MEMBRANE.

primary feather the quill feathers on the hand of the bird's wing—the outermost flight feathers.

primary focus see FOCUS.

primary follicle an immature OVARIAN FOLLICLE.

primary growth growth from the seedling stage of an ANGIOSPERM to produce the herbaceous structure of stems and roots. Many DICOTYLEDONS and a few MONOCOTYLEDONS carry out SECONDARY GROWTH to produce woody structures.

primary homonym either of two specific names proposed in combination with the same generic name at the time of publication.

primary intergradation a region of intermediate characteristics between two distinct phenotypic populations that has arisen through SELECTION.

primary oocyte an early stage in OOGENESIS.

primary production the production by living organisms (AUTOTROPHS) of organic material from inorganic sources. *Gross primary production* is the total amount of organic material synthesized in a given time, whereas *net primary production* is the amount of organic material formed in excess of that used in respiration. Compare SECONDARY PRODUCTION.

primary spermatocyte an early stage in SPERMATOGENESIS.

primary structure the linear sequence of amino acids in a POLYPEPTIDE CHAIN.

primate any member of the mammalian order Primates, including lemurs, tarsiers, monkeys, apes, and humans. These mammals have a placenta, possess nails rather than claws, and usually have a thumb and big toe that are opposable to the other digits, allowing objects to be grasped. All possess a relatively large brain and have well developed eyesight, often with BINOCULAR VISION.

primed cell a cell stimulated by an ANTIGEN that can produce more cells that respond to the antigen, mediate reactions of cell-mediated immunity, or synthesize immunoglobulin.

primitive streak a line of cells in the center of the embryonic disk of reptiles, birds, and mammals that forms the future axis of the embryo.

priority the precedence of the earlier of two published taxonomic names.

prismatic layer the middle layer of the three layers forming the shell of MOLLUSKS.

probability the likelihood that a given event will occur. Probability is expressed either as values between 0 (complete certainty that an event will *not* occur) and 1.0 (complete certainty that an event will occur) or as percentage values between 0 and 100. Probability is used widely in SIGNIFICANCE tests.

proband an individual considered as the starting point for the study of a family for inheritance of a particular condition.

proboscis 1. the elongated snout of a tapir or elephant. 2. the elongated mouthparts of some insects.

procaryote see PROKARYOTE.

process any method of operation in manufacture of a substance or bacteria.

proctodeum the inpushing of ectoderm in the embryo where it meets the endoderm to form the anus or cloaca.

procumbent or **prostrate** lying along the ground.

producer any AUTOTROPH capable of synthesizing organic material, thus forming the basis of the food web (see FOOD CHAIN). ANGIOSPERMS are the main producers in the terrestrial ecosystem, and PHYTOPLANKTON in the aquatic environment. Compare CONSUMER.

productivity the amount of material in terms of BIOMASS or energy generated in a given time in an ECOSYSTEM over and above the STANDING CROP.

proflavin a MUTAGEN that can initiate FRAMESHIFTS in the TRANSLATION of an mRNA sequence.

progeny test a method by which the genetic capabilities of an organism can be established by examining the performance of its progeny. For example, the milk yield genes of a bull can be estimated by measuring the milk productivity of its daughters.

progesterone a female sex hormone produced by the CORPUS LUTEUM and the PLACENTA. It is concerned with preparing the uterus to receive the fertilized OVUM and with maintaining pregnancy. Progesterone is secreted on the stimulus of the corpus luteum by the pituitary hormones LH and LTH (LUTEOTROPIC HORMONE).

proglottid one of the divisions or apparent segments of a tapeworm, formed by transverse budding in the neck region, that remain connected as they move backward, increasing in size and maturing. Eventually, the proglottid is cut off and is shed from the gut of the host. Each proglottid contains male and female sex organs.

prognathous (of apes or humans) having a protruding face or jaws.

prokaryote or **procaryote** an organism that is either a bacterium or a blue-green alga, its main characteristic being *prokaryotic cells* lacking a membrane-bound nucleus and no MITOSIS or MEIOSIS. Compare EUKARYOTE and see Fig. 150.

prokaryotic cell see PROKARYOTE.

prolactin see LUTEOTROPIC HORMONE.

prolegs the false legs present on the anterior part of the abdomen of caterpillars in the form of stumpy, jointless appendages.

proline one of 20 AMINO ACIDS common in protein. It has a nonpolar R group structure and is relatively insoluble in water. See Fig. 253. The ISOELECTRIC POINT of proline is 6.3.

Fig. 253. **Proline.** Molecular structure.

prometamorphosis the first stage of METAMORPHOSIS in amphibians.

promoter see OPERON MODEL.

pronephros the first excretory organ in the vertebrate embryo. Its duct (MULLERIAN DUCT) gives rise to the OVIDUCT in the female and degenerates in the male.

pronotum the covering of the first thoracic segment in insects.

propagule 1. an infective stage of a plant PATHOGEN, such as a fungal spore, by which the organism gains entry into a plant host. 2. any part of an organism that is liberated from the adult form and can give rise to a new individual, such as a fertilized egg or spore.

prophage a BACTERIOPHAGE chromosome integrated into the DNA of a bacterium.

prophase the first stage of nuclear division (MITOSIS and MEIOSIS) in which the chromosomes coil and thicken and become visible with the optical microscope, condensing onto the inner wall of the NUCLEAR MEMBRANE. As the stage proceeds, the NUCLEOLUS disappears from view and the nuclear membrane disintegrates, leaving a clear area at the edge of the nucleus that contains the CENTROSOME.

Meiosis has a much more complicated prophase than mitosis and can be summarized thus:

(a) meiosis has two prophases, the first one complex (see below), the second rather similar to prophase in mitosis.

(b) prophase 1 of meiosis can be divided into five substages: LEPTOTENE, ZYGOTENE, PACHYTENE, DIPLOTENE, and DIAKINESIS. The essential processes occurring are (i) pairing of homologous chromosomes and (ii) pairing of nonsister CHROMATIDS forming chiasmata with eventual CROSSING OVER.

proprioceptor a receptor structure linked to the nervous system of animals that detects internal changes, particularly around joints, and in tendons and muscles.

prostaglandins a group of lipid substances that exert a wide range of stimulatory effects on the body, the most important of which is enhancement of the effects of CYCLIC AMP. Prostaglandins are derived from many tissues, including the prostate gland—it can also be made synthetically—and have been used in the induction of labor and abortion.

prostate or **prostate gland** 1. a gland of male animals that produces substances that are added to the semen. ANDROGENS affect the size and secretion of the prostate gland, whose exact function is unknown. 2. the gland associated with the male reproductive system in ANNELIDS and CEPHALOPODS.

prosthetic group a nonprotein group attached to a protein. Such prosthetic groups are usually vital for the functioning of the protein. For example, many enzymes contain metallic ions, as in carboxypeptidase, which contains zinc, and HEMOGLOBIN contains HEME with an iron atom at the center.

prostrate see PROCUMBENT.

protagonistic muscles muscles that work together to produce a movement.

protandrous 1. (of male gametes) ripening before the female gametes. Compare PROTOGYNOUS. 2. (of plant flowers) possessing ANTHERS that ripen before the stigma can receive the pollen, thereby preventing SELF-POLLINATION.

protease any enzyme that splits proteins, such as PEPSIN, TRYPSIN, EREPSIN, or RENNIN.

protective coloration any patterning or camouflage that helps an organism blend into its background and thus gives it protection from predators.

protein a large complex molecule, mol. wt. from 10,000 to more than 1 million, that is built up from AMINO ACIDS joined together by PEPTIDE BONDS. All proteins contain carbon, hydrogen, oxygen, and nitrogen, and most contain sulfur. Proteins are produced in the cytoplasm at the ribosomes (see PROTEIN SYNTHESIS) and begin as long, unbranched POLYPEPTIDE CHAINS, the *primary structure*.

All protein molecules undergo a physical rearrangement to give a *secondary structure*. The most common type of shape is *alpha-helix* (right-handed), in which the coils are held in place by hydrogen bonds. Some proteins, such as keratin, remain at this stage. An alternative secondary structure is *beta-pleating*, in which parallel polypeptide chains are cross-linked by hydrogen bonds to form an extremely tough structure, as in silk. Proteins with these relatively simple two-dimensional secondary structures are called *fibrous proteins*.

PROTEINASE

Some proteins undergo even more complex folding, in which the secondary structure is arranged into a three-dimensional *tertiary structure* forming globular proteins held together by forces between side groups. Such molecules are, for example, ENZYMES, ANTIBODIES, most blood proteins, and MYOGLOBIN. Finally, globular proteins can be composed of two or more polypeptide chains loosely bonded together, for example, HEMOGLOBIN giving a *quaternary structure*.

proteinase see ENDOPEPTIDASE.

protein synthesis a complex anabolic process occurring in all cells by which genes control the precise structure of proteins manufactured in the cell. The following summary of events refers to a EUKARYOTE cell:

(a) DNA molecules in the chromosomes of the nucleus carry specific messages about how proteins are to be constructed.

(b) The DNA of each gene carries instructions about one protein chain (see ONE GENE/ONE ENZYME HYPOTHESIS).

(c) The two polynucleotide chains of the DNA molecule separate, and messenger RNA nucleotides become attached in complementary pairing, the process being called TRANSCRIPTION.

(d) The mRNA molecule leaves the DNA, which reforms a double helix.

(e) The mRNA leaves the nucleus via pores in the NUCLEAR MEMBRANE and enters the cytoplasm, where it becomes attached to one or more RIBOSOMES (see also POLYRIBOSOMES) near the ENDOPLASMIC RETICULUM.

(f) With the aid of transfer RNA, TRANSLATION of the message in the mRNA takes place, with the formation of a POLYPEPTIDE CHAIN that later becomes coiled (see PROTEIN).

proteolysis the splitting of protein molecules by HYDROLYSIS of their PEPTIDE BONDS.

proteolytic enzyme any enzyme concerned with PROTEOLYSIS. See ENDOPEPTIDASE, EXOPEPTIDASE.

prothacic glands the glands activated by a hormone from the neurosecretory cells in the brain that secrete the MOLTING HORMONE ecdysone. The glands have a cyclic activity within each INSTAR and break down on METAMORPHOSIS. They induce molting, which in most insects occurs only in the juvenile stage, and in the absence of JUVENILE HORMONE the glands stimulate metamorphosis.

prothallus a small thalloid structure produced by germination of the spore in ferns and related plants. It bears the ARCHEGONIA and ANTHERIDIA and is the GAMETOPHYTE generation.

prothorax the first thoracic segment in insects.

prothrombin see BLOOD CLOTTING.

Protista the kingdom containing all unicellular organisms but now expanded to include many algae, bacteria, fungi, slime molds, and Protozoa.

Protochordata a division of the phylum Chordata, including the Hemichordata, Urochorda, and Cephalochorda. The group lacks a vertebral column, cranium, and organs associated with the region of the head in other chordates.

protogynous (of female gametes) ripening before the male gametes. Compare PROTANDROUS (1).

protonema a haploid, branched, filamentous structure produced by germination of a moss spore. The protonema produces new plants by budding.

protonephridium see FLAME CELL.

protophloem see METAPHLOEM.

protoplasm the living contents of a cell, that is, the cytoplasm and nucleus. The entire cell is called the *protoplast*.

protoplast see PROTOPLASM.

protopod larva a primitive insect larva lacking abdominal segmentation and possessing only rudimentary appendages. Such larvae are usually found as ENDOPARASITES.

prototherian any mammal of the subclass Prototheria, including the MONOTREMES.

prototroch see TROCHOPHORE.

prototroph a strain of an organism that does not possess growth requirements in excess of those of the wild type.

protoxylem the first XYLEM to differentiate from the primary MERISTEMS, with annular (ringlike) and spiral bands of thickening on the walls. Although dead, the cells are able to elongate as the adjacent cells grow in length. Protoxylem differentiates eventually into METAXYLEM.

protozoan any member of the phylum Protozoa, sometimes regarded as a subkingdom of the animal kingdom, including unicellular or acellular organisms. The members of the group feed as HOLOPHYTES, SAPROPHYTES, or in a HOLOZOIC manner. They move by means of FLAGELLA, CILIA, or PSEUDOPODIA and reproduce by FISSION or CONJUGATION.

proximal situated at a point nearest to the body in any structure or nearest to the center of the system concerned. For example, the wrist is the proximal part of the hand, being nearest to the body. Compare DISTAL.

proximal tubule the convoluted tube between the loop of Henle and Bowman's capsule in the vertebrate kidney.

pruinose (of plant structures) covered with a whitish bloom.

pseudo- or **pseud-** *combining form* denoting false, pretended, unreal.

pseudodominance the appearance of a recessive PHENOTYPE due to DELETION MUTATION of a dominant allele in a HETEROZYGOTE.

pseudogamy the parthenogenetic development (see PARTHENOGENE-SIS) of an egg after penetration of the egg membrane by a male gamete.

pseudoheart any of the 10 enlarged blood vessels (5 pairs) in the earthworm, which have valves and act as hearts, pumping blood from the dorsal to the ventral vessel.

pseudopodium (*pl.* pseudopodia) a protoplasmic projection (a false foot) from the main body of a protozoan—especially rhizopods such as *Amoeba*—and from white blood cells. The cell moves in the direction from which the pseudopodium is produced, and the pseudopodium is also used to engulf particles, both as food (in protozoans) and in PHAGO-CYTOSIS. See AMOEBOID MOVEMENT.

pseudopolyploidy a set of chromosome numbers in related species of organisms that erroneously suggests that the organisms are POLYPLOIDS (2).

pseudotrachea any of the food channels resembling tracheae that cover the oral lobes of dipterans and some other insects. After converging, they eventually lead to the mouth.

Psilopsida a TRACHEOPHYTE subdivision that includes many extinct forms. Related to the ferns, living forms are placed in the order *Psilotales* and are tropical or subtropical EPIPHYTES.

psittacosis a contagious disease of birds such as parrots that can be transmitted to humans, in whom it may cause bronchial pneumonia.

psoriasis a noncontagious disease of the skin marked by scaly red patches, due probably to a disorder of the immune system.

psychrophile an organism showing optimal growth at temperatures below 20°C and down to below 0°C, for example, many bacterial species, yeasts, and some algae.

pteridophyte any plant of the division Pteridophyta, including ferns, horsetails, and club mosses. The group is now not normally given taxonomic status and is included in the TRACHEOPHYTA.

ptero- or **pter-** *combining form* denoting wing or feather.

pteropod or **sea butterfly** a small gastropod mollusk found in the plankton, with the foot modified into winglike structures used for swimming. Pteropods are known as sea butterflies because of the appearance given them by these expansions of the foot. See Fig. 254.

Fig. 254. **Pteropod.** General morphology.

Pteropsida a subdivision of the TRACHEOPHYTA, including the ferns, conifers, and flowering plants.

Pterygota a subclass of the class Insecta into which are placed most insects, including all winged forms and insects that have secondarily lost the power of flight, such as lice or fleas. Compare AMETABOLA.

ptyalin see AMYLASE.

puberty the period at the beginning of human adolescence when sexual maturity is attained.

pubescent (of plant structures) covered with fine hairs.

pubis the bone forming the anterior part of the PELVIC GIRDLE situated ventrally and projecting forward in most TETRAPODS.

puffs see CHROMOSOME PUFFS.

pulmonary relating to the lungs.

pulp cavity the cavity within the tooth of vertebrates, containing nerves, blood vessels, connective tissue, and odontoblasts. The cavity opens into the tissues in which the tooth is embedded.

pulse the expansion of an artery as the left ventricle contracts (see BLOOD PRESSURE) and which can be detected where the artery is close to the body surface, for example, the radial artery at a person's wrist.

pulvillus a cushion or pad between the claws on an insect foot.

pulvinus a mass of thin-walled cells at the base of the leaf petiole in certain plants, forming a swollen area surrounding the vascular tissue. The pulvinus is subject to large changes in TURGOR. In the runner bean, for example, the pulvinus is turgid during the day and supports the petiole, so that the leaf is held outward. At night the pulvinal cells lose turgidity and the leaf droops. These diurnal leaf positions are sometimes called *sleep movements*. The sudden change in leaf posture observed in *Mimosa sensitiva* when touched is also controlled by pulvinal cells.

punctate (of plant structures) dotted or pitted.

punctiform (of plant structures) similar to a dot, small and round.

punctuated equilibrium the theory that evolutionary change has occurred during brief periods of rapid change punctuated by periods of stability. Such a process would be characterized by absence of an infinite range of intermediate forms, and supporters of the theory point to the vertebrate fossil record as evidence.

pungent (of a plant structure) stiffly pointed to the extent that it will prick.

Punnett square a table devised by the British geneticist R. Punnett, in which all possible combinations of gametes and progeny are displayed in a grid structure. For example, in the cross:

$$♀ \text{ Aa, Bb} \times \text{aa, Bb } ♂$$

the Punnett square would be as in Fig. 255.

♀ gametes

		AB	Ab	aB	ab
♂ gametes	aB	AaBB	AaBb	aaBB	aaBb
	ab	AaBb	Aabb	aaBb	aabb

Fig. 255. **Punnett square.**

pupa a stage found in ENDOPTERYGOTES that occurs as an apparently inactive phase between the larva and adult insect. While locomotion and feeding are absent, extensive developments take place in the formation of adult structures within the pupa, which in LEPIDOPTERANS is also referred to as a CHRYSALIS.

pupil the central opening in the iris of the vertebrate eye through which light passes to the lens and retina. It changes in size as a result of muscle contraction and expansion that move the iris.

pure breeding see HOMOZYGOTE.

pure breeding line or **true breeding line** a strain of individuals that are all homozygous for the genes being considered, so that their progeny show no variation in those genes. See BREEDING TRUE.

purine one of two types of bases found in NUCLEIC ACIDS, having a double ring structure. (See ADENINE and GUANINE.) Purines always pair with PYRIMIDINES in the two strands of DNA, ensuring a parallel-sided molecule.

purinergic (of nerve endings) releasing PURINES as TRANSMITTER SUBSTANCES.

Purkinje cell a specialized NEURON of the CEREBELLUM, consisting of an axon, a large cell body, and a single, much branched dendrite, resembling a tree.

Purkinje tissue see HEART.

pus a yellowish fluid consisting of serum, white blood cells, bacteria, and tissue debris formed during liquefaction of inflamed tissue (*suppuration*).

pustule a blisterlike area on a plant structure from which emerges a fungal fruiting body.

putrefaction the decomposition of proteins, which gives rise to foul-smelling products.

pycno- *combining form* denoting thick or dense.

pycnosis the process of shrinking and becoming more dense in a cell nucleus, which results in its becoming strongly staining, usually as it dies.

pyloric of or relating to the end of the vertebrate stomach that opens into the intestine. The other end is called the *cardiac* area of the stomach.

pyloric sphincter a ring of smooth muscle surrounding the opening of the PYLORIC end of the stomach into the intestine. The sphincter prevents premature escape of food from the stomach into the intestine before the food is properly digested. Constriction of the sphincter (*pyloric stenosis*) is well known in young children, a condition recognized by explosive vomiting. Compare CARDIAC SPHINCTER.

pyogenic pus-producing.

pyramid, biomass see PYRAMID OF NUMBERS.

pyramid, ecological see PYRAMID OF NUMBERS.

pyramid, energy see PYRAMID OF NUMBERS.

pyramid of numbers a means of depicting TROPHIC LEVELS to illustrate the numbers of organisms at any one level. The broad base indicates the large numbers of PRODUCERS, the next (narrower) stage indicates the number of PRIMARY CONSUMERS, and a third stage (narrower still) the number of SECONDARY CONSUMERS, and at the apex the top PREDATORS. It is better expressed in terms of biomass or energy (see ECOLOGICAL PYRAMID), as in some cases—for example, parasites higher in the trophic levels than the host—greater numbers occur higher and do not produce a pyramid when numbers only are considered. See Fig. 256 and FOODCHAIN.

Fig. 256. **Pyramid of numbers.**

pyranose ring a monosaccharide with a six-membered ring structure.

pyrenoid a region of starch formation found in the CHLOROPLASTS of various algae, for example, *Spirogyra* and *Chlamydomonas*.

pyrethroid an artificially produced biocide, for example, permethrin, similar in structure and action to the natural insecticides, PYRETHRUMS.

pyrethrum an INSECTICIDE prepared from the dried flowers of the chrysanthemum plant, the active ingredient being called *pyrethrin*.

pyridoxine (B$_6$) a water-soluble vitamin of the B-COMPLEX found in fresh meat, eggs, liver, fresh vegetables, and whole grains. The vitamin acts as a coenzyme in AMINO ACID metabolism from carbohydrates, a deficiency of which causes dermatitis and, sometimes, motor impairment.

pyrimidine one of three types of bases found in NUCLEIC ACIDS, with a single ring structure. DNA contains CYTOSINE and THYMINE, and RNA contains cytosine and URACIL. Pyrimidines always pair with PURINES in DNA.

pyrogallol or **trihydroxybenzene** a soluble phenol $(C_6H_4(OH)_3)$ that in alkaline solution will absorb oxygen. It is used to estimate the volume of oxygen in a gaseous sample.

pyrogen any substance that alters the body thermostat of HOMOIOTHERMS to a higher setting, giving rise to fever.

pyrrole a porphyrin building block that has a five-membered heterocyclic structure and contains nitrogen.

Pyrrophyta the fire algae, of which the *Dinophycae*, or dinoflagellates, form the most important members of the PHYTOPLANKTON. They have a photosynthetic pigment that is yellow to golden brown in color, hence the name 'fire algae.' Most forms have two dissimilar FLAGELLA, but others lack them entirely.

pyruvic acid an important 3-carbon molecule formed from GLUCOSE and GLYCEROL in glycolysis (see Fig. 257). See also ACETYLCOENZYME A. Pyruvic acid is broken down further, the precise reactions depending on whether oxygen is present or not. See AEROBIC RESPIRATION, ANAEROBIC RESPIRATION.

Fig. 257. **Pyruvic acid.** Molecular structure.

Q

Q_{10} or **temperature coefficient** a measure of the rate of increase in METABOLIC RATE over a 10° range in temperature. Thus, if an organism has a metabolic rate at 10°C of T units, a rate of twice T units at 20°C, the $Q_{10} = 2$. A Q_{10} of 2 is the typical exponential increase in rate exhibited by enzymes up to a certain maximum rate, after which DENATURATION occurs faster than increase, causing overall reduction of the rate.

Qo_2 the oxygen uptake in microliters (μl) per milligram dry weight per hour.

Q technique a method of analysis used in taxonomic work in which there is an association of pairs of taxa in a data matrix.

quadrat an area of ground surface, often 1 m^2, used as a sampling unit in population studies.

quadrate a cartilage bone at the back end of the upper jaw in the majority of vertebrates. In mammals it becomes the INCUS of the ear, but in most other vertebrates it forms the articulation of the lower jaw.

quadrat sampling (in statistics) a method of examining the distribution of organisms by taking samples within squares of known size, normally 1 m^2. Such squares are selected at random and marked usually with wire outlines. A series of quadrats is usually sampled so that comparisons are possible between, say, the distribution of a given plant in two different areas. The mean number in each series of quadrats can be compared with other means. See SIGNIFICANCE.

qualitative inheritance a genetic system in which a usually small number of genes are involved in control of a particular CHARACTER. Qualitative characters show discrete forms rather than continuously varying forms (see POLYGENIC INHERITANCE) and are not normally affected by the environment to any large extent. The major genes in the system can often be detected individually and appear to obey the laws of MENDELIAN GENETICS. The proportions of the various forms of character observed in offspring can be compared with the expected proportions, using a CHI-SQUARE TEST.

quantasomes see CHLOROPLAST.

quantitative inheritance see POLYGENIC INHERITANCE.

Quaternary period the last 2 million years of the Cenozoic Era, from 2 million years BP—the end of the Tertiary—to the present time. During this period, the increase in the human population has had significant effects on the populations of other animals and the populations of plants.

quaternary structure of protein see PROTEIN.

queen substance see ROYAL JELLY.

quill 1. the hollow stalk of the feather of birds. **2.** a whole wing or tail feather. **3.** the spine of a porcupine.

quinone any of the various compounds derived from benzene.

R

---

r the theoretical intrinsic rate of natural increase of a population.

rabies an ACUTE viral disease of the nervous system in many mammals, particularly humans, dogs, cattle, and foxes, resulting in degeneration of the spinal cord and brain and leading to death. Entry of the virus usually is through a wound or skin abrasion caused by a rabid animal. The incubation period is usually 3—8 weeks, the first signs being increased muscle tone and extreme difficulty in swallowing. The spasmodic contractions of the throat muscles that cause swallowing may become extremely painful, and contraction may even be triggered by the sight of water. For this reason, infected individuals are described as *hydrophobic*. Despite recent advances, patients must be vaccinated in the first few days after infection for effective treatment.

race a population that can be distinguished from other populations of the same species by several genetic characteristics, such as frequency of genes or chromosomal arrangements. For example, in humans, different races have been found to have quite different frequencies of alleles for the ABO BLOOD GROUP locus. See FOUNDER EFFECT.

raceme an inflorescence in which the main stalk bears the flowers on stalks (pedicels), producing a conical form. For example, in the foxglove there is usually no terminal flower.

racemose being or resembling a RACEME.

race-specific resistance or **vertical resistance** a situation in which a small number of major genes in the host confer high levels of RESISTANCE to a specific attacking organism. Such a system is likely to be ineffective, however, if the attacking organism undergoes genetic change. Compare NONRACE-SPECIFIC RESISTANCE.

rachis or **rhachis** (*pl.* rachises or rachides, rhachises or rhachides) any central axis, particularly that of a feather.

radial symmetry an animal body structure in which any section through the mouth and down the body length divides the body into identical halves. Coelenterates, ctenophores (sea gooseberries), and echinoderms are all radially symmetrical. Compare BILATERAL SYMMETRY.

radiant energy see ENERGY.

radiation the electromagnetic energy that travels through empty space with the speed of light (2×10^8 ms^{-1}). All objects emit radiation, at room temperature mostly in the infrared range, whereas at high tem-

peratures visible radiation is produced. See ELECTROMAGNETIC SPEC-
TRUM, ULTRAVIOLET LIGHT, X-RAY.

radical (of plants) arising from the root or crown.

radicle the basal part of the embryo in a seed, developing into the
primary root of the seedling.

radioactive isotope see ISOTOPE.

radioactive label any substance emitting an ionizing radiation that is
detectable and can be used to locate it.

radioisotope see ISOTOPE.

Radiolaria a group of marine, planktonic protozoans, possessing siliceous
skeletons and forming benthic oozes (see BENTHOS).

radius the anterior bone in the lower part of the forelimb of vertebrates.
See PENTADACTYL LIMB.

radula a rasping organ of mollusks situated in a sac on the underside of
the BUCCAL cavity. It is used for tearing plant material by rubbing it
against the hardened surface of the mouth.

ragworm the common name of errant POLYCHAETE worms such as the
nereids.

rainfall the precipitation of fresh water from the atmosphere, through its
variability producing different vegetation in different regions.

Ramapithecus a genus of hominids present in Africa, Europe, and Asia
between 14 million and 8 million years ago. They largely replaced
DRYOPITHECINES in open country.

ramenta (*sing.* ramentum) the brown, flaky epidermis of ferns covering
young leaves and stems.

ramet a single individual from a CLONE.

ramus a branch.

ramus communicans the slender trunk carrying nerves from the ventral root of the spinal nerve to a ganglion of the sympathetic nervous
system (see AUTONOMIC NERVOUS SYSTEM). See REFLEX ARC.

random fixation the accidental loss of one allele resulting in the fixation
of another in a population.

random genetic drift (RGD) or **Sewall Wright effect** changes in
ALLELE frequency in a population from one generation to another due
to chance fluctuations. RGD is important in small populations, which are
subject to sampling error and in which an allele can be lost (0% frequency) or fixed (100%). See Fig. 258.

The phenomenon was first described by the American geneticist
Sewall Wright.

random mating or **panmixis** the selection of mates by chance so that
the choice of a partner is not influenced by the genotypes under study.
For example, it is normal for human beings to display random mating

Fig. 258. **Random genetic drift.** The frequency of one allele of a gene over many generations. The continuous line represents population A, the broken line population B.

with respect to the ABO BLOOD GROUP, but ASSORTATIVE MATING with respect to other genetically controlled characteristics, such as body shape.

range 1. (of a species) the extent of its distribution. 2. (in behavior) the area within which an individual normally lives.

ranking the arranging of a taxon in the appropriate position in the taxonomic hierarchy, for example, selecting the category as an order, rather than a class or family.

raphe a longitudinal slit or ridge as found in diatoms, or in some seeds where it marks the position of the FUNICLE (1).

raphide a calcium oxalate crystal present in bundles in some plant cells.

raptor any bird of prey. The term usually denotes a diurnal bird of prey, such as an eagle, hawk, or falcon, but it can also denote an owl.

Rassenkreiss see POLYTYPIC.

ratite any flightless bird that lacks a keel on the sternum, such as an ostrich, rhea, or emu.

Raunkiaer's life forms a system of classification of plant forms based on the positioning of perennating buds (see PERENNATION) relative to ground level. See PHANEROPHYTE, CHAMAEPHYTE, HELOPHYTE.

ray a band of PARENCHYMA cells in plant roots and stems leading out from the center along a radius and separating the vascular tissues, forming xylem rays and phloem rays in primary and secondary growth. Rays enable the transport of water and other materials across the stem or root. See SECONDARY THICKENING.

ray floret any of the small flowers radiating from an inflorescence.

Ray, John (1627—1705) English naturalist, regarded as the founder of British natural history, who originated natural botanical classification and the division of flowering plants into monocotyledons and dicotyledons. The Ray Society is named for him.

reactant one of the groups of molecules participating in a reaction, which act upon others to produce new molecules.

reaction a chemical process during which one substance is changed to another.

reaction chain a chemical or atomic process, such as combustion or atomic fission, in which the products of the reaction promote the reaction itself.

reaction time see LATENT PERIOD.

recapitulation the apparent repetition in the embryological development of an organism of stages similar to those of the ancestral adult forms that, in terms of evolution, preceded it. The concept is expressed as: *ontogeny recapitulates phylogeny*. For example, gill slits appear in the development of the embryo of a human.

receiving waters water bodies into which waste is emptied from treatment plants.

Recent epoch see HOLOCENE EPOCH.

receptacle 1. also called *torus* in flowering plants, the end of the stalk becoming the flower parts. 2. in ferns, the mass of tissue that becomes the SPORANGIUM. 3. in liverworts, the cup containing a GEMMA. 4. in algae, the swollen tip of a branch carrying the reproductive organs.

receptaculum seminis a sac-like structure present in some female or hermaphrodite invertebrate animals in which are stored sperm previously transferred from a male.

receptor any cell or organ of an animal capable of detecting a change in the external or internal environment, and which subsequently brings about a response in the behavior of the animal. The eye is an example of a receptor, receiving and transforming stimuli into sensory nerve impulses. See also CHEMORECEPTOR, REFLEX ARC.

receptor site a point or structure in a cell at which combination with a drug or other agent results in a specific change in cell function.

recessive allele or **recessive gene** an ALLELE that only shows its effect in the PHENOTYPE when present in a HOMOZYGOTE. When a recessive allele is paired with a dominant allele, the effect of the recessive is hidden. See RECESSIVE CHARACTER.

recessive character a character controlled by a particular allele of a gene and only displayed when the individual is homozygous for this allele. See DOMINANCE (1).

recessive epistasis a form of EPISTASIS in which a pair of recessive alleles of one gene can cause a masking effect on the expression of alleles at another locus. Such an interaction would produce a DIHYBRID (1) ratio of 9:3:4 instead of the more normal 9:3:3:1. Compare DOMINANT EPISTASIS.

reciprocal cross a pair of crosses in which the PHENOTYPES of the partners are reversed. Thus, in humans the following are reciprocal crosses:

$$\text{♀ colorblind} \times \frac{\text{normal}}{\text{vision}} \text{♂} \quad \Big| \quad \text{♀} \frac{\text{normal}}{\text{vision}} \times \text{colorblind ♂}$$

Different results from the two crosses indicate SEX LINKAGE of the gene controlling the character.

recombinant DNA DNA from PLASMIDS that can be treated to pick up foreign DNA—for example, from a EUKARYOTE—and carry it into a bacterial cell. Here the new DNA may express, coding for foreign proteins. Recombinant DNA has been widely used in GENETIC ENGINEERING.

recombinant gamete a GAMETE containing a new combination of alleles as compared with those found on the HOMOLOGOUS CHROMOSOMES of the parent, the alteration being produced by RECOMBINATION.

recombination a rearrangement of genes during MEIOSIS so that a GAMETE contains a haploid GENOTYPE with a new gene combination. Recombination can occur by INDEPENDENT ASSORTMENT of genes on different chromosomes, but the term is used normally to refer to genes linked on the same chromosome where recombination is achieved by CROSSING OVER. See Fig. 259.

Fig. 259. **Recombination.** The rearrangement of genes during meiosis.

recon the smallest genetic unit between two of which RECOMBINATION can take place—effectively a DNA base.

rectal gland a gland that opens into the rectum in many vertebrate animals and may produce PHEROMONES.

rectrix see FEATHER.

rectum the terminal part of the intestine of an animal, opening into the ANUS or CLOACA.

rectus a straight muscle, such as either of the two muscles that, together with the more anterior pair of oblique muscles, serve to move the eyeball. They are situated behind the eyeball in a posterior position.

recurrent laryngeal nerve a branch of the vagus nerve in mammals that loops around the DUCTUS ARTERIOSUS and then goes forward along the trachea. Its route results from evolutionary lengthening of the neck.

recurved (of plant structures) bent backward.

red blood cell see ERYTHROCYTE.

redia a larval stage of liver fluke that develops from the sporocyst larva. It has a mouth, suctional pharynx, and simple gut and gives rise to secondary rediae or to carcaria larvae.

red nucleus a ganglionic center in the midbrain of mammals that, if destroyed, results in decerebrate rigidity. It therefore plays an important part in controlling movement and posture.

redox potential a quantitative measurement of the willingness of an electron carrier to act as a *red*ucing or *ox*idizing agent. Redox potential is measured in volts. The more negative the value, the better the carrier will act as a reducing agent. Thus, in an ELECTRON TRANSPORT SYSTEM, the carriers are arranged in order of increasing redox potentials, negative to positive. For example, in Fig. 205, ferredoxin has a lower, that is, more negative, redox potential than plastoquinone, which has a higher value—less negative.

redox reaction a reaction in which *red*uction and *ox*idation occur.

red tide sea water discolored by a bloom of red dinoflagellates in such numbers as to kill other sea creatures, particularly fish, by the production of toxins.

reducing agent any substance capable of removing oxygen from a molecule or of adding hydrogen, that is, it is capable of contributing electrons to a process.

reducing sugar a sugar containing free aldehyde ($H - C = O$) or ketone ($C = O$) groups capable of reducing metal ions such as Cu^+ and Ag^+. Reducing sugars such as glucose and fructose will reduce solutions in BENEDICT'S TEST and FEHLING'S TEST.

reduction a change in an atom or molecule through losing oxygen, adding hydrogen, or gaining electrons.

reduction division nuclear division in which the daughter cells have half the genetic material of the parent cell. See MEIOSIS.

reductionism an erroneous belief that complex situations can be explained by reducing them to their component parts and explaining these.

redundant characters taxonomic characters so closely associated with other already used characters, for example, in a key, that they are of no use in subsequent analysis.

redwood see SEQUOIA.

reflex action see REFLEX ARC.

reflex arc the nervous connections between RECEPTOR and EFFECTOR that result in a simple response being elicited by a specific stimulus (a *reflex action*), such as a knee jerk, without involvement of the brain. The receptor is excited by a stimulus that induces a nerve impulse in the DENDRITE of a sensory (*afferent*) NEURON. This passes through the cell body in the dorsal root ganglion and on along with a sensory AXON to the SPINAL CORD. There it crosses a SYNAPSE, usually to an intermediate neuron that synapses with the efferent neuron and passes out of the spinal cord via the ventral root along the axon of the motor (*efferent*) neuron to the effector that produces the stereotyped response. Most reflexes involve more than one synapse; that is, they are *polysynaptic*. See Fig. 260. See RAMUS COMMUNICANS.

Fig. 260. **Reflex arc.** The arrows indicate the direction of impulse from receptor to effector.

refractory period the period of inexcitability, normally lasting about 3 ms, during which the AXON recovers after it has transmitted an impulse. During the refractory period, it is impossible for the axon to transmit another impulse, because the membrane is being repolarized by ionic movements. During the *absolute* refractory period, no NERVE IMPULSE can be transmitted; however, during the *relative* refractory period, an impulse can be transmitted provided that the stimulus is strong.

refugium an area that has escaped alteration during glaciation, for example, a *nunatak*—an area of isolated land such as a mountain peak—and in which relic communities may exist.

regeneration the replacement or repair of tissues or organs lost through damage. In animals, the degree of regeneration varies from group to group but is generally more extensive in the lower phyla. In plants, regeneration is common and is used extensively in VEGETATIVE PROPAGATION.

regression analysis (in statistics) a test in which the size of one variable (the dependent variable) is dependent on another (the independent variable). Often the relationship is a linear one, enabling a line of best fit to be drawn on a SCATTER DIAGRAM.

regressive character any character that is reduced during evolutionary change.

regular (of plant structures) exhibiting RADIAL SYMMETRY.

regulating factor a chemical secretion of the HYPOTHALAMUS associated with blood sugar levels that controls secretion of hormones. Secretion and inhibition of hormones involve negative feedback systems (see FEEDBACK MECHANISM).

regulation 1. (in embryology) the process of determining normal development, even in cases of damage, where a properly formed embryo may result even after loss of a large part. In many animals regulation after damage is possible only before fertilization, but in others it may take place in later development. **2.** the limitation of a population over a period of time by natural factors, such as DENSITY DEPENDENT FACTORS.

regulator gene see OPERON MODE.

regulatory heat production the component of STANDARD METABOLIC RATE additional to BASAL METABOLIC RATE produced by an animal exhibiting TACHYMETABOLISM at environmental temperatures below those of thermoneutrality (units $cm^3 O_2 g^{-1}$, $cm^3 O_2 g^{-1} h^{-1}$).

Reissner's membrane a membrane in the cochlea of the inner ear that separates the middle canal from the vestibular canal. Named for the German physiologist E. Reissner.

relationship the evolutionary connection between organisms in terms of distance from a common ancestor.

relative growth the growth of a structure in relation to the growth of another structure. For example, skull size in developing humans has a smaller relative growth than long bones.

releaser any stimulus that gives rise to an instinctive act. For example, the red breast of a male robin causes another male to attack it.

releasing factor a special form of REGULATING FACTOR that stimulates release of hormones into the blood. *Inhibiting factors* prevent release of hormones.

relic or **relict** any organism, community, or population surviving from an earlier age.

relic distribution or **relict distribution** the much-reduced distribution of organisms resulting from an overall environmental change, such as glaciation.

relict see RELIC.

remige see FEATHER.

renal pertaining to the kidney.

renal portal system the system of veins in fish and amphibians taking blood from the region of the tail or hind limbs directly to the kidneys. See Fig. 261.

Fig. 261. **Renal portal system.** The venous blood supply to the kidneys in (a) fish (renal portal system present), (b) mammals (renal portal system absent).

rendzina or **humus-carbonate soil** or **A-C soil** a shallow soil formed over limestone that usually shows a dark-colored organic horizon (A) resting directly on weathering limestone (C).

reniform kidney-shaped.

renin a protein-splitting enzyme, sometimes called a hormone, that is secreted into the blood by cells lining the efferent glomerular vessels of the kidney. Renin combines with a protein from the liver to form ANGIOTENSIN, which in turn stimulates the cortex of the ADRENAL GLAND to release ALDOSTERONE.

rennin or **chymase** an enzyme present in gastric juice secreted by the gastric glands of the stomach wall that coagulates caseinogen in milk to form casein, which forms an insoluble curd (a calcium-casein compound) that in turn is attacked by pepsin. It is important particularly in young mammals, because it increases retention time in the stomach and enables more efficient digestion of the primary food source.

replacement name a substitute name proposed in taxonomic work to replace a name given incorrectly. It takes on the original TYPE and TYPE LOCALITY.

replacing bone see CARTILAGE BONE.

replica plating a technique used in the indirect selection of bacterial mutants that involves the transfer of an organism, usually a bacterium or fungus, from one culture to numerous plates using a velvet pile or needles.

replication the production of exact copies of complex molecules during the growth of living organisms. See DNA, BASE PAIRING.

replum the central part that remains after the valves of a dehiscent fruit have been shed. See VALVE (4) and PLACENTA (2).

repression the state in which a gene is prevented from being transcribed, so no protein is produced. See OPERON MODEL.

repressor a substance, often proteinaceous, that prevents the function of a gene. See OPERON MODEL.

reproduction 1. the production of young. 2. the mechanisms by which organisms give rise to others of the same kind.

reproductive isolation the condition of a separated population in which gene flow between the population and other similar populations is either impossible or reduced to a minimum. This can be brought about by several factors, which may be geographical, ecological, seasonal, physiological, or behavioral.

reproductive phase the part of the life cycle during which reproduction takes place.

reproductive potential the population size reached as a result of the maximum possible growth rate under ideal environmental conditions and in the absence of predators and competition for food and space. Under these circumstances, there is no environmental resistance. See FECUNDITY.

reptile any member of the vertebrate class Reptilia, including turtles and tortoises (Chelonia), lizards and snakes (Squamata), crocodiles (Crocodilia), the extinct dinosaurs (Ornithischia, Saurischia), pterodactyls (Pterosauria), plesiosaurs (Plesiosauria), and the ancestors of mammals, the Therapsida. All reptiles are egg-laying, and present-day forms are POIKILOTHERMS although some dinosaurs may have been HOMOIO-THERMS.

repulsion an arrangement in a double heterozygote in which a WILD TYPE allele of one gene is adjacent to a mutant allele of another gene on the same HOMOLOGOUS CHROMOSOME. Such an arrangement of linked genes usually is referred to as *in repulsion*. Compare COUPLING.

reserpine an alkaloid extracted from a species of *Rauwolfia* that is used as a sedative and as an antihypersensitive agent to reduce hypertension.

reserves any stored food supplies that can be drawn on in times of food shortage.

residual volume the air remaining in the lungs after respiration, c 1200ml.

resilient (of plant structures) springing back into position after being bent.

resistance any inherited characteristic of an organism that lessens the effect of an adverse environmental factor, such as a pathogen or parasite, a biocide (for example, a herbicide, insecticide, or antibiotic), or a natural climatic extreme, such as drought or high salinity.

resistance factor see R FACTOR.

resistance transfer factor (RTF) a gene set that carries genetic information for the transfer of R FACTORS.

resolution the minimum distance between two points at which they can be seen as such rather than as a single point. With the light microscope, this is approximately half the wavelength of light used in illumination. Only with a shorter wavelength can greater resolution be achieved, as with the ELECTRON MICROSCOPE.

resolving power the distance apart of two objects at which they can be distinguished as two separate objects by the microscope.

resorption the taking back into an organism of any structure or secretion produced.

resource 1. any potential product of an area. 2. a food supply.

respiration 1. a process by which gaseous exchange—oxygen and carbon dioxide—takes place between an organism and the surrounding medium. See AERIAL RESPIRATION, AQUATIC RESPIRATION, BREATHING. 2. a form of CATABOLISM that takes place in all living cells. See ANAEROBIC RESPIRATION, AEROBIC RESPIRATION.

respiratory center see BREATHING.

respiratory cycle the sequence of events during which an animal inhales and exhales a given volume of air through the respiratory system. In humans some 500 cm^3 of air is taken in and expelled during the cycle, which lasts about 5 seconds. See BREATHING, VITAL CAPACITY.

respiratory enzyme any enzyme that catalyzes oxidation reduction reactions.

respiratory gas any gas that takes part in the respiratory process. The term usually denotes oxygen and carbon dioxide. See RESPIRATION.

respiratory movement any movement by an organism that aids RESPIRATION, such as the movement of air or water through lungs or gills.

respiratory organ any organ across the surface of which gases pass to and from the body fluids to the exterior, such as gills or lungs.

respiratory pigment a substance present in blood, usually in the corpuscles or plasma, that combines reversibly with oxygen and acts as a store for it. Oxygen is taken up in a respiratory organ such as the lung, and blood gives up oxygen where it comes into contact with tissues deficient in oxygen. Examples of such pigments include HEMOGLOBIN, HEMOCYANIN, CHLOROCRUORIN, HEMERYTHRIN. See also OXYGEN DISSOCIATION CURVE.

respiratory quotient (RQ) the ratio of volume of CO_2 produced to the volume of O_2 taken up in a given period of time. From RQ estimates, it is possible to deduce the type of food being oxidized. Carbohydrates have an RQ of 1.0, fats of 0.7, and proteins of 0.9. An RQ lower than 0.7 indicates that organic acids, such as malic acid, are being oxidized (see CRASSULACEAN ACID METABOLISM). An RQ greater than 1.0 indicates that ANAEROBIC RESPIRATION is occurring.

respiratory surface a special area developed in order to satisfy requirements for gaseous exchange in larger organisms. Examples include external gills, internal gills, lungs, and insect tracheae. The surfaces are thin and moist, with a differential gradient maintained between the air/water and the internal tissues.

respirometer any apparatus used to measure uptake of oxygen by organisms during AEROBIC RESPIRATION. Examples include the Warburg apparatus, Cartesian Diver apparatus, and Philippson electrolytic respirometer.

response see STIMULUS.

resting cell any cell not undergoing active division (mitosis).

resting egg any invertebrate egg that undergoes a period of dormancy, during which it is resistant to adverse conditions.

resting potential the electrical potential present between the inside and outside of a nerve or muscle fiber when in a resting state. The inside is negatively charged (-60 millivolts) and the outside positively charged. The membrane is polarized and the axon has a resting potential. Compare ACTION POTENTIAL.

restriction analysis a genetic technique for fine mapping of a gene using RESTRICTION ENZYMES.

restriction enzyme an endonuclease that recognizes specific DNA base sequences and cleaves both strands of DNA at the same time.

resynthesis the production of a substance that has previously been broken down.

rete or **rete mirabile** a system of arterial and venous capillaries in which COUNTERCURRENT EXCHANGE can occur. Such a network occurs, for example, in the wall of the swim bladder, enabling the wall to be supplied with blood without large loss of oxygen from the bladder into the blood.

reticular formation the part of the CNS that consists of small islands of gray matter separated by fine bundles of nerve fibers running in all directions.

reticulate evolution evolution dependent on repeated intercrossing between a number of breeding lines. The evolutionary process is thus both convergent and divergent at the same time.

reticulate thickening the strengthening of a XYLEM vessel or TRACHEID in the form of a network of lignin deposition.

reticulin fibers fibers found intercellularly in many vertebrate tissues, which they bind together. They consist largely of COLLAGEN.

reticuloendothelial system see MONONUCLEAR PHAGOCYTE SYSTEM.

reticulum 1. the second compartment of the ruminant stomach. 2. a network, particularly of PROTOPLASM.

retina the lining of the interior of the vertebrate eye, containing a concentration of photoreceptor cells known as rods and cones that are connected to the optic nerve via BIPOLAR CELLS. The retina lies immediately below the vascular choroid layer, which nourishes it.

retinaculum 1. a hooklike structure on the forewings of moths that contacts the bristlelike *frenulum* on the hindwing, thus linking the two. 2. the hooklike structure that retains the springing organ (*furcula*) in Collembola.

retinal convergence the sharing of a single nerve fiber by several rods in the retina of the vertebrate EYE. The rods share or converge into one nerve fiber. Rods are used particularly in low illumination, when the stimulus of light on a single rod may be insufficient to generate an ACTION POTENTIAL in the NEURON. However, the stimulus of several rods on one neuron will excite it more easily, and six rods stimulated together will fire a neuron. This is an example of SUMMATION. Cones show little or no retinal convergence.

retinene the main carotenoid pigment found in the retina of the eye. It turns yellow in light.

retinol see VITAMIN A.

retuse (of plant parts) blunt or truncate and slightly indented.

reverse mutation a genetic change occurring in a MUTANT (2) individual that restores the WILD TYPE phenotype. Such events are far less common than FORWARD MUTATIONS.

reverse transcriptase an RNA-dependent DNA polymerase that catalyzes synthesis of DNA from deoxyribonucleoside-5'-triphosphate, using RNA as a template.

revision (in taxonomy) the summary and reevaluation of previous knowledge, including new material and new interpretation if present.

revolute (of parts) rolled down.

R factor or **resistance factor** or **R plasmid** a transferable PLASMID of many enteric bacteria that carries genes for resistance to antibiotics. It is often associated with a transfer factor, which after conjugation results in transfer of the R factor to another bacterium.

RGD see RANDOM GENETIC DRIFT.

R genes the genes present on the R FACTOR that are concerned with resistance to antibiotics.

rhachis see RACHIS.

RHA see RHESUS HEMOLYTIC ANEMIA.

rhabdom or **rhabdome** a transparent rod that passes down the center of an insect or crustacean ommatidium. See EYE, COMPOUND.

Rhesus blood group a form of human blood variation in which about 85% of the US population possesses an *Rh factor* (D-ANTIGEN) on the surface of red blood cells. Such people are described as being *Rh-positive;* those without the factor are *Rh-negative.* Unlike the ABO BLOOD GROUP, there is normally no Rhesus ANTIBODY, unless an Rh-negative person is sensitized by a Rhesus antigen, for example, in a blood transfusion or when an Rh-negative mother receives blood cells from an Rh-positive fetus (see RHESUS HEMOLYTIC ANEMIA). The blood group factor is controlled by a single autosomal gene on chromosome 1, with two principal alleles. The allele for the Rh-factor is dominant.

Rhesus hemolytic anemia (RHA) a serious blood abnormality in newborn children in which LYSIS of red blood cells causes anemia. The condition arises from a reaction between Rhesus antigens and antibodies (see RHESUS BLOOD GROUP). RHA occurs when a second (and subsequent) Rh-positive child is born to an Rh-negative mother. The mother is sensitized to the Rhesus factor on fetal blood cells transferred from the first baby at PARTURITION and produces Rhesus antibodies in response. When she is pregnant again, her Rhesus antibodies pass to the fetus, resulting in RHA when the child is born. The condition can be prevented by giving the mother a large dose of Rhesus antibodies immediately after birth of her first child. These antibodies will destroy the fetal cells in her blood before she has time to become sensitized to them.

RH factor see RHESUS BLOOD GROUP.

rhizo- *combining form* denoting root.

rhizoid a hairlike structure that functions as a root in lower organisms, such as certain fungi and mosses. Rhizoids are important in penetrating a substance, giving anchorage and absorbing nutrients.

rhizome a horizontal underground stem, with leaves and buds, that serves as a storage organ and a means of VEGETATIVE PROPAGATION. Rhizomes are found in such flowering plants as *Iris.*

rhizomorph a densely packed strand of fungal tissue with the appearance of a root that is produced by some higher fungi such as *Armillaria*. In some cases HYPHAE can be distinguished in the tissue. Rhizomorphs enable fungi to spread.

rhizoplane the part of the RHIZOSPHERE made up of the root surfaces.

rhizopod any protozoan of the subclass Rhizopoda or *Sarcodina* including the ameboid protozoans that feed by means of pseudopodia and lack cilia or flagella.

rhizosphere the area immediately surrounding the roots of plants in which their exudations affect the surrounding microbial flora. Many exudations are nutrients that the microorganisms utilize and include carbohydrates, vitamins, and amino acids. Conversely, the plant roots may take up minerals released by the microorganisms. Bacteria may be present in the rhizosphere in numbers 50 times greater than in surrounding soil. Gram-negative rods predominate, whereas gram-positive forms are less common than in the surrounding soil. Fungi are usually present in the rhizosphere in similar quantities to those in the surrounding soil, although some plants encourage particular forms.

Rhodophyta members of the Thallophyta division Rhodophyta, in which the chlorophyll is masked by PHYCOERYTHRIN. Rhodophytes vary from filamentous forms to those with an extensive thallus and have nonmotile gametes.

rhodopsin or **scotopsin** or **visual purple** a purple pigment found in the rods of the retina of the vertebrate eye. Lack of rhodopsin causes night blindness. When bleached by light, rhodopsin liberates a protein called OPSIN and a yellow pigment called RETINENE. As a result of this reaction, energy is released that triggers an ACTION POTENTIAL. See also IODOPSIN, METARHODOPSIN.

rhomboid (of plant parts) diamond-shaped.

Rhynchocephalia a primitive group of DIAPSID reptiles that includes *Sphenodon*, a genus having a pineal eye in the roof of the skull.

Rhynchota see HEMIPTERAN.

rhythm the regular occurrence of strong and weak impulses of a particular phenomenon.

rhytidome bark consisting of alternating layers of cork and dead CORTEX or PHLOEM.

rib any of the long, curved bones forming the wall of the THORAX in vertebrates, attached dorsally to the VERTEBRAL COLUMN. The anterior ribs are connected ventrally to the STERNUM in higher vertebrates and form a protective rib cage around the contents of the thorax. Ribs are connected by intercostal muscles, which cause movement during breathing in terrestrial vertebrates.

riboflavin or **vitamin B$_2$** a member of the B-COMPLEX of water-soluble vitamins. Found in a wide variety of foods, riboflavin is required in the metabolism of all animals (acting as a carrier in the ELECTRON TRANSPORT SYSTEM) and is part of several plant pigments.

ribonuclease an enzyme that catalyzes the depolymerization of RNA.

ribonucleic acid see RNA.

ribose pentose sugar. See Fig. 262.

Fig. 262. **Ribose.** Molecular structure.

ribosomal RNA (rRNA) a form of RNA transcribed from DNA in the NUCLEOLI of EUKARYOTE cells or clustered ribosomal genes in PROKARYOTES, whose function is to join with various proteins to form the RIBOSOME. rRNA is produced in only a few forms of varying length, some of which have been completely analyzed, base by base.

ribosome a small particle (not an ORGANELLE) found in the cytoplasm of all cells, composed of protein and RIBOSOMAL RNA. Each ribosome is composed of two subunits of different sizes that sediment at different rates during centrifugation (see ULTRACENTRIFUGE). PROKARYOTES have ribosomes with 70 S size and mass; EUKARYOTES have ribosomes with 80 S size and mass. Ribosomes bind to the 5' end of MESSENGER RNA (see POLYNUCLEOTIDE CHAIN) and travel toward the 3' end, with TRANSLATION and POLYPEPTIDE synthesis occurring as they go along. Frequently, several ribosomes are attached to one piece of mRNA, forming a POLYRIBOSOME.

ribulose a pentose sugar found in syrup that is important in carbohydrate metabolism. Formula: $C_5H_{10}O_5$.

ribulose biphosphate (RuBP) or **ribulose diphosphate** a 5-carbon ketose that acts as a receptor of CO_2 in the Calvin cycle.

rickets a disease of young children and other mammals in which faulty calcification of bones produces bowed limbs. Rickets is due to a diet deficient in VITAMIN D and low in calcium and phosphorus. The condition is now rare in the US, although it is common in poor countries.

Ringer's fluids saline solutions made up of ions similar to and ISOTONIC with the tissue fluids of the organs to be studied, and in which physiological preparations can be kept alive in vitro. Named for the English physiologist Sidney Ringer (1835—1910).

ringing experiment a procedure in which the outer tissues of a stem are removed, leaving intact only the xylem and pith. Water transport up the stem is unimpeded by such a process, whereas food transport down from the leaves stops at the ring, thus demonstrating the respective roles of XYLEM and PHLOEM.

RNA (ribonucleic acid) a NUCLEIC ACID composed of a single POLYNUCLEOTIDE CHAIN of NUCLEOTIDES. RNA, a vital component of PROTEIN SYNTHESIS, occurs in three forms: (a) MESSENGER RNA, involved in TRANSCRIPTION and transport of a coded signal from DNA to RIBOSOMES; (b) RIBOSOMAL RNA, forming the site of polypeptide synthesis; and (c) TRANSFER RNA, carrying amino acids to the ribosomes to be inserted in the correct sequence during translation.

RNA polymerase one of several enzymes that catalyze the formation of RNA molecules from DNA templates during TRANSCRIPTION. See OPERON MODEL.

Robertsonian chromosome a chromosome produced as a result of fusion of two separate chromosomes.

rocky shore the coastline, usually marine, where outcropping rock at the surface forms at least part of the substrate.

rod or **rod cell** a rod-shaped, light-sensitive cell lying in the more peripheral parts of the retina in the vertebrate eye. Rods are associated particularly with vision under conditions of low illumination, and they occur in large numbers in nocturnal animals. They are not capable of color discrimination and their visual acuity is poor (compare CONE CELL). RHODOPSIN (visual purple) is found in rods. There are some 240 million rods in the retinas of a primate.

rodent any member of the mammalian order Rodentia, including gnawing mammals, which have chisel-like incisors and lack canines. Examples include rats, mice, and squirrels.

rogue 1. an unwanted individual in a crop, particularly plants, which usually is removed during a breeding program. **2.** an animal, particularly one of vicious character, that has separated from the main group and leads a solitary life.

Roentgen or **Röntgen, Wilhelm Konrad** (1845—1923) German physicist who discovered X-RAYS. A *roentgen* or *röntgen* is the quantity of X-rays or gamma radiation used as a unit of radioactivity. Abbreviation: R or r.

röntgen see ROENTGEN.

root the part of a plant that usually grows below ground. The root provides anchorage for aerial parts, absorbs water and mineral salts from the soil, conducts water and nutrients to other parts of the plant, and often stores food materials over winter. Root structure is variable among higher plants, but generally there is (unlike the young STEM) a central core of conducting tissue (the STELE), which also serves as a strong structural element, assisting the root as it pushes downward and resisting upward pressure from the aerial parts.

Roots can be classified into three main types: primary, secondary (see LATERAL ROOT), and ADVENTITIOUS (1). The primary root of ANGIOSPERMS develops from the radicle of the seedling. Later, secondary roots emerge from the top of the primary root and then farther down. At the apex of the root is a protective ROOT CAP. The typical root structure of a DICOTYLEDON is shown in Fig. 263.

primary xylem with narrow vessels
metaxylem with large vessels
pericycle
epidermis with root hairs (not shown)
parenchyma ⎱
endodermis ⎰ cortex
primary phloem

Fig. 263. **Root.** Cross section of a typical dicotyledon (buttercup) root.

In MONOCOTYLEDONS the number of xylem arms is usually much greater than in DICOTYLEDONS, 12 to 20 in monocotyledons, 2 to 5 in dicotyledons. Roots frequently undergo SECONDARY THICKENING in dicotyledons, but not in monocotyledons.

root cap a structure found at the apex of ROOTS, except those of many water plants, produced by the APICAL MERISTEM. The cap consists of a thimble-shaped collection of PARENCHYMA cells, which have a protective function. As the root pushes its way through the soil, the outer (older) cells of the root cap are sloughed off and replaced by new cells from the MERISTEM.

root crop any roots used for human or animal food. They usually are from plants that use their roots as storage organs, and with few exceptions they have tap roots, for example, carrots and parsnips.

root effect or **root shift** a change in blood oxygen capacity resulting from a change in pH.

root hair a hairlike outgrowth from the epidermis of roots. Root hairs occur in large numbers in a zone behind the growing tip. They are short-lived and greatly increase the absorbing area of the root.

root nodules see NITROGEN FIXATION.

root pressure a force exerted within a plant root that pushes water up toward the stem. The phenomenon is produced by the root cells having a solute concentration gradient that increases from outside the root toward the center of the root. Thus, by OSMOSIS, water passes from the soil, across the root, and into the xylem as a result of salt excretion by the ENDODERMIS into the xylem, creating pressure that can be observed in a plant with the aerial parts removed. See Fig. 264.

closed manometer

rubber sleeve with airtight seals

mercury

stump of healthy plant (e.g. *Pelargonium*)

Fig. 264. **Root pressure.** The mercury enables root pressure to be measured.

root shift see ROOT EFFECT.

root system the total below-ground vegetative system of vascular plants. See ROOT.

rotate (of a corolla of a flower) having petals at right angles to the axis and forming a wheel shape.

rotifer any minute aquatic multicellular invertebrate of the phylum Rotifera, containing the *wheel animalcules,* the smallest METAZOANS. They move and feed by means of an anterior ring of cilia.

roughage 1. the less useful part or refuse of a crop. **2.** any indigestible material eaten in food to stimulate the actions of the intestines.

rough endoplasmic reticulum see ENDOPLASMIC RETICULUM.

round window see FENESTRA OVALIS AND ROTUNDA.

roundworms see NEMATODE.

royal jelly or **queen substance** a substance produced by the pharyngeal glands in the early adult life of the worker bee that is used for feeding the young brood for up to four days and the larvae of queen bees for longer periods to ensure their development into queens. It contains 40% dry matter in the form of lipoproteins, neutral glycerides, free-fatty acids, sugar, amino acids, and all the B vitamins. It also has a high content of ACETYLCHOLINE.

RQ see RESPIRATORY QUOTIENT.

rRNA see RIBOSOMAL RNA.

r selection SELECTION for an opportunist strategy in which traits leading to a high rate of natural increase are selected for.

rubella see GERMAN MEASLES.

ruderal a plant living on wasteland in built-up areas.

rugose (of plant parts) wrinkled.

rumen a branch of the esophagus of ruminants in which unchewed food is stored temporarily and from which it is regurgitated to the mouth for chewing (see RUMINANT STOMACH). Some cellulose is digested and absorbed in the rumen, where bacterial action results in the synthesis of B vitamins. Cellulase is produced by bacteria, which may number 1 billion per cm^3 in the rumen.

ruminant any mammal of the suborder Pecora (deer, giraffes, antelopes, sheep, goats, cows) of the order Artiodactyla. They usually possess horns in the males, lack incisors in the upper jaw, and have a four-compartmented stomach that includes the RUMEN.

ruminant stomach a digastric stomach with four chambers of two divisions. The first division is composed of the RUMEN and reticulum, acting as a fermentation vat for unchewed vegetation. The second division is composed of the OMASUM and ABOMASUM, the latter being a true stomach, secreting digestive enzymes.

ruminate (of plant parts) appearing chewed.

rumination the chewing of partially digested food, retrieved from the RUMEN by reverse PERISTALSIS.

runcinate (of plant parts, leaves) having pinnate lobes pointing backward to the leaf base.

runner or **stolon** a long, slender stem running along the surface of the ground, arising from the axil of a leaf, whose function is to enable rapid VEGETATIVE PROPAGATION in an area. Along the runner are small scale leaves with buds from which roots emerge and enter the soil. The runner eventually withers, leaving many new daughter plants (a CLONE). Runners are found, for example, in strawberries and creeping buttercup.

rust fungal diseases of plant stems and leaves caused by members of the order Uredinales. Rusts are OBLIGATE parasites, their host plants often being cereals. For example, the fungus *Puccinia graminis tritici* causes black stem rust of wheat.

rut the period of maximum testicular activity in male mammals (compare ESTRUS CYCLE), particularly applied to the period of sexual activity in deer.

S

sac a baglike or pouched structure.

saccate baglike, pouched.

Saccharomyces a genus of unicellular fungi that is included in the order Endomycetales (class Hemascomycetes), most species of which ferment a wide range of sugars. Some forms are used in the manufacture of bread and as brewer's yeast in beer making. They may occur in the form of simple, budding cells or as a pseudomycelium (chain of cells). Each ASCUS contains one to four rounded or ovate SPORES.

saccule 1. any small sac. **2.** a membranous labyrinth joined to the UTRICLE and forming part of the vestibular apparatus in the inner ear.

sacral vertebrae the thick strong vertebrae of the lower backbone, some of which are fused together and attached to the PELVIC GIRDLE to form the SACRUM giving great strength to the hip region.

sacrum the collection of fused sacral vertebrae attached to the PELVIC GIRDLE.

sagittal (of a section through an organism) being dorsoventral and longitudinal in the midline, so producing mirror-image halves along the length.

sagittate (of plant structures) shaped like an arrowhead, with two backward-pointing barbs.

salinity the degree of saltiness that occurs, for example, in enclosed seas where salinity is great, or in estuaries where the normal salinity of the sea may be diluted by fresh river water. It is defined as the total amount of dissolved solids in water in parts per thousand by weight and in sea water is approximately 35%.

saliva a viscous, transparent liquid containing water, salts, MUCIN, and sometimes salivary amylase (see PTYALIN). Saliva is secreted by cells of the salivary glands, which occur in humans in three pairs, one in the cheek and two between the bones of the lower jaw. The amount of saliva produced depends on the type of food being consumed. Dry foods and acidic foods stimulate a copious volume of nonviscous saliva, while liquids, such as milk, stimulate small quantities of thick saliva. The amount of amylase can also vary, being high when meat is eaten.

salivary amylase see AMYLASE.

salivary gland any gland that secretes SALIVA.

salivary gland chromosome or **polytene chromosome** a giant chromosome present in the salivary glands of certain DIPTERANS, such as midges or fruit flies. The interesting feature of such structures is that, when suitably stained, their CHROMOMERES are readily visible, making it possible to map the physical presence of genes. Studies have shown clear correlation between the order of genes mapped by genetic RECOMBINATION and visible structures on the polytene chromosomes. At certain times it is possible to see CHROMOSOME PUFFS, which are thought to represent areas of gene action.

Salmonella a genus of bacteria containing a wide range of species that are pathogenic for man and other animals. Examples include *S. typhi*, which causes typhoid fever, and *S. typhimurium*, which causes severe gastroenteritis, or food poisoning.

salp a free-living planktonic TUNICATE with no larval stage. The nervous system is degenerate, and the gill clefts lack longitudinal bars.

saltation 1. any changes of an abrupt nature that occur in the thalli of fungi either through mutation or the occurrence of segregation of parts of the thallus with different genetic makeup (HETEROKARYONS and HOMOKARYONS). **2.** the movement of soil particles by wind.

salt gland a leaf hydathode (see GUTTATION) that secretes a saline solution.

salt marsh a community of salt-tolerant plants growing on intertidal mud in brackish conditions in sheltered estuaries and bays.

samara a one-seeded indehiscent fruit with a wall flattened into a membrane wing. It is found, for example, in ash and elm trees.

sample any portion of a whole, such as a small part of a population collected for examination.

sampling 1. the act of taking a fraction of substance to be tested or analyzed. **2.** the selection of some parts from a larger whole as in statistical sampling.

sampling error (in statistics) a statistical phenomenon in which the variation within a sample is inversely related to the size of the sample. In other words, the smaller the sample, the larger the sample error. Thus, if 100 people toss 10 coins each, the variation within each sample will be quite high, from perhaps 2 heads: 8 tails, to 8 heads: 2 tails. However, if the same 100 people toss 1000 coins each, the variation will be expected to be *proportionately* less, from perhaps 350 heads: 650 tails to 650 heads: 350 tails. The variation in a sample can be expressed, for example, as mean $\pm$ standard error.

Sanger, Frederick (1918—) English biochemist who carried out extensive research into protein structure and who determined the amino acid sequence of insulin.

sap a watery liquid found within the vacuole of a plant cell (cell sap) and within conducting tissues of the VASCULAR BUNDLES.

saprobiont any organism that feeds on dead or dying animals or plants. See also SCAVENGER.

saprophyte or **saprotroph** or **necrotroph** any plant or microorganism that obtains its nutrition from dead or decaying organic materials in the form of organic substances in solution. Such organisms are of great importance in breaking down dead organic material. See NITROGEN CYCLE.

saprophytic see NECROTROPHIC.

saprotroph see SAPROPHYTE.

sapwood the ring of living XYLEM tissue in a stem or root that has undergone SECONDARY THICKENING and is composed of VESSELS and PARENCHYMA cells. Sapwood lies outside the HEARTWOOD but inside the ring of PHLOEM.

sarco- *combining form* denoting flesh.

Sarcodina see RHIZOPOD.

sarcolemma the thin connective tissue sheath that occurs around a muscle fiber and extends and contracts with the contractile material enclosed.

sarcoma a cancerous growth derived from muscle, bone, cartilage, or connective tissue.

sarcomere the part of the muscle fiber that is contained between two Z-MEMBRANES and is the contractile element of the fiber. See Fig. 265. See MUSCLE, I-BAND.

Fig. 265. **Sarcomere.** Muscle fibrils consist of alternating groups of thick and thin filaments (dark and light bands), the distance between two Z-membranes being termed a sarcomere.

sarcoplasm the cytoplasm of a muscle cell.

sarcoplasmic reticulum the cysternae of a single muscle fiber.

saturated fats see FATTY ACID.

saturated vapor pressure the pressure exerted by a vapor when it is completely saturated and in equilibrium with its liquid form. For example, the evaporating surface of a MESOPHYLL cell is saturated with water and has a vapor pressure strongly affected by the ambient temperature. See Fig. 266.

Temperature °C	Water V.P. (saturated) millibar kPa
10	1.2
15	1.6
20	2.5
25	3.2

Fig. 266. **Saturated vapor pressure.** The effect of ambient temperature on the vapor pressure at the surface of a mesophyll.

-saur *combining form* from the Greek word for lizard, used in the names of extinct reptiles.

Saurischia an order of dinosaurs lacking a post-pelvic bone and having a normal PELVIC GIRDLE, unlike *Ornithischia*. The group includes the large four-footed dinosaurs, such as *Diplodocus*.

Sauropsida a nontaxonomic group including all reptiles and birds with the exception of mammal-like reptiles (*Therapsida*).

scab a symptom of various plant diseases in which there are local areas of surface roughening, for example, apple scab caused by the fungus *Venturia inaequalis,* a HEMIBIOTROPH.

scabrous having a rough surface.

scalariform ladderlike.

scalariform thickening the internal thickening of XYLEM VESSELS or tracheids in which lignin bands are deposited in a SCALARIFORM pattern.

scala tympani the lower chamber of the cochlea in mammals, filled with perilymph and ending in the fenestra rotunda. It connects with the scala vestibuli via the helicotrema.

scala vestibuli the upper chamber of the cochlea in mammals, filled with perilymph. It lies between REISSNER'S MEMBRANE and the wall of the bony canal and connects with the SCALA TYMPANI via the helicotrema.

scale any platelike outgrowth of the integument of an organism, each in the form of a flat calcified or horny structure on the surface of the skin. Scales are found in fish and in reptiles, such as snakes, where they are derived from both the epidermis and the dermis, and in insects (for example, *Lepidoptera*), where they are derived from hairs. See PLACOID, COSMOID, GANOID.

scape a flower stalk bearing no leaves and arising from a rosette of leaves.

Scaphopoda a class of primitive mollusks, possessing a tubelike shell open at both ends.

scapula the shoulder blade. See PECTORAL GIRDLE.

scarious (of plant structures) thin, with a dried-up appearance, especially at the edges and tips.

scarlet fever an ACUTE, contagious disease in humans, particularly of young children, caused by the bacterium *Streptococcus pyogenes* and characterized by inflammation of the pharynx, nose, and mouth and a red skin rash.

scatter diagram a graphic figure in which two axes are plotted at right angles to each other, the independent variable on the x (horizontal) axis and the dependent variable on the y (vertical) axis. Each individual or object is then measured for these two variables, for example, age (x) and weight (y), and the position is marked on the correct coordinates of the diagram, producing a series of scattered points. These may be given a line of best fit by REGRESSION ANALYSIS.

scavenger any organism that feeds on carrion, refuse, or material left unconsumed by other organisms. See also SAPROBIONT.

schistosomiasis see BILHARZIA.

schizocarp a dry fruit developing from a SYNCARPOUS ovary that splits into one-seeded portions as, for example, the fruit of fennel.

schizogenous (of secretory organs in plants) derived by spaces being created by separation of cells.

Schwann cell a type of cell occurring in the region of the nerve fibers of the peripheral nervous system of vertebrates. It produces the neurilemma, which encloses the MYELIN SHEATH (see Fig. 220), and is found in close contact with the nerve axons between each node of Ranvier. See SCHWANN, THEODOR.

Schwann, Theodor (1810—1882) German anatomist who first recognized the egg as a cell in 1838. He showed that all living organisms are composed of cells and that fermentation is brought about by living organisms. He discovered PEPSIN in gastric juice, and the SCHWANN CELL is named for him.

scientific method the way of approaching a problem by means of drawing up a hypothesis based on a series of observations, and then testing the hypothesis by means of experiments designed in such a way as to support or invalidate the hypothesis. On the basis of the experimental evidence, a theory is proposed to account for the initial observations. If the theory is found subsequently to be wanting in some respect, new hypotheses are sought and tested experimentally, so the process is a successive refinement, or iterative process, that in science never leads to absolute truth, but to more reliable knowledge.

scientific name the binomial or trinomial designation of an organism in the form of latinized (or Latin or Greek) words.

scion the part of a plant, usually a piece of young stem, that is inserted into a rooted STOCK (1) to produce a GRAFT.

sclera or **sclerotic** the outer coat of the vertebrate eye to which are attached extrinsic muscles for moving the eyeball. The sclera is lined with a vascular layer, the CHOROID, except for the forward-facing part, which is called the CORNEA and is transparent, having no underlying choroid.

sclereid a type of SCLERENCHYMA cell of higher plants, which is roughly spherical in shape with a thick wall that can be smooth or spiky and is always heavily impregnated with LIGNIN. Sclereids occur in the flesh of succulent fruits, such as pears, and are common in the shells of nuts.

sclerenchyma a plant tissue in which the cells have greatly thickened walls impregnated with LIGNIN and no cell contents. The tissue has a mechanical function of supporting the plant and consists of two types of cells: fibers and SCLEREIDS. Fibers are long cells with tapered ends, which are often grouped into bundles.

sclerite chitinous plates separated by thinner membranes in the exoskeleton of arthropods.

sclero- *combining form* denoting hard.

sclerosis 1. (in animals) a hardening of tissue due to excess growth of fibrous tissue or deposition of fatty plaques or degeneration of the myelin sheath of nerve fibers, as in sclerosis of the liver in humans, which can be lethal. 2. (in plants), a hardening of the cell wall or tissue, often due to the deposition of LIGNIN.

sclerotic see SCLERA.

sclerotium 1. a resting stage in many fungi. It takes the form of a ball of HYPHAE varying in size from a pinhead to a soccer ball, and usually has a hard, dark-colored exterior coating. Fruiting bodies may be formed eventually from the sclerotium (either sexual or asexual), or a MYCELIUM may form. Normally the sclerotium does not contain spores. 2. the firm resting condition of a MYXOMYCETE.

scolex the head of a tapeworm, being the part at the anterior end that bears hooks and suckers and is used for attachment to the gut wall of the host. See Fig. 267.

scotophase the dark phase of a dark/light cycle. Compare PHOTO-PHASE.

scotopsin see RHODOPSIN.

scrapie a disease of sheep with no certain cause, in which the animal develops intense itching and increasing weakness and eventually dies.

scrotum or **scrotal sac** a sac containing the TESTES of male mammals

Fig. 267. **Scolex.** The scolex of *Taenia solium*.

that is situated outside the posteriorly ventral part of the abdomen. The external location ensures that the testes are cooled to below body temperature, since heat can adversely affect development of sperm. In some organisms, such as bats, testes may lie protected inside the abdomen for much of the year, descending into the scrotum only during the breeding season.

scrub a habitat in which shrubs predominate.

scurvy a condition in which the blood capillary walls become fragile, leading to excessive bleeding and anemia, spongy gums with tooth loss, impaired wound healing, and eventually to death. Scurvy is due to a lack of ASCORBIC ACID in the diet, normal health being restored by administration of fresh fruits, particularly citrus fruits. (English sailors aboard ocean-going ships of the 18th and 19th centuries were supplied with citrus fruits to prevent scurvy, this habit giving them the nickname limeys.)

scutellum a platelike projection from the back of a dorsal plate of the thorax in insects.

scutum 1. the middle of the three dorsal thoracic SCLERITES of an insect. 2. one of the two lateral plates forming part of the carapace of a barnacle.

scyphistoma a larval form of COELENTERATE, arising from a planula larva. It may bud but in autumn and winter produces EPHYRA larvae by STROBILATION. See SCYPHOZOAN.

scyphozoan any marine medusoid COELENTERATE of the class Scyphozoa, containing the jellyfish. The medusa is the dominant and sometimes sole phase of the life history, the polyp being small (a SCYPHISTOMA) or absent.

sea butterfly see PTEROPOD.

sea mat see BRYOZOAN.

seasonal isolation any variation in breeding seasons that effectively keeps two populations of organisms from interbreeding.

sea zonation the divisions of the sea and sea floor for purposes of reference to specific areas as shown in Fig. 268.

Fig. 268. **Sea zonation.** The zones of the open sea and sea floor.

sebaceous gland one of many glands occurring in the skin and secreting oil, or sebum, into the hair follicles in mammals. This maintains an
oily coating of the hair and contributes to its waterproofing. Secretions
from sebaceous glands are the result of cell destruction.

secondary carnivore a carnivore that feeds on other carnivores.

secondary consumer a carnivore that feeds on the herbivores (PRI-
MARY CONSUMERS), which are sustained in turn by PRIMARY PRODUC-
TION, that is, by PHOTOSYNTHESIS.

secondary growth see SECONDARY THICKENING.

secondary homonym one of the two identical SPECIFIC NAMES that
were originally proposed for different genera but, as a result of revision,
have come to be included in the same genus.

secondary intergradation a zone of hybridization in which two previously separated populations have come together and interbred.

secondary meristem an area of cambial cells between xylem and
phloem of roots and stems in DICOTYLEDONS. The MERISTEMS give rise
to tissues causing lateral expansion or SECONDARY THICKENING.

secondary metabolite a product of microbial cells in culture when
growth is slowing down. While having no obvious role in the cellular
physiology of the producer, secondary metabolites are sometimes most
useful to humans, for example, as antibiotics.

secondary production any production (see PRODUCER, PRODUCTIV-
ITY) by organisms that consume organic material themselves. Secondary
production results entirely from resynthesis of organic matter, as distinct from its synthesis from inorganic materials as in PRIMARY PRODUC-
TION.

secondary root see LATERAL ROOT.

secondary sexual character any of the various features of a male or female animal produced when sexual maturity occurs. In humans, the female secondary sexual characters are induced by ESTROGEN at puberty and include mature genitalia, breasts, body hair, and feminine body shape, particularly broadening of the pelvis and fat deposition around the hips. The male human secondary sexual characters are induced by TESTOSTERONE at puberty and include mature genitalia, body and facial hair, muscular development, deep voice, and narrow pelvis. These characters are all excellent examples of SEX LIMITATION.

secondary structure of protein see PROTEIN.

secondary succession any SUCCESSION of plants arising after the clearing of the original vegetation, for example, after burning.

secondary thickening or **secondary growth** the growth in the girth of stems and roots in DICOTYLEDONS produced by division of the secondary MERISTEM, resulting in woody tissues. The growth begins with formation of a continuous cambial ring. In stems there is already a fascicular cambium between the xylem and phloem of the vascular bundles, which becomes joined by interfascicular cambium. The xylem tissues become divided into an inner heartwood (dead) and an outer SAPWOOD.

Secondary thickening can sometimes occur in herbaceous ANGIOSPERMS but is usually associated with woody types producing, for example, a stem that tapers upward. MONOCOTYLEDONS do not carry out secondary thickening. See Fig. 269.

Fig. 269. **Secondary thickening.** Secondary thickening in a typical dicotyledon.

In roots, a cambial ring is produced from parenchymatous cells between the XYLEM and PHLOEM.

second-division segregation the separation of chromatids carrying different gene ALLELES in the second cycle of MEIOSIS. Such an event can be detected by TETRAD ANALYSIS.

second law of thermodynamics see THERMODYNAMICS.

secretin a hormone responsible for secretion of bile from the liver.

secretion 1. the process by which a useful substance produced in a cell is passed through the plasma membrane to the outside. **2.** the substance itself. Secretions are usually produced by gland cells, but may be the results of cell destruction as in SEBACEOUS GLANDS. Glands of internal secretion (ENDOCRINES) pass their secretions directly into the bloodstream, whereas glands of external secretion (EXOCRINES) pass their secretions into special ducts.

secretor status an individual producing ABO BLOOD GROUP type antigen, including H-SUBSTANCE, in saliva, semen, and other body secretions, due to the presence of at least one dominant allele of an autosomal gene. Such fluids can thus be typed, a useful fact in forensic examination.

secund (of plant structures) all turned to one side.

seed the structure formed in the fertilized ovule of an ANGIOSPERM, consisting of an embryo surrounded by a food store for nourishment during germination, with an outer hard seed coat, the TESTA. The food store can be located either in a special area called the ENDOSPERM with an outer ALEURONE layer, or within the cotyledons—the number of which determines whether a plant is a MONOCOTYLEDON or a DICOTYLEDON. In some plants the so-called seed is really a fruit in which the PERICARP is fused with the testa. See Fig. 270 (b).

Fig. 270. **Seed.** Longitudinal sections of (a) broad bean seed and (b) a corn fruit seed.

seed dormancy see GERMINATION.

seed germination see GERMINATION.

seedling see GERMINATION and Fig. 166.

segmentation 1. the process of cutting off one part of an organism from another, as in CLEAVAGE of an OVUM. **2.** the production of metameres in METAMERIC SEGMENTATION. **3.** the cutting off by a cross wall of a multinucleate portion of a filament or HYPHA.

segregation the separation of HOMOLOGOUS CHROMOSOMES during anaphase I of MEIOSIS, producing gametes containing only one allele of each gene. Such an occurrence is the physical mechanism underlying the first law of MENDELIAN GENETICS and is particularly important when the two separated alleles are different.

selection the differential rate of reproduction of one phenotype in a population as compared with other phenotypes. Hence, an organism is at a selective advantage if it produces more offspring that survive to reproduce than are produced by another type. The environmental pressures causing selection can be either natural, for example, competition for food, or man-made (for example, insecticides). See DDT, DIRECTIONAL SELECTION, NATURAL SELECTION, STABILIZING SELECTION.

selection coefficient see SELECTION PRESSURE.

selection pressure a measure of the amount of relative reproductive disadvantage of one phenotype over another of the same species living together in the same area. Such pressure is usually represented by the *selection coefficients*, which can have a value from zero (no selective disadvantage, maximum FITNESS) to 1.0 (complete selective disadvantage leading to actual death or GENETIC DEATH, minimum fitness).

selective breeding the breeding of animals and plants to embrace desirable characters.

selective enrichment any technique that encourages growth of a particular species or group of microorganisms.

selective fishing any process by which individuals of a particular size of fish are caught, for example, with nets of large mesh to permit small fish to escape.

selective medium any medium that restricts growth of certain microorganisms but not others.

selective permeability or **differential permeability** the capacity of a membrane to allow some particles to pass through but not others. Such differentially permeable membranes (for example, CELL MEMBRANE, cellular organelle membrane, TONOPLAST) allow water molecules to pass readily through them, whereas solutes dissolved in water can pass less rapidly or not at all. The ability of molecules to travel across the membrane and the velocity with which they do so depend on the fat solubility, size, and charge of the molecules. An extreme example of differential permeability is a *semipermeable membrane*, which is almost completely impermeable to solute molecules but permeable to the solvent. Such membranes are rare. See ACTIVE TRANSPORT.

selective reabsorption the reentry of a specific material into body tissue to avoid a deficiency within the body of that material. This is one of the mammalian kidney's functions.

self-fertilization the fusion of male and female GAMETES from the same HERMAPHRODITE individual. Self-fertilization is fairly rare in animals—

occurring, for example, in some snails and nematode worms—but is common in some plant groups. See SELF-POLLINATION. Compare CROSS-FERTILIZATION.

self-incompatibility a condition in plants in which certain types of pollen will not form pollen tubes when deposited on the female stigma, thus preventing fertilization. Self-incompatibility prevents self-fertilization and promotes heterozygosity, the mixing of allelic forms. The system is controlled by an S locus with many alleles (see MULTIPLE ALLELISM), and pollen with the same allele as that in the stigma will not germinate to form a pollen tube. This is shown in Fig. 271. Self-incompatibility mechanisms are much used to produce HYBRID plants, for example, various brassica crops. See also COMPATIBILITY.

Fig. 271. **Self-incompatibility.** The process depicted results in the progeny being S_1/S_3 and S_2/S_3.

self-pollination the transfer of pollen from the stamen of a flower to either the stigma of the same flower or to another flower on the same plant. Since self-pollination leads to self-fertilization, which is a form of inbreeding, many plants have developed mechanisms that prevent its occurrence. For example, plants can be DIOECIOUS, show SELF-INCOMPATIBILITY, and have differential maturation times of male and female floral organs on the same plants (for example, see ARUM LILY). Compare CROSS-POLLINATION.

self-sterility the inability of some HERMAPHRODITES to reproduce sexually, that is, to form viable offspring by self-fertilization.

semen the ejaculate from the male reproductive organs, which in mammals contains the sperm together with SECRETIONS from the SEMINAL VESICLES and PROSTATE gland that are essential for maintaining sperm viability.

semicircular canals the fluid-filled canals present in the inner ear of vertebrates. Usually, there are three canals on each side of the head, one in each plane—two vertical and at right angles to each other, and one horizontal and at right angles to the other two. Any movement causes the fluid in the canals to stimulate the receptors in the ampulla at the end of each canal, so that the group of semicircular canals is sensitive to movements of the head and serves to maintain BALANCE.

semiconservative replication model a model of DNA duplication in which each new molecule of DNA contains one POLYNUCLEOTIDE CHAIN from an original molecule and one chain freshly synthesized from individual NUCLEOTIDES. See Fig. 272. That such a model could be tested experimentally was shown by Matthew Meselson and F. Stahl in 1958, using radioactively labeled DNA of *E. coli*. They employed two ISOTOPES of nitrogen of different weights, ^{14}N (light) and ^{15}N (heavy), the two types being distinguishable by DIFFERENTIAL CENTRIFUGATION. See Fig. 273. The semiconservative replication model has superseded the CONSERVATIVE REPLICATION MODEL.

Fig. 272. **Semiconservative replication.** DNA duplication.

Generation number	DNA grown in	DNA weight		
		light (^{14}N)	medium (^{14}N/^{15}N)	heavy (^{15}N)
1	^{15}N (heavy)	0%	0%	100%
2	^{14}N (light)	0%	100%	0%
3	^{14}N	50%	50%	0%
4	^{14}N	75%	25%	0%

Fig. 273. **Semiconservative replication.** Meselson and Stahl's results.

semigeographic speciation the separation of species along a geographical line of secondary intergradation or along an ecological boundary.

semilunar valve either of the tricuspid heart valves: (a) at the orifice of the pulmonary artery or (b) at the orifice of the aorta.

seminal fluid the fluid in which the sperms are bathed.

seminal vesicle or **vesicula seminalis** an organ present in male animals that often stores sperm and adds extra secretions to the semen.

seminiferous tubules coiled tubules in which SPERMATOGENESIS takes place in the testes of male vertebrates. They are made up of germinal epithelium, and hundreds are present in each testis. The germ epithelium proliferates, forms spermatogonia, and grows into spermatocytes that give rise to spermatids by GAMETOGENESIS. The spermatids mature to spermatozoa embedded in nutritive SERTOLI CELLS.

semipermeable membrane see SELECTIVE PERMEABILITY.

semispecies a taxonomic group intermediate between a SPECIES and a SUBSPECIES, usually as a result of geographical isolation. See SUPERSPECIES.

senescence the process of growing old, which occurs in all species and is typified by a gradual slowing down of METABOLISM and breakdown of tissues, often accompanied by endocrinal changes.

senior homonym the earliest published of identical names for the same or different taxa.

senior synonym the earliest published of synonyms for the same taxon.

sense organ any receptor of external or internal stimuli.

sensillum (*pl.* sensilla) any small sense organ or receptor, particularly in insects, used for detection of touch, taste, or smell and for perception of heat, sound, or light. While most sensilla respond to stimuli from outside the body, for example, taste organs in the feeding of many butterflies and flies, some sensilla act as proprioreceptors, detecting internal changes, such as the flexion of joints.

sensitive reacting violently to the effects of a PATHOGEN.

sensory cell 1. see SENSORY NEURON. 2. a modified cell adapted for acceptance and transmission of stimuli.

sensory neuron or **sensory cell** a neuron that conducts impulses from the periphery of an organ to the CNS.

sepal a modified leaf, usually green, forming part of the CALYX of the flower of a DICOTYLEDON.

sepaloid (of plant structures) like a SEPAL.

septicemia or **blood poisoning** an infection of the bloodstream by a variety of pathogenic microorganisms, such as *Salmonella* and *Pseudomonas,* usually from a nonintestinal source, leading to fever, lesions in body organs, and even death.

septum any dividing wall or partition that occurs between structures or in a cavity.

sequoia either of two huge coniferous trees, the redwood *Sequoia sempervirens* or the giant sequoia *Sequoiadendron giganteum*, which can reach heights greater than 100 meters. They are among the oldest living organisms in the world, taking perhaps 2000 years to reach their mature size.

sere a plant SUCCESSION; a progression of plant communities with time.

series the sample available for taxonomic study.

serine one of 20 AMINO ACIDS common in proteins. It has a polar R group structure and is soluble in water. See Fig. 274. The ISOELECTRIC POINT of serine is 5.7.

Fig. 274. **Serine.** Molecular structure.

serology the branch of biological science concerned with the study of SERUMS.

serosa 1. a SEROUS membrane such as the PERITONEUM that secretes a serum. **2.** an epithelial layer formed under the vitelline membrane in the development of the insect egg. It lays down the serosal cuticle of the egg.

serotonin a pharmacologically active compound derived from tryptophan, which acts as a vasodilator, increases capillary permeability, and causes contraction of smooth muscle.

serous of, resembling, or producing SERUM. See SEROSA.

serrate (of edges) with toothlike shape.

Sertoli cells large nutritive cells occurring in the wall of SEMINIFEROUS TUBULES, which serve to nourish the developing sperm. Named for the Italian histologist E. Sertoli.

serum 1. see BLOOD SERUM. **2.** clear, watery animal fluid, especially that exuded by serous membranes. **3.** also called *antiserum,* antitoxin containing large quantities of ANTIBODIES to a specific ANTIGEN, which confers quick-acting passive IMMUNITY when given to an individual who may have been exposed to the antigen. For example, tetanus antiserum is injected after the possible entry of tetanus bacterium in an accident. Compare VACCINE.

serum hepatitis see HEPATITIS.

servomechanism a control system that uses negative feedback (see FEEDBACK MECHANISM) to maintain a level of output or performance.

sessile 1. (of an organism) remaining sedentary. **2.** (of part of an organism) having no stalk.

seta 1. the erect aerial part of the spore-producing structure of mosses or liverworts. **2.** see CHAETA. **3.** a slender, straight prickle.

setaceous bristly.

seventy-five percent rule an arbitrary rule stating that a population can be considered subspecifically distinct from another if 75% of the individuals are distinct from all those of the other population.

Sewall Wright effect see RANDOM GENETIC DRIFT.

sex chromatin see BARR BODY.

sex chromosome or **heterosome** one of a pair of chromosomes that are different in the two sexes and are involved in SEX DETERMINATION. All remaining chromosomes in a KARYOTYPE are called AUTOSOMES. In most organisms, for example, mammals and DIOECIOUS plants, the female contains two identical X chromosomes and is the HOMOGAMETIC SEX, whereas the male contains one X and one Y chromosome and is the HETEROGAMETIC SEX. In birds, butterflies and moths, some fish, and certain plants, the situation is reversed in the two sexes. Genes located on sex chromosomes are described as showing SEX LINKAGE.

sex determination the control of maleness and femaleness by genes located on SEX CHROMOSOMES. The actual mechanism differs in various organisms but very often is through a HETEROGAMETIC SEX and a HOMOGAMETIC SEX. In humans the male is heterogametic, sex being determined by presence of a Y chromosome rather than presence of two X chromosomes (see KLINEFELTER'S SYNDROME and TURNER'S SYNDROME). In birds, reptiles, some amphibians, and lepidopterans, the situation is reversed, with females being the heterogametic sex. In fruit flies, sex is determined by the ratio of the number of X chromosomes to the number of sets of autosomes (A). When the ratio of $X/A = 1.0$, the individual is female; when $X/A = 0.5$, a male results. In other DIPTERANS, such as the yellow-fever mosquito, sex is determined by a single locus with two alleles, the heterozygote being the male (M/m) and a homozygote the female (mm). Plants can also have XX, XY sex determination when they are DIOECIOUS, but various other mechanisms can occur. For example, sex in asparagus is controlled by a single pair of alleles, with maleness dominant.

sex factor see F FACTOR.

sex hormones hormones capable of stimulating development of the reproductive organs and SECONDARY SEXUAL CHARACTERS in mammals. The hormones are ANDROGEN, ESTROGEN, and PROGESTERONE. Sex hormones are secreted by the ovaries, testes, adrenal cortex, and placenta. See ESTRUS CYCLE.

sex limitation the restriction of the expression of a character to one or other of the sexes, for example, lactation in female mammals and facial hair in male humans, even though both sexes may carry genes for such characters. Sex-limited genes are strongly affected by the level and types of sex hormones present in the body and are mainly carried on AUTOSOMES rather than SEX CHROMOSOMES.

sex linkage the location of genes on one or other of the SEX CHROMO-SOMES producing an inheritance pattern that is different from that shown by AUTOSOMES. See Fig. 275.

Autosomal Genes	*Sex-linked Genes*
1. RECIPROCAL CROSSES produce the same results.	Reciprocal crosses produce different results.
2. All individuals carry two alleles of each gene.	Males carry only one allele of each gene (= HEMIZYGOUS).
3. Dominance operates in both males and females.	Dominance operates in females only (see 2.).
4. Alleles passed equally to male and female progeny.	"Criss-cross" inheritance pattern produced: father to daughter to grandson, etc.

Fig. 275. **Sex linkage.** The inheritance patterns of autosomal and sex-linked genes.

Most sex-linked genes are located on the X chromosome (X-linkage), although some conditions are controlled by genes on the Y chromosome (Y-linkage) that are transmitted only through the males, for example, genes responsible for SEX DETERMINATION in mammals.

sex ratio the number of males in a group divided by the number of females, giving a value that is usually about 1.0. The ratio is controlled by the SEGREGATION of SEX CHROMOSOMES in the HETEROGAMETIC SEX during MEIOSIS (see SEX DETERMINATION). For example, in humans the situation is normally as shown in Fig. 276. In fact, in humans a few more males than females are born—105 males to 100 females is typical—due either to preferential fertilization of eggs by Y-carrying sperm, causing an unequal primary ratio, or to preferential survival of males during GESTATION. Whatever the reason, the sex ratio at birth (the secondary ratio) becomes altered to about 1:1 at sexual maturity in natural circumstances, due to slightly higher mortality of male children.

Fig. 276. **Sex ratio.** The ratio of male-to-female progeny in humans.

sexual behavior any behavior associated with courtship and reproduction.

sexual cycle the series of events in which generations are linked via GAMETES and in which MEIOSIS takes place. For example, in a DIPLOID

(1) organism such as a human, HAPLOID (1) gametes are produced by meiosis, and once fertilization has occurred the diploid number is restored in the ZYGOTE. In haploid organisms, such as many fungi, meiosis is postzygotic, occurring after fertilization and with the function of restoring the haploid number.

sexual dimorphism the presence in a population of two sexes, each with a different PHENOTYPE. This is a classic example of GENETIC POLYMORPHISM. The underlying mechanism varies in different organisms, but is often controlled by genes on special SEX CHROMOSOMES (see SEX DETERMINATION).

sexual reproduction a method of reproduction involving the fusion of haploid GAMETES (fertilization) to form a diploid ZYGOTE. The zygote develops into a new individual organism, in the life history of which MEIOSIS takes place to form the haploid gametes. In the life histories of some organisms, sexual reproduction alternates with ASEXUAL REPRODUCTION.

sexual selection the selection of a mate by female animals in which, for example, the most brightly colored is favored, thus maintaining brightly colored males in a population. Some authorities consider that sexual selection explains the existence of SECONDARY SEXUAL CHARACTERS.

shell any hard outer covering, such as the carapace of turtles and tortoises, the exoskeleton of crustaceans, the calcareous plates of echinoderms, the outermost membranes of an egg, the skeleton of Foraminifera, and the mantle secretions of mollusks.

shipworm any marine bivalve mollusk, such as *Teredo*, that bores into woodwork by rotary action of the two shell valves and swallows the sawdust, which is then attacked by special enzymes that enable digestion of cellulose.

shoot the part of a vascular plant above the ground, consisting of stem and leaves.

short-day plant one that requires a day length of less than a certain minimum value for inducing flowering. In fact, the term is somewhat misleading in that such plants, for example, strawberries and chrysanthemums, are really sensitive to periods of darkness rather than daylight, requiring a night length of more than a minimum duration, that is, these may be thought of as *long-night plants*. Compare LONG-DAY PLANT, DAY-NEUTRAL PLANT. See PHOTOPERIODISM.

shoulder girdle see PECTORAL GIRDLE.

shrub a woody plant less than 10 meters high, in which there are abundant side branches and no real trunk.

shunt vessel a type of bypass channel in the blood circulation. See ARTERIOLE.

sibling a brother or sister.

sibling species see SPECIES.

sickle cell anemia (SCA) a human abnormality in which defective HEMOGLOBIN molecules (Hb^s) cause the red blood cells to have a twisted sickle shape, resulting in major circulatory problems and eventually death. The condition is controlled by a single autosomal gene on chromosome 11, with two alleles, S and s. The mutant hemoglobin has one amino acid alteration in its beta chain, number six having changed from GLUTAMIC ACID to VALINE, possibly as a result of SUBSTITUTION MUTATION. Sickle cell anemics have an s/s genotype, while heterozygotes (S/s) have a condition called *sickle cell trait*, with a tendency for their blood to sickle at low oxygen tension. Although SELECTION operates strongly against individuals with SCA, the mutant allele has remained at fairly high frequency in some populations, for example, in Central Africa, probably because the heterozygotes are at an advantage relative to the normal (S/s) types in terms of resistance to the MALARIA PARASITE, producing a GENETIC POLYMORPHISM. In North America, however, SCA is a transient polymorphism among blacks of African descent since the malarial selection pressure has been removed and its frequency in the population is expected to fall.

sieve cell see SIEVE TUBE.

sieve plate see SIEVE TUBE.

sieve tube a series of long cells (*sieve cells*) lying end to end and forming a tube, found in the PHLOEM of ANGIOSPERMS. Each sieve cell loses its nucleus when mature but maintains the cytoplasm, which is continuous from one cell to another and crosses cell boundaries via perforations in the wall called *sieve plates*. Associated with the sieve tube are modified PARENCHYMA cells, each with a cytoplasm, nucleus, and many MITOCHONDRIA, called *companion cells*. It is considered that the companion cells may regulate TRANSLOCATION of materials within sieve tubes, since there are cytoplasmic connections between the sieve cells, and the companion cells and the sieve cells are anucleate.

sigma factor a subunit of RNA polymerase that determines the site where transcription begins.

significance (statistics) a description of an observed result that shows sufficient deviation from the result expected to be considered different from the expected result. Significance tests such as the CHI-SQUARE TEST can be carried out to produce a value that is converted into the probability that an observed result will match the result expected from a theory.

In biology there is a convention that, if there is more than a 5% chance ($P > 5\%$) that the observed result is the same as the expected, it is possible to conclude that any deviations are not significant, that is, they have occurred by chance alone. If, however, there is less than a 5% chance (P < 5%) that observed and expected results are the same, then it is concluded that the deviations are significant, that is, they have *not* occurred by chance alone.

For example, a coin is tossed 100 times with the result that there are 58 heads and 42 tails. The probability that 58:42 is similar to the expected 50:50 is greater than 5%, so we may conclude that there is no significant deviation between observed and expected results.

silicula a type of dry fruit in which the seeds are contained in a short broad structure that splits (dehisces) to allow the seeds to escape, for example, the fruit of shepherd's purse, a European weed.

silique a type of dry fruit in which the seeds are contained in a long, somewhat cylindrical structure that splits open (dehisces) to allow the seeds to escape, for example, the fruit of the wallflower.

Silurian period the period of the PALEOZOIC ERA lasting from 425 million BP to 405 million BP, during which trilobites declined. The first land plants appeared, although they probably evolved in the Ordovician. Armored jawless fish and eurypterids were common. See GEOLOGICAL TIME.

simple see COMPOUND.

sinoatrial node (SAN) see HEART.

sinuate (of plant structures) having a wavy outline.

sinus 1. (in plants) a depression or margin between two lobes of a leaf. 2. (in animals) a cavity within a bone, such as the human facial bone. 3. (in animals) a large blood-filled cavity such as the HEMOCOEL of ARTHROPODS or enlarged veins of fish.

sinus venosus 1. (in lower vertebrates) the chamber of the heart to which veins return blood. 2. (in mammals) a vessel of the embryonic heart, present in the tranverse septum, into which open the vitelline, allantoic, and cardinal veins.

Siphonaptera see APHANIPTERA.

siphonophore any marine colonial hydrozoan of the order Siphonophora, including the Portuguese man-of-war.

SI units the units of measurement forming the *Système International*, consisting of the meter, kilogram, second, ampere, kelvin, candela, and mole.

skeletal muscle see STRIATED MUSCLE.

skeleton any structure present in an organism that maintains its shape and supports structures associated with the body. It can take the form of an internal bony skeleton as in vertebrates, an external calcareous or chitinous exoskeleton as in arthropods, a hydrostatic skeleton as in jelly-

fish and earthworms, or that of a subcellular system of support (see
CYTOSKELETON).

skin the outer covering of an animal that is external to the main musculature, often bearing scales, hair, or feathers, and consisting of an EPIDER-
MIS derived from the embryonic ECTODERM and a DERMIS originating
from a MESODERMIS. The epidermis is often hardened and covered by
a cuticle, but may be only one cell thick.

The subcutaneous fat of the dermis acts as insulation and reduces
heat loss. Heat is also conserved by the skin in cold conditions by contraction of superficial blood vessels, which diverts blood to lower layers
of the skin. In some structures, such as the ear, special shunt vessels
occur that dilate in cold conditions and pass blood directly from arterioles to venules, bypassing the superficial capillaries. See Fig. 277.

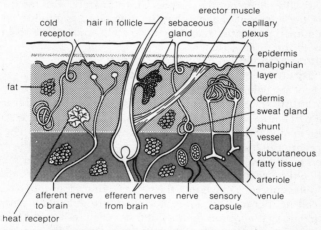

Fig. 277. **Skin.** A section of the human skin showing the dermis.

skull the skeleton of the vertebrate head.
sleeping sickness see AFRICAN SLEEPING SICKNESS, ENCEPHALITIS.
sliding filament hypothesis see MUSCLE.
slime molds see MYXOMYCETE.
small intestine a narrow tube over 7 meters long, divided into an anterior part, the duodenum (25 cm), a central part, the jejunum (5.6 meters), and a posterior part, the ileum (125 cm). CHYME from the stomach
stimulates secretion of PANCREATIC JUICE on passing into the duodenum. Bile is added from the liver and flows into the duodenum through
the bile duct. The jejunum, the main absorptive region, has a larger

diameter than the duodenum and larger VILLI than the rest of the intestine.

Large amounts of MUCUS are produced by the glandular cells, and a number of enzymes including maltase, peptidases, sucrase, lactase, enterokinase, and nucleotidases are also secreted. The enzymes are thought to be largely produced in the CRYPTS OF LIEBERKUHN. The secretions of the small intestine are collectively called the *succus entericus.* The entire intestinal lining in humans is replaced every 36 hours and is the main site of food absorption.

smallpox a contagious viral disease of humans characterized by pustules on the skin and scar formation. Smallpox was the first disease to be controlled by vaccination (see JENNER), and worldwide immunization programs organized by the World Health Organization are believed to have virtually wiped out the disease. Unfortunately, with the disappearance of the disease it is likely that the general susceptibility levels will rise in human populations, making wide-scale epidemics a real possibility should the disease return.

smooth muscle see INVOLUNTARY MUSCLE.

social organization the establishment among a group or colony of animals of set behavior patterns.

sodium pump the mechanism by which sodium is removed from inside the axon of a neuron, thus helping to establish the RESTING POTENTIAL. It is also involved in transfer of ions in the LOOP OF HENLE. The process requires energy from respiration and is an active process; the energy is derived from breaking down ATP. Sodium pumps occur in many cells and should, perhaps, be referred to as *sodium/potassium pumps,* because potassium ions move into the cell as sodium ions move out. However, cell membranes are more permeable to potassium ions than to sodium ions, so the former diffuse out faster than sodium diffuses in, and sodium is also pumped out faster than potassium is pumped in. This, together with the mobility of large negative organic ions to move out of the axon, maintains the resting potential.

soil the uppermost layer of Earth's crust, which supports the majority of terrestrial plant life together with many animals and microorganisms. Soil derives from erosion of the rock strata and contains minerals and variable amounts of organic material derived from organisms that live or have lived on it. Soils are affected by climate, living organisms, parent rock, relief, groundwater, and age and usually contain various horizons, the succession of which is called the soil profile. MULL soils tend to be alkaline and Mor soils acid. (*Mor* is a Danish word meaning acid.) Soils may be heavy, clay, loam (sand and clay), peaty (large amounts of dead plant material), light, or sandy.

soil water any water held in the soil as a vapor, liquid, or solid.

sol a suspension of colloidal particles in a liquid. See COLLOID. Compare GEL.

solenocyte a tubular FLAME CELL found in AMPHIOXUS and annelids that is much more elongated than the cells found in platyhelminths.

solifluction a slow movement of soil or rock debris down an incline, usually as a result of lubrication by its water content.

soligenous (of peat bogs) dependent on an inflow of drainage water.

solubility the amount of a substance that will dissolve in a given amount of another substance.

solute a substance that is dissolved in a SOLVENT.

solution a mixture in which a substance (solid, liquid, or gas) is dissolved in another liquid.

solvent a liquid in which another substance (a SOLUTE) may be dissolved to form a solution; the solvent is the larger part of the solution.

soma the body of an animal, excluding the germinal cells that give rise to the gametes.

somatic 1. of or relating to the SOMA. **2.** of or relating to the human body as distinct from the mind.

somatic cell any of the cells of a plant or animal except the reproductive cells.

somatic cell hybridization the process of fusion between different SOMATIC CELLS, such as human and rodent cells, to produce hybrid cells in which there is often one fused nucleus. Such a process occurs in cell cultures, and the products are useful in establishing the expression and location of particular genes.

somatic mesoderm a MESODERM with its embryonic origin on either side of the NOTOCHORD. It develops into (a) a series of blocks of SOMITES from which are derived MYOTOMES; (b) mesenchyme, which forms connective tissue; and (c) the vertebral column.

somatic mutation see MUTATION.

somatic nervous system the part of the nervous system that supplies the limbs and body wall and controls the voluntary activities of the body. See AUTONOMIC NERVOUS SYSTEM and NERVE IMPULSE.

somatostatin a hormone of the hypothalamus that inhibits release of growth hormone from the pituitary gland.

somatotrophic hormone (STH) see GROWTH HORMONE.

somite or **metamere** a serial segment of the animal body. See METAMERIC SEGMENTATION.

sorus a group of sporangia developed on the underside of SPOROPHYLLS (spore-bearing leaflets) of the SPOROPHYTE generation of a fern. See Fig. 278.

Fig. 278. **Sorus.** Transverse section.

spadix a massive, fleshy spike of flowers protected by a large, sometimes green, bract called a *spathe*. A classic example of a plant with such a structure is the ARUM LILY.

sparging the introduction of air into a microbial fermenter under pressure.

spathe see SPADIX.

spathulate (of plant structures) paddle- or spoon-shaped.

special creation a theory of evolution that postulates the formation *de novo* of species by an all-powerful creator.

speciation the process by which new species are formed. Speciation occurs when gene flow has effectively ceased between populations where it previously existed and is brought about by ISOLATING MECHANISMS. See GEOGRAPHICAL ISOLATION.

species the lowest (taxonomic) grouping of animals or plants that, at least potentially, forms an interbreeding array of populations unable to breed freely with other sorts of animals and plants. The species is the only natural unit (taxon) of CLASSIFICATION. It is usually recognized on the basis of morphological characters (a MORPHOSPECIES), but different species can be morphologically identical (*sibling species*), for example, *Drosophila pseudoobscura* and *D. persimilis* exhibit behavioral differences leading to REPRODUCTIVE ISOLATION. See BINOMIAL NOMENCLATURE.

species recognition the exchange of specific signals between individual members of a species, for example, during courtship.

specificity the selective reactivity of an ANTIGEN and its corresponding ANTIBODY.

specific name the second of two names in a binominal indicating the name of the particular species in that genus. For example, *rubecula* is the specific name of the robin *Erithacus rubecula*.

sperm or **spermatozoon** a small, usually motile male GAMETE. See ACROSOME.

spermatheca a sac for storage of sperm, a seminal receptacle that occurs in the female reproductive tract of many lower animals, such as insects and PLATYHELMINTHS.

spermatid a haploid stage in male GAMETOGENESIS.

spermatocyte a diploid or haploid stage in male GAMETOGENESIS.

spermatogenesis the form of MEIOSIS producing male gametes. See GAMETOGENESIS.

spermatogonium an early diploid stage of male GAMETOGENESIS.

spermatophore a packet of sperm that is transferred from male to female in certain invertebrates, such as crustaceans, mollusks, cephalopods, and in a few vertebrates, such as aquatic salamanders.

spermatophyte any plant of the division Spermatophyta, comprising all forms of seed-bearing plants, ANGIOSPERMS and GYMNOSPERMS.

spermatozoid see ANTHEROZOID.

spermatozoon see SPERM.

sperm bank a refrigerated source of male gametes (sperm), usually from males of proven breeding value, and used regularly by animal breeders. See ARTIFICIAL INSEMINATION.

Sphenopsida a subdivision of the Tracheophyta, including the horsetails (*Equisetum*).

spherule a thick-walled structure containing large numbers of fungal spores.

sphincter a ring of muscle surrounding a tube or the opening to a tube that controls the size of the aperture it surrounds and, thus, the movement through the tube, for example, pyloric and anal sphincters.

spicule 1. a small spiked structure in male nematode worms that assists in copulation. 2. any of the slender rods of calcium carbonate found in sponges supporting the soft wall.

spike a raceme of SESSILE (2) flowers, as found in the plantain and the spotted orchid.

spikelet a unit in the inflorescence of a grass consisting of one or more flowers surrounded by other structures, for example, one or more sterile GLUMES.

spinal column see VERTEBRAL COLUMN.

spinal cord a more or less uniform tube extending the full length of the body in vertebrates behind the head. It is enclosed in the backbone. Pairs of spinal nerves leave the cord in each segment of the body. The cord contains many NERVE CELLS and bundles of fibers, many associated with simple REFLEX ARCS, others with the brain. Coordination of movement of various parts of the body is brought about in the spinal cord.

spinal nerve any of numerous nerves that leave the SPINAL CORD, one pair in each segment, each being connected with the cord by a dorsal and a ventral root. They are mixed nerves, containing both sensory and motor fibers, and carry groups of AXONS to receptors and effectors in different parts of the body. See REFLEX ARC.

spinal reflex a reflex action whose pathway goes through the spinal cord, not the brain.

spindle or **spindle fibers** a network of fibers or MICROTUBULES formed during late prophase and early metaphase of MITOSIS and MEIOSIS, and which serves as an attachment point for chromosomes before they are pulled to the spindle poles during anaphase. Spindle formation is prevented by COLCHICINE.

spindle fibers see SPINDLE.

spinneret one of a number of tubular appendages in spiders and some insects that exude silk threads. In spiders the silk is used to make webs, and in insects is used for cocoons. Spinnerets in insects and spiders are not homologous structures.

spiracle 1. (in fish) a gill-like cleft that opens behind the eye and through which water is drawn in for gaseous exchange, as it is through the mouth, by expansion of the pharyngeal cavity. It is absent in many bony fish. 2. (in arthropods) the exterior opening of the tracheae, often possessing valves that can close to prevent water loss.

spiral cleavage the division of cells in the developing animal egg in a spiral manner (see Fig. 106). With the exception of echinoderms, protochordates, and a few smaller groups, most invertebrate groups exhibit this type of cleavage

spiral thickening a deposition of lignin on the inner surface of a XYLEM VESSEL, forming a spiral pattern.

splanchnic of or relating to the viscera.

splanchno- *combining form* denoting viscera.

splanchnocoel the perivisceral cavity lined on the inside by splanchnopleure and on the outside by somatopleure.

splanchnopleure the inner layer of embryonic mesoblast that contributes to the wall of the alimentary canal and parts of the visceral organs.

spleen an important part of the MONONUCLEAR PHAGOCYTE SYSTEM, made up of lymphoid tissue. It stores excess red blood cells, destroys old cells, and is capable of acting as a reservoir holding 20—30% of all blood cells. It produces LYMPHOCYTES and serves to regulate the volume of blood cells elsewhere in the blood system.

splicing the joining together of RNA chains, for example, after excision of INTRONS to link up the AXON segments and produce mature mRNA.

splitter a taxonomist who recognizes minute differences and as a result recognizes numerous separate taxa. Compare LUMPER.

sponge any member of the phylum Porifera. Sponges are multicellular organisms, although many biologists regard them as colonies of single cells. Several types of cells exist in a sponge, but they are functionally independent of one another and can exist on their own or in small isolated groups. They usually have an internal skeleton of separate crystalline spicules, irregular organic fibers (bath sponge), or both.

spongin a horny substance secreted by cells in the middle layers of the sponge that acts as a cement joining together the spicules in the body wall or forming a fibrous skeleton in other types.

spongy mesophyll see MESOPHYLL.

spontaneous generation or **abiogenesis** a discredited belief that living organisms can arise from nonliving things. It was finally shown to be untrue by PASTEUR in his famous swan-neck flask experiments.

spontaneous mutation a MUTATION occurring in the absence of a known mutagen. In humans, a typical rate of spontaneous mutation is between 1×110^{-5} and 1×10^{-6} mutations per gamete formed. The rate varies considerably between different organisms, perhaps reflecting different DNA repair systems at work.

sporangiophore a fungal HYPHA bearing one or more SPORANGIA.

sporangium (*pl.* sporangia) the structure within which asexual SPORES are formed.

spore a reproductive body consisting of one or several cells formed by cell division in the parent organism. The parent, when detached and dispersed, and if conditions are suitable, germinates into a new individual. Spores occur particularly in fungi and bacteria and also in Protozoa. Some have thick, resistant walls that enable them to overcome unfavorable conditions, such as drought. Usually, they are produced in very large numbers and occur as a result of either sexual or asexual reproduction.

spore mother cell a DIPLOID (1) cell in which MEIOSIS occurs to give four HAPLOID (1) spores.

sporo- *combining form* denoting a seed.

sporocyst a cyst producing asexual spores.

sporogonium (*pl.* sporogonia) the SPOROPHYTE generation of mosses and liverworts, producing asexual SPORES.

sporogony the formation of SPOROCYTES in a PROTOZOAN zygote by encystment and division.

sporophore any fungal structure that produces SPORES.

sporophyll a leaf bearing a SPORANGIUM. In some plants, such as ferns, the sporophyll is identical with ordinary leaves, but in others is considerably modified as in the stamens and carpels of flowering plants.

sporophyte the diploid generation of plants, which by MEIOSIS gives rise to a HAPLOID (1) generation of spores.

sporozoan any parasitic protozoan of the class Sporozoa, such as the MALARIA PARASITE.

sporozoite any of the very small mobile spores formed by multiple fission of a protozoan zygote, as in the MALARIA PARASITE.

sport an individual distinctly different from its parents in a way that was not expected, such as a mutation.

sporulation a form of asexual reproduction in which specialized cells become surrounded by a tough, resistant coat and then separate from the parent plant. These SPORES are able to withstand severe environmental conditions; when conditions improve, they germinate to produce new plants by repeated MITOSIS. Sporulation is common in fungi.

springtail see COLLEMBOLA.

spur 1. a short shoot on which flowers are borne. 2. an extension of a leaf base below its point of attachment to the petiole. 3. a hollow, conical projection from the base of a petal, as in the larkspur.

Squamata an order of reptiles containing the lizards and snakes, which have a skin with horny epidermal scales or shields. The movable quadrate bone makes it possible to move the upper jaw with respect to the braincase.

squamosal either of the paired bones that occur on each side of the skull of vertebrates. In mammals they take part in the zygomatic arch, and the lower jaw articulates with the squamosals.

squamous (of epithelium) flattened and platelike.

squid a 10-armed CEPHALOPOD (cuttlefish) with an internal shell that moves by means of jet propulsion through a muscular siphon.

S stage the synthesis phase of the CELL CYCLE.

stabilizing selection a type of SELECTION in which both extremes of a phenotypic range are selected against, producing a stable average PHENOTYPE with reduced variation in the range. See Fig. 279. A good example of stabilizing selection is human birth weight. Under natural conditions, babies are subject to selection pressure if they are too small at birth (due to immaturity of body system) or too large (due to difficulties in delivery related to the size of the mother's pelvis). Compare DISRUPTIVE SELECTION.

stable polymorphism see BALANCED POLYMORPHISM.

stable terminal residue material that is not broken down by natural means in the soil and remains as the last of the soil degradation products.

stamen the male organ in angiosperm flowers, consisting of a stalk, or filament, bearing an anther in which POLLEN grains are produced by MEIOSIS.

staminate (of flowers) having STAMENS but no CARPELS.

Fig. 279. **Stabilizing selection.** The mean represents the stable average phenotype.

staminode a rudimentary, infertile stamen that may be reduced in size.

standard deviation (S) a measure of the variation in a sample, calculated as the square root of the VARIANCE. When mean values are supplied, they often are followed by the standard deviation. See STANDARD ERROR.

standard error (SE) an estimate of the STANDARD DEVIATION of the means of many samples, calculated as the standard deviation(s) divided by the square root of the number of individuals in a sample (n), that is, $s/\sqrt{n}$. See Fig 280.

Values in sample (n = 7)	48, 27, 36, 52, 35, 41, 33
mean of sample	$\bar{x} = 38.86$
variance of sample	$s^2 = 76.48$
standard deviation	$s = 8.74$
standard error	$SE = 3.31$

Fig. 280. **Standard error.**

The SE can be used to assess any SIGNIFICANCE in the deviation of the mean of a sample from the true mean of the entire population.

standard metabolic level the total STANDARD METABOLIC RATE of an animal at a specified temperature divided by the body mass raised to the power of the metabolic exponent for the species or taxonomic group.

standard metabolic rate (SMR) the metabolic rate of a resting postabsorptive animal in a darkened chamber at a specified environmental temperature. For tachymetabolic animals, SMR is BASAL METABOLIC RATE plus REGULATORY HEAT PRODUCTION. Units: $cm^3 O_2 h^{-1}$.

standard temperature and pressure (STP) the standard conditions of 25°C, 1 atmosphere.

standing biomass the BIOMASS present in an ecosystem at a given time.

standing crop the mass of a particular organism or organisms present at a particular time within a given environment, that is, the total BIOMASS of that organism or organisms.

stapes the innermost of the three ear ossicles, which contacts the oval window of the ear. It is stirrup-shaped.

starch a polysaccharide carbohydrate consisting of two forms of GLUCOSE units, amylose and amylopectin, which are joined to form a helical molecule. Upon heating, the two components are separated, with amylose giving a purplish/blue color when iodine is added and amylopectin giving a black color—forming the standard test for starch. Starch is the principal storage compound of plants. See DEXTRIN.

starch sheath an ENDODERMIS containing starch grains.

starch test see STARCH.

statoblast an internal bud in a BRYOZOAN that develops into a new individual.

statocyst an organ of balance in which a STATOLITH (2) rests among hairlike projections of sensory cells. A change in position of the animal moves the statolith against a receptor, sending a nervous impulse to the central nervous system.

statolith 1. (in plants) a solid inclusion within a cell, such as a starch granule, by means of which the position of the plant in relation to the gravity is thought to be perceived. 2. (in animals) a granule that stimulates sensory cells in a STATOCYST as the animal moves. See OTOLITH.

stearic acid a saturated fatty acid having 18 carbon atoms, which occurs in animal fat.

stegosaur or **Stegosaurus** a quadrupedal herbivorous ornithischian dinosaur of the suborder Stegosauria, a large JURASSIC PERIOD reptile up to 9 meters in length. Stegosaurs had large neural spines that supported very large, vertical, triangular plates of armor.

stele or **vascular cylinder** the cylinder of tissues lying inside the ENDODERMIS of plant stems and roots, containing the vascular tissues.

stellate star-shaped.

stem the part of the shoot of vascular plants from which leaves and reproductive structures are produced at regular intervals. Stems are usually circular in cross section, but some are ribbed and others are square, for example, members of the family *Labiatae,* such as mint and lavender. The internal structure of stems can be herbaceous (nonwoody) or show SECONDARY THICKENING. See Fig. 281.

The forms adopted by stems are highly varied, ranging from the oak tree to climbing plants, such as *Clematis* and the pea. Stems are some-

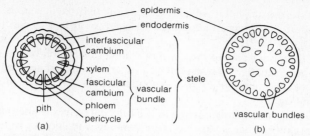

Fig. 281. **Stem.** Transverse sections of herbaceous stems: (a) dicotyledon and (b) monocotyledon.

times used as underground storage organs as in RHIZOMES, CORMS, BULBS (underground shoots with food stored in fleshy leaves), and TUBERS, while others are adapted for VEGETATIVE PROPAGATION, as in the strawberry RUNNER and suckers of mint.

stereoisomer one of two or more isomers that have the same molecular structure but differ in the spatial arrangement of the atoms in the molecule.

stereotropism see THIGMOTROPISM.

sterile 1. incapable of producing offspring. 2. free from living microorganisms.

sterile male release (SRM) a method of insect BIOLOGICAL CONTROL in which large numbers of sterile males of a pest species are produced and released into the pest population. Since many female insects mate only once, the idea of the technique is that females should mate with sterile rather than fertile males, thus dramatically decreasing the size of the next generation.

sterilization 1. the act of destroying all forms of microbial life on an object, making it sterile. 2. the act of preventing an organism from reproducing by removing the gonads.

sternite the skeletal plate(s) on the ventral side of insect and crustacean body segments.

sternum the breastbone that occurs in the ventral region of the chest and to which, in flying birds where the bone is keel-shaped, are attached the pectoral muscles associated with flight. Anteriorly, the sternum is connected to the shoulder girdle, and the ventral ends of the ribs are attached along its length.

steroid an important but unusual type of LIPID, formed of four rings of carbon atoms with various side groups, such as cholesterol, cortisone, and digitoxin, which forms part of the heart-stimulating drug digitalis.

sterol a steroid alcohol in which the alcoholic hydroxyl group is attached in position 3 and has an aliphatic side chain of at least 8 carbon atoms at position 17.

stigma the upper part of the pistil of a flower on which pollen is deposited. The stigmatic surface secretes a sugary solution that aids in germination of the pollen grain, unless a SELF-INCOMPATIBILITY mechanism is operating.

stimulus any detectable change in the internal or external environment of an organism that is capable of influencing a RESPONSE in the entire organism or parts of it.

sting an organ present in many different animal groups that is capable of injecting a poison into other organisms either as a defensive or offensive mechanism. Examples include the modified ovipositor in HYMENOPTERA, cnidoblasts in coelenterata, and the tail in a scorpion.

stipe 1. the stalk of the thallus of a seaweed. 2. the fruiting body of a fungus.

stipel one of two leaflike structures at the base of a leaflet in some compound leaves.

stiptate (of plant structures) having a stalk.

stipule one of a pair of leaflets found at the base of a leaf where it joins the stem. Stipules are common in many plant families, such as Rosaceae.

stochastic model any mathematical model of a system that is governed by the laws of probability and contains a randomized element, for example, a computer program that models a population controlled by the mechanisms of MENDELIAN GENETICS.

stock 1. a rooted stem into which a SCION is inserted for grafting (see GRAFT). 2. a mating group used in a breeding program.

stolon see RUNNER.

stoma (*pl.* stomata) an opening in the epidermis of leaves and, sometimes, stems that enables gaseous exchange. The size of the stomatal aperture is controlled by two guard cells whose shape can alter depending on internal turgidity. See Fig. 282. When flaccid, the thick inner wall causes the guard cells to straighten, closing the stoma. When turgid, the guard cells become curved, opening the stoma for gaseous exchange.

Fig. 282. **Stoma.** (a) Closed aperture. (b) Open aperture.

The mechanism of guard cell operation is not fully understood. An older theory proposes that high CO_2 values at night cause high acidity, which encourages enzymic conversion of sugar to starch, thus reducing OSMOTIC PRESSURE in the guard cell sap, with the result that water is lost and the stoma closes. During daylight, PHOTOSYNTHESIS uses up available CO_2. The pH rises, thus favoring conversion of starch to sugar, increasing the flow of water into guard cells by osmosis, and causing the stoma to open.

A newer theory, built on the older one, suggests that changes in osmotic pressure are caused not just by differences in levels of CO_2 but by levels of potassium ions (K^+) in the guard cells. According to this theory, K^+ ions are actively pumped into the guard cells during the day, thus increasing osmotic pressure and, hence, turgidity.

stomach the part of the vertebrate gut system that follows the esophagus. It is expanded to form a chamber, and its walls secrete pepsinogen, giving rise to PEPSIN, RENNIN (in young mammals), and hydrochloric acid. Gastric secretions also include mucin, which lubricates the food mass that is passed a little at a time to the SMALL INTESTINE via the PYLORIC SPHINCTER. The mixture of partly digested food and secreted fluids is known as CHYME. See DIGESTION, DIGESTIVE SYSTEM.

stomium the part of the wall of a fern SPORANGIUM with thin-walled cells that ruptures during dehiscence, facilitating release of spores.

stone cell a cell with thick walls reinforced with lignin, found in the flesh of succulent fruits such as pears.

stop codon see NONSENSE CODON.

storage material any compound that accumulates naturally within a cell, for example, the starch grains of potato tubers and glycogen in liver cells.

STP see STANDARD TEMPERATURE AND PRESSURE.

strain a group of organisms within a species or variety, distinguished by one or more minor characteristics.

stratification a process in which certain seeds are subjected to low temperatures for a period of time, enabling GERMINATION to occur. Natural stratification takes place when seeds are shed in autumn and become covered with soil, leaves, and the like in winter. The process can be reproduced artificially by alternating layers of seeds with layers of moistened substrate, such as sphagnum moss, and storing at a low temperature.

stratified epithelium see EPITHELIUM.

streaming see CYTOPLASMIC STREAMING.

Strepsiptera an order of insects containing very small parasitic individuals. The larvae parasitize bees and plant bugs, the females are wingless endoparasites, and the males are winged (hind wings only). Parasitized insects are said to be *stylopized* (after *Stylops,* one of the parasitizing genera) and cause the host sex organs to degenerate.

streptomycin an ANTIBIOTIC produced by a soil ACTINOMYCETE, which is active against many bacteria, particularly of the gram-negative type (see GRAM'S SOLUTION). Streptomycin works by causing a misreading of the GENETIC CODE during PROTEIN SYNTHESIS in the bacteria.

stretch receptor the receptor for detecting muscle stretch located in the muscle spindle organ. The receptor is situated centrally and consists of spiral nerve endings (branches of an efferent nerve) surrounding noncontractile muscle fibers. Efferent nerve fibers connect at each end with contractile muscle fibers. Stretching of a muscle causes discharge from spiral nerve endings to the muscle itself, thus causing contraction. The more the spindle is stretched, the greater the efferent frequency of impulses and consequently the more the muscle contracts. This is the *stretch reflex.*

Muscle spindles occur in numbers up to 30/g of muscle, shoulder and thigh muscles being spindle-poor and more distal muscles being spindle-rich. The largest numbers occur in the head and upper vertebral column. See Fig. 283.

Fig. 283. **Stretch receptor.** The stretch receptor of the muscle spindle.

stretch reflex or **myostatic reflex** the contraction of a muscle in response to a sudden longitudinal stretching of the same muscle.

striate (of plant structures) marked with parallel ridges or depressions.

striated muscle or **striped muscle** or **skeletal muscle** or **voluntary muscle** contractile tissue, in vertebrates consisting of fibrils with marked striations at right angles to the long axis. The muscle fibers are made up of a number of SARCOMERES (see MUSCLE, I-BAND). The muscle is capable of rapid contraction and is concerned with movement of skeletal parts, hence the alternative name skeletal muscle. Striped or voluntary muscle are additional alternative names, the latter because of its stimulation by the voluntary nervous system. Compare INVOLUNTARY MUSCLE.

strict (of plant structures) growing upward, stiff and rigid.

stridulation the sound produced by rubbing together part of the hind legs and the forewings by grasshoppers and locusts (see ORTHOPTERA). The sound produced is believed to result in the bringing together of males and females for mating.

striped muscle see STRIATED MUSCLE.

strobila a linear sequence of similar animal structures, such as the segmented body of a tapeworm.

strobilation asexual reproduction by division into segments, as in tapeworms and jellyfishes (see EPHYRA, SCYPHISTOMA).

stroma see CHLOROPLAST.

stromatolite a rocklike mound, often found in fossil form, created by blue-green algae. See CYANOPHYTE.

structural gene see OPERON MODEL.

strychnine a poisonous alkaloid obtained from *Strychnos nux-vomica,* used as a stimulus for the central nervous system.

style the stalk of the PISTIL of a flower connecting the STIGMA to the ovary.

sub- *prefix* denoting under or below.

suberin a complex of fatty substances present in the wall of cork tissue that waterproofs it and makes it resistant to decay.

suberization the deposition of SUBERIN.

subfamily a taxon immediately below the level of family and above genus.

subgeneric name a little-used taxonomic grouping below the genus, usually enclosed in parentheses when used in a scientific name, for example, *X-us (Y-us) britannicus.*

subjective synonym any of two taxonomic synonyms resulting from different TYPES, but considered to refer to the same taxon by those regarding them as synonyms.

sublittoral growing near the sea, but not on the shore.

subsoil the soil below the plow layer.

subspecies the division of the population of a SPECIES on the grounds of incomplete REPRODUCTIVE ISOLATION. In many groups of organisms, subspecies have been named on minor morphological differences that usually occur in different geographically defined populations. Often, in birds, for example, different parts of a CLINE have been given subspecific status. If clines are to be named, only the extremes should have subspecific names. Clearly defined populations, such as island forms, often merit subspecific names and may be thought of as species in the making. See ISOLATING MECHANISMS.

substitute name a taxonomic name replacing another preoccupied name and therefore taking on the same TYPE specimen and locality.

substitution 1. a reaction in which an atom or a group of atoms is removed and replaced by another atom or group. **2.** the replacement of one amino acid by another. **3.** the replacement of one base by another in a nucleotide or nucleic acid.

substitional load the cost of replacing one ALLELE by another during evolutionary change in a population.

substitution mutation a mutation affecting the base sequence of a DNA molecule, in which one base is substituted for another one, with no loss or gain of base and therefore no risk of a FRAMESHIFT.

A *transition substitution mutation* is the replacement of a PYRIMIDINE base by another pyrimidine—for example, thymine changing to cytosine—or a PURINE by another purine—for example, adenine replacing guanine. A *transversion substitution mutation* is the replacement of a pyrimidine by a purine or vice versa.

substrate 1. the medium on which an organism, especially a microorganism, can grow. **2.** the solid object to which a plant is attached, such as a rock forming the substrate for a seaweed STIPE. **3.** any substance on which an enzyme can act.

substrate-enzyme complex a chemical combination of a substrate molecule at the ACTIVE SITE of an enzyme.

substrate-level phosphorylation the direct transfer of a phosphate group of ADP thus forming ATP, without the presence of oxygen. The phosphorylation is thus independent of the ELECTRON TRANSPORT SYSTEM used in oxidative phosphorylation. See ANAEROBIC RESPIRATION, GLYCOLYSIS.

subulate (of plant structures) long, narrow, and pointed.

succession the progression from initial colonization of an area by organisms to the CLIMAX population. The term usually refers to plants.

succulent fruit one in which the PERICARP contains a fleshy mesocarp that often is good to eat, for example, peach, plum, cherry, and apricot, which are all DRUPES.

succus entericus see SMALL INTESTINE.

sucker 1. an axial shoot arising from an adventitious bud of a root and appearing separate from the mother plant. Such structures are common in the family Rosaceae. **2.** a new shoot on an old stem. **3.** a modified root in a parasite enabling it to absorb nutritive materials from the host.

sucrase or **invertase** an enzyme that catalyzes the hydrolysis of SUCROSE into GLUCOSE and FRUCTOSE. Sucrase is contained in the SUCCUS ENTERICUS.

sucrose a DISACCHARIDE nonreducing sugar used in sweetening, being obtained from the juice of the sugar cane and from sugar beet. Sucrose

($C_{12}H_{22}O_{11}$) is formed by a CONDENSATION REACTION between FRUCTOSE and GLUCOSE.

suction pressure see WATER POTENTIAL.

sudoriferous (of a gland or its duct) producing or conveying sweat.

suffruticose (of plants) being a dwarf plant, particularly a shrub, in which many upper branches die back after flowering.

sugar a simple CARBOHYDRATE, formed of MONOSACCHARIDE units. Such molecules can exist in either a straight chain or a ring form. The straight chain contains a $C = O$ group. If this group is terminal, the sugar has the properties of an aldehyde (aldose sugar). If it is nonterminal, the sugar acts as a ketone (ketose sugar).

Both aldose and ketose sugars can be oxidized and will reduce alkaline copper solutions (see FEHLING'S TEST, BENEDICT'S TEST). They are thus called REDUCING SUGARS. Several disaccharides such as maltose and lactose are also reducing sugars. Sucrose, however, is a *nonreducing sugar* in which the linkage of glucose and fructose masks the potential aldehyde group of glucose and the potential ketone group of fructose, so that no reduction occurs in Fehling's and Benedict's tests.

The backbone of the sugar can be of varying lengths, containing as few as three carbons (triose sugars) but, more commonly, five carbons (pentose sugar) and six carbons (hexose sugars).

sulcus a groove or fissure.

sulfonamide a class of organic compounds that are amides of sulfonic acids, some of which are sulfa drugs and act as powerful inhibitors of bacterial activity.

sulfur bridge the linkage between two sulfur atoms within molecules that enables complex folding to occur. For example, disulfide bridges often form between cysteine residues in proteins.

summation the production of an effect by repetition of stimuli, any one of the stimuli alone being insufficient to produce an effect, as in muscular contraction where summation brings about TETANUS, which results from a series of stimuli. See RODS and CONE CELL for the effect of summation in the eye.

super- *prefix* denoting above or beyond.

superfamily a taxon above a family and below an order.

superficial on or near the surface, for example, of an artery, vein, or ovule.

supergene a cluster of genes along a chromosome that, while located close to one another, may have unrelated functions. Supergenes may act as a single unit during RECOMBINATION in meiosis.

superinfection an infection added to one already present.

superior ovary a plant ovary in which the PERIANTH is attached to its base, leaving the ovary free.

supernatant the clear liquid above a precipitate that has settled out.

superoptimal stimuli any stimuli to which an organism responds more strongly than to those for which the reaction was originally selected.

superspecies a monophyletic group of species that occurs together in a single geographic location, but whose members are too distinct to form a single species. See SEMISPECIES.

suppressor mutation a MUTATION that acts to restore normal functioning of another gene located elsewhere in the GENOME, or another mutation at a different site in the same gene.

supra- *prefix* denoting above or over.

supraspecific above the species level.

surface area/volume ratio see BERGMANN'S RULE.

susceptible liable to attack by another organism (pest or pathogen) or a biocide.

suspension a system in which denser, microscopically visible, particles are distributed throughout a less dense liquid and maintained there, settlement being hindered or prevented either by the viscosity of the fluid or by the impacts of the liquid's molecules on the particles.

suspensor 1. (in higher plants) a mass of cells that pushes the developing embryo down into the nutritive tissues so it can obtain maximum nutrition for further development. **2.** (in mycology) a HYPHA that supports a ZYGOSPORE, GAMETE, or gametangium.

Sutherland, Earl Wilbur (1915—1974) American pharmacologist and physiologist awarded the Nobel Prize for Physiology and Medicine in 1971 for isolation of cyclic AMP (adenine monophosphate). With T.W. Rall, Sutherland discovered that hormones such as ADRENALINE act on their target cells by causing an increase in cyclic AMP.

suture 1. a thread or wire used to join together a wound in surgery. **2.** the seam formed after stitching two parts together. **3.** an immovable joint between bones of the skull. **4.** (in plants) the line of fusion between two carpels.

Svedberg (S) unit a unit of sedimentation velocity used to describe molecules of various sizes. See DIFFERENTIAL CENTRIFUGATION.

Swammerdam's glands amphibian glands that secrete calcareous nodules on each side of the vertebral column. Named for the Dutch naturalist J. Swammerdam (1637—1680).

swarm 1. a group of social insects, especially bees led by a queen, that has left the parent hive in order to start a new colony. **2.** a large mass of small animals, especially insects.

swarm cell a spherical cell in *Rhizobium* that penetrates the root hairs of legumes in order to establish the symbiotic relationship associated with NITROGEN FIXATION.

sweat gland a structure present in the skin of some mammals that secretes sweat containing sodium chloride as part of the cooling system. A typical human has about 2.5 million sweat glands. Dogs, cats, and rabbits are among the mammals that do not sweat, but use evaporation from the upper respiratory tract to lose excess body heat.

swim bladder see AIR BLADDER.

swimmeret any of the small paired appendages on the abdomen of crustaceans, used for locomotion or reproduction.

switch gene a gene that causes the total genetic developmental system to change to a different developmental pathway.

sym- see SYN-.

symbiont an organism living in a state of SYMBIOSIS with another.

symbiosis or **mutualism** a relationship between dissimilar organisms in which both partners benefit, for example, the hermit crab *Pagarus* and the sea anemone *Adamsia palliata*, which lives attached to the crab shell. The anemone obtains food scraps from the crab, and the crab is camouflaged by the anemone and defended by its stinging cells (NEMATOCYSTS).

sympathetic nervous system see AUTONOMIC NERVOUS SYSTEM.

sympatric (of a population of organisms) occurring together in the same geographical area. The term is used to describe the geographical distribution of organisms that either coincide or overlap. Compare ALLOPATRIC.

sympatric hybridization the occasional occurrence of hybrids between well-defined sympatric species.

sympatric speciation the occurrence of species formation without geographical isolation, genetic isolation occurring through other mechanisms.

sympetalous see GAMETOPETALOUS.

Symphyla a group of primitive millipedes possessing features, particularly mouthparts, that suggest a common ancestry with the insects.

symplast the part of a plant consisting of the PLASMALEMMA and the cytoplasm contained within the plasmalemma, outside which is the APOPLAST (2). The symplastic organization enables *symplastic transport* between live cells, via PLASMODESMATA.

symplesiomorphy the sharing of ancestral characters by different species.

sympodial (of a stem) growing in length by development of lateral buds, the terminal bud developing into an inflorescence or dying back each year.

symptom any change in normal function or activity associated with a particular disease.

syn- or **sym-** *combining form* denoting together or with.

synapomorphy the sharing of derived characters by different species.

synapse the point at which one nerve cell connects with another and at which transmission of an impulse takes place by chemical means. When an impulse arrives at a synapse, it causes a synaptic vesicle to move toward the presynaptic membrane. On contacting the membrane, it discharges the contained transmitter substance into the synaptic cleft, across which it diffuses to the postsynaptic membrane and causes it to depolarize. This causes a positive charge to develop (*excitory postsynaptic potential, EPSP*) because of sodium ions flowing into the postsynaptic nerve cell. When the positive charge builds up sufficiently, it generates an action potential that usually is unidirectional. See END-PLATE MOTOR and Fig. 143.

Synapsida (in the taxonomy of reptiles) a subclass fossil form having a single inferior temporal FOSSA on each side of the skull. These are the Theromorphs from which mammals probably evolved. The term is sometimes extended to include the mammals.

synapsis 1. the lying together of structures as in, for example, the junction of two nerve cells. 2. (in genetics) the pairing of HOMOLOGOUS CHROMOSOMES in prophase I of MEIOSIS.

synaptic cleft the narrow gap that separates the membrane of an axon terminal of a nerve cell from the membrane of another, across which TRANSMITTER SUBSTANCE diffuses to effect a stimulus of the postsynaptic cell.

synaptic knob the expanded distal end of the small terminal branches of a neuron. See ENDPLATE.

syncarpous (of an ovary of a flowering plant) having fused carpels. Compare APOCARPOUS.

synchronic (of species) occurring in the same periods in time.

synchronous muscle see FLIGHT.

syncytium a cellular structure containing many nuclei.

syndactyly having two or more digits fused together.

syndrome a group of symptoms that occur together in a disease or abnormality. Syndromes are often named after their discoverer. Examples include DOWN SYNDROME, KLINEFELTER'S SYNDROME, TURNER'S SYNDROME.

synecology the study of communities, rather than individuals. Compare AUTECOLOGY.

synergid either of two small cells present in the embryo sac of seed plants near the egg cell at the micropylar end.

synergism a chemical phenomenon in which the combined activity of two or more compounds is greater than the sum of the individual activities. For example, CYTOKININ and AUXIN act synergistically in promoting DNA replication.

syngamy the fusion of gametes.

synonym (in taxonomy) any one of a list of names for the same taxon.

synonymy (in taxonomy) a listing in chronological order of all the scientific names applied to a given taxon, together with dates and authors.

synopsis a summary of current knowledge.

synovial fluid a viscous fluid contained within a membrane enclosing movable joints, such as the elbow and knee. The fluid lubricates the cartilages that make surface contact between the bones at the joint.

synteny the assignment of genes to the same chromosome in SOMATIC CELL HYBRIDIZATION.

synthesis see ANABOLISM.

synthetic lethal a lethal chromosome resulting from RECOMBINATION after CROSSING OVER from nonlethal chromosomes.

synthetic medium a microbial growth medium in which all components have been chemically identified and quantified.

synthetic theory the theory of evolution generally accepted by scientists at the present time, which has resulted from a synthesis of parts of previous theories. MUTATION and SELECTION are basic components.

syntype or **cotype** any specimen of a series, in which no HOLOTYPE was designated, that is used to designate a species. The syntype may become the LECTOTYPE, if so designated.

syphilis a human disease of the sexual organs caused by the spirochete bacterium *Treponema pallidum* that is spread usually by sexual contact. The organism penetrates mucous membranes, giving rise within a few days to primary ulceration of the membranes. This may give way to a secondary stage of low-grade fever and enlargement of the lymph nodes. A final, tertiary stage can take place in which serious lesions occur in many organs, and blindness is common. The bacterium can also be transmitted from an infected mother to her fetus, resulting in congenital syphilis, which may be fatal.

Systema Naturae see BINOMIAL NOMENCLATURE.

systemic distributed throughout an entire organism.

systemic arch the 4th aortic arch of a vertebrate through which blood flows from the ventral to the dorsal aorta. Birds have only a right arch, and mammals only a left arch.

systemic biocide or **biocide** a chemical such as some insecticides or fungicides that are applied to the soil or leaves, and not directly to the target organism. The biocide is absorbed by plant roots to be translocated around the plant, or absorbed from the leaves.

The biocide has its effect when the plant is attacked by a pest organism, such as an aphid, that sucks up sap containing the insecticide. Compare CONTACT INSECTICIDE.

systemic mutation a form of MUTATION postulated by R. Goldschmidt that fundamentally reorganizes the GERM PLASM THEORY. It is suggested that such mutation could cause the origin of completely new types of organisms.

systole see HEART CARDIAC CYCLE.

syzygy the aggregation in a mass of certain protozoans, especially when occurring before sexual reproduction.

T

table, water the level at which all fissures and pores are filled with water, roughly following the surface of the ground. Where the water table comes above ground, standing water, such as a lake, appears.

tachy- *combining form* denoting swift.

tachycardia an increase in heart rate above the normal rate.

tachymetabolism the pattern of thermal physiology in which an animal has a relatively high BASAL METABOLIC RATE and is able to respond to a fall in CORE TEMPERATURE with an increase in REGULATORY HEAT PRODUCTION to maintain homoiothermy. Most tachymetabolic species are both homoiothermic and endothermic. The only extant (living) forms with this physiology are the birds and mammals.

tactile pertaining to touch.

tactor see TANGORECEPTOR.

tadpole the larva of an AMPHIBIAN or of sea squirts (tadpole larva). See TUNICATE.

tagma one of the divisions—head, thorax, or abdomen—of the body of an ARTHROPOD.

taiga the zone of forest vegetation lying on wet soils between the tundra in the north and steppe hardwood forest in the south. Taiga encircles the northern hemisphere.

tail 1. the rearmost part of an animal. **2.** (in vertebrates) the part behind the anus.

tailor's posture a form of muscular hypertonicity commonly observed in PHENYLKETONURIA.

tandem duplication a CHROMOSOMAL MUTATION producing identical adjacent segments. For example, A *B C D* E becomes A *B C D B C D* E.

tangoreceptor or **tactor** a receptor sensitive to slight pressure differences.

tannin a complex organic compound occurring widely in plant sap—particularly in bark, leaves, and unripe fruit—and used in producing leather and ink.

T-antigen an antigen found in cells infected by the oncogenic virus. See ONCOGENE.

tapetum a nutritive layer surrounding cells that will become MICROSPORES. The tapetum is found in a wide range of vascular plants, from

FERNS to ANGIOSPERMS. In the latter, a tapetal layer is found in the pollen sacs of the ANTHER.

tapeworm any parasitic flatworm of the class Cestoidea (phylum *Platyhelminthes*). The adults attach themselves inside the gut system of vertebrates by means of hooks and suckers on the SCOLEX, and the long, ribbonlike body made up of a series of proglottides may reach a length in excess of 10 meters in some species. Eggs develop into six-hooked embryos and pass out with the FECES of the host. If eaten by a suitable secondary host, the embryos may develop into a larval stage called a CYSTICERCUS. When eaten by the primary host, and this may take place in some species only after transfer through an additional secondary host, the tapeworm becomes sexually mature.

taproot a primary ROOT structure in which one main root forms the major part of the underground system. Taproots are often swollen, serving as storage organs of perennation. Many vegetable crops have taproots, for example, carrot, rutabaga, and sugar beet.

Tardigrada in taxonomy, a name that has usually been used to denote the following two different animal taxons: 1. (formerly) sloths (now Bradypodidae), 2. a group of small, transparent eight-limbed ARTHROPODS often classified as ARACHNIDS.

target cell any cell that responds to specific hormones.

tarsal bone or **tarsus** the bone of the hind limb of TETRAPODS that articulates with the TIBIA and FIBULA proximally and with the METATARSALS distally. See PENTADACTYL LIMB.

tarsier any arboreal, lemurlike primate of the genus *Tarsius*, of Southeast Asia, having large eyes and ears.

tarsus see TARSAL BONE.

tartrazine an AZO DYE that produces a yellow color widely used as a food additive (E102).

taste bud a receptor organ of taste containing groups of slender modified epithelial cells with hairlike microvilli clustered in a small external pore. Taste buds are usually associated with the mouth of most vertebrates, but in fish they also occur over the body surface and on the fins and appear as well on the tarsi of some insects, for example, DIPTERANS.

Humans distinguish between sweet, salt, sour, and bitter tastes, using taste buds in different locations on the tongue: sweet on the front, sour on the sides, bitter on the back, and salt all over. Tastes depend on the relative activity of neurons that innervate the taste buds and not on any structural differences on the buds. See Fig. 284.

Tatum, Edward see BEADLE.

tautomeric shift see BASE ANALOG.

taxis a behavioral response in which an animal orients itself toward or

Fig. 284. **Taste bud.** Cross section of the human tongue.

away from a given stimulus, for example, GEOTAXIS, PHOTOTAXIS. Compare KINESIS.

taxon (*pl.* taxa) any grouping within the CLASSIFICATION of organisms, such as SPECIES, GENUS,and ORDER.

taxonomic category the ranking of an organism within a hierarchical CLASSIFICATION.

taxonomic character any characteristic used to separate members of different TAXA.

taxonomy the study of the CLASSIFICATION of organisms. Classical taxonomy involves the use of morphological features, cytotaxonomy involves the use of somatic chromosomes, experimental taxonomy involves the determining of genetic relationships, and numerical taxonomy involves quantitative assessments of similarities and differences in an attempt to make objective assessments.

Tay-Sachs disease a lethal human condition in which children who are apparently normal at birth show signs within 6 months of marked deterioration of brain and spinal cord. By the age of 1 year the child can only lie helpless, becoming mentally retarded, increasingly blind, and paralyzed. Death occurs between 3 and 4 years, with no known survivors and no cure. The condition is controlled by recessive alleles of a gene located on chromosome 15, double recessives producing a deficient amount of the enzyme hexosaminidase A, which leads to accumulation of complex fatty substances in the CENTRAL NERVOUS SYSTEM.

T$_2$ bacteriophage a particularly virulent BACTERIOPHAGE that infests *Escherichia coli* and was used by HERSHEY and Chase to demonstrate that the genetic material of phages is DNA.

T$_4$ and T$_6$ bacteriophage, fever phages of *E. coli.* See T$_2$ BACTERIOPHAGE.

TCA cycle (Tricarboxylic Acid Cycle) see KREBS CYCLE.

T-cell or **helper T-cell** a type of LYMPHOCYTE produced in bone marrow and differentiating in thymus tissue that counteracts the presence of foreign ANTIGENS by a process of cell-mediated immunity in which the antigen is slowly destroyed by the T-cell or by a toxin released from the T-cells. The priming of the T-cell to a specific antigen and the long-term growth of activated T-cells are thought to be influenced by INTERLEUKINS produced by MACROPHAGES.

tectorial membrane a membrane present in the COCHLEA of the inner ear that runs parallel with the BASILAR MEMBRANE. Between the tectorial and basilar membranes, sensory cells span the gap, and these cells are connected with nerve fibers that join the auditory nerve. The tectorial membrane forms part of the organ of Corti.

teleost any bony fish of the subclass Teleostei, containing all present-day bony fishes except lungfish, sturgeon, and garpike. Teleosts are characterized by presence of an AIR BLADDER.

telluric of, relating to, or originating on or in the earth or soil.

telocentric chromosome a chromosome in which the CENTROMERE is terminal at one end, so that there is effectively only one arm.

telolecithal (of eggs) having the yolk aggregated at the vegetative pole.

telomere the rounded tip of a chromosome.

telophase a stage of NUCLEAR DIVISION in EUKARYOTE cells, occurring once in MITOSIS and twice in MEIOSIS. During telophase, the two sets of chromosomes aggregate at the spindle poles, each set having the same number of chromosomes as the parental cell in mitosis, but half the parental complement in meiosis. See Fig. 285.

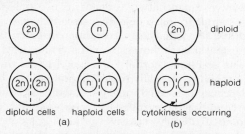

Fig. 285. **Telophase.** (a) Mitosis. (b) Meiosis.

The chromosomes uncoil, become extended, and cannot be identified individually. A NUCLEAR MEMBRANE forms around each set of chromosomes, and the NUCLEOLI are reformed. The process of cell division (CYTOKINESIS) is completed during this stage.

telson the terminal appendage of the last abdominal segment of some arthropods, such as the tail fan in many crustaceans or the sting in the scorpion.

temperate phage a BACTERIOPHAGE that may become a PROPHAGE by becoming integrated with the host DNA or by replicating outside the host chromosome and causing LYSIS. Compare VIRULENT PHAGE.

temperature the degree of hotness or coldness, usually related to a zero at the melting point of ice (Celsius scale) or absolute zero (Kelvin scale).

temperature coefficient see Q_{10}.

temperature regulation the maintenance of body temperature at a steady level. This occurs to some extent in all vertebrates and many invertebrates, but applies particularly to HOMOIOTHERMS. In humans, a constant body temperature of 36.9°C is maintained, and this is the optimum temperature for normal metabolic reactions involving enzymes.

Various mechanisms bring about temperature regulation. Hair and feathers of mammals and birds trap air that acts as insulation. Sweating acts as a cooling mechanism, and animals in cooler climates have a smaller surface area/volume ratio (see BERGMANN'S RULE). Subcutaneous fat also acts as an insulator. Superficial blood vessels constrict in response to cold and dilate in warm conditions, thus taking blood away from the skin surface when it is cold and to the skin surface when warm. The center for controlling body temperature lies in the HYPOTHALAMUS.

Plants also control their temperature and keep cool by transpiration, losing the latent heat of EVAPORATION. They wilt on loss of too much water, but this results in their leaves being moved (by drooping) from the direct rays of the sun. In effect, therefore, they remain cooled until sunset.

template the molecule that forms the mold for synthesis of another.

tendon a bunch of parallel COLLAGEN fibers making up a band of CONNECTIVE TISSUE that serves to attach a muscle to a bone.

tendril a modified plant structure used for attachment to a support. *Clematis* has tendrils that are modified PETIOLES (leaf stalks), and the vine uses a modified stem. In some species of pea, for example, *Lathyrus aphaca*, the entire leaf is specialized to form a tendril, with normal leaf functions performed by greatly enlarged STIPULES.

tensor tympanni the muscle connecting the MALLEUS to the wall of the tympanic chamber in the mammalian ear.

tentacle any long slender organ of touch or attachment.

tentaculocyst any of the numerous sensory tentacles surrounding the rim of coelenterate medusae. Tentaculocysts are associated with sense organs such as STATOCYSTS and light-sensitive pigment spots.

tepal a single member of the perianth of a flower, especially where sepal and petals are not clearly differentiated, as in the tulip.

terato- *combining form* denoting monster.

teratogenic producing malformation in a fetus.

teratology the study of abnormalities in structures, such as malformations.

terete (of plant structures) lacking ridges, grooves, or angles.

tergum the plate of thickened, often chitinous material on the dorsal side of an insect segment, forming part of the EXOSKELETON.

terminal (of plant structures) carried at the end of a stem.

terminalization the process of apparent movement of CHIASMATA to the ends of the chromosomes in late prophase of MEIOSIS.

termination codon see NONSENSE CODON.

termite see ISOPTERA.

terpene an unsaturated hydrocarbon of plant resins and oils.

terrestrial of the land as opposed to water or air.

territorial behavior see TERRITORY.

territory any area defended by an animal against members of the same species. During the breeding season, breeding territories may be defended, but territoriality may occur outside the breeding season, for example, in defending feeding territories. In breeding territories, the male usually defends the area against other males, and territoriality may last all or only a part of the breeding season. The term is not to be confused with HOME RANGE.

tertiary consumer see TOP CARNIVORE.

Tertiary period a period of the Cenozoic era lasting from 65 million years ago until the beginning of the Quaternary, 2 million years ago. This is the period of the emergence of mammals, following extinction of the DINOSAURS.

tertiary structure of protein see PROTEIN.

testa a protective coat around the seed, formed from the INTEGUMENTS of the OVULE. In one area on the testa is the hilum, at one end of which is often found the MICROPYLE. The testa sometimes is responsible for seed dormancy, a condition broken when the coat ruptures (see GERMINATION).

testcross a cross in which one partner is homozygous (see HOMOZYGOTE) for the recessive alleles of the genes being investigated. The testcross progeny will indicate the GENOTYPE of the unknown parent. See Fig. 286. Testcrosses are used extensively in experiments to establish GENETIC LINKAGE. See also BACKCROSS.

testis (*pl.* testes) the organ of the male animal, producing male gametes, or sperm. It also produces ANDROGENS—male sex hormones. See SCROTUM, SEMINIFEROUS TUBULES, GERMINAL EPITHELIUM, SERTOLI CELLS.

testosterone a steroid ANDROGEN produced by the LEYDIG CELLS, between the SEMINIFEROUS TUBULES of the TESTIS. It causes development

'X' x t/t | 'Y' x t/t

50% T, 50% t | 100% T
deduction: 'X' is T/t | deduction: 'Y' is T/T

Fig. 286. **Testcross.** A testcross to find the genotype of the unknown parent.

and maintenance of accessory sex organs, the genitalia, and the SECONDARY SEXUAL CHARACTERS.

tetanus 1. a sustained contraction of muscle due to fusion of many small contractions (twitches) that follow one another in rapid succession. **2.** a disease produced by toxins from the bacterium *Clostridium tetani*, which usually enters the body through a wound, producing spasm of the voluntary muscle, especially of the jaw (*lockjaw*). Bacterial tetanus can be treated by administering antitetanus serum containing ready-made ANTIBODIES or by administering antitetanus vaccine, which induces formation of antibodies in the recipient.

tetany an abnormal increase in nerve and muscle excitability resulting in spasms of the arms and legs, caused by a deficiency of PARATHYROID secretion.

tetra- *combining form* denoting four.

tetracycline an ANTIBIOTIC of the *broad spectrum* type, so-called because of its effect on a wide variety of bacterial types. Since tetracyclines can adversely affect host cells as well as bacteria, they are prescribed cautiously.

tetrad 1. the four homologous CHROMATIDS that associate during prophase (the PACHYTENE stage) and metaphase of MEIOSIS and are involved in CROSSING OVER. **2.** the four haploid cells produced by one complete meiotic division.

tetrad analysis a genetic analysis of events at MEIOSIS, as shown by the arrangement of cells in a TETRAD, the four products of a single meiotic cell. The technique usually involves determining the precise order of the eight ascospores within a fungal ASCUS. See FIRST-DIVISION SEGREGATION.

tetradynamous (of plant stamens) being six in number, two shorter than the other four.

tetraploid 1. having four times the HAPLOID (1) number of chromosomes in the nucleus. **2.** an individual with four sets of chromosomes per cell. See TRIPLOID.

tetrapod any vertebrate with two pairs of PENTADACTYL LIMBS.

tetrapterous having four wings.

tetraspore the product of MEIOSIS in many red and brown algae, being produced in fours in testrasporangia and forming the first cells of the GAMETOPHYTE generation.

thalamus the major sensory coordinating part of the vertebrate forebrain.

thalassemia or **Cooley's anemia** a type of human anemia in which there is a deficiency of either alpha or beta HEMOGLOBIN chains. Various causes have been found for the condition, including a recessive mutant allele for beta chain deficiency that is present in high frequencies in certain areas of the Mediterranean that are often associated with high incidence of mosquito activity. Named for the American pediatrician Thomas B. Cooley (1871—1945).

thallophyte any plant of the group (or former division) Thallophyta, containing the most primitive types of plants characterized by the possession of a THALLUS. They vary in size from unicellular types to giant seaweeds up to 75 meters long. The group includes Algae, Bacteria, Fungi, slime fungi (Myxomycetes), and lichens. Thallophyta clearly have several different evolutionary origins, and the term is not used in modern systematics.

thallus the vegetative part of simple plants, ranging from unicellular structures to large seaweeds. It shows no differentiation into root, stem, and leaves. See THALLOPHYTE.

theca 1. a sheath or case. 2. the protective sheath surrounding the GRAAFIAN FOLLICLE. 3. an obsolete term for ASCUS.

thecadont having teeth in sockets as in mammals and some reptiles.

thelytoky a form of PARTHENOGENESIS in which females give rise to more females without fertilization.

therapsid any extinct reptile of the order Therapsida, from which mammals are thought to have evolved.

thermocline a boundary layer, found in lakes or enclosed seas, between warm upper water and cooler lower water, which is usually maintained only under calm conditions in summer.

thermodynamics the science concerned with the relationships between heat and mechanical work. The laws of thermodynamics are:

(1st) When one form of energy is converted to another, there is no loss or gain.

(2nd) When one form of energy is converted to another, a proportion is turned into heat.

thermonasty a response of plants to a general temperature stimulus. See NASTIC MOVEMENT.

thermoneutral zone the range of environmental temperature across which a tachymetabolic organism (see TACHYMETABOLISM) is able to regulate CORE TEMPERATURE solely by modulating its thermal conductance. Within the thermoneutral zone, the STANDARD METABOLIC RATE (SMR) of an animal is at a constant minimum level, the basal metabolic rate (BMR).

thermophilic of or relating to heat-preferring fungi or other microorganisms whose optimum temperature for growth is above 45°C.

thermoreceptor a sensory nerve ending that is responsive to temperature change.

thermoregulation the control of body heat in HOMOIOTHERMS.

therophyte an herb that survives the winter, or other unfavorable conditions, as seeds—one of RAUNKIAER'S LIFE FORMS.

thiamine or **vitamin B₁** a water-soluble organic compound found in cereals (for example, rice) and yeast, whose main function is to act as a COENZYME in sugar breakdown by forming part of the NAD molecule. Thiamine is part of the B-COMPLEX of VITAMINS, and deficiency results in the disease BERIBERI.

thigmotropism or **haptotropism** or **stereotropism** a form of plant growth (TROPISM) in which the plant responds to contact. The response is usually positive—there is movement toward the contacted surface—and is best seen in climbing plants that use tendrils.

thoracic cavity the space within the THORAX.

thoracic duct the main collecting duct of the LYMPHATIC SYSTEM of mammals that leads into the left anterior vena cava.

thoracic gland see PROTHACIC GLAND.

thorax 1. (in vertebrates) the part of the body that contains the lungs and heart, and in mammals is divided from the abdomen by the DIAPHRAGM. 2. (in ARTHROPODS) the part of the body directly behind the head and in front of the abdomen. 3. (in insects) three segments bearing the legs and wings.

thorn a sharply pointed woody plant structure formed from a modified branch.

thread cell see CNIDOBLAST.

threat display a type of animal behavior in which aggressive postures are adopted or intimidating markings are revealed. Such displays are common in fish and birds involved in defense of TERRITORY and often result in the retreat of the threatened animals, thus avoiding direct conflict. See PECKING ORDER.

threonine one of 20 AMINO ACIDS common in proteins. It has a polar R group structure and is soluble in water. See Fig. 287. The ISOELECTRIC POINT of threonine is 5.6.

threshold the level at which a STIMULUS results in a response and below which there is no response despite application of a stimulus.

THROMBIN

Fig. 287. **Threonine.** Molecular structure.

thrombin see BLOOD CLOTTING.

thrombocyte see BLOOD PLATELETS.

thromboplastin see BLOOD CLOTTING.

thrombosis the formation of a clot of blood in a blood vessel.

thrush 1. an acute or chronic condition produced by the fungus *Candida albicans* in which lesions occur in the mucous membranes of mouth, vagina, and respiratory tissues. Thrush can occur also in skin areas that are subjected to long periods of immersion in water. **2.** a member of the PASSERINE genus *Turdus*.

thylakoid see LAMELLA.

thymine one of four types of nitrogenous bases found in DNA having the single-ring structure of a class known as PYRIMIDINES. Thymine forms part of a DNA unit called a NUCLEOTIDE and always forms complementary pairs with a DNA purine base called ADENINE. See Fig. 288. Thymine is replaced by URACIL in RNA molecules.

Fig. 288. **Thymine.** Molecular structure.

thymonucleic acid a NUCLEIC ACID that was first extracted from the THYMUS gland.

thymus an endocrine gland situated in the neck region of most vertebrates, but close to the heart in mammals. It produces LYMPHOCYTES, which then move to lymph nodes. The thymus produces a hormone called *thymosin*, which causes the lymphocytes to form antibody-producing plasma cells immediately after birth, but regresses in adult animals.

thyroglobulin a protein containing and storing THYROXINE and triiodothyroxine in the THYROID GLAND.

thyroid gland an endocrine organ situated in the region of the neck that produces THYROXINE a hormone containing iodine obtained from the diet. Thyroxine controls BASAL METABOLIC RATE (BMR) and also controls metamorphosis in amphibians.

Undersecretion during development causes *hypothyroidism*, reduced physical and mental development leading to CRETINISM in subadults. In the adult stage MYXEDEMA results and gives rise to general slowness of thought and action, coarse skin, and fatness. Overproduction (*hyperthyroidism*) causes *exophthalmic goiter,* in which the thyroid and thus the neck swells and the eyeballs protrude. Those so affected become restless and overactive, lose weight, and have an accelerated heart rate. Deficiency or excess of iodine in the diet causes malfunction of the thyroid gland. A deficiency was found to occur naturally many years ago in parts of Michigan.

thyrotrophic hormone or **thyroid stimulating hormone (TSH)** a hormone secreted by the anterior lobe of the PITUITARY GLAND that triggers the shedding of THYROXINE from the colloidal follicles of the THYROID GLAND into the bloodstream. Excess thyroxine inhibits production of TSH—an example of a negative FEEDBACK MECHANISM.

thyrotrophic releasing hormone a hormone secreted by the neurosecretory cells of the HYPOTHALAMUS that releases THYROTROPHIC HORMONE from the anterior lobe of the PITUITARY GLAND.

thyroxine a complex organic compound containing iodine, the main hormone produced by the THYROID GLAND.

Thysanoptera the insect order containing the thrips, major pests of cereals and fruits.

Thysanura the insect order containing the bristletails, primarily wingless insects inhabiting soil and leaf mold.

tibia the anterior of the two long bones articulating in the hind limb, proximally with the femur and distally with the tarsal bones. (See PENTADACTYL LIMB.) In humans, the tibia is the shinbone. In insects, it is the fourth segment from the base of the leg.

tibial of or in the region of the TIBIA.

ticks arthropods of two families of the ACARINA which are mainly ectoparasitic blood suckers, having an anticoagulant in the saliva and playing an important role in carrying disease.

tidal volume the amount of air taken into the lungs by an animal breathing normally, at rest, during each respiratory cycle (each breath). In humans this is about 0.5 dm^3 (500 cm^3).

tiller a branch that forms from the base of a plant or the axils of the lower leaves. Such tillering is common in cereal plants.

Tinbergen, Nikolaas (1907—) British zoologist, born in the Nether-

lands, who made animal behavior his specialty and, with Konrad LOR-
ENZ, is considered a cofounder of the science of ETHOLOGY.

tissue any large group of cells of similar structure in animals or plants
that performs a specific function, such as MUSCLE, PHLOEM.

tissue compatibility see IMMUNE RESPONSE.

tissue culture a technique in which individual cells grow and divide in
a bath of sterile, nutritive fluid. The method is used extensively in biological laboratories, for example, in cancer research (see HELA CELLS), plant
breeding, and routine analysis of chromosome KARYOTYPES. See AMNI-
OCENTESIS.

tissue fluid the intercellular fluid forming the internal environment
immediately surrounding cells. It is formed from blood by a process of
ULTRAFILTRATION.

tissue respiration see AEROBIC RESPIRATION, ANAEROBIC RESPIRA-
TION.

titer the concentration of a substance in a solution, for example, the
amount of specific antibody in a serum. The concentration is usually
expressed as the reciprocal dilution. For example, when 1:200 gives a
positive test and greater dilutions are negative, the titer is 200.

toadstool the common name for the fruiting bodies of Basidiomycete
fungi.

tobacco mosaic virus a rod-shaped viral particle consisting of an RNA
helix surrounded by a protein coat. The virus, the first to be purified and
crystallized, causes yellowing and mottling in the leaves of tobacco and
other crops, for example, tomato, which adversely affects the quality and
quantity of crop produced.

tocopherol see VITAMIN E.

tolerance 1. the ability of an organism to withstand harsh environmental
pressures, such as drought or extreme temperatures. **2.** the ability of an
organism to withstand the buildup of adverse factors, such as pesticides
or endoparasites within itself, without showing serious symptoms of
attack.

tomentum the dense covering of short cottony hairs on some plant
structures.

tongue a muscular organ on the floor of the mouth in most higher
vertebrates that carries taste buds and manipulates food. It may act as
a tactile or prehensile organ in some species.

tonoplast the CELL MEMBRANE surrounding the vacuole in the cytoplasm of a plant cell, controlling movements of ions into and out of the
vacuole. See SELECTIVE PERMEABILITY.

tonsil one of two large outgrowths at the back of the human oral cavity that have a lymphatic function. The tissue can become infected, resulting in considerable soreness and general ill health. The removal of children's tonsils by surgery (tonsillectomy) used to be common, but is not popular at present.

tonus the state of moderate contraction of muscle as a result of continuous low-level stimulation that maintains the posture of an animal. Tonus occurs because some cells in every muscle are in TETANUS (1) and the muscles feel firm. The condition continues without fatigue because some cells are relaxed while others are contracted.

tooth 1. one of a series of structures found in the mouth of vertebrates and associated with biting, tearing, and crushing food. Each tooth is a hard structure consisting of a very hard external enamel layer of minerals bound by KERATIN. Underneath this is dentine, which has a structure similar to that of bone but is harder, again due to mineral content. The dentine is perforated by fine channels containing processes of the odontoblasts (tooth cells). Centrally, the pulp cavity contains blood capillaries and nerve endings. The root is covered by cement and embedded in the jaw bone. See Fig. 289. See INCISORS, CANINES, PREMOLARS, and MOLARS. **2.** any structure with the general appearance of a tooth, such as a dogfish tooth (denticle), which is a modified scale.

Fig. 289. **Tooth.** Vertical section of a human molar.

tooth bud the germinal material from which teeth develop.

top carnivore or **tertiary consumer** an organism found at the top of the PYRAMID OF NUMBERS that preys on other organisms but is not itself preyed on.

topogenous (of peat bogs) dependent on landscape (topography) for its origins.

topotype any specimen of the same species collected in the type locality of that species.

topsoil the surface layer of soil to plow depth.

tormogen a cell in insects that secretes the socket for a bristle.

tornaria larva a HEMICHORDATE free-swimming larva having two bands of cilia.

torpor a state of inactivity into which some HOMOIOTHERMS enter in order to conserve energy. There is usually a reduction in temperature and general body metabolism.

torsion a phenomenon occurring in embryonic gastropods in which the visceral hump rotates through 180°.

torus 1. a central thickened area in the BORDERED PITS of GYMNOSPERMS. 2. see RECEPTACLE.

totipotency the ability of a cell or tissue to give rise to adult structures. The capacity is often lost in adult cells, particularly in animals. Having differentiated into one specific type, adult cells cannot change to another type of cell. See GURDON, CELL DIFFERENTIATION.

toxin a nonenzymic metabolite of one organism that is injurious to another organism. See TETANUS, BOTULISM.

toxoid a substance produced from a toxin but in which toxicity is destroyed while retaining the property of inducing immunity to the toxin.

trabeculae 1. a pair of cartilage bars in the vertebrate embryo that form the front part of the floor of the cranium, 2. the rod-shaped supporting structures of various plant organs.

trace element any element necessary in minute quantities for proper working of biological systems. Absence can cause disease and death. For example, boron deficiency causes heart rot in sugar beets, and cobalt deficiency causes coast disease in Australian sheep and cattle. See THYROID GLAND for iodine deficiency. See also ESSENTIAL ELEMENTS.

tracer any rare ISOTOPE, for example, radioactive forms such as ^{14}C, which is administered in some way to organisms so that its fate may be followed subsequently within the organism or in the products of its METABOLISM.

trachea 1. (in vertebrates) also called *windpipe,* the main tube leading from the glottis in the neck to the point at which the bronchia branch to the lungs. 2. (in insects) a series of TRACHEOLES by which air is conducted into the body from external openings called spiracles. See also TRACHEAL GILL. 3. (in plants) see XYLEM VESSEL.

tracheal gill the TRACHEA (2) of aquatic insects formed by slender outgrowths of the body into which TRACHEOLES project.

tracheid any of several structures found in XYLEM consisting of a cell that is long, slender, and tapered, with heavily lignified walls surrounding an empty lumen, the protoplasm having died.

The wall thickening can be continuous with BORDERED PITS, or else arranged in a variety of patterns—annular, helical, and ladderlike. See

Fig. 290. Tracheids form the water-conducting tissues of GYMNOS-PERMS, but are found also among the xylem vessels of ANGIOSPERMS.

tracheid cell

lignified ring of thickening

Fig. 290. **Tracheid.** General structure.

tracheole the small branching tubes from the TRACHEAE (2) of insects.

tracheophyte any plant of the division Tracheophyta, comprising all forms of vascular plants, PTERIDOPHYTES and SPERMATOPHYTES. The division includes the subdivisions PSILOPSIDA, LYCOPSIDA, SPHENOP-SIDA. and PTEROPSIDA.

Trachylina an order of hydrozoan COELENTERATES in which the hydroid stage is suppressed.

trachymedusa a medusa of the hydrozoan COELENTERATE order Trachylina.

tract a bundle of nerve fibers that may run within the CENTRAL NERVOUS SYSTEM or to the peripheral nervous system.

trans- *prefix* denoting across, beyond, or through.

transaminase an enzyme that transfers amino (NH_2) groups. See TRANSAMINATION.

transamination the process by which amino groups are transferred from one AMINO ACID to form another, using a keto acid as an intermediary. The mechanism takes place in the liver and is important in the breakdown of excess amino acids to form keto acids, and in the formation of new amino acids (perhaps not available in the diet) from keto acids. An example is shown in Fig. 291. ESSENTIAL AMINO ACIDS cannot be produced by transamination.

transcription the formation of RNA from a DNA template during PROTEIN SYNTHESIS. The process can be broken down into a number of steps (see Fig. 292):

(a) The DNA double helix unwinds.

(b) Only one DNA POLYNUCLEOTIDE CHAIN serves as a template (the *sense strand*) in any one region, although both chains will act as templates in different locations.

(c) The enzyme RNA polymerase catalyzes synthesis of an RNA molecule from RNA nucleotides with bases complementary to the DNA base sequence, starting at the promoter region of DNA. Growth of the RNA chain is in the 5′ to 3′ direction only, just as in DNA synthesis.

TRANSDUCTION

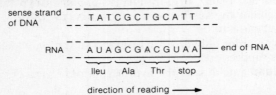

Fig. 291. Transamination. The transfer of an amino group to form a different amino acid.

sense strand of DNA — — — — T A T C G C T G C A T T — — —

RNA — — A U A G C G A C G U A A — end of RNA

Ileu   Ala   Thr   stop

direction of reading ⟶

Fig. 292. Transcription. Uracil replaces thymine in the RNA stage. See GENETIC CODE for details of triplets.

(d) Transcription carries on until a DNA stop signal is reached (see GENETIC CODE).

(e) The new RNA molecule leaves the DNA and moves to the cytoplasm, where it will function as TRANSFER RNA, MESSENGER RNA, or RIBOSOMAL RNA.

(f) The DNA molecule rezips.

transduction the transport of DNA from one bacterium to another, using a VIRUS as a vector.

transect a line across a habitat or habitats along which organisms are sampled in order to study changes that may occur along that line. Transects are most frequently used in studying changes in vegetation, often a particular species, across a physically changing habitat, such as a bog or sand dunes.

transferase any enzyme that catalyzes transfer of a chemical group, such as amino, methyl, or alkyl, from one SUBSTRATE to another substrate.

transfer RNA (tRNA) a form of RNA molecule with about 80 NUCLEOTIDES and a cloverleaf shape whose function is to carry specific AMINO ACIDS to the ribosomes during TRANSLATION. At one end (3′ end) there is attachment of the amino acid producing AMINOACYL-TRNA, with an unpaired region about half way along, called the *anticodon*, in which three bases are complementary to the codon on MESSENGER RNA. See Fig. 293.

Fig. 293. **Transfer RNA.**

transformation the incorporation of a piece of foreign DNA into the GENOME of a bacterial cell. The process is important historically since, following transformation experiments on the *Pneumococcus* bacterium by Frederick GRIFFITH, DNA was shown to be the genetic material of cells by AVERY, MacLeod, and McCarthy.

transfusion tissue tissue lying on either side of the vascular bundles in leaves of GYMNOSPERMS, which probably represents an extension of the vascular system. It is composed of empty parenchymatous cells with pitted and thickened walls.

transient polymorphism a temporary form of GENETIC POLYMORPHISM existing at a time when an ALLELE is being replaced by a superior one.

transition substitution mutation see SUBSTITUTION MUTATION.

translation the formation of a POLYPEPTIDE CHAIN in a RIBOSOME during PROTEIN SYNTHESIS, using a sequence that is contained in MESSENGER RNA.

The process can be broken down into a number of steps:

(a) The mRNA produced from the DNA during TRANSCRIPTION becomes attached to one or more ribosomes (see POLYRIBOSOME).

(b) The RNA passes through the ribosome, beginning with a start signal at the 5' end of RNA and ending with a stop signal at the 3' end (see POLYNUCLEOTIDE CHAIN).

(c) Surrounding the ribosomes are various TRANSFER RNA molecules, each attached to its specific AMINO ACID. As a triplet of RNA bases moves through the ribosome, it is read by the correct tRNA molecule, which leaves behind the correct amino acids.

TRANSLOCATION

(d) The amino acids become joined by PEPTIDE BONDS, forming a polypeptide chain. See Fig. 294.

Fig. 294. **Translation.** A polypeptide chain, formed by amino acids joined by peptide bonds.

See GENETIC CODE for details of polypeptide sequence.

translocation 1. the transport of organic substances in the PHLOEM of higher plants, the mechanism for which is not fully understood. A popular theory accounts for the movement by MASS FLOW, but there is evidence of active uptake of solutes into the sieve tubes of phloem involving use of ATP. There may also be movement of solutes along the protein filaments that stretch from one sieve element to the next via the sieve plates, using a form of CYTOPLASMIC STREAMING. 2. a type of CHROMOSOMAL MUTATION in which non-HOMOLOGOUS CHROMOSOMES break and exchange pieces. During the process, pieces of chromosomes can be lost or gained, causing serious problems, particularly with gamete viability. See TRANSLOCATION HETEROZYGOTE.

translocation heterozygote an individual carrying cells with one normal set of chromosomes and one set in which a reciprocal TRANSLOCATION has occurred between two non-HOMOLOGOUS CHROMOSOMES. See Fig. 295. Such an event causes pairing problems in prophase I of MEIOSIS when the chromatids undergo SYNAPSIS (2). These problems are solved by producing a cruciform configuration in which all chromosomal segments are correctly paired.

When the chromatids separate, they can do so either in adjacent or alternate disjunction. See Fig. 296. *Adjacent disjunction* produces gametes that have duplicated and deficient chromosomal segments, and therefore produces gametes that can cause death in the offspring. *Alternate disjunction,* produced by a twisting of the cross, results in a mixture of completely normal gametes and gametes containing a balanced trans-

Fig. 295. **Translocation heterozygote.** (a) Normal cell. (b) Reciprocal translocation heterozygote.

location. These types are both viable, and the progeny will all survive. The overall result of a translocation heterozygote is that about half of the progeny survive, a fact that has been used in experiments to control insect populations.

Fig. 296. **Translocation heterozygote.** Adjacent and alternate disjunction.

transmitter substance or **neurotransmitter** any chemical substance that is present in SYNAPSES and passes across the synaptic cleft, from the presynaptic membrane to the postsynaptic membrane it depolarizes, thus propagating the impulse in the postsynaptic axon. See ACETYLCHOLINE, ADRENERGIC, CHOLINERGIC.

transovarial passing infection from one generation to another through the egg.

transpiration the loss of water vapor from the inside of a leaf to the outside atmosphere, via STOMATA and LENTICELS. Transpiration exerts considerable upward pressure in the stem and is thought to be part of the explanation of how water ascends from roots to leaves.

TRANSPIRATION STREAM

The rate at which transpiration proceeds depends on several physical factors:

(a) Water vapor pressure at the MESOPHYLL cell surface inside the leaf. The evaporation surface is saturated and will have a VAPOR PRESSURE (WVP_{satn}) that is strongly affected by ambient temperature. For example, at 20°C the $WVP_{satn} = 2.5$ kPa, at 10°C the $WVP_{satn} = 2.5$ kPa.

(b) Water vapor pressure in the outside air (WVP_{air}), the maximum value being equal to WVP_{satn} at that temperature. If there is the same temperature inside and outside the leaf, the rate of flow of water vapor between the surface of the mesophyll cell and the outside is the difference between WVP_{satn} and WVP_{air}; that is:

$$WVP_{diff} = WVP_{satn} - WVP_{air}$$

Thus, the greater the WVP_{diff} value, the greater the diffusion gradient and the higher the transpiration rate.

(c) Size and number of stomatal pores per unit area of a leaf. The smaller the pore diameter, the greater the resistance to water vapor diffusion. The presence of vapor shells over each stoma creates a boundary layer of high water vapor pressure in still air, which will slow down transpiration since it increases the WVP_{air} value. This effect is most important when the pore diameter is large. In moving air, the vapor shells cannot form, so transpiration rates increase.

(d) Stomatal and leaf structure, which are modified in some XEROPHYTES to reduce transpiration rates.

(e) A constant supply of water from the roots.

transpiration stream the flow of water through a living plant as a result of water loss due to TRANSPIRATION through the leaves.

transplantation the transference of an organ or tissue from a donor to a recipient in need of a healthy organ or tissue. In recent years, kidney, lung, heart, and liver transplants have taken place. For successful transplantation to occur, similar tissue types must be involved (see HLA SYSTEM) and genetical similarity is one of the best ways of ensuring this.

Drugs that inhibit normal IMMUNE RESPONSES are used, but these also inhibit the body's defense against microorganisms. Rejection of foreign tissue is part of the normal response of the body, and the development of drugs that will prevent rejection but not affect the normal response to microorganisms is actively being pursued.

transport the movement of materials through a system, as in an ELECTRON TRANSPORT SYSTEM.

transposable genetic element or **mobile genetic element** any genetic unit that can be inserted into a chromosome but has the ability to become relocated.

In recent years phage, DNA, PLASMIDS, and certain regions of bacterial chromosomes have been shown to be transposable, but the phenomenon was first reported in the 1950s by Barbara McClintock, an American who was working on corn. She received a Nobel Prize in 1983 for her discoveries in this area. A transposable element in a bacterium carrying bacterial genes is called a *transposon*.

transposon see TRANSPOSABLE GENETIC ELEMENT.

transudate any substance that passes through a membrane, especially through the wall of a capillary.

transude to ooze or pass through interstices, pores, or small holes.

transverse process lateral projections from each node of the neural arch of tetrapod vertebrates to which ribs are attached.

transversion substitution mutation see SUBSTITUTION MUTATION.

trematode any parasitic flatworm of the class Trematoda, including the FLUKES.

Triassic period the first period of the MESOZOIC ERA immediately following the PERMIAN PERIOD. It lasted from some 230 million to 200 million years BP and was the age of reptiles in which the DINOSAURS emerged. Horsetails, cycads, *Ginkgo*, and conifers were common. Ammonites reached their peak, and the first primitive mammals and flies appeared.

tribe a taxonomic category between genus and subfamily, used mainly in the CLASSIFICATION of plants.

tricarboxylic acid cycle see KREBS CYCLE.

tricho- *combining form* denoting hair.

trichocyst a threadlike structure of uncertain function found in some PROTOZOANS, which is ejected from a pit on stimulation.

trichogyne a projection from the female sex organ of some ASCOMYCETES, red algae, and lichens that receives the male gamete before fertilization.

trichome an epidermal outgrowth on a plant, forming a hair or spine. For example, the hairs growing out from the epidermis of cotton plant seeds are unicellular trichomes with thick CELLULOSE walls.

Trichomonas a genus of parasitic protozoan occurring in the digestive and reproductive systems of humans and many other animals.

Trichonympha a flagellate PROTOZOAN capable of producing CELLULASE, a very rare enzyme in animals. It lives in the gut of termites, enabling them to digest wood.

Trichoptera the insect order containing the caddis flies. The larvae are aquatic, and the adults have reduced mouthparts and only feed rarely.

trichotomous (of a plant) branching into three divisions or shoots.

trichromatic theory the theory that all colors can be produced by mixing blue, green, and red. See COLOR VISION.

tricuspid a tooth having three cusps.

triecious see TRIOECIOUS.

trifid split into three.

trigeminal nerve the fifth cranial nerve of vertebrates, usually possessing ophthalmic, mandibular, and maxillary branches.

triglyceride see FAT.

trigonous having three prominent angles, for example, a plant stem or ovary.

trihydroxybenzene see PYROGALLOL.

triiodothyronine a minor hormone of the thyroid gland that has the same function as THYROXINE although it is present in smaller amounts. Formula: $C_{15}H_{12}I_3NO_4$.

trilobite a fossil arthropod of the class Trilobita from the CAMBRIAN and SILURIAN PERIODS.

trimethylamine oxide the compound found in marine TELEOST fish that is the end product of nitrogen metabolism. The compound has evolved because it requires relatively little water for its elimination as compared with ammonia, which is the nitrogenous end product in freshwater fish.

trimorphism the property exhibited by certain species of having or occurring in three distinct forms.

trinomial nomenclature the addition of a subspecific or trivial name to BINOMIAL NOMENCLATURE.

trioecious or **triecious** (of a plant species) having male, female, and hermaphrodite flowers occurring on three different plants. Compare MONOECIOUS, DIOECIOUS.

triose a monosaccharide that has three carbon atoms.

triose phosphate see PGAL.

triplet codon see CODON.

triploblastic having three primary embryonic cell layers: ECTODERM, MESODERM, and ENDODERM. All animals except PROTOZOANS, SPONGES, and COELENTERATES are triploblastic.

triploid 1. having three times the HAPLOID (1) number of chromosomes. **2.** an individual of this type. See TETRAPLOID.

trisaccharide an OLIGOSACCHARIDE whose molecules have three linked MONOSACCHARIDE molecules.

trisected cut into three nearly separate parts.

trisomy a state in which a DIPLOID (2) organism has three chromosomes of one type in a cell or in all cells. For example, DOWN SYNDROME individuals are trisomic for chromosome number 21, but have two of every other type of chromosome. See also EDWARDS' SYNDROME, PATAU SYNDROME.

tritium a radioactive isotope of hydrogen with an atomic mass of three (H^3).

trivial name the specific or subspecific name in CLASSIFICATION.

tRNA see TRANSFER RNA.

trochanter 1. (in insects) the second segment from the base of the leg. 2. (in vertebrates) one of several large processes near the head of the femur, to which muscles are attached.

trochlear nerve the fourth cranial nerve on vertebrates, which innervates the superior oblique muscles of the eye.

trochophore or **trochosphere** the characteristic larva of polychaete worms, mollusks, and some other invertebrates. It is more or less spherical, with a pre-oral ring of cilia called the *prototroch*.

trochosphere see TROCHOPHORE.

trophallaxis the exchange of regurgitated food that occurs between adults and larvae in colonies of social insects.

trophic of or relating to nutrition. See FOOD CHAIN, TROPHIC LEVEL.

trophic level any of the feeding levels that energy passes through as it proceeds through the ecosystem. For example, primary producers (see PRIMARY PRODUCTION) form the first level in most ecosystems, followed by PRIMARY CONSUMERS (herbivores), and up to the top predator level. See PYRAMID OF NUMBERS, BIOMASS.

trophic substance a hypothetical substance thought to be released from the terminals of neurons and to influence the postsynaptic cell.

trophoblast the outermost layer of cells surrounding the BLASTOCYST, consisting of embryonic epithelium, which subsequently encloses all embryonic structures of the developing mammal and forms the outer layer of the CHORION and the embryonic side of the placenta.

trophozoite the form of a protozoan of the class Sporozoa in the feeding stage, containing SPOROZOITES. In the MALARIA PARASITE this stage occurs in the human red blood cell.

tropic see TROPISM.

tropism a bending growth movement in a plant either away from or toward a directional stimulus. Tropic movements are brought about by unequal growth on the two sides of an organ, such as the stem, resulting from unequal distributions of AUXIN. See PHOTOTROPISM, GEOTROPISM, THIGMOTROPISM.

tropo- *combining form* denoting change, reaction, or turn.

tropomyosin a long protein molecule found in the grooves of muscle ACTIN filaments. It inhibits muscle contraction by blocking interaction between the filaments and MYOSIN.

troponin a complex of calcium-binding proteins that allows TROPOMYOSIN to move out of the myosin-blocking situation on muscle actin filaments.

tropophyte a plant unable to adapt to seasonal changes in temperature, rainfall, or the like.

tropotaxis the movement or orientation of an organism in relation to a source of stimulation, especially light.

true breeding line see PURE BREEDING LINE.

truffle any of various edible saprophytic ascomycete subterranean fungi of the order Tuberales.

truncate (of plant structures) terminating abruptly.

trunk 1. the main stem of a tree. 2. the torso, that is, the body excluding the head, neck, and limbs. 3. the thorax of an insect. 4. the elongated prehensile proboscis of an elephant. 5. the main stem of a nerve, blood vessel, and the like.

trypanosome any parasitic protozoan of the genus *Trypanosoma*, which is parasitic in the gut of tsetse flies and in the blood of vertebrates. Trypanosomes cause important diseases in horses and cattle, as well as AFRICAN SLEEPING SICKNESS in humans.

trypsin an enzyme secreted as part of the PANCREATIC JUICE, which breaks PROTEIN down into POLYPEPTIDES. It is secreted as an inactive precursor *trypsinogen*, which is converted to trypsin by ENTEROKINASE secreted in the SMALL INTESTINE.

trypsinogen see TRYPSIN.

tryptophan one of 20 AMINO ACIDS common in protein. It has a nonpolar R group structure and is relatively insoluble in water. See Fig. 297. The ISOELECTRIC POINT of tryptophan is 5.9.

tsetse fly any of various bloodsucking DIPTERANS of the genus *Glossina* that transmit AFRICAN SLEEPING SICKNESS. See TRYPANSOME.

TSH see THYROTROPIC HORMONE.

t-test (statistics) a test of SIGNIFICANCE that enables the means of two small samples—less than 30—to be compared, in order to judge whether they came from the same population or from populations with different means.

tube feet the locomotory organs of ECHINODERMS, which are protruded from the body by, and are retracted by, fluid pressure from the water vascular system.

Fig. 297. **Tryptophan.** Molecular structure.

tube nucleus one of two haploid nuclei within a developing POLLEN
TUBE, whose function may be control of tube growth.

tuber an enlarged underground root or stem containing PARENCHYMA
cells packed with STARCH for overwintering. An example is the stem
tuber of potato, which has buds in the axils of tiny leaves, forming the
potato eyes. Root tubers often have a fingerlike branched structure, as
in the lesser celandine, *Ranunculus ficaria*, an Old World plant.

tubercle a spherical or ovoid swelling.

tuberculate (of plant parts) warty, having small blunt projections.

tuberculosis a contagious human disease affecting particularly the
lungs, which is caused by the bacterium *Mycobacterium tuberculosis*.
Response to infection is varied among individuals, some showing no
signs while a few will die of the effects. These variations in host resistance are under genetic control. Tuberculosis is endemic in many parts
of the world but, since the introduction of drugs and immunization with
vaccines, the world death rate has declined dramatically. A typical Western country mortality rate in 1900 was 190 per 100,000. This has now
dropped to about 10 per 100,000.

tubule any small tubular structure.

tubuliflorous (of plants) having flowers or florets with tubular corollas.

tubulin a globular protein molecule, similar to ACTIN, that is the building
block of microtubules within the cytoplasm of cells.

Tullgren funnel a piece of apparatus for extracting animals from soil or
litter. The soil litter is supported on gauze, heated from above by a light
bulb, and organisms are collected in a container as they fall through the
funnel in moving down the heat/desiccation gradient.

tumor a swelling, usually a morbid growth.

tundra a type of vegetation found in arctic and antarctic zones, consisting
of lichens, grasses, sedges, and dwarf woody plants.

tunic the thin dry, papery covering of a BULB or CORM.

tunica any layer of tissue or membrane that encloses a structure or organ in either an animal or plant.

tunicate or **urochordate** any minute marine chordate of the subphylum Tunicata, containing the sea squirts. They feed by ciliary action and lack a NOTOCHORD, although one is present in the tail of the tadpole larva.

turbellarian any aquatic free-swimming PLATYHELMINTH of the class Turbellaria, the body of which is covered with cilia.

turbinate (of plant parts) shaped like an inverted cone.

turgor the state of a cell that has taken in a maximum amount of water, causing distention of the protoplast. The term is used mainly in connection with plant cells, which have a maximum size when turgid that is governed by how much the cellulose cell wall will stretch. See WALL PRESSURE, PRESSURE POTENTIAL, TRANSPIRATION.

turgor pressure see PRESSURE POTENTIAL.

turion a swollen bud of many water plants that contains stored food. It becomes detached from the parent plant, enabling it to survive the winter.

Turner's syndrome a human chromosomal abnormality in which the individual has 45 chromosomes, 44 AUTOSOMES, and one X CHROMOSOME.

The main features of the syndrome are (a) a female phenotype but with few or no SECONDARY SEXUAL CHARACTERS (b) a broad shieldlike chest, and (c) slight mental retardation. The condition is important in understanding SEX DETERMINATION in humans, since the fact that a single X chromosome produces a female rather than a male suggests that normal maleness (with XY) is not due to the possession of a single X but rather to the presence of a Y chromosome. See also KLINEFELTER'S SYNDROME.

turnover rate an assessment of the ability of an enzyme to catalyze a reaction, as measured by the number of molecules of substrate that react per second at one ACTIVE SITE when the enzyme is saturated with substrate. The turnover rate varies widely between different enzymes. The fastest known enzyme is CATALASE with a rate of 10 million molecules of hydrogen peroxide reacting per second at a single active site.

twins two offspring born at the same time of the same mother. See DIZYGOTIC TWINS, MONOZYGOTIC TWINS.

tylose or **tylosis** an outgrowth from xylem parenchyma in the XYLEM VESSELS, produced in response either to a severe water shortage or, more usually, to presence of pathogenic organisms. The growth of tyloses often causes the vessels to become blocked, thus preventing water transport. See Fig. 298.

xylem parenchyma

tylose

vessel

Fig. 298. **Tylose.** An outgrowth into the xylem vessel.

tympanic bone a bone homologous with the angular bone of reptiles that is found only in mammals. It forms the base of the auditory capsule and the external auditory meatus. See EAR.

tympanic cavity see EAR.

tympanic membrane or **tympanum** or **eardrum** a membrane situated at the end of the external auditory meatus at the junction of the outer and middle ears. Vibrations are set up in the membrane by sound waves, and these are transmitted by the ear ossicles to the oval window.

tympanum see TYMPANIC MEMBRANE.

type or **type specimen** or **onomatophore** the specimen that serves for the original description of a TAXON. Onomatophore means bearer of the name.

type genus the genus from which the name of the family or subfamily is derived.

type locality the locality in which a HOLOTYPE, LECTOTYPE, or NEOTYPE was collected.

type method the process of associating the name of a TAXON with a single specimen of that taxon.

type species the species from which the name of the genus is derived.

type specimen see TYPE.

typhlosole a dorsal unfolding of the earthworm's intestine along its entire length that increases its surface area for digestive purposes.

typhoid fever an acute intestinal disease caused by infection by the bacterium *Salmonella typhiosa,* which is characterized by high fever, skin spots, and abdominal pain. Treatment can be effected by administration of the drug chloramphenicol, although resistant strains have appeared in which other drugs must be used.

typhus an acute, infectious disease caused by intracellular rickettsial bacteria. It is characterized by high fever, skin rash, and severe headache. The bacteria are transmitted from human to human via the body louse *Pediculus humanus,* and control of the insect vector is a powerful means of preventing the spread of typhus.

typical having most of the characteristics of a particular taxonomic group.

typological thinking a CLASSIFICATION concept that disregards individual variation and considers all members of a population to be replicas of the TYPE.

tyrosine one of the 20 AMINO ACIDS common in PROTEINS. It has a polar R group structure and is soluble in water. See Fig. 299. The ISOELECTRIC POINT of tyrosine is 5.7.

Fig. 299. **Tyrosine.** Molecular structure.

U

ulna the posterior of the two bones of the forearm of TETRAPODS. The ulna articulates proximally with the HUMERUS and distally with the CARPALS. See PENTADACTYL LIMB.

ultracentrifuge a machine capable of spinning a rotor at speeds of up to 50,000 rpm, producing up to 500,000 g forces. The high speeds enable separation of tiny particles, which are identified by the rate at which they move down the centrifuge tube. The units of rate are called Svedbergs (S), after the inventor of the ultracentrifuge. Thus, RIBO-SOMES are found to consist of two subunits after ultracentrifugation, called 30S and 50S. See also DENSITY-GRADIENT CENTRIFUGATION, DIF-FERENTIAL CENTRIFUGATION, MICROSOMAL FRACTION.

ultrafiltration the process by which small molecules and ions are separated from larger molecules in blood to form the INTERSTITIAL FLUID.

ultraviolet light (UV) a type of electromagnetic radiation beyond the wavelength of visible violet light, ranging from 18,000 to 33,000 nm (see ELECTROMAGNETIC SPECTRUM). Unlike X-rays, UV light is not an ioniz-ing radiation and can only penetrate a few cells. However, it is used as a powerful MUTAGEN of microorganisms to cause formation of thymine DIMERS in DNA and can be harmful to the human RETINA. Some orga-nisms can detect UV light (see ENTOMOPHILY).

umbel an umbrella-shaped inflorescence that forms a RACEME in which the central axis has not elongated. Examples include the flowers of parsley and lovage.

umbilical cord the cord that joins the embryo of placental mammals to the PLACENTA (1), consisting of blood vessels supported by connective tissue. The cord is usually severed at birth.

umbo the pointed center of a clam shell, being the oldest part and around which are many concentric lines of growth.

unarmed (of plant structures) without prickles or thorns.

uncinate process a hooklike projection on each of the first four thoracic ribs of birds that overlaps the rib behind and serves to strengthen the thorax during flight.

uncini (*sing.* uncinus) the hooked chaetae of tubicolous polychaetes with which they cling to the sides of their tubes.

undulant fever a type of persistent human BRUCELLOSIS caused by *Brucella melitensis*, in which vague gastrointestinal and nervous symp-toms are common, together with enlarged lymph nodes, spleen, and liver. Most cases occur in people whose occupations may expose them to infected cattle.

undulate (of plant leaves) with up-and-down wavy edges.

unequal crossing over a CROSSING OVER event between HOMOLO-GOUS CHROMOSOMES that are not perfectly aligned, producing duplicated segments on one homologue and deleted segments on the other.

ungulate one of the numerous species of herbivorous mammals possessing hooves. See ARTIODACTYLA, PERISSODACTYLA.

unguligrade walking on the tips of the digits sheathed in cornified hooves, as in horses and cattle.

uni- *combining form* denoting one.

unicellular see ACELLULAR.

unilocular (of plant structures) made up of one cavity.

uninomial nomenclature the system of reference to a taxon by a single word—as in all taxa above the rank of species.

uniovular twins see MONOZYGOTIC TWINS.

unisexual having separate male and female organisms in a species. See DIOECIOUS.

unit-membrane model a model for the CELL MEMBRANE in which the membrane consists of a central lipid layer sandwiched between two layers of protein. See Fig. 300. The unit-membrane model was proposed in the 1950s by the American physician David Robertson, who found that his ELECTRON MICROSCOPE studies tallied with deductions reported by H. Davson and James Frederick Danielli in the 1930s. More recently, the FLUID-MOSAIC MODEL has come to be more generally accepted.

Fig. 300. **Unit-membrane model.**

univalent chromosome a chromosome that is unpaired during prophase I of MEIOSIS and fails to carry out CROSSING OVER with another HOMOLOGOUS CHROMOSOME. Univalent chromosomes occur often in POLYPLOIDS with odd numbers of chromosome sets.

univariate analysis (statistics) an analysis of a single character.

universal donor/recipient the ABO BLOOD GROUP compatibility between a donor and a recipient. Individuals with Group O have no A or

B ANTIGENS and are therefore called *universal donors*, because their blood type will not react with that of a recipient and thus can be given to *any* other ABO type. Individuals who are Group AB, with no anti-A or anti-B ANTIBODIES, are *universal recipients*, since they have no antibodies to react with any donated antigens. The terms do not apply to any other type of BLOOD GROUPING and, since these other groups are important in blood transfusion, the terms are rather misleading.

unsaturated fat see FATTY ACID.

upper critical temperature the environmental temperature defining the upper limit of the THERMONEUTRAL ZONE of a tachymetabolic animal (see TACHYMETABOLISM). Above this temperature, STANDARD METABOLIC RATE rises as a consequence of an increase in CORE TEMPERATURE.

upwelling an upward movement of water masses that results in nutrients being brought to the surface. Regions of upwelling are regions of high ocean productivity, occurring, for example, off the Peruvian coast, where there are major stocks of anchovies.

uracil one of four types of nitrogenous bases found in RNA, having the single-ring structure of a class known as PYRIMIDINES. Formula: $C_4H_4N_2O_2$. See Fig. 301. Uracil always forms complementary pairs with a base called adenine in DNA (during TRANSCRIPTION) or RNA (during TRANSLATION).

Fig. 301. **Uracil.** Molecular structure.

urceolate (of flowers) urn-shaped.

urea an organic molecule that forms the major end product of protein metabolism in mammals, being derived mainly from the ammonia released by deamination of AMINO ACIDS. Formula: $CO(NH_2)_2$. See ORNITHINE CYCLE.

urea cycle see ORNITHINE CYCLE.

urease an enzyme that catalyzes hydrolysis of UREA into carbon dioxide and ammonia. See Fig. 302.

Uredinales an order of basidiomycete fungi containing the rust fungi, which are important plant pathogens.

ureide any compound formed between urea and organic acids.

ureotelic (of animals) excreting UREA as the end product of the break-

$$H_2O + \underset{\underset{NH_2}{|}}{\overset{\overset{NH_2}{|}}{C}} = O \longrightarrow CO_2 + 2NH_3$$

Fig. 302. **Urease.** The hydrolysis of urea.

down of amino acids. Urea is produced by the ORNITHINE CYCLE and is characteristic of embryonic development, in which soluble urea can easily diffuse away.

ureter the duct that carries URINE from the kidney to the CLOACA or urinary BLADDER.

urethra the duct by means of which URINE is discharged from the BLADDER in mammals. In males the distal part of the duct also has a reproductive function, carrying semen from the VAS DEFERENS and voiding to the exterior via the penis.

Urey, Harold see COACERVATE THEORY.

uric acid an organic molecule that is the primary end product of protein metabolism in various animals, particularly those well adapted for life on land, such as insects, reptiles, and birds. Formula: $C_5H_4N_4O_3$. Uric acid is quite insoluble in water and thus nontoxic when released during embryonic development within the egg. Uric acid also permits removal of nitrogen with a minimum of water loss and is eliminated as a thick paste or even as dry pellets. See Fig. 303.

Fig. 303. **Uric acid.** Molecular structure.

uricotelic (of animals) excreting uric acid as the end product of the breakdown of amino acids. Such excretion is characteristic of embryonic development in a shell, where waste products must be stored.

uridine a molecule formed from a combination of a ribose sugar and the RNA base URACIL. Further addition of a phosphate group produces the NUCLEOTIDE.

urine an aqueous solution of organic and inorganic substances, the waste product of METABOLISM. In mammals, elasmobranch fishes, amphibia, tortoises, and turtles, nitrogen is excreted in the form of UREA, which in humans forms 2% of the urine on average.

uriniferous tubule the coiled tube that leads from the BOWMAN'S CAP-

SULE of the vertebrate kidney to the collecting tubes that convey urine to the ureter.

urinogenital system see GENITOURINARY SYSTEM

uro- *combining form* denoting urine *or* denoting tail.

urochordate see TUNICATE.

Urodela the amphibian order containing newts and salamanders. They usually have a well-developed tail and four limbs and have a larva with external gills.

urodeum the region of the CLOACA into which the genital ducts and URETERS open in birds and some reptiles.

uropygeal gland a large gland opening on the dorsal side of the UROPYGIUM in birds, from which an oily fluid is secreted that is used in preening.

uropygium the fleshy and bony swelling at the rear of a bird that supports the tail feathers.

urostyle a slender, pointed bone at the base of the backbone in amphibians, which is formed from fused vertebrae.

uterus the enlarged posterior portion of the OVIDUCT in which the embryo implants and develops in VIVIPAROUS (1) species. It is also called the *womb* in female humans.

utricle one of two connecting sacs from which arise the semicircular canals of the inner ear. The other sac is the SACCULE (2).

uvula a fleshy structure hanging from the back of the soft palate in humans.

V

***

vaccine a preparation containing inactivated (see ATTENUATION) or dead microorganisms used to stimulate an IMMUNE RESPONSE in the recipient, which affords IMMUNITY. Vaccines are thus not quick-acting, but rely on the recipient to build up a supply of ANTIBODIES gradually. For example, the Salk polio vaccine contains attenuated viruses. Compare SERUM (3).

vacuolar membrane the membrane surrounding the VACUOLE.

vacuolation the formation of a VACUOLE.

vacuole a space within the cytoplasm of a plant cell, containing cell sap. The vacuole is surrounded by the TONOPLAST.

vacuum activity an animal behavior pattern performed without apparent need or stimuli. See DISPLACEMENT ACTIVITY.

vagina the portion of the female reproductive tract (OVIDUCT) of mammals into which the penis is introduced during copulation.

vagus nerve the 10th cranial nerve of vertebrates, which arises on the side and floor of the brain MEDULLA and supplies the pharynx, vocal cords, lungs, heart, esophagus, stomach, and intestine. In the vocal cords and lungs it has a sensory function, but elsewhere in the parasympathetic nervous system (see AUTONOMIC NERVOUS SYSTEM) it has a motor function, including inhibition of the heartbeat.

valid name any name available to a taxonomist that has not been previously used.

valine one of 20 AMINO ACIDS common in proteins. It has a nonpolar R group structure and is relatively insoluble in water. See Fig. 304. The ISOELECTRIC POINT of valine is 6.0.

Fig. 304. **Valine.** Molecular structure.

valvate (of PERIANTH segments) having the edges in contact in the bud, but not overlapping.

valve 1. a piece of tissue that enables the movement of a liquid, for example, blood, in one direction only. **2.** the lidlike part of the shell of brachiopods and barnacles. **3.** either shell of a bivalve mollusk. **4.** the lid of some ANTHERS.

van der Waals' forces the weak bonds formed between electrically neutral molecules or parts of molecules lying close together. Such interactions are common in the secondary and tertiary structure of protein.

vane the part of a bird's feather formed by the barbs and excluding the RACHIS.

vapor pressure the pressure exerted by a vapor (gas) that is in equilibrium with its solid or liquid form. The term is particularly important in the diffusion of water vapor. See TRANSPIRATION.

variable (V) region an area of an IMMUNOGLOBIN molecule specific to that particular molecule. Compare CONSTANT REGION.

variance (s²) (in statistics) the variation around the ARITHMETIC MEAN. It is calculated as the average squared deviation of all observations from their mean value. The square root of variance is the STANDARD DEVIATION.

variant a particular form of a species or variety that has not been given a special name.

variation **1.** ecophenotypic variation in an organism caused by local factors rather than genetic factors. **2.** any differences, both genotypic and phenotypic, between individuals in a population or between parents and their offspring. See ECOPHENOTYPE, GENETIC VARIABILITY.

varicosities swellings that occur on a blood vessel or nerve fiber.

variegation color variation in various parts of the leaves or flowers of a plant. It can occur genetically, for example, by a somatic mutation affecting PLASTIDS or through disease, particularly viral infection.

variety a group of organisms that differs in some way from other groups of the same species. Botanically, this is often below the level of subspecies, but in zoology the term is often synonymous with subspecies or race. However, it is also used often for a morphological variant, for example, a form displaying MELANISM.

vasa recta one of a series of long loops of thin-walled blood vessels (efferent arterioles) that dip down alongside the loop of Henle in the vertebrate kidney. They pass blood into the interlumber veins and then into the renal vein.

vascular (of vessels) conducting fluid, for example, blood in mammals, water in plants.

vascular bundle a structure of vascular plants that runs up through the roots, into the stems, and out into the leaves, and whose function is transport within the plant. Water and ions are transported mainly by XYLEM, and dissolved organic solutes mainly by PHLOEM. Some vascular bundles are described as *open*, since they contain dividing CAMBIUM tissue between the xylem and phloem.

vascular cylinder see STELE.

vascular plant any member of the division TRACHEOPHYTA, possessing a specialized transport system formed of VASCULAR BUNDLES.

vascular system 1. (in animals) the blood circulatory system, including arteries, veins, capillaries, and heart. 2. the water vascular system of echinoderms, which serves to manipulate the tube feet for locomotion. 3. (in plants) the tissue that serves to conduct water throughout plants. The tissue is mainly XYLEM and PHLOEM and forms a continuous system that conducts water, mineral salts, and food nutrients and gives mechanical support.

vas deferens a duct conveying sperm from the TESTIS to the exterior in invertebrates or to the cloaca or URETHRA in vertebrates, and hence to the outside.

vasectomy a human operation involving cutting and separating the cut ends of the VAS DEFERENS so that they cannot rejoin. Effectively, the operation prevents sperm from mingling with secretions of the accessory glands and thus acts as a means of BIRTH CONTROL. The resulting semen, therefore, lacks sperm, and although a normal ejaculation can be produced, there is considered to be no risk of fertilization. Sperm is reabsorbed in the vas deferens, and there is usually no effect on sexual behavior.

vas efferens the tubules leading from the TESTIS to the VAS DEFERENS.

vasoconstriction a narrowing of the blood vessels, often in response to cold, which occurs through contraction of INVOLUNTARY muscles in the walls of the vessels brought about by a stimulus from the sympathetic nervous system (see AUTONOMIC NERVOUS SYSTEM).

vasodilatation the expansion of blood vessels by action of muscles mainly controlled by the sympathetic nervous system (see AUTONOMIC NERVOUS SYSTEM).

vasomotor (of sympathetic nerves) associated with constriction and dilatation of blood vessels.

vasomotor center an area of the stem of the brain that causes changes in blood pressure on stimulation of different parts, the pressor area giving a rise in pressure and the depressor area a fall.

vasopressin see ADH.

vector any organism that transmits a parasite. For example, the *Anopheles* mosquito transmits the MALARIA PARASITE.

vegetal pole the yolky end of the animal egg away from the cell nucleus.

vegetative of or relating to the nonsexual organs of a plant, such as root, stem, and leaves. See VEGETATIVE PROPAGATION.

vegetative cell one of two primary cells formed within the pollen grains of GYMNOSPERMS, which elongates to form a slender POLLEN TUBE.

vegetative propagation or **vegetative reproduction** a form of ASEXUAL REPRODUCTION in plants in which vegetative organs are able to produce new individuals. Natural methods of vegetative propagation are by means of, for example, RHIZOMES (stems), TUBERS (stems or roots), and RUNNERS (stems). Artificial methods include GRAFTING and CUTTINGS.

vegetative reproduction see VEGETATIVE PROPAGATION.

vehicle an inanimate carrier of an infection from one host to another.

vein 1. (in higher animals) the part of the BLOOD CIRCULATORY SYSTEM carrying blood back to the heart from the tissues. Veins are thin-walled, but have the same basic structure as ARTERIES, although veins are usually larger than the corresponding artery. Veins, unlike arteries, will collapse when empty, and are provided with a series of one-way valves that aid in maintaining the flow of blood back to the heart, assisted by skeletal muscles when moving. **2.** (in insect wings) the thickened parts of the CUTICLE, which resemble a pattern of veins and enclose tubular air sacs (tracheae) and blood sinuses. Pumping blood into these veins early in the adult stage causes the wings to take on their final form. **3.** (in vascular plants) any of the vessels within the blade of each leaf, made up chiefly of vascular tissue, that are continuous with the VASCULAR BUNDLES of the stem. The patterns of such veins are distinctive in each plant and are often used in classification.

velamen a layer of dead cells acting as water-absorbing spongy material and found on the outside of aerial roots of epiphytic plants.

veliger a larval stage of some mollusks, similar to a TROCHOPHORE, that develops a shell and other organs during later development. It is a ciliary feeder.

vena cava (*pl.* venae cavae) one of the major veins of the BLOOD CIRCULATORY SYSTEM.

venation 1. (in insects) the arrangement of veins in the wing. **2.** (in plants) the arrangement of leaf veins.

venereal disease any contagious disease transmitted usually during sexual intercourse, such as GONORRHEA or SYPHILIS.

venter the swollen base of the ARCHEGONIUM that contains the egg cell.

ventilation rate the rate of respiration in terms of the volume of air breathed per minute.

ventral of or relating to the underside of an organism, or the side normally directed downward in the usual stance or resting position. In bipedal primates, such as humans, the ventral side is the front, but would obviously be the underside if a four-legged gait were assumed.

ventral gland see PROTHACIC GLANDS.

ventral root any of the nerve roots issuing from the ventral side of the vertebrate brain or spinal cord, containing MOTOR nerves.

ventral tube an appendage of the first abdominal segment of collembolans (see COLLEMBOLA) formed by fusion of paired limbs. It may be associated with attachment or water uptake, and the name *Collembola* (glue stopper) is based on this structure.

ventricle 1. a chamber of the heart, having thick muscular walls, that receives blood from the ATRIUM and pumps it to the arteries. 2. four large spaces in the brain filled with CEREBROSPINAL FLUID. They occur in the CEREBRAL HEMISPHERES (lateral ventricles), FOREBRAIN (third ventricle), and MEDULLA OBLONGATA (fourth ventricle).

ventricular fibrillation see FIBRILLATION.

venule a small vein, differentiated from a capillary by possessing connective tissue and sometimes smooth muscle in the walls.

Venus flytrap a carnivorous plant, *Dionaea muscipula,* in which a hinged leaf snaps shut on insects from which the plant obtains nitrogenous compounds.

Vermes *obsolete collective term for* all worms of different phyla, ANNELIDS, PLATYHELMINTHS, NEMERTINES, etc.

vermiform appendix see APPENDIX.

vernacular name the common name for an organism, for example, robin for *Turdus migratorius.*

vernalin a substance similar to a hormone produced in VERNALIZATION.

vernalization a process, commonly called *forcing*, in which young plants are subjected to low temperatures (2—5°C) to induce a change to an older physiological state, thus shortening the interval between sowing and flowering. Vernalization can be reversed by high temperatures.

vernation leaf arrangement in a bud.

versatile (of ANTHERS) having the filament attached near the center so as to allow movement.

vertebra (*pl.* vertebrae) one of the bony segments of the VERTEBRAL COLUMN.

vertebral column or **spinal column** or **backbone** the series of vertebrae surrounding the SPINAL CORD. Each vertebra consists of a centrum that replaces the embryonic NOTOCHORD, plus a neural arch covering the spinal cord and often a hemal arch enclosing blood vessels. Transverse processes may also be present to which ribs articulate. Vertebrae are joined by the centra and often by projections of the neural arch. The column articulates with the skull by means of the atlas vertebra, with the ribs at the thoracic vertebrae, and with the pelvic girdle at the sacrum. See Fig. 305, LUMBAR VERTEBRA, ZYGAPOPHYSIS.

Fig. 305. **Vertebral column.** A lumbar vertebra of a mammal. (a) Front view. (b) Side view.

vertebrate any member of the subphylum Vertebrata (= Craniata) in the phylum Chordata, including all organisms that possess a backbone, such as fish, amphibia, reptiles, birds, and mammals. In addition, they are characterized by having a skull that surrounds a well-developed brain plus a bony or cartilaginous skeleton.

vertical classification a form of CLASSIFICATION stressing common descent and placing organisms in a single higher taxon to demonstrate PHYLETIC relationships. Compare HORIZONTAL CLASSIFICATION.

vertical resistance see RACE-SPECIFIC RESISTANCE.

vesicle any small sac-like structure.

vesicula seminalis see SEMINAL VESICLE.

vessel 1. a tubular structure that transports blood. 2. See XYLEM VESSEL.

vestibular apparatus the part of the inner ear that, together with the COCHLEA, forms the membranous labyrinth (see EAR).

vestibular canal the canal of the COCHLEA of the inner ear, which connects with the oval window.

vestibule any passageway from one cavity to another, such as the depression leading to the mouth in *Paramecium* or from the VULVA to VAGINA in the female mammal.

vestigial organ any organ that during the course of evolution has become reduced in function and usually in size. Examples include the pelvic girdle of the whale and wings in flightless birds. Such organs often have lost their original use and may be used for other purposes. For example, the penguin's forelimbs are adapted for swimming.

viability a measure of the likelihood that a ZYGOTE will survive and develop into a adult organism. For example, seeds become less viable as they get older, and a diminishing percentage actually germinate.

viable cell a cell able to live.

vibrissa or **whisker** any of the stiff sensitive hairs found around the mouths of mammals.

vicariad any of several species that are closely related but form an AL-LOPATRIC POPULATION.

Victoria mazonica the giant water lily, whose structure shows the close relationship between structure and function. The leaf has its edge up-turned to prevent inundation, and its underside greatly strengthened by ribbing.

villous (of plants) shaggy.

villus (*pl.* villi) a fingerlike outgrowth, as in the lining of the SMALL INTESTINE. Villi effectively increase the surface area of the gut wall and contain (a) blood vessels for absorption of carbohydrates and amino acids that pass into the hepatic portal SYSTEM and (b) lacteals that absorb fats into the LYMPHATIC SYSTEM.

vinegar a dilute, impure acetic acid, made from beer or wine.

viral pneumonia a form of pneumonia caused by an infection by a pneumovirus, which is closely related to the measles virus. Children are particularly vulnerable to attack by the virus, which can spread as an EPIDEMIC.

virion see VIRUS.

viroid a viruslike pathogenic structure consisting of an RNA molecule, but with no protein coat.

virulence the collective properties of an organism that render it pathogenic to another one, the host.

virulent phage a BACTERIOPHAGE that, following phage replication in the cell, results in LYSIS of the host. Unlike a TEMPERATE PHAGE, it cannot be integrated into the chromosome of the host.

virus the smallest organism known, ranging in size from about 0.025 — 0.25 μm. The mature virus, a *virion,* consists of nucleic acid (RNA or DNA) surrounded by a protein or protein and lipid coat. Viruses infect cells of bacteria, plants, and animals, and while they carry out no METAB-OLISM themselves, they are able to control the metabolism of the in-fected cell. In infection the virus first adheres to the cell wall and then penetrates the wall with its tail. The nucleic acid strand is injected into the cell, where it first replicates itself and then forms new viruses, which are released on rupture of the cell wall.

viscera the internal organs of the body cavity.

visceral arches the skeletal structures lying between adjacent gill slits in vertebrates, or the division between the gill slits.

visceral hump the dorsal part of mollusks, which accommodates the visceral organs. It is usually covered by the mantle and shell.

visceral muscle see INVOLUNTARY MUSCLE.

viscid (of plant parts) sticky.

viscosity 1. the property of stickiness by which substances resist change or shape. **2.** a measure of the ease with which layers of fluid pass each other.

viscus any organ lying in the VISCERA.

visible spectrum see ELECTROMAGNETIC SPECTRUM.

visual cortex the thin outer layer of gray matter in the occipital region of the CEREBRUM, which is concerned with interpreting information from the eyes.

visual purple see RHODOPSIN.

vital capacity the total amount of air that can be expired after a maximum inspiration (deep breath). This is calculated as the sum of:

(a) the *tidal volume,* the amount of air taken in with a normal breath.

(b) the *inspiratory reserve volume,* the amount of air that can still be taken in after a normal breath.

(c) the *expiratory reserve volume,* the amount of air that can be expelled after breathing out normally.

Typical results from an adult man at rest are shown in Fig. 306. Thus, the vital capacity of a normal man is between 3.5 and 4.5 dm^3, but can reach 6.0 dm^3 in a trained athlete.

Fig. 306. **Vital capacity.** The vital capacity of an adult man at rest.

vitalism a doctrine holding that biological phenomena cannot be expressed solely in physical and chemical terms.

vital staining the staining of cells while alive, which has been used particularly for studying the movements of parts of embryos.

vitamin an organic compound necessary in the diet for normal growth and health. Not all organisms require the same vitamins in their diet. For example, rats can synthesize vitamin C but humans cannot. Only small amounts of vitamins are normally required in the diet, as vitamins usually act as COENZYMES or parts of coenzymes. They are divided into two types: fat-soluble (A, D, E, and K) and water-soluble (B and C). See VITAMIN A, B-COMPLEX, ASCORBIC ACID, VITAMIN D, VITAMIN E, VITAMIN K.

vitamin A or **retinol** a fat-soluble hydrocarbon, closely related to CARO-TENOIDS, that occurs in liver, green vegetables, and storage organs, such as carrots. It is concerned with normal functioning of the mucous membrane of the eye as well as respiratory and genitourinary tracts. It also forms part of the photochemical reactions in the RODS of the eye. Deficiency of vitamin A leads first to *night blindness* and then to *xerophthalmia,* inflamed eyes and eyelids. The lining of the respiratory tract can become inflamed, and sterility results. Infants obtain a large supply of the vitamin in the mother's first milk (COLOSTRUM).

vitamin B complex see B-COMPLEX.

vitamin C see ASCORBIC ACID.

vitamin D a fat-soluble molecule found in fish liver oils and also produced in the skin when subjected to ultraviolet rays from sunlight. The main function of the vitamin is to increase the utilization of calcium and phosphorus in bones and teeth. A deficiency results in RICKETS in children and *osteomalacia* (bone-softening) in adults, particularly women after several pregnancies.

vitamin E or **tocopherol** a fat-soluble molecule found in many plants, such as wheat-germ oil, green leafy vegetables, egg yolk, milk, and meat. The vitamin is known as an antioxidant, enabling oxidation of, for example, unsaturated fatty acids and vitamin A in the body. A deficiency can result in sterility.

vitamin K or **phylloquinone** a fat-soluble molecule found in spinach, cabbage, kale, and pig's liver. The vitamin is essential for synthesis of prothrombin, which is used in BLOOD CLOTTING. A deficiency causes an increase in clotting time.

vitamin M see FOLIC ACID.

vitelline blood vessels the blood vessels that convey nourishment to embryos of vertebrates that have yolk.

vitelline membrane or **primary egg membrane** a FERTILIZATION MEMBRANE surrounding and secreted by the ovum. Secondary membranes are secreted by other structures, such as the OVIDUCT or OVARY.

vitreous humor the liquid jellylike material occupying the space within the eyeball behind the lens of the eye.

viviparous 1. (of animals) having the development of the young inside the body, as in placental mammals. Compare OVIPAROUS, OVOVIVIPAROUS. **2.** (of plants) having seed germinating in the fruit. **3.** (of plants) having shoots that serve for vegetative reproduction rather than forming flowers.

vocal cord the membranes that lie in the larynx of a mammal. Their vibration produces sounds that are altered by varying their position and tension.

voluntary muscle see STRIATED MUSCLE.

voluntary response a response under control of the will of an organism. Compare REFLEX ARC.

volutin granules of a highly refractile nature, made up of polyphosphates, which occur in many bacteria. Long chains may form storage material in some cells.

Volvocales an order of colonial green algae made up of flagellated cells embedded in spheres of mucilage.

vomer the thin flat bone forming part of the separation between the nasal passages in mammals.

von Baer's law see HAECKEL'S LAW.

vulva the external opening to the VAGINA in the female reproductive system of mammals.

W

waggle dance the behavior pattern by which bees convey information on the location of pollen supplies.

Wallace, Alfred Russel (1823—1913) British naturalist who was influenced by the ideas of MALTHUS and LYELL and corresponded with DARWIN about his ideas on natural selection. As a result he wrote a paper with Darwin that was read at the Linnaean Society in 1858 and led to founding of modern evolutionary thought.

wall pressure the pressure exerted by the cellulose cell wall of a plant, which is equal to the opposing PRESSURE POTENTIAL.

wandering cell any cell such as an amebocyte or macrophage that actively moves about during the life of an organism.

Warburg manometer an apparatus designed by the German biochemist Otto Warburg that measures aerobic respiration rates in tissues and small organisms. Carbon dioxide released from respiring material inside a flask is absorbed by potassium hydroxide, the resulting drop in pressure being measured by a manometer. The amount of CO_2 produced is equivalent to oxygen uptake by the tissue, assuming a RESPIRATORY QUOTIENT of 1.0. The respirometer apparatus is very sensitive to temperature, which is controlled by immersing the flask in a water bath whose temperature is regulated by a very accurate thermostat. Variations in atmospheric pressure do not affect the results, since the respirometer is a closed-circuit system.

warm-blooded animal see HOMOIOTHERM.

warning coloration or **aposematic coloration** any striking or conspicuous markings occurring on an animal that appear to indicate, presumably through learning, that the organism is distasteful to potential predators. The warning is to the predator, not to the zoologist. See MIMICRY.

water a colorless, odorless liquid that is the most abundant component of any organism, over 60% by weight in humans, for example. Life almost certainly originated in water, and water provides a medium for biological reactions to occur.

water culture see HYDROPONICS.

water potential or (formerly) **diffusion pressure deficit (DPD)** or **suction pressure** the tendency of a cell to draw in water from outside by OSMOSIS, the water moving from a higher to lower water potential. Since pure water at one atmosphere has a water potential of zero, cells drawing in water have a water potential of less than zero. Thus, water potential is measured as a negative value, which can be confusing. Readers should be careful when using the terms *higher* or *lower* water potential; *more negative* or *less negative* are more descriptive terms.

In mathematical terms water potential is the sum of the OSMOTIC POTENTIAL and the PRESSURE POTENTIAL of a cell:

$$\text{water potential} = \text{osmotic potential} + \text{pressure potential}$$

For example, when osmotic potential $= -9$ and pressure potential $= 4$, water potential $= -9 + 4 = -5$. See OSMOREGULATION.

waterproofing the process of preventing passage of water into and out of structures, usually brought about in a living organism by laying down LIPID layers, such as the insect cuticle.

water-soluble vitamin any of a group of vitamins soluble in water. Most are components of coenzymes, for example, those of vitamin B complex.

water stress any WILTING exhibited by plants that are losing more water by TRANSPIRATION than they are taking up through the roots.

water uptake the uptake of water into a plant through the roots. Water enters the plant only when there is a deficit in the XYLEM, normally caused by losses during TRANSPIRATION. The path of water from soil to leaf is as follows:

(a) movement of free soil water into the root hair by OSMOSIS.

(b) across the CORTEX of the root toward the STELE, by one of three methods: (i) via cell walls and intercellular spaces by hydration, (ii) via PLASMODESMATA by CYCLOSIS, and (iii) via cell vacuoles by osmosis.

(c) through the endodermis (see CASPARIAN STRIP) across the PERICYCLE and into the XYLEM VESSELS. These vessels contain ions that are actively pumped into the xylem to raise the concentration of solutes and thus the OSMOTIC PRESSURES.

(d) water moves up the plant in the xylem by a combination of (i) TRANSPIRATION pull and cohesion-tension (see COHESION-TENSION HYPOTHESIS), (ii) capillarity, and (iii) ROOT PRESSURE.

All water uptake is variable according to the type of plant, its age, the environment, and the time of year.

water vapor water in the gas phase, especially when due to evaporation. Vapor is important in maintaining the atmospheric humidity essential to living organisms.

water vascular system a system of canals found in ECHINODERMS that contain fluid and are open to the sea or the body cavity. This system supplies fluid to the tube feet for use in locomotion.

Watson, John (born 1928) American molecular biologist who, with

Francis CRICK and Maurice WILKINS, put forward a model for the structure and functioning of DNA in 1953, work for which they shared a Nobel prize in 1962. Their double-helix model for DNA is now universally accepted, together with their general ideas for DNA replication.

wavelength the distance between two successive points at which the wave has the same phase. For example, visible light has a wavelength of between 400 nm (violet) to 750 nm (red).

W chromosome the smaller of the two SEX CHROMOSOMES in female birds and LEPIDOPTERANS, being equivalent to the Y chromosome in male mammals. See also Z CHROMOSOME, SEX DETERMINATION.

Weber-Fechner law or **Fechner's law** a law stating that sensation increases arithmetically as the stimulus increases geometrically. Named for Ernst Weber (see WEBERIAN OSSICLE) and the German physicist Gustav Fechner (1801—1887).

Weberian ossicle a small group of bones, probably derived from the vertebrae, connecting the air bladder of the OSTARIOPHYSI with the ear capsule. Named for the German physiologist Ernst Weber (1795—1878).

weed any plant that competes for resources with a plant of importance to man. Weeds usually have a high VIABILITY and can use up disproportionate amounts of water, sunlight, and nutrients.

weighting 1. a method of determining the importance of characters in CLASSIFICATION by attributing different values to them. 2. the application of statistical loadings to data so as to enhance the value of some figures and reduce the value of others.

Weinberg, W. see HARDY-WEINBERG LAW.

Weismannism the theories of heredity, now considerably modified, proposing that germ cells are set apart at an early stage of development and not influenced by characteristics acquired during life. The known actions of chemicals and physical factors on chromosomes have resulted in modification of Weismannism into the CENTRAL DOGMA. Named for the German biologist August Weismann (1834—1914).

wen a sebaceous cyst, especially of the human scalp.

Went, Fritz Dutch biologist who identified the plant hormone AUXIN and devised a series of tests for the auxins. The BIOASSAY involves using an oat COLEOPTILE and an agar block containing the test substance to measure the possible effect of the test substance on growth.

wet rot a brown rot of damp timber caused by the fungus *Coniophora cerebella.* The fungus can be controlled by application of a wood preservative such as creosote.

whale see CETACEAN.

whalebone see BALEEN.

wheel animalcule see ROTIFER.

whisker see VIBRISSA.

white blood cells see LEUKOCYTE.

white fibrous cartilage any CARTILAGE containing white nonelastic fibers of COLLAGEN.

white matter the tissue of the CENTRAL NERVOUS SYSTEM, lying outside the GRAY MATTER in the spinal cord but internal to gray matter in the brain of some vertebrates, and which contains the myelinated AXONS of nerves. The MYELIN SHEATHS give the tissue its white appearance.

whole mount the preparation of an entire organism for microscopic examination.

whooping cough an infectious disease, common in children, caused by the bacterium *Bordetella pertussis,* in which the first symptoms are similar to those of the common cold. Severe coughing then develops, usually ending in a characteristic whoop as air is breathed in. There is frequent vomiting, and lung damage often occurs if ANTIBIOTICS such as erythromycin are not administered. In some cases, particularly in very young children, whooping cough can be fatal. Vaccination of young children is common, although this procedure carries a small risk of brain damage.

whorl a circular set (two or more) of leaves or SEPALS arising at the same level on the plant.

wild type the normal PHENOTYPE present in a natural or laboratory population, as distinct from a MUTANT (2) type, which often can survive only under artificial conditions. Wild type alleles are usually given a plus symbol $(+)$. For example, the wild type allele of the vestigial wing mutation (vg) in *Drosophila* is vg^+.

Wilkins, Maurice (1916—) English biophysicist born in New Zealand who carried out X-ray diffraction analysis of DNA, in collaboration with WATSON and CRICK, for which work they shared a Nobel Prize in 1962.

wilting a plant state in which a loss of TURGOR by cells of the leaves and other soft tissues causes drooping. The condition is caused by a lack of water (see WATER STRESS), either through drought in the soil or a disease, such as fungal wilt, which blocks the XYLEM VESSELS in the stem or leaves.

wing 1. either of the modified forelimbs of a bird that are covered with large feathers and specialized for flight in most species. **2.** one of the organs of flight of an insect, consisting of a membranous outgrowth from the thorax containing a network of veins. **3.** either of the organs of flight in certain other animals, especially the forelimb of a bat.

winkle a gastropod MOLLUSK of the genus *Littorina.*

wisdom tooth a 3rd molar in humans, which appears at about the age of 20 and often has to be removed as it crowds or distorts other teeth.

wobble hypothesis see CRICK.

Wolffian body see MESONEPHROS.

Wolffian duct the duct from the mesonephros in vertebrates. In fish and amphibia, it forms the urinary duct in females and the genitourinary duct in males. In reptiles, birds, and mammals, it forms the VAS DEFERENS in males and it degenerates in females.

womb see UTERUS(2).

wood louse any terrestrial member of the crustacean order ISOPODA, being dorsoventrally flattened arthropods with limbs of similar structure.

Woodpecker finch one of DARWIN'S FINCHES (*Geospinza*), which occurs in the Galapagos Islands and uses a cactus spine to remove insects from crevices. This is one of few known examples of birds using a tool.

work energy in which mechanical effort is involved, measured in joules. A joule is defined in work terms as a force of 1 newton moving its point of application through 1 meter. See SI UNITS.

XYZ

xantho- *combining form* denoting yellow.

xanthophyll see CAROTENOIDS.

X chromosome a type of SEX CHROMOSOME containing genes that always express when found in a male (XY). Examples of conditions controlled by X-linked genes are HEMOPHILIA (2 loci), Duchenne muscular dystrophy, color blindness (2 loci), and a form of diabetes. Compare Y CHROMOSOME. See SEX LINKAGE.

xenia the changes due to foreign pollen in the appearance of an ENDO-SPERM. For example, in corn, when a form with white endosperm is pollinated by a form having dark yellow endosperm, a pale yellow endosperm results.

xeno- or **xen-** *combining form* denoting alien, guest, strange.

xenograft see HETEROGRAFT.

Xenopus the African clawed toad that has been used to test for pregnancy in women. Injection of urine from a pregnant woman results in egg-laying by the toad.

xero- *combining form* denoting dry.

xeroderma pigmentosum a lethal genetic disorder of the skin in which affected individuals exhibit unusually heavy freckling and ulceration of skin after exposure to sunlight. Such individuals lack an endonuclease enzyme that normally repairs thymine DIMERS produced in DNA by ultraviolet light. Affected individuals are thought to be homozygous for a pair of recessive alleles on an AUTOSOME, although there may be up to five different genes involved in the condition. Heterozygous individuals are often heavily freckled. There is no treatment, and death occurs usually in childhood.

xeromorphy the condition of having the appearance of a XEROPHYTE due to possession of characteristics typical of such types.

xerophyte a plant adapted to growing in areas with low or irregular supplies of water. Various modifications can be noted that reduce water loss by TRANSPIRATION: sunken STOMATA (for example, *Pinus*); rolled leaves with the stoma·a on the inner surface only (for example, MARRAM GRASS); development of leaf spines (for example, gorse); and possession of small leaves (for example, many heathers). Compare HYDROPHYTE, MESOPHYTE.

xerosere a plant succession that begins on a dry site.

Xiphosura the group containing the king crabs, aquatic ARACHNIDS occurring as fossils as far back as the Paleozoic era.

X-ray an ionizing radiation that is a powerful MUTAGEN with wavelengths between 10^{-1} and 10^1 nm on the ELECTROMAGNETIC SPECTRUM. X-rays are produced by bombarding a metallic target with fast electrons in a vacuum and are capable of penetrating various thicknesses of solids. Having passed through a solid, they can act on a photographic plate, producing a light/shade pattern indicative of the solid structure.

xylem a woody plant tissue that is vascular in function, enabling transport of water with dissolved minerals within the plant, usually upward. Xylem is characterized as having TRACHEIDS, xylem fibers for support, xylem PARENCHYMA, and XYLEM VESSELS. The location of xylem is different in roots and stems, and the area of xylem is greatly increased by SECONDARY THICKENING.

xylem vessel or **vessel** or (rarely) **trachea** an empty tube formed from longitudinal fusion of several cells with strong walls reinforced with LIGNIN, whose function is mass transport of water for TRANSPIRATION. Vessels are aggregated into XYLEM tissue within the VASCULAR BUNDLES of ANGIOSPERMS.

xylose a PENTOSE SUGAR present in plant cell walls. Formula: $C_5H_{10}O_5$.

Y chromosome the smaller of the two SEX CHROMOSOMES, found in the male of mammals together with one X CHROMOSOME. Although Y chromosomes are responsible for SEX DETERMINATION in mammals, few specific genes have been located. Such Y-linked genes—a tentative example is a form of hairy ears in men—would only be inherited down the male line of a family.

yeast a collective name for those unicellular ASCOMYCETE or BASIDIOMYCETE fungi of economic importance in the brewing and baking industries (see SACCHAROMYCES). Yeasts secrete ENZYMES that convert sugars into alcohol and carbon dioxide (see ALCOHOLIC FERMENTATION), and it is the CO_2 that causes bread to rise.

yellow elastic cartilage any CARTILAGE containing a network of yellow fibers composed of elastin.

yellow fever an acute destructive disease of tropical and subtropical regions in which a virus causes cellular destruction in liver, spleen, kidneys, bone marrow, and lymph nodes. The effects of the disease are serious, with death occurring in about 10% of cases. The yellow fever virus is transferred from one human host to another via the mosquito *Aedes aegypti*. Control of the disease is principally by measures to reduce populations of the mosquito vector.

yellows any of a number of plant diseases in which there is significant yellowing of the leaves. Yellows can be caused by a wide range of microorganisms, for example, virus yellows of sugar beet.

yield 1. the part of the production of a crop that is removed by humans. 2. the actual amount of substance obtained during preparation of a substance, for example, in fermentation or in a manufacturing process.

Y-linked (of a gene located on the Y CHROMOSOME) transmissible only through the HEMIZYGOUS sex, that is, males in mammals.

yogurt a product of fermented milk. Boiled milk is inoculated with *Lactobacillus bulgaricus* and *Streptococcus thermophilus* and incubated at 45°C until the lactic acid content is 0.85—0.9%.

yolk the food store in the eggs of the majority of animals, made up mainly of fat and protein granules. Where yolk is present in the egg, as in chickens, there is meroblastic CLEAVAGE, but where it is absent, or nearly so, cleavage is holoblastic, as in *Amphioxus*.

yolk sac the sac-like structure that contains YOLK and is in direct contact with the gut of embryos in fish, reptiles, and birds. Though present in mammalian embryos, it does not contain yolk but absorbs uterine secretions until the PLACENTA (1) becomes functional.

Z chromosome the larger of the two SEX CHROMOSOMES in female birds and LEPIDOPTERA, being equivalent to the X CHROMOSOME in mammals. See also W CHROMOSOME, SEX DETERMINATION.

zeatin a CYTOKININ type of plant hormone extracted from the ENDOSPERM of corn kernels.

zero order reaction a chemical reaction in which the rate is independent of the concentration of the reactants.

zero population growth (ZPG) a state in a population in which births equal deaths, so that overall numbers remain in a steady state. ZPG and even negative growth has virtually been achieved in many Western countries, where the family size is low, but thus far has proven an impossible target for most third-world countries, ZPG being achievable only where there is widespread use of contraceptives (see BIRTH CONTROL, DEMOGRAPHIC TRANSITION).

Z-membrane a transverse membrane found in the light banding of skeletal muscle, at each end of a SARCOMERE.

zoea the larva of crabs and some other crustaceans.

zona pellucida a mucoprotein membrane surrounding the egg of mammals. It is secreted by the ovarian follicle cells.

zonation the division of a BIOME into zones that experience particular physical conditions. Zonation is clearly seen in the distribution of animals and plants on rocky seashores where, for example, the sublittoral zone (below low-water mark) is followed by the lower shore, middle shore, upper shore, and splash zone, all with their characteristic flora and fauna. See SEA ZONATION and Fig. 268.

zone any division or specific area. See SEA ZONATION, ZONATION.

zoo- *combining form* denoting living being, animal.

zoochlorella a unicellular green alga that lives in SYMBIOSIS with some sponges, coelenterates, and annelids.

zooid 1. any individual polyp of a colony of invertebrate animals that are linked together. For example, COELENTERATES have feeding polyps (gasterozoids), and reproductive polyps (gonozoids). **2.** a motile cell or body, such as a gamete, produced by an organism.

zoology the study of animals.

zoophyte an animal having a plantlike appearance, such as a sea anemone.

zooplankton the portion of the plankton made up of animal life. Compare PHYTOPLANKTON.

zoosporangium a SPORANGIUM in which ZOOSPORES are formed.

zoospore or **swarm spore** any of the motile, flagellated SPORES (asexual cells) found in green and brown algae and in PHYCOMYCETE fungi. They are produced within a SPORANGIUM.

Z scheme in photosynthesis the z-shaped passage of electrons in the LIGHT REACTIONS.

zwitterion the chemical form of an AMINO ACID with a dipolar ion state. The pH at which the amino acid exists as a zwitterion is called its ISOELECTRIC POINT, and at that pH it will not migrate in an electric field, produced, for example, by ELECTROPHORESIS. See Fig. 307.

$$H_2N - \overset{\overset{\displaystyle H}{|}}{\underset{\underset{\displaystyle (R)}{|}}{C}} - C \overset{\displaystyle O}{\underset{\displaystyle OH}{\diagup}}$$
(a)

$$H_3N^+ - \overset{\overset{\displaystyle H}{|}}{\underset{\underset{\displaystyle (R)}{|}}{C}} - C \overset{\displaystyle O}{\underset{\displaystyle O^-}{\diagup}}$$
(b)

Fig. 307. **Zwitterion.** Molecular structure of (a) undissociated amino acid, (b) zwitterion.

zygapophysis any facets of vertebrae that articulate with each other—usually two anterior zygapophyses that articulate with two posterior zygapophyses of the vertebra. See VERTEBRAL COLUMN and Fig. 305.

zygo- or **zyg-** *combining form* denoting yoke, yoked, yoke-shaped.

zygodactylous (of birds) having two toes pointing forward (second and third) and two backward (first and fourth), for example, the woodpecker.

zygomorphic (of flowers) exhibiting BILATERAL SYMMETRY.

Zygoptera see DAMSELFLY.

zygospore a thick-walled resting SPORE that is formed from the union of similar gametes.

zygote the DIPLOID (1) cell produced by fusion of the nuclei of male and female gamete nuclei at FERTILIZATION.

zygotene a stage of MEIOSIS near the beginning of Prophase 1, when the homologous chromosomes undergo SYNAPSIS so that identical genetic segments lie opposite each other, ready for CROSSING OVER. Although each chromosome is split into two CHROMATIDS, these are not usually visible.

zymase the yeast enzyme that brings about fermentation by enabling the breakdown of hexose sugars to alcohol and carbon dioxide.

zymogen an inactive precursor of an enzyme, particularly one concerned with protein digestion, for example, PEPSINOGEN and TRYPSINOGEN. Zymogens require ACTIVATION ENERGY to become functional.

zymogen granule a cytoplasmic particle surrounded by a membrane formed by the GOLGI APPARATUS. It stores and secretes zymogen.